COMPARATIVE POLITICS
A POLICY APPROACH

COMPARATIVE POLITICS

A POLICY APPROACH

MICHAEL J. KRYZANEK
Bridgewater State College

A Member of the Perseus Books Group

Copyright © 2004 by Westview Press, A Member of the Perseus Books Group

Published in the United States of America by Westview Press, A Member of the Perseus Books Group, 5500 Central Avenue, Boulder, CO 80301-2877, and in the United Kingdom by Westview Press, 12 Hid's Copse Road, Cumnor Hill, Oxford OX2 9JJ.

Find us on the world wide web at www.westviewpress.com.

Westview Press books are available at special discounts for bulk purchases in the United States by corporations, institutions, and other organizations. For more information, please contact the Special Markets Department at the Perseus Books Group, 11 Cambridge Center, Cambridge, MA 02142, or call (617) 252-5298, (800) 255-1514 or e-mail j.mccrary@perseusbooks.com.

Library of Congress Cataloging-in-Publication Data
Kryzanek, Michael J.
  Comparative politics: a policy approach / Michael J. Kryzanek.
  p. cm.
  Includes bibliographical references (p.) and index.
  ISBN 0-8133-4102-7 (hardcover: alk. paper)
  ISBN 0-8133-9792-8 (paperback: alk. paper)
  1. Comparative government. I. Title.
  JF51.K79 2004
  320.3—dc21
                                                  2003010006

Text design by Cynthia Young; set in 11 point Garamond 3.

10   9   8   7   6   5   4   3   2   1

To
ANNE WILUSZ

Contents

Preface

It is as difficult a matter to reform an old constitution as it is to construct a new one; as hard to unlearn a lesson as it was to learn it initially. The true statesman, therefore, most not confine himself to matters we have just mentioned; he must also be able to help any existing constitution. He cannot do so unless he knows how many different kinds of constitutions there are. As things are, we find people believing that there is only one sort of democracy or oligarch. This is an error. To avoid that error, we must keep in mind the different varieties of each constitution; we must be aware of their number, and of the number of different ways in which they are constituted.

—ARISTOTLE
Politics 4.1.7–8

One of the eternal wonders of education is the opportunity for students to ask questions about the subject matter, particularly what can best be described as the *whys*. As an undergraduate instructor in political science, I have been bombarded with a constant stream of "whys," from the earnest question of why politics is conducted in a certain way to the old standard, "Why do we have to know this stuff?" The first why question verifies student interest in the world of politics and makes the role of the instructor rewarding, but the second why question is equally legitimate.

Why an area of study is important in the college experience is often not immediately obvious. Students know the routine of general education requirements and courses in their majors that they simply cannot avoid. Often the requirement for taking these courses is justified by the assertion that they are essential to a liberal arts education or are foundational to a particular major. In the discipline of political science the course often called comparative government or comparative politics is usually one of the foundations of the major. As students make their way through the political science curriculum, they usually are steered into a "comparative" class with a kind of foggy understanding that they will be studying countries other than the United States.

At this stage in their academic career students become aware that politics and the public sector are organized differently outside of the United States. As the student travels through the governments of the industrial nations and developing countries, democracies and authoritarian regimes, the wealthy and the poverty-stricken states, it becomes increasingly clear that "Comparative" is a valuable course that opens new horizons and raises many new whys. Comparing constitutions, governments, parties and interest groups, elections, public policies, and a range of political values, political opinions and political behaviors complicates the study of the world around us. But comparison sharpens critical thinking skills as it forces students to see the world from new and exciting vantage points.

In many respects "Comparative" is one of the most important courses students can take during their college experience and is certainly the bedrock of the political science major. Aristotle is often viewed as the first student of comparative politics. Although Aristotle wrote his *Politics* over twenty-four hundred years ago, the challenge of trying to make sense of governing variety and difference remains the goal of modern-day comparativists. As Aristotle knew instinctively, the study of comparative politics opens up a broad vista of governing options and political processes. It helps the student of politics understand that the key elements of government—power and authority—are not one-size-fits-all arrangements; it examines the fundamental relationship between the people and the state as unique and constantly fluid.

A modern course in "Comparative" addresses issues that are more complex and perhaps messier than the ones Aristotle faced when Greece was organized around a number of small city-states. Today the world is populated by over 190 sovereign nations, each with its own governmental structure and political system. The world of government is not cookie cutter consistent, nor is it like the images gleaned from a travel brochure or from a casual sound bite on television. "Comparative" is rather the study of how governing is practiced in our world, at once a daunting challenge and an enormously rewarding experience. As comparativist Howard Wiarda correctly states, "Comparative politics is one of the most exciting and innovative fields in political science—indeed, in all of the social sciences, for students of comparative politics, the whole world is our laboratory—and that laboratory is constantly expanding, changing and becoming more interesting."

Besides opening up the world to us and stimulating our interest about the ever changing nature of government and politics, a course in "Comparative" also helps build our capacity for formulating theories about governing. The more we compare, the more we are able to see similarities and patterns. Governments may be different, but they face common challenges, common threats, and common expectations. Following a comparative approach will likely lead to an understanding of the basic theories of how governments work and how governments react to challenges, threats, and expectations. Taken one step further, the comparative approach and the theory building that follows from the approach can help predict how governments will act in certain situations. By comparing governments over time and defining those similarities and patterns, it is possible to bring some order to the messiness that is found in the world.

Many people from around the world have visited Disney World or Disneyland. A ride called It's a Small World is one of the most popular. When I took my children on this ride, they and I were fascinated by the colorful costumes and flags of the children of the world. The message is that we are all in this together; no matter what our differences, we share the same planet. The world is indeed getting smaller as satellite communications, the Internet, expanded transportation, global trade, an international consumer culture, and the increasing migration of people from one end of the earth to the other have created an endless number of linkages. What happens in one country far away and remote from our thinking can significantly affect our way of life. We no longer live in a closed world; we cannot surround ourselves with a fortress that keeps the rest of the world at bay.

Therefore it is incumbent on us to become students of the world to recognize and become familiar with the countries and the people who live beyond our borders. Although *Comparative Politics: A Policy Approach* does not touch all of the nation-states in the world today, it does look at a sampling of countries that will pique your interest in government and encourage you to expand your interests beyond the United States. The best answer to the question of why we have to know this stuff is that the world has grown smaller and closer and no one can afford to be ignorant of countries around the globe. It is a good educational investment in time and effort to get to know that small world around us.

Eventually a course in comparative politics gets around to the textbook that is used in class. Textbooks in "Comparative" not surprisingly are a little messy themselves. Although most of the texts follow a country study approach—the authors tend to choose a number of countries that they feel best represent the range of governing systems and governing environments found in the world. In many cases the choice of countries is a mix of European democracies, Third World developing countries and a sampling of former communist states, newly industrialized nations, and authoritarian regimes. In other approaches authors examine "Comparative" from a topical or functional angle by studying critical problems or conditions that governments face on a regular basis. These approaches, although different, nevertheless provide the student with the essential tools for understanding government and politics and for making solid and meaningful comparisons.

The approach taken in this textbook is more like a hybrid. Like the majority of texts, *Comparative Politics: A Policy Approach* examines countries from the advanced industrial world, the Third World, and the former communist world. The countries that will be examined are the United States, the United Kingdom, Russia, Japan, China, Mexico, South Africa, and Iraq. These countries were chosen because they exemplify major economic powerhouses and struggling developing states, established democracies and authoritarian regimes, complex political systems and centrally controlled dictatorships. The United States is included to provide a familiar baseline to the study of "Comparative" that students can use to make their own judgment on a range of governing issues. The United Kingdom was chosen because its parliamentary government has become a model throughout the world. Russia is one of the former communist countries, in fact the pillar of communism, that are in transition, while China remains a communist state, although one with newly capitalist leanings. Japan is the strongest Asian democracy that is currently coping with a transition to a more open economic system, while Mexico and South Africa are budding democracies facing severe economic and social challenges. And finally Iraq is a quintessential example of a centralized dictatorship, although after the U.S. invasion a transition to democratic rule will occur. Taken together, these eight countries "touch all the bases" of governing and provide diverse examples of how governments respond to a range of domestic and foreign challenges.

Its country approach places this text within the traditional mode of studying comparative politics; however, these eight nations are examined from an additional perspective. Accompanying each country study is a series of "policy briefs" that outline policy issues and policy debates in the forefront of the governing agenda. The text thus focuses on exploring the connection between the governing system and the policy process, between the decision-making system and the outputs of government. Including policy briefs in a comparative politics text is necessary not only because they provide a flavor of what government currently has on its agenda, but also because they allow students to understand these nations as more than just structure and process. The policy briefs help make the country real as they often reflect the conditions, the views, and the controversies of national life.

In order to establish a linkage between how government works and what government does, the text is organized around key functions and relationships in the political system. General comments about the current conditions within each country "set the scene" for a discussion of important political milestones that have shaped the political process, a presentation of the formal government as it is constitutionally organized, an assessment of the connections between citizen and state, a description of the various pathways to participation available in the country, a delineation of the important members of the power elite, an analysis of the realities of the governing process, an overview of the political economy, and a discussion of the critical governing challenges that lie ahead. The country section ends with a comparison that seeks to link the political and governing situation in the country with other countries in its immediate region as well as within the international community of nations. Interspersed throughout these sections are policy briefs that describe governmental efforts to respond to domestic and foreign problems.

These ten sections mix traditional approaches to studying the countries with some new ways of looking at politics and government. The more standard sections, such as the one on political milestones, highlight key events that shaped the body politic and the formal government, which provides the essential structure of governing. But there are some new approaches too, for example, the discussion of the power elite, which centers on identifying the key players in the political process and how those players influence the direction that government takes. The section on real government describes the policy process by looking at informal relationships and decisionmaking arrangements that are often not part of the formal governing structure.

The eight countries discussed in this volume do not exist in a vacuum. They are part of an international environment that in the last ten years has changed dramatically. Communism has faded into obscurity, democracy has emerged as the dominant governing philosophy, globalization provides the rules of commerce, development, and political economy, and terrorism has become a sad staple of national life. The world has been overwhelmed with new technological breakthroughs that are shaping and reshaping business, government, and personal lives. The term "global village" has become a reality as telecommunications, computerization, and transportation unify countries and people in ways never before dreamed of. Moreover, the concept of a global village has had a noticeable impact on the formation of a mass culture. As a result of the Internet, satellite television, heightened travel, and e-commerce governments can no longer ignore the fact that people have almost unlimited access to the world and all that the world offers.

Acknowledging the enormous influence of these trends and conditions, the study of the eight nations is presented in ways that underscore the role played by the end of communism, democratization, terrorism, globalization, technological advances, and international culture in shaping government and politics. Each of the countries provides a real-time microcosm of how these megatrends and megaconditions have changed the rules of politics and re-structured government. These megatrends and megaconditions provide the background and define the environment in which these eight countries function and, more importantly, help provide answers to the whys that the reader is certain to ask.

By presenting the eight countries in terms of nine explanatory sections, adding a series of contemporary policy briefs, and providing underlying themes that explain the context in which countries exist in the contemporary world, *Comparative Politics: A Policy Approach* touches all the bases. The study of "Comparative" has come a long way since the days when Aristotle studied 154 city-state constitutions. "Comparative" today must be more comprehensive, more sensitive to differences, and more appreciative of the influence of outside forces on the political system. *Comparative Politics: A Policy Approach* attempts to meet these challenges and in the process introduce you, the reader, to some very interesting and very important countries.

Although writing a textbook is a lonely experience, it is not done in a vacuum. A personal debt of thanks goes to my colleague and friend Howard Wiarda of the University of Massachusetts, Amherst, who introduced me to comparative politics and has been my guiding light ever since. I also want to acknowledge the influence of Gerard Braunthal and Anwar Syed, who provided me with a solid foundation in comparative politics. I want to thank my faculty colleagues at Bridgewater State College, especially Shaheen Mozaffar, who often serve as my sounding boards for discussions of comparative politics. Finally, and most importantly, I want to thank my wife, Carol, and my daughters, Laura, Kathy, and Annie, who over the years have been my loving support system.

This book is dedicated to my mother-in-law, Anne Wilusz, who is one of the wisest people I know. Over the years Anne has taught me patience, kindness, and the benefits of quiet humility. I owe her a great deal. This book is partial payment for all her loving gifts.

Michael Kryzanek
Whitman, Massachusetts

Introduction

There's an old line from the sports world that "you can't tell the players without a program." In a book on comparative politics that covers eight countries from historical and contemporary perspectives, that old line needs to be modified somewhat to state that "you can't understand the countries without defining the terms." Since each of these countries is a unique entity with its own way of doing politics, I try to provide some semblance of commonality by presenting the concepts, ideas, institutions, and processes that serve as the foundation on which these countries have developed and currently operate. Defining the terms provides a structure to the discussion of the eight countries and clarifies the manner in which government is run and political decisions are made.

The terms that are used in political science courses are critical to understanding how nations are organized, how politics works, and how governments operate. These terms bring specificity and precision to the study of political science and are essential in a course such as comparative politics. Because comparative politics is about determining whether there are linkages, similarities, and trends that exist in the countries being studied, it is important to establish an agreed-on "language." Words become the building blocks of comparison. Using them carelessly or without concern for their proper meaning weakens the process of making proper linkages, finding similarities, and determining the existence of common trends.

In order to present these terms in an orderly fashion and establish a "language" of comparative politics, a series of categories has been developed. These categories cover the "fundamentals," which are the basic terms of politics and government, the "ideas," which are the philosophies and ideologies that guide politics and government, the "systems," which establish the process of decisionmaking, the "institutions," which are the decisionmaking structures of politics and government, and the "worlds," which are the political and governmental settings created by and resulting from public policy decisions. With this language, the study of comparative politics thus becomes not just a description of eight individual countries but also a means through which the building blocks of political science can be understood and appreciated.

THE FUNDAMENTALS

Political science courses are concerned with describing and analyzing various aspects of politics and government. Oftentimes, however, the words "politics" and "government" are used haphazardly. There is an assumption that students know the difference between what politics is about and what government does. In order to properly lay the foundation for a discussion of the "language" of this text, I will define the two most central terms of that language.

Politics is connected to an activity that is at the core of organized society. Politics involves public decisionmaking and the means through which public decisions are made. When people form organized societies they eventually need to make decisions on a range of issues related to the general welfare. Issues of security, distribution of resources, conflict resolution, and problem solving are matters that become political. Politics is thus the activity that people engage in to run their societies.

Often politics requires that leaders be named or elected or self-appointed in order to take charge of the political process and bring order and direction to public decisionmaking. These leaders thus gain the political authority to manage the affairs of the society. Sometimes the relationship between the leader and the general public is based on participation and consent; other times the relationship between the leader and the general public is based on force and control. But whatever the relationship, political leaders are in charge of the process of politics and shape that process by using the authority that comes with their position.

Power and the use of power drive politics. Power is the ability to get things done. Those who have power possess the key to controlling the process of public decisionmaking. Political leaders are the ultimate power holders because they can use their authority to say yes and make a public policy happen or say no and stop a public policy from happening. But citizens have power as well. They can strip political leaders of their power by voting them out of office or forcibly removing them from office. While they are in office, however, political leaders wield considerable power to collect and allocate public resources, appoint other public officials, make and implement public laws, and solve disputes that affect public life. The power of political leaders is so great that in most organized societies they overshadow all other power contenders, although they may possess economic wealth, social influence, intellectual competence, or religious standing.

The activity of politics is best understood as occurring within a state. A state is a defined territory with established borders, a recognized governing structure, and a claim of independence. The designation that political scientists often use to properly identify the state is "nation-state," suggesting that this specific territory is occupied by people who have a common language, religion, tradition, and historical background. It is important in the modern era to distinguish between a state and a nation-state because not all national groupings that share these commonalities are organized into states. In fact, many of the trouble spots in the world today are places where distinct peoples are seeking to establish a separate state but either are under the control of another nation-state or are in the process of seeking to establish independence and governing autonomy. The ethnic and racial conflicts that have erupted in the world in the last ten to fifteen years have been over the efforts of breakaway movements to establish new nation-states.

Governments are the political and administrative structures that are created within nation-states. To form a government is to create institutions for decisionmaking and policy implementation. Governments usually are organized around three distinct institutions: a legislature, an executive, and a judiciary. Each of these branches of government has distinct decisionmaking and decision-implementing responsibilities. The legislature is charged with debating public policy concerns and responding to those concerns in the form of public laws, the executive is responsible for administering the laws and in the process managing those bureaucrats who must implement the laws, and the judiciary has the responsibility of guaranteeing that the laws are protected and implemented within the bounds of the law.

The ability of government to function properly requires two key ingredients. First, the government that heads the state must be capable of establishing sovereignty. Sovereignty is the power to control the governing process free of external intervention. States that are sovereign are not dominated by another state and the decisions that they make regarding public matters are not subject to approval by another state or outside governing force. Sovereignty can also be applied to internal control of the government. The term "popular sovereignty" suggests that the people of the state hold ultimate control over the government and the governing process and their will determines who has power and how that power is to be used.

The second ingredient in shaping government and its ability to function is legitimacy. To carry out its responsibilities a government needs to be recognized as legitimate. Legitimacy may come from winning an election or following the rules contained in a constitution or being recognized by other governments or international institutions. A government that does not possess this intangible commodity called legitimacy is likely to find it difficult to manage the political process. A loss of legitimacy may mean that groups of citizens or political parties or other organized segments of the population are working to replace the government with one that does possess this intangible commodity. Legitimacy is thus essential for governments. Having legitimacy means that a government has public support and that its decisions, while perhaps controversial or contested, nevertheless are recognized as valid.

One of the most effective means of establishing legitimacy is for a government to form and adhere to a constitution. A constitution is not just the basic law of a state that creates a structure and process of governing; it is also a system of rules and rights that defines the relationship between government and its citizens. A constitution can be a powerful document to define power, channel power, and limit power. However, a constitution can also be a piece of paper that the governing authorities use to create the illusion of legality and foster a climate of legitimacy. When a government and its citizens adhere to a constitution and the principles inherent in the constitution, they create a state where laws form the basis for societal order, where those with power are required to play by the rules, and where fundamental rights are guaranteed. When a government uses the constitution as a facade to enhance its image, the state becomes a mere extension of the rulers with no means of controlling the excesses of power and no recourse to ensure that the relationship between citizen and government is based on trust and participation.

A critical factor in forming a constitution and creating an environment of constitutionalism is the establishment of individual rights. To the citizens of a state, the relationship that is developed with the government is built on the freedoms, guarantees, and protections they receive from this basic law. Most constitutions provide their citizens with an array of rights from speech and religion to guarantees of workers' rights, cultural identity, and gender equality. In the modern world constitutions have become more than documents of structure and process; they assure citizens that the government is committed to maintaining individual freedoms, ensuring fairness and justice, and protecting diversity. But if constitutionalism is a sham, the listing of rights is weakened by language that limits what citizens can do and what they can expect from the government. In these governments the citizen has no individuality or autonomy but is a functionary in a large and often repressive state system.

THE IDEAS

Political activity and the operation of government do not exist in a vacuum. Every state has a political culture—a system of beliefs, values, and visions that shape the political process and direct the workings of government. While the political decisions and the public policies that result from those decisions are often made with cold, hard calculations and realistic assessments, there is always a linkage between action and ideas. Political leaders and government officials may be practitioners of the practical, but they come to public life with a philosophy of what the state should stand for and how the common good should be achieved. Ideas matter in politics, and government and public life are rarely devoid of an underlying philosophy or worldview. A political leadership cannot sustain itself in power without believing in something or at least paying lip service to a set of beliefs.

One of the most powerful ideas to shape politics and government since the time of the Greeks is democracy. Democracy, whose name comes from Greek and means rule by the people, was at first looked on with great suspicion and fear. The idea of placing governing decisions in the hands of ordinary people was considered dangerous and foolhardy. Government, it was thought, should be in the hands of the elite—those with property, social standing, and education. The great Greek thinker Plato abhorred democracy in favor of a philosopher king, while Aristotle could accept only aristocracy as the proper leadership group. It was not until the seventeenth century in Europe that the roots of modern democracy were formed. British thinkers such as John Locke began espousing the importance of consent and inalienable rights, and later the French thinker Jean-Jacques Rousseau introduced the concept of a social contract between citizens and the state.

With the American War of Independence and the French Revolution democratic pressures intensified as the old system of monarchies began to break down. Either by legislation or by gradual acceptance, democratic norms and practices began to be accepted in nineteenth-century Europe and North America. The vote was expanded, representative governance became accepted, and elections evolved into regular democratic events that were open, secret, and the final arbiter of political power. In the twentieth century, particularly after World War II, democracy exploded in the less developed world. By the end of the 1990s fully three-fourths of the world's countries were living under democratic rule. In 1993 alone forty-three elections were held in the less developed world, many for the first time.

Today democracy is the governing philosophy of choice. With a commitment to the rule of law, individual rights, restraints on power, toleration of opposition and dissent, majority rule and representative government democracy have overcome the suspicions and fear of the Greeks to become the best means of organizing public life and achieving a balanced relationship between citizens and the state. Democracy in the modern world is now viewed as creating the conditions for societal stability and economic development. Those states that opt for nondemocracy and accent societal control, centralized decisionmaking, repression of alternative views, and unlimited power in the hands of one person or an elite have become a small minority of the community of nations. They are governing outcasts who are themselves viewed with suspicion. In a real sense democracy has come full circle from the days of the Greeks. It is now the nondemocrats who are on the wrong side of history and have a difficult time defending their position.

Within the democratic tradition two additional philosophies have emerged regarding the proper role of the state and the process of change. The conservative philosophy, first articulated by the English statesman Edmund Burke, stressed that existing institutions of politics and society should not be subject to constant change. Burke viewed stability and continuity with the past as core governing values. Whatever change was introduced into society, conservatives felt, needed to be slow in application and achieved through extensive consensus. As the conservative philosophy evolved over time, its supporters questioned the role of government as an agent of change. Conservatives feared the growth of government and the taxation that was required to respond to that growth. There was also an insistence among conservatives that government should stay out of the marketplace and not engage in regulatory activity that hindered the ability of the private sector to function within the established economy.

In direct opposition to the conservative philosophy was liberalism. Developed during the eighteenth and nineteenth centuries, liberalism accented the individual and individual freedom. Liberals became associated with the efforts to use government to improve society. Unlike conservatives, liberals did not fear change or see it as a destabilizing force. They viewed change in the name of societal improvement as the supreme good. Liberalism took its views on change and societal improvement one step further by embracing government as the primary agent of change. Government action, government programs, and government spending in the name of societal improvement were accepted as necessary for freeing man from inequality, social injustice, and any number of problems that citizens might face. As liberal philosophy evolved over time, it became associated with the plight of the poor and minorities, those who were discriminated against, whose only relief from abuse or injustice lay in the power of government.

Conservatism and liberalism have been locked in a struggle for the hearts and minds of citizens in democratic society. Most issues that face government and most political debates among leaders are framed within the dynamic of conservatism and liberalism. These two contending philosophies have energized citizens and given them the basis for self-definition, and they are the root cause of deep divisions within the political arena and the governing system. Questions of how much government is necessary and how far government should intervene in people's lives have become central to the political process of making public policy. Whoever has the governing power will likely fashion the public policy agenda along either conservative or liberal guidelines. Of course a balance between the two is the ultimate solution, and many times such a balance is achieved. But along the road, politics is usually marked by a contest between proponents of using as little government as possible and proponents of using as much government as needed.

Without question, democracy is the dominant political and governing philosophy of Western civilization. Yet states are also guided by economic philosophies and economic systems that have developed from those philosophies. Capitalism, based on a laissez-faire theory of the marketplace and the manner in which individuals participate in that marketplace, has been the most influential economic philosophy in modern history. First developed by Adam Smith in England, capitalism limits government intervention in the market economy and accents private ownership of goods and services. A capitalist economy is structured around the principles of supply and demand. With the government acting only in a limited capacity to influence the economy, individual and corporate participants in the marketplace determine the price and the availability of goods through the interaction of supply and demand. Capitalism is a highly individual economic philosophy that allows those in the marketplace to reap the benefits of private ownership.

Since the Great Depression of the 1930s and World War II capitalism has undergone significant transformation as the role of government in the marketplace has deepened. Governments have become regulators of the economy and individual governing administrations have sought to manage national economies in order to respond to the downturns and the dislocations that arise when capitalist systems are not able to sustain prosperity. Adam Smith's "invisible hand" of capitalist self-correction has been replaced by increased government involvement in economic decisions. Today most economies of the world are mixed: a capitalist system with all its individual trappings and its private wealth generation functions side by side with a governing system that monitors economic activities, regulates economic decisions and institutions, and intervenes in the marketplace.

Capitalism and the economic systems that were formed in individual governing states faced stiff competition in the nineteenth and twentieth centuries from socialism and communism. Although capitalism can be a highly successful system of economic development and personal wealth accumulation, it can also create huge income gaps between those who own and control the means of production and those who do not. In Europe an alternative to capitalism, socialism, developed. Based on the principle of collectivism, it accented the importance of government ownership and control of the means of production. Under a socialist system the government runs the economy in the name of the people and works to achieve a more equitable distribution of the resources and the wealth generated from those resources. In many European countries socialism was linked with democracy to create what was viewed as a more humane governing and economic system. Democratic socialism became associated with nationalization of major natural resources and industrial sectors, government planning of economic development, comprehensive social welfare programs, and extensive intervention in private economic decisions.

A more radical offshoot of socialism was developed by the German theorist Karl Marx, who in the mid-nineteenth century wrote a critique of capitalism called *Das Kapital*. Marx believed that capitalism must be destroyed and replaced by communism. In a communist economy all land and capital are owned by the state and governing power is controlled by the people. To achieve a communist society, Marx advocated a class struggle against the capitalists, a revolution that would destroy the landowners and the managerial class. Eventually this revolution would lead to a classless society and a "withering away" of the state. Marx believed that communism would create a utopian society in which collectivism would conquer individuality, and a people's society would replace the inequality and injustice created by capitalism. The transition to the communist utopia would require an interim period called the "dictatorship of the proletariat" as the people were led by a revolutionary elite who made decisions for the good of the masses. This concept of the "dictatorship of the proletariat" would be the critical factor in establishing governments based on authoritarian principles and practice.

The Marxist philosophy became the basis for the Russian revolution of 1917 led by Vladimir Lenin and eventually dominated by Josef Stalin. It also became the guiding force in the Chinese revolution of 1949 led by Mao Zedong. Communism served through much of the twentieth century as the antithesis of capitalism, offering the less developed world the prospect of replacing the colonial system that was based on capitalist principles with a communist ethic that offered the masses a people's state. Wars of national liberation initiated by supporters of Marxist revolution or ardent nationalists who saw communism as a means of ridding their countries of Western influence erupted in a number of less developed nations. In Algeria, Cuba, Egypt, and Vietnam, to name some of the more prominent challenges to colonialism and capitalism, revolutionary movements led by Marxist guerrillas or nationalist forces led by military leaders replaced existing governing and economic systems with the communist alternative. These wars of national liberation, such as the Vietnam conflict, not only expressed the masses' discontent with the colonial and imperial presence of Western powers, but also became proxy wars that pitted the United States against communist archrivals, the Soviet Union and China. Throughout the post–World War II period the world was divided into two opposing camps as capitalism with its promise of individuality and private wealth generation competed with communism with its promise of an economy based on equality and social justice.

Over time communism proved to be an economic and social system with severe limitations. Communist countries were top-heavy in state bureaucracy, consumer goods were often shoddy and in short supply, inefficiencies and delays were everywhere, and the promise of equality was lost in a society of privilege for the elite and misery for the masses. By the late 1980s and early 1990s communism collapsed under its own weight as the Soviet Union turned away from its collectivist system and embraced democratic capitalism. As the Berlin Wall was torn down and former communists became instant capitalists, there was a mood of finality as Western democratic nations declared that the competition between state control of the economy and the private marketplace was over. Capitalism had emerged victorious. Although China and a few other nations such as North Korea and Cuba remained nominally communist, even these stalwart proponents of Marxism introduced capitalist elements into their economies to take advantage of the opportunities of a brand-new world.

THE SYSTEMS

Political activity and government action eventually are directed toward public decisionmaking. The public decisions that are made and the public policies that result from those decisions shape and direct a state. As a result, the act of making those decisions and formulating policies becomes a critical part of politics and government. All organized states have developed systems for public decisionmaking. In a democratic setting that system often involves the interaction between the legislative and executive branches with legislators formulating the laws and executive officials implementing them. In authoritarian or nondemocratic settings public decisionmaking is usually not placed under the authority of legislative and executive institutions but is controlled by a single person or an elite body not bound by rules of representative lawmaking or set procedures for implementing and administering public policies. Although the system of democratic and authoritarian decisionmaking varies from state to state, recognized decisionmaking processes are frequently found in these two governing settings.

The most prominent and most frequently used legislative-executive decisionmaking system is parliamentary government. Often called the Westminster system because of its connection to the British government and its heritage of democratic politics, a parliamentary system is based on the principle of legislative sovereignty. States that adopt the parliamentary process of public decisionmaking place supreme power in the hands of the legislative body. A parliamentary system fuses power with links between the legislative and executive bodies. The head of government, usually a prime minister or premier, is a member of the legislature whose political party or coalition of parties has gained a majority of the seats in the legislature. Parliamentary government thus functions on a strict majoritarian basis with the party or parties that gain the majority of the seats having the power to name the prime minister and cabinet and run the government. If that party or coalition of parties maintains its majority, it continues to control government and pass legislation. Minority parties have few opportunities to stop or overturn the public policies of the majority, unless the majority crumbles as members leave the fold.

Parliamentary government has been a popular form of government and the model for legislative-executive relations throughout the world because it has a simplicity of operation and offers an effective, efficient governing process. The party that wins the most seats in the legislature forms the government; that government earns the right to make public policy without challenge from the opposition or from an independent executive or powerful judiciary. The principle of parliamentary sovereignty means that decisions made by the majority government have the full weight of law. The decisionmaking process is changed when the voters elect a new majority, which forms a new government and utilizes parliamentary sovereignty to its programmatic advantage.

While the parliamentary system may seem to allow for majoritarian abuse, in reality control by the government requires a great deal of negotiation and consensus building behind the scenes and before the final vote is taken. The effectiveness and efficiency of the parliamentary system does not mean that alternative views are dismissed or that laws are made in a hurry. But when the majority government has the support that it needs and a public policy is agreed on, the lawmaking process proceeds with a high level of assurance and the implementation stage is conducted by a government that is part of the legislative majority.

Although the parliamentary system is by far the most popular democratic process for public decisionmaking, the presidential system offers another method of organizing the interaction between the legislative and executive branches of government. A presidential system is built on the principle of separation of powers and checks and balances. Three branches of government, the legislative, the executive, and the judicial, have specific powers. Spreading decisionmaking power among the three branches of government restrains political leaders from assuming too much governing control, and neither the legislature, the executive, nor the judiciary becomes a dominant force in government. What results is a check and balance process, with each branch wary of the power of the other branches. The process of public decisionmaking is complex and demanding in a presidential system because it is possible to have the executive come from one political party and the legislature controlled by another party. In a presidential system the chief executive is elected directly by the voting populace, which can lead to two opposing parties controlling two decisionmaking bodies. This fosters a natural partisan tension that further restrains power.

Because the presidential system separates powers instead of fusing them, public decisionmaking is often subject to delays, unpredictability, and even gridlock. The presidential system is not characterized by efficiency and effectiveness but depends on bargaining, compromise, and stamina as the interaction between the three branches of government creates a governing system in which success is not guaranteed and policy initiatives may take years to reach fruition. Although the presidential system guards against the possibility of majoritarian excess, it is not designed to respond quickly to problems or to assure voters that promises will be kept and acted on. Supporters of the presidential system emphasize that controlling governing power and fostering partisan tension subject the public policy process to intense scrutiny and cautious development.

Whether policymaking is done by party majority and parliamentary sovereignty or by separation of powers and partisan tension, the democratic process of arriving at public decisions is open, competitive, and guided by established rules. This is not the case with authoritarian political systems that reject democratic principles and practice. The authoritarian political and government setting places the state and state power above the individual. The political leadership is not committed to individual participation in the process of decisionmaking through elections, party activity, or dissent. The governing structure centralizes the executive and administrative functions. Authoritarianism is a top-down system that severely limits citizen involvement in the state and often punishes citizens for attempts to steer the system toward greater democracy.

The authoritarian model of public decisionmaking has a number of key characteristics. Authoritarian states often concentrate power in the hands of one individual or a group of individuals. The political leadership can be associated with the military, a single political party, a ruling family, or even a group of religious leaders. This leader and the elite that forms around him have little interest in using governing institutions to formulate public policies. They use politics and government to promote personal objectives, often simply to stay in power. Laws and rules are secondary to authoritarian leaders and governmental processes are mere window dressing. In an authoritarian state alternative viewpoints and persons promoting alternative viewpoints are not permitted. There is no concept of a loyal opposition, and those who challenge the existing leadership and leadership elite are subject to a range of sanctions, including violence and terror. Authoritarianism in short creates an armed state in which citizens have little if any political standing.

An authoritarian state creates a strange sort of efficiency and effectiveness. Debate over public policies is often a conversation between a few members of the elite or the direct order of the leader. There are no partisan wrangles, procedural delays, or concern over the view of the majority. Authoritarianism establishes the ultimate in streamlined governance as there are no institutional barriers and legal restraints are ignored. Authoritarianism does not guarantee that public policy decisions will be wise or necessary. Because the process is centralized and personalized around the whim of the leader, tragic mistakes can be made and the state led down a tragic road of failed policies and repression. But as long as the leader and his supporters can maintain order, the process is uncontested and free from reform. The Achilles' heel of an authoritarian system is the lack of a formalized agreement on succession. The political leader and the political elite stay in power as long as they can hold on to power. In some cases power may be informally handed down to relatives or close associates, but usually authoritarianism is the governmental equivalent to the old game of King of the Hill, where power is maintained by the leader who outlives his opponents.

Whether it has a parliamentary, presidential, or authoritarian system of decisionmaking, each country places its own mark on how these political arrangements and governmental structures are organized. These systems often end up as hybrids, unique mixtures that respond to the individual conditions and identity of each country. There is a vast gulf between decisionmaking in parliamentary and presidential systems and authoritarianism: parliamentary and presidential decisionmaking pulls citizens into the process of decisionmaking, while authoritarianism denies citizens the opportunity to be part of the political and governing system. This is a fundamental and critical difference.

THE INSTITUTIONS

Politics and governing come together in the various decisionmaking institutions created by the state. Institutions are the places where decisions are actually made. But institutions are not just the buildings or the people that occupy them; they are the rules, procedures, traditions, and informal arrangements that form the framework of decisionmaking. Public decisionmaking does not just happen. There must be an institutional method or mode of operation for making decisions that is guided by the above mentioned rules, procedures, traditions, and informal arrangements.

The institutional framework of politics and governing begins with the legislature. Although legislatures make laws, they also serve as great meeting and debating societies where legislators can freely present their arguments for or against a particular public policy. The meeting and debating function of legislatures flows from their responsibility to be a representative body that transmits the views and wishes of the citizenry into the decisionmaking arena. Also important, legislatures usually exercise an oversight function in which they ensure that legislation is properly implemented and that government officials carry out their responsibilities according to the law. Finally, legislatures serve as service institutions that solve constituency problems and assist constituents through the governing process. Lawmaking may be the highest calling of the legislature, but constituency service is the true representative function of legislators.

The constitution of the state usually mandates the structure and the responsibility of the legislature. In the modern world most legislatures are bicameral in nature, meaning that they are formed around two decisionmaking houses. How legislators populate these two houses varies from state to state, but the key ingredient in bicameralism is that it creates a competition and a tension that influences lawmaking. Often one legislative body has powers that differ from those of the other body. Constitutions are very precise in specifying the duties and responsibilities of each legislative body, granting them extensive lawmaking powers or a role in the lawmaking process. The differentiation of power between the legislative bodies lays the groundwork for eventual disagreements over public policies and the manner in which public policy becomes law. The bicameral nature of the legislature with its competition and tension fosters a dynamic environment that is not only representative but partisan. Because of this dynamic environment, public policymaking can be contentious and partisan. In many respects legislatures are the true democratic institutions where policies are debated, citizens are served, organized viewpoints are permitted to clash, and of course laws are made and monitored.

Executives compete with legislatures for decisionmaking power. Chief executives such as presidents or premiers are charged with seeing that public policies are properly executed or implemented. In order to accomplish this critical task executives are provided with specific constitutional powers.

These powers often include the ability to appoint key cabinet members and advisers, the general management of the economy and leadership of the military during time of war, and overseeing the foreign affairs of the nation. In some countries executives are given broader powers to issue decrees that have the force of law and to exercise emergency powers during periods of crisis. The primary responsibility of executives, however, is to run the government, in effect to be the CEO of the large public organization called the state.

The responsibility of running the state requires that the chief executive interact with the legislature. As mentioned earlier, in a parliamentary system the executive partners with the legislature in the policymaking process, while in a presidential system the executive often competes with the legislature. Whatever the arrangement and the process, the executive is the recognized head of the government; he or she represents the country to the outside world and leads the country in both domestic and external affairs. In the contemporary era chief executives have amassed great power and responsibility. Because problems facing a country require quick, decisive action along with one voice explaining the action, presidents and premiers have emerged as the dominant governing figure in most states. Legislatures may make the laws, provide the money, and monitor the implementation, but it is the executives who take the lead in managing public policy and ensuring that the country and the people they represent are well served.

Chief executives who have the skill to deal with legislative competition and provide inspirational and effective leadership can amass considerable power. They can use their position to rally public opinion to achieve a particular goal or to weaken the position of their legislative adversaries. Because chief executives are in the center of the public policy process and run government, they face enormous pressures to produce results and achieve the promises made to the general citizenry. Chief executives are in a real sense lonely warriors fighting to advance their agenda. They do not have the luxury of legislative bodies that are made up of hundreds of representatives and can blame the other party or one house or one ideological grouping. Chief executives in a democratic setting are the political and governing leaders. There are few places to hide from the responsibility that is placed on the shoulders of one individual.

Many times overlooked as a decisionmaking institution is the judiciary. A court system with a national responsibility and specific constitutional and statutory powers exists in most countries. These courts and the justices that make up the courts offer advisory opinions on key issues or exercise authority on matters that do not put them at odds with the sovereign policymakers. The judicial branch in most governing situations is limited in its ability to make public policy through its legal opinions or overturn decisions made by the legislative and executive branches. In a few countries such as the United States, Germany, and to a lesser extent France, judiciaries have the power of judicial review: the ability to declare existing laws unconstitutional and therefore null and void. Judicial review interjects the judiciary into the policy process and makes the courts powerful players in government.

In countries with a powerful judiciary the justices view the cases that come to them in terms of constitutional and statutory law. The justices interpret the law, apply it to the specific circumstances of the case, and make a determination that can retain the status quo, make an adjustment to existing policies, or throw out those policies. In countries with a powerful judiciary the separation of powers system or parliamentary sovereignty has been transformed into a more complex decisionmaking process. Existing laws or proposed laws cannot be assumed final or beyond review, since the courts may choose to exercise their power.

As the institutional framework of government developed over time, a distinction developed between the executive and bureaucratic branches. The executive has traditionally incorporated all sectors of government charged with implementing public policies and serving the needs of the nation and the people. But as government grew because its responsibilities multiplied, the bureaucratic sector of government came to be viewed as a separate entity. Today the executive branch is often thought of as the office of the president, premier, or head of state, while the bureaucracy has become the cabinet secretariats, independent agencies, regulatory bodies, and quasi-public corporations that form the administrative arm of the state. In many countries the bureaucracy has become a huge public organization, often the largest and most influential employer, with enormous power to affect the lives of the citizens and chart the direction of the state.

Bureaucracies in theory implement public policy, but their job description has changed dramatically in the modern era. As bureaucracies implement public policy, they have wide latitude to write the rules and regulations under which the policy will be implemented. The rules and regulations provide the details of the public policy and its implementation. Furthermore, the bureaucracy actually spends the money that lawmakers attach to the public policy. A law is a broad outline of policy, as well as a broad spending document that ensures implementation. By controlling the distribution of the money associated with a public policy, the bureaucracy further expands its power and influence. The power to fill in the blanks with the details of public policies and then to control the distribution of appropriations linked to the policy makes the bureaucracy a force to reckon with in government.

Then there is the regulatory aspect of bureaucratic activity. Some bureaucratic entities have been formed to regulate various key sectors of society and the state. Legislatures, responding to citizen pressure and recognizing the need for oversight, have established regulatory agencies and given them authority to set appropriate standards of practice and behavior. Regulatory agencies monitor the nuclear industry, food and drugs, the environment, banking, insurance, stocks, communication, and utilities. There are few key sectors of society, particularly in the advanced industrial world, that are not influenced by a regulatory body. Regulatory bureaucracies have powers ranging from setting common standards, inspecting facilities, licensing individuals or corporations, recalling consumer items, and punishing violators of existing rules. Those that interact with regulatory agencies or require their approval become part of an adversarial relationship as government intervenes in private sector ownership and activity. Despite the potential for disagreement and conflict over government regulation, the societal benefits of establishing a check on key sectors of the economy can outweigh the costs of intervention.

Another significant trend in decisionmaking institutions is the centralization of power in the national government. Again in large part because of the expanded role of government and the need to address societal problems on a national basis, many policies are developed and administered by the central authority. This centralization of policymaking authority has come at the expense of local government. Local governments continue to control key services such as fire, police, and education and serve as the grassroots source of public opinion and democratic participation. But increasingly the national bureaucracy or the provincial or regional government controls the financial resources and issues key regulations that determine the structure and direction of local services. In most countries a working relationship has been formed between the center and the local government to ensure that local needs are met and that centrally administered policies are properly implemented. The fact remains, however, that the ability to control, distribute, and utilize resources to support a system based on centralized administration and regulation clearly places the central authority in the policy driver's seat.

The relationship between the central government and local government has been established within certain systems of power and authority. The two most common systems are unitary and federal governance. The unitary system, as the word suggests, places most of the policymaking and implementing power in the hands of the central government. Local governments are well organized and active and play a role in key service areas, but it is the central government that controls the primary elements of policy, including tax collection, budget authority, and administrative guidance. In a federal system there is greater sharing of power and responsibility between the central government and governing units such as the states. In federalism the states and the central government have specific areas of policy responsibility that the other has a limited role in. There are also specific areas of policy that the states and the central government can exercise jointly. By spreading around the power and setting limits and specific responsibilities, federalism creates countervailing power, in effect limiting power all around and fostering competition for control of public policy. In a federal system local government engages in a power struggle with both central and state authority, which often controls the resources and issues regulations that affect towns and villages. In unitary and federal systems local government usually answers to a higher authority and has only marginal control over key public policy areas.

Establishing central governing control has become more difficult in the wake of growing ethnic, racial, tribal, and religious cleavages in many countries. The effort to create national governments from disparate regions or by unifying ethnic, racial, or religious enclaves has been a critical challenge facing political leaders in the modern world. Some countries have sought to form confederations, extending federalism to form nations in which individual states have a loose alliance with a central governing authority but retain significant public policy control. Confederations permit the retention of local control that is based on ethnicity, race, tribal affiliation, and religious belief but foster a parochialism that makes nation-state formation difficult, if not impossible. The proliferation of breakaway states formed on the basis of specific identity factors has rejuvenated local government and local authority but has weakened the central administration of the state and more importantly the power of the nation-state to establish unity from regions, peoples, and identities.

THE WORLDS

So far politics and government have been discussed in a rather abstract manner that does not tie terms, concepts, processes, and systems to the real world and real-world situations. The real world of politics and government is largely conducted within the confines of the nation-state and among nation-states. But the institutions of government exist within nation-states, and it is within nation-states that these institutions make policy decisions regarding a whole range of public issues and concerns. The nation-states that have established sovereign boundaries can be defined and described in numerous ways: land area, population, ethnic and religious makeup, natural resources, economic growth, level of individual prosperity, and structure of politics and government. If there is a word to describe the world of nation-states, it is "diversity." With 190 nation-states currently claiming sovereign status, formulating a precise definition is a major challenge.

During most of the Cold War period, from 1945 to the early 1990s, nation-states were organized around a series of worlds: the first world or industrial nations that were largely European and North American, the second world of communist countries led by the Soviet Union, and the third world of developing countries in Africa, Asia, the Middle East, and Latin America. This tripartite organization brought a semblance of order to the world of nation-states, even though there were countless distinctions within each of these worlds. But once the Cold War ended and communism lost its allure, the second world faded from view. The Soviet Union broke up and the countries aligned with the Soviet Union sought to divorce themselves from the communist system. The industrial world of democratic countries remained intact and became the model of national development. The remaining countries of the world, which were largely poor and in debt, were left to compete in a new world, a world increasingly defined in terms of globalization. A globalized world is one in which there is an ever widening array of contacts—corporate, trade, investment, cultural, and human—that form a more integrated world community and foster linkages that break down traditional nation-state barriers.

As globalization set in around the world and became the model for economic development, nation-states were identified in terms of the success they had achieved in adopting the new system within their borders. The distinctions that evolved to group or categorize nations were often based on whether they were high income, middle income, or low income or whether they provided their people with a high level of human development, a medium level, or a low level (with human development determined by indices such as education, literacy, and life expectancy). The world of nation-states thus evolved into a listing of which countries were "making it" in the new global environment and which nations had fallen behind in the race to acquire wealth and develop. Separate distinctions were made among the countries such as recognizing some nation-states as "newly industrialized," suggesting that they were breaking through their less developed status and approaching membership in the industrialized world.

Another approach to categorizing the nation-states of the world is through what has come to be called the "clash of civilizations." Harvard professor Samuel Huntington developed a view of the post–Cold War world in which he defined the diversity of nation-states in terms of cultural unity rather than sovereignty. Huntington identified nine separate cultural traditions: Sinic (Chinese), Japanese, Hindu, Buddhist, Islamic, Western, Latin American, African, and Orthodox (Russian and Eastern European). In Huntington's view these cultural groupings describe how the people of the world will identify themselves in the post–Cold War world. While nation-states will remain and citizens of nation-states will continue to hold nationalistic sentiments, the cultural linkages tied primarily to language and religion will become the dominant factors of identity. Furthermore, and more disturbing, Huntington believes that the conflicts of the future will be based on these cultural groupings and not on disputes between nation-states. The cultural approach to organizing the nations of the world has come under attack as too simplistic and failing to understand the power of allegiance to individual countries. Nevertheless, Huntington's cultural approach and the prospect of a clash of civilizations has remained a method of grouping nation-states and analyzing their potential behavior that has garnered a great deal of interest and support.

Although the post–Cold War world has generated a number of ways in which to make sense of the diversity of the 190 nation-states, at the core the most accurate approach to looking at these sovereign entities is in terms of wealth. A huge gap exists between the wealthy countries of the world and countries gripped by varying levels of poverty. Industrial countries in Europe and North America that provide data to international organizations like the United Nations number only 33 out of the 190. These wealthy countries have economies that generate gross national product per capita incomes from $9,200 to well over $30,000. This industrial elite is followed by the so-called middle-income countries (GNP per capita from $756 to $9,200) and includes a mix of Latin American, Eastern European, and Asian states. These middle-income countries number about 70. Finally there are the poorest of the world's nation-states with GNP per capita incomes of $755 or less. There are currently nearly 60 of these nations, mostly located in Africa and the Middle East.

Categorizing nation-states according to economic statistics provides only half of the analysis. A more serious distinction is the growing income gap that is developing between the industrial countries and all the rest. While the globalization system has brought a degree of prosperity to some countries, it has not closed the gap between rich and poor countries. In fact the growing divide between the rich and poor countries is becoming the most telling method of categorizing nation-states and understanding the real world of international politics and government. According to data from the United Nations Human Development Report (2001), the poorest 10 percent of the world's people had only 1.6 percent of the income of the richest 10 percent; further, the richest 1 percent of the world's people received as much income as the poorest 57 percent. It is estimated that 1.2 billion people live on $1 a day, and 2.8 billion on less than $2 a day.

This income gap is not just an issue of unequal distribution of the world's wealth; it can contribute to raising tension and conflict within countries where inequality is high and also between the industrial world and all the countries that reside in poverty. United Nations Secretary-General Kofi Annan has stated publicly that unless the rich countries of the world, along with the major multinational corporations, begin a massive redistribution of wealth, anarchy is likely to grow in less developed nations, as well as terrorist acts by persons who want to strike out at the sources of the inequality—the major industrial powers. Annan called for a massive foreign aid program at the World Economic Summit in 2002 that would provide $100 billion in new assistance to the less developed world to help alleviate inequality and the dangerous effects of inequality.

The most significant debate surrounding the issues of poverty, income inequality, and the countries of the world is the impact of the new globalized system based on free trade, foreign investment, private sector development, and contracted state involvement in the domestic and international economy. Globalization has replaced the Cold War ideological contest between capitalism and communism. In today's world nation-states have little option but to organize their internal economies around the principles, values, and structures of globalization. Although extensive evidence points to the benefits of a nation-state entering the global economy and abiding by its rules, there is also evidence that globalization has created uneven growth in the less developed world and has done little to correct the disastrous effects of the income gap. There are constant arguments over whether nation-states that remain mired in poverty have adequately adopted the global model of development or whether the model is flawed and actually perpetuates existing inequalities. But what is certain is that huge differences continue between an elite core of industrial nations and a large cohort of countries that have only experienced modest growth and modest prosperity.

The eight countries that are discussed in this text exist in a world of stark differences and enormous challenges. The political and ideological competition that marked the Cold War period has been replaced with economic and cultural competition brought on by the rise of the globalized system based on market capitalism. The process of comparison that serves as the framework of this text is thus carried out on a number of levels (i.e., comparisons of politics and governance, decisionmaking and policy implementation, citizen participation and state power). But these comparisons exist within a larger context of a new world system, a globalized system of countless financial and corporate interactions, endless movement of people and products, and an economic culture founded on the principles of individualism, privateness, and competition. As the discussion in this book moves from country to country, the global system is always in the background, influencing the function of politics and government, shaping the decisionmaking and policy implementation process, and directing the actions of citizens and states. All eight countries are fundamentally different and yet all are part of a similar global system. The task of describing these eight countries is to present the unique elements of their political and governing systems, while showing the common challenges that each faces in the new world of globalization.

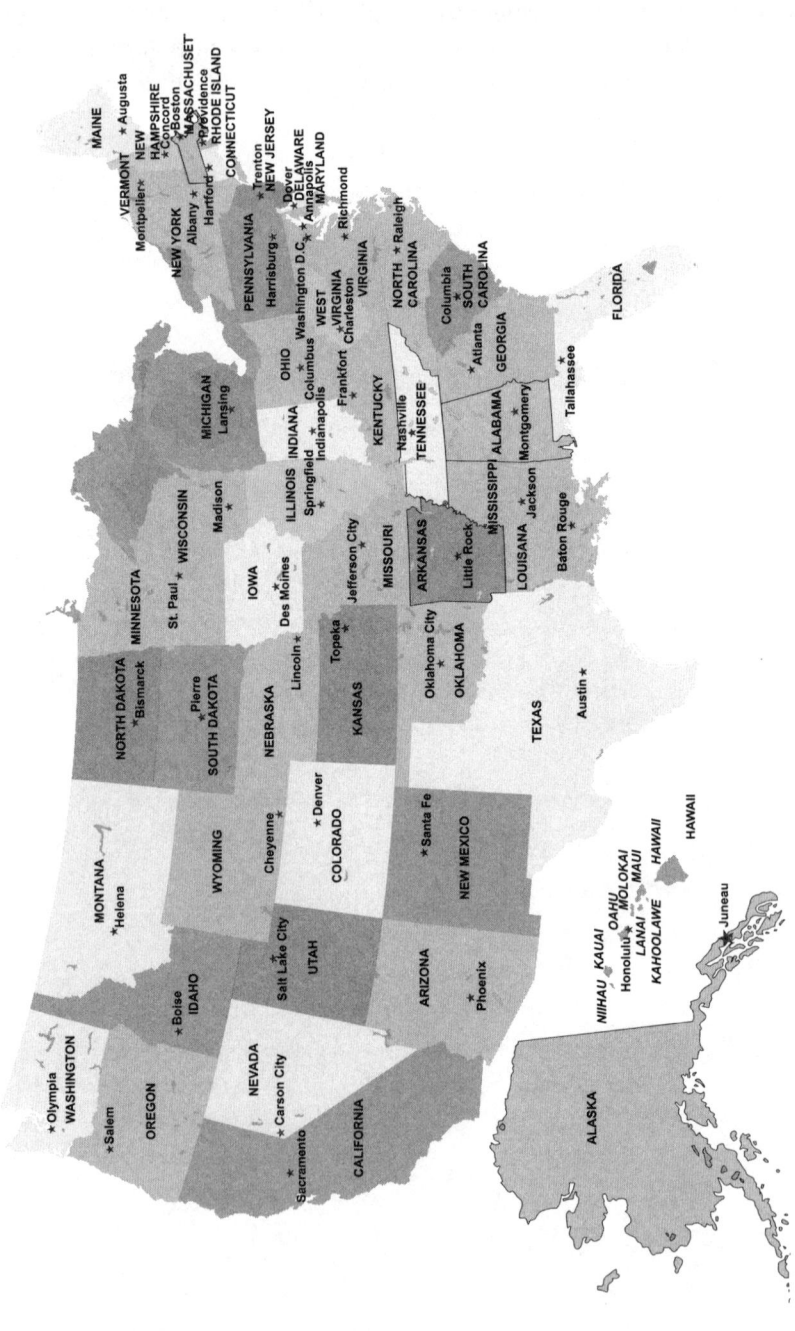

MAP 1.1 United States

United States of America

Data Bank

Area: 3,618,770 sq. miles
Population: 270,312,000 (2000 census)
Rural/urban population ratio: 24/76
Ethnic makeup: 69 percent white, 13 percent Hispanic,
   12 percent black, 4 percent Asian, 0.7 percent Amerindian
Life expectancy: Male, 74 years; female, 80 years
Adult literacy: 97 percent
Form of government: Federal republic
Head of state: George W. Bush
Per capita income/GDP: $37,600 (2002)
Exports: $663 billion; imports $912 billion
   (partners: Canada, Mexico, Japan)
Source: United Nations and World Bank

SETTING THE SCENE

Since this is a comparative politics text, it is perhaps best to begin discussing the U.S. government with a quote from a British observer, James Bryce. Writing in his commentary *The American Commonwealth* (1888), Bryce says this about American democracy and the American governing system: "There is in the American government . . . a want of unity. The Sailors, the helmsman, the engineer, do not seem to have one purpose or obey one will, so that instead of making steady way the vessel may pursue a devious or zigzag course, and sometimes merely turn round and round in the water."

To an outside observer the American political system may seem like a great seagoing ship with the capacity to forge ahead toward its destination, but for some reason the ship is unable to keep a steady course, occasionally floundering and then somehow reaching safe harbor. This giant ship of state that Bryce sought to make sense of was originally constructed so that travel through the sea of politics would not be direct, predictable, or speedy. The architects of American government envisioned their ship of state as characterized by caution, compromise, and gradualism. Although the ship has the capacity to move swiftly ahead, the captain, the crew, and the passengers have accepted the navigational rules and take pride in the fact that there are regular zigzags and an occasional aimless circling in the ocean.

To those unfamiliar with the American way of running public affairs, the maze of hurdles and obstacles that stand in the way of completing a policy initiative is puzzling. On the one hand the United States is a world superpower, a nation of wealth and prosperity. And yet it has a government that sometimes can't seem to make up its mind and certainly doesn't allow for quick decisions or efficient decisionmaking. Rather, it glories in creating extensive controls on power and moving cautiously when making public policy decisions.

The governing document that came out of the deliberations in Philadelphia in the summer of 1787 guaranteed that the manner in which this country conducted its public business would be guided by the principles of caution, compromise, and gradualism. This would not be a government that made quick decisions, centralized power, or permitted popular control of policymaking. This would be a conservative government concerned with abuse of office, protection of property, and potential excesses of the majority.

If the Founding Fathers had a primary objective as they wrote the Constitution, it was to find the most practical and acceptable way to preserve unity. In their mind the best way to accomplish that objective was to give something to everyone, but never to give someone everything. The government of the United States of America is thus a patchwork of powers and restraints, rights and restrictions, state and central governments, majorities and elites. But this patchwork is not designed to streamline decisionmaking or to respond efficiently to a national crisis or to paper over partisan or regional differences. This governing system is designed to frustrate power and the powerful, force bargaining between opposing camps, and attain policy solutions that are always "half a loaf."

While the governing climate in the United States is a reflection of the Founders' concern with unrestrained power, the character of politics that exists today is undergoing enormous change. The terrorist attacks of September 11, 2001, changed the status and the role of government in the United States. As Americans stood horrified at the human loss and physical devastation, they turned to government for answers and protection. In one sad day the government of the United States and public officials moved to center stage in national life. Trust and support of the government rose significantly during the aftermath of September 11. There was evidence of increased job applications for the Central Intelligence Agency, the Federal Bureau of Investigation, and the Federal Sky Marshals Office.

There was also a narrowing of personal freedoms as American citizens began to accept the reality of expanding security. Contrary to the wishes of the Founding Fathers, government post–September 11 became more powerful and more intrusive. Civil libertarians and human rights advocates questioned the extent to which individual liberties and legal protections were being quashed for those individuals who in some way were linked to terrorist groups. There were also numerous charges of arbitrary and prolonged detentions, increased surveillance powers, erosion of trial rights, and restrictions on foreigners and those seeking asylum. Although most Americans did not seem concerned with the clampdown on those who were being targeted by the government, there was no doubt that in post–September 11 America the rules established by the Bill of Rights had changed in the favor of government power. The need for heightened security and monitoring of foreigners intensified further after the Bush administration decided to invade Iraq. Terror alerts were elevated and photos of suspected operatives of al-Qaeda were published widely.

But September 11 did not change everything about American government. There are some political constants that will likely remain unaffected by the war on terrorism. In a matter of weeks the Congress passed the USA Patriot Act, a sweeping antiterrorism bill that gave the government new powers to deport foreign nationals who support terrorists, monitor money laundering, broaden surveillance powers, including e-mail, voice mail, and Internet, and expand intelligence-gathering capabilities. President Bush proudly signed the bill as an example of bipartisan cooperation. But a few weeks later the Congress was gridlocked over a proposal to federalize the security workers at the nation's airports. Although the Senate passed the bill to federalize the workers, House Republicans opposed the measure because it would increase the number of federal employees and strengthen the ranks of unionized workers in the government. The president was finally able to get the legislation passed but only after much partisan bickering and executive-legislative "zigging and zagging." Later in 2002 President Bush faced intense opposition from the Democrats over his Homeland Security Bill, which would streamline the organization of government to provide a more effective response to terrorism. Democrats, while agreeing with the intent of the bill, were concerned over federal worker rights and the paucity of money that was allocated for state and local responses to a terrorist attack. After much wrangling and give and take President Bush signed the bill, again after much "zigging and zagging."

While there is a long litany of examples in which the U.S. government was caught in partisan and institutional confrontations leading to gridlock or at best highly compromised solutions, there has been a high level of partisan agreement over the importance of money as the engine that drives democratic government. As has been said so often, "money is the mother's milk of American politics." The capitalist economy that serves as the foundation of American society has fostered a political environment where participation is often viewed as writing a check to a candidate or a political party, not in the traditional sense of voting, communicating, petitioning, and protesting. The federal courts have legitimized political giving by agreeing with the check writers that money is a form of free expression protected by the First Amendment to the Constitution. As a result American politics has become an endless quest for dollars: dollars for television ads, dollars to pay teams of consultants, dollars for travel, dollars for bumper stickers and silly hats, and dollars to pour into "war chests" to ensure that opponents will not have an edge in the race for public office. In 1996 the cost of all federal elections was $2 billion. Four years later in 2000 the bill for federal elections had increased to $3 billion.

In 2002 Congress, in the wake of the Enron financial collapse and evidence of substantial political contributions by the failed company members to both parties, passed a sweeping campaign finance reform bill that did away with "soft money" contributions to political parties but permitted increased private contributions (up to $4,000 per person, per candidate). Both houses of Congress struggled over the language of the bill and its implications for party effectiveness and interest group leverage. There were also lingering concerns about the impact of the legislation on freedom of speech issues and inevitable constitutional challenges. In the end Congress made the most significant reforms in the way money is collected and spent in the public arena since the 1970s, but not without heated partisan wrangling and grave reluctance to move to an uncertain process for campaign financing.

This campaign feeding frenzy of money, groups, and access is a long way from the concerns that James Madison expressed in his famous *Federalist 10* essay written to support ratification of the Constitution. To Madison the greatest fear of a popular government was the tendency toward faction and factional disputes. If Madison were around today, he would likely change "faction" to "group," but the real change would be in how he might interpret the danger that group behavior posed in the money-driven atmosphere of campaign politics. Madison originally thought that the federal constitution with its numerous restraints on power and power-sharing formulas with the states would provide a sufficient check on factions with their tendency to divide the nation. Madison, however, never envisioned thousands of groups using their dollars to attract the attention of political leaders with their own separate cause and separate agenda. Madison's concern over factional disputes involving religion, region, and class have in the modern era been transformed into interest groups using their financial resources to shape public policy to their narrow designs.

Lost in this modern, access-driven group politics is the concept of national interest, or more appropriately the common good. American politics is today a far cry from the classic interpretation of democracy, often termed pluralism. Pluralism defines democracy as an open and fair interplay of groups advancing the interests of the people. Pluralism means that group formation and participation are part of a level playing field as citizens seek to advance their interests through organizations that speak for them in the political arena. But the pluralistic vision of democracy has been coopted by the moneyed elite who use their financial resources to tilt the political process in their favor, often in ways that flaunt the national interest. Somewhere along the way popular politics with political equality and limitless political opportunity got lost. There are some who fight city hall alone or have the courage and perseverance to advance their cause without the luxury of campaign contributions. But these democrats are a dying breed.

An American political climate with a governing environment marked by caution, compromise, and gradualism combined with a democratic system that has been severely tainted by money and influence peddling and a citizenry that sees public policy made in self-interest, not national interest, is an unhealthy mix. Bringing fundamental change to the political system is inherently difficult given the power of entrenched interests and the power that money can bring to bear on politicians. With the system driven by narrow interests, the American people often throw up their hands in disgust and walk away from the political arena. The result is a governing system that functions, but not from a solid base of citizen support. The United States may be the world's greatest democracy, as Americans leaders often boast, but the greatness is more a result of wealth, military power, and entrepreneurial energy, rather than open access to government, citizen involvement in politics, and widespread respect for political leaders.

POLITICAL MILESTONES

The political development of the United States has, as in most countries, not been a smooth and agreed-on process of change. A combination of a diverse population, deep-seated regional differences, fundamental disagreements over the role of government in society, and of course a system of policymaking marked by the ever present zigzagging have had a profound impact on the U.S. response to internal and external challenges. Fortunately for the

United States, the evolution of its political system has been marked by only a few major crises that have called into question its approach to governance and its vision of the "good society." Nevertheless, there have been distinct periods in American political history when both the national leadership and the people were forced to make major institutional and policy decisions in order to protect the governing system and ensure that it retained the capacity to respond to a range of challenges and threats.

During these critical periods the American political system functioned in a manner that reflected the character and quality of the constitutional framework. Responses to crises and challenges were resolved through bargaining and compromise; gradualism and delay were important tactics of avoiding confrontation and fragmentation; the rule of law rather than of powerful individuals carried the day and the concept of incremental change, now termed "muddling through," became the first best option for consensus building. These systemic ingredients serve as the foundation of the American political system and the keys to political and social stability over time.

National Supremacy and the Civil War

The debates associated with writing the Constitution signaled the obstacles and challenges that lay ahead for the new nation. The core of the problem that would face U.S. political leaders was found in disagreements over national supremacy, states' rights, and slavery. It became obvious in Philadelphia that serious divisions existed between northern and southern states over the distribution of governing power and the appropriateness of maintaining and spreading a system of human bondage. The compromises that permitted the Constitution to be completed and ratified postponed the inevitable clash over who would have the edge in making national policy: the federal government in Washington or the individual state capitals.

While the political system in the early formative years of the 1800s concentrated on addressing federal issues such as taxation of the national banking system, control over domestic commerce, and the extent of executive power, there remained a constant drumbeat of controversy over slavery and its implications for governing power. Voices in the North favored a strong central government with the power to dictate policy decisions to the states. These voices were joined by the abolitionist movement that sought the complete eradication of slavery as a moral evil. Southern states' rights advocates bristled at the thought of the federal government intervening in local issues and defended slavery as an established and necessary part of the agricultural economy. Many Southern leaders felt that the North was anxious to cripple the region and impoverish its plantation system.

The battle over governing power between North and South was waged on a number of fronts. Southern political leaders like Senator John C. Calhoun of South Carolina attempted to introduce alternatives to the existing constitutional principle of national supremacy. Calhoun's doctrine of "concurrent majority" sought to create a relationship between federal and state government in which a region—the South—would have the right to veto the actions of the majority—the North. The Congress, on the other hand, sought to use its power to limit the expansion of slavery, despite the protestations of Southern politicians. In 1820 Congress passed the Missouri Compromise, which permitted slavery in existing states but stopped its expansion to new states. The Missouri Compromise, however, was declared unconstitutional by the Supreme Court (using its newfound power of judicial review for the second time) in its 1857 decision in *Dred Scott v. Sanford*. In the decision the Court stated that slaves were property and therefore protected, even in states that had outlawed slavery. As the country went back and forth over the issue of national supremacy, states' rights, and slavery, the North and South moved further and further apart and prepared for war.

With both sides in this great debate intensifying their efforts to advance the cause of federal control or states' rights, the customary culture of balance, compromise, and consensus that had protected the country from regimentation broke down. On April 12, 1861, the first shots of the Civil War were fired on Fort Sumter in Charleston, South Carolina. For the next four years the nation endured a bloody civil war as American fought American over a way of life and a method of governing. The Civil War, with the ultimate victory of the North and the devastating collapse of the South, put to rest, at least for a time, the issue of where the power would lie in the United States. The Union had been preserved, the promoters of states' rights had been silenced, and slavery was officially ended. Although the issue of states' rights had been pushed off the political stage, an underlying antagonism persisted between those who supported the unifying capacity of the federal government and those who maintained the level of local control that states' rights provided American citizens. This disagreement returned to the forefront of American politics during the civil rights era.

The Struggle for Women's Suffrage

The question of who should receive the right to vote was not a burning issue during the Constitutional Convention. The Founders operated from the position that men, particularly men of property and wealth, would likely make up the voting population. Ultimately the right to vote was awarded to the states, where again it was understood that suffrage would remain in the hands of males. In the early presidential elections, the Electoral College, with its elite nature, controlled who would become the chief executive. Only in elections for the House of Representatives was there some semblance of popular voting, again excluding women, Native Americans, and slaves. The era of Jacksonian democracy saw the expansion of male voting to the western states and the agricultural sector, but the movement toward real expansion of suffrage was slow and severely limited.

The first signs of political activism among women occurred at the Seneca Falls, New York, Women's Rights Convention (1848). Although the convention had a broad agenda, including the abolition of slavery, American women were willing to speak out loudly against being excluded from the political process. Unfortunately, the Civil War and the postwar era of economic development and industrialization put a damper on the women's suffrage movement. Furthermore, women continued to encounter roadblocks on the way to gaining the vote. For example, the language of the Fifteenth Amendment guarantees that the right to vote cannot be denied based on "race, color or previous condition of servitude" but fails to include gender as a protected category.

The effort to attain voting rights that started in Seneca spawned a number of women's political groups that actively campaigned for suffrage. Groups such as the National American Woman Suffrage Association and the National Women's Party, along with legendary women's advocates such as Elizabeth Cady Stanton and Susan B. Anthony, elevated the fight for voting rights to a national issue. On many occasions the effort to secure the vote ran into male opposition as members of Congress and state legislatures, particularly in the South, stood firm in their belief that women should not be permitted participation in the political process.

Voting rights for women received a boost from the unlikely state of Wyoming with its cowboy culture. Before Wyoming applied for statehood in 1890, it had given women the right to vote and serve in its legislature. Wyoming leaders faced congressional opposition based on their support for women's suffrage. Wyoming political leaders stood their ground and refused admission to the Union on congressional terms. Congress eventually relented and before long over half of the existing states had followed suit and granted women the right to vote. The state-by-state approach, although successful, was viewed by women's leaders as piecemeal and without national legitimacy. The goal became a constitutional amendment.

With the states taking the lead in permitting women's suffrage, the move to attain national recognition with an amendment was successful in 1920. The Nineteenth Amendment to the Constitution added the following language: "The right of citizens of the United States to vote shall not be denied or abridged by the United States or by any state on account of sex. Congress shall have power to enforce this article by appropriate legislation." The long struggle to gain the vote came to an end, but suffrage advocates recognized that women would have to be encouraged to participate and take active roles in the political process.

The Great Depression

The relationship between economic conditions and politics is often critical. The status of a national economy can spur political action, while political decisions can influence the direction of the national economy. In the late 1920s and into the 1930s a severe economic decline in the United States crippled the nation and also touched off a major political debate over the proper role of government. As the Great Depression spread and engulfed more and more Americans, the issue of how involved the federal government should be in responding to the economic crisis and correcting the fundamental problems that caused the crisis took center stage.

The stock market crash of 1929, which turned wealthy speculators into paupers overnight, is usually viewed as the beginning of the Great Depression. The Crash was emblematic of the unregulated, pro-business atmosphere of the Harding, Coolidge, and Hoover administrations. The Crash began a long period of economic decline that worsened throughout the administration of Herbert Hoover. Hoover, like many of the captains of industry and finance in the country, believed that the economy would self-correct and would not require outside intervention. By 1932 the United States was in a deep depression with huge unemployment, bankruptcies, and foreclosures. These were desperate times that required new leadership and new ideas. In 1932 Franklin Delano Roosevelt was elected and gave the United States both.

Franklin Roosevelt was an unlikely leader to shake up the capitalist system and usher in a new vision of government and the economy. The son of wealth and prominence, Roosevelt nevertheless believed that the Depression required a radical departure from past practice. As Roosevelt stated in his inauguration address, "The people of the United States . . . in their need . . . have registered a mandate that they want direct, vigorous leadership. The have asked for discipline and direction under leadership. They have made me the present instrument of their wishes. . . . May God guide me in the days to come."

And guide is what Roosevelt did. In his first hundred days in office Roosevelt redefined the role of government in the national economy. During those one hundred days Roosevelt closed the banks and reformed the banking industry, passed a series of agricultural laws that provided relief to impoverished farmers, created the National Industrial Recovery Act (NRA) to reform and regulate the nation's industries, and initiated long needed changes in the securities industries. This was only the beginning. Roosevelt was determined to give the American people a New Deal economy and respond to the human needs of those affected by the Depression.

Roosevelt continued throughout his first and second terms in office to expand the role of government in the economy. His programs to put people to work (the Civilian Conservation Corps) and provide a baseline of income security (such as Social Security) made him a topic of ridicule and suspicion among the business elite. The private sector saw his programs as akin to socialism and too close to the Marxist experiment being undertaken in Soviet Russia. Roosevelt's attempt at broadening the Supreme Court because it overturned his NRA program and the Agricultural Adjustment Act was symptomatic of the economic tensions that existed in the political system. Yet these setbacks did not deter Roosevelt or stall the movement toward a more aggressive government involvement in the national economy. The American people overwhelmingly returned Roosevelt to office in 1936.

Up until Roosevelt and his New Deal, the president of the United States was never really viewed as an economic manager. Managing the economy was a task for the "invisible hand" of capitalism. But the Great Depression changed the rules of governance and allowed Roosevelt to chart a new course for the nation. With the New Deal, presidents were looked to for economic leadership and entrusted with ensuring that the nation never returned to those dark days of 1932. Furthermore, the New Deal established the national government as the employer of last resort, the regulator of the capitalist system, and the initiator of economic and social reforms.

The Civil Rights Era

The 1960s was a period of enormous change and controversy in the United States. At the center of this change and controversy was the movement of African Americans to attain their civil and political rights. Despite the Civil War amendments that abolished slavery, guaranteed equal protection of the laws, and secured the right to vote to African Americans, the status of race relations in the United States was marked by discrimination and segregation. African Americans were widely denied political rights, forced to endure countless discriminatory practices, and required to live and work and go to school in either segregated or clearly unequal circumstances. Although African Americans had quietly accepted their condition, by the late 1950s and 1960s the mood of race relations shifted dramatically from resignation to active protest.

The target of most of the protest against racism was in the South with its open policy of segregation and its firm belief in states' rights. Southern politicians supported policies of separation as morally legitimate and used their belief in states' rights as a shield against federal attempts to bring about change.

But with landmark judicial decisions such as the *Brown v. Board of Education* decision, which mandated the integration of public schools, and the high-profile protests of Rosa Parks and Dr. Martin Luther King, African American leaders began to openly challenge the system of discrimination and segregation.

The push for civil rights in the United States was a mix of high-profile marches in the South, federal-state confrontations, and tragic incidents of murder of innocent protesters. The civil rights movement gave birth to a number of new organizations designed to arouse support for the cause and challenge of the existing system of discrimination and segregation. Groups like the Congress on Racial Equality (CORE) and Martin Luther King's Southern Christian Leadership Conference became widely visible in protest marches, lunch counter sit-ins, and demonstrations that often led to arrests. To complement the efforts of African Americans, the federal government during the Kennedy administration aggressively sought to integrate the South, particularly in the area of higher education. The confrontation between the states' rights governor of Alabama, George Wallace, and federal marshals at the University of Alabama became a symbol of the gulf that existed between Washington policymakers and Southern political leaders. Finally, the senseless killings of civil rights workers, the bombings and burning of churches, and the assassination of Dr. King in 1968 proved that social change and social justice would not come without sadness and loss.

The constant pressure of the civil rights movement eventually achieved success as major legislative measures were approved by the United States Congress. The Lyndon Johnson administration was noted for its civil rights achievements. These include the Civil Rights Act of 1964, which forbids discrimination in places of accommodation and ensures that all Americans will not be denied employment because of race, color, religion, or sex, the Voting Rights Act of 1965, which put the full force of the U.S. government behind voting guarantees for African Americans, and the Civil Rights Act of 1968, which extended prohibition of discrimination to housing. While Southern political leaders railed against the expansive powers of the federal government in largely local if not private business matters, the tide had clearly turned against those who used the power of government to maintain a separate system of political rights, social relations, and economic opportunity.

The Reagan Presidency

Although change in the area of civil rights came as a result of public protest and political action, the normal route to change in the United States is the electoral process. Certainly the election of Franklin Delano Roosevelt in 1932 brought about a new response to the Great Depression and a new role for government. A similar watershed event in terms of the role of government in American society occurred with the election of Ronald Reagan in 1980. After almost fifty years of ever expanding government in the tradition of Roosevelt's New Deal, the presidency of Ronald Reagan created its own governing revolution, only this time big government was the target with its ingrained philosophy of taxing, regulating, and spending in the name of providing social programs and controlling business.

Ronald Reagan entered office in 1981 with a mission to rein in government and lessen its hold on the pocketbooks and business decisions of Americans. To Reagan the federal government had become bloated, mismanaged, costly, and interventionist. More importantly the government had become a drain on the American economy with its big-program, big-tax, big-regulation philosophy. The answer, according to the new president, would come to be called "supply-side economics," an approach that advocated significant tax cuts, rolled back government programs, and liberated business from costly regulations, all with the express purpose of increasing the "supply" of money and resources in the hands of Americans. Although critics of "supply side" viewed this as a thinly veiled attempt to lessen the tax load on business and the rich while weakening government, President Reagan sensed that the country was overwhelmed by the scope and the cost of modern government.

Once in office Reagan immediately went to work to craft a major tax cut, trim a number of programs from Medicaid to foreign aid, cut the employment rolls in government agencies, relax regulations on business, and generally create an environment where the private sector set the national agenda rather than the federal government. After years of liberal democratic programs added layer on layer of spending and regulation, Reagan not only introduced new approaches to government but new threats as well. The Reagan presidency became a battleground between the conservative supply-siders and the liberal New Dealers as every piece of legislation that restructured government and every regulation that strengthened business and every tax cut that limited resources for the Treasury became a contest over national values and political priorities.

Ronald Reagan, like Franklin Roosevelt, had an enormous talent for getting his message out and for convincing even liberal Democrats of the merit of his proposals. Despite facing a Senate and House controlled by Democrats, Reagan was successful in pushing through his supply-side agenda. The tax burden was reduced (mostly for the rich and corporations) and business benefited from fewer regulations and regulators. Reagan expanded the military to prove American willingness to compete with the Soviet Union and fired the striking federal air traffic controllers in an obvious attempt to send a message to the unions. Reagan did not control the federal deficit, as spending continued while federal revenues decreased. The size and role of government were in decline, but the IOUs that allowed the government to function skyrocketed.

There is considerable debate among liberals and conservatives over how history will judge the Reagan presidency. Liberals see Reagan as the great dismantler of government social and regulatory programs who increased the gap between rich and poor. Conservatives see Reagan as a modern-day Franklin Roosevelt—a visionary leader who used his office to chart a new course for the nation. A debate such as this comes to no conclusion, but it does offer an opportunity to examine the role of government in American society. With Reagan, as with Roosevelt, Americans saw firsthand two different approaches to public problem solving and national development. Although the governing policy environment is usually a mix of both approaches, the emphasis of one over the other can have a profound impact on how the United States responds to the needs of the nation.

Timeline

1775	American Revolution begins
1776	Declaration of Independence is issued
1787	Constitutional Convention is convened
1789	George Washington is inaugurated as president
1812	British invade the United States and destroy the White House
1861	The Civil War begins with secession of Southern states
1864	Lincoln announces the Emancipation Proclamation
1898	United States enters Spanish-American War
1917	United States enters World War I
1929	Stock market crash
1933	Franklin Delano Roosevelt becomes president and announces New Deal
1941	Japan attacks Pearl Harbor
1945	United States drops atomic bombs on Hiroshima and Nagasaki
1963	President John F. Kennedy is assassinated
1964	President Lyndon Johnson announces his Great Society programs
1974	President Richard Nixon resigns in wake of Watergate crisis
1980	Ronald Reagan is elected president
1990	President George Bush leads multinational coalition to liberate Kuwait
1999	President Bill Clinton is impeached
2000	George Bush defeats Al Gore in closest presidential election in history
2001	Terrorists attack the World Trade Center and the Pentagon
2003	U.S. troops invade Iraq

IMMIGRATION

In December 1999, six-year-old Elián Gonzáles was found floating alone off the coast of Florida. Elián's mother had taken him from Cuba by boat in a desperate attempt to reach the United States and a new life. For months the case of little Elián occupied center stage in the United States as his relatives in Miami fought to have him remain in the country, while his relatives in Cuba, including his father and grandparents, demanded his return. Although a unique case in that the dispute pitted the Cuban American community of South Florida against the communist government of Fidel Castro, the controversy over Elián Gonzáles nevertheless underscored what has become one of America's most pressing public policy issues, the migration of millions of immigrants to the United States.

Every year nearly a million foreign-born persons are admitted legally into the United States as lawful "permanent residents" or in some cases as "political refugees." An additional 25 million are permitted entry into the United States for limited periods of time as students, businesspeople, or tourists. Currently there are 20 million foreign-born persons living in the United States, which is approximately 9 percent of the population. In recent years the number of legal immigrants coming into the United States has been expanded in large part because of the need for skilled workers. However, the current policy debate is concerned with the number of illegal entrants who crawl through the fences that separate Mexico from California, wade the Rio Grande River in Texas, or, like Elián, board creaky boats and head out from Cuba or Haiti or the Dominican Republic to the United States.

Official estimates place the number of illegal immigrants in the United States at over 400,000 a year, while groups dealing with immigrant placement state the number may be as high as 3 million. In total the number of illegal immigrants in the United States may be as high as 10 million. Most of the illegals are Mexican nationals who move regularly across the 2,000-mile border that stretches from Texas to California. Most of the immigrants come to the United States to work in low-end, low-pay jobs from house painting to gardening to apparel assembly. The lure of working in the United States with its burgeoning economy is enough to spur foreign nationals to take the risk and cross the border illegally. Moreover, countries like Mexico, Haiti, the Dominican Republic, and others are unable to control their own borders and often silently consent to the mass migration as a kind of human "safety valve" that diminishes population pressure on jobs, education, and housing.

The movement of illegal immigrants into the United States has forced the government to expand its Border Patrol, Immigration and Naturalization Service, and Coast Guard. Over the years the U.S. government has passed sweeping legislation designed to control migration. The most recent act of Congress was the 1986 Immigration Reform and Control Act, which placed heavy fines on employers who knowingly hired illegal immigrants, beefed up the Border Patrol, and offered amnesty to certain illegals who had been living in the United States for an extended period of time. Despite the restrictive measures put in place by the United States, the human flow of immigrants continues. But now that flow has fostered a backlash from Americans who are more vocal in criticizing immigration policy and the presence of illegal immigrants in the United States.

At the forefront of these problems is the reaction to undocumented immigrants in border states such as Florida, Arizona, Texas, and California. Citizen groups have organized to complain about the drain on social services and education that illegal immigration places on government budgets. Other groups have complained about language issues, in particular the failure of government to mandate that English is required in schools, businesses, and government offices. In 1994 California, for example passed Proposition 187, which prohibited access to public services to illegal immigrants, including education and nonemergency health care. Groups in Arizona have taken the lead in forming the English First movement, which promotes making English the official language of the United States. Although both of these initiatives are no longer in the mainstream of the public policy debate, they reflect the antagonism that exists toward undocumented aliens and foreign-born persons in general.

The critical immigration issue on the front burner of American politics relates to putting restrictions on Arab people either currently in the United States or seeking entry to the United States. Since September 11, Congress, the president, and the Immigration and Naturalization Service were involved in policy discussions over how to safeguard the country from terrorists. Arab people became natural targets of immigration policy, especially those on student visas, work permits, or tourist cards. Since a number of the attackers who crashed into the World Trade Center and the Pentagon were in this country illegally, pressure mounted for government to tighten up immigration rules. ⊕

FORMAL GOVERNMENT

The best place to start describing the government of the United States is to give a brief description of the Constitution. The preamble begins famously, "We the People," along with a series of pledges or mission statements. The Founding Fathers were not big on grand philosophical dissertations but realized that the government must stand for something. So they decided to promise "to form a more perfect Union, establish Justice, insure domestic Tranquility, provide for the common defense, promote the general Welfare and secure the blessings of Liberty to ourselves and our Posterity." Obviously these big promises are open to interpretation, but they nonetheless lay out what this country stands for and what it intends to achieve.

The preamble is followed by a series of articles, which provide the framework for the American governing system. Articles 1–3 introduce the separation of powers relationship that is at the core of the Constitution. Each article details the organization, powers, and responsibilities of the governing branch and clearly sends a message that this new government would not tolerate power centralized in the hands of one individual or one institution. Moreover, the manner in which each branch of government is organized and the character of the powers and responsibilities create a system of checks and balances to ensure that no individual or institution can accumulate control of the governing process.

Article 1 describes the legislative branch, the Congress of the United States of America. This is the longest of the articles and shows that the Founding Fathers were convinced that real governing power would reside in the Congress. In this article the Congress that is formed is bicameral or composed of two houses. The House of Representatives was established as the most democratic of the Congress, with members directly elected by voters in their home state. Because members represented electoral districts based on population, larger states with more people gained more representatives and thus more voices in the Congress. The population imbalance created in the House of Representatives was offset by the composition of the Senate, which allowed each state two senators. These senators were to be nominated by the state legislature without citizen participation. Because of the elite nature of governance during the early days of the republic, the Senate evolved as the "upper house" with more prestige and visibility, while the House of Representatives became the "lower chamber."

The initial sections of article 1 describe the characteristics of the bicameral Congress, thereby providing an organizational framework to the legislative branch. Section 8 presents the powers and responsibilities of the legislature. Section 8 is in effect a "power list" in which the Congress is charged with a wide range of governing tasks from laying and collecting taxes to borrowing money to regulating commerce to declaring war. The specificity of section 8 makes it abundantly clear that the Congress would make the vast majority of policy decisions in the new United States. Furthermore, at the conclusion of section 8, the Founders added a key power when it granted the Congress the right "To make all Laws which shall be necessary and proper for carrying into Execution the foregoing Powers and all other Powers vested by this constitution in the government of the United States." This so-called Elastic Clause (because it stretches the powers of the Congress beyond what is written in section 8) leaves no doubt that governance of this new republic would reside in the legislative branch.

Constitutional Language

The most powerful language in the constitutional heritage of the United States does not come in the body of the document but in the First Amendment added a few years later. This language is bold and clear and provides American citizens with personal liberty and individual rights. As stated in the First Amendment: "Congress shall make no law respecting an establishment of religion, or prohibiting the free exercise thereof; or abridging the freedom of speech, or the right of the people peaceably to assemble, and to petition the Government for redress of grievance."

Where article 1 overwhelms the reader with details of organization, powers, and responsibilities, article 2 on the executive branch is much less expansive. Article 2 has only four sections (compared to ten in article 1), and only in section 2 do the Founders provide a glimpse of how they envision the role of the president. Section 2 provides the president with control of the army, navy, and the state militias, responsibility for running the executive branch (which at that time was a minuscule number of bureaucrats), the right to negotiate treaties (with the advice and consent of the Senate), and lesser responsibilities to grant pardons and reprieves and appoint public officials. There is also in section 3 a responsibility to provide for a State of the Union address and an impeachment process in section 4 should the president, vice president, or any civil officer be found to have committed treason, bribery, or other high crimes and misdemeanors. These powers are not insignificant, particularly those that grant the president control over the armed forces and the responsibility to conduct foreign policy. But compared to the "power list" of the Congress, the president was initially viewed as a facilitator of the policy process and not a maker of policy.

Article 3 on the judicial branch seems almost an afterthought. Just three sections long, article 3 details the organization of the federal court system (a Supreme Court and "inferior courts as the Congress may from time to time ordain and establish"), the power of courts (extended "to all Cases, in Law and Equity, arising under this Constitution, the Laws of the United States, and Treaties made," along with specialized areas of federal laws such as cases affecting ambassadors and public officials, cases of admiralty and maritime jurisdiction, and cases involving state disputes and individual disputes with states), and a definition of treason, which at the time of the writing of the Constitution was a critical issue of governance and the law. The placement, structure, and responsibilities of the judicial branch as written in article 3 strongly suggest that the role of the Court in government was to be narrow and restrained with little or no connection to the policymaking process.

The remainder of the constitutional document is taken up with issues of relations between the states and the central government, the amendment process, and ratification. Article 4 presents a series of rights and guarantees that citizens hold in the various states. The Constitution guarantees "full faith and credit" to all public acts and documents in every state, provides that citizens of each state are entitled to all "privileges and immunities" of citizens in all other states, describes the process of admitting new states, and guarantees a "Republican Form of Government" to every state. Article 5 sets out the amendment process for changing the Constitution. Although there are four options for amending the Constitution, in reality a process in which two-thirds of each house of Congress and three-fourths of the state legislature must consent to a change is the most common.

Critical language in the later part of the Constitution is contained in article 6. This article is often termed the supremacy article, for in it is found the language that sets the federal government above the state governments. As stated, the "Constitution, and the Laws of the United States which shall be made in Pursuance thereof; and all Treaties made, or which shall be made, under the authority of the United States, shall be the supreme Law of the Land." This language carried the potential for deep political divisions, since the unity that the founders so desperately sought to achieve hinged on the creation of an equitable relationship between the states and the central government. By forming a federal system of states and central government (with some powers shared, some powers held exclusively, and some powers held concurrently) and then establishing the supremacy of the federal government, the Founders set up a relationship that was destined to be contentious and divisive.

The Constitution ends with article 7, the ratification article, which required that nine of the thirteen colonies agree to the document before it became operational. After a long struggle, with some narrow victories and a few recalcitrant colonies (North Carolina and Rhode Island), all thirteen colonies agreed to the Constitution and the United States of America was officially formed. But almost immediately, the states agreed to add ten amendments because the Constitution was strangely silent on providing personal guarantees and limitations on the power of the government. As a result, by 1790

Americans had a Bill of Rights that granted such critical guarantees as freedom of speech, religion, press, and assembly, along with protections from unreasonable searches and seizures. There was also a range of judicial guarantees such as a speedy trial, trial by a jury of peers, and protection against cruel and unusual punishment. Although the Constitution was correctly lauded as a work of governing genius that has survived the test of time, it is the Bill of Rights that has become a powerful agent of change and a consistent restrainer of excessive government power.

Describing the essential elements of the Constitution, article by article, and then highlighting key language, however, does not really tell why this is a unique governing document and why the United States of America emerged from the constitutional process as a democratic nation. A short list of the key values and principles that are the basis of American government is in order.

- The Constitution established a republican form of government, which means that public policy decisions would be made by representatives elected by the people in regular elections with a secret ballot. The Constitution further guaranteed that the individual states would also provide republican government. From the start this would be an imperfect republican form of government with restrictions on voting rights and representation. Despite its flaws the United States moved into uncharted and risky governing territory by opening up the political system to an ever expanding number of citizens.
- The Constitution created a governing culture where the rule of law was held in high regard and applied equally to those of power and those without power. Although the federal court system was not originally intended to be a major player in the governing structure, it quickly became a protector of the Constitution and an interpreter of its meaning. With the key ruling in *Marbury v. Madison,* in which Justice John Marshall enunciated the doctrine of judicial review and created the power of the Court to overturn an act of Congress, it became increasingly clear that the United States was becoming a country of laws, not men.
- The Constitution fashioned a governing system of separation of powers and checks and balances that controlled official power and forced political leaders to seek compromise. By spreading governing powers over three branches the Founding Fathers not only distributed the responsibility for national policymaking, but diluted the ability of one individual or one institution to dominate national policymaking. By creating numerous opportunities for one branch of

government to check the actions of another branch—presidential veto, Senate ratification of treaties, court protection of the laws—the policy process was destined to be painstakingly slow but properly deliberative. Separation of powers permitted multiple access points to the policy process, while checks and balances permitted multiple means of ensuring caution, compromise, and gradualism, the watchwords of the American system.

- The Constitution developed a workable relationship between the states and the central government, one of the most difficult obstacles in the way of achieving national unity. Federalism spread around public power by granting states the right to control many of the basic services at the local level, while retaining critical defense, foreign policy, and public responsibilities at the national level. Addressing the wide differences among the thirteen colonies and the inclination to retain power at the state level rather than cede control to Washington required sensitive balancing skills. A loose union of colonies, as was the case under the Articles of Confederation, was judged to be weak and leaderless. But to move to a strong national union with expanded federal powers as the Constitution provided was looked on by some with trepidation. Yet because of the balance and fairness included in federalism, the concept of union became the law of the land.

- The Constitution placed into writing individual rights and guarantees that celebrated freedom and protected the people from their government. The Bill of Rights, despite its addition after the ratification of the Constitution, is often thought of as an integral part of our governing document. In fact many Americans have more familiarity with the contents of the Bill of Rights than with the structure of government contained in the Constitution. Although the Founders were little interested in providing rights and guarantees in the Constitution, they were pressured by those such as Jefferson and Hancock to recognize that a governing document that established a democratic republic but did not include mention of personal freedoms and individual guarantees was a shallow exercise.

One of the most significant aspects of the document that created the government of the United States has been its capacity for change. Many scholars refer to the work of the Founders as the "living Constitution," suggesting that the values, rules, and procedures that make up our system of government are not static but have the ability to adjust to the times. As a result of an amendment process and more importantly the interpretation and application of the Constitution by the federal courts, the document written over two hundred years ago has not been replaced, as has been the case in many countries. Rather, it has undergone regular refinements and adjustments that keep it relevant while preserving its unifying character. The claim that the United States has the longest existing constitution among democratic countries attests to the "living" quality of the document and its durability in the face of wars, depressions, assassinations, scandals, impeachments, social movements, and regular partisan conflict.

ABORTION RIGHTS

In 1973 the Supreme Court announced its decision in the abortion rights case, *Roe v. Wade*. Justice Harry Blackmun, writing for the majority, stated that women have a right to an abortion during the first trimester of their pregnancy. In *Roe v. Wade* the High Court rendered one of the most controversial and highly charged decisions in its history. Since that decision the right to an abortion has remained at the forefront of the national issue agenda. Highly visible interest groups have formed to attack or support abortion rights, political parties have made abortion a key plank in their platforms, and politicians have been pressured to articulate their position on a woman's right to control her reproductive process. Amendments to the Constitution have been proposed to overturn the *Roe v. Wade* decision, and countless demonstrations in Washington and throughout the country have highlighted the issue of abortion. There have also been numerous acts of violence against abortion clinics and doctors who perform abortions. Outside of the civil rights struggle, no other issue has so galvanized public opinion and action and so separated the American public.

Since *Roe v. Wade* the Supreme Court has sought to place certain limits on abortion rights. In 1989 in the *Webster v. Reproductive Health Services* decision, the Court agreed with a Missouri law that public facilities and public employees cannot perform or assist in abortions. The Webster decision supported Missouri's right to "protect human life when viability is possible." In 1992 in a case out of Pennsylvania the Court further limited abortion, while upholding a woman's right to have the procedure performed. In a close 5–4 decision Justice Sandra Day O'Connor upheld the Pennsylvania restrictions, which included requiring the doctors who perform abortions to advise women of the risks involved, a twenty-four-hour waiting period after requesting an abortion, and parental consent for minors or, barring that, the consent of a judge. Pro-life advocates hailed the decision as another set of limitations that would make abortions more difficult to attain, but abortion rights groups emphasized that the Court continued to support the right to have abortions performed as part of a woman's reproductive rights and privacy rights.

While the abortion debate has been played out in the Supreme Court and the halls of Congress, interest groups on both sides of the issue have attracted attention with their efforts to shape public opinion and pressure members of Congress. Abortion rights activists are the Planned Parenthood Association and National Abortion Rights Action League. Opponents of abortion are centered in groups such as the National Right to Life Organization, Operation Rescue, and various groups associated with the Catholic Church and other religious denominations who oppose abortion. Representatives of these groups work the offices of representatives and senators and face off against each other during street demonstrations and confrontations at abortion clinics.

Despite Court decisions upholding the right to an abortion, the fight over abortion is by no means over. The new battle that has taken center stage concerns the partial birth abortion, a medical procedure done during the last trimester for women who face life-threatening problems associated with childbirth. In 1996 President Clinton vetoed the Partial Birth Abortion Act on the grounds that it violated a woman's right to an abortion and jeopardized the health and safety of women who sought the procedure. Conservatives in the Congress who passed the bill saw the procedure as a kind of medical infanticide. Although the veto was upheld, conservatives in Congress continue to work to revive the act and aggressively end the procedure.

The emotion associated with both sides of the abortion debate may have subsided as political attention has moved elsewhere, but the issue of a woman's choice versus the right of the fetus remains viable and always threatening to candidates for public office and those who already hold office. The groups associated with the debate remain some of the most well organized and active in the political process. It is unlikely that they will be silenced, no matter where abortion policy moves in the coming years. ⊕

POINT OF FACT
The United States was the first country to have a formal, written bill of rights as part of its fundamental law.

THE CITIZEN AND THE STATE

The relationship between the American people and the U.S. government can best be described as one of contradiction. Public opinion polls over the years point out a profound sense of patriotism, an appreciation of fundamental

freedoms, and a desire to engage in democratic politics. In the weeks following the attack on America, the National Opinion Research Center found that
97 percent of Americans polled said that they would rather be citizens of the
United States than of any other country. Patriotic feelings among a wide
spectrum of Americans were found to be at a thirty-year high. The terrorist
attack on the Twin Towers and the Pentagon also inspired new levels of confidence in government. In public opinion polls done two weeks after the attack, 64 percent of Americans polled said that they trusted the federal government "nearly always" or "most of the time," while 35 percent said they
trusted government "only some of the time." The results on trust in government marked the first time since 1966 that confidence in government
showed such a significant increase.

Renewed patriotism and trust in government have come none too soon. In
recent years there has been consistent evidence of a decline in expressions of
patriotism and especially in the levels of trust in governing institutions.
Although Americans may love their country and love what their country
stands for, they have shown little faith in their government and, worse yet,
little understanding of how their government works. Also, the ability of
many Americans to sustain their level of trust in government is weak. Six
months after the terrorist attack, public opinion polls showed a decline in
levels of trust, which nearly wiped out the "spike" in trust achieved immediately after September 11. Americans were returning to their old ways.

There are numerous reasons for Americans' estrangement from their governing system, including the scandal-plagued nature of the recent political
scene. Starting with the Watergate scandal that forced President Richard
Nixon to resign in 1974 and ending with the impeachment of President Bill
Clinton in 1999, American politics has seen a progression of presidents and
presidential administrations face charges of illegality, impropriety, and unethical behavior. Recent studies have shown that nearly 70 percent of Americans feel that public officials are not interested in their political concerns and
the policy demands of the average citizen.

Reading the political mind of the American people and documenting the
growing estrangement of the general public has become a burgeoning industry in the United States. Over two hundred polling organizations in the
United States employ thousands of poll takers and poll analysts who are in
the business of providing their clients with the most accurate sense of the nation. The relationship between citizen and state is now filtered through the
questions, mathematical computations, and expert analysis of the polling
companies. The United States has become so poll driven that there is mounting evidence of a reaction of the American public against polls and even lying
to poll takers as a quiet form of revenge for the constant invasion of privacy

that poll taking creates. Despite the poll overkill and the evidence of negative views toward polls, the political scene in the United States remains one in which public opinion is a critical ingredient in campaigning, elections, and public policy debates. The relationship between the citizen and the state may not be as direct as democratic purists would like, but the public opinion polling that is now an integral part of the process provides a linkage that cannot be ignored or downplayed.

The next wave of citizen-state relations is without question the Internet, which has created a revolution in democratic practice in the United States by offering the American people direct access to the political process. E-mail allows citizens to directly contact their elected representatives, chat rooms provide citizens with opportunities to contact others with similar concerns and opinions, and Web pages permit candidates, groups, government agencies, and individuals with visual presentations of their views, objectives, and visions. While television changed the nature of American politics by connecting the voice of policy and the face of policy, the Internet has allowed citizens to become involved in the political process. The Internet has helped groups organize, stimulate grassroots support, pressure members of Congress, and get their message across to millions who are online.

The Internet is also changing the manner in which Americans are educating themselves about politics. Fifty years ago a discussion of how Americans learn about politics and acquire their political values and beliefs—often termed political socialization—concentrated on family, school, neighborhood, peer relations, and other organizations such as the church. Then along came television with its power to attract and mesmerize its viewers. The family, which was losing its grip, schools, which were no longer effective socializers, and the neighborhood and the church, which were in retreat, got pushed aside by the television. Television had an enormous impact on shaping the opinions of Americans during the Kennedy-Nixon debates, the Vietnam War, and the presidency of Ronald Reagan, also known as the Great Communicator.

Although television was touted as the ultimate political socializer, the Internet was quietly positioning itself as a new source of information and contact. Recent studies show that more and more Americans are looking to the Internet for news and commentary. The nightly news programs are no longer the sole source of world events and cultural trends. The news commentators—Brokaw, Jennings, and Rather—now must compete with hundreds of Web sites with their own commentators, analysts, and muckrakers. When many Americans get up and get ready for work, they boot up their computers and log onto the Internet rather than turn on the news; at work they keep up with the news of the day from their computer terminals. When they arrive home and have some time to relax, they don't necessarily sit down with the newspaper in front of the television, but they continue the process of surfing the Net that started in the morning.

While the Internet has revolutionized the relationship between citizen and the state, it has also contributed to a culture in which Americans are content to stay at home rather than venture out at night to interact with neighbors. This tendency to remain in the home "bunker" and not participate in the public life has been termed by Harvard political scientist Robert Putnam as the "bowling alone" syndrome. Putnam in his study noticed a decline in the number of Americans who were joining civic groups from the Parent Teacher Association to the Veterans of Foreign Wars to bowling leagues. Putnam was concerned over this lack of interest in civic involvement primarily because it weakened the very foundations of democratic practice. Democracy is a participatory form of governance. If Americans are not interested in leaving their bunkers to participate in the civic life of their communities, then, according to Putnam, this democracy, this country, is in trouble.

Putnam's "bowling alone" thesis has been the source of extensive investigation and criticism. Many critics state that new groups are being formed regularly and that Putnam was just looking in the wrong place when he developed his disturbing evaluation of American democracy. Other critics state that the Internet has created a new kind of relationship between citizens and the state, perhaps best described as "virtual participation" where citizens need not leave their homes and physically join their neighbors in a civic pursuit, but can use their computers to participate and effect change. In light of the events of September 11, Putnam has stated that civic society in America may have entered a "turning point" as citizens become more involved in public life. But whether civic life is on the decline or merely going through a major shift, Putnam's "bowling alone" thesis forced a dialogue over the state of citizen-government relations in the United States. The term "civil society" has moved to the front lines of this dialogue about democratic practice in the United States.

The relationship between citizens and the state in the United States is without question multifaceted. It involves, as we have seen, a range of interactions. At the core of the interaction is the proper role of government. Americans may not always pay attention to matters in the public domain, but they usually can be counted on to offer their views on the extent that government should be involved in their lives. These beliefs about the proper role of government in American society have been linked to the terms "liberal" and "conservative." Although precise definitions of liberal and conservative remain elusive, there is a general consensus that liberals tend to support an expanded role for government in responding to the needs of society, even if that means more taxes, more bureaucrats, and more spending. Conservatives, on the other hand, worry about the expanding role of government with its regulations, programs, and of course taxes.

Public opinion data has regularly monitored the beliefs of Americans toward the proper role of government. The most recent data from 2000 show that 18 percent of Americans identified themselves as liberals, 32 percent identified themselves as conservatives, and 50 percent took the middle way and identified themselves as moderates. While the conservative point of view clearly outdistances the liberal, the key piece of data from this opinion poll is the number of Americans who prefer to see themselves as straddling the fence. Americans have historically been "middle of the roaders" seeing the merit on occasion of an intrusive and active government, but at the same time fearing the excesses of government power. This fence straddling may be seen as revealing a lack of commitment to principle. But with so many citizens in the middle, American politics has avoided extremism and the ideological domination that can divide a country and its people.

Much of the discussion regarding citizen interaction with government in the United States appears to be one way. Americans define their democracy as offering them opportunities to get something from government, whether rights or benefits or power or merely attention. Civil-governmental relations, however, can also be examined as a reciprocal arrangement where citizens have responsibilities and are expected to contribute to the common good. In the United States this reciprocity is viewed as paying taxes, obeying the laws, serving on juries, voting, and generally being a "good" citizen. While these responsibilities are substantial, new initiatives are being forwarded to expand citizen responsibilities to incorporate public service. The Clinton administration, for example, introduced a Youth Corps program designed to get young people involved in community service. After the terrorist attacks President Bush touted the USA Freedom Corps, a major volunteer program designed to get the American public involved in a range of civic duties, including homeland security. At the local level, many school districts in the country require some form of volunteering in the community to instill values of civic responsibility. The rationale for these initiatives is that because the United States does not have mandatory military service, American citizens, particularly the young, need to recognize the importance of giving back to their community and their country. Building on the idealism that was part of the Peace Corps generation in the early 1960s, programs that teach civic responsibility have now become a part of citizen-state relations. Although in their infancy, they signal the growing recognition in the United States that citizenship is a two-way street.

POINT OF FACT
Over a thousand talk shows offer Americans an opportunity to speak their mind.

CAPITAL PUNISHMENT

Interpreting the Constitution and the amendments to the Constitution has never been a simple exercise. The language used by the Founders and later Congress has often been purposely vague to allow for broad application over time and to avoid placing the courts in an interpretative "straitjacket." There is perhaps no better example of the interpretation challenge associated with the Constitution and its amendments than the Eighth Amendment. It states that "excessive bail shall not be required, nor excessive fines imposed, nor cruel and unusual punishments inflicted." It is the last phrase forbidding "cruel and unusual punishments" that has become the focal point for judicial interpretation and for intense political debate. The issue surrounding "cruel and unusual punishments" is the legal and moral appropriateness of instituting the death penalty by the federal government and particularly by state legislatures.

The sanctioning of murder by the state for those who have been convicted of capital crimes has become a deeply divisive issue in the United States. At present there are approximately 3,650 people on death row in thirty-five states. As a result of the landmark Supreme Court decision in 1972 in *Furman v. Georgia*, over three hundred convicted criminals have been put to death, with Texas and Florida leading the way in the number of executions. It is noteworthy that in the *Furman v. Georgia* case the Supreme Court struck down the Georgia death penalty law because it was deemed too "random." But as a result of the signal sent by the Court to states that they needed to rewrite their laws if they expected support from the federal judiciary, states immediately passed new laws that met the Court's concerns. In a subsequent challenge to the death penalty in a 1976 case, *Gregg v. Georgia,* the Court upheld the death penalty, stating that capital punishment "is an expression of society's outrage at particularly offensive conduct," and that the death penalty "is an extreme sanction, suitable to the most extreme crimes."

While the Supreme Court has been the focus of the constitutional debate over capital punishment, the American public has also been engaged in a debate that has approached the issue from the standpoint of justice, deterrence, and economics. Proponents of capital punishment often bolster their case by stating that executing individuals who have committed a heinous crime is an act of justice. Citing the biblical admonition of "an eye for an eye," supporters of the death penalty state that the victims of capital crimes deserve closure and a feeling that justice has been done. Politicians and police officials often cite the benefits of capital punishment as a deterrent. Although studies of the link between capital punishment and deterrence are questionable, it is argued that putting a criminal to death certainly does not allow him or her to commit another crime. Finally, some have argued that keeping a convicted criminal on death row is costly. Estimates place the cost of maintaining death row as upwards of $35,000 a year. When the arguments become emotional, some proponents of capital punishment use the defense that it is far cheaper to execute someone than to keep that person alive for twenty years or a lifetime.

The opponents of capital punishment are not without their arguments as well. The primary arguments against the death penalty are associated with the humane approach to punishment, the failures of the judicial system, and the prospect of making a mistake. The case against capital punishment is at its core an attack on the inhumanity of state-sanctioned murder, of the state playing God and taking a life in a revenge-filled act. The argument is made that it is far more humane to put someone in jail for a lifetime than to take a life. The humane position is further bolstered by the data associated with the *McClesky v. Georgia* case, which showed that a preponderance of death row inmates are minorities, particularly African Americans. Opponents state that African Americans often do not benefit from the best legal counsel because they lack funds, especially to sustain the long appeals battle to fight execution. Finally, the death penalty is viewed as wrong because there is regular evidence that people have been accused and convicted of a capital crime and have spent time on death row or were executed for crimes unjustly. With the use of DNA evidence increasing, a number of successful challenges to death sentences have been served on particular individuals, further supporting the position taken by opponents of capital punishment. In 2003 outgoing Illinois governor George Ryan commuted the sentences of all death row inmates to life in prison because of his belief that the criminal justice system in his state was deeply flawed.

The United States has consistently been at odds with the rest of the industrial democracies of the world with its support of capital punishment. European countries in particular have often criticized the United States for sanctioning state executions. The 2001 execution by lethal injection of Timothy McVeigh, the convicted bomber of the Murrah Federal Building in Oklahoma City, was supported at home but vilified in Europe. There remains a large reservoir of support for capital punishment despite the foreign criticism and the new DNA testing that has found innocence where there were claims of guilt. But with every police officer and every child murdered, public opinion reveals its outrage and calls for the execution of the criminal. ⊕

Election Data

The results of the 2000 presidential election:

Al Gore, Democratic Party	48.3 percent (266 electors)
George Bush, Republican Party	47.8 percent (271 electors)
Ralph Nader, Green Party	2.7 percent (0 electors)
Pat Buchanan, Reform Party	0.4 percent (0 electors)
Harry Browne, Libertarian Party	0.3 percent (0 electors)
Howard Phillips, Constitution Party	0.09 percent (0 electors)
John Hagelin, Natural Law Party	0.08 percent (0 electors)
David McReynolds, Socialist Party	0.01 percent (0 electors)
James Harris, Socialist Workers Party	0.01 percent (0 electors)
Write-ins	0.02 percent (0 electors)

Others receiving votes:

L. Neil Smith, Libertarian Party
Monica Moorehead, Workers World Party
Cathy Gordon Brown, Independent
Denny Lane, Vermont Grassroots
Randall Venson, Independent
Earl Dodge, Prohibitionist
Louie Yongkeit, Unaffiliated
None of the above

PATHWAYS TO PARTICIPATION

The United States is called the land of opportunity. This is certainly true in regard to opportunities for political participation. The number of pathways that exist for citizen involvement in the political process range from the more common methods of voting and communicating with public officials to the more time-consuming and focused methods of joining interest groups and political parties. These participatory opportunities, however, have not attracted large segments of American society. Although the United States is a country with thousands of interest groups (with millions of members), hundreds of millions of dollars in campaign contributions, and some of the most competitive national elections in the world, evaluating political participation often returns to the dismal voting turnout numbers that register in national, state, and local elections.

In voting turnout among voting-age population in the industrialized world, the United States resides near the bottom, usually just ahead of Switzerland. In the 1996 election 49.5 percent of the voting-age population cast their ballots, while in the 2000 election the turnout was just over 51 percent. When turnout is viewed in terms of registered voters, the United States has a solid record of citizen participation, usually in the 80 percent range, which places the country in the middle of the pack of the industrial democracies. Despite this more positive view of voting, the critical factor is that turnout has stabilized at or near the 50 percent range with no sign of significant improvement. The last presidential election with over 60 percent turnout was in 1960 with the Kennedy-Nixon contest. Since then the trend has been downhill. The situation is even worse in off-year elections for members of the House of Representatives and the Senate or in state and local elections. Usually these elections bring out about a third of the voting-age population, and in some states that number has begun to fall below 30 percent.

Public officials and political scientists have been wrestling with the low voter turnout for years and have come up with a number of ways to increase the level of participation. In 1993 Congress passed the Motor Voter Bill, which was designed to make registration easier by offering citizens the opportunity to complete the necessary forms at the state motor vehicle and licensing center. While increasing the level of registration somewhat, the Motor Voter Bill has not been the panacea that advocates of expanded participation had thought. Now the answer seems to be in computer participation. In the Arizona presidential primary in 2000 as many as 50,000 citizens in Arizona were permitted to vote by Internet. Other states are also investigating online voting, while still others see the answer in direct mail of ballots. Both Internet and direct mail voting have inherent security problems that could jeopardize the one-man, one-vote concept that is the underpinning of our democratic system, but public officials continue to look for ways to draw people into the political process. New opportunities for voting do nothing to turn around the major sources of low turnout, which are lack of interest, displeasure with politics, and a sense that voting does not really matter.

If voting is in trouble in the United States, there are some signs of life in other forms of participation. Contacting public officials either by phone, letter, and e-mail has increased significantly in recent years. There is evidence that Americans are more willing to sign a petition or demonstrate openly for or against a cause than their counterparts in other democratic countries. And perhaps most importantly, the United States remains a nation of joiners as the number of interest groups continues to mushroom. If voting turnout were removed as a variable used to describe the level of participation, the United States would likely rise close to the top of the list as a country with an active, engaged citizenry.

What has replaced voting as a growth area of participation is interest group formation and activity. There are over 30,000 interest groups organized and functioning in the United States, with 7,000 of those in Washington, D.C. These groups range from trade associations representing specific industries or products to professional societies to trade unions to a multiplicity of so-called single-issue groups that advocate anything from a cleaner environment to anti-abortion to gun control. The political system is literally awash in these interest groups and their representatives, the lobbyists. The political process in the United States is now one in which elected officials and bureaucrats regularly interact with lobbyists at key points in public policy formation and implementation. While elected politicians and government officials state categorically that they make up their own mind on legislation or regulations, there is no doubt that interest group information, pressure, and various kinds of support influence the outcome. Interest group activity has become the modern method of democratic practice in the United States. Rather than fight city hall alone, the group with a large budget, professional staff, and aggressive lobbying techniques has defined the new method of participation.

There is one other important means that interest groups employ to get their message across—campaign contributions. Just like individual supporters of candidates, interest groups are also permitted under the law and its various judicial interpretations to provide campaign contributions to influence the policy process. But in order to comply with the law, interest groups and corporations are required to form political action committees (PACs), which serve as the official conduits for the campaign contributions. Through the PACs millions of dollars are filtered to the candidates and the political parties each year and become a tidal wave of giving when election time approaches. Currently there are over 4,000 PACs (1,500 in national politics), with many concentrated in the business, union, and professional sectors. With this large number of PACs there is no doubt that their financial contributions are considerable. In the 1996 elections PACs gave out over $200 million in campaign contributions. In the 2000 election business-oriented PACs contributed $88 million to House and Senate candidates, trade association PACs contributed $66 million to candidates, and labor PACs contributed just under $50 million to candidates.

Although it would be easy to make the connection that all this money translates into votes and government action, the reality is that the PAC money opens doors and provides opportunities to make a case. Interest group lobbying remains a concerted effort to sway the policy process in the direction of the organization and its membership. Money is now an integral part of that swaying process, but the real story is in the growth of the PACs and the heightened reliance that interest groups are placing on using money as means of access. There is a critical factor of inequality in campaign contributions and PAC activity. A sizable portion of the money goes to incumbents rather than challengers, thus making incumbents not only the beneficiaries of the largesse but the constant targets of pressure. Members of Congress often bemoan the pressures they face from interest groups and PACs with generous checkbooks. They nevertheless accept the contributions.

The growth and influence of groups and their PAC organizations comes at a time when political parties are in a period of declining visibility and power. The party machines that dominated American politics at the turn of the century and even into the 1960s have given way to personal campaign organizations run for the candidates by high-priced political consultants. The Democratic and Republican parties and a number of lesser third parties remain viable, but their ability to dominate electoral politics and the governing process has waned considerably. Party membership has plummeted, party identification has also declined, and party cohesion within government remains low. Even more serious, the campaign finance reform bill passed by the Congress is viewed as a boon to interest groups and political action committees and a further blow to the political parties. With "soft money" outlawed, the political parties will no longer have access to hundreds of millions of dollars to distribute to candidates, thus weakening their role and influence in the campaigns and likely expanding the influence of interest groups.

Despite their reduced role and influence, political parties in the United States provide critical support services for the candidates and the elections. The parties participate actively in the primaries and contribute valuable organizational and financial assistance to the candidates during primaries and elections. Once in government, parties help identify policy differences between candidates through a range of educational and opinion-shaping activities. Political parties will likely have to adjust to the new world of campaign finance and carve out a new role and develop new means of influencing the electoral process. But at present the parties are on the defensive.

Because of the weakness of political parties, candidates for public office now rely on consultants who provide most of the electoral services necessary for victory, including electoral strategy, fund-raising, field organization, speech writing, polling, and general campaign management. Today candidates anticipating a run for public office first sign on a political consulting firm and then seek out party leaders to determine how the organization can assist the consultant-run campaign. The political parties become a valuable source of local organization and campaign finances, but local, state, and national party organizations are relegated to a secondary role in the development and implementation of the campaign. The days of political bosses sitting in smoke-filled rooms maneuvering to name the Democratic or Republican nominee for president of the United States are long gone.

The confluence of voting, group activity, and political parties is best seen at election time and during the campaigns for public office. The electoral process in the United States is like no other in terms of length, media coverage, and expense. The campaign for the White House often begins a year before the first primary. Candidates crisscross the nation seeking to get out their message and convince prospective voters that they have the presidential "right stuff." Defining the right stuff is usually the job of the political consultants who describe the unique characteristics of the candidate and package that candidate in a manner that will be attractive to the voters. Campaigns thus become media driven as candidates search for the photo opportunity or the sound bite that will get them on the nightly news and provide them with that all-important edge. Not surprisingly, a long campaign with consultants, travel, television ad buys, polling, mass mailings, and all the minutiae of a campaign is a costly venture. The Bush-Gore election of 2000 officially cost nearly $167 million (which includes spending by the Buchanan and Nader campaigns), but that figure only represents public funding money, not money raised by political parties, interest groups, foundations, and other sources. Most estimates of the total cost of the 2000 presidential election approach $600 million.

Amid all this time, media glitz, and money, it is difficult for issues to make their way into the election process. Candidates of course present their policy platforms in speech after speech, in public debates, and in television commercials, but public policy issues often are complex and confusing, which leads voters to look for something else. It can be the strength or weakness of the economy, the leadership qualities and experience of the candidates, or simply the image that the candidate exudes. James Carville, President Clinton's campaign manager during his successful 1992 election, hammered home the now famous phrase, "It's the economy, stupid," to emphasize that his candidate and the entire campaign must constantly emphasize economic issues and economic vision.

Increasingly leadership qualities and character have become critical ingredients in campaigns. The sexual affairs of President Clinton that led to his impeachment prompted candidates in the 2000 campaign to claim that they would bring a new sense of personal responsibility to the White House. George Bush, in particular, stressed the importance of integrity in the campaign, while Al Gore found it difficult to separate himself from Bill Clinton. Both candidates sought to convince the American voter that, while issues were important, personal values, intelligence, common sense, and decency were equally critical in choosing a president. Polling data from the 2000 election revealed that George Bush benefited from the public perception that he was more honest than his opponent and that he was a more "likable" individual.

Voter preference, no matter what the source, eventually finds its way into the voting booth. Candidates view the American electorate not as a mass of voters, but as men and women, whites and blacks, professionals and laborers, young and old, wealthy and poor. The campaign for public office thus is geared toward convincing these various segments that the candidate has the right approach to solving their specific concerns. Bill Clinton's victory in 1996 was closely tied to his ability to gain the women's vote. Through a careful use of polling, the Clinton campaign was able to determine that women's concerns on health care, education, and Social Security were quite strong and quite different from men's issues, which focused on taxes, the economic climate, and defense. In the 2000 election George Bush was ultimately successful not because of the issues he supported or the demographic groups that he aligned with, but because Al Gore did not effectively link himself and his party with the strong economy during the two Clinton terms. While Bush was able to make inroads into traditional demographic areas of Democrat support (women, Catholics, Hispanics, young people), it was Al Gore's failure to link prosperity to the Democratic Party and his candidacy that carried the day.

This enormous expenditure of effort leads up to the drama of Election Day. On the first Tuesday after the first Monday in November the American people cast their ballots. Continuing the complexity of the electoral system in the United States, the choice for president is achieved in an indirect manner through the Electoral College. A vestige of the Founding Fathers, who feared giving citizens direct election of the chief executive, the Electoral College is a device that makes states the key participants in the democratic process. Candidates for the presidency are victorious when they pass the 270-electoral-vote mark, which is attained by winning the vote in states and acquiring the electoral votes of that state (determined by adding the number of U.S. representatives and the two U.S. senators). Individual votes help a candidate win a state, but campaign strategies are geared toward winning states, especially the larger states such as California, Texas, New York, Florida, Illinois, and Ohio that have large blocs of electoral votes. In many respects campaigns for the presidency take on the quality of a military campaign as candidates seek to "take" California and "battle" to gain the electoral votes of Texas. Each vote is important, but only as it contributes to "capturing" the state.

This was especially true in the 2000 election, when the determination of the victor hinged on the vote total from Florida and the critical twenty-six electoral votes that would provide either candidate with the victory. After Al Gore initially decided to concede, the closeness of the vote in key counties in Florida made him retract his decision and wait for final vote totals to be announced.

The waiting turned into a month-long marathon as Gore and Bush battled over vote counts, ballot irregularities, and interpretations of voters' intentions. The battle over Florida's electoral votes became a test of our constitution and the manner in which we elect public officials. The battle eventually was decided by a 5–4 Supreme Court vote which stopped a recount effort in some Florida counties. Bush won Florida and the presidency, but Al Gore won the popular vote by over 500,000 votes. He was only the third presidential contender in our nation's history to lose the election even though he won the popular vote.

There is much that deserves criticism in the way the United States has developed its democratic system. There is too much money and not enough voting; there is too much influence in the interest groups and not enough in the political parties; and there is far too much emphasis on image, advertising, and media in electoral campaigns and not enough emphasis on issues, policies, and vision. Reformers of the American system are never without suggestions on how to expand participation and make campaigning less costly and more serious. In 2002, for example, President Bush signed the Help America Vote Act, which along with funneling federal money to states to upgrade their voting procedures also set a series of standards for conducting elections from new rules to avoid voter fraud to guarantees that voting places will be handicapped accessible. Although the Help America Vote Act provides hope that a repeat of the 2000 election will never happen, fundamental structural problems continue to exist. Change is difficult because so much money is around, so many jobs are involved, and most importantly so much power is at stake. All those involved in the electoral process, from candidates to consultants to party officials to PACs, are reluctant to take the steps that would bring the voters back and make the process more intelligent rather than more visual. Meanwhile the voting curve continues its downward spiral and the cost of campaigning skyrockets.

POINT OF FACT
There are 525,000 elective offices in the United States.

GUN CONTROL

Since its early revolutionary days with the Minuteman standing ready with his long rifle, the United States has been a nation of gun owners. Many Americans point proudly to the Second Amendment to the Constitution, in which the Founders signaled their support of gun ownership by granting citizens the right to bear arms. Although critics of the Second Amendment are quick to point out that the right to bear arms only applies to a "well regulated Militia," gun ownership has become akin to a sacred privilege that legislatures, presidents, and courts have been either unwilling or unable to terminate.

But each act of random violence involving a weapon elicits louder calls for gun control. There have been some successes, in particular the 1993 Brady Bill (named after James Brady, who was disabled by a bullet during the Reagan assassination attempt), which required a five-day waiting period on the purchase of handguns. The antigun lobby experienced success in 1994, when President Clinton signed the Violent Crime Control and Law Enforcement Act banning the manufacture, sale, transport, or possession of nineteen semiautomatic assault weapons. But each initiative of the antigun lobbies such as Citizens Against Handguns (a group started by James Brady's wife, Sarah) brought a vigorous response from the National Rifle Association (NRA), the main group seeking to limit restrictions on gun ownership and gun availability. The NRA has a long record of convincing members of Congress to resist legislation that would compromise what it believes to be the constitutional right to bear arms.

With a Republican-controlled House in 1994, gun control was not a high public priority. Republican leaders stressed the need to enforce existing laws and to punish lawbreakers as the most effective way to control the use of weapons. Republicans even amended the Violent Crime Control and Law Enforcement Act law to require convicts to compensate their victims who were injured or disabled by gun use. The Republican position on guns was that laws regulating ownership and availability would not work. Criminals would find ways to buy illegal guns, and restricting gun ownership and availability would needlessly punish law-abiding Americans who wanted to possess weapons. Gun supporters got a lift from the Supreme Court in 1997 when it struck down the congressional mandate that the chief law enforcement officer in the local community be required to conduct a background check of gun purchasers. Although the Court ruling in this case was based primarily on the issue of states' rights versus federal mandates, it nevertheless weakened the linchpin of the Brady Bill.

While gun advocates gained some solace from the actions of the Supreme Court in the 1997 decision, they have had an uphill battle since then to shape favorable public opinion. The arguments of the NRA and its allies in Congress often collided with those of President Clinton, who used each tragic killing spree as a platform to advance tougher gun control legislation. To off-set these attacks by the president, supporters of gun rights began to embrace so-called safe guns, which included a lock or code device that prevented unauthorized use, particularly among young people. While this proposed change was seen in a positive light by the antigun lobby, its goal remained to

Photo 1.1 U.S. President George W. Bush waves to journalists upon returning to the White House. (Reuters NewMedia Inc./Corbis)

George W. Bush was born on July 6, 1946. He was raised in Midland and Houston, Texas. He earned an undergraduate degree from Yale University and master of business administration from Harvard Business School. He began his business career in the oil and gas industry in Midland. He was also a partner in the Texas Rangers baseball franchise from 1989 to 1994. In 1994 he was elected governor of Texas and was reelected in 1998. In the presidential election of 2000 he became the forty-third president of the United States.

limit gun availability at gun shows, make background checks more thorough, and provide the government with more regulatory powers.

The campaign for the presidency in 2000 saw gun rights play a prominent role. George Bush aligned himself with the gun lobby, while Al Gore took the traditional Democratic position of expanding control. Gore particularly targeted gun shows, which offer opportunities for unregulated purchases of weapons. George Bush became entangled in a controversy in which he suggested that the NRA would play a prominent role in his administration. The remark set off a firestorm of controversy as critics of the gun lobby felt that a Bush presidency would embolden the NRA to weaken existing

laws. With George Bush capturing the White House, advocates of gun ownership felt they had a sympathetic ear in government. As to gun ownership,
the attack on America spurred a new round of purchases by Americans fearful of terrorism. ⊕

THE POWER ELITE

The best place to begin searching for the power elite in American government is at the White House. Public opinion polls consistently show that
Americans view the president as the most powerful man in the United States.
In terms of the Constitution, the president's powers are considerable. He is
the chief executive of the federal bureaucracy, commander in chief of the
armed forces, negotiator of foreign treaties, and partner with the Congress in
the legislative process. Along with the constitutional powers granted to the
president, he is at the center of the decisionmaking process in government.
As chief executive, he is the point man for many of the policy initiatives
taken in the United States and the target of partisan battles that accompany
the lawmaking process. As chief executive, he takes the credit and the blame
for the policies that emerge during his time in office.

Although the president is enormously powerful and responsible for national
policymaking, his base of power is part of a larger policymaking elite of White
House advisers, counselors, and staff members. It is more appropriate when talking about power in the White House to use the term "Office of the Presidency,"
which connotes that power emanates from a number of sources that flow into
the ultimate decisionmaker and power holder, the president of the United
States. Even though we often see the president making a speech, signing a bill,
or carrying on the duties of his office, he is performing these functions as part of
a larger elite that has power to direct, shape, and control public policy.

At the core of this presidential elite is the president's inner staff—his chief
of staff, who often controls the day-to-day flow of policy issues along with access into the Oval Office; his national security adviser, who is the point person on global affairs, international crises, and foreign policy options; his congressional liaison, who has responsibility for advancing the president's
legislative agenda; and his economic adviser, who provides the president with
assessments on the current state and future direction of the nation's economy.
On issues that have a global and national security component the inner circle
includes the vice president and the secretaries of state and defense. On economic and financial concerns the secretary of the Treasury plays a critical
role. In recent years presidents have relied more heavily on the secretary to be

the chief architect of sustaining growth or dealing with the threat of recession. One key player in the domestic economy who is not part of the president's inner circle is the chairman of the Federal Reserve. Although he is appointed by the president and approved by the Senate, the chairman of the Federal Reserve is an independent voice on economic matters. With his capacity to influence monetary policy, the chairman of the Federal Reserve is a critical voice in shaping the national economy.

This inner circle of advisers, cabinet members, and agency heads is responsible for providing the president with the most accurate information available along with their best assessments of issues and problems. The president relies on his inner circle for an endless stream of policy advice. This dependency on the inner circle translates into the capability to shape public policy. The president makes the final yes or no, but governing power can be defined more broadly to include the ability to provide information, manage the policymaking debate, and shape the final decision.

The Founders never anticipated the power that the president would accumulate and certainly had no idea that the Office of the President would include an elite body of advisers who would also become powerful (the government of the United States under George Washington had three employees). The early vision of power was in the Congress with its mandate to raise taxes, make war, and pass legislation in response to pressing national problems. But as the United States developed and as presidents redefined their role to one of national leader rather than follower of the Congress, power politics became a contest between the Chief Executive with his advisers and the Congress with its team of legislative leaders.

Power in the United States is also congressional power, specifically, partisan power. The positions of legislative authority are distributed based on which political party controls a majority of seats in the House of Representatives and the Senate. At the top of the power elite is the Speaker of the House of Representatives, who besides being second in line to succeed the president, is master of the legislative agenda and the legislative process. But like the president, the Speaker of the House is not a lone legislative decisionmaker. Power in the Congress is held by a partisan team that includes the majority leader, the majority whip (charged with whipping up votes and support for legislation), and key committee chairmen such as Appropriations, Ways and Means (responsible for tax and Social Security laws), and Budget. The Senate is also organized around party lines and a leadership team, but there is no equivalent to the Speaker (there is an honorary president pro tempore who heads the Senate but without the power). Ultimate power resides in the majority leader, who also relies on a partisan legislative team.

But just as there are visible power holders, there are also those with power who work behind the scenes. In the legislative system of the United States staff members, who work for the leadership or on committees, have become a power unto themselves. The power of legislative staffers is knowledge based. Staffers have a handle on what is in the details of the legislation and what will be necessary from a legislative standpoint in order to move the legislation through the tangled process. Staffers meet regularly with interest group lobbyists, bureaucrats, and other players in the legislative process to assist the members of Congress in writing the laws, defending the legislation, and ensuring that the laws meet the political and constituent needs of the individual member of Congress. With thousands of pieces of legislation coming before the Congress each session, the leadership and individual members rely heavily on staff members to provide them with details of the legislation and the rationale for supporting or opposing the legislation.

If the power elite in the Congress is partisan in nature, the power elite in the third branch of government, the judiciary, is restricted to the nine justices of the Supreme Court. The Court is at the pinnacle of the federal judiciary. The members of the Supreme Court are appointed by the president (subject to Senate approval) for life. Justices can be impeached. They meet in secret sessions to determine the vote and to debate the legal underpinnings of the vote and pronounce their decisions as fiat. In a democratic country like the United States the Supreme Court stands out as a visible elite body that is clearly apart from the other popular-based legislative and executive branches.

The Court's responsibility to uphold the Constitution has allowed the justices to carve out a large piece of public policy formation as they interpret the laws and apply the Constitution to specific areas of American life. The Court has amassed the power to overturn legislative and state laws through judicial review, a function that is not mentioned in the Constitution but is inherent in the Court's responsibility to interpret the Constitution and the amendments to the Constitution in order to ensure that the original intent of the Founders and Congress is upheld. In doing so the Court has ventured into controversial territory as it has made new law and developed new rights.

One of the most interesting aspects about the Supreme Court is that the nine justices head their own mini-law firms with their own staffs who assist them in determining which cases to review and how best to defend a judicial position. Like congressional staffers, the law clerks who work for the nine justices exercise considerable influence in the judicial process of the Supreme Court. They may not be in the regular weekly meetings where the nine justices debate a case, but they are critical participants in shaping the opinions of the justices. The justices rely on them to provide the history of case law, write outlines of decisions, and serve as sounding boards for their thinking. In the end, the decisions that are made and announced to the American public are by the nine justices, but they are decisions that were developed by another behind-the-scenes elite.

When looking for power and a power elite in the U.S. government, many observers have said that the first place to start is the "fourth branch of government," the bureaucratic establishment. From an organizational standpoint the bureaucracy in the United States is under the control of the chief executive. But in real terms a bureaucracy is not under the control of the chief executive. The cabinet-level bureaucracies, regulatory bodies, and independent agencies, in addition to commissions and public corporations, act as separate entities that a president often finds impossible to manage, much less control. Each high-level official in the bureaucratic establishment functions as a kind of master over a governing fiefdom with control over budget, personnel, and administration, as well as the ability to make policy by implementing the laws of Congress. Congress may make the laws and the president may sign the laws, but the bureaucrats implement the laws, which means they transform the general wishes of Congress and the president into the specific rules and regulations that individuals, corporations, and other entities must follow.

The power elite that runs the United States is not limited to the government buildings in Washington, D.C. They are also in the prestigious law firms that represent clients doing business with the government. In recent years "superlawyers" have surfaced among Washington insiders. They are often nationally known attorneys, some former members of Congress or cabinet officials, whose reputation and skill at working the political process has elevated them to positions of prominence. These superlawyers are more than paid lobbyists; they are men and women with unusual access to the corridors of power. They are consummate negotiators and deal makers, and they are experts at knowing how to move legislation forward or change a regulation. Clients, whether from a Fortune 500 company or a foreign government, pay the superlawyers handsomely for their services with the expectation that they are paying for the inside track to government. The fact that law firms continue to grow in size and the regular movement of government officials from the public sector to superlawyer status attest to the power that these attorneys have in the Washington political scene.

While the superlawyers must be considered members of the power elite because of their insider status and their ability to attract high-priced and high-visibility clients, the superlobbyists are part of the power elite because of their success at advancing the interest of their organization. As already noted, interest groups are growing in numbers and influence in the political process, but not all groups are created equal and not all lobbyists carry equal weight when they speak with a member of Congress or a government official. Of the seventeen hundred interest groups that have offices in Washington (along the famous K Street corridor), only a handful are viewed as major players in the political process and only a select few of the lobbyists among that handful of groups reach the status of superlobbyists. In 1997 *Fortune* magazine sponsored a survey of 2,000 Washington insiders and asked them to rank the most powerful lobbying groups. The top five most powerful groups were the American Association of Retired Persons, the American Israel Public Affairs Committee, the AFL-CIO, the National Federation of Independent Business, and the Association of Trial Lawyers of America. These top five lobbying groups have established a track record of getting Congress and the executive branch to embrace their positions and achieve their objectives. These five don't win all the time but have shown that they wield considerable power in Washington and throughout the country.

Also part of the power elite mix is what President Dwight Eisenhower called the military-industrial complex. In his farewell speech in 1961, Eisenhower, a distinguished military man, warned about the Pentagon's relationship with major weapons suppliers, suggesting that close ties between the two would lead to sustained (and often unnecessary) escalations in military spending, as well as excessive influence in the policymaking and budgetary areas of national government. Unlike law firms and lobbying groups, there is no organization called the military-industrial complex. But there is the enormous procurement program of the Pentagon and hundreds of defense-related industries whose profitability, if not existence, depends on government contracts. With the war on terrorism expected to last years rather than months and expenditures related to the war mushrooming into billions of dollars, the generals charged with running the war and the weapons suppliers called on to provide the military with the capability to win the war will likely remain at the core of the Washington power elite.

AFFIRMATIVE ACTION

In 1965 President Johnson signed Executive Order 11246, which required all government agencies at the federal level and all private businesses with federal contracts to abide by affirmative action practices. With the signing of that order, President Johnson set in motion programs in the public and private sectors that would seek to overcome past unequal treatment of minorities or women by providing preferential treatment in admissions to college or professional schools, hiring and promotions in the workplace, and other practices that denied minorities and women equal access or equal advancement. In the heyday of civil rights legislation Johnson did not anticipate the controversy that would be associated with affirmative action and the tension that it would generate between whites and blacks, women and men.

Once affirmative action was promulgated as a federal program with private sector responsibilities, government agencies, colleges and universities, corporations, and other private entities began developing guidelines that would meet the intent of the executive order. With the power of the government behind it, affirmative action became an integral part of the workplace as admission, hiring, and promotion policies became more sensitive toward minorities and women. Later, it would be the task of regulatory agencies such as the Equal Employment Opportunity Commission (EEOC) to monitor compliance and require those in violation of the program to make appropriate changes in their policies and practices.

Although the intent of affirmative action was clear, the application of the program and the attainment of the objectives became the source of numerous court challenges. In one of the most important cases, the *University of California Regents v. Bakke* (1978), the Supreme Court found that a special admissions program which targeted minorities for entrance to the state medical school was in violation of the Equal Protection Clause of the Fourteenth Amendment. While the Court agreed with the intent of the affirmative action admission program in California, it stated that a separate program for minorities which excluded whites and in effect set up a quota system was against the Equal Protection Clause. In a case one year later the Court held in *United Steelworkers of America v. Weber* (1979) that a program designed to place more blacks into technical positions was within the guidelines of the Civil Rights Act of 1964. Weber, a white man, challenged the preferential jobs program on the grounds that it excluded whites, many of whom had more seniority.

Both the Bakke and the Weber decisions introduced the terms "quota" and "reverse discrimination" into the lexicon of American politics. Critics of affirmative action stated that many of the admissions, hiring, and promotion decisions made by public and private entities merely fulfilled a quota, in effect satisfying government regulators whose responsibility it was to implement the program. Whites, in particular white males, became associated with the term "reverse discrimination." It suggests that affirmative action guidelines and quotas foster a new kind of discrimination in which white males are passed over in order to increase opportunities for minorities and women. Both the concept of meeting race quotas and creating a new kind of discrimination would serve as the basis for the attacks on affirmative action and intensify the pressure on government to make changes in the program.

Although affirmative action continued to retain the support of liberals in Congress and the overwhelming endorsement of the black community and women's groups, the Supreme Court began to chip away at the program. In the late 1980s the Court began to strike down so-called set aside programs that guaranteed minority companies a set percentage of construction projects, this time using the Equal Protection Clause to limit the scope of affirmative action. Moreover, the Court began questioning the broad-brush approach used by affirmative action proponents to implement programs so as to remedy past discrimination or injustice. The Court often stated that affirmative action programs must show clearly that they are designed to remedy a specific instance or pattern of discrimination.

The attempt to bolster affirmative action against legal and legislative challenges, however, has run into increased opposition at the state level. In 1996 California voters passed Proposition 209, which forbade government agencies to pursue policies based on preferential treatment. California, especially in its college and university system, had taken the lead in questioning the fairness of affirmative action and the use of race as key factor in admissions policies. The California Civil Rights Initiative, as Proposition 209 was called, survived court challenge leading to other states following suit with similar changes to their laws. Affirmative action as a program designed to enhance opportunities for minorities and women remains in place, but it is facing more challenges and more restrictions as state governments react to the backlash from voters who see in the concept of preferential treatment "reverse discrimination." ⊕

Composition of the United States Congress, 2003

House of Representatives	Senate
Republicans, 228	Republicans, 51
Democrats, 205	Democrats, 48
Independents, 2	Independents, 1

REAL GOVERNMENT

The crowning achievement of the democratic process in the United States is the formulation and implementation of laws. Legislatures are entrusted with enormous powers to make public policy decisions, some that affect the lives of individual citizens and others that affect the nation as a whole. It is no exaggeration to state that a legislature is the key focal point for examining how a nation defines its politics and sets its priorities. In the United States the legislative process is a long and arduous journey through a maze of hurdles, some institutional, some partisan, and some personal, that requires the utmost patience, perseverance, and political savvy to ensure that what starts out as a bill becomes a law.

The process begins with the introduction of the proposed law into both the House of Representatives and the Senate, a step which guarantees that two different bodies will likely have two different approaches to the same problem or issue. A new legislative proposal is assigned to a committee and subcommittee in both houses where members of Congress with the expertise and interest can determine the worthiness of the bill, the cost of the bill, and the chances of the bill seeing the light of day. Survival beyond this point is often difficult because of partisan infighting and the realities of working in a complex and inefficient system. But should the bill emerge from the committee process, it then enters the debate stage with strict rules for discussion in the House and few limitations on discussion in the Senate. This is the time of passionate speeches, amendments, partisan wrangling, and eventually a vote. But with two bodies involved in the process, there are often two pieces of legislation directed at one issue or problem. This duality requires a conference committee made up of leaders from each body to iron out differences and in many cases create a brand-new bill. The work of the conference committee then goes back to both bodies, where passage is more than likely to occur because the bill has gone through numerous stages of partisan compromise. Then it is off to the president for his signature or veto. Since the American legislative system is one of checks and balances, the process is not over if the president chooses to nix the bill. Congress can override the veto by a two-thirds vote, a difficult task but not impossible.

Although the steps of the legislative process are fairly predictable, the movement through these legislative steps is achieved only because the key players in the House and the Senate have been able to use their political skills to maintain the momentum and successfully clear a series of obstacles. The powers of persuasion, the art of deal making, and the ability to build coalitions all have a hand in determining whether a bill becomes a law. But political skills are not enough, since the fate of a piece of legislation is also connected to how responsive members of Congress are to the dictates of party leaders, pressure from interest groups, and of course constituents' demands. There are many factors that shape the legislative process, including doing nothing or saying no. This process of legislation works in the reverse in that the key players in the House and Senate have the skills to ensure that a bill never moves forward or is delayed.

The spirit of cooperation in Congress has been severely challenged in recent years. The House and Senate have been the site of intense and personal partisan wrangling. The days when members of Congress would leave the partisan battles of the floor debate and meet socially over drinks or for golf are largely gone. Today Republicans and Democrats are more wedded to their ideological positions than to a bygone culture that accented civility and camaraderie. The partisanship that pervades the Congress makes it easier to identify policy positions and separate Democrats from Republicans, but at the same time the emphasis on ideology makes bargaining, compromise, and conciliation difficult. The 106th Congress, which ended its session in late 1999, was criticized for its lack of lawmaking production, and the aforementioned gridlock of the aviation security bill in 2001 underscored the permanence of the ideological and partisan division. While Democrats and Republicans will blame each other, the spirit of cooperation and the drive for consensus have declined markedly in the Congress. Skills that in the past lay at the core of the legislative process are not used often. Congress is still a place where the laws of the nation are made, but the way the business of Congress is conducted has led to gridlock and partisan attack.

Washington, D.C., is a city where relationships matter, and there is no more critical relationship than the one between the president and the Congress of the United States. It is said the president proposes and the Congress disposes, a simplistic definition of how public policy is made in the United States. The president and the Congress interact in a number of ways. The president may indeed propose legislation as is customary, for example, during the yearly State of the Union Address, but the president does not leave the proposals and sit by idly. He and his staff follow the proposal as it winds its way through the legislative process, acting as a lobbyist for the bill, drumming up public support for the bill, and suggesting ways to modify or enhance the bill so as to ensure passage. As for the Congress, the manner in which it disposes of the president's proposals can range from forging a bipartisan consensus that creates a new law to partisan bickering that leads to delay, numerous amendments, or a veto. Members of Congress are conscious of the president's influence, particularly his ability to shape public opinion and cast his initiatives in the context of national interest, but that does not mean that members of Congress are helpless in the face of presidential power. Not only do they have their own agendas and ideological persuasions that may conflict with the White House, but they possess powers in their own right to counteract the White House.

Part of the problem for the Congress as it interacts with the president is its composition. There are 535 members of the House and Senate from fifty states and two different political parties, which means that the views of one president may not always coincide with a legislative body that has a proclivity for fragmentation. There may be a meeting of the minds over a particular presidential proposal, but it is likely that what the Chief Executive wants will undergo intense scrutiny, extensive revision, and partisan disputes in a Congress made up of so many different voices. When the nightly news shows the president surrounded by members of Congress signing a piece of legislation, their smiles and handshakes reflect the relief and satisfaction that accompany the knowledge that both governing bodies have finished a long and tortuous route that too often leads to failure rather than success.

The keys to success in presidential-congressional relations include an ability to define a centrist position that is acceptable politically, a willingness to keep working to maintain the relationship despite differences, and a level of trust and respect that creates a conducive atmosphere for deal making. But this is enormously difficult to attain. Defining the extremes of an issue is often easier than finding a proper balance. Working to maintain a relationship between the two centers of power is difficult because of the egos involved and the penchant to fall back on ideology and party loyalty. And finally, developing trust and respect in the political world is asking a great deal of politicians who are naturally distrustful and see their competitors as threats to their power base and popularity.

The tension that is created between the president and the Congress is ultimately a factor of leadership and power. Because the president is elected nationally and is the chief executive, it is natural for him to take the lead and exercise power. Although the Constitution does not expressly state it, the president has increasingly been defined as the nation's chief legislator responsible for creating a policy agenda and working with Congress to make that agenda into law. But from the Congress's point of view, leadership and power also should reside in the House and Senate. Both bodies are closer to the American people, both bodies have significantly expressed powers to make laws, and both bodies have the ability to counteract the president. Thus it is no surprise that presidents and Congresses vie for national leadership and national power. It is what the Founders wanted, but it has created monumental struggles.

In his classic work of political science, Richard Neustadt described presidential power as the power to persuade:

The power to persuade is the power to bargain. Status and authority yield bargaining advantages. But in a government of "separated institutions sharing powers," they yield them to all sides. With the array of vantage points at his disposal, a President may be far more persuasive than his logic or his charm could make him. But outcomes are not guaranteed by his advantages. There remain the counter pressures those who he would influence can bring to bear on him from vantage points at their disposal. Command has limited utility; persuasion becomes give and take. It is well that the White House holds the vantage points it does. In such a business any President may need them all— and more.

RICHARD NEUSTADT, *Presidential Power:*
The Politics of Leadership (New York: Wiley, 1960)

The interplay between the president and the Congress may obscure the enormous influence of the bureaucracy on the policy process. There is a story about President Harry Truman that tells volumes about the power of the civilian bureaucracy in the U.S. governmental system. It seems that Truman was contemplating the ascension of Dwight Eisenhower to the presidency in 1953. Eisenhower, a military man, was used to giving orders and having orders obeyed. Truman was heard to say about Eisenhower, "He'll sit behind that big desk and say, 'Do this' and 'do that.' And do you know what will happen? Nothing." Truman may have been a bit extreme in his characterization of the bureaucracy as a wholly independent force in government and the president as completely ineffectual in getting the bureaucracy to respond to his commands, but there is a nugget of truth in Truman's observation. The bureaucratic establishment in the United States is difficult to control, but it possesses power in its own right as the implementer of public policy.

The power of the bureaucracy touches all phases of life in the United States. Government agencies and the bureaucrats who run those agencies set standards for food and drugs, issue licenses for television and radio stations, inspect businesses to determine their safety for workers, regulate a vast array of industries from nuclear power plants to the stock market, and, perhaps most importantly, spend trillions in government budget money. There are few areas of personal, institutional, or corporate life in the United States that are free of bureaucratic oversight or regulation. Powerful bureaucratic agencies such as the Environmental Protection Agency set standards for water and air quality, the Bureau of Land Management controls millions of acres of federal lands, the National Security Agency spies on the world from powerful satellites, and the Internal Revenue Service collects the nation's taxes. The list of agencies, bureaus, and regulatory bodies is long, with fourteen cabinet departments that employ nearly 2.6 million workers and over fifty independent establishments and corporations that employ nearly 1 million workers. Needless to say, this is a costly operation. It is estimated that the federal government spends $1 billion every six hours, 365 days a year.

At the center of the power of the bureaucracy is its rulemaking authority. When Congress passes legislation, it drafts in effect a general policy statement with objectives and the money to attain those objectives. Because the legislation is an outline of legislative intent, it requires that the cabinet department and the various subcabinet bureaus responsible for implementing the legislation go to work and draft regulations that will properly meet the goals of the legislation and of course wisely spend the money that Congress appropriated. Although rulemaking begins with the bureaucracy, it is not an authoritarian exercise. Rules must be published in the Federal Register and the individuals, institutions, and corporations that will be affected by the rule have an opportunity to influence the rule. The Negotiated Rulemaking Act of 1990 authorizes bureaucratic agencies that are responsible for writing and monitoring the rules to permit those affected by the rules to participate in negotiations that eventually lead to an agreed-on rule or set of rules.

The negotiations involved in rulemaking have led to the formation of a helpful model of how bureaucracies work and how they interact with other sectors of the government. The Iron Triangle model of governance shows that public policy results from the interaction of legislative staff, who represent members of Congress; lobbyists, who are seeking to advance the interests of their particular group; and bureaucratic officials, who write the rules, enforce the regulations, and spend the budget dollars associated with legislation passed by Congress and signed by the president. The term "Iron Triangle" suggests that this relationship forms a tightly knit group of power holders who are often at the core of writing legislation, advancing legislation through the Congress, and implementing the legislation.

In many ways the bureaucracy is the dominant side of the triangle, in large part because it controls the output of government, the laws that define the policy, the rules that implement the policy, and the money that funds the policy. The bureaucratic establishment has been the target of those who see government as too large, too expensive, and too intrusive. The rallying cry for those opposed to the reach of the government has been deregulation. Since the Carter administration and most visibly in the Reagan presidency the push was to weaken the bureaucracy by budget cuts, personnel cuts, and the dismantling of government agencies or at least the limiting of their ability to regulate. Deregulation has meant that businesses have had fewer government inspectors visit their plants, airlines have been able to open new routes without government permission, and long-standing regulatory bodies like the Civil Aeronautics Board and the Interstate Commerce Commission were eliminated. Critics of deregulation cite growing concerns that lack of government oversight and enforcement has led to irresponsible business practices.

While the bureaucratic establishment remains a big, intrusive giant that costs billions and regulates our lives, Americans are not in the mood to dismantle the administrative arm of the government. Public opinion polls indicate support for certain government agencies such as the National Aeronautics and Space Administration, the Food and Drug Administration, and the Social Security Administration. There are also surprising admissions that government may be user-friendly and that government bureaucrats are not the ogres that the traditional image presents. Presidential initiatives such as the Clinton administration's National Performance Review, commonly called "reinventing government," have had some success in reducing needless paperwork, ending some of the outrageous purchasing practices (the $435 hammer for the Defense Department), and creating new customer service practices that make dealing with the government easier.

Reforming the federal bureaucracy will remain high on the agenda of Congress and the White House. For example, there is increasing discussion of privatizing certain government functions or permitting government agencies to compete with the private sector. Also, advances in communications are certain to have an impact on the government, as they have on the rest of American society. But the critical factor involving the American bureaucracy is how its customers, the American people, view it. While there are signs that Americans do not oppose the bureaucracy, they nevertheless remain suspicious of its power and the scope of its involvement. When government touches the lives of its citizens, it is usually not the president or a member of Congress but a bureaucrat—administering a regulation, requirement, or penalty. Bureaucrats are on the front line of government service and regulation, which will align them in an adversarial position with many Americans.

WELFARE REFORM

Americans are universally recognized as generous people who are willing to contribute to a wide variety of charitable causes. Although generosity is part of American culture, government-sponsored welfare programs for the poor and needy have rarely received popular support. Public opinion polls that seek to clarify views of the welfare system and work requirements for recipients consistently point to broad disenchantment. For example, polls taken in 1994 for the *Los Angeles Times* and CNN showed that 71 percent of Americans felt that the welfare system does more harm than good because it encourages the breakup of the family and discourages work. This disenchantment with the welfare system has been the catalyst for reform initiatives at the state and national level.

Starting in 1992, President Clinton pledged to "change welfare as we know it." Clinton was not alone in calling for an overhaul of a system that was not moving people off state support and into the world of work. State governors such as Wisconsin's Tommy Thompson had since the late 1980s been implementing new welfare requirements that accented work and stressed the importance of time limitations for welfare recipients. In order to further advance the welfare reform agenda, both the Bush and the Clinton administrations granted waivers to states, which freed them to experiment with new programs and institute new regulations. By 1995 thirty-two states had been granted these waivers and governors moved quickly to dismantle their welfare systems.

Many of these state-initiated welfare reform measures were controversial, requiring recipients to find work, forcing teenage mothers to live with adults, and setting a two-year limit on welfare payments. Because of unrelenting pressure from government agencies on people to move off the welfare rolls and a strong economy that offered abundant jobs, states registered significant progress in reducing the number of people on welfare. In Wisconsin the welfare rolls dropped by 27 percent, and the state saved an estimated $210 million. Other states such as New Jersey and Michigan made similar progress as state money was shifted from cash payments to individuals to funds targeted to child care and employment training.

With the states taking the lead, the issue of welfare reform shifted to the federal government, where President Clinton took the lead. Although he received criticism from welfare advocates, minorities, and liberals in his own party, the president worked with Republicans to pass the Personal Responsibility and Work Opportunity Act (1996). The legislation sought to achieve a number of objectives: ending the Aid to Families with Dependent Children (AFDC) program, which guaranteed assistance to families of poor children;

providing block grants to states to finance the welfare system; requiring that welfare recipients find work within two years or lose benefits; limiting access to welfare benefits to legal immigrants for the first five years in the United States; and restricting the eligibility of poor people to receive food stamps. The last two provisions of the law were deemed too harsh by the president and he had them removed in an agreement with Congress in 1997.

Although public attention to welfare reform legislation centered on the work requirement, the shift toward state control of the welfare system was key. The legislation in effect permitted fifty different welfare systems in the United States, with states allowed to use block grants as they wished. The result of this shift in power was that many states developed markedly different welfare requirements and welfare allocations. California developed more liberal regulations, allowing recipients to stay on the rolls for up to five years, while Connecticut requires recipients to find work within twenty-one months. The variations in the state programs have been targeted by welfare advocates who feel that the poor and needy will migrate from states with restrictive guidelines to states that take a more liberal approach. It is still too early to test out this assessment, especially since the American economy has provided a wealth of opportunities for welfare recipients to find work and meet the imposed deadline.

To date, welfare reform has been deemed a success by Congress and state leaders. Welfare rolls are down nationally by 18 percent, and the number of recipients finding work and turning their lives around are steadily increasing. But there are some caveats associated with welfare reform. Many welfare recipients who have moved into jobs are not pulling themselves out of poverty. Many of the jobs available to welfare recipients offer minimum wage and few benefits. These economic conditions make it difficult for those in the welfare system to find adequate housing and provide basic necessities for their families. Homelessness has again reared its ugly head in most urban areas, in large part because of the inability of the poor to make ends meet. The most worrisome problem of the new welfare society in the United States, however, is the challenge that may arise should the economy not perform as it has over the last ten years. If the United States enters a period of recession, many welfare advocates fear that the safety net, which is already narrow and porous, may completely collapse. ⊕

POINT OF FACT
In fiscal year 2002 the Bush administration spent $880 million on counterterrorism measures as part of an overall defense budget of $317.5 billion.

THE POLITICAL ECONOMY

One of the reasons for government's size and intrusiveness is that it has taken on increased responsibility to manage and direct the nation's economy. It is estimated that nearly 35 percent of gross domestic product in the United States is accounted for by public spending at all levels. Moreover, despite the fact that principles of private ownership and a market system based on consumer demand serve as the underpinnings of the economy, a wide variety of government institutions are involved in setting policies on the supply of money, the personal and corporate tax burden, trade rules, incentives and regulations for businesses, and protection for workers. The three most influential forces affecting the American economy—inflation, interest rates, and unemployment—are never far from the policy arena as politicians and government officials have the power to make adjustments to ensure that these forces do not threaten the stability of the economic system. While "capitalism" may be the term used to describe the economy of the United States, in reality the economy is best defined as a balance of private and public sectors.

The role of the government in the national economy is demonstrated in its use of fiscal and monetary policy; recently trade policy has been added to the mix. Fiscal policy involves the government's policies relative to budgetary spending and taxation. What and where government spends its money and how much or how little government collects from its citizens and its corporations are powerful means of influencing the economy. Increases or decreases in the budget and tax collections can stimulate or restrain an economy. Monetary policy involves decisions made by the nation's bank, the Federal Reserve, which can influence the flow of money in the economy and ultimately the interest rates that are charged for the use of money. A decision to increase or decrease interest rates by the Federal Reserve can put a brake on spending by making the cost of money go up or push spending forward by making it cheaper to borrow money. Finally, trade policy has in the last ten years moved to the forefront of what the government is doing to manage and direct the economy. As free trade and globalization have come to dominate the economic agenda of the United States, the government has heightened its efforts to negotiate favorable terms of trade with countries and regions. By negotiating these agreements, the United States has signaled the growing importance of worldwide trade.

Of the three policy areas, fiscal policy has been the most politicized. For much of the last twenty years Congress and the president have been locked in often acrimonious debate over how much and where government should spend its money and how much and from whom government should collect the revenue that it uses to fund its programs. This debate began during the administration of Ronald Reagan, who advocated cutting budgets and taxes in line with his supply-side philosophy. While Reagan lowered marginal tax rates for individuals and secured tax incentives and tax benefits for the business sector with the Tax Reform Act of 1986, the budget side of fiscal policy became a tug-of-war between liberals and conservatives.

President Clinton became the political beneficiary of budget surpluses, which began in 1998. Although the surpluses resulted in part from the conclusion of successful budget negotiations with the Republican-controlled Congress that set limits on spending, a positive balance sheet was attained as a consequence of near full employment with attendant increases in tax collections. As the United States finished the twentieth century, the debate in Washington was not on how to cut the budget in order to avoid ever growing deficits, but rather how to properly spend the current surplus and the anticipated surpluses in the coming years. There was some general agreement that the surpluses would be used to shore up Social Security and Medicare, although the actual amount of the surplus was in doubt. Beyond this tentative consensus, there was little agreement. Republicans were convinced that surplus revenues should be returned to the American taxpayer as a kind of bonus for a vibrant economy, while Democrats talked about the need to invest the surplus in areas of the public sector that had been ignored, such as education, health care, and the environment.

When George W. Bush entered the White House, he made comprehensive tax relief a centerpiece of his administration. With bipartisan support Bush was able to push through Congress a major tax package that included one-time rebate checks to the American taxpayers. While the rebates were widely popular, the remainder of the Bush tax package was more controversial as it provided for reductions in marginal tax rates and capital gains tax, and an eventual end to the estate tax. These changes alarmed Democrats who claimed that they benefited only those at the upper ranges of the tax code.

Much of the attention directed at the tax package was superseded by the terrorist attack on September 11, 2001. The attack crippled the American economy and set the stage for a economic downturn. The Bush administration was forced to use fiscal policy as a stimulus to recharge the sagging economy. Furthermore, the surplus that was building steadily during the Clinton years and into the first year of the Bush administration became the basis for expanded federal spending on recovery efforts in New York, homeland security and public health, and the prosecution of the war in Afghanistan. There was growing realization that during the remainder of the Bush presidency deficit spending would dominate the world of fiscal policy. Once the war in Iraq began, estimates of the federal deficit for 2003 were placed at between $300 billion and $400 billion.

While fiscal policy is more open in that it is formed by presidential and congressional interaction, monetary policy is in the hands of an appointive and often secretive body, the Federal Reserve. Monetary policy, which in effect is the action by the Federal Reserve to change the amount of money in circulation and thereby affect interest rates, credit, the level of inflation, and the condition of unemployment, has become a vital part of what government does to manage and direct the nation's economy. The Federal Reserve Banking System, established by Congress in 1913, consists of a board of seven governors, including a chairperson, who meet monthly to set monetary policy. Because of the board's highly critical role in shaping economic policy, the chairman of the Federal Reserve and the other governors of the various federal banks are protected from the vagaries of national partisan politics. Although the president appoints the members of the Federal Reserve, the board of governors, and particularly the highly visible and important chairperson, is an independent body.

The current chairman of the Federal Reserve, Alan Greenspan, was appointed to the post during the first Bush administration and remained at the post throughout the Clinton presidency. Greenspan has become an enormously powerful figure in the American economy; his decisions on interest rates are watched carefully by American businesses, the stock market, and individual citizens. Greenspan's words when he briefs Congress are analyzed for any hints that may signal whether the board of governors is contemplating a rate change. Such a change would likely have a profound effect on the borrowing habits of corporate and individual America and the short-term movement of stocks on Wall Street.

During 2000 and 2001 Greenspan dropped interest rates on ten separate occasions in an attempt to use monetary measures to stimulate a stagnant economy. By making money "cheaper," Greenspan and the Federal Reserve relied on an expanded money supply as the critical ingredient in combating a recessionary trend. Relying on monetary policy as a frontline strategy for stimulating the American economy during a downturn is widely accepted, but Greenspan's reduction of rates in 2000–2001 could not stave off the recession brought on by a general decline in consumer confidence associated with the events of September 11.

The third area of economic policymaking is trade. The role of government on issues relating to trade has expanded dramatically in recent years. Although trade relations with other countries and regions have been a part of public policy since the days of Thomas Jefferson and the Barbary pirates preying on American merchant ships, it was not until the 1970s that trade became an issue of national interest and national security. The Arab oil embargo threatened the economic security of the United States and the economic power of Japan, served as a wake-up call on the vulnerability of the American economy to outside forces, and focused attention on the growing interconnect-edness of the world economy and the importance of trade as an engine of growth. By the 1970s it was becoming clear that U.S. economic domination, which began after World War II, was coming under challenge as a revitalized Europe, an aggressive Japan, and Third World countries such as Korea, Brazil, Mexico, and China developed more sophisticated and competitive economies.

These developments in international trade occurred in an emerging global economy, where trade barriers were viewed as antithetical to economic growth and new trading regimes were being negotiated to further link countries through their exports and imports. Free trade became the watchword of political leaders and corporate executives as they touted the wonders of open economies not fettered by cumbersome regulations and high tariffs. In order to advance the free trade agenda, the administrations of George H.W. Bush and Bill Clinton took significant steps that signaled government's role in ensuring that the United States would be a leader in the global economy.

In 1992 the first Bush administration signed the North American Free Trade Agreement with Canada and Mexico. The NAFTA signing, in the words of President Bush, would "begin the process of creating a hemisphere-wide free trade zone; increase investment . . . to create a new flow of capital in the region and further ease the burden of debt with important benefits for the environment." With over 360 million people and $6 trillion in output, a free trade zone that stretched from "the Yukon to the Yucatan, from Anchorage to Argentina" would create a dynamic economic zone that generated corporate profits, new jobs, and an ever expanding regional economy. Bush's successor, Bill Clinton, shared his predecessor's enthusiasm for NAFTA. Although facing stiff opposition from labor unions that saw NAFTA as a means of sending manufacturing jobs to less developed countries, Clinton made NAFTA and free trade a hallmark of his administration.

With NAFTA in place, the United States moved quickly to advance its trade policy on the global stage, signing in 1994 the so-called Uruguay round of trade negotiations sponsored by the U.N. General Agreement on Tariffs and Trade (GATT). Over one hundred representatives from around the world signed the trade agreement, which significantly liberalized trade relations and set up a new organization, the World Trade Organization (WTO), with broad powers to further liberalize trade (a 40 percent cut in tariffs worldwide) and arbitrate trade disputes between countries and trading blocs involving unfair subsidies and regulations that limit access of goods. Since the 1994 agreement establishing it, the WTO has been the source of controversy. In a 1999 WTO meeting in Seattle huge, violent demonstrations erupted to protest the organization and the impact of free trade on the working class, the environment, and human rights. Protesters pointed out that although free trade brought prosperity to some, it brought inequality, environmental degradation, and human rights abuse to many in the less developed world.

The free trade juggernaut is not about to be stopped, nor is the push to create economic integration. The global economy is here to stay, but trade policy will increasingly become a political issue rather than arcane decisions made by faceless WTO negotiators. Today the assets of the two hundred richest people in the world are greater than the combined income of more than 2 billion people. Inevitably the power of the few and the inequality inherent in the world economy will require that the United States fine-tune a system it fostered. Even though the impact of globalization and the new rules of trading have created enormous prosperity, the concentration of wealth and the level of inequality are causing heightened anti-Americanism in the less developed world.

POINT OF FACT

The World Economic Forum designated the United States as the country having the highest level of innovation and business creativity. The International Institute for Management Development likewise named the United States as having the most competitive business environment.

The United States and the Global Economy

The global economy is not the invention of one person or country, but the United States has been the most influential participant in setting the guidelines and establishing the rules under which countries interact in the international marketplace. Often these guidelines and rules are termed the "Washington consensus" to establish the impact that the United States has had on globalization. The key elements of the Washington consensus that now form the basis for globalization are as follows:

Establishment of the private sector as the source of economic growth
Elimination of tariffs on imported goods
Expansion of exports
Openness to foreign investment
Privatization of state enterprises
Deregulation of bureaucratic controls
Balanced state budgets
Reduction in the number of state workers
Maintenance of low rate of inflation
Elimination of corrupt practices in public and private sectors

CHALLENGES

Because the events of September 11 changed everything in the United States, the challenges facing the government and the American people have been re-defined. Combating terrorism worldwide, protecting the homeland from ter-rorist threats, expanding the governmental infrastructure relating to airport security, public health, and intelligence gathering are now top priorities. In many respects the United States was underprepared for the September 11 ter-rorist attacks. Although the government knew that terrorists associated with Osama bin Laden and his al-Qaeda organization were behind the bombings of the U.S. embassies in Africa and the attack on the USS *Cole* in Yemen, it never anticipated the scale of the attacks against the World Trade Center and the Pentagon. The CIA and the FBI received intense criticism from Congress for failing to adequately assess the terrorist threat and warn the nation.

Since September 11, the United States has shifted attention from more tra-ditional domestic issue areas and policy concerns to placing the country on a wartime footing. Legislation designed to give law enforcement stronger tools to fight terrorism was passed, along with the compromise airport security bill. More difficult challenges involved the fine line between an open society that protected individual rights and a nation that was fighting threats from terrorists in its midst. The U.S. government was forced to deal with requests of Middle Eastern residents seeking entry from foreign countries as students and workers, the call for police profiling of Muslims as part of a general secu-rity policy, and the rights of those detained by the police as material wit-nesses because of their association with known terrorists. The question raised by civil libertarians was how far the United States was willing to go in regard to counterterrorism before it began to weaken fundamental principles con-tained in the Bill of Rights.

The most critical challenge the government faced was creating a climate of confidence and security for the American people. In the wake of the anthrax deaths that followed the attack on the Twin Towers, it became clear that the American people feared domestic terrorism and that government agencies were not adequately prepared to protect the country. From the U.S. Postal Service to the Center for Disease Control to the Immigration and Naturali-zation Service, there was widespread concern that a new way of operating was necessary if counterterrorism was to be successful. These government agen-cies and entities moved rapidly to put new security measures in place, but in the process showed the American people that life had indeed changed after September 11 and that the role of the government had expanded. As the war on terrorism moved forward, the American people came to a greater understanding that more changes in lifestyle, rights, and government responsibility would be forthcoming.

The national security agenda became even more complicated in 2003 when the Bush administration made the decision to invade Iraq to remove the regime of Saddam Hussein. Despite intense opposition from the United Nations and the reluctance of European allies (except Britain) to join another multilateral coalition, the Bush administration maintained its resolve that Iraq, with its weapons of mass destruction, posed a threat to the United States as well as the region. A solid congressional majority, including many Democrats, joined President Bush in supporting a resolution granting him the authority to use military force to overthrow Saddam Hussein. While there was concern over the ramifications of such a military move for stability in the Middle East and rising anti-Americanism, the Bush administration held to its position that the war on terrorism must be extended to include the overthrow of Saddam Hussein.

Although national security has become the number one priority of the United States, it is incorrect to assume that issues deemed critical before September 11 have disappeared. The attack on America deepened the challenges facing the United States and complicated the policy agenda. For example, the United States is currently in the midst of a national debate over how it will meet the needs of the baby boomer generation as it begins tapping into Social Security and Medicare in the next few years. The two programs will be subjected to enormous pressure and will require significant injections of dollars to remain solvent.

Projections from various government and independent sources show that by the year 2013 the number of Americans retiring will be so large that the cost of providing monthly checks to seniors will far outstrip the money coming into the program. By 2032 some prognosticators predict that the Social Security system will be bankrupt and unable to meet its financial obligations to the American people. Since its inception in 1935, Social Security has become one of the most popular social welfare programs instituted by the government. Currently Social Security recipients include over 27 million retirees, 5.4 million widows and widowers, 4.4 million disabled, and 3.8 million children of deceased or disabled persons. By the year 2030 the number of Americans eligible for Social Security will have risen to over 70 million, and $1 trillion (in today's dollars) in additional taxes will be necessary to fund the program.

Despite the disturbing demographic projections, public opinion polls regularly show unyielding support for Social Security, a fact not lost on national political leaders who see the program as untouchable in terms of budget cuts or policy compromises. One potential problem area for Social Security, despite its popularity, is the tax burden that young Americans will bear to take care of the Social Security needs of the baby boom generation. At present it takes 2.7 workers paying Social Security taxes to support the system, but by 2013 it will take 3.3 workers to provide the same support. But that support, with a price tag of $1 trillion, will be provided by a generation that may not take too kindly to seeing their payroll taxes increase dramatically to provide a benefit that they will not enjoy.

While Social Security and its solvency in the next thirty years receives the lion's share of attention, the future of the Medicare program is also in jeopardy, in large part because of the aging of America. Medicare, the health care program for seniors receiving Social Security, is financed by a mix of payroll taxes and monthly fees. In 1994 Medicare costs were $163 billion; in 2000 those costs jumped to nearly $250 billion and projections for future years show costs skyrocketing. Seniors are now living longer and as a result are using the Medicare program and the resources of the Medicare program. Hospitals, health maintenance organizations, and insurance companies are struggling to remain profitable while providing care for those requiring medical attention. At the center of the problem is the Medicare system, which covers hospitalization, some nursing home care, and home health services, along with optional payments for physician services and many outpatient and diagnostic services. The health care industry in the United States is currently going through a period of internal restructuring, financial uncertainty, and in some cases bankruptcy, in large part because of government caps on Medicare payments to hospitals at a time when a growing senior population is making greater use of hospital services.

The challenges facing the United States are not just domestic ones. Also of critical importance to the United States is properly defining and implementing its role as superpower and world leader. Since the Soviet Union broke up and communism collapsed, the United States has been the lone superpower. With its nuclear arsenal, high-tech weapons, and well-trained troops, the American military overshadows all other armed forces. But with the Soviet Union no longer around to offer an alternative to Western democratic capitalism, the United States has solidified its position as leader of the free world and the most influential diplomatic force in times of crisis. But with superpower status and its leadership role come increased demands to use its military strength and its diplomacy as peacekeeper and peacemaker. The U.S. military has become the peacekeeper of first recourse in the world today. Responding to small wars, ethnic and racial flare-ups, difficult democratic transitions, and humanitarian missions has become commonplace for the U.S. military as its role has been redefined in the postcommunist era.

Furthermore, instead of concentrating on Cold War grand strategy involving nuclear deterrence, military containment, and diplomatic chess games, the United States has become the world's problem solver, moving to trouble spots such as Somalia, Bosnia, Haiti, Kosovo, Afghanistan, and Iraq.

Responding to heightened demands to use its superior military strength and its diplomatic clout to manage crises has created a wide-ranging debate in the United States. Questions have been raised concerning the appropriateness of the United States' accepting responsibility to secure peace in a troubled world. The doctrine of isolationism with its America-first views has gained greater support from those who feel that the United States has overextended its presence in world trouble spots and too quickly assumes a leadership role in peacekeeping operations. Military and diplomatic intervention is costly, and it places U.S. troops in harm's way. The involvement of U.S. troops in anarchic conditions in Somalia (where one U.S. helicopter pilot was dragged through the streets of Mogadishu) and the ethnic wars in Bosnia and Kosovo (where the United States contributed the lion's share of troops to the conflict) during the Clinton presidency prompted widespread criticism of U.S. policy. In the invasion of Iraq, U.S. troop levels approached 300,000, with an initial cost of over $70 billion.

Critics in Congress questioned whether American interests were at stake in these wars and whether sending U.S. military forces as peacekeepers placed them in jeopardy for no good reason. Supporters of the U.S. peacekeeping role in these localized wars cited humanitarian considerations (the high civilian death toll and the tragic refugee problem) as the basis for extending national interest considerations to countries and conditions not directly connected to security concerns. The divide between the isolationists and the interventionists was not bridged in large part because the postcommunist world with its small wars and humanitarian missions poses a new set of international conditions that has yet to bring forth a policy consensus.

But then came September 11 and the insertion of American troops in Afghanistan to hunt for the Taliban and al-Qaeda terrorists. With Congress and the American public nearly united on the need for ground troops in Afghanistan, past concerns over intervention were forgotten, although the antiterrorist campaign could not be defined as a small war or a humanitarian mission. Nevertheless, the United States has left behind, at least for a time, its reluctance to use its military muscle. In his 2002 State of the Union speech President Bush targeted Iraq as part of an "Axis of Evil" (along with Iran and North Korea). Since that speech he and various members of his administration have been publicly and privately laying the groundwork for an expanded use of U.S. military might against the so-called Axis of Evil.

The widening use of American ground troops and the bold targeting of the Axis of Evil mirror the extensive efforts within the United States to bolster homeland security. The Bush administration has shown that it takes the potential for future terrorist strikes seriously and is expending billions of dollars on strengthening the institutional framework in areas such as chemical and biological warfare, airport security, emergency preparation, and law enforcement. The view that the war on terrorism will be long and that security and preparation measures will become part of everyday life is evident in the American political arena and among the American public.

COMPARISONS

For all its stellar reputation for longevity and stability, the governing system that serves as the foundation of the American political system has not become the model for democratic development in the world. Although many Latin American countries have adopted variations of key constitutional constructs such as the presidential system and federalism, the British Westminster system of parliamentary governance and unitary organization has attracted the founding fathers of new democracies or countries seeking to move away from an authoritarian past. The idea of a president separate from the majority party or coalition of parties in the legislature has found little support as nations seek to streamline governance. The idea of numerous powerful subnational entities such as the states that can challenge the authority of the central government has not been a dominant method of internal organization. The American political system with its constitutional mechanisms for restraining power and requiring extensive gradualism and compromise has often been viewed as a quaint exception that works for the United States, but not for countries anxious to make their democracy work in an efficient and effective manner.

Although the American constitutional system has remained an unattractive governing alternative, some key elements of the American political arena have filtered into the mainstream of public life in many developed and developing countries. For example, in many Western democracies interest groups have begun to challenge political parties for influence on the policy process. Elections are not simple ideological contests between competing parties, but elaborate and expensive media extravaganzas with sophisticated media campaigns, high-priced consultants, endless public opinion polls, and candidates more interested in their image than their policy platforms. Although the United States maintains a commanding lead in campaign expenditures, many Western nations are spending at rates unheard of twenty years ago. But this Americanization has not increased popular participation in Western democracies. Like the United States, many European countries have witnessed sharply declining voter turnouts in the past ten years. It is of course impossible to make a connection between the Americanization of European politics and the decline of democratic practice, but the connection is not lost on critics in these countries who long for a return to a time when political parties mattered, money and the media were insignificant factors, and elections brought out high percentages of eligible voters.

Comparisons between the American political system and others in the world reveal that the most essential linkage is in the area of economic management. Most of the countries of the world have put into place the privatized, market-based, global economic approach that has evolved in the United States since the Reagan administration. Less government, tax cuts, deregulation, privatization, free trade, low interest rates, and a pro-business attitude have become the elements of national development. Government has become a partner in economic modernization and growth rather than the driving force behind modernization and growth. The relationship between government and the economy in the United States has in a real sense set off a revolution of profound proportions in the countries of the world. The American model has not been universally accepted, and policies or positions taken by the United States to promote its vision of a new relationship between government and the economic sector have been extensively criticized. But the economic model put in place since the 1980s has become the key force in defining the world we live in.

Because the United States is the most powerful and economically dominant nation in the world, what its government does and how its politics play out will have an impact on other countries, whether rich or poor. At the core of American influence are the democratic values of freedom, equality, fairness, rule of law, tolerance, and openness. Although these values have not been perfectly attained in the United States, they nonetheless serve as the model for nations that seek to establish democracy. Newly emerging nations may not copy the most complicated and difficult elements of the American governing system, but it is hard for the political leadership in these countries to claim to form a democracy without building it on the core values of freedom, equality, fairness, the rule of law, tolerance, and openness. Just like the United States, where there are imperfections in securing these values, those countries in Asia, Africa, Latin America, and the Middle East that are struggling to deepen democratic principles and practice nevertheless have accepted the importance of establishing a political culture founded on American values.

CONCLUSION

The key to understanding the governing system is to remember that it is linked with an economic system that remains the marvel of the world. The 1990s witnessed the longest period of economic prosperity in the history of the United States. This prosperity compensated for a series of disturbing events in the political system, including the impeachment of a president, a government shutdown, weak levels of citizen participation, and disturbing signs of Americans turning away from government. Now that a new century has dawned and the United States is facing its most serious foreign and domestic crisis since World War II, questions can legitimately be asked as to whether the political system has the capacity and the American people possess the willingness to make the governing puzzle work.

The American economy seems to work best when government recedes into the background and the American government seems to work best when the economy needs assistance. When the two grand forces of American capitalist wealth and democratic power work in tandem and play off each other, the country gathers the benefits from each. Americans have come to accept the half solutions and the muddling through that defines the public policy arena. As one commentator stated, "Somehow it works."

A FEW BOOKS YOU SHOULD READ

Joseph Nye, *The Paradox of American Power* (New York: Oxford University Press, 2002). Seeks answers to the questions, What role should the United States play in the world and How should Americans define their national interests?

David Mayhew, *America's Congress: Actions in the Public Sphere: James Madison Through Newt Gingrich* (New Haven: Yale University Press, 2002). Contains everything you ever wanted to know about how Congress works.

David O'Brien, *Storm Center: The Supreme Court in American Politics*, 5th ed. (New York: Norton, 1999). A key source on the federal courts.

Stephen Wayne, *Is This Any Way to Run a Democratic Election?* (New York: Houghton Mifflin, 2002). Examines the key components of electoral politics from money to the media.

Gary Wills, *A Necessary Evil: A History of American Distrust of Government* (New York: Simon & Schuster, 1999). A disturbing examination of why Americans are wary of politics and politicians.

A FEW WEB SITES YOU SHOULD VISIT

www.cq.com. *Congressional Quarterly,* the most informative and nonpartisan news about the Congress.

www.whitehouse.gov. The White House Web site. Send the president an e-mail.

www.gallup.com. The Gallup Organization Web site provides a wealth of data on America and American politics.

www.c-span.org. C-SPAN is one of the more respected sources of news on American government.

www.yahoo.com/government. The Yahoo government index is an essential search engine for everything you ever wanted to find out about American government and politics.

Norwegian
Sea

Faroe Is.

Shetland
Is.

Scotland

North
Sea

IRELAND

Nothern
Ireland

Dublin

UNITED
KINGDOM

England
Wales
London

English Channel

SOURCE: Michigan State University Map Library, Data Source ESRI
MAP 2.1   United Kingdom

United Kingdom of Great Britain and Northern Ireland

Data Bank

Area: 94,525 sq. miles

Population: 59.1 million (1999)

Rural/urban population ratio: 11/89 (1999)

Ethnic makeup: 81 percent British, 9.6 percent Scottish, 2.4 percent Welsh, 1.8 percent Irish, 4.7 percent West Indian and South Asian

Life expectancy: Male, 75 years; female, 80 years

Adult literacy: 99 percent

Form of government: Constitutional monarchy

Head of state: Her Majesty Queen Elizabeth II

Head of government: Prime Minister Tony Blair

Per capita income/GDP: $29,360 (2002)

Exports: $267 billion; imports $311 billion (partners: Germany, United States, France)

Source: United Nations and World Bank

SETTING THE SCENE

Great Britain is frequently thought of as a country steeped in tradition and history, a country of royalty and civility, a country where policemen are known as bobbies and a huge clock is called Big Ben. The British place a premium on preserving the past and take pride in the pomp and circumstance of the monarchy. Travelers to Great Britain follow the course of Western civilization with Roman ruins, gigantic castles overlooking battlefields, and the burial places of kings, queens, generals, and prime ministers.

This is a country of Shakespeare and Shelley, Oxford and Cambridge, West-minster Abbey and Trafalgar Square, Robin Hood and Mary Poppins.

Great Britain is also a country where government is a defining characteristic of national life. Although democracy was born in ancient Greece, it acquired its modern form in Great Britain. The Magna Carta, the first democratic governing document, was written here; the first parliament and the first prime minister, Sir Robert Walpole, were installed here; some of the great thinkers of democracy such as John Locke and John Stuart Mill were born here; and much of the common law tradition that serves as the basis for the modern legal system was promulgated here. Walking through the British House of Commons and House of Lords provides a history lesson on democratic governance. Famous men such as Winston Churchill and Benjamin Disraeli spoke in these chambers, and heated debates over going to war and making peace were conducted from the front benches. For over three hundred years decisions on how to manage a vast global empire were made by ministers, lords, and commoners.

Great Britain, however, is not just an old country with a long and illustrious past. The Great Britain of today is a nation that has been transformed. The nation that gave birth to the Industrial Revolution is now known as a high-tech investment and communications hub with growing ties to Europe. Furthermore, with the new engineering marvel, the Chunnel, linking it to France and the rest of Europe, Great Britain is an important participant in the European Union, the economic and trade bloc that has lowered tariffs and allowed free access of goods and services. Since the 1980s Great Britain has sought to shed its image as an old industrial power dependent on coal, shipping, and automobiles. In its place Great Britain has moved forcefully into the computer age with hundreds of start-up companies that cater to the demands of the information age. While old northern cities like Liverpool, Newcastle, and Birmingham remain tied to heavy industry and mining, in the south of the country power, population, and wealth are clearly in evidence. A new generation of entrepreneurs has turned small, sleepy hamlets into booming suburban communities. London, the capital, remains at the center of political, economic, and cultural power, but it too has been transformed with large skyscrapers, an affluent consumer class, and the hustle and bustle of a city that has become the crossroads of modern Europe.

Great Britain has also been transformed in its political life. The traditions that lay at the core of the country for centuries are gradually undergoing change. The House of Lords, once the bastion of privilege, has been reconstituted to limit the number of hereditary peers. The royal family no longer commands the adulation of the British people, as they are subjected to endless reminders of the death of Princess Diana and the personal failings of other members of the family. The current prime minister, Tony Blair, modeled his electoral campaigning and subsequent governing style after that of American politicians (primarily Bill Clinton) with astute use of television, public opinion polling, and image-enhancing advertising. The Parliament building with its stately spires and its ornate halls remains for the tourists, but government in Great Britain is thoroughly modern.

Perhaps the biggest transformation that the British face is the reality of "small power status." Since the conclusion of World War II Great Britain has reduced its presence in the world. In 1939, before the outbreak of World War II, Britain was the second wealthiest country in the world (the United States being the wealthiest). By the 1970s Britain had fallen behind many of its European neighbors, thus earning the title "poor man of Europe." In the early 1990s Britain fell further behind, being surpassed by some of the emerging Asian "tigers" such as Hong Kong and Singapore. In recent years, Britain has rebounded somewhat due to a vibrant economy but still lags behind countries such as Norway, Belgium, Sweden, Iceland, Germany, and Austria.

As its international power and standing have diminished, Britain has given its imperial outposts independence, one by one. From India in 1947 to the Bahamas in 1973 to Hong Kong in 1998 Great Britain has returned its possessions, in some cases because of opposition to its rule but mostly because holding on to them was too costly. Moreover, Great Britain is no longer able to compete militarily with other superpowers. Although Britain continues to play an active peacekeeping role and has taken the lead with the United States in supporting the military response to remove the regime of Saddam Hussein, its involvement has been largely in a supportive role. For a nation where, in Kipling's words, "the sun never sets on the British empire," the change to "small power status" has been difficult.

But transformations in economic life, sovereign control, and global power status have not detracted from the reputation that Great Britain has developed as a nation of good government. The Westminster model of executive-legislative relations that is the cornerstone of the British political system has been transferred around the world to newly emerging nations. The concepts of parliamentary sovereignty and majority rule that the British have honed to perfection are widely viewed as the most efficient means of governing and national decisionmaking. The British party system with its emphasis on issues rather than personalities, disciplined voting, and structured policy platforms has become a textbook example of the organization and functioning of partisan power. As a result, the Conservative and Labour Parties have earned the reputation as two of the leading political organizations in Western democracies. Finally, the "world's greatest debating society," the House of

Commons, has reminded all democrats of the importance of regular inter-change between differing political viewpoints. The vigorous verbal repartee between front benchers and back benchers and the occasional humorous and boisterous exchanges between members of Parliament make viewing Commons and the process of democratic lawmaking both informative and entertaining.

It is inevitable that the British system will be placed side by side with the American system to explore strengths and weaknesses, benefits and draw-backs. Most observers would agree that the British governing system is more streamlined and efficient, while the American system is complex and slow moving. The key to understanding and evaluating the British govern-ing system is not to engage in comparisons but to appreciate the unique characteristics of parliamentary democracy. British government has much to offer the student of lawmaking, executive-legislative relations, political party systems, electoral behavior, and public policy. In many respects Great Britain is the place to begin when studying democratic governance and pop-ular politics.

POLITICAL MILESTONES

It is no easy task to take the length and breadth of British political history and condense it into a set of important milestones. Since the history of Britain is a chronicle of many of the formative events in the development of Western democracy, singling out the key ones poses a problem. Nevertheless, amid the wide expanse of British history there are some watershed events that have shaped the constitution and governing process along with leaders who have left their mark on national life. The manner in which the British have responded to these events reflects their capacity to bring forth change in a manner that does not destroy the fabric of politics, but rather brings the country to a new level of modernity and maturity.

The dominant theme in British historical development is evolutionary change. In marked departure from some of its European neighbors, Britain has been able to fashion a democratic culture and political system in a man-ner that avoided revolutionary measures and destabilizing movements. Governing reform has served as the basis for British political development. Political elites have recognized that the way to avoid internal disorder and political fragmentation is to pursue incremental change and build societal consensus around national public policy. British political development has in no way been ideal in the sense of smooth transitions and public acceptance of change, but a positive undercurrent of reform has served the nation well.

The Glorious Revolution

A substantial portion of British political history is associated with the relationship between Parliament and the monarchy, in particular the definition of power holders and the demarcation of where power lies among the power holders. The critical struggle to define and demarcate power in British government occurred during the seventeenth century, specifically between 1642 and 1689. This was the period of the Civil War with its endpoint as the Glorious Revolution. The period begins with Charles I (1625–1649) dissolving two Parliaments and making unpopular financial decisions. The antagonism between king and Parliament eventually led to war between the peers, the Anglican Church and Catholics supporting the king and urban dwellers and the Puritans supporting Parliament. Charles was executed by the pro-parliamentary forces in 1649 and four years later Oliver Cromwell, taking the title Lord Protector, assumed power under Britain's only written constitution, the Instrument of Government. Despite being a proponent of parliamentary rule, Cromwell amassed power and ruled in an authoritarian manner. His death in 1658 allowed the restoration of the monarchy under Charles II.

Charles worked with Parliament and remained on the throne until his brother James II became king in 1685. James, a Catholic, moved quickly to restore the Catholic Church and strip the Anglican Church of its influence within government and society. James's efforts to reestablish Catholic supremacy forced the parliamentary forces to drive him out of the throne in 1688 in what is often called the Glorious Revolution. The victorious parliamentary forces transferred power to James's daughter, Mary, and her husband, William of Orange. The removal of James and the ascension to the throne of William and Mary effectively ended the ongoing conflict between Parliament and the monarchy. To ensure that future monarchs would not challenge Parliament, the Bill of Rights was promulgated, which clearly stated that Parliament was the legislative authority. The Bill of Rights also stated that the king was not permitted to levy taxes without parliamentary consent and that the monarch was not allowed to maintain an army without legislative approval.

The Glorious Revolution firmly established Parliament as the governing power in Britain. In 1701 Parliament further secured its position by passing the Act of Settlement, which transferred the monarchy from the Catholic descendants of James II to the Protestant House of Hanover and forbade the monarch from removing judges without the consent of Parliament. The transfer of the throne to the House of Hanover was most significant in that it required the monarchy to be affiliated with Anglican Protestantism.

During the reigns of George I (1714–1727) and George II (1727–1760) the monarchy gave up more responsibility to the Parliament and the majority party within Parliament. It became common practice for the monarch to choose cabinet ministers from the majority party rather than rely on personal preferences. By 1721 George I was working with Sir Robert Walpole who, although he did not have the title of prime minister, was viewed as leader of the Parliament. When Walpole lost the support of Commons in 1742, he resigned, showing that he could no longer function in a legislative body that was responsible for managing the affairs of state.

When George III rose to the throne in 1760, Parliament's supremacy was unquestioned. The British system had evolved with little disruption into one in which the monarch was viewed as weak and dependent on the direction of the Parliament. The Parliament became the decisionmaking body of the nation and possessed the sovereignty to make laws for the nation. Kings and queens would remain in the forefront of British life, and some monarchs such as Queen Victoria would exert considerable influence on British political life. But the transition of power from monarch to Parliament that became known as the Glorious Revolution forever changed the way in which Britain is governed and the way it is led.

The Great Reform Act of 1832

The Industrial Revolution, which had its roots in England, led to a number of important developments. The wave of industrialization expanded the wealth of the business and managerial class, increased the movement of people to the urban centers, and heightened class tensions between workers and their bosses. There was also a political component to this transition from an agricultural to a factory-dominated economy. In many of the industrial cities middle-class males, who had prospered as small business operators or factory supervisors, gained influence. As Britain entered the nineteenth century and it became clear that this new industrial middle class was anxious to become part of the democratic process, there was growing pressure to extend suffrage as well as a realization among governing elites that a change of electoral laws was a prudent political move.

Just as middle-class suffrage rights were being debated, there was concern in Commons over the corruption of representative democracy. Before 1832 large municipalities were poorly represented and many members in Parliament gained their seats by making financial payments to party leaders. It was estimated at the time that as many as half of the seats in the House of Commons came from "rotten" boroughs (Commons seats from areas that had lost population but still commanded representation) and "pocket" boroughs

(Commons seats under the control of a landed aristocrat who sold the right to participate in Parliament). The distinguished member of Parliament William Pitt the Younger castigated the "rotten" borough system on the floor of the House of Commons: "This House is not the representative of the people of Great Britain; it is the representative of nominal boroughs, of ruined and exterminated towns, of noble families, of wealthy individuals, of foreign potentates." Reform was clearly needed to rid the British parliamentary system of what came to be called the Old Corruption.

Parliament reluctantly, after considerable political infighting, passed the Great Reform Act of 1832. It abolished the "rotten" boroughs by creating new constituencies in unrepresented or underrepresented areas. It also established a single system of property qualifications for voting and also a voter registration procedure. Although it did not address specifically the "pocket" borough problem of buying seats in Commons, the expanse of the legislation and the support of key elites such as Lord Grey in the House of Lords did much to turn the tide against the Old Corruption. The most significant change brought about by the Great Reform Act was the extension of suffrage rights to over a million members of the male middle class. Although this appears to be a large bloc of new voters, suffrage rights covered only approximately one-fifth of the British population. A first step had been made to make Britain more democratic.

The act did set in motion a process of democratization and legislative representation that would bear fruit. In 1867 and 1884 Commons passed the People's Act, which further enfranchised the urban middle- and working-class male population. In 1885 Commons passed the Redistribution of Seats Act, which created a fairer process of drawing the district lines for purposes of representation. Throughout this period Commons gradually worked on ridding the political process of corruption. As was the case in most industrial democracies, women had to wait until the twentieth century to become full participants in the British political process. In 1918 Commons extended suffrage rights to married women and to single women over thirty. In 1928 it extended full suffrage rights to all women over the age of twenty-one.

The Great Reform Act of 1832 fits into the description of British politics as an evolutionary rather than revolutionary process. Governing elites recognized that political and social stability would be threatened if Commons continued to be the domain of the rich and the well connected. This was no altruistic gesture on the part of Commons, but a clearheaded understanding of the need for reform before the entire governing system was weakened by corruption and undemocratic behavior. The governing stability that the British have enjoyed throughout their political development is a direct result of the kind of enlightened conservatism inherent in legislation like the Great

Reform Act of 1832. The word "great" has been added over time to describe the legislative and electoral reforms agreed to in 1832. The term is certainly appropriate because with this legislation Britain made a great leap toward democracy and extended it by following a careful, step-by-step approach that never caused serious disruption to the body politic.

Winston Churchill and the Battle for Britain

In the words of Winston Churchill, the Battle of Britain went down in history as England's "finest hour." In May 1939 Hitler's troops had all but overrun Belgium, except for nearly 450,000 allied troops, mostly French and British, in the port city of Dunkirk. In one of the most dramatic rescue missions in the history of warfare, the British, using every seaworthy ship available, brought home nearly 380,000 troops to fight the Nazis another day. Britain would need every soldier and sailor it could muster in the next two years because the island nation stood virtually alone against the Germans. The Battle of Britain was largely an air war with the German Luftwaffe engaging the Royal Air Force (RAF) in countless skirmishes over the country. But in September 1940 the Germans changed their strategy and began bombing civilian population centers. This began the period known as the "Blitz," when cities like London and Coventry were heavily damaged by German bombing raids. The RAF and military antiaircraft batteries fought back, but there was enormous damage to buildings and considerable loss of life. At the end of 1940 civilian casualties were put at 13,000 killed and 20,000 wounded. By 1941 the RAF was able to establish firm control over the air space and the Nazis backed away from their strategy of bombing Britain and turned toward the eastern front and the Russians. After Pearl Harbor was bombed in 1941, the United States, which had been militarily neutral (but had supplied military equipment to Britain through the Lend-Lease Act), entered the European war and bolstered the opposition to Hitler's Germany.

During the Battle of Britain Prime Minister Winston Churchill embodied the spirit of resistance and national pride that developed among the British people. After Churchill's predecessor, Neville Chamberlain, conceded the Sudetenland to Hitler, it became clear that the only way to stop the Nazi war machine was to stand firm and fight. Winston Churchill was just the man. During the dark days of the Blitz, Churchill was on the radio, at civil defense positions, among the rubble of burned-out buildings, and with the pilots of the RAF urging them on and sending a signal to the Nazis that Britain would fight them alone if necessary. Although there is much disagreement among historians about the administrative skill and military planning prowess of Churchill, there is no disagreement over Churchill's single-minded ability to move a nation toward a single goal and to rouse their nationalist passions. Churchill recognized the danger of Nazi domination in Europe and took the lead against Hitler despite overwhelming odds. To say that he saved England is not an understatement.

When the war was over, Winston Churchill turned his attention to the new threat from the Soviet Union. In a famous speech given in President Truman's home state of Missouri Churchill warned about an "Iron Curtain" that was developing in Eastern Europe, a curtain that was separating the democratic countries from those controlled by Soviet communism. When Churchill left office in 1955, his legacy was secure as the symbol of opposition to tyranny and authoritarian expansionism. Never one to mince words or downplay the challenge, Churchill will be remembered for promising his fellow countrymen "blood, toil, tears and sweat," and for letting the Nazis know that "we shall fight on the beaches" in order to end the Germany quest for European domination.

Social Welfare and Nationalization in the Postwar Period

The aftermath of a major war often fosters significant social and economic change. Although Great Britain emerged victorious from World War II, its economy and numerous public policy areas were in serious need of revitalization and reform. Although the British economy was vigorous with high employment and production, there were deep-seated problems connected to the devastation caused by years of German bombing, Britain's outdated industrial base, and its declining overseas presence. Moreover, Britain needed to address serious health problems among its population, along with expanding educational opportunities and providing adequate housing. The slogan of Britain during this postwar period was, "We are up against it: we work or we want."

In 1945, the Labour Party reentered government under the leadership of Clement Attlee. Labour, with its solid union support and socialist leanings, moved quickly to address the reconstruction needs of the nation. The government's economic plan was based on two major initiatives—central planning and nationalization. The Labourites believed strongly that the only way to properly utilize the resources of the nation in this reconstruction period was to institute a system of national planning that managed national income, manpower, and raw materials. To achieve a centrally planned economy, the Attlee government introduced plans to nationalize or put under government control basic industries such as coal, gas, electricity, rail transportation, steel, and other key resources. Once completed, the nationalized sector of the British economy made up 25 percent of the country's GDP. The Labourites held true to their socialist principles, but they were unwilling to create a completely planned state economy. Rather they maintained a modified free-enterprise system with private corporations existing side by side with nationalized industries. These private industries, however, would be part of the national planning system and were expected to conform to the national economic plan.

With the planning and nationalization initiatives in place, Attlee and his Labour majority set about to make changes in the area of social services. Relying on a 1942 white paper authored by Liberal leader Lord Beveridge entitled "Social Insurance and Allied Services," Labour began a great social experiment in providing British citizens with an expanded safety net of health, education, housing, and retirement legislation. The centerpiece of the social safety net package was the 1948 passage of the National Health Service Act. The government acquired all hospitals except teaching hospitals and placed restrictions on doctors, including where they could set up their practices. The attractiveness of the National Health Service was that it provided free medical care, including hospital and dental services, for each British citizen. For a modest contribution and small fees for services, the British were able to receive health care without concern for cost. Critics of the program pointed to the high cost of the program and the restrictions on doctors selling and moving their practices, but in the postwar period there was a great need for medical attention. Despite the criticism, the National Health Service became one of the most popular social programs in the history of the country.

The Attlee government also moved on the education and housing front. Building on the Education Act of 1944, the Labour government expanded schooling opportunities, especially for those among the working class, and increased spending on higher education. In housing the Labourites built numerous temporary housing units for those whose homes were destroyed by war. The government made unused homes available for rent and initiated a range of public subsidies for housing. With health care, education, and housing, along with expanded retirement benefits, the Attlee government was beginning the formation of a "cradle to grave" social welfare system that provided assistance to British citizens from birth to death. This system proved to be a costly one and the tax burden on the wealthy made the Labourites a target of criticism in Parliament.

In the 1950 election Labour lost eighty-one seats and maintained only a threadbare two-seat majority. With little cushion in Commons and public opinion moving against its planning, nationalization, and social welfare initiatives, new elections were called in 1951 and the Conservatives regained power with a 321–296 margin of seats in Commons. The defeat of Labour, however, did not mean the end of its economic and social policies. A policy consensus had been established around a central government that managed the economy, controlled vital natural resources, and provided extensive social welfare programs. The National Health Service, for example, expanded its reach under Conservative governments that continued in power from 1951 to 1964. Britain became a nation guided by economic planning and social welfarism. Furthermore, Britain became a model of economic restructuring along statist lines that was followed by other European nations. The attraction of a more balanced system in which free enterprise existed side by side with state enterprises and state programs would become commonplace in the advanced industrial world for the next thirty years. It would take another critical election, much like the one that brought Attlee and Labour to power in 1945, to again reshape British economic and social policy.

The Thatcher Revolution

The term "revolution" is used sparingly in describing the scope of British political history, and even when "revolution" is attached to an event or an era, it is not associated with a bloody overthrow of the government. The ascension to power of the Conservative Party and its leader Margaret Thatcher in 1979, however, does qualify as a revolutionary event in that British government, economy, and society were transformed. Margaret Thatcher was destined to become one of the most powerful and feared prime ministers in the modern era. Her program of narrowing the scope of government, advancing the interests of the business community, and revitalizing the domestic spirit and international standing of Britain is likely to remain a source of praise and criticism for years to come.

When the Conservatives took power in 1979, Britain was deep into an economic slide. Unemployment was nearly 14 percent, real GNP growth was nonexistent, inflation pushed into the double-digit region, and the industrial base continued to crumble with strikes, low productivity, and bankruptcies. Thatcher, who quickly earned the title "Iron Lady," instituted a range of austerity measures designed to jump-start the economy by cutting back on government regulation, government subsidies, and government employees. Thatcher's target was the nationalized industries and government social welfare programs such as the National Health Service. Her solution for the nationalized industries was to begin privatization of state assets in which the government would sell to private buyers government enterprises that it had controlled since the Attlee era. The Thatcher government initiated the sale of British Telecom, the government-owned telephone and telecommunications company, and similar offerings were made for British Air and British Gas. As to the social welfare programs, Thatcher used the ax approach as she cut deeply into appropriations for the National Health Service, reduced the stock of public housing by permitting residents to buy their government-subsidized homes, and weakened government's commitment to public higher education.

A key objective for Thatcher was weakening the unions, which had expanded their power and economic influence during the previous years of Labour Party rule. A major confrontation between Thatcher and the unions occurred in 1984, when the government decided to close unproductive and unprofitable coal mines, with the loss of 20,000 jobs. Coal miners, who made up some of the most militant unionists in Britain and in the Labour Party, staged a year-long strike. Thatcher, however, would not budge, and eventually public opinion shifted away from support of the miners to disillusionment with their constant attacks on the government and their willingness to jeopardize national economic stability in the name of worker power. After a year, the miners ended their strike and Thatcher moved legislation through Parliament to weaken the power of union leaders to call strikes. The prime minister had outlasted the unions and turned public opinion to her side. The defeat of the miners' strike began a period of decline in union membership and union control of the Labour Party.

Despite the austerity measures and attacks on labor, Margaret Thatcher and the Conservatives increased their seats in Parliament. In 1983 Thatcher called an early election soon after the victory over Argentina in the Falkland Island War and saw the Conservative majority expand to more comfortable levels over Labour. British voters, particularly the middle class, were impressed with Thatcher's no-nonsense approach to politics and the economy. Even the working class found the Thatcher program attractive, further eroding union power. More importantly, by the mid-1980s there were some signs that "Thatcheromics" was beginning to show signs of success. Thatcher's monetarist approach, which raised interest rates, brought down inflation, and contributed to an increase in economic growth, was widely praised. But despite these successes, there were still numerous signs that the Thatcher approach was not working, especially in the areas of unemployment and income inequality.

By the second parliamentary election in 1987 the British had begun to tire of Margaret Thatcher, and the Conservatives lost twenty-one seats. The decline was attributed to the Labour Party's effectively challenging government economic measures, including the poll tax, a new revenue source that replaced the property tax. The poll tax actually increased the number of citizens required to pay taxes to the government from 18 million to 38 million. The introduction of the tax created a firestorm of protest and forced Thatcher to call back the tax initiative. Also during the mid-1980s there was controversy over Thatcher's abolition of London's local government, the Greater London Council, which had become a hotbed of anti-Conservative activity and according to the prime minister the center of the so-called loony left. In both the poll tax issue and the abolition of the Greater London Council Thatcher was viewed as a vindictive ideologue who was unbending in her program to place a free-market, conservative agenda in place.

In 1990 it became clear that Margaret Thatcher had lost significant support within her own party. There was division over how to deal with a new round of inflation and the social unrest that was building in the nation among the unemployed. Thatcher, sensing that her base of support was declining, resigned as leader of the Conservatives and worked to place her protégé, John Major, in the leadership position. Margaret Thatcher had the distinction of serving as prime minister longer than any political leader in the last hundred years. Moreover, Thatcher put into place a policy agenda that ended the collectivist state that had been in place since the postwar years. Thatcher moved Britain into the free market system, where the private sector pushed aside the public sector. It is safe to say that Margaret Thatcher changed the face of Britain.

Timeline

1215	Magna Carta
1265	First Parliament
1642	Outbreak of Civil War
1688	Glorious Revolution and Bill of Rights
1721	Sir Robert Walpole, first prime minister
1832	Great Reform Bill
1911	Parliament Act; House of Lords loses power
1939–1941	London under siege
1946–1950	Nationalization Acts and formation of National Health Service
1947	India granted independence
1949	Second Parliament Act; House of Lords further loses power
1955	Churchill retires
1960–1965	Independence granted to nations in Asia, Africa, and the Caribbean
1974–1979	Labour Party in power
1979	Conservatives and Margaret Thatcher elected
1982	Falkland Islands war
1985	Coal strike collapses; Thatcher at peak of power
1990	Thatcher resigns as Conservative leader; John Major becomes prime minister
1997	Tony Blair and New Labour assume power
2001	Labour wins again in national elections and Tony Blair remains prime minister
2003	Britain joins the United States for an invasion of Iraq

CROWN POLICY

There is more to Queen Elizabeth II, the British monarch, than the carriage rides from Buckingham Palace, the tradition-bound speech from the throne opening Parliament, and the countless ceremonial duties and royal visits to Commonwealth countries. The queen, her family, and some other members of the aristocratic class are part of British government and as a result are subject to a number of laws, tax obligations, and political responsibilities that define their role as participants in the British constitutional monarchy. While the public role of the monarch and the royal family often gain the attention of the media, it is the lesser-known budget appropriations, support infrastructure, and real estate holdings of the Crown that are rarely discussed.

The queen (and those acting on her behalf) is funded from four sources: the civil list, which meets official expenditures relating to her role as head of state, the grants in aid from Parliament, used primarily to maintain the royal palaces and travel, the Privy Purse, the so-called traditional income for the queen's public and private use, and the queen's personal income from inheritance, landholdings, and other financial resources. In 1992 the queen offered to pay income tax and capital gains tax on a voluntary basis. Since that time the queen has paid tax on her personal income and any capital gains that may accrue from her investments. The civil list and the grants in aid are not taxable because they are used in her role as head of state. The Privy Purse is taxable, but deductions for official expenditures are allowed.

The most politically charged aspect of the queen's sources of income is the civil list, which is set by Parliament as a fixed amount each year. Currently the allocation is £7.9 million, which is largely for the expenses related to the staff working for the queen. The civil list also meets the cost of social functions hosted by the queen, such as royal garden parties and dinners with visiting foreign dignitaries. The queen meets nearly 50,000 visitors each year. During the 1960s and 1970s, when Labour was in power and leftists dominated the party, there were regular calls to end the civil lists and disband the monarchy, largely because of the expense associated with the royal duties. These efforts were never successful in large part because the monarchy continued to retain broad popular support. But the civil list remains a political issue, especially among MPs who feel that the queen and the royal family are outdated and too costly.

The grants in aid expenditures fund the property services and royal travel of the monarch. With a budget in excess of £15 million, the queen's palaces, which include Buckingham Palace, St. James Palace, Clarence House, Marborough Mews, the residential and office areas of Kensington Palace,

Windsor Castle, and over 285 other properties available for residential use by staff, are maintained. Also the grants in aid allocation paid for the restoration of Windsor Castle after the tragic fire in 1997, although most of the cost was provided by surplus revenues from the summer opening of the state apartments in Buckingham Palace. Part of the grants in aid expenses are those related to royal travel. The royal family conducts nearly 3,000 engagements, both domestically and abroad. Expenses related to the use of the Royal Air Force aircraft and the royal train take up a large part of this budget.

What has gained the most attention regarding the queen and her tax obligations and official expenditures is the private wealth that she controls. The Privy Purse Office manages the queen's income from the Duchy of Lancaster. The duchy is a landed estate held in trust. The income from the duchy is private, but the queen often uses the money to defray expenses related to the royal family. This income is taxable. The other side of the queen's personal wealth is the income derived from her real estate holdings (Balmoral and Sandringham Castles), investments, and inheritance. There has been much speculation regarding the wealth of the queen (with some estimates climbing to £100 million). The income from these assets is taxable, although the full extent of the queen's wealth is unknown.

The British monarchy is thus not just crowns and jewels and palaces; it is a government institution. As a government institution the monarchy is a budget line item, a part of the tax code, a system of official residences, and a bureaucratic staff. The queen is a ceremonial head of state with symbolic power and tangential influence, an integral (and costly) part of the organizational structure of the British government. ⊕

FORMAL GOVERNMENT

The United Kingdom of Great Britain and Northern Ireland is the official title of this island nation of 57 million people. Although more frequently called the United Kingdom or simply Britain, the name reveals the complexities of the governing structure. The United Kingdom is a nation of distinct governing units, each with its own heritage and culture, held together in a tenuous relationship. England forms the largest land and population sector of the United Kingdom with more than 50 percent of the landmass and over 80 percent of the population. Wales, the second largest of the governing regions, has 30 percent of the total population and has been linked with England since the Middle Ages. As a result of legislation passed in 1997, Wales has an assembly that widens local autonomy. Scotland, the third of the governing regions, has been the most nationalist. Scotland has its own local government, legal system, and educational structure apart from England and as a result of the same legislation in 1997 now has its own parliament. The final unit is Northern Ireland, which remained under British rule in 1926 after Ireland (more specifically southern Ireland) became independent. Northern Ireland is certainly the most disputed region of the United Kingdom with serious internal differences over whether it should remain tied to Britain or become integrated with Ireland.

Together these regions and governing units form a nation with great diversity and a strained alliance. The Welsh have their own language; the Scots, the most clearly defined national identity; and the Northern Irish, the hatred between the Protestant majority and the Catholic minority. Although England with its power center in London provides the governing "glue" that holds this governing diversity together, there are serious strains that call into question the ability of the United Kingdom to remain united. The Welsh, although less strident about autonomy, nevertheless take pride in their uniqueness and are less and less enamored of England. Scotland, with its new parliament, is poised to exert increased autonomy and some say sovereignty. Northern Ireland continues to be torn between London and Dublin as Protestants and Catholics fight over its future. In the coming years the governing shape of the United Kingdom of Great Britain and Northern Ireland will likely be a critical national issue.

While the governing structure of the United Kingdom is diverse and in transition, the political system is more secure and predictable. The British political system is formally a constitutional monarchy that exists under parliamentary rule. The use of the term "constitutional" in the formal political title is somewhat misleading, since the British do not have a document that lays out the structure and procedures of government. Rather, the British version of a constitution is a series of important historical documents and legislative statutes that together form a body of governing rules. From the Magna Carta, which established a relationship between monarch and Parliament, to the Bill of Rights, which instituted parliamentary sovereignty, to the parliamentary reforms of 1911, which shifted power from Lords to Commons, the British constitution has been an ever expanding document that reflects the decisions and actions of the Parliament. Stated simply, the legacy of British laws that form the constitution firmly establishes parliamentary sovereignty, and Parliament uses that sovereignty to change the British constitution.

Fundamental to the British constitution is the concept of the Crown. The connection between monarchy and Crown means that the king or queen, who serves as the monarch, is the head of state or ceremonial leader of the country.

The Crown also means that the king or queen provides the governing authority and legitimacy for those in political power. For example, it is the monarch who establishes a new government and names the new prime minister after a national election. The monarch has no choice but to name the leader of the majority party or majority coalition that was victorious in the election, but British custom and tradition makes the Crown a formal participant in the governing process. Also, at the beginning of each new session of Parliament the monarch makes the speech from the throne in the House of Lords, since monarchs are not permitted in the democratic House of Commons. The monarch reads a speech written by the prime minister. In that speech the monarch outlines the policies and policy proposals that the government has placed on the legislative agenda. There is no personal commentary—the monarch reads what the government wants to be read. British constitutional scholar Sir Walter Bagehot has said, referring to the monarch and the concept of the Crown that underlies British government, the monarch "reigns but does not rule."

While the constitution and the monarchy provide the foundation of British government, it is the parliamentary system that provides the structure and the process for defining power and making public policy. Parliamentary democracy as practiced in Britain is based on the principles of majority rule, fusion of power, and open debate. At the center of the British system is the understanding that the political party (or parties) which captures a majority of the seats in the House of Commons during an election has the opportunity to claim victory and assume governing power. Elections currently are held every five years in Britain, with 659 legislative seats at stake. The number of years between elections was set at five as a result of the parliamentary reform of 1911 and the number of seats in Commons changes periodically due to population increases and the redrawing of legislative boundaries. What remains constant in the parliamentary system is the principle of majority rule.

Majority rule is a function of political party strength and popularity. The British electorate travels to the polls with the intent of putting a political party into office, not a specific individual. In Britain party candidates for the legislative seats need not live in the district that they represent or make public policy promises to the voters. Elections determine which political party is able to win a majority of seats in Commons. The members of Parliament, therefore, are not servants of their constituents but a political number separating majority from minority. Numbers drive the British parliamentary system and political parties look to the numbers to claim victory and run the government. Currently the Labour government of Prime Minister Tony Blair has a sizable majority (410 Labour seats to 163 Conservative seats) as a result of the party's victory in the 2001 national elections and other party shifts resulting from by-elections in 2002 and 2003.

Once the Labour Party is formally recognized as the government, the prime minister has the responsibility of forming the cabinet and managing the affairs of Parliament. In Britain the governing cabinet is large, with as many as twenty-five members. Individual cabinet portfolios range from key positions such as Treasury, Foreign Affairs, Defense, and Home Secretary to less critical appointments, such as the national heritage secretary who is in charge of national preservation. Many of the members of the cabinet are members of the majority party leadership who are given high-level positions as a means of solidifying party unity and ensuring party loyalty. These cabinet members make up the front bench of the House of Commons. They are called on to define government policy and respond to questions from their own party and the opposition. Since the House of Commons dates back to the sixteenth century, when membership in the legislative body was small, there is not enough room in the back benches to accommodate all the members of the majority party. At first this may seem to be a major problem in a democratic body, but a seat is not a critical ingredient of representation in the British system. The back benchers are there to vote and specifically to vote the party line. Occasionally the leadership will allow the members to vote their conscience, but the legislative process eventually gets around to the vote and the principle of majority rule remains dominant.

When a vote in Commons is imminent, the party whip is responsible for getting the vote out and reminding back benchers of their responsibility to maintain party discipline. An especially important vote receives a three-line whip, and back benchers are advised that their presence and their vote is essential. The role of the whips underscores the importance of party discipline and vote cohesion in a parliamentary system like Britain's. Although the success rate of proposed legislation varies in each legislative session, the discipline within the governing majority usually guarantees that what the party promises during election time or throughout their time in power will likely be enacted into law. Legislative proposals undergo some modification as cabinet members, back benchers, and even the House of Lords add amendments or change wording, but rarely is legislation proposed by the majority government defeated.

Her Majesty's loyal opposition (the minority party or parties) tries to use the legislative process to cast doubt on the proposed legislation and perhaps win some concessions in the form of amendments or changes to the language. Only in situations where the majority holds a slim lead over the minority does the opposition have a chance to influence the outcome of the legislative debate. In 1974, for example, the Labour government held a slim majority of 301–297 over the Conservative opposition. The Labour government of James Callaghan had an extremely difficult time passing legislation because of the uncertainty of its majority. After eight futile months of trying to govern with only a slight advantage over the Conservatives, Callaghan was forced to call new elections with the hope of increasing the numbers in Commons. Fortunately for Labour, the majority increased to 319, permitting some breathing room and weakening the ability of the Conservatives to check the government's program.

The dominance of the majority in the British parliamentary system ensures that the legislative agenda proposed by the government will encounter only minor obstacles. A factor that contributes to the efficiency of parliamentary rule is the principle of fusion of powers. British government does not have to endure the complex interplay of checks and balances that is the hallmark of the American system of separation of powers. In Britain the prime minister and his cabinet are both legislators from electoral districts and members of the front bench with the responsibility of running the government. There is no veto power in the hands of the queen, the courts do not possess the power of judicial review to overturn acts of Parliament, and there is no fear that a government will have its prime minister from one political party and its legislature controlled by a different party. Fusion of power means that the governing system is simple and streamlined with power not only in the hands of the majority, but the critical executive-legislature relationship that determines public policy working in unison.

Majority rule and fusion of power give to the British system what would appear to be awesome, uncontested capability to do whatever the government wants. There is, however, no evidence of governments abusing their power and passing laws that have narrow party or public support. The British parliamentary system may be efficient, but it has not shown a willingness to be radical and politically unwise. There was no doubt that when Margaret Thatcher and the Conservatives took power in 1979, a new legislative agenda would be presented to Commons. Because of their solid majority and their party cohesion, the Thatcher government was able to make sweeping changes in a range of economic, social, military, and foreign policy areas. But these changes were grounded in the will of the electorate as expressed in their vote preference for the Conservatives.

The principle of fusion of power in British parliamentary rule contributes to governing efficiency in large part because one legislative body has been stripped of its ability to counteract the will of the other legislative body, as is often the case in the United States Congress. Parliamentary sovereignty rests solely in the House of Commons. The House of Lords is no match for the power of Commons, even though it is a part of the legislative process. Parliamentary reforms in 1911, 1949, and 1999 have stripped Lords of most of its powers. The House of Lords can offer amendments to legislation in Commons (although the amendments need not be accepted), it can delay the legislation in Commons for up to a year (although this often appears to be a petty maneuver), and it can use its time in debate to raise questions about the appropriateness of legislation (although the British public is not easily influenced by the positions taken by Lords).

The recent Labour government legislation, which reduced the number of hereditary peers, may be the death knell of this legislative body. Before the legislation, the House of Lords had a membership of approximately twelve hundred, although in most proceedings of the Lords only 200 members took an active part (there are now approximately 700 members in the House of Lords). The composition of the Lords was heavily weighted toward the hereditary peers, with as many as two-thirds of the members holding aristocratic titles (the remainder of the body was made up of bishops of the Anglican Church, retired Lords of Appeal, and various life peers). Little power remains in this body, a series of proposed reforms hold out the promise of an expansion of responsibility.

The third principle of the British parliamentary system drives the relationship between the party majority and executive-legislative relations: the vital role of debate in forming a public confrontation between government and Opposition. In once recent visit to Commons I viewed a debate over the decommissioning of weapons by the Irish Republican Army in Northern Ireland. Because Commons is set up so that the two opposing camps face each other, the debate became a substantive interchange of views and a rapid-fire dialogue. Although the debate happened to be quite reserved, often the exchanges among members become heated and boisterous, with frequent catcalls, laughter, and mocking criticism. The Speaker of the House of Commons has his hands full in managing the verbal confrontation.

The debate atmosphere becomes even more charged during the question hour, as the prime minister and cabinet take the hot seat. Question hour is a once-a-week meeting of the full House of Commons in which back benchers from all parties are permitted to quiz the government on virtually anything. British television and C-SPAN broadcast the question hour regularly. It is the closest thing to real-life political drama with a little bit of political circus thrown in for good measure. Unlike the American legislative system in which members of Congress talk to an empty chamber or to a few party supporters, question hour creates an atmosphere where both sides of the

Commons must defend their positions. Moreover, in the American system the president is never subjected to the scrutiny directed at the British prime minister, who has to endure the verbal abuse of the loyal opposition.

The principle of parliamentary sovereignty that is so pervasive in the British system means that the judicial branch of government does not play a political or constitutional role. British courts are primarily concerned with civil and criminal cases. The High Court of Justice hears civil cases, the Crown Court is concerned with criminal cases, a Court of Appeal hears both civil and criminal cases on appeal, and the House of Lords, also known for judicial purposes as the Judicial Committee of the Privy Council, acts as the court of last resort. Both Scotland and Northern Ireland have their own court system, but the House of Lords remains as the final arbiter of appeals from both Scotland and Northern Ireland. Also in cases involving capital punishment appeals from members of the Commonwealth (which are the former colonial possessions of Britain), the House of Lords has appellate power. Finally, now that Britain is part of the European Community, British citizens can appeal rulings to the European Court of Human Rights, which is based in Strasbourg, France.

The main point to emphasize about the British judicial system is that justices in England are not called on to render judgment on an interpretation of a legislative statute or a constitutional principle. Moreover, as mentioned above, the British courts have no power of judicial review and thus cannot challenge the decisions made by Commons. Consequently, British courts know their limitations and do not concern themselves with matters of national policy.

One area of the British governing system that also needs to be addressed is the structure of local administration. Local government in Britain is unitary, which means that many of the key domestic policy matters are controlled by the national administration. Local governing units handle the day-to-day issues of town and village life but depend on the taxing power and the distribution of budget resources of the central government. Since 1996 Britain has reorganized its local governing units by creating 20 regional authorities instead of the two-tier structure of 36 counties and 274 district councils. At the center of the new local governing system are five metropolitan councils situated in the largest cities. London, which had been administered by the Greater London Council (GLC) until 1986, when Margaret Thatcher abolished it, has acquired a new governing structure as a result of Prime Minister Tony Blair's policy of devolving or returning power to local governments. London now is governed by an American-style mayoral system.

In the coming years British government will undergo substantial restructuring and reform. Besides the changes brought about in the House of Lords and the devolution initiatives, there are also proposals advanced by the Labour government to establish a bill of rights, adopt a proportional representation electoral system, institute a national referendum, and pass a freedom of information act. The British parliamentary system, which has become the standard of good governance worldwide, is destined to become more democratic, more open, and more responsive to its citizens. The forces of change appear to be holding the upper hand in Britain, and constitutional reform has received wide endorsement. Polls have consistently shown that the British are growing increasingly displeased with the Westminster system and overwhelmingly support many of the changes, particularly the bill of rights and national referenda. There is even evidence that the British would favor a written constitution over the current evolutionary compendium of documents, bills, and traditions.

Although change may move more efficiently through the parliamentary system, there are pitfalls in the current push for substantial institutional reform. Making the British system more democratic, open, and responsive is certain to have an impact on the ability of the governing majority and particularly the prime minister to control the legislative agenda and the legislative process. Moreover, these reforms could also affect the long-standing reputation of British politics as stable and flexible as parliamentary sovereignty is challenged by popular sovereignty. It is too early to judge the ramifications of these changes and proposed changes, but they are sure to make British governmental reform the central focus of parliamentary action.

Constitutional Language

The Magna Carta is Britain's most prestigious governing document. Written in 1215 by a group of landed barons, the Magna Carta attempts to address a series of grievances dealing with ownership of land, debt obligations, and inheritance. More than a list of complaints, the Magna Carta is a serious effort to stake out power for the barons under the monarchy of King John. Below is an excerpt from the original document, which highlights the language of the barons as they sought to establish a governing role in early England:

The barons shall elect twenty-five of their number to keep, and cause to be observed with all their might, the peace and liberties granted and confirmed to them by this charter. Any man who so desires may take an oath to obey the commands of the twenty-five barons for the achievement of these ends, and to join with them in assailing us to the utmost of his power. We give public and free permission to take this oath to any man who so desires, and at no time will we prohibit any man from taking it. Indeed, we will compel any of our subjects who are unwilling to take it to swear it at our command.

POINT OF FACT

The British commitment to tradition is nowhere more in evidence than at the beginning of the House of Commons. The Speaker, in wig and gown, marches into the chamber as one of the sergeants at arms shouts, "Hats off strangers." Those in the procession carry a sword and a mace, which symbolize royal protection. The Speaker climbs onto his throne and reads Psalm 67 and three other prayers. Once he finishes, the doorkeeper announces, "Mr. Speaker in the Chair, the mace is laid on the table," and the session begins.

SCOTTISH DEVOLUTION

In 1707 the Scottish Parliament gave up its sovereignty and joined England to create Great Britain. Although the union was motivated by Scottish financial insolvency and a fear of Catholicism, Great Britain has remained in control ever since with little hint of separation. But the union of Scotland and England is currently undergoing restructuring as a result of the Labour government's support for devolution, a returning of local autonomy. In May 1999 the Scottish people voted favorably in a referendum to begin a process of devolution that would ultimately create a popularly elected Parliament and an executive office. That Parliament and executive are now in place.

While the election of the Scottish Parliament caused street celebrations and a renewal of nationalist pride, devolution of power from London to Edinburgh remains modest. The Parliament in Scotland will vote on a range of public policy matters such as health, education, and welfare and determine the allocation of budget resources in these areas, but the bulk of the money that will be spent in Scotland will come from English taxpayers as a result of decisions made in Westminster. The issue of extracting taxes in England and then redistributing them in Scotland is a matter of significant debate in Britain. Currently spending rates for Scotland are fixed under a formula (often called the Barnett formula, after a finance minister) that is very generous to the Scots. For every British pound collected from English residents, £1.25 is spent in Scotland. This distribution formula is a sore spot for many in England, but for the Scots it is a budgetary windfall that may temper any thought of moving completely toward nationhood.

Also militating against any final separation is the large presence that Scotland has in the British Parliament. At present there are seventy-two Scottish MPs in Parliament, a contingent well beyond an equitable distribution of seats in terms of population. Moreover, the Scots have considerable presence in the Labour cabinet of Tony Blair—five members of his cabinet, including the chancellor of the Exchequer, the defense minister, and the foreign secretary. Blair himself is Scottish by birth, descent, and schooling. This Scottish presence in Parliament and the cabinet is not lost on the English people, who have become increasingly distressed that their countrymen to the north have such a dominant role in their government.

Although the Labour Party is the party of choice in Scotland, the future of Great Britain may be in the hands of the Scottish Nationalist Party (SNP). The Labour Party leadership is clearly concerned about the growing popularity of the SNP and also its public pronouncements about nationhood, including emphasis on the usage of the Gaelic language, the flying of the Scottish flag, and even more mundane matters such as wearing the traditional kilt and tam by noted public figures. The resurgence of Scottish nationalism by the SNP has led to growing tensions by anti-English and anti-Scottish jokes, rabble-rousing speeches by politicians on both sides, and frequent demonstrations in favor of nationhood. The Scottish are not blind to Ireland, which achieved its independence from Britain and is enjoying a sustained period of economic prosperity and membership in the European Union. The Irish model serves as the model for the SNP and other Scottish nationalists as they seek to lay the foundation for a future break with England.

The future of Scotland within Great Britain is uncertain. The new Parliament with its limited powers may be enough to quench the thirst of the nationalists, especially when separation would end the special economic benefits that Scotland has enjoyed. Nevertheless, Scotland has entered a new era of local autonomy with the accompanying national pride. These two forces may place Scotland on the track toward independence at some future date. ⊕

THE CITIZEN AND THE STATE

The relationship between citizen and state in Britain is founded on a very simple yet critical principle: the British people accept the government as the legitimate authority. While there is abundant evidence that British politicians and British institutions receive their fair share of criticism and ridicule, there is no question that British citizens remain loyal to the governing authority and take enormous pride in parliamentary democracy. Often this loyalty and support are associated with deference, meaning that the British are willing to defer to the judgment of their elected and appointed public officials. Walter Bagehot commenting on the British constitution stated that democracy was possible in England because of "mutual confidence of electors, a calm national mind and a gift of rationality," and that democracy was destined to fail in nations that reveal "diffused distrust and indiscriminate suspicion." Bagehot's confidence in the British people may be a bit excessive and ethnocentric, but it does present a core truth: solid and unyielding support of the governing system is the key to stability and consensus, the watchwords of British society.

Loyalty to governing authority is manifested in the strong adherence to the rule of law by the British, in particular their respect for officers of the law. Britain has a long tradition of low crime, peaceful protest, and general compliance with the laws of the land. The fact that the number of British law enforcement officers is significantly lower compared with France and Germany is a testament to the high level of legitimacy that the governing system enjoys. British police officers do not carry weapons (except under certain conditions such as when dealing with terrorist threats) because gun availability and gun use are almost nonexistent in the country, and because the British people are not prone to challenge authority in a violent way.

Associated with loyalty to the lawful authority is the support given the parliamentary system. Despite Britain's periodic economic woes, which have had a deleterious effect on citizen trust in government, there nevertheless remains a strong sense of civic duty and responsibility among the people. For example, British voter turnout for parliamentary elections consistently holds at the low to mid 70 percent mark. Turnout in the 1997 parliamentary elections was 71 percent, which was somewhat lower than in past elections, but is still within the range of countries like Germany (84 percent) and Italy (91 percent). In the 2001 parliamentary elections turnout dropped to 59.4 percent, in large part because of the enormous popularity of Tony Blair and the weakness of the Conservative Party.

Although the British hold their system in high regard because of its long and illustrious history and its international reputation, they are unwilling to become involved in the political process, other than to cast their ballot every five years. This condition of civic pride linked with sporadic political interest is not out of order with a country that has a strong underpinning of governing legitimacy, respect for authority, and confidence in the law. There is general satisfaction with the governing system and therefore political involvement beyond voting is not viewed as a pressing national concern. Outside of politics, however, the British are a nation of joiners, participating in a broad range of local groups that are largely social in nature. There is participation in British society, but not necessarily political participation.

Just as the legitimacy of the political system in Britain serves as the foundation of citizen-state relations, social class and social class distinctions define the manner in which citizens interact with the state. Perhaps the most visible sign of the link between class and politics is the political parties. Labour historically has been the party of the working class. Since the late nineteenth century, when the working class was given the vote and organizations like the Fabians sponsored working-class power, the Labour Party has extended its hand to the powerful Trades Union Congress and has worked to build voter support in the industrial North. The Conservative Party, on the other hand, is the bastion of the British middle class. The Tories appeal to business owners, professionals, and managers who are concerned with issues such as taxation, welfare spending, and government regulation. Many Conservative MPs in Parliament are members of the aristocratic class, educated at the elite boarding schools, and committed to counteract union and working-class power.

The connection between class and politics must be guided by a significant caveat. The Conservatives have been the most dominant political party in Britain since the end of World War II, in large part because it has been able to attract working-class voters. The Tories have been more successful in gaining the class crossover vote than the Labour Party has in attracting middle-class support. It was only when Labour sought to expand its reach by moving away from its socialist roots and its Marxist antagonism to business that it was able to move to victory in 1997. Today the link between class and voting behavior has changed. Less than half of the electorate votes consistently with their class; that leaves a great deal of room for movement of working- and middle-class voters to support either Labour or the Tories. Class is important in explaining party allegiance and party programs, but it is no longer the defining variable of British political life.

While social class has faded somewhat into the background as a key factor in British political behavior, race has become increasingly important in defining the British people and creating pressure points in the policy process. Race became part of British national life in 1948, when the British Nationality Act was passed. The act stated that any citizen of the United Kingdom, its colonies, or a Commonwealth country (sovereign nations formerly under the control of Britain) were "British subjects" and possessed the right to enter the United Kingdom at any time, enjoy suffrage rights, and become a member of Parliament or a civil servant. The passage of the Nationality Act served as a catalyst for the migration of thousands of British subjects from countries such as India, Pakistan, Kenya, and the Caribbean ministates. With the entry of nonwhite British subjects from the less developed world, Britain slowly became a nation that was no longer homogeneous. The changing racial and ethnic makeup of Britain unleashed a backlash against immigration and began a sustained period of legislative restrictions designed to limit access to the United Kingdom.

Immigration laws have limited entry into the United Kingdom, but those who meet the letter of the law have changed the face of British society. Currently it is estimated that 6 percent of British citizens are nonwhite, with most coming from Asia, Africa, and the Caribbean. Indians make up the largest percentage of nonwhites, with Pakistanis second and Caribbean residents third. Many of these immigrants have assimilated into British society, particularly the Indians who have become prominent as small shopkeepers and skilled professionals. Others, such as those from Africa and the Caribbean, remain mired at the bottom of the economic ladder. In recent years there has been an influx of Muslim people from the Middle East, which has further transformed Britain into a culturally diverse society. The Muslim population is estimated at over 1 million, and mosques now stand side by side with Anglican cathedrals in many British neighborhoods.

The integration of the nonwhite population into British society has not always gone smoothly. During the 1960s and 1970s there were a number of race riots in neighborhoods such as the Braxton section of London. Claims by blacks of discrimination in housing, employment, and police abuse forced the government to pass a series of civil rights laws designed to respond to the charges of the rioters. In 1965 and 1968 legislation was passed to outlaw discrimination in housing and jobs. In 1976, again as a result of racial violence, Parliament passed laws that made it an offense to incite racial hatred and created a Race Relations Board that would facilitate bringing the races together. A Commission for Racial Equality was inaugurated to hear complaints of racial discrimination. During the Thatcher administration there was regular evidence of race and race issues entering the political arena with Conservatives often taking a hard line against immigrants. In 2001 a series of ethnically based conflicts erupted in the towns of Bradford, Oldham, and Burnley between white and Asian youths, which renewed debate in the country over whether Britain had adjusted to its newfound heterogeneity and was capable of maintaining a multicultural society.

While racial incidents have forced the British to examine the level of tolerance that exists in society, it is the debates over class-based politics that have provided the clearest evidence of the national political culture. Perhaps one of the best examples of this debate and its impact on the political culture is the struggle within the Labour Party to define its fundamental principles and its national objectives. The source of the debate was the vision of the party as stated in Clause 4 of Labour's constitution. Clause 4 boldly laid out the socialist commitment of the Labour Party and its pledge to fight for the rights of the working class. Clause 4 stated that the goal of Labour was "securing for the workers by hand or by brain the full fruits of their industry, and the most equitable distribution thereof that may be possible, upon the basis of common ownership of the means of production, distribution and exchange." With Labour in power, Clause 4 became the rallying cry of government as it aggressively sought to advance union power and distribute tax and budget resources from the rich to the working class. This was the era of "soak the rich" taxation and "living on the dole" social programs. The Labour Party opened up its national conference by singing "L'Internationale," the socialist anthem celebrating union solidarity against the onslaught of capitalist greed.

Needless to say, Clause 4 was anathema to the business and managerial class in Britain. The idea of redistributing wealth and having unions use their power of the strike to cripple the economy in the name of worker solidarity caused deep fissures in society. Rock stars Elton John, Paul McCartney, and Mick Jagger established residences outside the country to avoid stiff tax payments. As it was intended, Clause 4 made a statement to the British people and to the world that the Labour Party was firmly under the control of those who saw government as the agent for taking money from the rich and distributing it to the working class.

When Margaret Thatcher entered government in 1979, she immediately challenged the language of politics and the values and principles that created the language. As a fierce proponent of business and an archenemy of unions, Thatcher expressed a vision of society and government that was in stark contrast to that of Labour. To Thatcher, liberty and personal responsibility were the watchwords of her administration. Thatcher, in classic conservatism, wanted her fellow citizens to leave their dependency on big-taxing, big-spending, and big-distributing government behind and embrace personal freedom and personal responsibility. Thatcher made sure that public policy initiatives were driven by freedom and responsibility as she cut government programs, cut taxes, and cut government regulations. To many in British society, who had become used to the benevolent arm of the state in their lives, Thatcher became a cruel and uncaring threat. But for those who had seen their wealth redistributed to others and their businesses regulated by an intrusive government, Thatcher represented a long awaited savior who was determined to end the socialist attack on the market.

The conflict over public values and public principles has by no means ended in Britain. As head of a New Labour party, Tony Blair has sought to shed the stigma of Clause 4 and replace it with a more inclusive and more communitarian brand of citizen-state relations. Blair has said frequently that he wants every British citizen to be part of the political solution and does not want to return to the days when Labour took pride in worker power and showed open contempt for the middle class. Blair often makes mention that a communitarian ethic that breaks down class barriers is absolutely necessary if British society is to deal with the challenges of a new global economy. For Blair, Britain cannot maintain its unity and stability in the rough-and-tumble new economic order unless it leaves behind the class tension inherent in Clause 4 and the harsh atmosphere of freedom inherent in the message of Margaret Thatcher.

POINT OF FACT
In 2002 all secondary schools in Britain required citizenship training.

GAY RIGHTS

In the U.S. military, the policy toward homosexuals is described with the slogan, "Don't Ask, Don't Tell." Members of the armed forces are told to ignore a person's sexual orientation and go about their business. In Britain homosexual rights in the military have become an issue that is far more fundamental than whether soldiers should respect an individual's privacy. As a result of a ruling by the European Court of Justice in 1999, Britain has been forced to suspend the ban against homosexuals in the military. Over the years the British military has developed a very stringent policy against homosexuals. Officially, it has stated that gays in the military are an "unwelcome social experiment" that could harm discipline and weaken morale. As a result, over a thousand gay men and women have been expelled from the armed forces. British courts have supported the military ban, but the European Court in its ruling stated that the ban violated the soldiers' right to privacy. The military ban on homosexuals was based "founded solely upon the negative attitudes of heterosexual personnel toward those of homosexual orientation."

The decision of the European Court is seen by many civil libertarians in Britain as a major development; under British law there is no guaranteed right to privacy. Furthermore, the decision is seen as the first step in the process of change in common law that comes as a result of the incorporation of the European Convention on Human Rights into British law in October 2000. The British will be required to make domestic laws compatible with the European Convention and mandate that British judges interpret human rights according to the Convention. Compared to other European countries, Britain has lagged behind in the area of privacy rights and homosexual protections. The Netherlands lifted its ban against gays in the military in 1972, the Danes in 1979. Italy has a ban, but it is not enforced, and Germany does not have a ban.

Although Britain is not required to accept the decision of the European Court, it has abided by previous rulings in large part because of its desire to smooth the integration into the European Union. In the future, should Britain ignore or countermand a decision of the European Court, it could mean expulsion from the European Union. Civil libertarians in Britain are convinced that this ruling on homosexuals in the military will open the doors to other rulings that will protect private behavior and individual freedom.

Of particular interest as the next challenge for the homosexual community is the abolition of Section 28, which is a clause in the 1988 Local Government Act that prohibits "the intentional promotion of homosexuality" by local authorities and "the teaching of homosexuality as a pretend family relationship" in schools. Section 28 has become a partisan issue with the Labour Party taking up the cause of abolition and the Conservatives supporting the retention of the language in the act. In Scotland the Clause 28 debate has turned into a crusade with the Catholic bishop, the Conservative press, and business leaders demanding that the language be retained. The public mood in Scotland and indeed throughout Britain values tolerance of personal lifestyles, but the abolition of Clause 28 with its teaching of homosexuality as acceptable for children is going too far.

The issue of homosexual rights is important in Britain, but many citizens are concerned that the European Court will amass enormous judicial power and rewrite British common law. One of the lawyers for the gays who challenged the military policy described the decision of the Human Rights Act as the "most significant legal reform ever in the history of the United Kingdom." This may very well be, but the growing power of the European Court is certain to force a debate on the issues of sovereignty, European integration, and individual guarantees. Traditionalists are likely to emphasize that the power of the European Court usurps the sovereign rights of Parliament to make public laws, while civil rights advocates will stress that the judgment of the European Court is certain to force Britain to move more quickly to promulgate a bill of rights or at least pass legislation that meets the intent of the Court's judgment. The Court's ruling on gays in the British military is thus an opening salvo in a battle over the constitution, the prerogatives of Parliament, and the rights of individuals in the new Europe. ⊕

What the Experts Say

Andrew Sullivan, writing for the *New York Times Magazine* on his impression of England in transition, stated in 1999:

It is possible to talk about the abolition of Britain without risk of hyperbole.

The United Kingdom's cultural and social identity has been altered beyond any recent prediction. Its very geographical boundaries are being redrawn. Its basic Constitution is being gutted and reconceived. Its monarchy has been reinvented.

Half its Parliament is under the ax. . . . And its role in the world at large is in Radical flux.

New York Times Magazine,
FEBRUARY 21, 1999

PATHWAYS TO PARTICIPATION

The heart of the British political system may be parliamentary democracy, but it is the political parties that provide the democratic energy to sustain parliamentary democracy. Political parties are at the center of the British governing process as they organize the citizenry, recruit leaders, articulate issues, conduct elections, and manage the decisionmaking apparatus of the nation. The British people have accepted the political parties in their country as the agents of participation and rely on them to conduct the business of governing. As noted earlier, since British participation is limited primarily to voting and does not include other forms of political activism, the parties have become the focal point of democratic involvement. Where Americans, for example, constantly zero in on candidates and the image that they cultivate, the British pay more attention to the ideology, organizational alliances, and platform planks of the political parties. British political party activity is controlled by three electoral and parliamentary organizations: Labour, the Conservatives, and the Liberal Democrats. Like many European countries, Britain has a wealth of minor political parties. At the most recent count forty-two political parties were active in the United Kingdom. These include parties such as the environmentally conscious Green Party, the Islamic Party of Britain, the anti–European Union Referendum Party, and the Monster Raving Loony Party led by (Screaming Lord) David Sutch. The largest grouping of parties is on the extreme left, with various Communist, Socialist, Marxist, Trotskyite, and militant parties. But in terms of parliamentary parties that hold seats in the House of Commons, there are only ten parties.

The Labour Party currently is the dominant political organization in British politics. Founded in 1900 as a vehicle for expressing the views of trades unions and intellectuals disenchanted with the shortcomings of the capitalist system, Labour (or as current party leader Tony Blair prefers, New Labour) has sought to shift its appeal to the middle and white-collar managerial class and downplay its reliance on unions and the working class. For most of its history, the Labour Party was overshadowed by the Conservatives. The Conservatives have held power more than any other party in the twentieth century. Labour controlled government in the post–World War II era with Clement Attlee, during the 1964–1970 period under Harold Wilson, again in the 1974–1979 era under Wilson and James Callaghan, and now under Tony Blair since 1997.

Labour, following its departure from government in 1979 to the election of Tony Blair's New Labour in 1997, went through a series of wrenching internal disputes over the very soul of the party after Thatcher's departure. Party leader Michael Foot of the pro-union wing of the party sought to retain the leftist purity of Labour by opposing the European Union, supporting unilateral disarmament, and advancing a broad agenda of socialist programs. Foot's leftist bent forced a number of more moderate MPs to leave the party and form the Social Democratic Party, which eventually evolved into the Liberal Democrats. Foot was defeated as Labour sought to move the party toward the center. Neil Kinnock took over the party organization but retained many of Foot's positions and moved Labour through two embarrassing defeats in 1983 and 1987. Eventually Kinnock made a bold break with the leftist positions of Labour by weakening union power and removing the Trotskyite elements in the party known as the Militant Tendency. Kinnock's efforts to reform the party did lead to ever expanding voter totals and seats in Parliament, but no majority victory. In 1992 Kinnock and Labour were defeated by John Major, Margaret Thatcher's protégé.

Kinnock's replacement was Scottish lawyer John Smith. Smith led Labour to a number of local elections, but he died unexpectedly in 1994, opening the way for the appointment of Tony Blair as party leader. Blair continued the slow advance of Labour in European Parliament elections in 1994 and later in a series of by-elections. Blair's most significant contribution to Labour resurgence was his success in eliminating Clause 4 from the party constitution and promoting a new image of the party as a mainstream organization in the party platform entitled "Labour into Power." In 1997 Labour under Blair won a significant electoral victory, relegating the Conservatives to the position of loyal opposition for the first time since 1979. The most interesting aspect of the Labour victory was that 101 women assumed seats in the new majority as Blair presented "women only" lists in a number of safe constituencies to tap into the women's vote and to broaden the appeal of the party.

Tony Blair's capacity to bring change to both the Labour Party and Great Britain was substantially advanced by his landslide victory in the 2001 parliamentary elections. The electoral victory of New Labour gave Blair the mandate to move forward on key issues such as embracing the euro, renationalizing the nation's railway system, and increasing income tax rates. Critical to his and his party's continued popularity will be addressing the declining state of public services, especially transportation, and moving the country through the downturn in the economy. The two objectives are intertwined as revenue streams dry up and battles over budget priorities intensify. Despite his popularity, Blair has begun to face heightened criticism from circles within his own party in Commons for the extent of his support for U.S. policy in Iraq. In a crucial vote in Commons over sending British troops to Iraq, over 120 Labour MPs voted against their prime minister in an astounding rebuke. Tony Blair prevailed in the vote (with support from Conservative MPs), but clearly his position as party leader was damaged and his political future jeopardized to some extent. Britain's involvement as a critical partner of the United States in the war against Iraq has provided a real test of Blair's ability to maintain his hold on British politics and unity in the Labour Party.

The current opposition party, the Conservative Party, has been the mainstream party in British politics. It has not had to deal with many of the internal struggles over ideology, program, and citizen base that the Labour Party has. The Conservatives (or Tories) dominated British electoral and parliamentary politics, in large part because of their ability to meld a winning coalition of business, middle class, farmers, and on more than one occasion elements of the working class. The Conservative Party is the party of college graduates, the white professional class, women, and seniors. Conservative candidates for office are heavily connected to the Oxbridge educational background (educated at Oxford or Cambridge), and their strength in Commons is situated in the southern region of the country. The organizational foundation of the Conservative Party is its National Union of Conservative and Unionist Associations, which is a federation of over six hundred constituency associations designed to provide the party with support, candidates, and votes.

The heyday of the Conservative Party occurred during the Thatcher era, when it became a parliamentary force for a market-based approach to national development. Thatcher and the Tories, however, planted the seeds of their own decline. Throughout her administration Thatcher faced internal dissension between moderate factions opposed to the stringency of her market approach (the "wets") and supporters of the prime minister who were convinced that radical reforms were necessary ("drys"). This factionalism eventually led to Thatcher's resignation in 1990 and the election on the second round of party voting of her chancellor of the Exchequer, John Major.

Although the Conservatives won the 1992 parliamentary elections, the fortunes of the party among the British electorate continued on a downward spiral. A series of by-elections in 1994 and 1995 signaled that the party was in deep trouble among voters and that Major was not able to command respect as a national leader. The Tories were increasingly viewed as harsh on the working class and too focused on bringing economic reforms that cut into the National Health Service and education. By 1996 the Conservative majority in Parliament was close to minority status, in large part because seventy-four MPs voted in favor of a referendum in support of the European Union, a position that was against Thatcherite policy.

The resounding election of Labour in 1997 precipitated a shake-up in the Conservative Party. John Major resigned and after three ballots William Hague, the former Welsh secretary, was elevated to the position of party leader. Hague at thirty-six became the youngest Tory leader in the twentieth century. Hague's election did not silence the factionalism within the party as battles over the new European currency erupted with many of the "wets" group, like former deputy Prime Minister Michael Haseltine, criticizing Hague for continuing party opposition to the new currency. Hague in return pushed through party regulations that were designed to discipline members who challenged the authority of the leadership.

But Hague never was able to garner support from the Tory party or, for that matter, British voters. He was seen as too bland and lacking a vision for the Conservative Party and the British nation. When Labour and Blair won another overwhelming electoral victory in the 2001 elections, the Conservatives pushed Hague out of the party leadership. But replacing Hague was not easy and revealed deep divisions within the party, especially over the position the Conservatives would take on matters related to membership in the European Union. The party split between Iain Duncan Smith, a right-wing Euro-skeptic, and Ken Clarke, a leftist who supported strong links to Europe and the European Union. Eventually Smith rose to Tory leadership. Smith's victory, however, did not help the Conservative Party rejuvenate its once great popularity and regain its dominant role in British politics.

Although British politics is dominated by two major parties, a third party, the Liberal Democratic Party (LDP), has remained a viable alternative to Labour and the Conservatives. As some have said, the LDP plays the role of the one-half party in a strong two-and-a-half-party system in Britain. The roots of the Liberal Democrats go back to 1859 and the founding of the party as a nonsocialist, reform organization espousing traditional liberal positions. The Liberals have had their day in the sun under the leadership of such illustrious prime ministers as William Gladstone and David Lloyd George. After World War I the fortunes of the Liberal Party declined as a result of the union alliance with Labour and the popularity of the Conservatives. Since that time the Liberals, acting under different party labels, have become the third party in British politics, winning on average twenty seats in Parliament and attracting 16–24 percent of the popular vote. In the 1997 elections the Liberal Democrats gained a record forty-six seats in Parliament on the basis of 16.7 percent of the popular vote. In the 2001 elections, the Liberal Democrats under a new leader, Charles Kennedy, increased their representation in the House of Commons to fifty-two MPs and a wider share of the electoral vote.

The Liberal Democratic Party in the modern era was formed from the union of the Liberal Party and the Social Democratic Party. The union created the Social and Liberal Democratic Party, which was shortened in 1989 to the LDP. Before the formal unification of the two parties the Liberals joined the Social Democratic Party in a series of electoral and parliamentary alliances during the 1980s. The SDP, as already noted, was a breakaway movement of dissident Labour party members who opposed the radical bent of the party under union domination. The alliance was a rocky one as members of the SDP objected to the formal unification of the two parties. When some of the dissidents left the SDP and formed another party, the merger was approved and the Liberal Democratic Party moved forward under the leadership of Paddy Ashdown. With Ashdown at the helm, the Liberal Democrats increased their electoral and parliamentary support. The high point of Liberal Democratic resurgence came in 1995 and 1996, when the party overtook the Conservatives in local elections and ended up controlling forty-six local councils. Building on that support the Liberal Democrats took forty-six seats in the 1997 elections and were invited by Prime Minister Blair to participate in special cabinet committees for regular consultations in areas of "mutual interest."

The Liberal Democrats historically have suffered under the first-past-the post electoral system in Britain, which is the British version of a winner-take-all arrangement that penalizes parties finishing second. As a third party, the Liberals have gained a respectable percentage of the vote, only to come in second in many of the electoral district races. Much of the clamor in Britain in recent years for an electoral system of proportional representation has come from the Liberal Democratic Party, which would likely gain a larger number of seats under a system that was tied to overall voter strength and not simple victory. Despite their lack of ability to win more representation in Commons, the Liberal Democrats have used their small numbers to gain access to power and influence in governing circles. The Liberal Democrats have consistently been linked with the Labour Party and have shown willingness to vote in Commons as part of an informal alliance.

The Liberal Democrats have been associated with a range of issues but have made their reputation as a party of reform. In recent years the Liberal Democrats have called for a fixed term for the House of Commons, replacement of the House of Lords, a bill of rights, an independent and powerful Supreme Court, greater decentralization, and devolution for Scotland and Wales. The Liberal Democrats have also been the party of greater integration with Europe calling for increased powers for the European Parliament and a stronger European Union. In the 1997 election the Liberal Democrats sought an increase in the basic income tax and stronger environmental laws. These positions put them at odds with Labour, creating tension between two traditional allies. The future of the Liberal Democrats is murky as a result of the 1999 resignation of Paddy Ashdown. Without his forceful and charismatic leadership, many observers feel that the Liberal Democrats may eventually lose the electoral momentum that they achieved as a result of their showing in the 1997 and 2001 parliamentary elections.

Any discussion of party representation in Commons must include the Scottish Nationalist Party and the Welsh Plaid Cymru. The Scottish Nationalist Party was founded in 1934 on a platform of Scottish independence. In its 1992 manifesto the SNP called for an autonomous Scottish Parliament elected by proportional representation. Since 1979, when it lost nine of its eleven seats in Commons, the SNP has been working diligently to regain a foothold in Scotland around the issue of a Scottish Parliament. During Conservative rule the SNP trailed Labour as the second most popular party in Scotland, but by the 1997 parliamentary elections it had won a total of six seats and was again poised to take a leadership role in the transition to a new Scottish Parliament. In the 2001 elections the SNP representation dropped to five seats, but the loss was not critical since the attainment of the Scottish Parliament was a key victory. The SNP has relied on its ties to Labour to make the Scottish Parliament a reality. In a 1997 referendum on the Parliament the SNP aligned with Labour and the Liberal Democratic Party to win a yes vote on devolving powers to Scotland.

In Wales the Plaid Cymru (Party of Wales) has also been linked with issues of devolution. Since its founding in 1925, the Plaid Cymru has pushed for local governing authority within a social democratic framework. Because of the similarity of their objectives, the Plaid Cymru has worked closely with the Scottish Nationalists to advance devolution. Currently it has four seats in

Commons and, like the SNP, has generally cooperated with the Lab
Like the SNP, the Plaid Cymru worked with Labour and the LDP t
"yea" vote in the 1997 referendum on a Welsh regional assembly. T
assembly differs from the Scottish Parliament in that it has fewer powers
than the body in Scotland and faces greater veto powers from the government
in London.

All the parliamentary parties plus the scores of nonparliamentary parties
meet at election time in Britain, creating a complex pathway to participation. Elections, as mentioned earlier, must occur every five years, but can be
called at any time by the prime minister (formally through the Crown) in order to advance a strategic party objective, which usually translates as a perceived opportunity to increase seats in Commons. With the date of the election set (usually six to eight weeks from the time of the announcement), the
British begin a short, serious, and relatively inexpensive campaign to determine the will of the people. While campaigns in Britain, like those in the
United States, increasingly use television, polling, and slick advertisements,
they are tame compared to the raucous candidate slugfests between the
Democrats and the Republicans.

Britain, like many European countries, has developed a system of public
financing of elections, although private contributions are growing and similarities to the U.S. system of financing elections are in more in evidence.
Political parties rely on contributions from business, labor, and individuals.
There are no limits on the amounts that national party organizations spend
on campaigning. Parties may spend what they wish on party political broadcasts, visits by party leaders, and general publicity. The general income of
the Conservative Party is made up of contributions from corporate and small
business sources, along with financial support from grassroots party associations. Business firms are required to publish their political contributions
over £200. Fifty percent of the Labour Party's income comes from annual
fees paid by trade unions, socialist groups, and other supportive associations.
Increasingly, Labour has received financial support from individual contributions as it has entered the political mainstream and its links to trade
unions have been less secure. As British electoral politics becomes more like
American politics, individual contributions are growing and candidate so-
licitation of individual contributions is intensifying.

Although the British are not as committed to public financing as countries
such as Germany, Austria, and Sweden, they nevertheless have put into place
a number of reforms that diminish the role of money in campaigns. For example, Britain bans the purchase of media time by the candidates. The presentation of candidates and their positions in the media in Britain is a function of the party organization. This centralization of media exposure helps

control the excesses of spending and ties the candidates to the party rather than to a specific group or economic sector. Candidates in Britain can spend their own funds on campaigns, but they require approval by government oversight bodies of so-called independent expenditures. Television and outdoor advertisers provide free advertising for candidates, thereby further lowering the cost to the candidate and the party. These limits and controls have prevented the overarching influence of money on the campaign. With the election period short and the parties rather than the candidates the focus, expenditures are dramatically lower than in the United States.

Every British citizen over eighteen years of age is eligible to vote. Local officials are responsible for the registration procedures and the voting stations, which are in abundance throughout the country. Candidates for Parliament must pay £500 to register as candidates for the election and receive the money back if they win 5 percent of the vote. Votes for members of Parliament occur in electoral districts that have approximately 65,000 citizens per district. Winners in the single-member-plurality system (or as the British refer to it, the first-past-the-post system) assume the 659 seats available in the House of Commons. In recent years the electoral process has yielded more diverse members of Parliament with gradual increases in minority representation (nine Asian and black MPs) and a dramatic increase in women (119 female MPs).

A major difference between British and American political participation is the diminution of interest group influence. Because political parties dominate the political arena, interest groups have taken a backseat and are not critical to the outcome of public policy. On the business side the Confederation of British Industry (CBI) represents medium-sized manufacturing. Now that Tony Blair has talked about the importance of building business-government partnerships, the CBI has increased its visibility and importance in governing circles. On the labor side the Trades Union Congress (TUC) remains the core of union representation in government. But as labor unions weakened during the administration of Margaret Thatcher and now under Blair's more broad-based approach, the TUC is no longer the key player in developing social and economic policy that it was during the heyday of Labour power during the 1960s and early 1970s.

A range of new social movements represent policy concerns such as environmentalism, nuclear disarmament, race relations, religion, and feminism. Although not as established or politically connected as the business and labor groups, the new social movements nevertheless are becoming more vocal in presenting their positions to the British public. One cannot open a newspaper in London or walk through a public place such as Trafalgar Square and not see a demonstration by at least one of these social movements. The growth and visibility of social movements may signal a critical adjustment in the manner in which interest group politics is conducted in Britain, especially now that Tony Blair is seeking citizen commitment to make contributions to societal improvement. His concept of a stakeholder society is based on citizen involvement in order to make the entire nation a better and more just place to live. As Blair says about community participation, "the key is to recognize that we owe duty to more than self. Responsibility applies from top to bottom of society: from the responsibility to pay taxes to fund common services, to the responsibility of fathers to their children after a divorce, to the responsibility of people to respect the lives of their neighbors." For a nation where citizens have become used to political parties playing the key role in public policy development, Blair's challenge to become more involved is significant and worthy of close monitoring.

Election Data

Results of the 2001 Parliament election:

Labour Party	40.7 percent
Conservative Party	31.7 percent
Liberal Democrats	18.3 percent
Scottish National Party	1.8 percent
United Kingdom Independence Party	1.5 percent
Ulster Unionist Party	0.8 percent
Plaid Cymru/Party of Wales	0.7 percent
Democratic Unionist Party	0.7 percent
Sinn Fein	0.7 percent
Social Democratic and Labour Party	0.6 percent
Kidderminster Hospital and Health Concern	0.1 percent

BRITISH ANTI-IRA POLICIES

The movement of Irish Catholics to end British rule in Northern Ireland has had many defining moments, but none more influential than the Bloody Sunday massacre—the killing of thirteen unarmed civilian demonstrators by the British Army's First Parachute Regiment on January 30, 1972 (one other man later died of illnesses attributed to the shooting). The demonstrators were protesting what they viewed as the illegal internment of over 3,000 Irish Republican Army (IRA) activists and other protesters of British military occupation of Northern Ireland. The Bloody Sunday killings changed the face of the Northern Ireland conflict as public protest and civil disobedience were replaced with armed struggle led by the IRA and other nationalist groups committed to force the British military out of the country.

For the next twenty years Northern Ireland was beset by brutal sectarian violence between Catholics and Protestants with the British seeking to stabilize the situation. The British, however, were not viewed as neutral peacemakers by Catholics, since they aligned with the local Protestant police force, the Royal Ulster Constabulary (RUC), in rooting out IRA terrorists and sympathizers. The British along with the RUC and the locally recruited Royal Irish Regiment (RIR) put in place a heavy military presence numbering over 32,000 troops (20,000 British troops). At the high point of its presence during the 1970s and 1980s the British Army controlled 135 installations and used those installations to put in place a wide range of security restrictions. The violence between Catholics and Protestants continued despite this presence, with over 2,700 deaths by 1990. The British were not immune from the carnage as the IRA targeted the troops on patrol and at various checkpoints through the countryside.

As the fighting continued, the British changed their policy approach in the late 1970s to what was called Ulsterization and criminalization. Ulsterization involved replacing British soldiers with a more heavily armed Royal Ulster Constabulary and the part-time Ulster Defense Regiment. The criminalization strategy was based on removing the equivalent of prisoner of war status for terrorists in British jails and replacing it with criminal status. Criminalization backfired when IRA activist Bobby Sands conducted a hunger strike in prison and died along with nine other IRA inmates. His death caused renewed violence in Northern Ireland and in Britain. In fact, Margaret Thatcher narrowly escaped being killed by a terrorist bomb that blew up a hotel she was staying at during a Conservative Party conference.

The violence continued into 1990, when more concerted peace efforts were initiated and the IRA agreed to a series of cease-fires. But the talks between the British and the political arm of the IRA, the Sinn Fein, broke down at various times during this period largely over issues related to the decommissioning of weapons in the hands of the IRA and the model that would be used to form a government once the British left Northern Ireland. With the failure of the peace talks, the IRA took their terrorism to the heart of London. During the 1990s London was the target of numerous IRA bombings in the populated financial district, the subway system, and residential areas. Even a British military base in Germany was hit by a terrorist bomb.

The path to a more sustained peace process was begun in 1996, when former U.S. Senator George Mitchell was able to convince the British and the new Labour government of Tony Blair that talks with the IRA and its representatives from Sinn Fein should not be contingent on the surrender of arms. Although British political leaders were apprehensive about the IRA commitment to the peace process, the Good Friday Agreement was achieved in 1998 and approved by voters in the North and in Ireland. But this approval did not stop the violence. In August, terrorists associated with a splinter group of the IRA called the "Real IRA" detonated a bomb in Omagh, killing twenty-eight people. It was the worst single act of terrorism since the "Troubles" began in the 1960s.

Despite continuing sporadic violence, the Protestant Ulster Unionists and the Catholic Sinn Fein Party have established a power-sharing arrangement under the auspices of the Good Friday Agreement. Both sides have participated in the North-South Council ministerial meetings that have brought together representatives from Northern Ireland and Ireland along with a Northern Ireland Assembly. But the power-sharing arrangement has been subject to breakdown, as both sides continue to accuse the other of violent acts and terrorism. David Trimble, the Ulster Unionist leader, and Gerry Adams of the Sinn Fein engage in regular confrontations and threaten to end peace negotiations. In 2000, 2001, and 2002 the British government had to suspend the Northern Ireland Assembly because of various crises between the two parties ranging from decommissioning of IRA weapons to an alleged Sinn Fein theft of confidential materials from the government. After the 2002 suspension British officials stated that the only resolution of the crisis in Northern Ireland was to disband the IRA and remove IRA sympathizers from any participation in a power-sharing arrangement. The antipathy of the IRA and Sinn Fein toward the Ulster Unionists and their British backers is so deep that the prospect for creating a long-term solution in Northern Ireland is bleak. A return to the days of sectarian violence is thus always a possibility. ⊕

THE POWER ELITE

Because power is centralized in Parliament and more specifically in the majority party in Parliament, that is the logical place to begin the search for the British power elite. Within that party majority the cabinet formed by the prime minister is the core of the power elite. The first among equals in the British cabinet is Tony Blair, whose official title is Prime Minister, First Lord of the Treasury, and Minister for the Civil Service. As prime minister, Tony Blair holds considerable power. As the chief executive of British government, he appoints and dismisses all ministers, manages the governing process through the cabinet, and makes

PHOTO 2.1   BRITAIN'S PRIME MINISTER TONY BLAIR
ADDRESSES JOURNALISTS DURING A NEWS CONFERENCE.
(REUTERS NEWMEDIA INC./CORBIS)

*Tony Blair was born in 1953 and was educated at schools in Durham,
England, and Edinburgh, Scotland. He studied law at St. John's College in
Oxford, England. His specialty in the legal profession was trade union and in-
dustrial law. In 1983 Blair was elected to Parliament as a member of the
Labour Party. He rose quickly in the Parliament through his association with
party leaders Neil Kinnock and John Smith. When John Smith died in 1994,
Blair assumed the leadership of the Labour Party and in 1997 led the party
to an electoral victory over the Conservatives.*

public policy decisions as the head of the cabinet. He is the chief legislator in
that he presides over the majority party in Commons and speaks for that majority in debate and during the question hour. He is the leader of his party, which
includes monitoring the day-to-day organizational issues of the party and determining the policy and electoral strategy of Labour. He is the traditional representative of the government to the Crown, fulfilling those tasks by meeting regularly with the queen. He is the chief representative of Britain to the world and
therefore conducts the foreign policy relations of the government. And finally

Blair, like many of his counterparts throughout the world, is the manager of the economy with responsibility to ensure that Britain has a healthy growth rate, low inflation and unemployment, and expanding prosperity.

In post–World War II Britain, the power of the prime minister has steadily expanded, while the cabinet, which historically has been the center of decisionmaking, has seen its power diminish. The cabinet may collectively make major policy decisions, but it is the prime minister who conducts the business of government. The prime minister names the members of the cabinet, sets the meeting dates, controls the agenda, and announces the results of the ministerial deliberations. The power of the prime minister is such that students of British politics have concluded that modern-day chief executives function much like the president of the United States. As British historian Humphry Berkeley states quite accurately, "If the cabinet discusses anything it is the Prime Minister who decides what the collective view of the cabinet is. A minister's job is to save the Prime Minister all the work he can. But no minister could make a really important move without consulting the Prime Minister, and if the Prime Minister wants to take a certain step the cabinet minister would either have to agree, to argue it out in cabinet or resign." Cabinet power in modern Britain is thus not collective but singular, and cabinet decisions often ratify the decision made by the prime minister. Moreover, the British media and certainly the British people increasingly view the prime minister, not the cabinet, as having the authority and the responsibility for leading the country.

Yet the cabinet has not moved outside the boundaries of the British power elite. While prime ministers may exercise ever expanding power, they nevertheless work closely with cabinet ministers who control vast bureaucracies and wield considerable power in their own right to formulate and implement policy. No prime minister can manage all facets of government and must of necessity depend on the advice and the leadership capabilities of those ministers that are appointed to the cabinet. The fact that the British cabinet meets regularly with the prime minister to discuss public policy issues is a distinct departure from how the cabinet is used in the United States, where meetings are often photo opportunities rather than collective policy discussions.

Compared to the American cabinet, the British cabinet is much larger and more specialized. In July 2001 after the last election, the cabinet was constructed of twenty-three ministers. Prime Minister Blair relies on an inner circle of cabinet secretaries for regular policy consultation. John Prescott, Blair's deputy prime minister, Gordon Brown, the chancellor of the Exchequer, Jack Straw, the secretary of state for Foreign and Commonwealth Affairs, David Blunkett, the secretary of state for the Home Department, and Geoff Hoon, the secretary of state for Defence, form the key members of the

Labour government. These ministers sit prominently in the front benches of Parliament, lending support to the prime minister and fielding many of the questions that come from the back benchers of both their own party and the opposition.

The modern evolution of the prime minister into a quasi-president has influenced the advisory networks that have been put in place. There is growing evidence that recent prime ministers have borrowed from the American chief executive and formed an internal inner circle of advisers that is separate from the key members of the cabinet. Prime Minister Blair has assembled an inner circle of personal advisers who are senior civil servants from Whitehall—the center of the bureaucratic establishment—and from within his own party and a wide range of experts from academia and business. Blair relies heavily on this personal inner circle of the "best and brightest" of the British policy elite to advise him on domestic and foreign issues.

The principal bureaucrat with day-to-day responsibility for implementing public policy is the permanent secretary. The permanent secretary sits just below the cabinet secretary and a junior minister and works in unison with them as a liaison with the larger bureaucratic establishment. The permanent secretary has his or her own hierarchy of support, including a principal private secretary who is often an individual with potential to move up the administrative ladder. The number of these senior-level bureaucrats is approximately 75,000. Of course, not all of them are members of the power elite in British government, but senior-level administrators, such as junior ministers and permanent secretaries, wield tremendous policymaking and implementing power since they define the details of the laws that Commons passes.

The power elite in British government also includes the top leadership of the nationalized sectors, such as the National Health Service (NHS). The NHS is the core of the British welfare state system. The most interesting aspect of the NHS is that despite the efforts of Margaret Thatcher and John Major to move Britons away from dependence on the state for health care, expenditures for the NHS rose steadily from about £30 billion at the start of Thatcher's administration to £40 billion in 1996, the last year Conservatives controlled Commons. The administrative leaders of the NHS have seized on the fact that 87 percent of the British people rely on nationalized health care and see cutbacks as a distinct threat to gain ever larger increases in government funding.

Other key agencies are the so-called quangos—quasi-nongovernmental agencies. The strength of the quangos is found in the local communities, where they are often responsible for areas such as education and public health. Currently there are over 6,000 quangos employing 50,000 people. The level of spending by the quangos has increased dramatically in the

1990s, accounting for one-third of all public spending. The influence of quangos is likely to continue as Tony Blair pursues his plans for decentralizing British government. Moreover, since quangos often have a public-private component, they fit nicely into Blair's vision of a more cooperative relationship between government and the corporate sector. The heads of the various executive bodies and agencies that are designated quangos can be expected to play a heightened role in government in the future, thus further solidifying their status as members of the British power elite.

Other forces that influence the public policy process include the press. The British are one of the most literate and well-read people in the modern world. Although in recent years newspaper readership has slipped considerably, newspapers continue to be a vital part of national life and the most consistent source of analysis and criticism of political leaders and government policy. The center of newspaper publishing in England is Fleet Street in London. In the last few years a spate of acquisitions and mergers have reshaped the British press, but it has not toned down the competition between the more serious-minded newspapers such as the venerable *Times* and the more tabloid publications such as the pro-Labour *Mirror* and the pro-Conservative *Sun*.

Also part of the media power elite is the broadcasting services provided by the British Broadcasting Corporation (BBC) and a growing commercial sector. Founded in 1922, the BBC is a publicly financed entity that operates two national television channels, three satellite channels, five national and four regional radio services, and thirty-eight local stations. Increasingly the BBC is facing competition from the commercial stations, in particular Rupert Murdoch's British Sky Broadcasting. While the BBC has moved away from its news, commentary, and educational formats to more entertainment, commercial stations like British Sky Broadcasting are gaining popularity. Nevertheless the BBC remains the primary source of television and radio news about politics and government. BBC positions on leaders and legislation are taken seriously by the government. The British are not television watchers on a par with the Americans, but with 25 million viewers in the country, the BBC and the commercial stations are a force to be reckoned with in presenting the news and analyzing events.

Queen Elizabeth II, who is certainly a more public presence than Tony Blair and is on any organizational chart describing the British governing system, cannot be included in the power elite. The queen has regular visits with the prime minister in which she has an opportunity to voice her opinion on matters of state and thus could be an influential force in the country. But the relationship between monarch and prime minister is largely courtesy rather than substance. Tony Blair apparently has a cordial relationship with Queen Elizabeth, although his reform of the aristocratic Lords and his party's traditional public

criticism of the monarchy would likely mean that the weekly discussion between the two is perfunctory. Support for the concept of the monarchy and
party preference, however, does not always predict the tenor of the relationship
between the queen and the prime minister. Margaret Thatcher's relationship
with Queen Elizabeth was frosty. Observers of the two women leaders re-
marked at the tension in the room as the queen expressed her opinions to the
prime minister, whose abrasive and no-nonsense style of governance was not
conducive to the formality of the conversation.

Also in a diminished role are the members of the House of Lords.
Although the leader of the House of Lords is a member of Tony Blair's cabinet, he, along with the other aristocratic and church leaders who make up
Lords, are not in the mainstream of public policy formation or political influence. Now that Tony Blair has achieved the first step in reforming Lords by
stripping 759 hereditary nobles of their right to sit in the House of Lords,
while permitting 9 to win seats through an election by their colleagues, there
is speculation that the "new House of Lords" may become more of a legislative force. Lord Strathclyde, the Conservative leader in Lords, has already
stated that the "new House of Lords" should become a constitutional watchdog and pay more attention to legislation that comes out of the European
Union.

Membership in the European Union will likely create a new group of leaders and policymakers with considerable impact on the country. The most
powerful institution of the European Union is the European Commission.
The Commission's responsibility is to make the policies in twenty-three economic, financial, and trade areas that together define the mission of the
European Union. The Commission has twenty members, five of whom come
from Great Britain. Since the Commission acts as the executive arm of the
European Union, the commissioners are key decisionmakers determining
where the fifteen-nation economic and political entity is headed. The five
British commissioners will become increasingly important in representing
the interests of their country. Although Tony Blair has stated emphatically
that he staunchly supports Britain's involvement in the European Union,
deep concerns remain over issues such as sovereignty, the implementation of
the euro, and various trade matters.

There is also concern in Britain over the European Parliament. Currently
Britain holds eighty-seven seats in the European Parliament, the political arm
of the European Union. But it is a weak institution, since most of the decisions are made by the Commission in conjunction with the Council of
Ministers (representing the governmental leaders of the fifteen countries).
Increasingly, however, the European Parliament has begun to acquire more
power and more visibility as an active participant in the policymaking

process. Britain's eighty-seven legislative representatives, a number equal to that of Italy and France but fewer than Germany (ninety-nine seats), will become a key voting bloc as the Parliament takes on ever more difficult decisions concerning a united military force, peacekeeping operations, and the potential for transforming the European Union into a sovereign political entity.

Because Tony Blair has made a high priority of restructuring the United Kingdom and its constitutional framework, the power elite in Britain will certainly undergo significant changes in the coming years. The core power relationship of prime minister–cabinet–Whitehall will in all probability remain in force, but new power elites may emerge, particularly as Britain solidifies its relationship with Europe. Because it is impossible to predict the outcome of the constitutional and political reform initiated by Blair, defining with precision the British power elite may become difficult.

POINT OF FACT

Queen Elizabeth is not only queen of the United Kingdom but also head of the Commonwealth, a voluntary association of fifty-four independent countries. The Commonwealth serves to foster international cooperation and trade links. Queen Elizabeth is also queen of a number of Commonwealth realms, including Australia, New Zealand, and Canada.

Legislative Composition as a Result of the 2001 Parliamentary Elections (not including by-elections in 2002 and 2003)	
Labour Party	413 seats
Conservative Party	166 seats
Liberal Democratic Party	52 seats
Scottish National Party	5 seats
Ulster Unionist Party	6 seats
Plaid Cymru/Party of Wales	4 seats
Democratic Unionists Party	5 seats
Sinn Fein	4 seats
Social Democratic and Labour Party	3 seats
Kidderminster Hospital and Health Concern	1 seat

REAL GOVERNMENT

Britain's parliamentary system with its majority rule and power centralized in the cabinet, particularly the office of the prime minister, is more predictable and less complex than that found in the American presidential system.

Nevertheless, the process of making public policy in Britain is not a cut-and-dried affair devoid of partisan differences, personal disputes, group influence, public debate, institutional scrutiny, and political compromise. Because the lawmaking function is centered in the House of Commons with the front bench of the majority party controlling the proceedings, there is less of the wrangling, deal making, and delay that characterize the American legislative system. But the streamlined nature of British policymaking does not mean that Commons, the cabinet, the prime minister, Lords, and Whitehall are mere governing robots with little opportunity to move from the party script. Public policymaking in Britain has many of the characteristics found in the American system. The difference, however, is that in the parliamentary system those characteristics are not as pronounced and do not create an environment dominated by gridlock.

The public policy process in Britain is rooted in the yearly party conferences. All the major parties conduct conferences that choose the leadership, ratify the platform, and give activists an opportunity to present their views on the direction the party should take in the coming year. The Labour Party Annual Conference and the Conservative National Union Conference are large gatherings (1,200 for Labour and 4,000 for the Conservatives) that are part political rally and part policy sounding board. The leadership of both major parties uses the annual conference to gauge the opinion of activists and shape that opinion where it is deemed necessary. The annual conference has changed somewhat into a forum that determines whether the leadership correctly matches the views of the membership. If those views do not mesh, then the conference becomes a place where fences are mended and views are more clearly articulated. At the completion of the conference, the leadership moves forward and takes the government or the opposition to the parliamentary stage, where ideology and initiatives are changed into action.

The key stage in the policy process occurs at Number 10 Downing Street, the prime minister's residence. With the power of the majority behind him and no real concern over a threat from Lords or the monarchy, the prime minister and his closest aides, key party leaders, and Whitehall ministers begin the task of drafting legislative proposals and preparing those proposals for introduction into the lawmaking process in Commons. Throughout this preparatory stage the prime minister stays above the internal debate among his advisory team over the specifics of the legislation such as language, cost, and the scheduling of debate. Despite holding the majority and benefiting from party discipline, the prime minister and the advisory team are always alert to the opinion of back benchers and the potential for opposition attacks. It is also at this preparatory stage that the internal team consults appropriate interest groups and representatives of affected social or economic sectors to drum up support for the policy, or to include changes in the policy that would enhance support and passage. Of course a larger parliamentary majority and strong party support for the policy make the preparatory stage easier and more streamlined. But if the party in power holds government by a slim margin and faces internal dissension over the policy, then this preparatory stage becomes a time of extensive compromise, bargaining, and public opinion formation.

Once the government is satisfied that it has taken the necessary preparatory steps, the proposed policy would come before the cabinet. Each prime minister has his or her own style of interacting with the cabinet. Margaret Thatcher was known for her low threshold of tolerance for cabinet dissension. John Major, on the other hand, followed a more accommodating posture toward his cabinet and sought a variety of viewpoints on the shape and direction of public policy initiatives. To date, Tony Blair has taken a less caustic but more Thatcher-like view of the cabinet. He expects support and quick ratification of his legislative proposals. Cabinet meetings over policy are usually pro forma exercises in cabinet responsibility where ministers follow the wishes of their prime minister. If debate occurs over the policy, it happens much earlier in the process and within a tightly knit circle of Tony Blair's advisers.

With the policy formulated and supported by the cabinet, the next stage is the introduction into Commons. Traditionally, legislation in the British parliamentary system moves through five stages in Commons, a similar process in Lords, and then the royal assent. The core of the process in Commons comprises three readings—a first reading that is a nominal exercise akin to formal introduction into the process, a second reading on the principles and purposes of the bill, which often includes the debate between the government and the loyal opposition, and a third reading in which verbal changes are permitted and the final draft is either approved or rejected. A committee stage examines the manner in which the bill will be implemented and a report stage considers proposed amendments.

The central feature of the British legislative process is the debate during the second reading. On major government initiatives the prime minister will lead the debate and present the arguments in favor of the bill. Government ministers with responsibility for the implementation of the bill will also speak. Television cameras and the viewing audience are attracted to the interchange between the government and the loyal opposition. Because the opposition is in the minority, party leader and members of the shadow cabinet will use their oratorical skills to poke holes in the government's proposal. Margaret Thatcher made much of her reputation as the Iron Lady with her steely responses to opposition charges. Tony Blair has taken a less combative mode in parliamentary debate and relies on his relaxed sense of humor and his self-confidence built on the fact that he commands a huge majority.

The debate in Parliament is not purely an exercise to showcase oratorical skills. It can raise concerns about a specific policy that prompts the government to go back to the drawing board and add amendments or change the language of the bill. The government is always concerned about how the proposed bill will be received by its own back benchers, and the debate often provides an opportunity to determine the opinions of the majority. Moreover, with the debate covered on television and in the newspapers, it can muster public opinion for or against the bill. The loyal opposition is always looking for an opening in which to insert its own views and make the government's legislative agenda less secure. But if the prime minister and his cabinet have a secure hold on the majority and are confident about the proposed bill, then there is little that the debating skills of the loyal opposition can do to deter the final outcome.

Although the British legislative process requires that a bill passed in Commons must move on to the House of Lords, this body has little power to influence legislation. If Lords plays a constructive role in the legislative process, it is in the amendment process and attracting public attention concerning a bill through the amendment process. The Lords during the 1990s took very visible action in legislation regarding local police power and in the initiatives related to the European Union. In so doing, it was able to modify the proposals of the government and have its amendments become part of the final legislation. In most legislative matters, however, Lords is an ornate rubber stamp for the government. There may be a need after Lords has acted to reconcile the work of the two legislative bodies, but the House of Commons decides to accept or reject modifications or amendments to the government's bill.

The British legislative process has similarities to the American congressional system—lively debate between proponents and opponents of legislation and the prospect that the minority party can exert some influence on the final outcome of the legislative process. There are also significant differences between the two systems. One of the most obvious is the minor role that standing committees play in the British system. There are eight such committees in Commons. The Speaker makes appointments to the committees and names from twenty to fifty members from Commons, based on party strength. These committees are not grounded in a specific policy specialization but receive a bill based on where it is in the legislative timetable. The committees are not charged with examining the purpose of the bill and therefore do not conduct hearings or call witnesses. There are no staff members, no specialized office or conference space, and no independent budget. The major purpose of the committees is to determine the proper manner for implementing the legislation. Service on the committee is thus confined to examining the details of the legislation and not writing or rewriting the law. Not surprisingly, committee members often view membership on the committee as a chore rather than an opportunity to wield power.

Another difference between the American congressional system and British parliamentary rule is the method of handling the budget. Since 1911, all money bills must be introduced by the House of Commons. Lords has no power to reject a money bill. The chancellor of the Exchequer begins the budget debate when he or she "opens the budget" before the Commons. Immediately the provisions of the budget are put into effect by a vote of Commons, thus ending a brief and highly centralized budget process. In the United States in recent years, budget deliberations have created dramatic confrontations between Congress and the president, but the British dispense with the budget by circumventing the Parliament. It is important to stress that Commons has not totally abandoned its role in the area of public budgeting. It has over the years established committees whose responsibility is to determine where economies can be made in the expenditure of money and search out waste and corruption in the implementation of public laws.

Perhaps the most significant difference between the American system and the British system of lawmaking is in the role played by the individual legislators. Legislators in Britain rarely have an opportunity to introduce legislation on their own. That is the responsibility of the government. Moreover, legislators in Britain are not likely to speak for or against a piece of legislation. Back benchers in Commons follow the directives of the whips and ensure passage of government bills. Occasionally the government "withdraws the whip" and permits back benchers to vote on bills, for example, on capital punishment or gay rights, according to their conscience. These opportunities are few and far between. Back benchers may utilize the question hour to participate in the legislative process, but even then there is no guarantee that the Speaker of Commons will recognize a back bencher.

The weakness of the back benchers as key participants in the legislative process is reinforced by their low salary. Compared to legislators in countries like Japan, Germany, France, and the United States, British legislators are paid poorly. The high cost of living in London forces many MPs to take other jobs to supplement their income. Most MPs do not have a staff or adequate office space. Because the committee system is weak in the British system and because there is less emphasis on constituent service, the legislators do not control the multimillion-dollar operations that their counterparts in the United States have at their disposal.

Once reconciliation has been accomplished, the bill is sent to the queen for the royal assent. This is a formality in which the queen attaches the royal seal to the legislation. Because Britain is a constitutional monarchy, the queen participates in the process of lawmaking. But the monarch is permitted no legislative input at this stage. What is important is that the queen maintains the traditions of British constitutional monarchy by adding the symbolic royal seal to the legislation. With that royal seal the proposed law, which began with the majority party leadership seeking to implement its electoral promises, was transformed in a fairly efficient and orderly legislative system into an act of Parliament.

A critical policy relationship is developing in the British system between the cabinet ministry and various policy networks. For example, the Ministry of Health and Social Security may develop close ties to a policy network that includes the British Medical Association, grassroots health care advocates, members of the academic world interested in health policy, and authors or journalists with a professional interest in the area of national health care. This network then forms the structure on which the prime minister and his staff develop their health care proposals and agenda. This network also interacts with party leaders and back benchers to expand their reach and ensure that their proposals gather political strength. Thus when party conferences are held and the cabinet meetings are conducted, these policy networks have already secured a place for themselves at the policymaking table. Once a policy proposal is scheduled for action in Commons, the network moves into high gear to further inform the party leadership and the back benchers of any changes or amendments that may be necessary to achieve passage. In the end it is Commons and the majority party in Commons that control the destiny of any piece of legislation, but the preparatory stage of public policy is increasingly in the hands of these networks, whose numbers are growing and whose reach into the core of government decisionmaking is expanding.

Real government in Britain is highly centralized in the relationship between the government and Commons. But as British government evolves, "pockets" of personal and institutional power outside of the cabinet and the Commons actively participate in the policy process and make significant contributions to the passage of national legislation. Not only are the policy networks gaining influence in shaping real government, but major city councils, the rapidly developing quangos, and in some instances the courts have broadened their involvement in the governing process. While all these "pockets" of power depend in some way on the party leadership and on the decisionmaking process that exists between the government and the Commons, they nevertheless have staked out a claim to governing by simply taking action where there was a need or filling a void that may have existed through inaction by the government of Commons. British citizens have looked to these new "pockets" of power in recent years for leadership and for resolution of public policy concerns. The government and Commons for their part seem willing to distribute governing power and follow through on the promise to decentralize Britain's public policy process.

POINT OF FACT

As of the election of 2001 and the formation of the government by Prime Minister Tony Blair, 18 percent of the seats in the House of Commons were held by women. As of 1999, 33 percent of the ministerial appointments were held by women.

THE NATIONAL HEALTH SERVICE

As an American, I was introduced to the British National Health Service (NHS) through my roommate in graduate school. About a month before the winter break, he got a terrible toothache that kept him (and me) up at night. As a citizen of the United States schooled in the realities of private sector insurance, I wondered why he did not pay the modest premium for the college medical insurance and get his tooth fixed. He looked at me incredulously and stated that he was going home soon and would get the tooth fixed free of charge by the government. Why would anyone, he asked, accept a personally funded health insurance program when the government provides the service free?

My roommate and millions of other Britons have enjoyed the benefits of the National Health Service since its founding in 1948. The British government made the NHS the centerpiece of the collectivist consensus that emerged after World War II. But over the years, and particularly since the Conservatives took power in 1979, there has been a noticeable erosion of the National Health Service. Although the Conservatives regularly criticized the NHS for its "money pit" character (a royal commission at the time termed the capacity of the health service to absorb resources "almost unlimited"), it nevertheless doubled real expenditures during its time in power. Despite continued support for the NHS, Britain began to fall considerably behind the rest of Europe in its contributions to health care, and service began to deteriorate.

The NHS developed a reputation for long waiting lists, uneven service, low-tech medical care, and health care facilities in desperate need of modernization. Those who could, because of their income, moved away from the NHS and signed up for private health care plans in order to avoid the hassles and the uncertainty that became commonplace. There is growing concern over the capability of British health care to address serious illnesses. While the life expectancy in Britain is seventy-seven years, which is similar to those of most of its European neighbors, survival rates for cancer and heart disease are some of the worst in Europe. Many experts cite the fact that Britain has one of the lowest doctor-to-patient ratios in the advanced industrial world and a highly inefficient and overly bureaucratized method of assigning patients to specialists. The limitations of the NHS, coupled with the disturbing data on the overall health of the public, have created an element of dissatisfaction with health care that has forced political leaders to take bold action.

In March 2000, Prime Minister Tony Blair announced that his government would support a significant budget increase for the NHS. The increase, equivalent to $31 billion, would bring health spending up to 7.6 percent of GDP, which is still below the average for the remainder of the European Union (8–9 percent). Currently Britain spends US$1,454 per person on health care. The EU average is US$1,884, and the U.S. expenditure per capita is $4,000. Blair's announcement, while welcomed by those who have long pressed the government to increase spending on health care, may only help Britain keep pace with rising medical costs and an aging population. Moreover, since this increase in spending will need time to filter through the health care system, estimates are that the new money will not make an impact on the quality of care until 2004. The NHS is planning to make significant spending increases of as much as £40 billion by 2007, which would raise health care spending to 9 percent of GDP, equal to that in France.

Like many countries, Britain is struggling to keep up with rising costs for prescription drugs and advanced medical procedures. For example, the NHS has seen a 50 percent increase in prescriptions in the last twenty-five years, and new drugs coming on the market will further heighten government expenditures. Paying for nursing home care has continued to gobble up scarce budget resources. These economic pressures have prompted growing talk of health care rationing. The government is currently reviewing what kind of procedures it is willing to fund and at what rate. A new government body, the National Institute of Clinical Excellence (NICE), has been formed to set uniform standards for the delivery of medical treatment.

The key challenge for the National Health Service in the coming years will be cost containment. Despite the public nature of its health care system, Britain will be forced to follow the principles of managed care that are the foundation of the medical system in the United States. The current debate in Britain is over defining which medical procedures or services the National Health Service makes available to patients and which ones the government does not include on its health care "menu." In many respects Britain has come late to this debate. Political leaders have invested most of their political energy in the area of budget appropriations, but now they realize that new approaches are necessary. One thing is certain: as Britain engages in this debate, the outcome will profoundly change the National Health Service and the way it serves the British people. ⊕

POLITICAL ECONOMY

Britain's economy and the role of government in the economy have been shaped by the ongoing transition from an aging industrial society to a more diversified, global approach to national development. After leading the world's economy because of its manufacturing base and its superior trading relations, Britain found itself by the 1960s in a steep decline. New competitors were emerging, particularly Japan and Germany; the industrial framework that had served Britain so well was giving way to more modern and efficient modes of production; and the entrepreneurial and innovative spirit that was fueling the new global economy was lacking. Add to this mix the class antagonism between workers and managers that led to debilitating strikes and regular governmental intervention, and Britain found itself facing an economic downturn. High unemployment, high inflation, low growth, trade imbalances, weakened currency, plant closings, bankruptcies, and general economic malaise gripped the country. For example, from the mid-1960s to the mid-1970s the British economy grew by a modest average of 2 percent a year. Inflation in 1975 reached an all-time high of 26 percent, and unemployment during most of the 1970s was in double digits.

For most of the 1960s and 1970s Britain was unable to respond effectively to the new economic challenges that it was facing. Governments during this period never received a clear electoral mandate and were forced to make policy with slim majorities and informal coalitions. Consequently no bold initiatives were taken and no leaders were willing to risk losing their shaky majorities by antagonizing either business or labor. Britain lurched from crisis to crisis. Union strikes in areas such as mining, transportation, and manufacturing further weakened the economy and called into question the ability of the government to move the country out of the mess. The 1973 Wage Control Act by the Conservative government of Edward Heath and the subsequent miners' strike in response to the act were symptomatic of the sharp divisions in the country over economic policy. Even when the Heath government lost the election in 1974, the new Labour government of James Callaghan overturned the wage policy and began another period of inflation. By the end of the decade Britain was experiencing stagflation, a dangerous mix of low or no growth mixed with ever higher inflation rates.

Economic policy took a markedly different turn when Margaret Thatcher was elected in 1979. The Thatcher approach to the British political economy can be divided into three periods with three different policy agendas. From 1979 to 1983 Thatcher pursued a monetarist policy. She and her ministers were most concerned about the skyrocketing inflation rate. To battle inflation Thatcher cut public expenditures and raised interest rates. By pursuing a policy of reducing the money supply, Thatcher was able to significantly reduce the rise in prices, although a sluggish world economy contributed to low growth rates and continued high unemployment. The Thatcher government also began restructuring the nationalized industries, requiring them to operate according to market principles. Increased public expenditures by the nationalized industries were frowned on. Most importantly, Thatcher began her crusadelike mission to weaken unions and lend support to failing industries such as British Leyland and British Steel.

The second phase of Thatcher's economic policies from 1983 to 1987 stressed a frontal attack on the unions coupled with full-scale privatization of state enterprises. During this period Thatcher won legislative approval to end secondary picketing of firms that were not party to a strike. She also won approval for legislation that required secret ballots in strike votes and the election of union leaders. Finally, the "closed shop" provision in which the workforce was required to join a union was held to a higher standard of approval (four-fifths support by the union membership). During this period nearly 60 percent of the nationalized industries were put out to bid. Thatcher made it clear in public speeches that she would not follow an income policy of responding to inflation with wage increases or any type of economic planning that intervened in business decisions.

In the final period of Thatcheromics, the Conservative government turned its attention to issues such as employment training, deregulation, employment zones, privatization of public housing, and renewed pressure on the unemployed to move off the welfare roles. The goal of this phase of economic policymaking was to inculcate the values of a private market economy on a British society that become dependent on the security and safety net of the state. In this period of her rule Thatcher became more strident in lashing out at big government, while emphasizing the benefits, both personal and monetary, of embracing the market system. Thatcher paid particular attention to building support for the enterprise zones and encouraging public housing residents to purchase their own homes.

When Thatcher ended her rule as prime minister, one of the most hotly debated subjects in Britain and indeed the industrial world was the impact that her economic policies had on pulling the country out of its downslide. There was general agreement that Thatcher's market-based approach had strengthened the finance and service areas of the economy, especially in the South and East of England. Moreover, it was clear that Thatcher had begun to position the country to take advantage of the emerging global marketplace by freeing business of government intervention and stressing the importance of innovation and investment. Where the debate became the most heated was in the area of how Thatcheromics benefited the working class and the old industrial sectors of the economy. Although there was some decline in unemployment and certainly a reduction in inflation, overall economic growth remained modest. Union power, however, was weakened, the safety net provided by the states was compromised, and the old industrial cities with their mining and manufacturing were not revitalized.

Economic policy during the government headed by John Major was focused on issues of budget shortfall, taxation, and the question of integration into the European Union. Prime Minister Major's approach to the British economy suffered in part from the leftover party factionalism that forced Margaret Thatcher to resign and also from a deteriorating economic climate. Major faced regular internal party criticism over his economic management, but by the time he assumed office Britain's inflation rate had risen to 9 percent and the trade deficit had reached dangerous levels.

Prime Minister Major's difficulties in trying to manage the British economy and his own party faithful stemmed in large part from the rapidly changing global business environment. The Conservative economic strategy had sought to turn the country away from the socialist consensus of the postwar period. But Major was not able to command the authority that Thatcher had, nor was he able to bring about a quick jolt of economic growth. As the critical 1997 elections approached, Major promised more modest goals of a steady recovery, broader deregulation and privatization, and more aggressive efforts to move Britain into the new global economy. While perhaps offering a more responsible approach to economic development than the boom-and-bust approach taken by Thatcher, Major was nevertheless viewed as a mediocre economic manager who led a party that was deeply divided over how to respond to economic stagnation and European integration.

Tony Blair's approach to British economic policy has been based on his Third Way program and his belief in proving that his "New" Labour Party is not wedded to its socialist past. Early in his administration, Blair pledged that he would not entertain any proposals to increase the income tax in Britain and would continue to embrace the market principles espoused by his Conservative predecessors. The Labour prime minister, however, did not forsake his traditional working-class base in the formation of economic policy. He moved quickly to push through Parliament a windfall profits tax on privatized industries, along with a hike in the minimum wage. Also, he established a job program for unemployed youths that placed 50,000 young men and women in just seven months.

With respect to the ongoing debate over European integration, Blair has placed himself the middle of the road. He has expressed support for integration with Europe and declared that participation in the European Monetary Union is inevitable. But Blair will likely not entertain a referendum on moving to the euro until his third term (should that occur), which would mean not until 2006. Blair's position on European Union and the euro is far more mainstream than that of the Conservative Party, which has become increasingly belligerent in its opposition to integration. Britons are apparently becoming more comfortable with European integration, although the issue of replacing the pound with the euro is linked with concerns over the loss of sovereignty and national identity.

The key story about the British economy is its growing strength and its reputation as a leader in Europe. In early 2000 the British unemployment rate was 4 percent, second only to the United States among the major industrialized countries. Inflation was a very attractive 2.6 percent and growth was a solid 3 percent. Prime Minister Blair was successful in managing the budget deficit, which shrank to 2 percent of GDP. Controlling the budget deficit had a number of positive spillover effects, including strengthening the pound and building business and consumer confidence. Although Britain experienced a downturn in the economy in 2001—GDP slowed to 2.3 percent, unemployment rose to 5.1 percent, and industrial production registered negative growth—there were some positive signs, especially in consumer confidence as retail spending enjoyed a robust 6 percent increase over 2000. The critical challenge for the Blair government was the global slowdown and the expected impact on British exports. British exporters expressed serious concern over the prospects for growth, and the terrorist attack in the United States, the war in Afghanistan, and the invasion of Iraq did nothing to assuage their concerns.

In the coming years Blair is likely to focus more on bread-and-butter issues such as education, health care, and transportation in order to show the British people that his government is doing something positive with the wealth that is being generated by the economic boom. This is where Blair's partnerships come into play. Blair has stressed the importance of working with private foundations to develop public research laboratories, building ties with corporations to raise school standards in so-called education action zones, and modernizing the London tube (subway), always popular with British citizens. It will be in the area of reforming the National Health Service and the social security system that Blair will find his true tests. Both these huge governmental programs continue to require considerable attention and budget money in order to sustain their service. But with promises of no new taxes and lean budgets already in place, Blair will face a difficult challenge.

Like most advanced industrial economies, Britain has entered the vast unknown of the global marketplace. While it has prospered to date because of its effective transition away from its socialist roots, uncertainty remains about Britain's ability to sustain its level of growth in the face of heightened competition not only in Europe but in North America and Asia. Tony Blair has captured the right image and the right language that coincides with the global marketplace. In the coming years he will be asked to make good on his promise that the Third Way approach to economic policymaking is the means to maintaining the current boom.

Britain in the Global Economy

Off the southern coast of Britain are a series of channel islands: the Isle of Man, Jersey, and Guernsey. The British government has allowed them to make their own business laws and direct their domestic economy. As a result, these islands have emerged as one of the world's prime centers of offshore banking and commerce. In the global economy banks that are established offshore from a major nation or region provide tax havens to corporations and individuals. These offshore sites have expanded as they attract billions of dollars and other currencies from not only Britain but most of the industrial world. The Isle of Man has consistently been viewed by independent financial advisers as having the top offshore finance center. Its 73,000 residents have prospered as employees of the numerous banks and brokerage houses that are housed there. On Jersey the island's banks now hold deposits exceeding £100 billion. Guernsey boasts over seventy international banks and a thriving fund management industry.

POINT OF FACT

In the 1960s Britain won eleven Nobel Prizes in chemistry, physics, and physiology or medicine, thirteen prizes in similar areas in the 1970s, four in the 1980s, and two in the 1990s. The steady decline has not been lost on British educators and officials who are struggling with a reduction in funding for the country's institutions of higher learning.

CHALLENGES

As Britain looks to the future, there is no doubt that constitutional reform will dominate the public agenda. The Labour Party under Tony Blair is committed to a broad reform of the British governing system, a process of change that has not been attempted since the early 1900s. Blair, however, is not just a bold reformer intent on radically reshaping the British constitution. Blair and the Labour Party have been concerned about finding issues that will distinguish them from the Conservative Party and also maintain their lead in electoral popularity.

The reforms advanced by Blair and Labour have caused extensive debate and division in Britain not only for what they propose, but also for what some see as the consequences they would create for the process of governing and the use of political power. Devolving power to assemblies in Scotland and Wales has been the bedrock of the Blair constitutional reform package, the first step in the decentralization process that is certain to weaken London's hold on national public policy.

No one can predict where all this decentralization is headed. There is now wide agreement that centralization created a governing system that was too rigid, too uniform, and too prone to what has been called "the universalization of error." Although centralization of power in London meant that it was easy to establish responsibility, the British now seem anxious to move away from parliamentary sovereignty and institute a new system of local responsibility.

Tony Blair has also gone on record favoring a review of electoral procedures, but he has been noncommittal in endorsing change. Before he became prime minister, Blair stated that he was "personally unpersuaded" that proportional representation would be beneficial to Commons. Blair set two tests that he felt had to be passed in order to gain his support—whether the change reflects public opinion and whether the change gives disproportionate influence to splinter groups. Once in office, Blair formed an Independent Commission on the Voting System headed by former Labour minister Lord Jenkins to examine the benefits and drawbacks of moving to proportional representation and to make a recommendation on alternatives to the current electoral system. In October 1998 the commission recommended an "alternative vote plus" system in which the single-member district would be retained. But instead of casting their ballot for one candidate, voters would be provided with a list of preferences.

Despite Blair's acceptance of the commission's report and his pledge to engage in a countrywide debate and eventual referendum, the proposed changes to the electoral system and the prospect of a new form of proportional representation has not been embraced by either Labour or Conservative parties. The Conservatives under their former leader William Hague promised Blair "the fight of his life" over the changes, since the Tories feared that proportional representation would jeopardize their presence in Commons and likely lead to smaller parties picking up new seats. Even Labour ministers were not supportive of the commission recommendations, feeling that any new system would be untested and could suffer from unintended consequences that would weaken the hold of the party in Commons. As Britain struggles with the prospect of a new electoral system, over one-third of legislation that affects the country is now being made in the European Parliament, where British electoral reform is not a factor.

The area of governmental and political reform that has the potential to significantly change British society can be found in individual rights, in particular a bill of rights. Only recently has Britain incorporated the European Convention on Human Rights into domestic law. Before the Labour government passed legislation complying with the European Court, Britain had one of the worst records of the European nations, with decisions rendered against it on a range of abuses such as telephone tapping, discriminatory immigration rules, denial of rights to prisoners and homosexuals, restrictions on press freedoms, and limitations on rights for the mentally ill. These decisions against Britain helped move Parliament to join the Convention. Now British judges determine whether the country is in compliance with the Convention, but Parliament retains the power to determine whether Britain will implement their judgment.

Much of the problem in complying with the European Court of Human Rights is that Britain does not have a detailed bill of rights which provides legally enforceable protections for its citizens. Although the British people overwhelmingly support a bill of rights, there has been opposition to promulgating a bill of rights. Written guarantees might challenge the sovereignty of Parliament and place power in the hand of judges. Unlike the Americans, the British do not have a tradition of strong and active high courts. Consequently there is fear that an unelected judge might reverse what an elected member of Parliament accomplished in a democratic legislative chamber. Despite this concern many in Britain are disturbed that there is no bill of rights to guide courts or reassure the general populace. Proponents of a bill of rights state that such a document detailing individual liberties would make redress of grievances faster and cheaper than relying on the parliamentary process.

Also connected to the issue of a British bill of rights is the proposal to pass a Freedom of Information Act. Modeling it after a similar law in the United States, the British have for years debated the necessity of creating legislation that will permit citizens to open up the decisionmaking process in government. Currently public access to meetings and documents is closed by virtue of the Official Secrets Act. Efforts to inform the public about governmental actions have on many occasions brought criminal charges against journalists, academics, and political activists who want to end the climate of secrecy that pervades British government.

Not all of Britain's governing challenges are constitutional in nature. Integration with Europe is sure to occupy Britain's foreign policy agenda for years to come. The Thatcherite opposition to European integration has been replaced by a willingness to accept the new system that has been put in place over the past twenty years. Tony Blair and Labour moved quickly on taking office to accept the EU Social Charter on worker benefits and the Convention of Human Rights. The realization that integration with Europe is here to stay has begun to sink in and the clamor over losing decisionmaking power and perhaps even moving away from the pound has begun to weaken. The Conservative Party remains the bastion of anti-European sentiment, but their minority status in Commons is a testament to the questionable support for their position.

However, participation in the European Union is fraught with disputes over trade regulations and economic policies. Many in Britain still recall the EU ban on British beef that resulted from the mad cow disease scare and the host of negative judgments of the European Court of Justice regarding individual rights. It is likely that decisions made by the institutions of the European Union will continue to cause controversy, especially since there remains an undercurrent of support for national sovereignty and a wariness of the bureaucratic and judicial establishment in the European Commission and the European Court of Justice. The critical test will come when Blair and Labour begin to take Britain further along the path of integration and the issues of joining EU and the euro become more than just debating points.

Perhaps one of the greatest challenges facing Tony Blair and his Labour government is keeping the support of its labor union base. In 2002 there was mounting evidence that Blair's union ties were fraying as key federations such as Amicus elected leaders who were clearly not willing to blindly support the government. Labor union leaders were sending a message that wages were not keeping pace with inflation and that unions were not going to sit by idly while their membership was forced to live on less. During 2002 there was also heightened strike activity. One-day strikes by transportation workers, postal workers, and firefighters showed that Blair could no longer count on labor peace. The changed atmosphere in the area of government-labor relations showed that Blair would have to mend fences among union leaders and respond to the wage requests of powerful worker organizations. Blair still had the hearts of the working class in Britain, but he was gradually losing their unqualified support. Such weakening of support from unions can contribute to a general weakening of Blair's political base and give hope to the Conservative opposition.

THE EURO

Great Britain is a reluctant member of the European Union. At the heart of Britain's reluctance is the euro, the European currency that has replaced the currency of eleven EU countries. In 1999 the eleven countries that accepted the euro as their official currency began basing exchange rates on the new legal tender. The British have chosen not to participate in the transition to the euro and have made the protection of the pound sterling the foundation of their "Euro-skepticism." Since 1999, much of the currency trading in Europe, and even in London's financial centers, has been conducted in terms of the value of the euro. On January 1, 2002, the European Union introduced the euro as the common currency for everyday use. At present there are no plans in Britain to trade in euros in international currency markets or to give up the pound as the official legal tender of the United Kingdom.

Britain's opposition to the euro is a mixture of national pride and apprehension over linking a new and untested currency to the economies of Europe. The British are concerned that embracing the euro may lock them into a currency union with countries that are less economically secure and productive, thus laying the groundwork for recession and unemployment. Prime Minister Tony Blair has skillfully put off the euro issue for now, but his public pronouncements hinting that at some future date Britain may accept the new currency have become increasingly guarded. A major part of Blair's and Britain's reluctance over the euro is that since its introduction in 1999 it has performed poorly compared with other currencies, especially the U.S. dollar. Moreover, public opinion in Britain has begun to show serious reservations about moving toward the euro. A reliable poll in early 2000 showed 69 percent of Britons opposed to the euro. Major economic organizations such as the Confederation of British Industry have come out expressing concerns over the euro.

The euro has become more of a political issue in Britain than an economic and financial one. The Conservative Party has taken the lead in opposing the euro and has stated forcefully that Blair and his allies in pro–European Union organizations such as Britain in Europe are trying to ramrod popular support for the new currency and playing down the dangers of withdrawing the pound from circulation. Former Tory leader William Hague reinvigorated the Conservative Party with the euro issue, sensing that opposition is growing in the country toward the new currency. His successor, Iain Duncan Smith, has carried that opposition forward. The Tories have started a "Save the Pound" campaign that has generated attention and support. The success of the Conservative Party in the 1999 European Parliament elections was viewed by many as an early signal that British voters are wary of the euro and of their prime minister's support for it. Blair and his cabinet have begun to recognize that the move toward the euro need not be inevitable and that pushing for a national referendum in the future could be politically disastrous.

But politics aside, British opposition to fully joining the European Union by accepting the euro has its pitfalls. Supporters of the euro state that failure to accept the currency may limit Britain's influence within the European Union. At present the chancellor of the Exchequer does not attend the meeting of the eleven euro-zone finance ministers who discuss key economic decisions that have an impact on British companies and British voters. There is also mounting concern that failure to accept the euro may have a detrimental effect on Britain's ability to attract foreign investment as companies prefer to deal with a common currency as they make decisions about a range of business issues. At this time the investment issue is not critical because the pound is a solid currency and the euro has had its problems. But the question becomes, What might happen in the future if the pound weakens and the euro becomes firmly established as a dominant and secure currency?

If there is one issue that may dominate the political process for the coming years, it is the euro controversy. The political parties constantly watch public opinion and plan their electoral strategies. The countries and supporters of the European Union want Britain to become a complete member rather than a reluctant member. Britain's future as a member of the European Union may hinge on how the euro controversy is resolved. ⊕

COMPARISONS

The Westminster or parliamentary government in Great Britain has had enormous influence throughout the world. When Great Britain controlled a vast colonial empire, it could easily graft its public decisionmaking structures and practices onto the indigenous people in countries from Asia to Africa to the Middle East to the Caribbean. The Commonwealth, as mentioned earlier, represents the countries formally under British control. In each Commonwealth country, whether India, Ghana, Egypt, or the Bahamas, the British brought the tradition, institutions, and procedures of parliamentary government. Even today many of these countries retain the pomp and circumstance of the British system and the essential elements of party majority—fusion of powers, the question hour, and votes of no confidence. Even though the British Empire is only a memory, the British way of governance has left an indelible mark on scores of countries. In many respects the Westminster system is the lasting legacy of a once grand world power.

In modern British politics the influence of American politics is quite evident. Prime Minister Margaret Thatcher and President Ronald Reagan worked closely during the 1980s to transform their economies. Although Thatcher can be credited with providing a critical impetus to the new economic order, it was Ronald Reagan, with the enormity of the U.S. economy behind him, who defined the terms and made the case for the new economic order. Prime Minister Tony Blair has taken a number of pages from the political handbook of former president Bill Clinton. Blair's electoral success and the rejuvenation of the Labour Party resulted from following the Clinton approach of moving to the center of the political spectrum (even though it may alienate hard-line elements in the party), concentrating on public relations techniques that attract voters rather than ideological purity, and relying heavily on polling and focus group analysis as a key means of determining support and charting electoral strategy. Blair faces mounting criticism from within his party and from traditional political practitioners in Britain for employing his American strategy, but his success in moving Labour into the mainstream and holding the party in power has only fortified the justification for using and continuing the strategy.

Because Britain is no longer a world power and its ties to the United States are generating increasing criticism, expanded linkages to Europe are now in vogue. Britain is currently undergoing a sort of identity crisis as it debates the extent to which it should become European. The debate is not only about the extent to which Britain should become tied to the European Union but about whether Britain should become less associated with the United States, in terms of foreign and defense policies. Tony Blair's decision to send British troops into Iraq only heightened the debate. Britain exists in a kind of triangle, one side accenting its proud colonial past with its contribution to parliamentary governance, one side accenting a long relationship with the United States that has transformed the policy and political scene, and one side accenting its new alliance with Europe with its natural and beneficial associations. This triangle can be viewed as providing Britain with a healthy mix of linkages that can energize the country and advance its interest. But the triangle can also be the source of significant political, economic, and social tension as the British leaders and the British people define themselves and create an identity that will respond to the needs and challenges of the twenty-first century.

CONCLUSION

The dominant theme that runs through the discussion of British politics and government is change. From the reform of the House of Lords to the devolving of power to Scotland and Wales, Britain has entered the millennium with a new national consensus to move away from its tradition-bound system and toward a more modern constitutional framework. Prime Minister Tony Blair has had much to do with forging this new consensus. If Blair and his re-vamped Labour Party remain in power for the foreseeable future, it is likely that Britain will be transformed. The governing institutions will shed their aristocratic image, public policy decisions will become more decentralized, elections will better reflect voter opinions, the public and private sectors will become less estranged, and the state will move further aside to permit the market economy to carry the burden of providing for the general welfare of the British people.

Although Tony Blair has emerged as the architect of change, other forces are at work that have contributed to this national transformation. Certainly the advent of a united Europe with its core missions of integration, free trade, and financial uniformity has influenced Britain's commitment to remake it-self. Governing changes such as decentralization of administration and pro-portional representation have long been a staple of public decisionmaking and electoral practice in Europe. While Britain may have resisted aligning with Europe, and may still have reservations about complete integration, there is no doubt that national political and economic elites, as well as the general public, are convinced that it is time to become European. As the British are often heard saying, "There will always be a Britain." But the New Britain is not isolated in its island fortress anymore. It is now part of Europe, which plays by different rules and demands different behavior.

The change that is fueling governing reform and Europeanization is the re-sult of significant social, cultural, and psychological trends that are increas-ingly in evidence. Britain is no longer the white, Protestant, stodgy, old country that it was for centuries. Britain today is a country with growing racial, religious, and ethnic diversity, high-tech entrepreneurs, sexual libera-tion, cell phones, and high fashion. There is still the venerable corner pub, the changing of the guard, and beautifully tended gardens. But these tradi-tions now stand side by side with modern art museums, trendy boutiques and restaurants, and high-rise condominiums. A generation of Britons that came to adulthood during the Thatcher and Blair eras has introduced a new way of life to the country. The governing and political reforms that are in place today are merely the extension of that new life into the public realm.

A FEW BOOKS YOU SHOULD READ

Tony Blair, *New Britain* (Boulder: Westview, 1997). The British prime minister presents his views and philosophy on a range of public policy issues.

Steven Driver and Luke Martel, *New Labour: Politics After Thatcherism* (Cambridge: Polity, 1998). Provides an excellent linkage between two different approaches to British development.

Roy Jenkins, *Churchill* (New York: Farrar, Straus & Giroux, 2001). The definitive biography of one of the great British political leaders.

Anthony King, *New Labour Triumph: Britain at the Polls, 2001* (London: Seven Bridges, 2002). A comprehensive study of why Labour won in 2001 and why it remains a popular political party.

Colin Pilkington, *Issues in British Politics* (New York: St. Martin's, 1998). A fine overview of the challenges facing modern Britain.

A FEW WEB SITES YOU SHOULD VISIT

www.parliament.uk. The official Web site of Commons and Lords.

www.labour.org.uk. New Labour presents its organization, policies, and leaders on the site.

www.number–10.gov.uk. The prime minister's Web site.

www.conservatives.com. The loyal opposition's site.

www.ukonline.gov.uk. General-interest site with accent on government and politics.

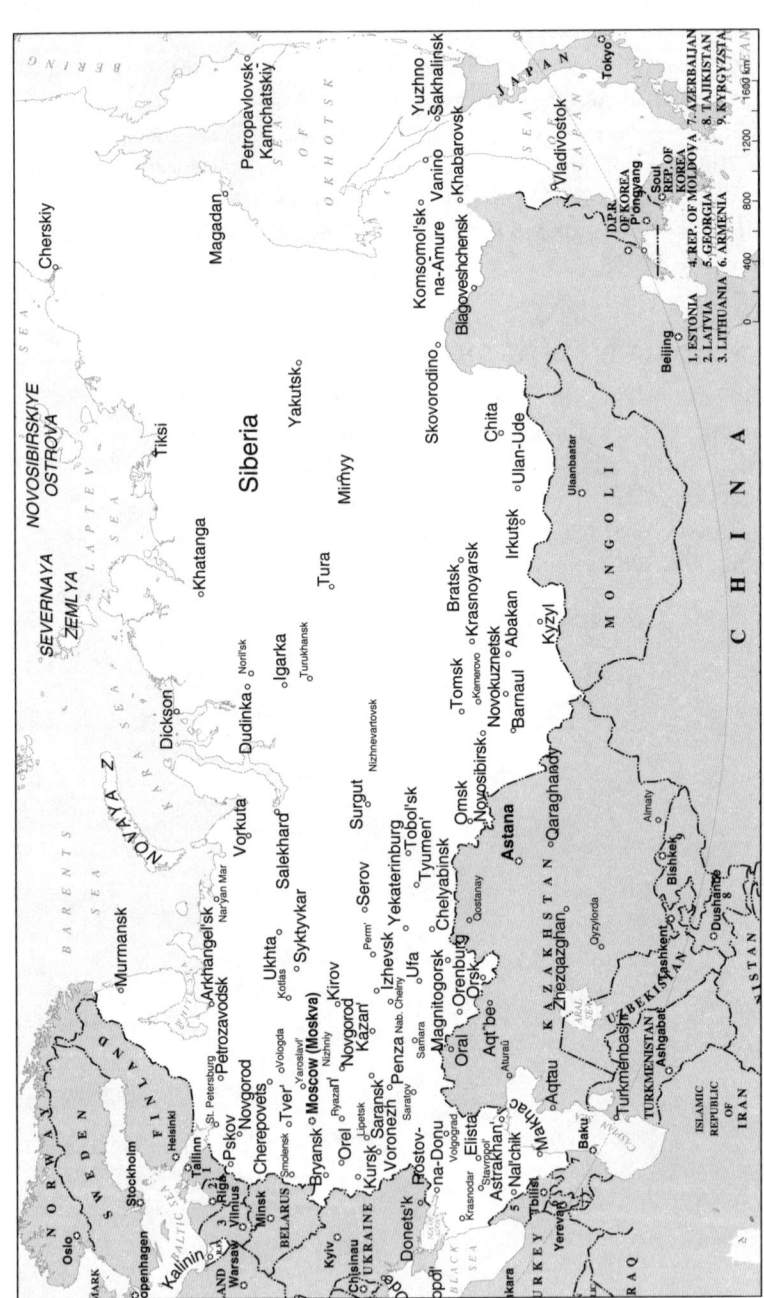

MAP 3.1 Russian Federation

3

Russian Federation

Data Bank

Area: 6.5 million sq. miles

Population: 157.5 million (1997)

Rural/urban population ratio: 23/77 (1999)

Ethnic makeup: 81 percent Russian, 4 percent Tatar, 3 percent
 Ukrainian, 12 percent other

Life expectancy: Male, 58 years; female, 72 years

Adult literacy: 98 percent

Form of government: Federation

Head of state: Vladimir Putin

Per capita income/GDP: $2,730 (2002)

Exports: $74 billion; imports $41 billion (partners: European Union,
 United States, China, Japan)

Source: United Nations and World Bank

SETTING THE SCENE

The fall of communism will always be remembered in the West as beginning
on that joyous night in 1989 when Germans of all ages began popping cham-
pagne bottles and sending off fireworks into the sky as they used sledgeham-
mers to break down the Berlin Wall. Since the 1960s, the Wall had been a
stark symbol of the separation between democratic West Berlin and communist East Berlin. For the Russian people, the event that will always be remembered as the symbol of communism's fall was Boris Yeltsin standing on top of a
tank with microphone in hand, the red, white, and blue Russian flag waving
behind him. The crowd listened intently as the former Communist Party
leader urged his supporters to defeat hard-liners in the government who

135

wanted to preserve the Soviet Union. Within hours Yeltsin was able to convince key military units to join his side and repel the coup that had already put Soviet President Mikhail Gorbachev under house arrest and was moving to crush the movement to create a sovereign and democratic Russia. Eventually, the Russian military supported Yeltsin, the coup fizzled, and Gorbachev was released; but there was no stopping the historic movement to create a new Russia and to end communist rule. Within a month Gorbachev reluctantly came to the realization that his power to control events had disappeared and that Boris Yeltsin and the forces of democracy had taken over. Thus in 1991 the Soviet Union and with it Soviet communism came to an end.

The communist state in the Soviet Union seemed an impregnable fortress of control. The party apparatus, the government ministries, the KGB security forces, the military, and the all-encompassing bureaucracy had dominated the political scene since the Russian revolution in 1917. The Soviet Union became a textbook case of a totalitarian state: all power was centralized within the party and all opposition to the wishes of the party was quashed. But the impregnable fortress of control eroded as the world changed and the Soviet Union found itself out of step with the unrelenting waves of democratization, growing domestic demands for a better life, and communism's inherent inability to provide freedom, equality, and opportunity. Mikhail Gorbachev valiantly attempted to reform communism with his call for glasnost and perestroika (openness and restructuring), but it was too late. Communism had already sowed the seeds of its own destruction with a bloated and inefficient state machine, an economy that paid little attention to the consumer, and a political process led by aging party leaders.

Since the end of Soviet communism, Russia has moved through its most contentious period since the revolution of 1917. After a period of euphoria following the fall of communism, Russia began a long transition from a centrally planned economy to one that accented market principles. The new system sought to totally revamp the Russian economy by stripping it of artificial pricing, central control, cumbersome bureaucracy, and antipathy toward private property and competition. The "shock therapy" programs forced enormous price increases, shortages, and unemployment as the subsidies, price controls, and guarantees that had provided the average worker with an economic safety net were systematically destroyed.

Replacing the old system of central control with Western-style economic structures and values challenged the resourcefulness and the patience of the Russian people. The ruble experienced wild swings and at one time in the 1990s was nearly worthless. Workers often went unpaid for months and the resulting strikes and confrontations with the authorities heightened the climate of disorder. Homelessness, malnutrition, and disease became commonplace. Suicide rates doubled and alcoholism, always a problem, skyrocketed. More significantly, the population rate began to decline and the life expectancy rate dropped dramatically. Between 1989 and 1999 the life expectancy of the average Russian fell from sixty-four years to sixty-one years. While an estimated 10 percent of the population benefited from the new economic regime, upwards of 40 percent of Russians experienced a drastic reduction in the quality of life.

The economic instability and uncertainty that dominated the Russian economy throughout much of the 1990s was unfortunately matched by political instability and uncertainty. Boris Yeltsin, the savior of Russian democracy, became increasing erratic in his behavior and suffered long periods of illness that took him away from his responsibilities as national leader. Russian government was marked by a succession of prime ministers and senior cabinet officials. During the economic collapse of 1998 Yeltsin named and then fired three prime ministers, one of whom lasted three months. In place of recognized governmental leaders, Yeltsin permitted policy to be made by shadowy figures tied to his family and his close friends and benefactors. When he did make policy, it was often without consulting his ministers and advisers.

Thus there was great relief when Vladimir Putin assumed power after Boris Yeltsin resigned on New Year's Eve in 1999. Putin became Yeltsin's prime minister earlier in 1999 and was given extraordinary powers to run the government. The Russian people saw in Putin the proper mix of a modern, democratically based leader who exuded power, strength, and competence in a manner that was in the tradition of czarist and Soviet rule. Putin's popularity, however, did not diminish the challenges that he faced. The Russian economy continued to require close monitoring and deft management in order to avoid a kind of wild west character of rampant lawlessness, weak or nonexistent economic rules, and looted state enterprises. There was also the issue of Russia's place in a new world order, as the United States and Europe dominated the political landscape and left Moscow on the fringes of influence. And perhaps most importantly, the Russian people, especially members of the younger generation, were demanding a better life and a place in the new global economic system. How would the government respond to their expectations?

Establishing a new identity after over seventy years of communist rule is no easy chore. Russian politicians have little background in democratic politics and parliamentary practice, Russian businessmen are new to the rigors and the responsibilities of a market economy, and the Russian people have become so dependent on the income security provided by the state that to fend for themselves has been a struggle. Russia is in a kind of in-between place in its political and economic development, which has made this transition period a daunting national challenge.

So much has changed in Russia since Boris Yeltsin stood atop that tank in 1991 that it is difficult to state with a degree of certainty where the country and its people are headed. Russia today is best described as a nation that is in the process of defining itself. But national definition is no easy task, especially in an environment in which the rules are changing and the rulers are themselves unsure of where the nation is going. Russia is a work in progress, experiencing the excitement of making itself anew while facing the unnerving prospect of an unknown future.

THE RUSSIAN SPACE PROGRAM

The high point of Soviet communism came on October 4, 1957, when the first satellite, *Sputnik I,* was launched into orbit. *Sputnik I* weighed only 183 pounds, but its impact on the world, and especially Soviet-U.S. relations, was enormous. The launch of *Sputnik* started the space race and established the Soviet Union as a world power with the capability of building nuclear weapons and developing sophisticated technology. While the United States remained in a state of shock, the Soviets continued their space successes with a number of additional "firsts." On April 12, 1961, Yuri Gagarin became the first human to orbit the Earth. On June 16, 1963, cosmonaut Alexi Leonov became the first person to walk in space. In April 1966 *Luna 9* became the first satellite to make a soft landing on the moon, followed five years later by *Salyut I,* the first manned space station to orbit around the Earth. All these "firsts" brought great pride to the Soviet people, and the political leadership used them to tout the benefits of communism and the strength of the Soviet Union.

But thirty years after *Sputnik I* the Soviet space program was a shambles, the victim of a crumbling economy and the government's inability to provide the necessary resources to keep pace with the United States. The Soviets were forced to fashion imaginative financing agreements in order to keep their program afloat. One such agreement was a $12 million deal to allow a Japanese journalist to go into space with Russian cosmonauts. Also, the postcommunist Russian government signed various contracts with foreign governments and private enterprises for use of the *Mir* space station. The desperate financial condition of the Russian space program meant that the *Mir* space station was allowed to remain in orbit well beyond its original life span of five years because it produced revenue. *Mir* has been dubbed the "flying garbage can," but its age is no joke as astronauts from other countries who have trained on the space station express concern about the real possibilities of fire and decompression, two problems often associated with aging space vehicles.

Today the Russian space program is a mere shell. Although the Russians are an integral part of the International Space Station (ISS), providing the key modules that will be used to construct the station, Western experts express deep concern that the government will not be able to sustain its involvement. As American space expert James Oberg stated in an analysis of the Russian capability to remain a key member of the ISS project, "the Russian space effort has been coasting on strategic reserves, winding down from the higher energy levels of former times and cannibalizing the last pieces of redundant equipment—in short, eating the seed corn." Key to the problems of the Russian space program is the shift of engineers and designers out of government service and into the private sector. Because the government is unable to pay its employees and because there are opportunities in the private sector, the once proud men and women in Russian mission control have not been replaced by a new generation of space-minded designers and engineers.

The ISS project is being advanced as the next step in space and a valuable means of achieving cooperation among the Western countries participating in the space program. But Russian leaders worry about the short-term payback of the station and whether the Russian public will tolerate the expense associated with the project while the economy is tottering. From its once proud position as the leader of space exploration, Russia is now making decisions on space travel based on the potential for profit. ⊕

POLITICAL MILESTONES

Among the political milestones leading to the formation of modern-day Russia, two major themes stand out. The first is the inability of the Russian state to follow Western models of economic development and political reform. Situated on the fringes of Europe, Russia trailed behind its neighbors in embracing intellectual trends, economic modernization strategies, and popular governing structures. Throughout its history Russia has been isolated from the mainstream of national development with strong anti-Western views among its people and an unwillingness to create a state system incorporating popular rule and decentralized decisionmaking. Some analysts use the term "backward" to describe Russian national development. Russian national development seems to be frozen in time as it nurses a romantic attachment to its past.

The second theme of Russian national development is the propensity of the political system to gravitate toward authoritarian rule. Russia has shown a consistent pattern of authoritarianism throughout its history with repressive governments, secret police, weak or nonexistent constitutional guarantees, and central political control. Such authoritarianism does not exist in a vacuum. The Russian people show a preference for strongman rule and the cult of personality. They seem to favor one individual who has the power to rule instead of supporting an open process of leadership selection, which would bring uncertainty and perhaps weakness.

Failure to keep pace with the Western tradition and deep-seated authoritarianism are key to understanding the evolution of Russia and its political system. At important points in Russia's historical development these characteristics have defined Russia and the Russian people. Although Russia is now seeking to become a modern, prosperous democracy, the past is not easily buried. As the following political milestones show, the story of modern Russia is one of trying to break out of a legacy that has kept the country tied to a troubled past. Previous attempts to break out of its past usually resulted from a struggle that tore the country apart.

Lenin and the Revolution of 1917

The Russian revolution of 1917 was actually two revolutions. In March 1917, with Russia hopelessly enmeshed in World War I, the country was coming apart. Russia was in a deep recession, troops were deserting by the thousands, and severe shortages had begun to create massive unrest. A group of democrats under the leadership of Alexander Kerensky led a coup that deposed the czar and initiated a provisional government along liberal democratic lines. These liberals, however, made one fatal mistake—they kept Russia in the war—and the economic and military problems intensified. The liberals' failure to offer a solution to Russia's domestic problems opened the door to the communists, who were commonly known as the Bolsheviks.

The Germans, seeing an opportunity to disrupt the Russian war effort, allowed communist leader Vladimir Ilyich Lenin to cross Germany en route from Switzerland to Sweden with the understanding that if he eventually gained power, the Germans could expect a peace agreement. Ever the astute political leader, Lenin saw his chance to capitalize on the weakness of the liberal government. His Bolsheviks were a minority party in Russia, but they were the best-organized political force and a ruthless force as well. Using his base in Petrograd, Lenin put together a revolutionary army of Bolsheviks, soldiers, students, and workers to bring the government down. Kerensky and his liberals were no match for the Bolsheviks, but consolidating the revolution in a country as large as Russia would not be easy. Lenin quickly made peace with Germany by signing the Brest-Litovsk treaty in 1918 and promising the

Russian people "Land, Bread, and Peace," a slogan designed to gain immediate support from a population that had had enough of war and aristocratic neglect.

Spreading Bolshevik influence throughout the country would take another three years. Lenin at first had to contend with Western allies who were opposed to the Russian communists. The United States sent a small force into Russia at the end of World War I in a vain attempt to stop the revolution. Lenin eventually defeated the Western threat and the opposition from the White army, a mixture of liberal democrats, royalists, and disgruntled military units. By 1921 the Bolsheviks were securely in power and on the way to building their communist state. Lenin emerged as the international symbol of communist change and the architect of a new society. But remaking Russia into an ideal Marxist society, now called the Soviet Union, would be a daunting challenge, especially since the country had endured the ravages of World War I, as well as three years of a divisive civil war.

Lenin's program to bring communism to the Soviet Union was called the New Economic Policy (NEP). Surprisingly, NEP was not a communist plan. Lenin, realizing that Soviet Russia was economically devastated, permitted a measure of private industry and private ownership. However, Soviet leaders placed heavy industry in the hands of the state and began a number of huge public sector infrastructure projects designed to get the people back to work and involved in national development. The NEP, while a modest attempt to introduce communist practices into Russia, was never fully implemented, in large part because of Lenin's health problems and eventual death in 1924. The Soviet Union made only minor progress during these early years of communism, and Lenin will be remembered more as a communist agitator than a nation builder or economic planner.

Many historians of Western civilization state without reservation that the Russian revolution of 1917 was the most critical event of modern times. The overthrow of Czar Nicolas and the Bolsheviks' rise to power destroyed Russia's aristocratic heritage and transformed the country into a working version of a Marxian workers' paradise of equality and harmony. With communism in place, Russia offered the world an alternative, a different means of organizing factories, governments, and countries. The once fringe country that sought to emulate the rest of Europe was now in the hands of communists who were dedicated to remaking Russia into a classless society, a people's state, and a totalitarian system of control.

Stalin and Stalinism

Lenin's death initiated a power struggle within the Communist Party. A number of revolutionary leaders struggled to move to the top of the power structure in the Soviet Union, but Josef Stalin proved that he shared Lenin's ruthlessness in removing any who challenged his power. A Georgian by birth, Stalin (Russian for "man of steel") rose quickly in the Bolshevik movement. After the revolution Lenin named him first general secretary of the party, and after his death Stalin consolidated his hold on the party by removing his main challenger, Leon Trotsky. Stalin had his agents follow Trotsky to his exile in Mexico and assassinate him.

With his command established, Stalin set about building a communist state. In 1928 he introduced the first of many five-year plans, which set in motion his vision of industrial development designed to move the Soviet Union to the forefront of world power. Achieving this vision demanded much from the Russian people. Stalin's Soviet Union became a vast work camp with twelve-hour workdays seven days a week. Those who were not willing to participate in this forced industrialization were sent to concentration camps or worse. The forced industrialization was complemented by collectivization plans for the agricultural sector. Wealthier farmers known as kulaks saw their land expropriated by the state and turned into collective farms. If they resisted, the state used its heavy hand to ensure compliance. By the 1930s Stalin's Soviet Union had become a communistlike society with workers contributing to the goals of industrial and agricultural development. It was also a huge prison run by an ever expanding totalitarian state completely controlled by its leader.

Never satisfied that his enemies were silenced, in the mid-1930s Stalin engaged in a political "cleansing" process known as the Great Terror. During this period Stalin either summarily executed or exiled over a million party activists who he felt posed a danger. This was the period of regular show trials in which party leaders like Nikolai Bukharin were brought before party tribunals, falsely charged with crimes, and then executed. The Great Terror quickly spread beyond the party as an estimated 10–15 million Russians were sent into exile in Siberia or to a series of gulags (political prison camps). Most of these Soviet citizens never made it back to their homes or families.

Stalin's obsession with liquidating his enemies took a backseat to the German threat in World War II. The purges, which included members of the high military staff, jeopardized the Soviet capability to fight off the German threat. Following the brutal victory in the central city of Stalingrad in 1942, Stalin led his nation to victory, ultimately entering Berlin in 1945 to seal the Nazi defeat.

Stalin emerged after World War II as a major player in international affairs. The pictures of Roosevelt, Churchill, and Stalin meeting at the crucial Yalta conference in the waning days of World War II underscored the value placed on the Russian military defeat of Nazi Germany and the power of the Russians to control Eastern Europe. Despite tremendous losses in the Great Terror and the war, the Soviet Union in 1945 was a major industrial and military power. Moreover, it gathered increasing support from Western intellectuals, who were impressed with the concept of a workers' state and the prospect of a classless society. Years later, after communism declined, Alexander Solzhenitsyn documented the horrors of the Stalin regime in his Nobel Prize–winning book *The Gulag Archipelago*. From the beginning of the Great Terror to the conclusion of World War II, over 20 million Soviet citizens perished as enemies of the state or in defense of their homeland.

In 1953 Josef Stalin died, possibly, as some believe, poisoned by his enemies. Stalin's legacy is one of totalitarian rule and the cult of personality. The man of steel lived up to his name in maintaining rigid control of his regime from 1928 to 1953. During that time he transformed the Soviet Union into a world power with control over its own territory and much of Eastern Europe. Communism became not just a revolutionary threat, as in the days of Lenin, but a major force in world affairs. This transformation was achieved over the bodies of tens of millions of citizens who simply got in the way of Stalin's plans.

The Soviet Union in Ascendancy

Stalin's death ushered in a period of renewal and rejuvenation. After some bitter and violent internal maneuverings among members of the Communist Party elite, Nikita Khrushchev rose to the position of first secretary of the party and eventually chairman of the Council of Ministers. Khrushchev made his mark early in the post-Stalin era by delivering a speech in which he denounced the former Soviet leader as a despot. This speech began the de-Stalinization process in Soviet politics in which all mentions of Stalin were removed from public view (the city of Stalingrad, for example, was renamed Volgograd). This was also the time in which millions of political prisoners were released and greater controls were placed on the secret police. While not really liberalizing the Soviet Union, Khrushchev allowed for some relaxation of personal restrictions and greater contacts with the West.

The emphasis on healing the wounds that Stalin inflicted was replaced by a new emphasis on competition with the capitalist countries, in particular the United States. Khrushchev debated Vice President Richard Nixon at a Moscow trade show on the benefits of communism over capitalism, and the Soviet Union shocked the world by placing the first unmanned satellite, *Sputnik,* in orbit in 1957, thereby beating the United States into space. Finally, a boastful Khrushchev pledged to the world that communism would bury capitalism.

These were heady days for the Soviet Union. Its economy, while not nearly as strong or consumer oriented as the U.S. economy, was nevertheless powerful, especially in the areas of heavy industry and military technology. The Soviet Union was capable of matching the United States and the NATO alliance step for step with new nuclear weapons systems and in the area of conventional weapons had a decided lead. Furthermore, Khrushchev's Soviet Union was gaining valuable allies in the less developed world. Its aggressive foreign aid and technical assistance programs were providing communism with a new legitimacy in Asia, Africa, and Latin America, where countries had experienced years of foreign intervention and exploitation.

In 1962 Khrushchev entered into an agreement with the communist leader of Cuba, Fidel Castro, to place offensive nuclear missiles in that country. The Kennedy administration learned about the missile placement and called on Khrushchev to remove the nuclear threat. The confrontation between the Soviet Union and the United States over the missiles escalated into the most dangerous period in the Cold War. The Kennedy administration imposed a naval blockade on Cuba and demanded that the missiles be removed. After days of tense negotiations, Khrushchev removed the missiles from Cuba (the Kennedy administration also pledged to remove missiles from Turkey) and the Soviet Union was seen as backing down from this episode of nuclear brinkmanship. For his part, Nikita Khrushchev never recovered his reputation as a leader within the Politburo of the Communist Party. Faced with some embarrassing problems in the agricultural sector and the rise of the Chinese to the forefront of leadership in the communist world, Khrushchev was replaced in 1964 by a three-man collective leadership.

During the 1960s and 1970s the Soviet Union expanded its competition with the West in terms of missile supremacy and influence in the less developed world. After numerous maneuverings behind the scenes, Leonid Brezhnev emerged as the key leader in the Soviet Union. Brezhnev was not the boisterous ideologue and foreign policy risk taker that Khrushchev had been. Rather, he concentrated on steadying the Soviet Union domestically and working out a relationship with the United States to avoid further episodes of nuclear brinkmanship. Brezhnev is best known for signing the first Strategic Arms Limitations Treaty (SALT) with the United States and for fostering a period of normality in diplomatic relations, often termed détente. But on the domestic scene Brezhnev was unable to maintain the enthusiasm that was generated by Khrushchev during the 1950s. Brezhnev introduced economic policies designed to make the Soviet system more efficient, but by the 1970s growth had slowed to a trickle. The sheer weight of the Soviet command economy with its huge bureaucracy and central control was becoming a brake on growth.

Despite the disturbing signs of economic decline, Brezhnev and his supporters in the Kremlin managed to maintain a facade of stability and success. The Soviet Union remained a superpower, its allies in Eastern Europe and the Third World continued to promote the revolutionary struggle, and people's grumbling over shortages, long lines, and poor-quality goods were considered part of the Soviet way of life. Meanwhile, many of the 14 million members of the Communist Party enjoyed the benefits of being part of the power elite. New and expensive dachas (summer homes) were built in the Moscow suburbs, and athletes and other friends of the government were given generous stipends and awards for performance. Those with connections always got the best health care, were permitted to travel abroad, and shopped in special stores controlled by the government. It was a good life for those who were connected.

When Brezhnev died in 1982, his system of maintaining stability and the appearance of success through party rewards continued under the leadership of his successors, Yuri Andropov (1982–1984) and Konstantin Chernenko (1984–1985). But the Soviet system was badly in need of repair. The aging leadership was out of touch with a new generation of Soviet citizenry. The command economy was no longer being tolerated by the average person. Most importantly, new leaders were emerging from the ranks of the party who were convinced that reform was absolutely essential in order to save communism. One such leader was Mikhail Gorbachev.

The Soviet Union in Decline

Mikhail Gorbachev may be remembered by historians as a dedicated communist reformer who did not realize that the system he wanted to change was finished. Gorbachev tried diligently to change communism, but as he tinkered with the centralized economic and political machinery of the state, the entire communist structure began to crumble. Gorbachev's efforts to save communism lend credence to some of the classic observations about nations in the throes of revolutionary change. Once the old regime has been weakened and has lost its legitimacy, efforts to restore faith in it or to reform it only lead to a sustained movement to replace it. Gorbachev was on the wrong side of history.

Gorbachev became the general secretary of the Communist Party after Chernenko died. At the age of fifty-four Gorbachev was a marked departure from the elderly men who had led the nation through the Brezhnev years. Once secure in office, Gorbachev started retiring the aging leadership of the party. By the end of the Twenty-seventh Party Congress in 1986, Gorbachev had successfully replaced almost one-third of the party elite and over one-half of the ministerial positions. Gorbachev brought in younger technocrats who he felt would begin the process of taking the Soviet Union in a different direction. With a new leadership in place, Gorbachev began to make significant structural changes in the Soviet Union. A new parliamentary system was launched along with new elections and a more independent judiciary. Gorbachev prevailed on the party to rescind article 6 of the Soviet constitution, which denied opposition political parties the right to organize and participate in elections. These changes were part of Gorbachev's overall strategy of introducing a new spirit in the country that emphasized openness and public debate (glasnost) and restructuring of the centralized economy (perestroika).

The creation of a new Congress of People's Deputies and the first competitive elections for that body resulted in an embarrassing defeat for the Communist Party in 1989. Gorbachev responded to the defeat by removing from the ranks of the Central Committee the "dead souls" who had held their positions for over thirty years. On the economic front all was not going well either. Reluctant to embrace the Western market model, Gorbachev instituted a series of minor reforms that did nothing to energize the economy. The state retained control of pricing and distribution, which led to continuing shortages of key consumer goods. The most problematic challenge Gorbachev faced was growing unrest in the various republics of the Soviet Union. The spirit of glasnost he advocated created a tidal wave of new activism at the republic and regional level. A new civic society was developing in the Soviet Union that opposed centralized rule and the command economy.

The major impetus for revolutionary change in the Soviet Union came from the union republics, which intensified the pressure for local autonomy and later separation. Because Gorbachev was unable to hold the center, he began talks that would lead eventually to a new union treaty. The Soviet Union was coming apart. The Baltic republics of Estonia, Latvia, and Lithuania were the first to challenge Moscow's authority and seek independence. Later the republics of Armenia, Georgia, and Moldova sought to break away. Gorbachev worked to hold the union together by introducing a plan to create a "Union of Soviet Sovereign Republics." Gorbachev's efforts to reconstitute the Soviet Union only divided the country further. In August 1991 hard-liners in the party and the military placed Gorbachev under house arrest and attempted a coup. Ultimately Boris Yeltsin emerged as the undisputed leader of Russia and the champion of communism's demise.

With the Soviet republics declaring independence, the Eastern European bloc rejecting communism for democracy, and Boris Yeltsin emerging as the de facto head of what was left of the Soviet Union, the end of Gorbachev's effort to save communism was imminent. The formal collapse occurred at the end of 1991, when Yeltsin signed a pact with the Ukraine and Belorussia to form the Commonwealth of Independent States, a loose association of the last remaining republics in the Soviet Union. With the agreement signed,

Mikhail Gorbachev was no longer the president of a country. Gorbachev, who had won a Nobel Peace Prize for his efforts to negotiate a lessening of tensions with the West and had earned the respect of many world leaders because of his reform efforts, was pushed off the governing stage by Boris Yeltsin. The last Soviet leader left power a defeated communist, only to appear a few years later as a pitchman for Pizza Hut.

The Yeltsin Years

While Mikhail Gorbachev will go down in Russian history as the man who failed to save communism, Boris Yeltsin will be remembered as the man who brought democracy and capitalism to Russia and almost lost them in the process. Boris Yeltsin took the Russian people on a wild ride through constitutional crisis, controversial reforms, near national bankruptcy, war, and numerous failed experiments to jump-start the faltering economy. The man who presided over the demise of Soviet communism and became a living symbol of change left the Kremlin a broken leader who had alienated and embarrassed his people with erratic behavior and poor judgment. Yeltsin was both a hero and a failure who left an indelible mark on modern Russia.

The rise of Boris Yeltsin to the heights of Russian political power began when Mikhail Gorbachev brought him into his leadership circle in 1985 as head of the Moscow party organization and a nonvoting member of the ruling Politburo. Soon Gorbachev realized that he had not appointed a yes man. Yeltsin began to publicly criticize party elites who were abusing their positions and engaging in corrupt practices. Yeltsin posed such a threat to the status quo that he was removed from his position in 1988 and demoted to a minor ministerial position in the construction sector. But the more the party leadership sought to censure or quiet Yeltsin, the more popular he became among the Russian people. It was inevitable that Yeltsin and Gorbachev would face each other for the leadership of a fast evolving Russian state. Yeltsin was the impatient reformer determined to remake Russia into a Western-style capitalist democracy, Gorbachev the gradualist fearful of taking the Soviet Union too far away from communism's roots.

Yeltsin astutely sought to develop his power base in the Russian Republic, rather than face Gorbachev within the Communist Party or the Supreme Soviet, the legislative body representing the fifteen republics. Riding the crest of immense popularity, Yeltsin moved the Russian Republic toward sovereignty in June 1990, and in 1991 he was elected Russian president by popular vote. Democratic legitimacy, however, did not protect Yeltsin from challenges to his authority. In 1991 Yeltsin encountered intense resistance from the Communist Party and other nationalist opponents to his economic reforms. When Yeltsin sought to advance a national referendum that would establish a new constitution, the stage was set for a showdown. Yeltsin boldly suspended the congress and scheduled new elections for both congress and president. Yeltsin's action precipitated an impeachment vote by the congress and the beginning of an armed challenge to the president. The ensuing battle for control of the government shifted to the White House, where parliament was held. In a stunning display of power Yeltsin brought in 2,000 troops and engaged the dissidents in a battle that claimed 140 lives, hundreds of injured, and the parliament building in flames. Yeltsin came out of the conflict with renewed power, a new constitution, and an opposition in disarray.

Although Yeltsin successfully removed his political adversaries, he was never able to establish an economic program that took Russia from a centrally planned system to a market economy. Yeltsin constantly faced opposition from a recalcitrant legislature, which was dominated by leftovers from the old Communist Party. Furthermore, his economic reforms brought enormous financial pain to the Russian people. Yeltsin's popularity quickly plummeted, as did his patience. Ministers and economic advisers came and went as Yeltsin sought the right strategy for applying Western models and the right technocrats to apply the models. Yeltsin's problems multiplied in 1994, when he challenged Chechen separatism by sending in Russian troops. But after two years and the loss of 100,000 lives on both sides, Yeltsin was forced to negotiate a cease-fire that was widely seen in Russia as a defeat.

By the 1996 presidential election race Yeltsin was no longer the democratic hero. Although he emerged victorious (in large part because he faced weak opponents), he had lost the spark to push the Russian state forward. Within months Yeltsin was hospitalized for heart problems and was in and out of office for over two years. The Russian state and the Russian economy stumbled along while its leader remained out of the public eye. When Yeltsin emerged from the hospital, it was usually to shake up his cabinet or to name a new prime minister. Western banks, investors, and economists were uneasy with the lack of leadership in Russia and the failure of Yeltsin to articulate a clear economic program. Moreover, the Russian people were tired of the uncertainty that they faced every day. Although Russia had stabilized politically in that there were no constitutional challenges to the president, the Russian economy continued to limp along with either no growth or meager growth rates. Lacking strong leadership, Russia became a haven of official corruption and private sector illegality. A tiny group of oligarchs emerged as the real power elite, with the existing government often acting as a compliant supporter.

When Yeltsin appointed Vladimir Putin prime minister in 1999, it was clear that a new transition was in the works. Putin quickly put his mark on Russian government by reigniting the Chechen war. Yeltsin remained in the background and allowed Putin to carry the war forward. As the Russian military entered the destroyed Chechen capital of Grozny and declared victory, Putin's support soared and Yeltsin became a nonfactor. When Yeltsin resigned on December 31, 1999, Russians felt a sense of collective relief. Putin represented the next stage of Russian development, while Yeltsin represented the struggles involved in moving the country to the present stage of development.

Timeline	
1917	March revolution overthrows monarchy; liberal government installed
1917	November revolution brings Lenin and the Bolsheviks to power
1917–1921	Civil war: Bolsheviks defeat White army of moderates and monarchists
1921–1928	Lenin's New Economic Policy
1924	Lenin dies and Stalin emerges as supreme leader
1930s	Stalin's reign of terror
1942	Siege of Stalingrad
1945	Cold War competition with the United States begins
1953	Stalin dies
1957	Khrushchev emerges as Soviet leader
1962	Cuban missile crisis
1964	Khrushchev removed from power and replaced with troika leadership
1966	Brezhnev named general secretary of the Communist Party
1968	Soviet troops invade Czechoslovakia to put down uprising
1982	Brezhnev dies
1982–1985	Leadership by gerontocracy
1985	Gorbachev appointed general secretary of Communist Party
1991	Coup attempt against Gorbachev
1991	Soviet Union dissolves
1992	Russian Federation formed
1993	New constitution
1994	War in Chechnya
1996	Yeltsin reelected president
1999	Yeltsin resigns
2000	Putin elected president
2002	Forty Chechen terrorists hold 700 hostages in Moscow theater
2330	Russia opposes war with Iraq in United Nations

RELIGION AND RELIGIOUS FREEDOM

Russia has a long tradition of religious belief and religious practice. The Russian Orthodox Church with its bearded patriarchs, ornate icons, and stunning cathedrals with the unique onion-shaped domes is an integral part of national life. But Russian religion also comprises Jews, Protestant Baptists, Muslims, and a wide range of smaller sects, such as Jehovah's Witnesses and Mormons. Under Soviet rule those who sought to express their religious views were subjected to imprisonment, repression, and death. Communist leaders had no tolerance for religion because it offered the people an alternative source of inspiration, leadership, and values. Even though the last Soviet constitution established freedom of religion as an inalienable right, the guarantee was a shallow promise as the government did all in its power to deny its citizens the right to believe in God and the right to belong to any faith or denomination. Gorbachev's glasnost policies included greater religious freedom and allowed churches and seminaries to reopen, but there remained an undercurrent of opposition among party members and the KGB, who intimidated those who chose to be religious.

As with most of Russian life, the state of religious belief and practice changed after the end of communism. The number of religious entities openly organizing the Russian people increased dramatically. Small sects with a charismatic or missionary approach began to surface with greater regularity. In the regions that bordered Central Asia, scores of Muslim groups formed. Many of these religious groups had a clear political perspective and contributed to the antigovernment fervor that spread throughout regions such as Chechnya. The linchpin of religious freedom in postcommunist Russia was a 1990 law that guaranteed religious rights while requiring religious organizations to register with the government. Many critics of the government saw this as a clear attempt to keep tabs on church groups and to deny official status to groups that were viewed as potentially dangerous. Nevertheless, the climate for religion in Russia was markedly different under democratic rule. Boris Yeltsin offered the Russian Orthodox patriarch, Alexy II, an official role in the 1996 presidential inauguration, a practice that had not been seen since the days of the czar.

The electoral victory of Vladimir Putin in 2000 ushered in what many believed would be the next phase of Russian religious freedom. Putin openly admitted that he was a practicing Russian Orthodox believer. Since Russian Orthodoxy is the most popular religious organization in the country, this was seen as a positive development, but those who practiced other religions, especially the minority sects, expressed concern over the establishment of an official religion at the expense of others. Putin put some of the minority religious groups' fears to rest when he insisted on a secular inauguration without the representation of the Russian Orthodox patriarch. But the real issue of religious freedom and practice that faced Putin early in his administration was a 1997 registration law that required reregistration of church groups. Groups such as evangelical Christians and Pentecostals saw this as a veiled attempt to liquidate their organizations because they were unpopular in the eyes of the government. Putin endeared himself to the proponents of religious freedom by extending the deadline for reregistration. This extension was supported by religious organizations with less than fifteen years of existence, which in most cases are the newer evangelical and Pentecostal groups. The membership of these groups exceeds 70,000.

Despite the extension and the favorable statements coming from Putin, Russian religious leaders are apprehensive. In January 2000 Putin signed a national security decree containing the following language: "the spiritual and moral education of the population should be regulated by the state." There is also language referring to the "negative influence of foreign missionaries." All this suggests to religious leaders that Putin is seeking to place greater controls on churches and is siding with regional and local officials who are placing more restrictions on the smaller sects.

Although Russia has made significant progress toward establishing true religious freedom, concerns remain that go beyond the language of Putin's decree. Anti-Semitism is still operative in the country, evidenced by the 1999 bombing of two synagogues. Members of the Jehovah's Witnesses were barred from practicing their religion in Moscow, and attempts have been made to weaken and discredit Wahabism, an Islamic movement that the Russian leadership believes is behind Chechnyan separatism. Putin's reputation as a cold, calculating technocrat who does not tolerate forces that would weaken his plan for centralized rule are wary of the promises of religious freedom. The coming years will be a true test of whether Putin intends to continue to expand religious freedom or whether his quest of national control puts him at odds with Russians who are experiencing a rebirth of religion. ⊕

FORMAL GOVERNMENT

The Russian governing system operates under the 1993 constitution, which was approved by a national referendum. The constitution created a hybrid decision-making structure with a president who "determines guidelines for the domestic and foreign policy of the state" and a prime minister, who is appointed by the president and serves as the chairman of the government. The president is clearly the center of the government with full appointment capability, control over the armed forces, the ability to dissolve the legislature, and extensive decree powers. Moreover, the Russian president has additional powers to declare martial law, call referenda, grant pardons, and suspend the actions of state agencies. But it is his decree powers that have made the Russian president a powerful chief executive. In the area of economic reform measures, for example, President Yeltsin invoked his decree powers and then waited for the legislature to pass laws legitimating his actions. In some cases the president has taken action without any concern over legislative support for his actions. In the area of foreign policy President Yeltsin initiated the Chechnyan war by utilizing his decree power without any legislative approval.

The power of the Russian president has limits. The president is directly elected for no more than two consecutive four-year terms and is subject to a vote of no confidence by the legislature, although he can reject the vote and retaliate by invoking his dissolution power. There is an impeachment clause in the 1993 constitution, but when the Communist Party sought to advance the removal of Yeltsin over his health issues and erratic behavior, the Constitutional Court did not endorse the action. The fact that there is no vice president in the Russian government assisted Yeltsin during his frequent health problems. With no constitutional successor to the president, even Yeltsin's enemies were concerned about the power vacuum at the top. Finally, the Russian constitution favors the power of the president in that it is difficult to amend. The difficulty of introducing amendments that would change the executive-legislative relationship or streamline removal from office has dissuaded opposition forces from using this avenue of change.

The Russian legislature is formally termed the Federal Assembly. It is made up of the Federation Council and the State Duma. The Federation Council is a representative body that encompasses the entire Russian Federation with two representatives from each territorial unit (there are currently 178 members in the Federation Council). The State Duma, a much larger body of 450 representatives, is made up of legislators, half of whom are elected by proportional representation from party lists and half from single-member districts. Although the State Duma is viewed as the lower house because of the Federation Council's national makeup, it nonetheless is the center of legislative activity and the counterweight to the power of the president. The Federation Council, because of its geographic makeup, has been primarily focused on ensuring that legislation beneficial to the eighty-nine regional districts is approved. The State Duma rose to legislative prominence during Yeltsin's administration because of its power to approve the president's choice of prime minister and other high administrative positions. The State Duma also has legislative responsibility over the budget and a range of domestic and foreign policy concerns, but it must face the power of the president, who has the veto. Overriding a presidential veto in the Russian

Duma / Federation Council

system is quite difficult. A two-thirds vote is required, and the override must be taken on the original bill without any amendments or word changes.

The Russian judicial system is organized around a Constitutional Court. The nineteen members of the court are appointed by the president and approved by the Federation Council. The Constitutional Court, as is the case in many European countries, has the power to hear cases involving the constitutionality of federal and regional laws, as well as disputes associated with various governing institutions. Besides the Constitutional Court, Russia has a full complement of national courts that are similar to those found in the United States. There are lower and appellate courts and a Supreme Court acting as the final arbiter of judicial disputes. These national courts are primarily concerned with civil and criminal cases and leave political and governing disputes up to the Constitutional Court. There is also a Superior Court of Arbitration in Russia that is designed to handle economic disputes between commercial entities or individuals with a commercial disagreement. The Russian court system has been slow to develop. Even though it became operational as a result of the 1993 constitution, it was not until 1995 that the courts began to function.

One area of Russian government that has seen extensive change is in the bureaucracy. Under the old Soviet system the state was a behemoth of ministries, agencies, and public bodies. In effect, everyone in the Soviet Union worked for the state, although in the waning days of communism more and more private enterprise was permitted if not encouraged. With the demise of the Soviet Union and the push to a market economy, a strange mix of restructuring has dismantled segments of the bureaucracy, while also building new state organizations. A good deal of the change has involved renaming and reappointing, abolishing a bureau in one policy area and then establishing a new bureau in another policy area. The result of downsizing, restructuring, and privatizing many former state bureaucracies has thus far been disappointing. One of the key reasons for the mixed record of bureaucratic reform is the opportunities for patronage. The prospect of using a bureaucratic appointment as a means of rewarding loyalty or service is a tool of power that political leaders in Russia are unwilling to relinquish.

The governing institution that has undergone the greatest change is the Russian military. Like much of the Russian government, the military was forced to cut its budget and its ranks, moves that were resisted by defense ministers and the military high command. In 1997 Yeltsin removed the minister of defense, Igor Rodionov, because of his reluctance to make further budget cuts and to downsize the ranks of the military. Rodionov's successor got the message from the president and discharged over 300,000 soldiers. Despite the cuts, the Russian military remained loyal to President Yeltsin.

This support, however, masked the deep problems that affected the military in the late 1990s. There were disturbing reports of horrible conditions for Russian soldiers, including lack of pay, miserable living conditions, and a steep decline in morale. These problems showed up on the battlefields of Chechnya, where reports documented desertions and severe problems in leadership. The decline of the Russian military caused concern in the West, especially with respect to command and control of nuclear weapons in the field.

The ascension to power of Vladimir Putin, himself a former military colonel, raised hopes in the ranks of the military. As prime minister, Putin transferred an extra $100 million to the defense budget, which was used to modernize the Russian military. The real challenge for Putin, however, was in the area of reformulating the military's mission. Top Russian generals have resisted conducting a thorough restructuring of the military through downsizing, developing more mobile forces, and moving toward an all-volunteer army. Putin has placed himself in the midst of a struggle between the Ministry of Defense and the General Staff over the future of the military. The ministry has traditionally stressed the development of nuclear weapons, while the General Staff has concentrated on conventional weapons. There is little evidence of an emerging consensus in the Russian defense establishment. The picture is of a military in deep trouble.

The final area of Russian government that has been touched by extensive change is the regional and local administrative units. The Russian Federation is made up of twenty-one ethnically defined republics and sixty-eight administrative regions, which include six territories (kraias), forty-nine regions (oblasti), the Jewish autonomous region of Birobijan, ten autonomous areas (obruga), and two cities that have been declared "of federal importance" (Moscow and St. Petersburg). In these republics and regions reside hundreds of ethnic groups, including Tatars, Ukrainians, Byelorussians, and Moldavans. The ethnic diversity in the Russian Federation has been a source of regular challenges to the authority of the central government. In the days after the collapse of the Soviet Union, Tatarstan declared itself a sovereign state, Ingushetia separated from Chechnya, Dagastan became a haven for Chechnyan rebels, and Tyva, after much negotiation, was given the right to secede (although it has not exercised this option).

These challenges call into question the viability of the Russian Federation. Many fear that the two wars in Chechnya are the first signs of the disintegration of the Russian Federation, as tiny ethnic republics and regions seek to establish local control. For years during the Soviet era, the central government used its overwhelming military might and its political control to keep up the facade of national unity amid ethnic diversity. But with the military in retreat and political controls absent, long-standing disputes and hatreds have risen to the surface. The Russian government has made national unity one of its top priorities and seems willing to use extraordinary force in order to stop the secessionist movements. But with such diversity at the far reaches of its nation and such weakness at its center, the prospect of continued redefinition of what Russia is remains likely for years to come.

Constitutional Language

The preamble to the Russian constitution of 1993 says much about what the country stands for and what it hopes to achieve:

We, the multinational people of the Russian Federation, united by a common destiny on our land, asserting human rights and liberties, civil peace and accord, preserving the historic unity of the state, proceeding from the commonly recognized principles of equality and self-determination of the peoples, honoring the memory of our ancestors, who have passed on to us love of and respect for our homeland and faith in good and justice, reviving the sovereign statehood of Russia and asserting its immutable democratic foundations, striving to secure the well-being and prosperity of Russia and proceeding from a sense of responsibility for our homeland before the present and future generations, and being aware of ourselves as part of the world community, hereby approve the Constitution of the Russian Federation.

POINT OF FACT
The western city of Vladivostok has found it difficult to convince voters to participate in elections. Some twenty local elections had to be invalidated due to turnout that was less than the legal minimum. As a result the government started a public relations campaign offering citizens lottery tickets for cars, televisions, VCRs, refrigerators, washing machines, and food baskets.

ALCOHOLISM IN RUSSIA

Finding alcohol and alcoholism in a public policy discussion may be unusual, but hard liquor has played an important role in national life and politics. From the days of Peter the Great and his drunken, destructive travels through Europe to Boris Yeltsin's inebriated performance directing a concert orchestra on a state visit to Germany, the link between alcohol and the Russian national character has been inescapable.

Alcohol is an integral part of Russian culture, and alcohol abuse has had a far-reaching impact on worker productivity, domestic relations, life expectancy, and even political decisionmaking. Alcohol and alcohol-related problems in Russia have often been the target of public policy initiatives and societal reforms. Unfortunately, little progress has been made in solving this national health problem.

Today Russia is experiencing its most dramatic increase in alcohol consumption and alcohol-related problems. In the ten-year period from 1988 to 1998, alcohol consumption rose sixfold and the number of deaths associated with alcohol increased dramatically. According to data from the Russian Ministry of Health, 40 percent of Russian men are alcoholics and 17 percent of women have dangerous alcohol problems. Russians consume about fourteen liters of alcohol in a year, placing them at the top of the world in this category. Most disturbing about the alcohol consumption in Russia is the death rate. Data from 1995 show that 500 Russians per 100,000 die as a result of alcohol use, while in the United States the rate is 77 per 100,000. This has had a significant effect on life expectancy in Russia. A study by the British journal *Lancet* found that from 1990 to 1994 Russian life expectancy declined by 6.2 years: "although factors such as nutrition and health services may be involved, the evidence is that substantial changes in alcohol consumption over the period could have caused the dramatic changes in mortality."

Sadly the current increase in alcohol consumption and alcohol-related deaths comes after the last Soviet government of Mikhail Gorbachev made serious efforts to control the abuse of liquor. As part of the perestroika program of national restructuring, Gorbachev used the power of the state and the party apparatus to crack down on the production and sale of liquor, especially the highly dangerous Russian moonshine that can contain anything from aftershave to diluted jet fuel. The Gorbachev government raised the price of vodka as a means of deterring consumption and jailed public drunkards. The results of this crackdown were impressive. The National Academy of Sciences in a study in the late 1980s stated that as many as 600,000 lives were saved and the number of violent deaths and domestic altercations decreased markedly. But the program, like Soviet communism, fell into a state of limbo as the government turned its attention to political survival.

Since the collapse of communism and Yeltsin's rise to power, alcoholism and alcohol-related problems have resurfaced, in large part because of government inattention and the sad model of the president abusing alcohol. Anecdotal stories of Yeltsin's actions in office while under the influence of alcohol caused real concern among Western leaders fearful that the Russian president would make major decisions or threaten aggressive measures while in a stupor. Yeltsin's aides made excuses for him, stating that the Russian leader was "ill" or "tired and emotional" and as a result could not attend a state function or a critical meeting. In reality Yeltsin was incapacitated due to excessive alcohol consumption.

Russia during the Yeltsin presidency took a casual attitude toward the mounting evidence of alcohol consumption and alcohol abuse. Vodka, the drink of choice for Russians, remains inexpensive and widely available. There were no major public health or public safety campaigns during the Yeltsin years to combat the effects of alcoholism and only silence when data from outside the country pointed to the detrimental impact of alcohol on national health. Vladimir Putin's rise to office has encouraged Russians who fear heightened levels of alcohol consumption. Putin is not a drinker in the Yeltsin mold and has stated publicly that he recognizes the dangers alcoholism poses for social stability. Most disturbing, the rate of alcoholism among teenagers is soaring as a new generation of Russians follows in the footsteps of their fathers and mothers. It is interesting to note that the Russian government is more concerned with drug use among young people than high levels of alcohol consumption; it has instituted stern policies for drug offenders and drug dealers, while generally ignoring the alcohol problem. ⊕

THE CITIZEN AND THE STATE

One of the most difficult challenges for the Russian people during this era of transition is the formation of a new civil society. For over seventy years following the communist revolution the Soviet people were part of a grand social experiment designed to create a "new man" and "new woman" in the image of Marx and Lenin. Now that communism has fallen into disrepute, that social experiment has also been rejected and replaced by a new vision based on democratic principles and market values. But rejecting the old and introducing the new are not easily accomplished. Today Russian society is moving through a difficult blending process as it seeks to shed its communist roots and embrace its democratic and capitalist future. The creation of this new civil society is one of the most exciting movements in contemporary Russia. It is also one of the most important. If the country is to attain stable democracy and a prosperous capitalist economy, it must first build a foundation of beliefs, associations, behavior patterns, and mores that can withstand the pressures to return to the past or, worse yet, fall into political and economic disarray.

Building a new Russian civil society will be difficult because of the pervasive nature of Soviet civil society. One of the key supports of the Soviet system was an elaborate socialization and public opinion formation apparatus, in which Marxist-Leninist ideology played a major role. To advance Marxist-

Leninist thought, and perhaps most importantly prevent opposition ideologies and movement, the Communist Party developed a number of programs and organizations. The Young Octobrists and Young Pioneers were geared toward educating grade school children, and the Komsomol was oriented to young adults. These socializing organizations were assisted by an educational system that stressed the value of the Communist Party and the benefits of the communist revolution. For the adult population the Soviet Union developed a media system that saturated the airwaves and the newspapers with pro-Soviet propaganda. Government newspapers such as *Izvestia* and the party newspaper, *Pravda,* were used effectively by the Soviet elite to announce policy initiatives and reinforce party decisions.

The Communist Party further strengthened its control over Soviet society by forming an intricate system of party organizations at each administrative level. At the local level, primary party organizations (PPOs) were present throughout the country and were the key means of advancing political indoctrination. These party organs were linked to a vast network of other functional organizations such as labor unions and agricultural associations, along with groups for artists, athletes, writers, and the like. Party activists were responsible for spreading the word, defining policy, and keeping a watch out for those who strayed from the ideological line. The Soviet system was all-encompassing as it sought to ensure that the citizenry would be tied into Marxist-Leninism and supportive of the Communist Party.

What is most interesting about the establishment of the postcommunist civil society is not how quickly the Soviet apparatus came tumbling down, but how long it has taken to rebuild a new democratic civil society. The Communist Party organization was dismantled in 1991 and the national and regional soviets (legislatures) were done away with in 1993. But new citizen-based institutions have been slow to emerge in Russia. There are certainly a wide array of political parties and electoral movements, but many have been short-lived. Civic organizations, however, have not developed as quickly as many in the West had hoped. What has grown in postcommunist Russia is a sense of alienation from government and political leaders. Russians are suspicious of government, the level of trust in political institutions is minuscule, politicians are roundly criticized, and there is little evidence of a national consensus on democratic values and democratic practice. There is a profound gap between the rich and the poor in Russia, which feeds into this sense of alienation, especially when those at the lowest economic levels see daily evidence of corruption and illegality among the elite.

If Russia is to create a new civil society it will likely be built on a set of moral principles that are in stark contrast to the current malaise of official corruption, heightened crime and violence, and general ethical deterioration.

One of the first priorities articulated by Russian president Vladimir Putin on taking office was the need for measures to combat "the corruption of morals in Russia." Putin elaborated on this theme of reviving Russian morals when he stated early in his administration that "for a Russian citizen, what is important are the moral principles which he first acquires in the family and which form the very core of patriotism. This is the main thing. Without it, it is impossible to agree on anything; without it, Russia would have had to forget about national dignity, even about national sovereignty. This is our starting point."

Corruption, both public and private, has soured the Russian people on the new Western model of government and economy. From skimming tax collections to illegally selling state assets to smuggling everything from drugs to nuclear materials, Russians have sadly come to accept corruption as part of the normal way of doing business. Rampant public illegality has consistently put Russia among the world's most corrupt countries. The international watchdog group on corruption, Transparency International, gave Russia one of its lowest scores. Even more damaging, Russia is viewed negatively by international business in regard to the honesty and integrity of the government. In a survey of businesspeople and academics, Russia was ranked the seventeenth most corrupt nation in the world out of ninety-nine nations.

The corrupt environment that exists in governing circles has led to an explosion of crime and violence. Criminal activity in Russia is organized around gangs, which, borrowing a term from American culture, have come to be called the *mafiya*. In 1995 an estimated 8,000 criminal gangs were operating in Russia, a figure that proportionally matches Italy. Russia even has its "dons," such as the notorious Vladimir "the Poodle" Podiatev, who controls the city of Khabarovsk through his own political party and television station. *Mafiya* gangs have in recent years branched out into computer-related crimes, hacking into bank accounts and other business transactions. There is also disturbing evidence that the *mafiya* have become major arms dealers, even to the extent of posing a threat to international security because of their ties to terrorist groups and their willingness to trade in small nuclear weapons. The Russian police are overwhelmed by the gang activity and have responded to the crime and violence with frontier justice. There is little in the way of due process and criminal rights in this war against the *mafiya*, and of course underpaid police are easy targets for gang payoffs.

In order to restore faith in government and inject a new moral code into Russian society, Putin has returned to some common themes. Being a man of the military, Putin has begun to stress the need for "military preparedness" and links military preparedness with patriotic obligation. Putin seems convinced that Russia must return to the values of a time when society recognized its responsibilities to the Motherland and the need for a vigorous moral code of behavior. Putin is waging a national crusade to save Russia from itself and to stop the decay that is turning the nation into a criminal enterprise and criminals into the real power holders in the country.

The concept of Motherland and patriotic zeal are deeply embedded in Russian culture. The writer Alexander Solzhenitsyn has often commented that the strength of Russian society lies in its ties to the land and its spiritual and romantic qualities, which are apart from the consumerist, money-fixated values that drive Western nations, particularly the United States. Putin's emphasis on linking the military and patriotic sentiment, however, appears to be more centered on the importance of discipline and rigid acceptance of the rule of law rather than the spiritual/romantic qualities identified by Solzhenitsyn. Nevertheless, Putin is convinced that Russians must address the corruption of morals and be willing to go to extraordinary lengths to achieve his goal. He has even made open overtures to the Russian Orthodox Church. Putin announced to the surprise of many that he was secretly baptized as an infant and that he is an "observant Christian." Putin's newfound Christianity is seen by many as another means of rebuilding the moral foundation in Russia.

While the moral and patriotic transformation of Russia is clearly ascendant, other forces are shaping the evolving civil society. Russia today is a country where new associations, organizations, clubs, political parties, and interest groups are beginning to take hold. Some of this civil activity is a holdover from the communist days when the party organized at the neighborhood, factory, and school level. Labor unions, for example, remain important conduits of worker views and interests. The successor to the Soviet-style union is the Federation of Independent Trade Unions (FITU), which continues to be the largest union organization, although it has run into stiff opposition from sector unions such as the coal miners' union. Union activity has been especially aggressive in light of the fact that the government during the late 1990s was unable to pay the workers. This led to massive strikes and public protests. Strikes have also been initiated by teachers and other government employees in the various regions of the Russian Federation.

The key area of vitality in Russian civil society is in the business sector, where there has been an explosion of trade and professional associations. These associations have been developed for the express purpose of lobbying government and the international investment community for lucrative contracts and trade relationships in the new market economy. Also with billions of dollars in foreign humanitarian assistance, technical expertise, and multilateral loans entering the economy, there has been a significant growth in nongovernmental organizations (NGOs), which have contributed significantly to the deepening of civil society. Finally, with the state bureaucracy reduced, a number of social welfare and environmental groups have formed. From groups that deal with the impact of the Chernobyl nuclear accident on the populace in the Kiev area to the mounting problems of homelessness, alcoholism, and spousal abuse, Russia has become a country of self-help associations.

Despite evidence that Russian civil society is weak, Russia has made significant gains in the formation of a democratic environment since the fall of the Soviet system. A poll in 2000 asked Russians how they adapted to the changes of the past few years. Fifty percent stated that they adapted well to the changes, while 28 percent said they would never adapt. Sixteen percent said that they will adapt in the near future. These are encouraging signs about the prospects of taking Russia further toward democracy and a market economy, but there is a long road ahead.

PATHWAYS TO PARTICIPATION

One of the legacies of Gorbachev's glasnost policy of greater openness in Soviet society was the formation of new political parties. By the time Boris Yeltsin stood on the tank in front of the White House, Russia had as many as two hundred political party organizations. Although many of these parties were one-person operations with a narrow policy focus and limited popular support, the existence of so many political organizations pointed to the huge undercurrent of participation in the crumbling Soviet system. Since those early days of unbridled political party activity, there have been constant realignments, factional divides, and new formations. The political parties that carried the banner of reform and the market approach to national development were more prone to experience internal change and reformulation. If there was a semblance of stability in the emerging political party system in the early days of Russian democracy, it was at the far left of the spectrum, where the nationalist parties resided, and the far right, where the "new" Communist Party was entrenched. In between those extremes the Russian political party system was awash in diversity with organizations that sought legislative representation in order to advance the interests of peasants, women, workers, Muslims, Orthodox Christians, small businessmen, military leaders, environmentalists, and even beer drinkers. Russian democracy has been anything but dull in terms of providing the voters with variety and alternative viewpoints. The growth in parties has made the political and electoral process cumbersome, fragmented, and nearly impossible to draw effective ideological distinctions.

To identify the key political party organizations that have stayed afloat during this survival of the fittest process and to show the important realignments and reformulations within the key party organizations, it is helpful to examine the 1999 legislative elections and the 2000 presidential election. Despite the diversity and resultant complicated nature of political party participation in contemporary Russia, these two critical elections reveal some commonalities and consistencies that serve to bring clarity to an otherwise hyperpluralistic democratic process.

The 1999 Duma Election

The 1999 Duma election was conducted in the waning days of the Yeltsin administration. The campaign for the 450 seats in the Duma was conducted in an atmosphere of economic decline and significant apprehension over Western liberal models of national development. A consensus was emerging in Russia in 1999 that governing institutions like the Duma would have to support policies that moved Russia away from Yeltsin's market approach and toward variants of state capitalism. Russians in 1999 had grown tired of the path that Yeltsin had put the country on and were ready for more familiar approaches. As in past elections for the Duma, a number of political parties organized their supporters and developed their platforms, some of which were new to the process, some reformulations of previous party organizations.

The Communist Party again headed the list of political organizations seeking to control the Duma. But after four years as the opposition, the Communists had failed to tap into the discontent that was pervasive in Russia. By 1999 the Communists had seen some of their allies in the Duma, like the Agrarian Party, leave the fold and join other political parties such as the Fatherland–All Russia bloc. The Communists continued to have a solid organization and their message of opposition to economic reforms did resonate in the country. The Communists, however, lacked the ability to expand their base to the young, the educated, and to those who were prospering economically.

The rising political party that was capable of challenging the Communists was the Fatherland–All Russia bloc. Centered in Moscow and led by the mayor of the capital city, Yuri Luzhkov, along with former Prime Minister Yevgeny Primakov, Fatherland–All Russia benefited from Luzhkov's popularity in bringing a semblance of prosperity to the city. In August 1999 Fatherland united with All Russia, a movement of regional leaders, to form what many observers felt was the most potent political party organization in Russia. The united party advanced its prospects by making Primakov the head of the bloc's party list. Primakov was viewed by many Russians as the most trusted and responsible leader during the dark days of Yeltsin's second term.

The third party to contest the election was Yabloko. Despite its poor showing in the 1995 Duma vote, Yabloko developed a reputation as a strong voice against government policies and a firm advocate of democracy. The Yabloko representatives in the Duma earned high praise for their intelligent, professional efforts to deal with the economic crisis of 1998 and the constant struggles with Yeltsin. The addition of former Prime Minister Sergei Stepashin to the party list gave Yabloko increased visibility and respectability.

Also playing a role in the Duma election was a hastily formulated coalition of three groups that took the name Union of Rightist Forces. The bloc was made up of privatization head Anatoly Chubais and former Prime Minister Sergei Kiriyenko. Since both Chubais and Kiriyenko were viewed as closely associated with radical market reforms, their popularity among voters was suspect. But as the campaign developed a group of regional governors were added to the leadership team, thus holding out hope that the new "political party" would reach the threshold of 5 percent of the vote necessary to gain seats in the legislature.

The final main participant in the Duma election was the Unity group associated with Vladimir Putin. As with many of these temporary political parties, Unity was a movement formed within the walls of the Kremlin as a means of providing Putin and his allies with the organization necessary to win seats in the Duma. Unity was without question a personalist party that played on the enormous popularity of the prime minister accruing from his Chechnyan policies and his authoritative control of government in Yeltsin's absence. As the campaign for the Duma progressed, it was becoming clear to Russians that Putin would be more than a figurehead prime minister and as a result Unity gained more and more support.

The election on December 19, 1999, reinforced the dominant perception in Russian society that Putin and Unity were on the ascent. Although the Communists gained the largest number of seats (114), their total was a steep decline from their seats in 1995 (157). Putin's Unity group won seventy-three seats. Fatherland–All Russia came in third with sixty-six seats, the Union of Right Forces was fourth with twenty-nine seats, and Yabloko was fifth with twenty-nine seats. Vladimir Zhirinovsky's Nationalists Party and Our Home Is Russia brought up the rear of the Duma vote with seventeen and eight seats respectively. What is interesting about the Putin/Unity vote is that in exit polls conducted during the Duma vote 50 percent of the Unity vote was attributed to "liking the leader," while 41 percent of the Communist vote was attributed to the party "program" or because voters had "always voted" for the party.

Although the Communists gained the largest number of legislators in the Duma, by the opening of the first session in January 2000, the Unity delegation picked up support from nine other legislators, while the Communists lost the support of twenty-four legislators. This gave the Communists only a 90–82 edge over Unity. The Communists won the speakership, nine committee chairs, and two deputy speakers, but Unity took seven chairmanships and the first deputy speaker. It was becoming increasingly clear that Vladimir Putin, the prime minister and soon to be acting president, would have a Duma where his supporters edged closer to control, while the once powerful Communists were in retreat.

The Presidential Election of 2000

With the war in Chechnya reinvigorating national pride and Boris Yeltsin resigning from power, the presidential election of March 2000 became more an elevation to power of Vladimir Putin than a competitive election. Putin acted the part of the next president. He was the clear favorite of the Russian media and the politician the wealthy oligarchy wanted in the Kremlin. His no-nonsense image brought confidence to many Russians, particularly the young. There was little in the way of campaigning for the presidency, other than Putin acting presidential as he awarded medals to soldiers back from the Chechnyan front or spoke on state television about his plans to make Russia a world leader again. Putin just rode the wave of popularity and acted as if the election was a necessary part of his meteoric rise to power.

There was opposition to Putin. Again Gennady Zyaganov of the Communist Party led a list of competitors along with Grigory Yavlinsky of Yabloko and Vladimir Zhirinovsky of the Liberal Democrats. But the parties that had been active just a few months earlier in the Duma elections were noticeably absent. There was no candidate from Fatherland–All Russia, while the candidate of the Union of Right Forces was not officially endorsed by the party. Politicians like Primakov, Luzhkov, Lebed, and Kiriyenko, who figured so prominently in the 1999 Duma elections, chose not to challenge the Putin juggernaut. The remaining candidates in the field were minor players with no national recognition and no organization. Putin won election on the first ballot with a majority of 52.9 percent of the vote to Zyaganov's 29.2 percent. Grigory Yavlinsky came in a weak third with 5.8 percent. Nearly 69 percent of the eligible voters in Russia participated in the election, a testament to the support that democratic practice held in Russia and also the growing popularity of the frontrunner. It is important also to state that 1.4 million voters, nearly 2 percent of the Russian voters, chose "Against all" on the ballot.

In polling done at the time of the election it became obvious why Putin won handily. Russian voters saw Putin as "bringing order to the country," "strengthening state regulation of the economy," and pursuing a policy of "national self-reliance." They also saw Putin as a leader who would "guarantee freedom of speech," which shows the importance that Russians give to this cornerstone of democratic practice. Most of all Russian voters expressed trust and confidence in Putin and saw him as a change from the weak, erratic Boris Yeltsin. If there was a downside to the support for Putin, poll results showed a concern that the new president might be too beholden to Western investment and banking interests, a sign of lingering anti-Western, antiliberal feelings among Russians. Overall, however, Putin was viewed favorably by the Russian people, although it is important to remember that his election was not of landslide proportions.

With the election of Vladimir Putin, Russia entered a new phase of its democracy. The hyperpluralism of the last ten years has been replaced with the growing centralization of a popular autocrat. The Communist opposition was substantially weakened and there were no other adequate replacements. Anti-Putin forces in the country are so divided and disorganized that prospects for a workable opposition coalition are remote. On many levels Russian participation has been simplified with the rise of Vladimir Putin. Russians are either for him or against him; there are no second or third or fourth options. This makes the political process easier to understand, but it is a marked departure from the "untamed" democracy of the last ten years.

Electoral Data

In the 1999 elections for the Duma the following political parties received more than 1 percent of the vote:

Communist Party of the Russian Federation	24.3 percent
Interregional Movement Unity	23.3 percent
Fatherland–All Russia	13.3 percent
Union of Right Forces	8.5 percent
Zhirinovsky Bloc	6.0 percent
Yabloko	5.9 percent
Communist Workers	2.2 percent
Women of Russia	2.1 percent
Pensioners Party	2.0 percent
Our Home Is Russia	1.2 percent

AGRICULTURAL POLICY

The state of Russian agriculture and agricultural policy is best summarized by the conclusions of a 1998 report from the Organization of European Community and Development (OECD): "The story of Russian agriculture since the collapse of the Soviet Union has been one of sharp declines in production, share of GDP, labor productivity, capacity utilization, food consumption and wages." Although the report stated that Russia has vast land resources that favor farming and a sizable percentage of its population (14 percent) that have remained on the land, the agricultural sector has not made a smooth transition during the postcommunist period. Farming in Russia was devastated by the removal of price controls in 1992, which created a huge inflationary spike that led to a precipitous drop in consumer demand. But the fundamental problem in Russian agriculture was the difficulty in moving away from the Soviet-style policies that emphasized state procurement of foodstuffs and heavy subsidies to the aging and inefficient state farms. In 1989, for example, a study by American agriculture expert John Carlson showed that subsidies for main food products amounted to one-third of the Russian budget and the share of subsidies in the retail price of basic products reached 89 percent.

Even before communism collapsed, the Gorbachev government recognized the heavy involvement of the state in agriculture and instituted a series of reforms that accented privatization of the state farms *(sovkhozes)*. In 1989 and 1990 the Soviet government formed nonstate enterprises as cooperatives *(kolkhozes)*, denationalized the land and transferred ownership to the cooperatives, and established the legal right for Russians to form private or family farms. This privatization initiative was opposed by many of the local communist administrators, who feared a loss of power, as well as many of the Russian peasants, who showed little interest in moving away from decades of involvement in the state farm system. Besides the lack of individual capital to run private farms and uncertainties about the prospects for generating a profit, there was simply no tradition of family farming in Russia.

Throughout most of the 1990s the government made numerous attempts to restructure and reform the agricultural sector, but little change was achieved. Family farming made up about 6 percent of the total agricultural land in use, while the vast majority remained in the reconstituted cooperatives, which in most cases operated in a manner similar to the old state farms. While it is clear to government officials in Moscow that the agriculture sector must continue to implement policies that utilize land and produce foodstuffs in a more productive manner, there are major obstacles to reform, especially at the regional level. There is little in the way of a national agricultural policy in Russia. Instead there are regional policies with differing levels of government support, interregional trade barriers, and dissimilar restructuring policies that create wide discrepancies in productivity.

Amid all the problems in Russian agriculture, there are some positive developments. The heavy importation of food during the early 1990s has declined significantly, although Russia remains a net importer of agro-food products. There have also been some promising signs that foreign investors are beginning to take an interest in Russian agriculture. According to OECD data, foreign investment in the areas of baby food, ice cream, confectionery sugar, and tobacco has brought not only new capital but also technology and market-based expertise. Russia has also negotiated a number of new trade agreements, including the Partnership and Cooperation Agreement with the European Union and various bilateral arrangements with the former republics of the Soviet Union. Russian officials are working aggressively to integrate their agricultural sector into the global marketplace and view trade in agricultural products as the key to the restructuring and reform of farming.

But Russian agriculture will not be restructured and reformed unless peasants and regional officials are properly trained to participate in a highly competitive market economy. Like much of Russia's industrial sector during the postcommunist period, workers and managers in agriculture have little understanding of how to function in an open economic system. They have scant personal resources, little understanding of pricing mechanisms, and a legacy of reliance on price supports and other subsidies that deter the movement to a market system. A combination of time to adjust to a radically different way of farming coupled with aggressive efforts on the part of the government to attract foreign investment and foreign trade should in the coming years move Russia away from its dependence on imported food. Furthermore, economic revival of Russian agriculture will go a long way toward addressing serious poverty and income inequality in the rural areas. Because so much attention was placed on urban centers and the new economy of natural resource extraction, the rural areas moved deeper and deeper into economic and social decay. If Russian economic revitalization is to be truly national in character, the agricultural sector must not be forgotten, nor the peasants who work in agriculture. ⊕

THE POWER ELITE

Russia historically has valued strong leadership. Russian political culture is steeped in an appreciation of the man who will make the Motherland great and create the stability and normalcy valued by the citizenry. As a result leaders from Lenin and Stalin to Yeltsin and now Putin have all been expected to control the reins of government and shape Russia in their image.

PHOTO 3.1 RUSSIAN PRESIDENT VLADIMIR PUTIN SPEAKS DURING A RECEPTION IN MOSCOW. (REUTERS NEWMEDIA INC./CORBIS)

Vladimir Vladimirovich Putin was born on October 7, 1952, in St. Petersburg. He studied law at the State University in St. Petersburg and graduated in 1975. He worked first in the foreign intelligence service of the KGB, mostly in Germany. In 1990 he joined the staff of St. Petersburg mayor Anatoly Sobchak having responsibility for external relations. Later he became deputy mayor. In 1996 he was appointed by Deputy Prime Minister Anatoly Chubais to be part of the presidential administration of Boris Yeltsin. He quickly rose to the position of deputy chief of staff and later assumed the leadership of the new security service, the FSB. When Boris Yeltsin dismissed Prime Minister Sergei Stepashin in 1999, Putin became Russia's prime minister. On New Year's Eve 1999 Yeltsin resigned and named Putin acting president. In 2000 Putin was formally elected president of the Russian Federation.

Therefore this discussion of the power elite begins with the individual at the top of the political ladder, Vladimir Putin.

Vladimir Putin is in many respects the antithesis of Boris Yeltsin. Putin is the faceless former KGB agent who spent much of his formative years of government service as a low-level agent in East Germany spying on foreigners, while Yeltsin is the gregarious party official who risked all to take on the communist system. Putin is cautious and quiet, but with a steely demeanor that sends the signal that this Russian leader will be a tough negotiator. Yeltsin, on the other hand was blunt and gruff with occasional outbursts of clownish behavior that led many in Russia and the West to question his ability to govern. Finally, Putin, unlike Yeltsin, is not willing to remake Russia into a mirror image of the West; instead, he is an ardent nationalist who has promised to reevaluate the liberal reforms, financial arrangements, and military policies put in place by his predecessor.

As a candidate for president and now as sitting president, Putin has put on the face of a Western politician mingling with the Russian people and making trips to Europe and the United States. Although he has emphasized the need to make Russia great again, Putin has sought to make Russia a partner with the West. He became an early member of the Western coalition against terrorism in Afghanistan and provided the United States with access to former Soviet republics such as Tajikistan and Uzbekistan. Putin has also been willing to combine the missile reduction policies of Gorbachev and Yeltsin. In 2001 he negotiated an agreement with the Bush administration that further reduced each country's nuclear arsenal. But Putin has remained intransigent with respect to the Bush administration's efforts to scrap the 1972 Antiballistic Missile Treaty. Putin, like other European leaders, was uneasy about agreeing to destroy the treaty and allow the United States to build a missile shield system that would change the balance of nuclear power. He was outspoken in his condemnation of the Bush administration's invasion of Iraq.

Although Vladimir Putin fits into the Russian legacy of strong leadership and aggressive central control, there have always been other "pockets" of power in the country, whether in the former Communist Party machinery or in various state institutions such as the KGB and the military. But now that the political process has opened up and the economy is free of many of the systemic restrictions of Soviet communism, there are more of these "pockets" of power outside the Kremlin walls.

During the Yeltsin years key governmental leaders and top corporate heads, the so-called oligarchs, developed a kind of symbiotic relationship in which public policy decisions were made for the express purpose of advancing personal wealth and expanding the influence of business enterprises. The oligarchs included Boris Berezovsky, the multibillionaire who commands a banking, oil, and media empire, Pavel Borodin, who manages the Kremlin's huge property holdings, Rem Vyakhirev, who runs the huge gas company Gazprom, Mikhail Khodorkovsky, who acquired control of the Yukos oil company, one of the world's largest, and Vladimir Potanin, whose Uneximbank has been at the forefront of many of the loan agreements between state enterprises and private corporations. These and other members of the corporate and financial oligarchy in postcommunist Russia reaped enormous profits from their associations with the government, and in the process they raised serious questions about the appropriateness and legality of these associations. Despite these measures to reduce their influence, the oligarchs continue to wield power. Currently eight oligarchic groups control 85 percent of the value of Russia's top private firms. Putin may have reduced the level of criminality associated with the oligarchs, but he has recognized the need to work with them to advance national economic development.

By 2001 the government had taken a series of steps to remove the oligarchs from political and economic influence. Boris Berezovsky was forced into exile along with Victor Gusinsky, whose media outlet often challenged Putin and his policies. Pavel Borodin was charged with bribery by the Swiss government and was fired by Putin, along with two deputy prime ministers who were linked to corruption. And Rem Vyakhirev was pushed aside at Gazprom into a powerless directorship. Oligarchs who remain in either government or private sector positions no longer exercise the kind of influence that they once had, nor are they capable of engaging in financial dealings that stretch the boundaries of legality.

One government agency that weathered the internal dislocations in government and continues to maintain political influence is the KGB, the infamous Committee for State Security. During its heyday the KGB was the most feared arm of the government, a secret police responsible for ensuring that Soviet communism was able to keep pace with its adversary, the American Central Intelligence Agency, and also maintain political order through a wide range of oppressive measures. The demise of the KGB began when its chairman, Oleg Kruchkov, was implicated in the 1991 coup attempt. When the coup failed, a consensus emerged among governing officials that the KGB would be reorganized. As a result, the once feared secret police was stripped of its military role and denied domestic surveillance responsibility. To add insult to injury, the pro-Yeltsin allies after the 1991 coup attacked the Communist Party headquarters, took incriminating KGB files on thousands of operatives, and then tore down the statue of Felix Dzerzhinskii, considered the founder of the modern-day KGB.

The new KGB leadership pledged to follow the rule of law and to open up its vast archives, which have provided a window on the world of Cold War spying and political control. Eventually the KGB was renamed the Federal Security Service (FSB). The FSB today acts with much greater restraint and within an atmosphere of more domestic control over arrest powers. Since its reorganization, unfortunately, the agency has been wracked by charges of corruption rather than praised for its crime control. It has been linked to smuggling and shakedowns of prominent businesspeople. Nevertheless, the FSB under Putin has gained stature as key operatives have risen to positions of prominence in the new president's inner circle. The ability of the FSB to maintain a prominent position in Russian government is viewed by many in the country as resting on its vast databank of information (often compromising material) that can be used to intimidate officials.

With the breakup of the Soviet system, considerable power has shifted to the regions and to the governors of the regions. The Federation Treaty permits the various regions and other entities to enter into agreements and even treaties with foreign governments and other bodies as long as they do not violate the Russian constitution. As a result fifty-five Russian regions have developed political relations with former republics of the Soviet Union. Moreover, Russian republics can also become involved in foreign trade without receiving permission from central ministries in Moscow. This has opened the door for these regional entities to pass legislation regarding foreign investment and the opening of trade offices.

The aggressiveness of the local governors and administrators is the direct result of the inability of the central government to establish control of the vast Russian Federation. Local leaders sensed, especially during the waning years of the Yeltsin presidency, that there was weakness at the center of Russian government and that opportunities existed to establish great autonomy and expand local power. For example, during the 1998 meltdown of the Russian ruble many of the regional heads used their growing power to develop bilateral agreements with other regions and even foreign governments to stabilize their economies. Although most of the attention in the Russian Federation has been on separatist Chechnya, many of the local governors and administrators have chosen not to follow the example of the Chechens. Rather, they have opted to work within the existing weakened Federation to chart their own foreign, defense, and economic policies.

Russian political leaders like Boris Yeltsin and Vladimir Putin have recognized the increasing power and importance of local governmental officials. After the White House was attacked in 1993, Yeltsin issued a decree dismantling local governments and requiring that new elections be held. Yeltsin viewed the local governments as centers of opposition to his reform policies and threats to his efforts to maintain the cohesiveness of the Russian Federation. Although Yeltsin hoped to fill these regional bodies with his supporters, the elections brought many leaders opposed to him into office. Moreover, the direct election of regional governors has provided them with a greater degree of independence from both the president and the local legislative bodies. The president still retains the power to appoint his representatives to these regions and he can suspend decisions of regional government pending a court ruling. But these powers have not limited the ability of the regional governors to control the policy process. The national government still holds power with respect to budgetary transfers. Because local taxing powers are unclear or prohibited, the regions have had to depend on Moscow for critical resources.

The growing competition for power between the central government in Moscow and the subnational governments has allowed the Federation Council, the second house of the Russian legislature, to emerge as a key forum for issues relating to the regions. The Federation Council is an assembly of the chief executives and legislative leaders from the eighty-nine regional units that make up the Russian Federation. This body ratifies the federal budget and also ratifies treaties after they have moved through the Duma. Although budget and treaty powers are important, the Federation Council functions most importantly as a site for negotiations between the central government and the regions over conflicts, reform initiatives, and the distribution of financial resources. The Federation Council was a valuable ally of the Duma in its frequent confrontations with Boris Yeltsin. This alliance was effective in overturning presidential decrees and overriding presidential vetoes.

The administration of Vladimir Putin has aggressively sought to diminish the power of the Federation Council and place greater controls over the regional governors. In May 2000 Putin successfully pressured the Duma to pass legislation stripping the governors of their guaranteed seats in the Federation Council and having the members of the Federation Council elected by regional legislatures. The Duma also passed legislation allowing the president to fire regional governors and the governors to fire local administrators. These reforms came on the heels of Putin's issuing a decree that would create seven large superdistricts designed to bring more central control to the growing autonomy of the eighty-nine regions. The legislative initiatives, which are only in their early stages and will require extensive political bargaining, are Putin's attempts to crack down.

In terms of the current relationship between the central government and the subnational units, the governors and the various ministries in Moscow are constantly involved in a lobbying process over the division of authority, the allocation of resources, and the responsibility to provide key services. Because Russia has been faced with enormous economic and financial burdens, this lobbying process has dominated the relationship between center and periphery, especially in regions that have few natural resources or lack the political clout to influence policy decisions or the distribution of budget money. As a result of these resource and political discrepancies there is great diversity in terms of how the regions have applied market reforms and democratic governance. There is also great discrepancy in terms of the level of public corruption and governmental effectiveness among the eighty-nine administrative units. Because the subnational governments are so diverse and are at various stages of political development, the task of managing the affairs of the Russian Federation will likely remain uneven and irregular.

Power is indeed changing in post-Yeltsin Russia. Not only does the country have a new leader with new ideas, but the elites that matter represent the changes that have come to Russia since the breakup of the Soviet Union. As President Putin takes Russia forward, new elites may emerge. But because the Russian president has promised to take tough, aggressive measures both at home and abroad, old elites like the state security apparatus and the military will likely play a more prominent role. In any major change and transition new power emerges, but old power has a way of remaining resilient. In Russia, however, one segment of the power elite is finished. The Communist Party is now only an opposition party. It no longer recruits elites, formulates policy, or implements the communist system.

Composition of the Duma After the 1999 Election

Communist Party of the Russian Federation	113 seats
Interregional Movement Unity	72 seats
Fatherland–All Russia	66 seats
Union of Right Forces	29 seats
Yabloko	21 seats
Liberal Democratic Party of Russia	7 seats
Our Home Is Russia	7 seats
All-Russian Political Movement in Support of the Army	2 seats
Pensioners Party	1 seat
Congress of Russian Communities	1 seat

POINT OF FACT

In order to fulfill his promise to establish in Russia what he called a "dictatorship of the law," President Putin has begun taking the necessary legislative steps to introduce jury trials into the legal system.

What the Experts Say

Michael McFaul of the Carnegie Endowment for International Peace is one of the foremost scholars studying Russia today. In the following excerpt from an article in *Current History*, McFaul gives his views on the future direction of Russia under Putin.

Putin's political reforms have illuminated how weak societal checks on state power remain in Russia. Russia today has no effective political opposition. Political parties are weak, economic elites appear seemingly unwilling to challenge the power of the president, and regional leaders are on the defensive. Yet the people still firmly support Putin and his reform. Alternative sources of power may reorganize, especially if an economic crisis or an expansion of the war in the Caucasus erodes Putin's popularity, but these events are unlikely in the near future.

MICHAEL MCFAUL, "PUTIN IN POWER,"
Current History, OCTOBER 2000, PP. 307–314

REAL GOVERNMENT

Yulia Latynina, an analyst at the Institute of the Economy in Transition, summed up the reality of governing in Russia when she made the following observation in an interview with the *Washington Post*, "Russia lives not by law, but by understandings. When I say not by the law, I mean not by those formal rules and regulations that are written into our constitution and civil code, but by some informal rules, which are something in between a bandit's code and feudal code." Ms. Latynina was describing a governing process in Russia that is not only extraconstitutional and extralegal, but also highly personalistic, familial, ad hoc, and often mysterious. The Russians have put into place a governing system that is Western in structure and process, but the actual power relations that are responsible for making public policy and running the country are centered elsewhere.

The democratic revolution that transformed Russia, at least on the surface, established a rule of law and a system of decisionmaking based on a Western model. Russia has a democratic constitution, a civil code, and family and criminal codes, but it does not have the rule of law or strong legal institutions to enforce the rule of law. At the core of the problem of Russian law is lack of familiarity with the concept that rulers must subordinate themselves to a body of law and cannot place themselves above the law. Russia has had a tradition over hundreds of years that has relied on the personalistic authority of the czar or the powerful communist leader. Now under democratic rule the Russian people and their political elites are simply uneasy with the Western concept of a "country of laws rather than of men." To overcome the beliefs and practices of the past, the Russians are engaging in a comprehensive reform of the judiciary and court system.

President Putin has taken the lead in this reform effort by characterizing the current system as "shadow justice." As part of the reform initiative more judges would be brought into service, salaries would increase, and those judges who were tainted by corruption would be dismissed.

Critical to the reform of the Russian judicial system is reducing the influence of prosecutors. Prosecutors have accumulated immense power to arrest and convict those they see as breaking the law. Prosecutors have emerged as a power unto themselves and as a result are often linked to legal excesses and official corruption. The prosecutorial system in Russia is a leftover from the Stalinist days and has been immune from reform. Many prosecutors have stated publicly that they oppose the implementation of Western-style legal organization and procedures, in large part because such changes would drastically reduce their powers and influence. Putin, however, has made it known that he wants to rein in the prosecutors and limit their ability to define the law and engage in practices that reflect Stalinist authoritarianism.

While reform of the legal system is being touted as critical to modernizing Russian government, it is the administrative bureaucracy that is the key sector in need of a massive overhaul. Governmental ministries remain isolated fiefdoms with little accountability and gross inefficiency. The ministries are more often associated with corruption than providing services. The tax and customs bureaucracies are infamous for running extortion schemes against businesses and individuals. There remains an arbitrariness in commercial relations, and often public officials flaunt the law at the highest levels of government. Examples of the Russian failure to establish a rule of law offer a key to understanding how government operates. The powerful mayor of Moscow, Yuri Luzhkov, has been known to ignore rulings of the Constitutional Court regarding residence permits (*propiskas*), even though the rule is codified in Russian law. Instead, Luzhkov has decided to provide permits to those who are willing to give his administration a "fee." Interpreting the law to gain financial advantage is the way Russia works in the postcommunist era.

Putin's attempts to target administrative corruption have achieved mixed results. Ministers have been replaced and safeguards put into practice to create a culture of honesty and efficiency. But change at the top of the administrative ladder has not filtered down to lower-level bureaucrats who come in regular contact with Russian businesses and citizens and engage in criminal activity. Those seeking a more responsible bureaucracy are pressing for a freedom of information law that would force government agencies to show how budgets are being spent and how revenue is being collected and wasted. Pilot programs have been put into place in some provinces, but there is no national policy designed to allow Russians to see how their government works. There have also been some programs, again at the provincial level, to form antibribery pacts between government and the business community in order to restore confidence. But the Russian bureaucracy is so vast and its officials so entrenched that change is likely to come slowly. Perhaps the best prospect for reform of administrative practices is the privatization of state enterprises, which has brought a measure of competency, honesty, and efficiency to Russian business relations.

Bloated bureaucracy, patronage connections, bribery, and administrative fiefdoms are legacies of the vast Soviet system that still affect governance today, but so too are personalistic and familial relationships. One of the best examples of the personalistic and familial character of Russian decisionmaking occurred during the Yeltsin years. A closely knit group of advisers called The

Family worked behind the scenes to formulate public policy and direct the Russian Federation. The members of The Family were Yeltsin, his daughter, Tatyana Dychenko (who served as his "image adviser"), Yeltsin's chief of staff, Alexander Voloshin, Yeltsin's biographer, Valentin Yumashev, and Boris Berezovsky. The Family met on numerous occasions during the period of prime minister "musical chairs" in 1998 to direct the various personnel decisions associated with dismissal and appointment. With Yeltsin ill and unable to function, The Family fought over who should hold the prime minister position during the ruble crisis. The Family ultimately settled on Vladimir Putin in 1999, although Yeltsin appeared to play a dominant role in naming his ultimate successor.

Once Putin assumed power, he did not immediately dismantle The Family. He appointed Alexander Voloshin as his presidential chief of staff. Voloshin has become one of the few indispensable men in Russian government. Putin also retained a key Yeltsin insider, making Sergei Ivanov secretary of the Security Council. One member of The Family who did not survive was Yeltsin's daughter, Tatyana. Putin dismissed Tatyana within days of the transition. Although the term "The Family" is not currently used in Russia, Putin has formed his own "family," which includes many of his close associates from the KGB.

Putin faces a daunting task in trying to make Russia work in a manner comparable to Western democracies. In his state of the nation address in 2001, Putin presented the governing goals that must be met if Russia is to become a government that is capable of consolidating its power among its vast territory and providing effective administration to its citizens. Putin stated that his top objective was to strictly define power relations between the federal government and the regional administrations. As Putin stated in his address, "Neither the federal nor the regional [administrations] can exceed their power limits." While Putin talked about defining specific powers at the federal and regional level, it was clear that he wanted to shift more control to the center of national power. He elaborated in his address that there is too much duplication of power in Russia and that it was necessary to "restore order to the territorial structure of the bodies of executive power." This was a clear signal that provincial governors and administrators will see their powers and responsibilities reduced. Finally, Putin emphasized the need to further hone the distribution of tax revenue flows between the federal government and the local administrative units. High levels of inefficiency and corruption at the provincial and local levels led Putin to demand that the central government have greater control over budgets and the manner in which those budgets are used.

In an attempt to ensure that the federal government controls the levers of power in Russia, President Putin appointed seven "supergovernors" whose task is to oversee the provinces and control the excesses of the existing governors. Putin also pushed through parliament laws, which allow him to fire governors and reposition them in a lower order of prominence within the governing structure. If Putin is to be successful in his governing objectives, control over provincial affairs and provincial leaders will be critical. Putin has been reluctant to create local tensions by firing provincial leaders, who often are popular officials and whose support is important for his own political ambitions. As a result Putin has made grand speeches about reforming government and restructuring federal-provincial relations, but enormous roadblocks to achieving these objectives remain, in large part because of entrenched power holders and a governing culture that resists change.

Governance in Russia in the coming years will depend on Vladimir Putin—whether he is a dynamic modernizer or a cautious advocate of gradualism. Examples of Putin's desire to push Russian government forward include his willingness to shake up his cabinet and his vigorous restructuring of the gas entity Gazprom. But there are also examples of Putin being slow to move from past practice as he appoints cronies from the KGB to top governing positions and acts as a vindictive autocrat in his dealing with those who oppose his policies. While Putin's government has successfully reformed the tax laws and brought needed changes to land ownership, deregulation, and the legal system, two major challenges remain: administrative efficiency and public corruption. In these areas Putin has made cosmetic changes while leaving the old system in place.

POINT OF FACT
When the McDonald's in Pushkin Square in Moscow opened in January 1990, it set an opening day record for the number of customers served. After more than twelve years, it continued to be the busiest McDonald's restaurant in the world.

RUSSIAN HEALTH CARE AND HEALTH CARE REFORM

Russia's economic disorder has had a serious impact on the general health of the people and on the ability of the health care system to meet the growing needs of the people. During the Soviet era health care was one of the more effective areas of public policy; however, the shift to a more open economy has created a serious deterioration of care. In today's Russia there are many stories of long waiting lines, unavailability of some critical procedures, high physician and hospital costs, and in some instances requirements that patients provide their own bandages and medications. The crisis in the Russian health care system has been a factor in the disturbing data on infant mortality (twice that of Western Europe), the steep rise in tuberculosis (up 90 percent in the last five years), and the increase of deaths over births since 1966 (an increase of 60 percent).

Russia's new health care system, which mandates compulsory individual health insurance policies and regulates private health insurers and providers, has been riddled with general inefficiency and a severe shortage of financial resources. Many medical workers, particularly those outside the major urban centers, are poorly paid or go unpaid for months at a time. One estimate places the government's debt to the health care system at 17 trillion rubles, or $3 billion. With such financial shortfalls and payroll problems, the Russian health care system is being held together by the sheer dedication of medical professionals and federal prohibitions against work stoppages. Viewed from a comparative perspective, Russia spends about 3 percent of its gross national product on health care, while most of its European neighbors spend in the 8–12 percent range.

At the core of the health care crisis in Russia is the payment relationship between the governing authorities at the federal and regional level and the insurance companies that were formed as a result of the transition to a market economy. The financing of the Russian health care system was founded on a payroll tax allocation that employers were required to pay for their workers to both the regional and federal governments. Municipal authorities were required to pay for nonworking Russians such as children and the elderly. As a result of the funding mechanism, private insurers were licensed to provide the health care and bill the various regional funds. Since 1993 over 500 insurers have been licensed to provide health care to more than 110 million Russians. The problem was the inability of the regional funds to adequately compensate the health care providers. According to Judith Twigg, an American researcher who has studied the Russian health care system, the key problem is the inability of the municipalities to fund the nonworking citizen part of the health care system, which makes up about 60 percent of the population. Also, employers have been lax in making their contributions, in large part because of their financial weakness.

The funding problems associated with the Russian health care system have led the government to propose a recentralization of the financing of the medical insurers. Health ministry officials take the position that the market approach has led to a chaotic situation that requires governmental intervention. As one health ministry official stated about the financing crisis, "not everything about socialism was bad." Because private insurers are now firmly part of the health care system and have their own lobbying arm, there are other proposals that seek to strengthen the market approach. These proposals call for patient copayments, require municipalities to pay their share of the costs of nonworking citizens, and remove government from its role in licensing health care providers. Although the debate over public versus private involvement in health care is common in industrialized countries, it takes on added impetus in Russia, which in the last ten years has moved away from the Soviet-style system of socialized medicine and bureaucratic control.

Russian health care reforms will likely bridge the public and private sector divide with greater government involvement in the financing of the system but enhanced involvement of the private sector in providing a more efficient delivery of medical services. Russia remains committed to the privatization of health care as part of its overall movement toward a market economy. The disturbing data on the state of national health, however, have forced the government to rethink its role in planning, financing, and structuring the health care system. What is interesting about the health care crisis in Russia is that the country is not without doctors and other key health professionals. The last census on doctor/patient ratios in Russia had 45 doctors and 138 hospital beds per 10,000 patients, while Western European nations had 25 doctors and 83 hospital beds per 10,000 patients. The key to utilizing these medical professionals is a system that is efficient and financially secure. But like many other aspects of the Russian economy, the reforms associated with health care will require extensive cooperation between the old state and the new private sector and of course years of patience by the Russian people. ⊕

POLITICAL ECONOMY

During the transition from the Soviet system to a Western-style market system Russia has made many significant public policy decisions. These policy decisions initiated a radical restructuring of the Russian economy and in many cases caused significant uncertainty and hardship for the Russian people. Nevertheless, Russian leaders went forward with this restructuring confident that the old Soviet command economy would have to be forsaken and replaced with a free-flowing demand-generated economy. During the period from 1991 through 1999 the Russian government introduced countrywide elimination of government price controls and subsidies, privatization of the all-encompassing state enterprises, radical devaluation of the national currency, the ruble, and a series of multibillion-dollar loan deals with international agencies and private banks. Each of these policy initiatives and the changes that were brought about reveal not only the internal dynamics of the new Russian system but more importantly the enormous shift in the way Russians think about their economy and their personal economic life.

Market Reform

One of Boris Yeltsin's first initiatives after the collapse of the Soviet state was the introduction of market reforms. This was a radical departure from communist management of the economy. At its core, market reform in Russia meant that prices were allowed to find their natural market level free of government control, and huge state ministries that controlled most of Russian economic life were placed in the private sector. As a result, the practice of the state providing huge subsidies to certain key areas of Russian life in order to stabilize prices was ended. Furthermore, the shift from public enterprises to private enterprises generated huge sales of government assets that were used to modernize Russian society. Although the Russian state still controlled areas of national life such as defense, education, and health care, the move to a privatized economy was to be as complete as possible.

The key to introducing market reforms into the Russian economy was the speed of the transition. Yeltsin and his advisers were aware of the severe shock that the changes would create, but they felt that the old communist system needed to be completely destroyed and a Western model introduced as quickly as possible. The pain associated with the changeover was predicted to be temporary and would not seriously impact the living conditions of average Russians. As a result the government paid close attention to ensuring that the monetary system remained stable and that a period of runaway inflation would not occur with a drastic decrease in the value of the ruble. With this in mind, Yeltsin lifted price controls on most goods in Russia in early 1992. Almost overnight the inflation rate soared to levels above 1,000 percent as Russians crowded into stores in disbelief at the new prices for basic foodstuffs such as milk, bread, and eggs.

Although the hyperinflation of basic goods declined, Russian citizens experienced a significant loss of purchasing power. The pricing initiative caused a major dispute between Yeltsin and his economic advisers and legislators. Supreme Soviet Chairman Ruslan Khasbulatov warned in a speech that the entire Russian Federation could encounter "a catastrophic decline in living standards, famine, and social upheaval." In response, Yeltsin's cabinet resigned and the president was forced to step back from the radical reforms. Yeltsin, however, remained undeterred about introducing market reforms. He reappointed his key adviser on economic reform, Yegor Gaidar, but for most of 1993 Gaidar faced challenges to this authority from legislative hard-liners. Eventually Gaidar resigned in a dispute involving Central Bank policies that were fueling new rounds of inflation. By 1994 market reforms had slowed considerably as Yeltsin sought to stabilize the economy. Economic data showed that the Russian economy was mired in a depression with negative growth rates and a sizable shrinkage of the gross domestic product. Some estimates placed the contraction of the economy during this period as high as 10 percent.

Although replacing the vacuum created by the demise of communism with a new economic system was inevitable, Yeltsin and his advisers misjudged the impact of the changes and the wisdom of moving quickly to market pricing, private enterprise, and a reduction in the role of state subsidies. During the early days of the new Russian democracy, the Yeltsin government put in place an economic system that nearly destroyed the country and fostered a political climate of intense opposition and treasonous attacks on the presidency.

Privatization of State Enterprises

The move to privatize state enterprises began as part of Gorbachev's perestroika program to restructure the Soviet economy. This privatization, however, was limited to certain selected enterprises and remained in the hands of government bureaucrats. In 1992 the first official privatization law was passed, which spurred the movement to transfer state assets over to private owners and shareholders. Without much fanfare, the process of privatizing many of the small business operations in Russia was placed in the hands of individuals or families. Restaurants and grocery stores, which had been run by the communists, were transferred in many cases to employees who worked there and had the financial resources to purchase the property. In a very short period the economic environment in Russia changed from one of state control to a competitive marketplace of entrepreneurs.

Larger-scale state enterprises that were involved in manufacturing took a more complex road to privatization. Because Russians in most cases did not have the capital to purchase the huge factories left over from the Soviet days, the privatization process was driven by a voucher system. Many state enterprises were transformed into joint stock companies where individuals, either Russians or foreign nationals, or other entities such as trade unions could form the joint stock companies. To facilitate the formation of the joint stock companies, the Russian government issued vouchers worth 10,000 rubles. Russians were encouraged to use the vouchers to buy shares in newly privatized companies. Many Russians actually invested in the former state enterprises where they worked. There was a great deal of uncertainty and suspicion among the Russian people over the voucher plan, especially since the value of the vouchers was at that time the equivalent of $25.

The privatization of Russian state enterprises quickly became an opportunity for managers and members of the communist elite to gain control of state assets and in the process concentrate wealth among a few new capitalists. This concentration of wealth funded the formation of politically connected conglomerates in areas such as oil and natural gas and enabled the economic oligarchy to amass huge fortunes. State enterprises also attracted some foreign involvement. Before the Russian ruble crashed in 1998, yearly foreign investment in these enterprises was estimated to exceed $100 billion.

One downside of the privatization process in Russia has been the effect on employment. Thousands of Russian workers have lost their jobs to downsizing, a term that did not exist in the Soviet lexicon. Every citizen was virtually guaranteed a job in the huge, inefficient state enterprises. The downsizing has created a huge pool of unemployed and underemployed. Official figures suggest that 12–15 percent of the Russian population is unemployed but that number is often disputed. What is certain is that privatization, like the introduction of market pricing, has changed the face of the Russian economy. Russia is now a country of private corporations, stock markets, and foreign investors. But privatization has also led to great hardship and growing income inequality. Russians having the skill and the insider knowledge of privatization have reaped huge profits and amassed great economic power, while the remainder of the Russian population has become impoverished.

The Ruble Crisis

The Russian economy had endured much since the transition to a market approach, but the 1998 financial crisis, which required the devaluation of the ruble, was the most daunting challenge for the government since the collapse of the Soviet system. The crisis began in early 1998, when oil prices began to plummet. Since Russia was one of the world's largest producers of oil and its foreign monetary reserves were dependent on revenues from oil, the drop in prices set off a chain reaction of financial woes. Besides losing oil revenues, the Russian government failed to meet its target for collecting taxes. The government was unable to collect the taxes due to poor administration and high levels of evasion, and many Russians were paying their tax bill in forms other than cash. The weakness of the economy caused a barter system to emerge in the country, which even included the payment of taxes. The tax shortfall approached 50 percent of projected revenues and had a devastating effect on the government's capacity to meet its budget obligations. The financial situation further deteriorated when the Asian crisis kept foreign investors from injecting new capital into the Russian economy.

All these revenue and investment shortfalls forced the Russian government to borrow in the international bond market and to issue short-term Treasury bills known as GKOs. But as the year progressed, many investors who held the GKOs became concerned that the government was not going to be able to honor them. This growing confidence problem forced the government to raise interest rates on the GKOs to levels as high as 120 percent. In the summer of 1998 it was becoming increasingly clear to the international lending community that Russia was unable to meet its financial obligations. As word spread of the impending collapse of the GKOs, the Russian stock market lost 50 percent of its value in six months. The Russian government was forced to take radical action to regain the confidence of lenders and to head off an internal financial panic.

The government at the time was headed by Prime Minister Sergei Kiriyenko. He was forced to convert the GKOs into longer-term debt obligations, a move that wiped out the debt market as investors became convinced that the government would not honor its notes. The Kiriyenko government also imposed a thirty-day moratorium on payments of hard currency loans to Western banks, and in the most visible sign of its resolve to avoid a financial meltdown, the government announced that the ruble would be devalued by 30 percent. While the devaluation made Russian products more attractive abroad and showed that the government was serious about getting its financial house in order, the impact on the average citizen was devastating. The devaluation may have helped on the export front, but it made the price of many imported goods increase substantially, thus cutting the purchasing power of the Russian consumer. Also by government decree banks limited personal withdrawals, which forced many small businesses to shut down temporarily and some to go out of business.

The political fallout from the devaluation was huge. Yeltsin fired Kiriyenko and nominated former Prime Minister Chernomyrdin to the post of prime minister. When the Duma twice rejected the nomination, Yeltsin named Yevgeni Primakov to the position. While the political jockeying was going on, the economic crisis continued unabated. The ruble lost even more value, prices of many basic goods soared, and the Russian people began hoarding foodstuffs. Investor confidence both domestically and internationally was dismal. The Russian stock market became a mere shell and a number of banks shut their doors. Russia slowly regained its financial stability by late 1999 as the inflationary spiral eased and the ruble began to regain some of its value. But the ruble crisis of 1998 showed how close the Russian economy came to bankruptcy. Needless to say, the financial crisis did little to restore confidence in the ability of the Russian government to manage the economy and provide a semblance of stability and security for the general population.

Loan Arrangements with the International Monetary Fund

One of Boris Yeltsin's talents as leader was his ability to convince Western nations and particularly international lending agencies to provide his administration with foreign assistance and loans as a means of smoothing the transition from communism to capitalism. Early in his administration Yeltsin made numerous appeals to the West for assistance but was generally unsuccessful as the emphasis in lending circles was on repaying the Russian debt rather than developing assistance or financial loans to address budget deficits. Once it became clear that the shock therapy initiatives of the government were running into trouble and that Yeltsin himself was in jeopardy of not being reelected, the West went into action. Russia received approximately 60 percent of its assistance from a wide range of Western nations, with Germany, the United States, and the United Kingdom leading the way. Much of this aid was technical in nature and designed to provide the Russians with expertise necessary to build a more modern market-based economy.

In the area of financial assistance designed to address budget and currency issues, it was international lending agencies such as the International Monetary Fund and the World Bank that took the lead. In 1995 the International Monetary Fund began a series of multibillion-dollar loans to Russia. The first series of loans were designed to decrease the government's budget deficit to 5 percent of the gross domestic product, a move that had a positive impact on the inflation rate. Later in 1996 the IMF provided a $10 billion, three-year loan that many observers felt had few strings attached and was mainly a means of showing the support the West had for Yeltsin. The IMF loan commitment had the corollary benefit of attracting billions in foreign capital as investors saw that Yeltsin retained the confidence of Western nations and financial institutions.

From 1992 through 1999 Russia received an estimated $138 billion in aid from the IMF, the World Bank, the United States Agency for International Development, and several Western countries. At the same time an estimated $250 billion left Russia in capital flight as both corruption and fear associated with the ruble crisis led to a massive exodus of money. The IMF was embarrassed by making enormous contributions to the Russian economy without gaining meaningful structural reforms or control of public corruption. The IMF in later 1999 announced that it would end loans to Russia and concentrated on managing its existing debt, which approached $3 billion.

The End Result

With the resignation of Boris Yeltsin and the ascension of Vladimir Putin to the Russian presidency there is a general sense of relief mixed with a lingering anger over the economic restructuring policies of the government. While many Russians continue to support the market approach to national development, this process of change has had a devastating impact on their lives. The economic woes endured by the Russians during this transition have been enormous: the economy shrank by 50 percent between 1989 and 1999, the ruble was devalued to near worthlessness, there were regular bouts of hyperinflation, huge income inequalities, massive unemployment and underemployment, 60 million people living below the poverty level, staggering bankruptcies and foreclosures, and corruption that robbed the public sector of its assets.

Although Russian leaders see the country as part of greater Europe and a worthy participant in international gatherings of the industrialized powers, the fact remains that the economic collapse of the last ten years pushed Russia closer and closer to Third World status. Russia is far from matching the health, education, and income levels of the European, Asian, and North American industrial powers. There are pockets of prosperity in urban areas and in some resource-rich regions along with a wealthy elite, but overall the Russian economy is only now beginning to emerge from its restructuring nightmare.

There are signs of hope in the Russian economy. There was modest growth in 1999, 2000, and 2001, and 4 percent growth in 2002. Inflation pressures stabilized (inflation remains in the 15–20 percent range), the ruble has regained some of its lost value, and consumer confidence appears to have rebounded. As a result of an improving economy, Russia has paid down its foreign debt from $17 billion to $14 billion. Although much of this good economic news was based on high oil prices and a strong Western economy, Russia nevertheless has turned the corner. Gone are the days of stock speculation, unregulated management of former state enterprises, wasteful spending of international loans, and gross public sector corruption involving the illegal transfer of as much as $300 billion out of the country.

There is in Russia today a more mature approach to the economy. President Putin has brought a sense of stability to the country that has carried over into the economy. Putin has convinced key Russian elites to make an effort to rein in the excesses of the oligarchs and adopt business practices that attract Western investment. They know that to succeed in the global marketplace they must establish the rule of law in the business community and make government operations more transparent. This is a tall order but is essential for the future health of the Russian economy. *Allt för snabb övergång*

If there is a lesson in the legacy of the Russian transition to capitalism, it is that leaders relied too heavily on the "shock therapy" approach to push the country toward the market model, while completely abandoning the state system with its capacity for providing stability and predictability. The transition to capitalism was inevitable and necessary, but the speed and comprehensiveness of the transition created a volatile vacuum in the country that opened the way for the corrupters and those whose only interest was in cashing in on the dismantling of the state. As one Russian legislator stated during the ruble crisis, "We pinned all our hopes on the free market, which we believed would cure the country and rectify all wrongs. . . . Instead we ended up with utter anarchy and disorder." Perhaps the most revealing observation about the Russian political economy during the postcommunist transition was a joke that circulated through Moscow. One Russian says to another, "Everything the communists told us about communism was a complete and utter lie. Unfortunately, everything the communists told us about capitalism turned out to be true."

Russia in the Global Economy

Thomas Friedman in his book *The Lexus and the Olive Tree* describes how the global economy has touched Russia in some unusual ways:

NBA basketball today has begun to rival soccer as the most global sport. How global is it? You know those Matrushka dolls that they sell in Russia—the wooden dolls with one doll inside a larger doll inside a larger doll. Well, when I visited Moscow in 1989 the hottest-selling Matrushka dolls were those of the different Soviet leaders and the last Czars. You could get Lenin inside Stalin inside Khrushchev inside Brezhnev inside Gorbachev. But when I visited Moscow for the Russian presidential election in 1996, I found that the hottest-selling Matrushka doll outside the Kremlin was Dennis Rodman inside Scottie Pippen inside Toni Kukoc inside Luc Longley inside Steve Kerr inside Michael Jordan! You don't like the Chicago Bulls? Hey, no problem. Street vendors in Moscow were selling every NBA team as a set of Matrushka dolls that year.

THOMAS FRIEDMAN, *The Lexus and the Olive Tree*
(NEW YORK: FARRAR, STRAUS & GIROUX, 1999), P. 248

CHALLENGES FOR RUSSIA

For Russia, which has undergone a massive transformation of its political and economic system, enduring along the way great uncertainty, conflict, and hardship, the challenges for the future are indeed daunting. Many of these challenges can be found in the nexus between government policymaking and economic development. Russia today continues to feel the effects of the end of communism and the "wild capitalism" that replaced it. But if Russia is to rebound from negative growth and the rape of state assets, the government will need to make major changes in the way the political economy is organized and operates. There is a growing consensus of recommendations that have emerged both within the country and from abroad concerning what must be done to get the country back on track.

President Putin has targeted the banking sector as a critical ingredient in sustaining a vibrant economy. After the financial collapse of 1998 the Yeltsin government made a weak attempt to introduce Western banking practices to Russia. But in Russia there is a strange mix of banks, with giant state-controlled institutions sitting side by side with so-called pocket banks, tiny banks with a few owners who often conceal the sources of their holdings and serve as conduits for money laundering. In 2002 Putin took the unprecedented step of ousting the chairman of the central bank for his failure to move quickly on major reforms. Putin appears determined to transform the banks so that deposits are guaranteed and banks provide more opportunities for Russian citizens and entrepreneurs to borrow money and thus spur economic growth.

While Putin is concentrating on the banking industry, many opposition leaders in the Duma and critics of the government have suggested that a large-scale public works program is necessary at this stage. The vote of no confidence that Putin was able to beat back in 2001 resulted in large part from grumbling in the Duma over his failures to address social welfare issues at the expense of reducing the foreign debt. There is growing unease in the country as Russians see the government taking bold steps to address investment, deregulation, and currency stability but failing to pay adequate attention to the basic needs of the population, particularly the old, the young, and the infirm. Putin's attention to macroeconomic policy and global market concerns wins praise in the West but could be troublesome at home.

Putin will also have to face the emerging conflict over privatization and national control of natural resources. While Russia will never return to the days of the communist command economy, there are many in the country, particularly in the Duma, who feel that the government must regain control of its natural resources. With the scandals, the sale of assets, and the absence of effective controls on the production and sale of oil, the idea of renationalizing the oil industry has been discussed. Since this is a radical proposal that emanates from those who are outraged by the recklessness of the powerful oligarchs, there are many obstacles in its path. Nevertheless, the Russian governing leadership has begun to think of ways to ensure that it is gaining the tax revenues from the oil and other natural resources companies, that stockholders are not being bilked by unscrupulous owners, and that some centralized planning and regulation is associated with the former state enterprises.

There is also a renewed emphasis on domestic economic development. Since 1991 the Russian economy has focused on the external sector with international financing, export-generated income, multinational corporate investment, and development models that have stressed the importance of integrating Russia with the global economy. The sad result of this emphasis on the external sector was that Russian agriculture deteriorated markedly, the industrial infrastructure nearly collapsed, and the consumer economy became anemic. To help Russia regain its economic footing, the Putin government has begun to place greater emphasis on key aspects of the domestic economy that have long been neglected. This will not be an easy task. So much attention and resources have been placed on transforming Russia into a "modern" economy that the political and economic elite has forgotten how to feed its people, produce manufactured goods, and provide basic necessities to its people. *89 regioner, rasism, etc*

2 A second category of challenges facing the Russian government is in the area of its relationship with the eighty-nine regions and the scores of ethnic, racial, and cultural groups that live in those regions. The Russian Federation is unquestionably in a state of flux as new problems arise regularly involving issues of autonomy, corruption, budget and revenue, leadership, and economic development. The Russian political leadership will be challenged by conditions and events in the far reaches of the Federation, and the very unity of the Russian nation will be called into question. For example, after a period of tense but peaceful conditions in Chechnya, in 2002 rebel elements reignited their war with the Russian military by shooting down a helicopter, killing 115 soldiers. Even more seriously, in October 2002 forty Chechen terrorists forced their way into a crowded Moscow movie theater and held seven hundred people hostage, threatening to blow up the entire building. In a controversial move Russian security forces injected a form of sleeping gas into the theater, which allowed them to enter the building and kill the terrorists. But in the process they killed over one hundred Russian civilians. The two Chechen incidents awakened Russia to the seriousness of the

Chechen situation and the prospect for continued fighting, not only in that disputed territory but in Moscow as well. *Nationell identitet*

The spirit of national pride and "Russianness" has become a dominant force in the centers of governing power. The public reaction to the Chechen war and the terrorist attacks is evidence of the mood among ethnic Russians that breakaway movements must be crushed. Russia, however, is a country in which the central government has not developed the means to effectively establish control short of war. A middle way needs to be fashioned that permits varying degrees of autonomy and ethnic identity without compromising the need for Moscow to hold the Federation together. Government leaders will be required to formulate new methods of accommodating the natural tendencies of non-Russians to seek "separateness" rather than "Russianness."

Although Russia's challenges remain largely internal, its future relationship with the United States cannot be ignored. Since the collapse of communism and the economic chaos of the Yeltsin years, Russia is no longer on the same power level as the United States. But Russia retains a nuclear capability along with a substantial arsenal of conventional weapons, and the United States, the NATO countries, and neighbors such as China must remain vigilant. The transition from Yeltsin to Putin has raised concerns in the West, particularly the United States, that superpower relations must once again become part of the international agenda.

Now that Putin has made it clear that he intends to make Russia a major player in international affairs, the government will need to channel scarce public resources toward that end. It is popular in Russia to take such a stance after years of backpedaling in the world arena and seeing its influence, both military and diplomatic, decline. There are risks, however, in rejuvenating the Russian superpower role. Russia has fallen so far so fast that any attempt at renewal will be a significant undertaking. There is also the prospect that Putin and his allies in the military may want to reestablish their reputation by challenging U.S. hegemony. It is difficult to predict how Russian relations with the United States will play out in the coming years. Putin's strong support for the United States during the Afghanistan war and his solid relationship with President Bush show that he is treading carefully and not seeking to create a climate of antagonism. Putin's criticism of Bush's Iraq policy in 2003 cast doubt on the strength of the relationship. Russian leaders know that they are no match for the United States in military power and diplomatic influence, yet national pride and the memory of past greatness may be strong enough to spur a renewal of the competition. At that stage some very hard decisions will have to be made both in Moscow and Washington on how to respond to a new superpower competition.

Now that Russia has made the transition to a form of capitalism and democracy, one of the next steps is to become more fully integrated into Europe. This objective will not be easy to accomplish. Boris Yeltsin made valiant efforts to include Russia in the yearly G-7 talks of the major industrial powers, which include the key European nations, but he was often relegated to a kind of observer status. Vladimir Putin began early in his presidency making the rounds of meetings with European leaders (including the pope) in hopes of showing that Russia could play a constructive role in security issues such as the antimissile defense issue, which the Europeans and Russia view in similar ways.

While membership in the European Community is impossible in the short term, Russia views itself as becoming part of a so-called Grand Europe from the Thames to the Volga. But integration with Europe is fraught with apprehension on the part of key countries such as England and Germany over security issues and the instability and unpredictability of the Russian economy. The extension of NATO membership to former East European nations such as Poland, the Czech Republic, and Hungary has caused concern over whether integration is possible in an atmosphere of mutual distrust and the lingering memories of the Cold War. But in an age in which regional economic and security arrangements dominate the international landscape, the likelihood that Russia will continue to pursue policies of integration is strong.

POINT OF FACT
Ronald Englehart, a political scientist at the University of Michigan, published a study (2000) in which he sought to determine the level of well-being or happiness in a number of countries in the world. He found that Russia, along with former Soviet republics like Moldova, Belarus, and the Ukraine, had extremely low well-being scores: "subjective well-being was already extremely low in Russia in 1990, but life satisfaction and happiness have fallen even lower since the collapse of the Communist system and the Soviet Union to such a degree that Russia, Belarus and Ukraine show the lowest levels of subjective well-being ever recorded."

SIBERIAN DEVELOPMENT

The name "Siberia" conjures up visions of endless icy tundra with virgin forests and political prisoners banished to oblivion for their "crimes" against the state. Siberia matches the above description.

The Siberian region spans over 3 million square miles and stretches 22,500 miles from the eastern Urals to the Far East and the regional economic hub at Novosibirsk. It is not only a place of great beauty and potential but a tragically perfect site to send political opponents in hopes that the harsh conditions and the distance will combine to destroy their will. Today, however, Siberia has a much different vision as a result of the Russian government's economic development programs that place a high priority on opening up this region to foreign investment and international trade. The barren oil, natural gas, and timber outposts that mixed with thousands of Stalin's gulags have been transformed into the seventh most economically active region in Russia.

In many respects the Siberian region is reminiscent of the frontier atmosphere in the United States during the late 1800s. Novosibirsk has attracted capitalist entrepreneurs from all over the world seeking to tap into the enormous natural resource potential of the region. Since the 1990s Novosibirsk has grown to a city of 2.8 million people with two hundred heavy industry plants, 11,000 privatized enterprises, and fifty commercial banks. Siberia boasts the highest concentration of industry between the Urals and the Pacific. The boom in economic activity has begun to attract foreign investment. The region is home to nearly four hundred foreign-based joint ventures with China, Korea, and Germany. The United States is new to the region with only thirty enterprises (Pepsi, Eastman Kodak, and 3M), although an American Business Center has been opened in Novosibirsk to assist investment.

Although Siberia is emerging as an industrial center, its lifeblood is the extraction of natural resources. Oil and natural deposits in the region account for over three-fourths of Russia's hard currency receipts. Coal deposits, which exceed 600 billion tons in the region, are critical for the power needs of the nation. Lake Baikal holds one-fifth of the world's supply of fresh water and has enormous hydroelectric potential. And Siberia's 800 square miles of forests with the potential to make 40 billion cubic meters of timber are increasingly being viewed as holding the key to the region's development. There is literally no limit to the opportunities that Siberia affords to the adventurous entrepreneur and foreign investor.

A problem for Siberian development is a deficient infrastructure. Telecommunications are weak, housing is of the crumbling Soviet style, Western amenities are few and far between, and trained personnel are at a premium. Foreign business people constantly complain about the lack of an effective business culture in the region, which is often traced to the absence of effective communications. The common perception of Siberia as the land of ice and political prisoners has contributed to the slow pace of American and European investment. Yet businesspeople who are willing to work through the obstacles have found both opportunity and profit.

Because Siberia has become the Russian economic frontier with rapidly expanding development of key resources and industries, there are disturbing examples of environmental destruction. There is considerable air, water, and soil pollution, as well as dangerous toxic waste dumps near populated areas. Much of the environmental problem is connected to obsolete technology and a lack of governmental regulation. The region's officials and its entrepreneurs are too busy reaping the benefits of an open economy to pay sufficient attention to ecological concerns. Nevertheless, Siberia is fast becoming the region with the greatest potential for environmental decay and serious health problems associated with that decay.

The future of Siberia is summed up in the words of James Whitman, who runs the American Business Center in Novosibirsk: "There is a huge consumer market here for Western branded goods, there are production plants waiting to be upgraded, and there are technologies and know-how here with immense commercial potential. I would encourage serious business people to take a look at Siberia." Apparently Whitman's words are being heeded. ⊕

COMPARISONS

As a nation that has made the transition from a centrally controlled, authoritarian political system to one that is at least structured as a democracy, Russia is not unique. All of its neighbors in Eastern Europe that once made up the Warsaw Pact have followed a similar course, as have the fourteen other communist national entities that were part of the Union of Soviet Socialist Republics. All of these former communist governments have publicly embraced democracy by promulgating constitutions, holding elections, encouraging the formation of parties and interest groups, and expanding individual and group rights; all this as they dismantled the old system with its restrictions and its concentrations of power. Mix

Russian government is a mix of American presidentialism and British parliamentarianism, but there is a strong residue of communist authoritarianism and even a touch of prerevolutionary czarism with its attachment to strong individual leadership and a compliant citizenry. Boris Yeltsin and Vladimir Putin may talk about integration with the West and proudly proclaim that they lead democratic governments similar to those in Washington and London. Yet there is regular evidence that Russia remains tied to its centralized, authoritarian past, valuing strong, individual leadership and looking down on the intricacies of democratic process. As already mentioned, the problems that Russia has faced in establishing a vigorous civil society based on individual initiative and group organization and the weakness and flux within the political party system are clear signs that democratic structure has not been linked with democratic practice.

There is evidence pointing to both elite and popular interest in establishing a workable democracy like those in Western Europe and North America. In a survey conducted in 1999 and 2000 by the Russian Institute of the Academy of Sciences, for example, a cross-section of citizens were asked their views on democracy. Sixty percent responded that democracy was a fairly good or very good form of government in Russia, 87 percent responded that it was important that their leaders be elected, and 85 percent stated that freedom of conscience, expression, and the press were important. Clearly democratic values sit side by side with the remnants of the old way of politics and the old practices of government.

Time and stability are the keys to Russia emerging as a full-fledged democracy with a political and governing system that matches those in North America and Europe. But at the moment Russia is still transitioning away from its past and adjusting to a new mode of public decisionmaking and public power. The Russian governing system may evolve into a Slavic form of presidentialism with weak legislative, judicial, and local institutions headed by an all-powerful central leader. In an emerging democracy like Russia's this kind of compromise form of popular rule and authoritarian action is not unique. Many Latin American countries that moved from repressive military regimes to democratic ones found that the transition was slow and not without pitfalls and reversals. During this transition into the mainstream of Western industrial democracy Russia can be expected to revert to its past even as it focuses on the future.

CONCLUSION

The key responsibility of the Russian Federation is managing and preserving the new democracy. Democracy, despite its tentativeness and its limitations in the postcommunist era, has secured a foothold in the Russian body politic. After over ten years of crisis in government, Russia has entered a new phase of political development. With new leadership at the top and a calming of the political antagonism that nearly destroyed democracy, Russia appears ready to take the next step in its democratization. Perhaps the most serious of the new responsibilities is restoring the Russian people's confidence in their government. While Vladimir Putin has gone a long way in rebuilding the presidency and developing a spirit of national renewal, the Russian president will need to prove to his people that government is not the private enterprise of the oligarchs and that popular opinion and popular sovereignty have meaning. So far Putin has the support of the Russian people. In a poll conducted by Russian academics in 2003, 42 percent of the respondents stated that Putin's work as president was excellent, while only 10 percent gave him a negative rating. Eighty-two percent of the respondents who voted for Putin in 2000 said that they had made the right decision, while only 6 percent regretted their electoral choice.

Convincing the Russian people that their cynicism toward government and their apprehension about the nature of the political process are no longer necessary will be no easy task. Limiting public corruption, building institutions that work, and responding to citizen demands must be linked with government programs that build a democratic tradition in the country. Democracy in Russia now can use a solid shot of good government and the common good. This is not an unattainable ideal but an absolute necessity if Russia is to take the next step forward without falling back into its old ways.

A FEW BOOKS YOU SHOULD READ

Mikhail Gorbachev, *Gorbachev: On My Country and the World* (New York: Columbia University Press, 1999). The last leader of the Soviet Union gives his views on how the communist system ended.

Harry Eckstein et al., *Can Democracy Take Root in Russia? Explorations in State-Society Relations* (Lanham, Md.: Rowman & Littlefield, 1998). As the title suggests, a study in one of the key sectors of public life on which the future of democracy hinges.

Geoffrey Hosking, *Russia and the Russians: A History* (Cambridge: Harvard University Press, 2001). As described by the reviewer in *Foreign Affairs*, this is the "King James version of Russian history."

Michael McFaul, *Russia's Unfinished Revolution: Political Change from Gorbachev to Putin* (Ithaca: Cornell University Press, 2001). One of the best contemporary studies of Russia.

Peter Raddaway and Dmitri Glinski, *The Tragedy of Russia's Reforms: Market Bolshevism Against Democracy* (Herndon, Va.: U.S. Institute of Peace, 2000). A critical examination of the transition from communism to a market economy.

A FEW WEB SITES YOU SHOULD VISIT

www.moscowtimes.ru. An English-language Web site that provides daily news items about Russia.

www.russiatoday.com. A comprehensive site on business and economic concerns in English.

www.fednews.ru. Moscow's most important press conferences, speeches, newspaper articles, and TV reports.

www.rferl.org. Radio Free Europe/Radio Liberty Web site with excellent analysis of the contemporary Russian scene, particularly politics and public policy.

www.nns.ru. National News Service site with solid reporting and analysis.

Sapporo

Sendai

Tokyo
Kawasaki ★
Nagoya Yokohama
Kyoto
Kobe
Okayama Osaka
Hiroshima
Kitakyushu
Eukuoka

Kagoshima

MAP 4.1   Japan

4

Japan

Data Bank

Area: 145,856 sq. miles
Population: 126.2 million (1998)
Rural/urban ratio: 22/78
Ethnic makeup: Japanese; 0.6 percent Korean
Life expectancy: Male, 77 years; female, 83 years
Adult literacy: 99 percent
Per capita income/GDP: $30,990 (2002)
Form of government: Constitutional monarchy with a parliamentary
    government
Head of state: Emperor Akihito
Head of government: Prime Minister Junichiro Koizumi
Exports: $413 billion; imports $306 billion (partners: United States,
    China, Taiwan)
Source: United Nations and World Bank

SETTING THE SCENE

What is Japan? That is a question without an easy answer. Japan is an Asian nation that is allied with the major industrial democracies of the West. Yet Japan differs from North American and European countries in a number of societal characteristics from work habits to lifestyle to business practices to value systems. Its philosophical, cultural, and historical roots make it far different from the three countries examined in earlier chapters. As a result Japan is pulled between West and East, which makes a simple definition of Japan and the Japanese people difficult to formulate. Westerners are comfortable with the Japan that is like them, but the aspects of national life that stem from Japan's "other side" create mystery and accent differences.

Unfortunately, much of what Westerners know about Japan comes as quick images from television, movies, and popular culture. Too often stereotypes and gross caricatures have made their way into the common consciousness. There is a general recognition of the Japanese flag with the red circle on the white background, Godzilla movies, Nintendo games, and Pokemon cards, and of course the cars, VCRs, pianos, motorcycles, and electronic games that have "Made in Japan" stamped on them. Much of what we know about Japan is obtained from bits and pieces of information—World War II footage of Pearl Harbor and Hiroshima, the regimented environment of grade school and high school classrooms, and the traditional bow used as a greeting by the sararimen, the ubiquitous company man of Japanese business. There is familiarity with the surface minutiae of Japan, but not a great deal that would help answer the question, What is Japan?

The most familiar observation about Japan is that it has become an economic giant, and achieved this status in a phenomenally short period of time. Despite the devastating economic and psychological impact of losing World War II, the Japanese quickly rebounded, thanks in part to the domestic needs of the United States and its allies during the Korean War. Between 1954 and 1970 growth rates in Japan were consistently in the 10 percent range. In 1967 Japan showed its economic muscle by becoming the world's third largest producer of crude steel and aluminum and the largest shipbuilder. By 1980 Japan had surpassed the United States in automobile production. Throughout most of the 1990s Japan established itself as the world's third largest trader (after the United States and Germany), enjoyed the second largest gross domestic product (ranking after the United States), and led the world in providing foreign assistance to the developing world.

General discussions of Japan make little mention of politics, government, and political leaders. One of the mysteries of Japanese national life is how the great prosperity the country has enjoyed could have been achieved in a governing atmosphere of weak institutions, scandal-ridden politics, and ever changing political leaders. Japan is not known as a place where statesmen or politicians shape the national landscape. Nor is Japan known for its model legislature or court system. Japan appears to have moved to the front lines of world economic power through means other than the established political and governmental processes. As we will see, in Japan government power is substantial and critical, but it is not located in the places where one would normally look.

An answer to the question, What is Japan? may be found by viewing the country as a place of contrasts and contradictions, where appearances hide reality and all is not what it seems. Japan is a country that reveres the old and the traditional while embracing the new. Japan is also a country that steeps itself in isolation and fear of Western influence while reaching out to the world. And Japan is a country that resists change but engages in major upheavals and transformations that are reshaping the face of this island nation. In every area of national life these contrasts and contradictions create a society that is seeking to find the proper balance and avoid the confusion and conflict that come with an inability to strike that balance.

This strange mix of East and West, old and new, is everywhere in Japan. Postcard images of Japan often show the impressive Shinto temples where the Japanese quietly pray to their ancestors, the orderly and simply decorated homes where age-old customs such as leaving the shoes outside the door are followed, and the beautiful grounds of the Imperial Palace with their finely manicured water gardens and their traditional chrysanthemums. But side by side with these signs of beauty, serenity, and tradition exists the garish commercialism of the Ginza district, the ruthless and secretive trade and business practices of Japanese corporations, and the embarrassing financial scandals that constantly grip the political scene. A visitor to Japan may marvel at the contrasts and the contradictions as signs of effective blending, when in reality Japan is a nation in the throes of a difficult self-definition that is dividing all sectors of national life.

Political leadership is handled differently in Japan. The position of prime minister is akin to a game of musical chairs with political leaders coming and going while the real power resides in key ministries and corporate groupings. For all the apparent political change in Japan, the governing system is inherently conservative and unwilling to engage in substantive reform or major restructuring. If the governing system is responsive, it is to the large corporate groups, or *keiretsus,* that often advance their interests by illegal campaign financing deals, special contract arrangements, payoffs, and bribes. The image of the respectful Japanese politician runs contrary to the frequent scandals that have tarnished the political process.

It is in the economic realm that Japan shows its most pronounced contrasts and engages in its most painful introspection. Japan is nominally capitalistic in that private enterprise is the core of the economy; in reality Japanese capitalism is state supported and state directed. Ministries such as MITI, the Ministry of International Trade and Industry, play a pivotal role in developing new industries, protecting existing industries, raising investment capital, providing trade assistance, and formulating national strategic plans. The heavy involvement of state bureaucracies in the economy and the penchant for the bureaucracies to employ numerous protectionist methods has been a sore point for foreign countries and businesses seeking to enter the Japanese market. In a global economy, where free trade and easy access to markets are the watchwords, Japan is viewed as slow to break down barriers and unwilling to make the tough political decisions necessary to pry the economy away from its parochialism and protectionism.

Searching for an answer to the question, What is Japan? has become more difficult as a result of the recession that began in the early 1990s. Japan's economic troubles have not only spawned a serious societal malaise but intensified calls for a major overhaul of the economic and political systems. Unemployment, once almost invisible in the Japan of company men who earned lifetime jobs, has reached 5 percent in 2002 and 2003. Moreover, the concept of seniority has been weakened significantly as companies seek to improve their balance sheets. At present it is estimated that one in eight Japanese families has been hit by unemployment. Joblessness and a lack of a secure future have also affected a number of other areas of Japanese national life. Suicides have increased 53 percent since 1991. Homelessness is now a visible scourge on society, where a few years ago the problem was nonexistent. Crime, particularly youth crime, is on the rise with a number of gruesome murders perpetrated by teenagers. Finally, prostitution has become rampant, with "telephone clubs" attracting teenage girls anxious to make extra money in an increasingly difficult economic climate.

The old balances that kept Japan secure and stable are being challenged with greater regularity. The elites are facing hostile public opinion from a generation that does not accept the systems that have been in place since 1945. New economic entrepreneurs are cropping up and alternative political movements are starting to form. The staid economic and political elite is desperately seeking a formula that allows them to remain in power by tinkering with their systems instead of embracing a major overhaul or permitting a Japanese version of Margaret Thatcher to take over the reins of power. This push and pull between the old and new, the conservative and the reformer, is not about to subside. It will remain at the heart of Japanese society for years come. The side that wins the push and pull will be able to answer the question, What is Japan?

POINT OF FACT
Japan is one of the world's most densely populated nations. It ranks fifth, with 337 people per square kilometer.

POLITICAL MILESTONES

The political history of Japan is best approached from the perspective of a recurring theme involving a struggle between isolation from the outside world and acceptance of Western modernization. Throughout its history, dating back to some of the first recorded signs of a distinct Japanese society and culture in 660 B.C. (the year in which Jimmu, Japan's first emperor, was enthroned), Japan has been defined in terms of responding to external forces. The tribal clans, who most likely had their origin in Korea, succeeded in establishing the beginnings of a recognizable state that was often wary of what lay beyond its border. But the insular character of Japan did not isolate it from foreign ideas and philosophies like Chinese Confucianism, explorers and traders from Portugal and the Netherlands, and the whole range of inventions and technical know-how from Western countries outside its protective cocoon. At key points in Japan's evolution into a modern nation-state this need to keep the outside world at a distance despite external pressures and opportunities has been a determining factor in shaping political development.

Japanese leaders have responded to outside forces and pressures by seeking avenues of change that mesh with their culture and value system. The Japanese have become masters of giving the appearance of accommodating Western demands and grafting on Western economic and political models, while maintaining control of the change process. At times this reluctance to be pushed into rapid and comprehensive restructuring of societal norms and business practices served the Japanese well and allowed elites and institutions to avoid compromising their power base and their mode of operation. But this fundamental drive to manage what comes from the outside world also comes with a downside as Japan, particularly in recent years, has been faced with a serious economic downturn. Japan is at a historic crossroads as it seeks to maintain its traditional control of the external world in the face of a new global economic system that is unforgiving and does not recognize or tolerate the age-old reluctance to change.

The Tokugawa Shogunate

Throughout most of Japan's early history there was little centralized political control. Japan was a loose network of feudal estates controlled by warrior/administrators called samurai. In 1192 one of these samurai, Minamoto Yoritomo, was successful in unifying the country and in the process declared himself shogun (translated as "barbarian-subduing generalissimo"). Minamoto set the tone for political organization in Japan by forming a military-style regime that accented discipline and obedience to the various feudal lords and the shogun. When the Mongol leader Kublai Khan invaded Japan in the thirteenth century, the samurai repelled the attack, but all semblance of centralized rule was destroyed. Japan returned to its feudal roots and withdrew into isolation as it shut off all contact with the outside world. It would take the forceful campaign of Tokugawa Ieyasu to bring Japan back together again.

The Tokugawa shogunate, which existed from 1603 to its collapse in 1867, was profoundly influenced by the arrival of U.S. Commodore Matthew Perry in 1853. Tokugawa was a master of balancing competing interests, which was essential in a governing environment made up of numerous feudal lords, or *daimyo*. Tokugawa moved the capital city to Edo (now Tokyo) and required the *daimyo* to reside in the new capital throughout much of the year, thereby reducing their capacity to challenge central rule. Tokugawa transformed the emperor into a largely ceremonial role, thus eliminating a potential threat to his power. The identifying characteristic of the Tokugawa shogunate was a rigid social system. Similar to a caste system as practiced in India, the Tokugawa hierarchy placed nobles at the top of the system followed by the samurai, farmers, artisans, merchants, and a bottom caste (the Japanese referred to these people as the "filthy horde" and the "nonhumans").

The rigidity and isolation of the Tokugawa shogunate could not be sustained indefinitely. The event that precipitated the downfall of the Tokugawa family was the arrival of Commodore Matthew C. Perry. Sent by President Millard Fillmore to explore the possibilities of opening trade relations with Japan, Perry entered Tokyo harbor in 1853. Perry was not a welcome visitor to Japan as the Tokugawa leaders maintained their animus toward Western influences. Perry, however, entered Japanese waters with a flotilla of warships that struck fear in the government. The Tokugawa government sought to put off Perry and his trade demands by asking the Americans to return in a year. During that year Japanese elites engaged in a crucial domestic debate over whether to hold fast to the centuries-old policy banning contact with foreign countries. Faced with the returning firepower of Perry's navy and internal dissension, the Tokugawa rulers agreed to the American demands and lifted the ban. Japan would never be the same.

The arrival of Commodore Perry in Japan set off an internal revolution in the country led by a new generation of samurai loyal to the sixteen-year-old emperor of the Meiji clan in 1867. The Meiji Restoration began a new era in Japan as the governing elite sought to open the country to Western ideas, education, and technology. The Tokugawa shogunate with its fierce isolationism came to an end, although underlying concern over Western impact on Japanese values and culture remained in the national psyche. Japan was suspicious of the West and looked for ways to retain its traditions, despite the attractiveness of what external forces brought to its shore.

The Meiji Period

The ascension to the imperial throne of Emperor Meiji spelled the end of the shogun, the *daimyo,* and the feudal system. The capital was officially established at Edo and renamed Tokyo, and the feudal estates with the peasant class were returned to the authority of the emperor. Most importantly, Japan began the process of ending its ban on all things Western. Many of the reconstituted samurai took advantage of the opening with the West to embrace modernization initiatives in industry and commerce, education and the military. Foreign interests eagerly arrived in the country and brought with them the latest Western inventions and techniques such as steelmaking, shipbuilding, medicine, and weaponry. The Japanese recognized that the isolationist policy of the Tokugawa period had put them far behind the Western world. Consequently they moved with determination to modernize not only the economic sphere but also the governmental organization.

One of the significant accomplishments of the Meiji period was the promulgation of a constitution. In 1889, through the leadership of Count Ito Hirobumi, Japan further westernized by establishing a parliamentary system with a bicameral legislature (the Diet) and a prime minister. The Diet was organized around a House of Peers made up of aristocrats and a House of Representatives. The Diet was narrowly representative as the members were elected by wealthy taxpayers. The introduction of a Western governing system was severely restricted by imperial control and by a small group of elder statesmen, or *genro*. The prime minister was appointed by the emperor, and the Diet had little power to challenge the decisions of the emperor or the *genro*. The emperor also asserted his complete control over the military, thus stripping the armed forces of any civilian democratic oversight. In typical Japanese fashion, the introduction of Western-style parliamentary democracy was severely compromised by the powers given the emperor and the behind-the-scenes influence of the *genro* and the military. Japan modernized itself while maintaining its tradition of central control.

As the Meiji period evolved, the Japanese governing system took on more democratic characteristics. During the Taisho period (1912–1926) political parties came on the scene. The most significant party, Sieyukai, was at the center of government formation and became a model for the Liberal Democratic Party of the modern era. It was also during the Taisho period that the Manhood Universal Suffrage Law was passed. The law moved Japan away from its reliance on national tax payments as the source of suffrage and extended the vote to adult males. Tradition-bound Japan did not extend suffrage to females. The formation of political parties and the extension of suffrage, however, did little to change the underlying character of Japanese government, which became increasingly authoritarian and elitist. The Japanese people did not protest the weakness of the democratic institutions and the limitations of democratic practice. Rather, they had great confidence in the emperor's judgment and agreed to having public policy decisions made from the throne.

The Meiji period is remembered as a time when the Japanese entered the world. Not only did Japan allow Western nations access to its economy, but it sent government officials and business leaders to the United States and Europe to examine the manner in which these countries modernized. This was an exciting time in Japan as the nation and its people were introduced to a level of newness that they had never before experienced. Economic data from the period show that during the thirty years from the late 1800s to the conclusion of World War I Japan made major economic strides. Relying on low labor costs and a disciplined business climate, the Japanese became a formidable economic force. Giant corporate groupings called *zaibatsu* working cooperatively with government bureaucrats gave Japan the order, focus, and planning necessary to become competitive in the world economy. However, macroeconomic growth levels in Japan did not translate into social mobility. In fact the push toward Western modernization had little impact on the average Japanese. Fortunately for the elite, with a supportive and obedient population, Japanese leaders did not have to be concerned about social instability or political uprising.

Japanese Militarism

During the Meiji period the nationalist slogan that became the watchword for modern Japan was "rich nation, strong army." Although Japan focused on strengthening its economy by opening up to the world, it was also building a substantial military machine. Powerful army and navy staff offices were given nearly complete authority (subject only to limits placed by the throne) to develop an armed force equal to the Western ones. With such authorization the Japanese military became a force independent of civilian political control. The military became bolder and more antidemocratic, especially after its victories in the Sino-Japanese War (1894–1895) and the Russo-Japanese War (1904–1905). There were coup attempts, assassinations of cabinet members, and weak prime ministers. Military leaders occupied key ministerial positions and often exercised veto power over domestic and foreign policy. The imperial throne, occupied in 1926 by the youthful Hirohito, did little if anything to control the excesses of the military.

In 1931 the Japanese military initiated its expansionist policy by seizing all of Manchuria and establishing a collaborationist government. Manchuria was seen by the military as a vital economic center for Japanese goods and suitable as the first step in its grand scheme of dominating all of Asia. The invasion of Manchuria was condemned by the international community, but Japanese military leaders were unfazed. In fact Japan left the League of Nations, signaling that it did not intend to be bound by international agreements or subject to international diplomacy. Tensions heightened in the region when Japan and China went to war in 1937. In one of the most deplorable acts of Japanese aggression, the Chinese capital city of Nanking was invaded and thousands of civilians killed. The "rape of Nanking" remains a source of ill will between China and Japan.

Japan was now in full-scale expansionist mode. By the beginning of 1940 Japan controlled eastern China, Southeast Asia, Korea, Taiwan, and the Philippines. The military leaders allied the nation with the fascist governments of Germany and Italy and promised a "new order" in both Europe and Asia. The only major power left in its sphere of control was the United States with its major naval base in Hawaii and its formidable fleet docked at Pearl Harbor. If Japan wanted to complete its dominance of Asia, it would have to drive the United States out of Hawaii and destroy its navy. The initial dispute between the Japan and the United States was over access to petroleum. In 1939 the United States ended its trade agreement with Japan, which denied the Japanese a steady supply of oil. When the Japanese continued its expansionist policies in Indochina, the United States froze privately held assets. The Japanese, sensing that the United States was a threat to its economic security and its designs on the region, prepared to retaliate.

On December 7, 1941, the Japanese attacked Pearl Harbor and destroyed most of the naval vessels docked there. The Roosevelt administration immediately declared war on Japan and began a bloody four-year struggle to end Japanese hegemony. From a military perspective the attack on Pearl Harbor was the zenith of Japanese expansionism. From that point on Japan experienced stinging defeats at the hands of the United States and other allied powers. The culmination of the Japanese defeat in the Pacific was the decision by the Truman administration to drop atomic bombs on Hiroshima and Nagasaki in 1945. American leaders rejected an invasion of Japan as too long and too costly in human lives in favor of dropping the two bombs in hopes that the devastation would bring the Japanese military to its knees and end the war. In August 1945 the only two atomic bombs ever used on mankind were dropped from U.S. bombers, creating widespread destruction and killing 80,000 civilians. Within days Emperor Hirohito went on Japanese radio to inform his people that "developments in the war have not necessarily gone so well as Japan might have wished." On September 2, 1945, Japan surrendered.

The surrender marked the end of the war as well as the end of Japanese militarism and the tacit support of the military by the imperial throne. Japan was devastated economically, and its ambition of becoming a "rich nation" with a "strong army" was shattered. The atomic bombs and the unconditional surrender brought Japan to another critical juncture in its history. This time, however, change came in the form of outside control rather than outside contact.

Emperor Hirohito met with the American version of an emperor in General Douglas MacArthur. MacArthur and his occupiers ensured that the Japanese military held a severely diminished position in the hierarchy of government power. But most importantly, democratic values, practices, and institutions, which had received lip service since the Meiji period, began to play a more substantial role in national life. After centuries of authoritarian control by emperors, shoguns, and the samurai class, Japan belatedly entered the world of popular participation and pluralistic decisionmaking.

The Occupation

The American presence in postwar Japan had an enormous influence on government and politics. Japan's unconditional surrender meant that the occupying forces had almost unlimited power to shape both domestic and foreign policy. To oversee the postwar transition, President Truman appointed General Douglas MacArthur supreme commander of the allied powers (SCAP). MacArthur's authority was extensive. Although Emperor Hirohito remained on the throne (but not as a "living god") and the government continued to function through bureaucratic directives, real power resided with MacArthur. In many cases MacArthur issued an order that the Japanese government implemented. While such complete control over a nation's sovereignty would normally create tensions between the occupied and the occupiers, there was little in the way of conflict in U.S.-dominated postwar Japan. General MacArthur, in fact, was a popular figure who worked diligently to ensure that the occupation would be a peaceful and productive process.

The most visible change effected by MacArthur and the American occupiers was the demilitarization of Japan. Japanese military and naval forces were disarmed and military personnel were discharged from duty. For approximately five years Japan had no military establishment, except for a modest 75,000 National Police Reserve. But by the 1950s and with the outbreak of the Korean War, a self-defense force was developed with modest personnel levels and budget appropriations. The most troublesome aspect of the postwar demilitarization of Japan was the International Military Tribunal for the Far East, which brought to trial Japanese military officials charged with violating the Geneva Convention regarding the laws of war. Many Japanese command staff members were brought before this tribunal, along with members of militaristic organizations. These Japanese leaders were also declared unfit to hold public office. All together some 200,000 officials were purged as a result of this tribunal process.

In one of MacArthur's more controversial decisions, Emperor Hirohito was not targeted for his involvement in the war and his participation in military decisionmaking. Despite pressure from some in the United States who viewed the emperor as deserving of inclusion in a war crimes tribunal, MacArthur was reluctant to take that step, since he appreciated the deep feelings of reverence that the Japanese people had for Hirohito and the monarchy's importance as a symbol of Japan. Instead, MacArthur transformed the emperor into a ceremonial figurehead and separated him from the center of policymaking power.

The centerpiece of the American occupation was the creation of a constitution. Early in the occupation, Japanese government officials were reluctant to endorse a new constitution or accede to American pressures for significant constitutional reform. The Japanese were of the opinion that major constitutional reform or a new constitution would bring wholesale changes to the established governing system. Japanese foot dragging forced MacArthur's hand, and in 1946 the Government Section of the SCAP drafted a constitutional document that firmly established democratic sovereignty and basic human rights, and transformed the emperor into a "symbol of the State and of the unity of the people," rather than a head of state with specific powers and responsibilities. Although MacArthur placed his mark on the Japanese constitution, he retained the British parliamentary system of executive-legislative relations and the prefecture system of local government.

The occupation of Japan ended in 1952. By then General MacArthur had already made a new and controversial reputation in the Korean War theater. The allied occupation of Japan had a profound impact on national life. The SCAP had introduced reform in a number of areas, from the government to the economy to agriculture to education. It had developed a constitution that gave the Japanese an expanded role in their country and guarantees of personal liberties. It also laid the groundwork for Japan's economic resurgence through financial assistance and management of economic policy, as well as providing a stabilizing influence at a time when the country was near collapse. Critics of the American occupation were upset by the weakening of the emperor and the demilitarization. But Japan never developed an anti-Americanism or complained about having a system imposed on them. Rather the Japanese accepted the American system, copied what they liked, and worked to limit the influence of the characteristics they found offensive or against their interests. Japan became a Western-style nation with a market economy linked to a democratic government. The process of westernization moved forward on its own terms and at its own speed.

Liberal Democratic Dominance

Modern Japanese politics in the postwar period has been democratic in the sense that all the signs of popular participation have been in evidence. But the near total domination of the Liberal Democratic Party since the American occupation moved the country into a "special" category of democracy. From 1955 to 1993 the Liberal Democratic Party had either a solid majority or a substantial plurality in the Diet, permitting it to attain uncontested control over the policy process. In the 1993 general election the Liberal Democrats endured their most stunning defeat as the Japanese electorate turned against them due to continued campaign and government scandals. But within three years the Liberal Democrats were again in control, although short of an outright majority in the more important legislative body, the House of Representatives. The Liberal Democrats remain at the core of political and governing power, and in order to understand the postoccupation period, it is necessary to examine the impact that one-party democracy has had on the development of Japan.

In the early years of their control, the Liberal Democrats paid close attention to Japan's relationship with the United States. In 1960 the government sought to renegotiate the U.S.-Japan Mutual Security Treaty to make some adjustments to the relationship with the United States but keep the agreement in force. The revision initiative sparked one of the most serious political crises that the Liberal Democrats faced while in power. Socialists in the Diet joined by leftist unions and student groups challenged the renegotiation effort as a sham that would maintain U.S. military influence in Japan. But the Liberal Democrats, using their overwhelming numbers in the Diet, pushed the new treaty through even though it faced widespread public opposition. This was one of the first signs that the Liberal Democrats saw themselves as occupying a "special" position in the political process that allowed them to ignore the public will.

Stung by the virulence of the opposition to their foreign policy initiative with the United States, the Liberal Democrats concentrated on economic policies that would advance Japan's growing trade status and deal with recurring problems associated with the price and availability of imported oil, the lifeblood of the country's resurgence. In 1973 and 1979 Liberal Democratic governments faced "oil shocks" as a result of the Arab oil embargo and the Iranian revolution. These shocks posed a challenge to the capability of the Liberal Democratic government to manage an economy that depended almost exclusively on imported oil.

Although the "oil shocks" did not shake the popularity of the Liberal Democrats, recurring scandals involving party leaders, ministers, and even prime ministers created a groundswell of opposition that led to a general downturn in support. In 1974 Prime Minister Kakuei Tanaka resigned his position in the wake of charges that he accepted a $1.6 million bribe from

Lockheed, an American airplane manufacturer. In 1988 a number of Liberal Democratic party officials and government officials were charged with illegally reaping profits from the acquisition of shares in a real estate subsidiary of the publishing conglomerate Recruit. Former Prime Minister Nakasone admitted to an $800,000 return and Prime Minister Takeshita acknowledged a $1 million benefit. Overall forty-three politicians, ministers, and businessmen resigned their posts (including the chairman of the Clean Government Party) in the scandal, and eventually Prime Minister Takeshita left office.

As Japan entered the 1990s, the trail of scandal in the Liberal Democratic Party widened even further. In 1992 the government of Miyazawa Kiichi was hit by the most serious financial scandal in Japan's history. Over two hundred politicians in the Liberal Democratic Party were accused of accepting payments totaling $650 million from a parcel delivery firm. The scandal forced the resignation of the party's most powerful insider, Shin Kanemaru, and a general weakening of the Liberal Democrats in the Diet. The Miyazawa scandal is often viewed as the triggering factor in the 1993 electoral defeat of the Liberal Democrats. But when the party regained power in 1996 after weak and ineffective coalition governments, the corruption scandals continued.

The Liberal Democrats won again in the 2000 elections, but the party no longer commanded the respect of the Japanese people. Voter turnout was a low 62 percent; 50 percent of the Japanese electorate stated that they had no particular preference for a political party, an astounding turnaround from past overwhelming support for the Liberal Democrats. Moreover, in a public opinion poll at the time three out of four Japanese citizens stated that they had no expectations about the ability of the new Prime Minister Yoshiro Mori to accomplish any significant policy initiatives. The result was that the Liberal Democrats and the entire Japanese political establishment were wracked by self-doubt and immobility. After a less than lackluster performance as prime minister, Yoshiro Mori was replaced by Junichiro Koizumi, a nonconformist politician with long hair and a penchant for baseball and rock music. Koizumi was not supported by the old-line establishment in the Liberal Democratic Party, but reform elements were successful in overcoming opposition to the new Prime Minister. Koizumi immediately brought a level of energy to Japanese politics that had been missing, and many hoped that he would be able to break the hold of the party establishment. Koizumi, however, had his work cut out for him as the deepening recession and resistance to reform by key sectors of the economy such as banking and construction posed an enormous challenge for the youthful prime minister and indeed for all of Japan.

Timeline	
1600–1868	Tokugawa dynasty; isolation from West
1868–1912	Meiji Restoration; Western modernization
1912–1945	Period of militarization
1937	Invasion of China
1941	Attack on Pearl Harbor
1945	Japan surrenders
1946	New constitution; influence of General MacArthur
1951	Japanese Peace Treaty restores sovereignty
1955	Liberal Democratic Party formed
1976	Prime Minister Tanaka arrested in Lockheed scandal
1980s	"Bubble economy" period of dramatic economic growth
1990	Emperor Hirohito dies; Prince Akihito ascends throne
1993	LDP loses control of House of Representatives
1997	Japanese economy begins long period of recession
2000	Prime Minister Koizumi assumes power

AGRICULTURAL POLICY

Although Japan is commonly thought of as an urban society with huge population centers and massive overcrowding, there is a second Japan, the Japan of rural life where tiny farms dot the landscape (on average only 2.5 acres) and hardworking farmers toil in their rice fields. Today about 6 percent of the Japanese population is engaged in farming. While Japan has more farmers than most industrial societies have, the farm population is shrinking and the ability of farmers to make a living is being threatened. Ninety percent of the farmers in Japan work part-time, forced to supplement their income with nonfarm employment because the profit margin from the yield of their rice crop has dwindled considerably in the wake of deregulation policies. Just like the rest of the Japanese economy, globalization, with its emphasis on free trade and competition, has had a significant impact on the agricultural sector.

At the heart of Japanese farming is the yearly 10 million ton rice harvest, which has been the primary source of agricultural income as well as the target of foreign pressure to end protective tariffs and government subsidies. The Japanese government has over the years bowed to powerful farming interests, such as the nationwide agricultural cooperative organization, Nokyo, and set prohibitive tariff barriers to keep out foreign rice. In addition, the government has fostered a compulsory program to set aside 30 percent of the paddy rice each year in order to limit the crop and keep prices artificially high. The government program was so rigid that if individual farmers refused to set aside 30 percent of their crop, the entire farming community in the village would not benefit from the price support program. These policies have created a pricing system for rice that has made this staple commodity extremely expensive for the Japanese consumer and the source of ongoing tension between rice-producing nations such as the United States, Australia, Uruguay, and Argentina that want to gain access to the lucrative Japanese market.

Change in the agricultural sector and in the availability and pricing of rice came in 1994 when the government, pressured by the Uruguay Round of the General Agreement on Tariffs and Trade (GATT) treaties, passed the New Food Law. This law restructured the food control system in Japan governing rice production and distribution. As a result of this law private companies can now serve as rice collectors, wholesalers, and retailers, and the government's role was reduced. The end result was that domestic competition in rice production and distribution increased. Although the agricultural sector has seen the beginning of deregulation, the powerful farm lobbies and pro-farm politicians in the LDP and the ministries continue to seek prohibitive tariffs against foreign rice. In 1999 the European Union joined Australia and other Latin American countries in protesting the imposition of a 390 percent supertariff on rice imports as a violation of the GATT agreement. Furthermore, although Japan agreed to import rice equal to 8 percent of total consumption, it has been delaying implementation of this agreement, again in large part because of pressure from the powerful farm lobby.

The efforts of the Japanese government to protect its farmers and control the price of its prized rice crop may be difficult to sustain. Because of the GATT agreement 150 agricultural products that heretofore had been protected by import restrictions were eliminated. Only a dozen farm crops, including rice, received some protections. Also the agricultural sector is undergoing major restructuring as is evidenced by revisions to the Farmland Law, which has defined farm ownership. New language in the law allows corporate ownership of farming, a move that has changed the character of rural life in Japan as huge business entities have begun to buy up land and in the process have pushed the small farmer out. Most importantly, competition is now the watchword of farming in Japan. No longer will farmers have the security of government tariff protection and subsidies. The marketplace now rules, which has brought down prices for agricultural crops such as rice but has begun the impoverishment of the farmer and the destruction of the family farm. ⊕

FORMAL GOVERNMENT

In many ways the most significant change in the structure of the Japanese government in the postwar period was the SCAP decision to convert the country from an absolute monarchy to a constitutional monarchy. In the constitution that was promulgated on November 3, 1946, and put into operation on May 3, 1947, the transformation of the throne meant that the imperial authority, which was based on divine association and emperor worship, was replaced by the American principle of separation of church and state. The Shinto beliefs that formed the basis of the emperor's divine authority were removed from public life. Power and governing responsibility shifted as the new constitution established sovereignty in the Japanese people and made clear that all the emperor's decisions required the advice and consent of the governing cabinet.

Since the promulgation of the new Japanese constitution, the monarchy has kept a low profile in matters of politics and government. In fact the royal family is perhaps one of the most isolated in modern times. It is only in recent years that the Japanese press has sought to inform the Japanese readers about the family life of the monarchy. The current emperor, Akihito, who is the son of Emperor Hirohito, has been reluctant to assume a visible role in national affairs. He makes an occasional public speech and confers with the government, although not as a decisionmaker. Although the emperor is officially out of the governing stream, his standing in Japanese society has not diminished. There are still monarchist elements in Japan that yearn for a larger role for the emperor. Prime Minister Yoshiro Mori got into a political controversy in 2000 when he called Japan a "divine country with the emperor at the center." Although Mori stated that he was merely emphasizing the role that the emperor has played in Japanese history and culture, opposition leaders immediately jumped on the comment and asked for his resignation, underscoring the fact that Japan is a country with a new tradition of popular sovereignty.

The constitution entrusted governing power to the legislative branch, the Diet. The Japanese Diet is a bicameral legislative body made up of the House of Representatives (which dates back to the Meiji period) and the House of Councillors, which replaced the House of Peers (the new constitution abolished the peerage). The constitution specifies that the Diet is the "highest organ of state power." The House of Representatives is the key legislative body. It consists of five hundred legislators, three hundred elected from single-member districts and two hundred named as a result of proportional allocation of seats from party lists in eleven regions. The House of Representatives is the body from which the Japanese prime minister is selected in traditional parliamentary fashion. The House of Representatives has the power to pass a motion of no confidence against the cabinet, whereupon the government must resign or take an equally serious measure and dissolve the legislature. The House of Representatives has greater power than the House of Councillors in that it has the capability to override opposition to budget and treaty bills. Also, the House of Representatives has the responsibility to investigate matters of general government importance, a power that has been used extensively in recent years as campaign and ministerial scandals have rocked the Liberal Democratic Party.

The other legislative body, the House of Councillors, is made up of 252 members who are elected for six-year terms; 152 councillors are elected from Japan's forty-seven prefectures, while an additional 100 councillors are elected in national party preference elections. The House of Councillors has been forced to take a backseat to the power of the House of Representatives, particularly in budgetary matters. Because its membership is skewed toward rural and small business interests, the House of Councillors has gained a power status that cannot be ignored. The House of Councillors has found legislative influence in the power of delay. Much like the House of Lords in Britain, the House of Councillors exercises its influence by ensuring that legislation from the House of Representatives is not pushed through quickly or without careful examination. There is also some evidence that the House of Councillors, given a weak governing environment, can exercise power. In 1998 the councillors passed a motion of censure against a cabinet minister who was involved in an arms procurement scandal. The vote had no legal authority, but it embarrassed the government and forced the prime minister to revise his legislative strategy.

The Japanese Diet has elements from both the Westminster parliamentary and the American legislative system. The Diet has the power to require cabinet ministers to come before it and answer questions about government policy in a manner similar to the British question hour. Like the American legislature, the Japanese Diet is organized around a number of standing committees, which accent expertise and develop power centers that can initiate legislation and challenge bills that emanate from the cabinet.

As in many other parliamentary systems, the Japanese prime minister and the cabinet compose the formal core of the governing system. Differing from many parliamentary systems, the prime minister and the cabinet have become indistinguishable and interchangeable parts in the political process. Because of factionalism in the ruling Liberal Democratic Party, periodic scandals, and recent economic problems, Japan has changed prime ministers regularly and shuffled its cabinet continuously. Japan is now on its twenty-sixth prime minister since 1945 and the cabinet changes are too numerous to count. In Japanese government the chief executive is weak, as party leaders, key government ministers, and the heads of the corporate groupings often carry more political weight than the prime minister. The constitution of 1947 eliminated many of the key participants in making national public policy like the emperor, the *genro*, and of course the military high command, but the prime minister has not evolved into a position of preeminent power. The prime minister has become more of a political caretaker and administrator than a national leader. Few Japanese prime ministers have risen to the level of prominence enjoyed by their counterparts in Europe.

Despite the political weakness of Japanese prime ministers, they exercise a range of constitutional duties and responsibilities. The constitution states that the prime minister holds the power of commander in chief and has the responsibility to declare a state of national emergency. Furthermore, the prime minister has the power to appoint and remove ministers and to serve as chief executive by supervising the bureaucratic establishment. He reports to the Diet on the state of the nation and approves or disapproves public laws and cabinet actions. In Japan the prime minister names the Supreme Court chief justice along with lower court justices, calls the Diet into emergency session, and advises the emperor on public policy issues.

As for the cabinet, the constitution authorizes a number of important powers and responsibilities including preparing the budget, conducting the affairs of state, and engaging in foreign relations. The appointment of cabinet members is closely tied to party politics rather than expertise. Because of the factionalism in the Liberal Democratic Party, prime ministers are constantly seeking ways to shore up their position and power by new appointments, shufflings, and dismissals. As in the Westminster system, the prime minister and the cabinet are part of a fusion of powers arrangement with all members of the government holding seats in the House of Representatives and being subject to a vote of confidence originating in the House of Representatives. Although the numbers of cabinet positions can change with each new prime minister, in the modern period there have been twelve ministerial rank offices and eight cabinet-rank agencies. A major administrative reform implemented in 2001 streamlined Japan's ministerial configuration from its present status at twenty-one to twelve superministries.

The Japanese judicial system has been heavily influenced by American judicial structure and jurisprudence. The constitution of 1947 made a number of significant changes to Japanese courts, which allowed them to become more independent and more coequal with the other two branches of government. The Japanese judicial system is centralized under the authority of the Supreme Court. There are no local or prefecture courts in Japan. The Supreme Court has the power to interpret laws and to engage in judicial review. Like their counterparts in the United States, Supreme Court justices are appointed for life, but after ten years they are subject to a national referendum on their continuation in office. Justices also have the power to forward the names of justices for the lower courts to the cabinet. These justices serve ten-year terms. Besides their responsibility to interpret and protect the constitution, the justices of the Supreme Court ensure that Japanese civil rights and liberties are secure. Under the constitution the Japanese have extensive guarantees of freedom of thought and conscience, freedom from censorship, and protections against sexual and racial discrimination.

The national bureaucracy provides the greatest insight into the critical center of governing power. In recent years five ministries have formed the core of the governmental bureaucracy. The Ministry of Agriculture, Forestry, and Fisheries (MAFF), the Ministry of Construction (MOC), the Ministry of Finance (MOF), the Ministry of International Trade and Industry (MITI), and the Ministry of Posts and Telecommunication (MOT) are generally recognized as having substantial policymaking, regulatory, and implementation power. Also part of the cabinet are agencies with specific areas of responsibility such as the Economic Planning Agency and the Management and Coordination Agency, which have concentrated on deregulation and administrative reform, the Science and Technology Agency, which takes the lead in developing Japan's most critical economic sector, and the Self-Defense Agency, which in demilitarized Japan replaces the more formal Defense Ministry. There are two high-level development agencies in the cabinet dealing with the islands of Hokkaido and Okinawa, which face unique economic development problems (Hokkaido because of its underpopulation and Okinawa because of its poverty and links to the U.S. presence).

The Japanese bureaucratic sector employs over a million people (about 2 percent of the workforce) and spends approximately 16 percent of the gross domestic product (which is less than that of Britain and the United States). In recent years the national bureaucracy has lost much of its elite status as the Japanese have become attracted to employment in the private sector, although employment in the top five ministries remains prestigious and highly competitive. Nevertheless, the nearly 20,000 bureaucrats who hold positions at the executive level in the ministries, especially in the Ministry of Finance and the Ministry of International Trade and Industry, continue to be viewed as elite members of Japanese society and highly influential policymakers.

Alongside the government ministries are a number of public and semipublic agencies that perform critical functions in Japanese society. There are public financial institutions such as the Bank of Japan and the Japanese Development Bank, along with about a dozen specific funds or foundations. The banks, funds, and foundations receive budget allocations from the government and use their resources to assist various economic sectors with loans and grants. There are also public corporations that provide funds for large construction and infrastructure projects. These public corporations have become increasingly important as the Japanese government seeks to jump-start the economy with huge public works projects. Finally, there are specific businesses that are public or semipublic in nature. The government funds that these businesses receive may assist them in developing new products or engaging in research that is vital to the national interest.

One of the more interesting characteristics of Japanese government is the organization and function of local administrative units. Japanese local government is a mix of feudalism and French-style rural organization. Currently Japan is organized as a unitary system with extensive powers, especially budgetary and taxing powers centralized in Tokyo. The major population centers of Tokyo, Osaka, and Kyoto function as metropolitan districts. The lightly populated island of Hokkaido in the north is run as a single administrative unit, and the remaining areas of Japan are organized into forty-three prefectures. The prefectures are similar in nature to the French departments—local and increasingly urban governing bodies with a governor and an elected assembly that make decisions on numerous policy concerns such as roads, education, police, and health. The relationship between the prefectures and the central government in Tokyo has been a source of tension in Japan because of the allocation of budgetary resources and the "strings" that are attached by the central government to local use of the resources. Prefecture governors and legislators are constantly at odds with the government in Tokyo over inadequate budgets and their inability to make policy decisions without the approval of the ministries or the Diet.

A discussion of Japanese government would be incomplete without mention of the role that the military plays in the current institutional setting. Article 9 of the Constitution states that "land, sea and air forces, as well as other war potential, will never be maintained." The antiwar, antimilitary position of the Japanese government was modified over time. As a result of the Korean War in 1950, the Japanese government approved (with support from the United States) a remilitarization program. In 1954 Japan developed the Self-Defense Forces (SDF), which replaced a modest national "police reserve." In a 1959 case involving the constitutionality of the security treaty with the United States, the Japanese Supreme Court permitted the government to establish policies designed to defend the nation. Since that time there have been challenges to the constitutionality of article 9, but there has never been a definitive ruling on the SDF.

The Japanese SDF has grown dramatically to its present state as the military spending leader in Asia. Although China has many more men and women in its armed forces (3 million military personnel as opposed to Japan's 250,000), Japan outspends its chief rival in the region (Japan spent over $50 billion in

1995 compared to China's reported expenditure of $35 billion). Yet despite its remilitarization, Japan remains reluctant to extend the reach of its armed forces beyond its shores. During the Gulf War in 1991, Japan was heavily criticized by the international community for providing money for the war but no troops. Japan eventually provided two supply vessels for the Gulf War and has sent a small contingent of soldiers to United Nations trouble spots.

The governing model put into place in 1947 by General MacArthur was a means of satisfying the American need to make Japan an Asian version of the United States. From the Japanese perspective, governing institutions and processes were less important than the ability to retain those aspects of their culture, economic networks, and social relations that were fundamental to the maintenance of a unique national identity. Americans left Japan with a new constitution and a democratic governing system, but the Japanese got what they wanted—a political environment that could be manipulated in ways that allowed the governing elites to advance their economic interests. Japan became part of the democratic club, but Japanese democracy would be markedly different with weak political leaders, one powerful political party, and a critical alliance between the bureaucracy and age-old business networks that determined the course of national development.

Constitutional Language

One of the changes in the Japanese governing system was to place severe limitations on the emperor and transform him into a ceremonial leader. Chapter 1 of the Japanese constitution clearly lays out the status and role of the emperor:

Chapter 1, Article 1
The Emperor shall be the symbol of the State and of the unity of the people, deriving his position from the will of the people, with whom resides sovereign power.

Chapter 1, Article 2
The Imperial Throne shall be dynastic and succeeded to in accordance with the Imperial House Law passed by the Diet.

Chapter 1, Article 3
The advice and approval of the Cabinet shall be required for all acts of the Emperor in matters of state, and the Cabinet shall be responsible therefor.

WORKING WOMEN AND FAMILY POLICY

Japan is a society known for its commitment to hard work and long hours in the workplace. This societal commitment has played a key role in Japan's economic development. But in recent years a critical tension has surfaced involving work, women, and the birthrate. Japan's birthrate has been sliding since the postwar years from 4.4 children per woman in 1947 to the current 1.3 children. From a comparative perspective Japan is at the low end of the birthrate scale, along with countries such as Russia and Germany. As a result of the declining birthrate, population projections for Japan show a precipitous drop from the current figure of 125 million people to as low as 100 million by 2050.

At the center of this issue is the changing role of women in Japanese society and the inability of government and business to create a family-friendly environment for women and men. Japanese women are increasingly choosing work over family, in large part because the corporate culture in Japan is so demanding and rigid that it is simply too difficult for women to balance family and work. In 1980, 19 percent of Japan's working women had been employed for more than ten years, but in 2000 that number jumped to 32 percent. Moreover, 57 percent of married women now make up the female workforce, up from 32 percent in 1960. This feminization of the Japanese workforce is anticipated to increase as the labor shortage related to low birthrates expands in future years.

Faced with the movement of women out of the house and into the workplace and the accompanying decline in the birthrate, the Japanese government has begun taking steps to encourage women and men to have larger families. In 2000 the government doubled the time, to age six, that parents can receive subsidies for raising children. Also, a new law mandates that companies provide parental leave until a child turns one year old. The policy states that a woman who takes the leave receives 25 percent of her salary in unemployment compensation. This subsidy is on top of an existing benefit whereby mothers can take an eight-week maternity leave and receive 60 percent of their salary through a program administered by a national insurance plan. While these programs provide a means for women to be with their children, they are not as popular as the government anticipated. The most sought-after change in family policy, as expressed by Japanese women, is extending the hours of government-operated child care facilities. Currently these child care centers are open to 6:00 P.M., but in most Japanese corporations the workday lasts well beyond 6:00 P.M., especially for professional women on a career track.

Japanese men are not excluded when it comes to demanding changes in family policy. Many corporations think nothing about transferring their male employees to other regions of the country or abroad, thus splitting up families and creating marital tensions. Some Japanese men have begun to speak out against corporate policies that limit their time at home with their wives and children. Lawsuits have been filed against Japanese corporations for engaging in personnel policies that deny men an opportunity to be with their families. While males are demanding changes in the workplace, women have joined their husbands in following similar work patterns, at the expense of having children and spending more time with the children. As a means of balancing work and family life, most Japanese couples rely on grandparents to provide extended baby-sitting.

The Japanese government has been slow to recognize the changing character of female employment in the country and its impact on the birthrate, but it is now taking steps to deal with the problem. Ministries are allowing a spouse to take a leave of absence when the other spouse is transferred, and the concept of flex time has begun to be introduced into public administration. What has not changed in Japan is the demands that the business culture place on the Japanese worker, whether that worker is a woman or a man, a mother or a father. Japanese workers are reluctant to seek four-day work weeks or shorter work hours for fear of antagonizing their bosses, and they receive little encouragement from the government, which is reluctant to push for change, particularly at a time when unemployment is at its highest since the postwar era. Because of the combination of a business culture resistant to change and a government that is slow to address a serious social and demographic problem, Japan is likely to remain an unfriendly country for families. ⊕

THE CITIZEN AND THE STATE

In order to understand the relationship between the Japanese people and their government, it is essential to examine the belief and value system that forms a distinct political culture. Confucian philosophy, which dates back to the sixth century, has played a significant role in shaping the way the Japanese interact with one another and with their government. In 604, Crown Prince Shotoku issued his "Sixteen Article Constitution," a document that had as its foundation a series of Confucian principles such as the importance of societal harmony, obedience to governing authority, diligence and hard work, and honesty. The Confucian philosophy served to bolster the emerging centralized and bureaucratic regime under the divine monarchy. By accenting Confucian values, Japanese government leaders were able to establish social order and create a political environment where cooperation and acceptance of imperial dictates were firmly entrenched. Moreover, Confucianism also had a significant impact on social relations with its emphasis on strict class hierarchy, ancestor respect and worship, and male dominance in economic and political affairs. As Japan moved through the Tokugawa shogunate, these values deepened. Alternative value systems were not introduced in Japan until the Meiji Restoration and the attendant westernization. Those Western values, however, were no match for Confucianism. Japan had become a society of order and the maintenance of order.

The Confucian value system took on many different forms as Japan developed. The importance of societal harmony led to emphasizing the group and downplaying individualism. The Japanese are a people of strong group loyalty, hierarchy, and cooperation. Conformity and avoidance of controversy are the watchwords of the Japanese psyche. Personal relations are defined by the domination of superiors over their clients and the respect that clients show (with the traditional bow) their superiors. In all aspects of Japanese life—family, work, and education—there is a hierarchical relationship designed to create harmony and cooperation and in the process avoid messy disputes and violent conflict. But this emphasis on harmony and group cooperation can also have its downside. The Japanese often think of themselves as one national family that is not only different from other nationalities but superior to them. Centuries of isolation mixed with group identity have created a kind of national arrogance that on occasion borders on racism.

The high premium placed on social order and obedience in Japan has put a damper on individual expression, innovation, and critical thinking. The Japanese are a people schooled in rote memorization and socialized not to take risks or express opinions. One of the examples of this lock-step blandness can be found in higher education. College life in Japan is four years of quietly going through the motions without upsetting the status quo. Students attend classes, take notes, and remain silent (if not asleep) while their professors lecture. There is little classroom discussion, and students rarely offer their opinions to the professors. There is little reward in Japanese society for the outspoken or the critic. A common Japanese phrase, "It is the nail that sticks up that gets pounded down," best sums up Japanese obedience and unwillingness to challenge established authority.

This national attitude of quiet compliance and avoidance of controversy shows up in studies related to citizen-government relations. Data from cross-national surveys has found that the Japanese do not join political groups or communicate with public officials. They vote in numbers that are respectable, but other examples of connections to the political process are scant. This culture of passive acceptance of authority carries over into the political world, where the Japanese are best characterized as political observers and supporters, not activists. Although Japan has its rebellious elements, there is no real tradition of civil disobedience in the country and only scattered incidents of national protest. The Japanese prefer to settle disputes quietly and work behind the scenes. In many cases, especially those involving trade negotiations with foreign countries, the Japanese have been known for their intransigence and delaying tactics. Rather than engage in a public dispute that would upset harmony and create controversy, the Japanese often politely smile, ask for more time to study the issue, and hope that they can outlast their adversaries.

However, the Japanese have not remained silent on certain political issues. Relations with the United States have often been the springboard to protest. Since the end of World War II there have been numerous protest marches on Okinawa against the 40,000 American troops stationed there. In the late 1990s, after episodes of violence and rape directed against Japanese residents, the people of Okinawa heightened their protest, demanding that the United States reduce its presence on the island and questioning the necessity of continuing the military alliance.

Political protest in Japan has also included incidences of terrorism. In the most dramatic act against the government a Japanese cult called Aum Shinri Kyo staged a gas attack on the Tokyo subway system in 1995 in which twelve people were killed. In response to the attack the Japanese government passed legislation that gave it sweeping powers to control such groups. Although cult-related terrorism is only tangentially political in nature, it nevertheless was viewed by the government as an attack on the political and social order.

The lack of political activism also carries over into patriotic expressions. In recent years the Japanese have struggled with the playing of the national anthem, "Kimigayo," and the flying of the national flag, the Rising Sun. The Japanese parliament in 1999 passed a law naming the flag and the anthem as official symbols of the nation. Until 1999 the Japanese had been reluctant to express their allegiance to the state by displaying the flag or singing the anthem. Both the flag and the anthem are associated with the period of Japanese militarism and the divine authority of the emperor, which are no longer held in high regard by the average citizen. There have been signs that the Japanese, particularly in the public schools, are slowly displaying the flag and standing at attention while "Kimigayo" is played. But there is opposition. In the Hiroshima prefecture in 1999 a high school principal committed suicide when he was unable to convince his staff to play the national anthem.

Recent developments regarding Japanese admission of guilt for war crimes during World War II shed further light on the political culture. The Japanese have been reluctant to accept responsibility for a range of atrocities and heinous actions, from the rape of Nanking in which hundreds of thousands of innocent civilians (according to the Chinese, 35 million) were killed to the use of Korean "comfort ladies" (sex slaves) by the military. Japanese political leaders have resisted public apologies and have denied that military officials engaged in war crimes. It was only in the 1990s that the Japanese began to take steps to acknowledge what the Germans had done forty years earlier. Emperor Akihito began a kind of national confessional when he apologized to both South Korea and China for the aggressive occupation of their countries during World War II. In 1998 Prime Minister Obuchi issued a rather bland apology to Chinese Premier Jiang Zemin for Japan's occupation during World War II. The Chinese wanted a written apology that was more detailed and conciliatory, but the Japanese refused.

Currently the Japanese are locked in an international battle over reparations for the use of slave labor by the military and the giant financial and industrial conglomerates. It is estimated that well over 1 million American servicemen, Koreans, Chinese, and other Asians were enslaved in mines, factories, and construction projects characterized by high death rates and rampant physical abuse. In typical Japanese style, political leaders refused to acknowledge responsibility for the slave labor, stating that the 1951 peace treaty in San Francisco absolved Japan of reparations. So far scores of cases have been brought in Japan seeking restitution and a new wave of litigation is making its way through the courts in the United States.

Japanese reluctance to admit responsibility for World War II war crimes is anchored in the Japanese view of guilt and shame. Guilt, which has its roots in the Judeo-Christian tradition, has little influence in the moral thinking of the Japanese. Rather, they are drawn to shame as a moral foundation of their thinking and their actions. The Japanese are conscious of how their actions affect the national, corporate, or family group. To bring shame to these groups is the most serious "crime" that Japanese can commit. The bank executive who commits suicide for leading his institution into bankruptcy is spurred on by his sense of shame. Military leaders during World War II who committed *seppuku,* commonly known as *hara-kiri*, were following an ancient ritual of samurai honor that stemmed from their belief that they had brought shame and dishonor to the country. The Japanese are a people with a deep sense of morality, but it is a morality that is foreign to the West. It is a morality that ignores war crimes against innocents but accepts suicide as an appropriate act when business enterprises, family members, or national pride has been shamed.

A discussion of the relationship between citizen and state in Japan must include the issue of work and leisure. When Prime Minister Keizo Obuchi suffered a stroke and eventually died in 2000, Japan once again examined the impact of work on national health. Obuchi, like many Japanese men, was a workaholic, getting little sleep, holding endless meetings, and carrying the weight of economic policymaking on his shoulders. With his passing, Obuchi became another victim of *karoshi*, the unique Japanese condition best described as death from overwork. Each year one-third of the 35,000 Japanese men who die of cardiovascular disease succumb to *karoshi*. The situation has become so serious that the government passed legislation to compensate the families of workers who die from job-related illnesses, including overwork. The government even extended benefits to the families of workers who commit suicide as a result of overwork. In recent years the government established cabinet-level offices designed to promote leisure and leisure-time activities. But true to form in Japan, the ministers in charge of the program worked exhausting hours developing leisure policies. Increasingly, though, the Japanese are becoming aware of the dangers associated with overwork. Top-level ministers, including Obuchi's immediate successor, Yoshiro Mori, urged men in particular to take more time off and enjoy their leisure hours.

Despite the order and harmony that provide the foundation of Japanese society and political culture, there are significant signs of change in the relationship between citizens and the state. The Japanese are showing heightened displeasure with their government and the ruling Liberal Democratic Party. In the aftermath of the 1995 Kobe earthquake the Japanese people were highly critical of the government's response. Ministries associated with disaster relief and reconstruction seemed immobilized and uncaring about the suffering and loss of the people. The Japanese bureaucracy, which is often held up as a symbol of national efficiency and the epitome of group cooperation, could not muster the resources or the leadership to address the crisis, forcing many to rely on their own initiative. Then came the East Asian financial crisis of 1997 that began Japan's serious economic slide into recession. Successive governments since 1997 have only tinkered with the economy as political leaders showed great reluctance to implement significant reforms. This reluctance has built to the point where Japanese voters are becoming increasingly independent (only 50 percent of the voters show allegiance to a specific party, a marked decrease) and voicing their frustrations with the governing status quo.

Dissatisfaction with the current governing climate in Japan has brought about a gender shift in politics. Women are now playing a much wider role in the political process and speaking out openly about the need for a fundamental reorganization of the governing culture. Historically Japanese society has been male dominated, and the political system has been no different. Japan has for years ranked low in terms of the number of women in the legislature and government positions. But in the late 1990s a major shift occurred. In

1993 the House of Representatives named Takado Doi as its first woman Speaker. Although the position is more of an administrative duty than a political plum, Doi nevertheless captured the attention of the country and took a critical first step toward injecting women into the political process. In 2000 Makiko Tanaka, whose father had been prime minister during the 1970s, was named foreign minister by Prime Minister Koizumi and immediately became embroiled in conflicts with the male Liberal Democratic establishment and top-level bureaucrats. Tanaka, like a growing number of women politicians, was dissatisfied with the corruption scandals and the antireform mind-set of the male political elite. But there was a price to pay. Tanaka's outspokenness led to her removal by Prime Minister Koizumi in 2002. Today political parties such as the Clean Government Party and the Liberal Party of Japan are attracting women to their ranks, setting up the prospect that in the coming years the demographics of the Diet and the government will be substantially different.

The most significant change in the citizen-state relationship in Japan is the new generation that is emerging. Japanese youths, or *shin jinrui,* hold attitudes toward government and national life that differ from those of their elders. The younger generation of Japanese is less wedded to work, less tolerant of government corruption and inactivity, and less respectful of age-old traditions. They are more westernized and more demanding that their leaders take the necessary steps to restructure the political and economic systems. Japanese young people are no longer enamored of public service as bureaucrats in the elite ministries and seek employment in the private sector. This break with the past has both energized the political process and created new problems for Japan, such as youth violence, teen prostitution, and widespread drug use. The male political elite now has two major problems on its hands—dealing with the growing disenchantment with the status quo among youthful voters and protesters and coping with the social disorder created by a new generation that is not bound by the traditions of harmony, groupism, and quiet acceptance of one's place in a hierarchy.

Japan in the coming years will likely experience a redefinition of the relationship between citizen and state. There is much talk in the country about the need for a "third opening": a complete restructuring of the economic and political systems and the cultural environment that supports those systems. In a manner similar to the changes brought about by the Meiji dynasty and the American occupation, the "third opening" would be a major break with the past. The Japanese appear to be ready for this "third opening" as they express dissatisfaction with their government, the business elites, and the World War II generation that continues to dominate national life. In many ways the air of serenity that exists in Japanese society is beginning to disappear. There is an obvious tension in the country between the people and their government. The people want a change, but their government is fearful about what that change might be or become. The result could create a severe political chasm in a country where order and harmony are highly valued.

AGING POLICY

Japan has a senior citizen (over sixty-five) population that is the largest in the world. In 2000 the elderly population in Japan was 17.2 percent. But with a yearly increase of 0.5 percent the government estimates that in the year 2030 the senior population will increase to 29 percent. Japan is an aging society that faces problems and challenges common to senior citizens such as providing adequate health care, ensuring that social security is sufficiently funded, and responding to unique issues such as the high rate of suicides among the elderly (one-third of all suicides in Japan are people over sixty). The weakness of the Japanese economy has compounded the problems and challenges of its aging society as housing costs for seniors have become prohibitive and budget contributions to key supportive services such as nursing homes and treatment centers have not kept pace with needs.

Perhaps the most serious problem facing the elderly in Japan is the cost of health care. During the years of high growth in the 1980s and 1990s medical expenses for seniors increased 6 percent a year. More specifically the cost of medicine has increased dramatically. Currently the Japanese spend three times more on outpatient medicine than seniors in the United States. This situation will only become more serious since the government estimates that the elderly who will need caregiving will increase from the current 1.8 million to over 3 million by 2025. It is thus not surprising that when Japanese seniors commit suicide one of the key reasons given is the "pain of sickness" caused by the unavailability of care, the cost of medicine, and the general ineffectiveness of the caregiving system.

In 1995 the Japanese government passed a sweeping legislative package designed to address the needs of an "aging population." But the demographic spike in the number of senior citizens has become overwhelming and the traditional reluctance of the Japanese to accept welfare payments and other social insurance compounds the problem. Japanese seniors still hold to the belief that it is the family's responsibility to care for elderly relatives. Yet as Japan moves to a work culture in which women are in the office or the factory rather than taking care of parents or grandparents, providing care for seniors has become more difficult. In the past three or four generations would live in one household, but the dynamics of a new economy in

Japan has forced seniors to reside in their own homes and rely on nonfamil-
ial caregivers, both expensive propositions.

The Japanese government recognizes the needs of the elderly population
and is engaged in a series of policy initiatives to make the price of medical
treatments and medicine more reasonable. Steps are being taken to develop
an insurance plan that would permit elderly persons to make payments into a
plan that would help defray the cost of medical care when it becomes necessary. Most importantly, the government in 2001 launched a home care insurance plan to assist families with elderly relatives. For a modest cost, seniors
who need home care will have access to health aides and day care facilities.
The Japanese are also developing a number of specialized health care initiatives for the elderly such as a medical treatment welfare card that will contain
personal medical information about the individual that can be used in emer-
gencies and a space age tracking system that will allow hospitals to locate
impaired seniors who may wander away from a hospital or home.

Despite these initiatives the aging problem in Japan is only beginning. The
challenge posed in midcentury, when nearly 30 percent of the population will be
over sixty, is staggering. The costs related to taking care of a huge nonworking
population that requires medical and other health-related assistance are almost
incomprehensible. For a nation that has a relatively low tax burden, the demands of an aging society may require significant increases in taxation and major allocation of budgetary resources. The days of families taking care of family
members—the new generation looking out for the previous generation—have
ended in Japan. And as in other industrialized nations, the government has been
forced to step in to become the caregiver of last resort. ⊕

POINT OF FACT
*Prime Minister Koizumi is an avid baseball fan and a passionate rock 'n'
roll aficionado. He is especially fond of the Beatles.*

PATHWAYS TO PARTICIPATION

The Liberal Democratic Party has dominated politics since 1955 and has re-
linquished power only once. There are many pathways to participation in
Japan, as there are in other industrial democracies, but the Liberal Democrats' nearly complete control of the political system provides a clear starting
point for the discussion of how the Japanese structure and implement their
democracy. However, the Liberal Democrats' stranglehold is beginning to
weaken. Japan has always had opposition parties, some of which participated
in coalition governments during the 1990s. But the Japanese opposition is

becoming empowered as the reputation of the Liberal Democrats declines and the electorate looks for new leadership and new policies. As a result, the pathways to participation have begun to widen and multiply. The arena of participation in Japan is increasingly fluid, with the venerable Liberal Democrats facing new challengers who sense that the time for change is near. It is against this backdrop of Liberal Democratic dominance and opposition challenge that Japanese participation is best understood.

The Liberal Democratic Party (LDP) was formed in 1955 as a result of the merger of two conservative parties from the post–World War II era. The LDP has remained a party that sits on the right of the political spectrum in terms of not only its general policy stances (which can be described as pro-business) but also its reluctance to engage in internal reform and bold policy initiatives. Its party platform stresses a standard commitment to economic growth but addresses some unique problems such as deindustrialization, unemployment, and the appreciation of the yen. The platform also highlights smaller government, deregulation and decentralization, moral education of Japanese youth, cooperation between men and women, and meaningful lives for what it terms an "aged society."

The LDP has built its reputation over the years on bringing peace and prosperity to the country in the postwar and occupation period. Its guiding principles are freedom, democracy, and peace. It has pursued those principles by accenting the benefits of a capitalist economy and electoral reform and by maintaining a protective security umbrella through establishing solid ties to the United States. These platform positions and principles have served the LDP well as it gathered support from a wide range of demographic groups. Although its traditional base remains in the rural areas, it has been able to widen its net by attracting white-collar and professional groups. It has fared less well among women, labor groups, intellectuals, and the young. Its frequent scandals and its inability to effectively address the economic problems created when the bubble economy of the 1980s and 1990s burst have put it on the defensive, and as a result it has lost support among its core groups.

The power of the LDP in Japanese politics may be a bit misleading. Since 1963 the party has not been able to win a majority of the popular vote. Although it has won a majority of the seats in the Diet in numerous elections, it has increasingly relied on coalition support, especially after the disastrous defeat in 1993. In that election Prime Minister Kiichi Miyazawa's government lost a vote of no confidence in large part because he was reluctant to initiate a series of political reforms. When new elections were called, a number of LDP legislators left the party and formed new parties, thus sealing the defeat. Fortunately, the chaos created by the LDP defeat resulted in a reconfiguration of the Diet one year later in which the LDP, relying on coalition help from the

Social Democratic Party of Japan and the New Party Sakigake, participated in the government. In 1996 the LDP regained control of government as the head of a three-party coalition. In the 2000 election the LDP lost the majority status that it had built up since 1966 but still gained the largest number of seats in the Diet. As in the past the LDP had to rely on coalition partners, this time the Buddhist-backed New Komeito Party and the small Conservative Party.

The key to understanding the LDP lies in its factions. The LDP is a party of four groupings. Each faction has its own leadership, organizational structure, and, most importantly, source of campaign funds. These factional groupings hold the same platform positions of the larger LDP and their members benefit from the opportunity that electoral victory provides to gain ministerial positions and legislative leadership roles. But the factional groupings are akin to political clans with a leader who holds power by his ability to distribute campaign funds and make recommendations on patronage. The factional character of the LDP has created frequent competition and tension as these clan leaders jockey for power and influence within the broader organization and the government. Critics of the factions in the LDP point out that they are a remnant of Japan's feudal past and that multiple centers of power only create conflict and deadlock in the party's ranks. Yet the power of the factional leaders is so great in areas where it counts (money and jobs) that a more centralized organizational structure is unlikely to emerge.

Where the Liberal Democratic Party remains a stable but fragmented political force, the opposition parties in the Japanese system are in constant flux. Perhaps the only political party that has shown a semblance of continuity over time is the Japan Communist Party (JCP). A minor player in the political and electoral process, the JCP has consistently gained seats in the Diet (twenty-six seats in 1966 and twenty in 2000). Like most communist political parties that function in a Western democratic setting, the JCP has been hampered by its ideology and its advocacy of a discredited economic system. Nevertheless, the JCP remains an option for Japanese voters who are feeling the pain of growing unemployment and economic recession.

The other party that has been able to avoid the constant factional disputes and restructuring is the Social Democratic Party (SDP). Founded in 1955, at the same time as the LDP, the SDP, like the Communist Party, has held steady at around twenty seats in the House of Representatives. Unlike the Communist Party, the SDP has experienced a significant drop-off in support. In the 1993 election the Social Democrats gained seventy-three seats in the House of Representatives, while in the 2000 election its legislative contingent was reduced to nineteen. The Social Democrats have had a difficult time finding issues that stimulate electoral support. In the past they have been the party most critical of Japanese defense policy and ties to the United States. But with growing support for a remilitarization of the country, the Social Democrats have become the party of anti-Americanism, particularly with respect to U.S. troops on Okinawa.

The most substantial opposition parties in the Japanese political system have been subjected to regular factionalism and have resurfaced with new names and new leaders. The current opposition party is the Democratic Party of Japan (DPJ), which in the 2000 election garnered 127 seats in the House of Representatives. The DPJ is an offshoot of the New Harbinger Party, which itself broke away from the Liberal Democratic organization. The corruption scandals and internal bickering that dominated the LDP in the early 1990s and led to its first defeat in the Diet in 1993 caused a number of disgruntled party leaders to leave the party and form opposition organizations. During the remainder of the 1990s these parties further split and reconfigured, causing great confusion among the electorate and those outside of Japan trying to make sense of electoral politics.

The Democratic Party builds itself as a centrist organization much in the tradition of the British "third way." The party philosophy stresses the importance of achieving a just, fair society based on *kyosei,* which is defined as "living and working together for the common good." The party has also taken positions in favor of decentralization of government, equal opportunity for each individual, and pacifism. Party leader Yukio Hatoyama has become an active behind-the-scenes player in Japanese politics seeking to forge ties with other smaller parties such as the Liberal Party in an attempt to develop a solid alternative to the LDP.

The other major political party organization that has played a role in the electoral process is the Clean Government Party, or Komeito. Founded in the mid-1960s by members of the Soka Gakki Buddhist movement, Komeito has staked out the policy area of Japanese politics associated with campaign reform and progressive change in the manner in which Japan conducts politics. It has also championed a more equitable welfare system. Because of its roots in the Soka Gakki movement, which has been viewed by some as evangelical, if not fanatical, the Komeito in recent years has distanced itself from the Buddhist sect and has renamed itself New Komeito. The party has become more mainstream in its policies, actually joining the governing coalition in 1999. In the 2000 election the New Komeito gained thirty-one seats in the House of Deputies, third behind the LDP and the DPJ. It again joined the governing coalition with the LDP and the much smaller Conservative Party.

While political parties in Japan provide the key pathway to participation, it is the relationship between the parties and money that forms the centerpiece of the political system. Japanese politics is awash in campaign contributions, corporate gifts, payoffs, and various other forms of illegal payments to candidates and incumbents. The linkage between political parties and money goes back to the days before 1994 when the Japanese changed the methods by which legislators were elected. Until 1994 two or more members from the same party could run against each other in one electoral district. This competition created a process in which candidates formed organizations, called *koenkai,* that marshaled support in the district. One chief tactic of the *koenkai* was to spend money to win votes. Candidates raised huge amounts of money and spent lavishly on campaigns and other forms of constituency service in order to differentiate themselves from their party opponent. This spending spree led to numerous campaign illegalities as candidates flouted the law in order to win seats. Japanese politics became a sea of questionable campaign spending practices.

After the Liberal Democrats lost in 1993, the electoral system was reformed, with the multicandidate approach being replaced by a mix of single-member districts and proportional representation. Other campaign reforms were put in place, such as limits on corporate contributions and public subsidies. Current Japanese law prohibits contributions by corporations that receive capital or equivalent sources of financing from the government. The law also bans political contributions by business corporations that receive subsidies from the government and lawmakers' receipt of political contributions from these corporations. These reforms, however, have done little to stop the culture of linking money and politics.

Japanese banks, construction companies, high-tech firms, and other corporate entities continue to "interpret" the laws to their advantage and provide the political parties, especially the ruling LDP, with huge campaign contributions. Japanese businesses are quite open about their gifts to politicians and are unconcerned about the legal ramifications of their contributions. In one of many such instances in 1998 a number of Japanese banks received government loans totaling $18.2 billion. Two months later three of the major banks made campaign contributions to the LDP totaling $108,000, in what appeared to be a clear violation of the law. Both the banks and the LDP leadership admitted the linkage but stated that they were not covered by existing Japanese law. Although Japanese law states that violators of the campaign contribution statutes are subject to three years in prison or a penalty of no less than $5,000, prosecution of businesses and politicians is infrequent. Illegal contributors occasionally face judicial sanction and politicians have lost their seats or voluntarily resigned from office. Despite these controls Japanese businessmen and politicians continue linking politics with money. Campaigns are quite expensive and the public subsidies are inadequate to cover expenses.

While Japanese politics has become Americanized in the sense that campaign contributions dominate and define the electoral process, the character of participation is different in the sense that interest group activity takes a backseat to the parties. In Japan interest groups are vital and numerous, but they are less powerful in the policy process than their counterparts in the United States. Umbrella groups such as the Federation of Economic Organizations (a business group), the Japanese Trade Union Federation (labor's arm), the Central Union of Agricultural Cooperatives (the voice of the powerful rural interests), and professionally based organizations such as the Japan Medical Doctor Association and the Japan Teachers Union are active in the political process and make hefty contributions to the parties. But in Japan interest groups take cues from the governing ministries instead of trying to shape the ministries. In Japan the bureaucracy dictates policy and groups follow.

The influence of interest groups in Japan, although less successful in the ministries, has become increasingly associated with electoral politics. For example, the Japan Medical Doctor Association (JMDA) has emerged as a key player in the election strategy of the LDP. Critics have referred to it as a "machine for collecting votes." The LDP relies heavily on groups such as the JMDA to engage in grassroots organizing and the rather mundane but important campaigning activities. This active involvement in the electoral process, however, has reaped some policy benefits for the interest groups in both the legislature and the bureaucracies.

While the role and power of parties, money, and groups is expanding in Japanese politics, the relationship between the voter and the electoral process has taken a disturbing turn downward. The Japanese have sought to reform the election of members to the Diet, reducing the number of seats in the House of Representatives from 511 to 480 and eliminating the competition between party candidates for individual seats. At the present time 300 legislative seats are open for election every four years in a single-member, winner-take-all format. An additional 180 seats are elected by proportional representation in eleven regional blocs. These 180 are elected in a party list-based system. Candidates are permitted to run for both the single-member seat and the party-based seat.

These reforms, though, have not had a marked impact on rejuvenating interest in voting in Japan. Turnout in postwar Japan had been quite high, ranging from the high 60 percent range to nearly 80 percent. This level of electoral involvement lasted until the 1980s, when signs of voter confidence in the LDP led to slow but steady declines in turnout. In the 1996 election turnout dropped to 60 percent in the House of Representatives and hit a disappointing 46 percent in the House of Councillors. Today, voter turnout hovers around 60 percent with the 2000 election garnering a 59 percent share of the electorate in a lackluster campaign. Voting analysts in Japan are concerned about the drop-off but not surprised, in light of the woeful image that the ruling LDP has in the country and growing consensus that political reform is essential.

If Japan is to usher in a new era of political reform, it will need to begin with the relationship among the parties, the groups, and the campaign contributors. Again, using the comparison with the United States, Japanese democracy is slowly deteriorating as the voting population becomes increasingly concerned that the popular will is being pushed aside by a small coterie of wealthy interests who have coopted the political parties. In Japan the linkage between the parties, the groups, and money may be even more damaging to the political process simply because there are more scandals and more high-level corruption than there is in the United States. The corruption associated with the LDP and LDP government has begun to take its toll on the body politic after years in politics. The Japanese are not only participating less in national elections but also expressing their displeasure with their government more frequently. They have yet to translate that displeasure in more significant ways, such as rejecting the LDP. They have chosen rather to quietly resist by withholding their vote or quietly complaining.

Election Data

The June 2000 national parliamentary elections gave the LDP a solid victory, despite continued scandals and policy gridlock. The results from the House of Representatives (Shugi-in), with 480 seats contested, were as follows. (Note that Japan has a two-pronged process of choosing its House of Representatives: 300 members from single-seat constituencies and 180 from proportional representation in eleven regional blocs.) The following results show the single-seat vote percentage followed by the proportional vote percentage.

Liberal Democratic Party	41 percent/28 percent
Democratic Party	27.6 percent/25.1 percent
Komeito (Clean Government)	2 percent/13 percent
Communist Party of Japan	12.1 percent/11.2 percent
Liberal Party	3.4 percent/11 percent
Social Democratic Party	3.8 percent/9.4 percent
Liberal League	1.8 percent/11 percent
Conservative Party	2 percent/0.4 percent
Independents' Party	1.1 percent/0.3 percent

Photo 4.1 Junichiro Koizumi. (AFP/Corbis)

Prime Minister Koizumi was born in Yokosuka, Japan, in 1942. He graduated from Keio University with a degree in economics. He was elected to the House of Representatives in 1972. In 1979 he became state secretary of finance and one year later assumed the position of chairman of the Finance Committee of the Liberal Democratic Party. In 1988 he was named minister of Health and Welfare and in 1992 became the minister of Posts and Telecommunications. In 1996 and 1997 he reassumed the position of minister of Health and Welfare under two different prime ministers. He ran unsuccessfully for president of the LDP in 1995 and 1998. In 2001 he became president of the LDP and prime minister.

THE POWER ELITE

On the surface, a discussion of Japanese political leaders appears rather simple and straightforward. Since electoral popularity and governing responsibility have been controlled by the Liberal Democratic Party for most of the postwar era, the obvious place to look for the power elite is in the ranks of the LDP. But Japanese politics is a lot more complicated and subtle than it appears on the surface. The LDP is indeed the center of political power, but the power elite is not found in the positions that normally would yield the capacity to make public policy. Yes, the position of prime minister is an important post and the person who occupies that position is a force to be reckoned with. But Japan has a history of weak and colorless prime ministers who were both unable and unwilling to exercise their governing authority in order to effect change. There are no dominant figures who have occupied the position of prime minister.

The two prime ministers before Junichiro Koizumi, Keizo Obuchi and Yoshiro Mori, were viewed as lackluster leaders with little ability to address the economic problems facing Japan. Obuchi even apologized to the Japanese people when he made his victory speech before the LDP stating that he was an "inferior" to other party leaders and would have to make efforts to prove his leadership capacity. He traveled around the country to introduce himself saying at one point, "I know now that popularity among the people and popularity in the party should match each other." After Obuchi's death, Mori emerged as the new prime minister but quickly was dismissed by those in his own party who viewed him as a temporary replacement. Public opinion polls at the time revealed that over 75 percent of the Japanese people saw Mori as unprepared for the task of leading the nation.

The inability of the Japanese prime ministers to instill public confidence comes from the culture of the LDP, which breeds bland and cautious leadership. Political power is seen as a means of maintaining control, not an instrument of accomplishing change. Therefore the Japanese move through prime ministers with great regularity. As for cabinet ministers, their stay in office is even more precarious. The average stay in a cabinet position is one year. Like the position of prime minister, cabinet-level appointments are not viewed a political plums and are often subject to the machinations of the various factional leaders within the LDP.

The obvious question thus becomes, Who are the political elite in Japan? The answer to that question begins with the factional leaders of the LDP. There is no question that the leaders of the major factions within the LDP wield enormous power, not just in terms of patronage and distribution of campaign resources but in recruiting potential ministers and prime ministers. The term "kingmaker" is appropriate for the factional leaders who work quietly within the party hierarchy to make or break political leaders.

One reason that Japanese prime ministers find it difficult to exert decisive leadership is that they must first deal with the factional kingmakers in the party. Each kingmaker heads his own mini-LDP and pursues an electoral and policy agenda that may be different from that of the prime minister. The factional kingmakers also have considerable influence in constructing governing cabinets. In many cases Japanese coalition governments are in reality coalitions within coalitions. The makeup of the government must be formed not only to placate party partners but also to satisfy factional leaders anxious to advance their own ministers. Many observers of Japanese politics stress that prime ministers and cabinet ministers are mere front men who do the bidding of the powerful factional leaders and can be removed from their positions if they incur the wrath of the leaders.

The power elite within the LDP becomes even more complicated when another layer of influence is added to the mix. The LDP has a number of key councils and committees that exercise considerable power in terms of policy development and legislative strategy. In many instances these committees and their heads are power centers in their own right with the capacity to scotch reform efforts championed by the prime minister or to work with factional leaders to ensure that the position of the prime minister matches that of the committee head. The head of the Policy Research Council is in effect the party's chief policymaker and an expressed foe of the economic reforms that many Japanese agree are essential if Japan is to rebound from its long recession. Another critical body in the LDP is the Administrative Reform Promotion Committee, the primary body charged with making policy regarding deregulation. The head of this committee is in a position to limit or stop changes that would further deregulate the economy. Finally, a third leadership position in the LDP is the head of the Financial Reconstruction Commission, which oversees the banking industry and banking reform initiatives. The head of the commission has often been instrumental in limiting the reorganization of the banking industry and demanding more efficient procedures for handling outstanding debts and protecting citizens against default.

Outside of the factional leaders and the key committees of the LDP, ministers and subministers in key bureaucracies such as the Ministry of Finance, the Ministry of International Trade and Industry, and the Ministry of Posts and Telecommunications are vital members of the power elite. The MOF has substantial influence because of its control of the treasury and its involvement in developing and implementing economic policy. MITI, as the title suggests, is responsible for a range of governing functions including commerce, national resources, technology, and scientific research, but its involvement in trade policy has placed its chief ministers at the highest levels of national decisionmaking. The MPT has become important because of its responsibility in the area of telecommunications, but its ministerial leadership also controls the nation's largest savings bank and the postal service, an enormously lucrative bureaucracy that funds the Fiscal Investment Loan Program, the colossal public infrastructure agency that distributes billions to various projects. Because Japan has chosen to stimulate its economy through huge infrastructure projects, the Fiscal Investment Loan Program and its administrators have become important members of the power elite. Sometimes forgotten as a key player is the Ministry of Construction, which oversees public works projects. At present the construction budget is about 30 percent of the public works outlays with most of that money going into road building. The Ministry of Construction has grown dramatically in recent years and has become a more visible bureaucracy in the government.

Within each of the major ministries real power often lies with the vice minister, usually a career civil servant who comes to the position with years of expertise and a savvy ability to remain in office. Because the top minister in a cabinet position usually has a short stay due to factional infighting and political posturing, the vice minister holds the real power. Despite declining interest in public sector jobs, there is still stiff competition for positions in the key ministries at subministerial levels. Tokyo University is the primary recruiting source for up-and-coming Japanese bureaucrats. Students at "Todai" see the tough entrance exam as the entrance into the governing elite. In recent years only about 7 percent of students taking the exam were given positions in the ministries and placed on the administrative fast track.

Also part of the leadership mix in Japan are the thousands of so-called semipublic organizations that serve as regulatory arms of the government. These entities monitor various economic sectors of the economy to ensure that the government's regulatory policies are being followed. They have become havens for retired bureaucrats anxious to increase their salaries and find a safe employment haven once they leave government service. In Japan this process is termed *amakudari,* or "descending from heaven," a regular movement of ministers to these semipublic entities and also onto the boards of directors of the private sector corporations that they are charged with regulating. This incestuous relationship is highly lucrative and sought after by government ministers. Once these ministers have "descended from heaven," they continue to exert influence on economic and regulatory policy as they move easily between the government and the private sector.

Political power in Japan is not solely in the hands of the LDP or the ministries that are part of the LDP governing structure. The corporate sector has long been a major force in Japanese politics largely through the relationship of the government with the six business groups, or *keiretsu.* The *keiretsu* are large, complex networks usually comprising one of the major banks, a number of manufacturing entities, and various other enterprises from construction to shipping. The *keiretsu* are organized in different ways, some structured with equal and cooperative units while others form the equivalent of a pyramid with large corporations interacting with scores of smaller firms. The six *keiretsu* are founded on the key industries in the Japanese economy such as Sumitomo, Sony, Mitsubishi, and Toyota. These *keiretsu* are so large and encompass so much of Japanese business that they cannot be ignored by the government. In fact, most macro- and microeconomic policy decisions are made by the government ministries after extensive interaction from the representatives of the *keiretsu.* In important policy areas such as foreign trade, the six *keiretsu* often play a critical role in defining the official approach of the government as it negotiates agreements with foreign countries.

At the heart of the *keiretsu* system are the major banks. In Japan the banking industry has been the driving force of the "bubble" economy that propelled the country into the front ranks of the industrial world. But in recent years the banks have also been the source of its economic distress with bad loans and resistance to institute reforms. Japanese banks are heavily regulated by the government and as a result have close ties to the Ministry of Finance and the LDP Financial Reconstruction Commission. When the "bubble" economy burst in the mid-1990s, the long relationship with the government paid off in that many of the banks were bailed out of their enormous debts. In 1996 the LDP government of Prime Minister Hashimoto agreed to a five-year guarantee of all deposits made at failed banks. But in a policy reversal that showed the power of the banks, the government refused to limit the cap on protected deposits, which would have forced the banks to reform and institute more efficient lending policies.

Although the power elite in Japan is largely populated by representatives of traditional groups, it is important to point out that there are the beginnings of a power shift in the country. In the corporate sector the *keiretsu* system is showing signs of weakening as foreign investment and internal restructuring are causing the large business groupings to break apart or engage in mergers that limit group cohesiveness. The much heralded merger of the Sumitomo and Sakura banks in 2000 along with a series of lesser mergers showed that the *keiretsu* system is not above change and that heretofore conservative bank presidents are willing to redefine the way their institutions function in the new global economy. Also Japan is developing a new class of high-tech entrepreneur. Like Silicon Valley in the United States, Japan has its own Bit Valley, which has attracted a new generation of Japanese students anxious to make their mark in a nontraditional manner. Power and influence are beginning to be defined less in political and governmental terms and more along lines of risk-taking entrepreneurship and connections with foreign investors and multinationals. As real competition heats up in Japan and the old-boy *keiretsu* network recedes, the concentration of power among a few groups is likely to to be replaced by new members of the power elite.

The key to reform is Junichiro Koizumi. After overcoming opposition to his party leadership by the old guard, Koizumi emerged as an immensely popular leader and a symbol of a new LDP. While Obuchi and Miro were mired in dismal poll ratings, Koizumi racked up approval ratings of 80 percent in 2001. More importantly, he led his party in the July 2001 elections for the House of Representatives to a stunning victory that revitalized the party. The LDP share of the electoral vote in the House of Representatives increased from 28 percent in 1997 to 40 percent in the 2001 election. With the newfound popularity and rebound of the LDP, enormous pressure was placed on Koizumi to deliver results in revitalizing the economy and bringing sweeping structural reforms to the way in which Japan organizes its banking and business sectors. Koizumi was viewed as an outsider both in his own party and in the ranks of the bureaucracy. While outsider status originally was seen as providing Koizumi with an opportunity to shake up the system and bring about significant reform, by 2002 the Japanese prime minister was languishing, with popular support sagging and reform efforts in banking and bureaucratic restructuring rejected by powerful elites in the LDP and in the key ministries.

POINT OF FACT

The longest-serving prime minister was Sato Eisaku, who held power from 1964 to 1972. Three Japanese prime ministers served two months or less.

URBAN LIFE AND HOUSING SHORTAGES

Japan is frequently imaged in terms of large, crowded urban centers. Japan's population of 125 million people is concentrated in its major cities, with eleven Japanese cities of over 1 million people. Since 1900 the Japanese urban population has grown from 12 percent of the total to nearly 80 percent, according to 1990 census data. Currently, over half of the Japanese population lives in the metropolitan areas of Tokyo, Osaka, and Nagoya. This movement of people into the urban areas has created special problems for the government in the areas of proper infrastructure planning, land use, housing, and environmental considerations. The extent of these problems is made clear every day in Japan with subway and road congestion, dwindling open space, housing shortages, and severely polluted air. Massive growth compromises the quality of life in Japanese urban centers. There is widespread grumbling about the problems of urban life, and some evidence that the Japanese people are moving out of the major urban centers.

Yet Japanese cities continue to be a magnet for business, banking, and education. For example, 31 percent of the Japanese GNP is produced in the Tokyo metropolitan area, 91 percent of bankers and employees in the non-Japanese financial institutions operate in Tokyo, and 40 percent of students studying in institutions of higher learning reside in Tokyo. Japanese young people in particular continue to view urban life as a plus in terms of access to goods and services and the level of freedom and leisure activities that abound in the urban setting. Moreover, because of the heavy concentration of business, banking, and education in the great metropolitan areas, it is difficult to persuade people not to move to the cities. The Japanese government has done little to limit urban growth as it continues to build superhighways, bullet trains, and other public works projects designed to ease the burden of living and working in the cities.

Perhaps the most serious problem associated with urban life is in the area of housing. Japan has an urban housing shortage brought on by the sustained movement of people into the cities. Problems related to housing include the high cost of housing, the space available in housing, and the need for major renovations of the housing stock. In many of the large metropolitan areas small homes and apartments were built in the postwar era to accommodate population movements. But many of these structures were hastily built and fall below code standards. There is great fear in Japan that a major earthquake affecting the three major urban centers—Tokyo, Osaka, and Nagoya—would cause serious loss of life due to poor housing construction. Of the 40 million houses and apartments in Japan, it is estimated that 40 percent face onto narrow roads or pathways. This poses health and safety problems for ambulance and fire equipment.

Rapid, sustained urbanization in Japan has also led to serious environmental problems. Although the Japanese Diet in the 1970s passed major antipollution laws designed to address hazards associated with large industrial plants situated near densely populated areas, environmental protests have heightened in recent years. Japanese urban dwellers are concerned over issues of noise pollution from airports, land appropriations for major highway projects, and the general dislocations that are part of urban life. In 2000 residents in suburban Tokyo began a campaign to end the use of a public address system that has been installed by the government to provide regular messages to residents. Messages such as "Children, go home, it's getting dark" to "Don't use water, it hasn't rained in recent days," have begun to test the limits of patience of many Japanese. While minor compared to other forms of pollution, the constant Orwellian reminders, although consistent with the Japanese dependence on authority, add to the decline in the quality of urban life.

Japanese government officials do not have what can be termed a national strategic plan for urban problems, even though it is arguably the most serious quality of life issue, other than the stagnating economy. Perhaps because of the enormity of the problem, the government has settled for piecemeal solutions. It would be easy to state that the answer to Japan's urban problem is for people to move out of the cities, but that is not a plausible solution considering that Japan is an island nation with a scarcity of livable land space. Although there is some movement out of the cities, the answer may lie with more creative ways of dealing with the crush of people in urban areas. ⊕

Legislative Composition as of April 9, 2002	
Liberal Democratic Party	240 seats
Democratic Party	125 seats
Clean Government Party	31 seats
Communist Party	20 seats
Liberal Party	22 seats
Social Democratic Party	18 seats
Liberal League	1 seat
Conservative Party	7 seats
Independents Party	5 seats
Nonpartisan	11 seats

REAL GOVERNMENT

The process of making public policy decisions in Japan lies in the relationship of bureaucrats in the ministries, big business leaders, and top LDP politicians. Although the bureaucracy is relatively small compared to those in other countries and does not expend huge levels of budgetary resources, it clearly controls the governing system in Japan. Japan is best described as having a state-directed economy and a ministry-driven policy process (the term "Japan, Inc." is commonly used to describe the policy process because of the heavy involvement of the government and business in the economy). In this state-directed economy and ministry-driven policy process the bureaucracy engages in a cooperative relationship with the LDP and the *keiretsu* to advance national interests that are often defined by the ministries. The result is a policy climate in which the ministries "guide" the LDP and the *keiretsu* so that they follow the "correct" path toward solving national problems or advancing national interests.

Since the Japanese bureaucracy has amassed great governing power and has dominated the policy process, a question arises as to how it achieved this control. During the American occupation of Japan (in contrast to the occupation of Germany) there was little, if any, purge of the existing bureaucracy. The American occupiers were more interested in shaping the political system and stripping it of its authoritarian culture. They thus left the bureaucracy intact and in the process elevated the ministries to the highest level of decisionmaking. As Japan moved through its postwar development, it was the cohesive ministries, rather than the squabbling political parties within the Diet, that led the country. The public policy process thus became one in which the ministries initiated legislation that was then voted on by the Diet. The Diet, because it was overshadowed by the expertise and the high level of national respect of the ministries, usually passed legislation that was broad in scope and general in language. Consequently, the bureaucracy defined public policy and implemented the policy as it interacted with the complex corporate groupings, LDP politicians, and foreign interests.

The domination of the Japanese public policy process is best demonstrated by the Ministry of International Trade and Industry (MITI) and its involvement in directing the development of key industrial sectors. Japanese ministries like MITI have been credited with formulating what has come to be called industrial policy, an approach to national economic development in which the government works hand in hand with businesses and politicians to build new industries or to guarantee that existing industries have sufficient resources to compete in the domestic economy and the global economy. The Japanese have honed their techniques for implementing industrial policy since the early 1950s and have met with phenomenal success. They have earned the praise of their competitors for their visionary understanding of how government can assist economic development. But they have also created enormous tensions with foreign businesses and governments over their use of protectionist policies to launch a new industrial sector.

MITI officials in the postwar period utilized the close relationship with the various corporate groupings and their penchant to "guide" the economy to jump-start new industries such as steel and shipbuilding. MITI worked with the banks to provide the seed money for these nascent industries and limited competition to ensure that foreign companies in these sectors would not hamper the growth of these new business enterprises. Using tariffs, MITI effectively shut out foreign competition for a number of years. It then provided generous tax incentives, infrastructure development, and other subsidies to ensure that these industries would have not only the time but also the resources to compete with established foreign firms. Throughout this process of industry building MITI worked closely with the LDP in the Diet and the *keiretsu* to guarantee that all the key players and interests were focusing on national economic interests and strategic business plans.

MITI's broad-based industrial policies helped Japan move into the front ranks of the world's industrial powers, but at the same time it received frequent criticism for the manner in which it sought entry into export markets. In one particular area, semiconductors, Japanese industrial policy was highly successful but stimulated protest from foreign competitors like the United States. Beginning in the 1980s Japanese semiconductor manufacturers, with extensive help and encouragement from MITI, were able to become major suppliers of computer chips. MITI developed a marketing strategy anchored in long-term development rather than short-term profit. Computer chip companies in Japan were encouraged to sell their products at lower prices than competitors such as Motorola in the United States. These pricing policies, often termed dumping, incurred the wrath of both American companies and the U.S. government, but they allowed the Japanese firms to grab a larger share of the market. Furthermore, MITI established firm protectionist policies that made it difficult for American firms to build semiconductor factories in Japan, thus further limiting their ability to enter the Japanese market and compete with Japanese firms. The result was that through the cooperation of the semiconductor industry and MITI a key sector of the Japanese economy emerged as a solid international competitor.

The Japanese "way" of building and advancing domestic industries through cooperation and a healthy dose of protectionism has often frustrated foreign, especially American, businesses. The Japanese government has historically resisted approving applications from foreign businesses to establish a subsidiary or joint venture operation where the foreign business would hold a major share. This forced American businesses to license their products to Japanese firms. With licensing arrangements the Japanese continued to control domestic production while shutting out foreign direct involvement. It was only after the Japanese had gained the upper hand in the production of a particular product such as semiconductors that they eased the rules for foreign involvement.

There is no question that policymaking power resides in key ministries such as MITI, but that does not mean that the ruling LDP, particularly key factional leaders, are left out of the mix. In the LDP there are various informal policy groupings called *zoku*. *Zoku* members represent important economic sectors such as construction, telecommunication, transportation, and agriculture. They are also active in social policy sectors such as welfare. The primary function of the *zoku* is to advance the interests of their particular group in the highest levels of the party and the various ministries. *Zoku* gain influence for their interest by providing campaign funds and guarantees of votes from their base of supporters. One of the most powerful *zoku* is in the construction industry, which is one of the reasons that the public works budget, especially in road construction, is so high. *Zoku* politicians make sure that their interests are well protected and advanced and that attempts to reduce budget allocations are quashed.

In the Japanese Diet the *koenkai* groupings act as informal interest advocates, pressuring the ministries on behalf of their particular economic or social sector. Where the *zoku* are interested in budget allocations and regulations, the *koenkai* are formed by LDP politicians to ensure that their constituent groups receive patronage positions in the ministries and more mundane favors such as business permits, subsidies, and contracts. The *keonkai* groups can become powerful voices within the Japanese policy process because they too provide campaign funds to the LDP politicians along with a range of campaign-related support. One of the more interesting aspects of the *koenkai* is their longevity. There is considerable evidence that *koenkai* groupings are handed down through generations of LDP politicians and are utilized to guarantee electoral victory along with consistent influence within the ministries. In the 1996 general election 122 sons, daughters, sons-in-law, and grandsons of former Diet members won seats in the House of Representatives. The resiliency of the *koenkai* is a testament to the value the Japanese place on these informal electoral-policymaking arrangements.

Because the *zoku* and the *koenkai* are formidable forces within the public policy process and can effectively limit efforts to bring reform, recent prime ministers have attempted to establish new structures that seek to speed up change. So-called special advisory councils have been established in the key policy areas of deregulation and administrative reform. Prime ministers have appointed distinguished business leaders and academicians to these councils. In many respects these "councils" act in similar fashion to blue-ribbon commissions in the United States as they survey a problem area, gather data and testimony, and then issue a series of policy recommendations. The only problem with the "special advisory councils" is that they rely heavily on cooperation from the ministries that control the flow of information and even influence the makeup of the "councils." The result is that the well-intentioned efforts of the prime ministers are less than effective in bringing about change. The Japanese bureaucracy continues to hold most of the policy power, despite the illusion of aggressive change that the "special advisory councils" provide.

What the Experts Say

Japanese scholar M. Diana Helweg, writing on the movement of the country away from principles and practices that have limited the prospects for reform, states:

The revolution underway in Japan will recreate the nation from the inside out. Slowly but surely, Japan is shifting from state direction to a free market. Indeed Japan's social and political structures already reflect some of these changes. For example, the bureaucracy in various ministries now holds less control over the prime minister's office and the parliament than ever before. Newly elected Diet members are drafting reform legislation with the input of foreign businesses and government officials rather than bureaucrats.

"JAPAN: A RISING SUN," *Foreign Affairs*,
JULY–AUGUST 2000

There is, however, an alternative view. Another school of thought is built on the view that Japanese ministries and the key factional leaders in the LDP are merely offering window dressing reforms that either do little to change traditional governing practices or are revised shortly after implementation. Like the reform argument made above, there is adequate evidence to show that following a brief period of change after the 1993 electoral debacle and the Asian financial crisis of 1998, the Japanese government instituted reforms that opened up the trading system, restructured existing governmental institutions, and provided for more economic competition. But as Japan entered the new millennium and found that reforms threatened existing power bases, particularly in the banking and construction industries, changes were quietly and efficiently dismantled.

What the Experts Say

Aurelia George Mulgan, another respected Japan scholar, sees the prospect for change in a much more pessimistic manner:

Despite the fact that the Japanese economy has repeatedly shown that old methods and policies do not work, the push for reform has been vetoed by bureaucrats and LDP politicians. The modest injection of dynamism into the economy effected by corporate restructuring, the information-technology boom, the explosion of e-commerce, and the dissolution of traditional keiretsu corporate groups . . . is not enough to offset the drag of vested interests and myopic, self-serving bureaucrats and politicians.

"JAPAN: A SETTING SUN," *Foreign Affairs*,
JULY–AUGUST 2000

The direction that Japanese governance takes in the coming years depends in large part on how the state-business relationship evolves. There is no question that Japan is a country that resists change and values traditional practices and informal arrangements. But this is a crucial time for Japanese bureaucrats, businessmen, and politicians. Sustained recession and globalization have upset the normal stability of the state-business relationship. The normal modus operandi of Japan, Inc. faces a clear challenge as a result of its faltering economy and the outside pressures of a new international marketplace. If history is a proper guide, the relationship of bureaucrats, businessmen, and politicians will seek the course of least resistance and make as few adjustments as possible to the modus operandi. The key members of this relationship are of the mind-set that the economy will improve and that the impact of the global economy can be managed through the traditional tools of delay, controlled access, and the appearance of reform.

FOREIGN AID POLICY

Although Japan is experiencing a decline in its economy, it continues to rank number one in the world in bilateral development assistance, better known as foreign aid. Since 1991 Japan has held the number one position without interruption. In 1998 Japanese bilateral assistance totaled $8.606 billion and disbursements to multilateral institutions totaled another $2.125 billion, for an overall commitment of $10.731 billion. Japan leads the United States, which as a result of budgetary cutbacks during the second term of President Clinton has experienced a sharp drop in foreign aid. In Japan public opinion toward the heavy budgetary allocations for what is officially called Overseas Development Assistance (ODA) has also weakened in recent years in large part because of the faltering economy. But there is a large residue of support and pride for the contributions that the country has made in the area of ODA. Japan has stark memories of the destruction it experienced in World War II and the huge influx of foreign assistance that helped the country get back on its feet. World Bank assistance financed the Fourth Kurobe Dam and the Tomei and Meishin expressways, which are lasting reminders of the value of foreign assistance.

Japan's ODA program is not the result of national altruism. It has been subject to extensive pressure from the United States and other European powers to take measures that redirect national resources from its huge trade imbalance and small defense commitments into foreign assistance. There has also been a prevalent view in government and business circles that because Japan depends on foreign energy and raw materials, it should use foreign assistance as a means of ensuring access to those needs. Finally, there is a growing recognition that as the global economy plays more of a role in shaping the Japanese economy, it is simply good business to provide generous ODA as one means of expanding business. Japanese *keiretsu* are becoming increasingly aware that development projects offer numerous opportunities. In practical terms, ODA is one way that Japan can become a world leader and even outdo the West, especially the United States. As a 1999 report on official development assistance states, "Japan can win the confidence and appreciation of the international community" and also ensure its "own stability and prosperity by contributing to sustainable social and economic development in developing countries."

Japan now provides official development assistance to 150 countries in a number of forms—grant aid, technical cooperation, loan assistance, and contributions to international organizations. Japanese ODA has included specialized contributions to assist disaster victims, refugees from ethnic conflicts, and those that have been hospitalized because of land mine injuries. Japan has also not shied away from using its ODA in areas that are hotly controversial. It provided disaster assistance to communist Vietnam and contributed over $360 million to the Palestinian Authority, the largest contribution by any single donor country. In the Asian region Japan uses assistance as a means of advancing its own strategic and corporate objectives (Sri Lanka, for example, receives 40 percent of all its foreign and international assistance from Japan). Elsewhere there are pockets of assistance, such as in Peru, where the past president was of Japanese ethnicity.

Because of its large ODA contributions and its growing presence in the developing world, Japan is becoming the target of groups opposed to foreign assistance. In 1999 Japanese aid personnel were abducted in the former Russian republic of Kyrgyzstan, and there have been a number of lesser incidents targeting Japanese development officials. There have also been problems associated with language and cultural differences that have impeded the delivery of Japanese assistance. The dangers and the problems posed by aid work in less developed countries have not hindered the desire of the Japanese government to maintain its status as the number one donor of bilateral assistance in the world. Japanese aid officials in the 1999 ODA report expressed the position that providing foreign aid offers an opportunity to "maintain its vitality within the global community . . . and win the confidence and appreciation of the international community." Providing foreign assistance has clearly become a key means of playing an important role in international affairs. ⊕

POINT OF FACT
Japan's post office, more than the agency responsible for delivering the mail, is the world's largest financial institution. The Japanese have placed over $2 trillion in the post office bank, and 40 percent of life insurance is written by this agency.

THE POLITICAL ECONOMY

In the 1980s the Japanese economy was red-hot and poised to become an even more influential player in the industrial world. As a result of the 1985 Plaza Accord among the United States, Japan, West Germany, France, and Britain, which was designed to lower the value of the dollar, the Japanese yen appreciated in value. To avoid crippling its export sector, Japanese officials introduced liberal monetary policies and increased public spending and public investment. With capital cheap and available, Japanese banks began lending money with reckless abandon, which created huge borrowing opportunities and extensive speculation, particularly in real estate and stocks. The combination of a strong yen and easy money created a level of economic activity of enormous proportions. Caution was thrown to the wind as large and small firms rode the bandwagon of speculation and profitability.

This was the time when land prices in Japanese cities tripled and made instant millionaires, the Tokyo Stock Exchange outpaced the venerable New York Stock Exchange, and Japanese tourists, flush with a strong yen, traveled the world and stayed in newly purchased Japanese hotels and resorts. There was enormous confidence in Japan and widespread unease in the United States and Europe. The Japanese were clearly the dominant force in the international economy. They seemed unstoppable and their system of state-directed capitalism and communitarian economic culture was viewed as the wave of the future.

Then the bubble burst. In 1990 the Bank of Japan increased the discount rate (effectively increasing interest rates), creating a cascading impact on stocks, land, real estate holdings, and business ventures. Banks were saddled with huge debts and businesses collapsed into bankruptcy. The excitement and confidence that the "bubble economy" fostered was replaced by a kind of national paralysis as the Japanese government and business community frantically looked for ways out of the financial morass.

Since the mid-1990s Japan has experienced a long, difficult recession period accompanied by a political struggle in the ruling LDP and government bureaucracy over the most effective measures to revitalize the faltering economy. The Japanese have been unable to find the right mix of policies, both public and private, to move the economy out of recession. The result has been a painful political and economic period with Japan no longer being viewed as possessing a model economy worthy of following. Since the "bubble" days, Japan's competitors have made major adjustments in the way they organize their economies and conduct international trade. Japan, on the other hand, has been reluctant to restructure its state capitalist system, relying instead on its traditional cooperative, regulatory, and protectionist policies. Coupled with the Asian financial crisis that weakened some of its key trading partners in the region, the Japanese have had to endure over ten years of negligible growth, unemployment, huge bank debts, and government budget deficits.

At the heart of the economic malaise in Japan is the sluggish growth rate compounded by over $1 trillion in bad bank loans. For most of the 1990s the Japanese economy registered anemic growth figures in the 1 percent range. Then in the late 1990s Japan experienced a sharp drop-off in GDP. In 1999 Japan's "growth" was -1 percent. As Japan entered the twenty-first century, there was evidence of moderate growth in the 1–2 percent range, still not terribly dynamic. A report from the Japanese government in August 2000 remained cautiously optimistic about economic growth, stating that "although the Japanese economy has not yet got out of the severe situation, activities continue to improve moderately." But in 2001 and 2002 Japan was stilled mired in recession with a shrinking economy and few signs of a quick recovery. The more serious challenge in 2001 and 2002 was deflation, as prices continued to drop and caused fears that the economy could enter a more serious phase of decline.

Negative growth rates and bad debts have had a devastating impact on business bankruptcies and worker unemployment. Bankruptcies rose steadily in the late 1990s from nearly 15,000 in 1996 to a high of 20,000 in 1998. By 2000, business failures had dropped to 13,000, signaling a stabilizing economy. The unemployment rate in the country has historically been either nonexistent or very low (around 2 percent). But starting in 1994, the unemployment rate skyrocketed to 3 percent and then to 5.4 percent in 2002. As Japanese companies cut payrolls and engaged in long overdue restructuring, workers became one of the first victims of the economic decline. Between 1997 and 2000 up to 1 million Japanese workers were "restructured" out of their jobs.

Unemployment in Japan touched off a steep decline in spending in a nation that already had a reputation for thrift and high savings rates. Workers' real disposable income by household dropped precipitously in 1998, 1999, and 2000 to pre-1990 levels, further pushing the economy downward. Although Japan has a fully functioning social welfare system that provides unemployment insurance and workers' compensation, the high cost of living in the country has made it difficult for those "restructured" out of a job to live adequately. Japan now has homelessness and abject poverty that was unheard of during the "bubble" days.

In areas of the economy at which Japan has normally excelled—foreign trade and maintaining a positive budget balance—the bursting of the bubble had a devastating impact. Trade with its Asian neighbors dropped off dramatically, falling nearly 20 percent during the lowest point of the recession in 1998. Trade with the United States reversed as the trade imbalance surged upward in 1998 and 1999. There were some signs of a new vibrancy in Japanese trade in 2000, especially as its Asian neighbors rebounded from their own crises and exports of personal computers, telecommunications equipment, and other high-tech products combined to improve the trade balance. But the U.S. economic downturn in 2001 contributed to an overall slowdown of the economy that limited the ability of Japanese businesses to regain the trade dominance they held in the 1980s and early 1990s. At the close of 2001, industrial production in Japan shrank by 15 percent from the previous year, which moved Japan into a recession for the fourth time in ten years.

Attempting to move the country out of its economic morass, the government introduced a series of public works spending programs that injected $124 billion in 1998 and $85 billion in 1999. Between 1992 and 1999 government stimulus packages totaled $1.2 trillion. This public works spending, however, had a downside as the national debt ballooned to 150 percent of the GDP in 1997 and has remained high since then. In 2000 long-term debt, a combination of national and local borrowing, was pegged at $6 trillion, which translated into $48,000 per capita. The Japanese, who during the glory days of the economy prided themselves on their positive balance sheet, were forced to admit that they were a debtor nation. Prime Minister Obuchi called himself "the world's largest debtor." There is now deep concern in Japanese society that future generations will be saddled with the debt created by massive government spending.

Attaining a new economic environment will require structural adjustments in the way Japan interacts with global partners. For much of the postwar period Japanese businesses and Japanese workers were shielded from the impact of foreign competition, particularly in terms of wages and prices. But as Japanese industries faced increased competition from abroad, it quickly became clear that domestic firms would have to reduce their prices, their profitability, and the wages they paid to workers in order to survive in the harsh global marketplace. Japanese businesses and the Japanese government must intensify their efforts to heighten productivity and become more competitive if they are to increase profits and remain solvent. In the meantime Japanese workers are left with declining paychecks or, worse yet, forced unemployment as the impact of globalization hits home. The Japanese are involved in retraining programs to move the unemployed into new industries and areas of economic vitality, but this is a slow process, especially since the business community has been reluctant to engage in the kind of entrepreneurship and "creative destruction" found in the United States.

A key structural problem contributing to the Japanese recession is the relationship between savings and domestic investment. Currently Japan has one of the highest levels of savings in the world. Household savings in 1999 totaled 1,300 trillion yen. The enormity of savings has contributed to a high level of capital accumulation in Japan. The high level of savings is not just a factor of traditional Japanese conservative consumer buying habits. Rather, savings are associated with what has been called "double savings," which means that in an aging society like Japan with a declining birthrate, older people are saving more in preparation for the costs associated with senior status (nursing home care and medical bills), while younger people are saving because of their concern over the future of an unsteady economy. The "double savings" problem is compounded by the fact that Japanese savings are largely deposited in low-risk

assets such as bank passbook accounts and postal savings. Such savings, for example, comprise 55 percent of total assets in Japan, while in the United States
such deposits account for only 15 percent. In the United States savings are increasingly being shifted into stocks and bonds, which make up 43 percent of
household assets, while in Japan the amount is only 7 percent.

The savings glut in Japan has led to a decline in capital productivity. There is
currently a severe shortage of risk capital in Japan. Investors both in Japan and
abroad are reluctant to bring their capital to Japan because the amount of fixed
assets necessary to produce the same gross domestic product has been increasing.
In simple terms, the productivity of Japanese capital has been declining.
Japanese businesses and investors recognize this condition and understand the
need to create a high profitability environment in the country by creating new
industries and reallocating capital and labor to those new industries. There have
been some promising signs in the area of capital investment in recent years.
Foreign direct investment in 1998 totaled $10.5 billion, with over 60 percent
coming from U.S. sources. In the first six months of 1999, $11.3 billion in for-
eign capital entered the country, with increasing interest from European sources.
There are no signs to suggest this trend will end, but foreign investors stayed
away from Japan for years and it will be a slow road back. Moreover, Japanese
government officials have a major challenge to change the monetary habits of
the people. The sluggishness of consumer spending and consumer debt has put a
damper on government efforts to get the economy moving. In Japan how much
people save, where they save it, and how foreign investors look at the savings climate are vital ingredients in the process of economic revitalization.

The revitalization of the Japanese economy is not devoid of optimism.
Most economists and economic analysts agree that Japan in the coming years
will experience slow but steady growth. There is no grand bubble that will
emerge to spring the economy forward, but rather 2–3 percent growth rates,
diminishing unemployment rates, and a decline in bankruptcies and foreclosures. After ten years of recession and sluggishness Japan has started to learn
the lessons of the global marketplace and a deregulated and competitive domestic economy. Change is everywhere. Japanese accounting practices have
been reformed to follow international standards, a change that will force the
closing of loopholes used by business to avoid taxes and investors to hide
profits and losses. This reform will also strengthen the pension system, which
companies avoided paying into and in so doing created major liabilities.
Japanese banks are also undergoing change. Tough new regulations will require banks to provide documentation on the basis for their loans, using standards such as a company's credit worthiness. Moreover, bank loans will be set
at rates that are internationally competitive. Gone are the days of the sweet-
heart deals in the *keiretsu* groups that were ill advised and eventually unpro-

ductive. Prime Minister Koizumi appointed Heizo Takenaka in 2002 to be Japan's financial czar with the express task of requiring banks to dispose of bad loans and to ensure that there is no repeat of unprofitable lending in the coming years. In return for these strong measures Takenaka developed a plan to use public money to bail out many of the underperforming banks. Only time will tell if this bargain between the government and the banks will provide the impetus for a rejuvenated economy.

It is fair to state that the Japanese economy has entered a new phase. It is still in the process of transition from its regulated, protectionist, ministry-dominated economy to one that is deregulated, global, and more privately directed. Since the end of World War II Japan has looked to the United States for guidance on a whole range of issues and concerns while putting its own mark on the ideas and models that have been imported. Since the 1950s Japan has resisted American economic models, choosing instead to create a corporate and financial system that shields its businesses and its people from external competition. But the global economy is so pervasive and so unforgiving that the Japanese have been forced to play by new rules, rules that it cannot control with any degree of confidence. There is still a Japanese-style economy and there remains the Japanese way of doing business, but there is also a global version of the Japanese economy and a global way of doing business that is grudgingly being accepted. The Japanese will no longer be able to hold back the tide of the globalization. There will be attempts to delay it, tinker with it, run around it, and ignore it, but the new generation of Japanese business leaders and the younger generation of Japanese are now clamoring for an end to the old system.

POINT OF FACT
Tokyo is the world's costliest city to live in and to visit.

Japan in the Global Economy

In recent years Japan has begun restructuring its economy to allow for greater access to foreign firms and heightened imports. There has also been a movement away from the small "mom and pop" stores and toward major international retailers. A study by the *Economist* found that many foreign retailers such as The Gap, Starbucks, Gucci, and Bulgari have made significant inroads in the Japanese economy. Moreover, in the last eight years imports have been up over 60 percent, while exports have only risen 25 percent. A country that once was export driven is now accenting import-based consumerism.

WHALING POLICY

The dietary habits of a people seldom become a public policy issue. But Japan has a long-standing love affair with whales and whale meat. Strangely, this love affair has created an international controversy over how many whales the Japanese will be permitted to kill in order to continue an important tradition. Whales and whaling in Japan have evolved into a policy struggle pitting the dietary and cultural proclivities of a nation against the proponents of species preservation fishing limits. First, a little background on how whale meat became a public policy issue.

In postwar Japan, when the economy was still a shambles, whale meat, which was abundant, became popular, especially among the poor. At its peak in 1962, whale meat consumption hit 220,000 tons, creating a whole new segment of the fishing industry and a number of ancillary businesses such as restaurants featuring whale meat and delicacy stores offering specialized whale products. Eventually, even whale museums and mini-amusement parks catering to the Japanese passion for the whale were built in response to the growing interest and near worship of the giant mammal. Then in 1986 the International Whaling Commission banned commercial whaling and allowed whales to be killed only for research purposes, such as gathering information on migration, eating patterns, and pollution levels. The Japanese complied with the restrictions but have used the scientific loophole as a way to kill as many as 500 minke whales and over 150 Baird's beaked and pilot whales each year since 1986.

In 2000 the Japanese began a major challenge to the whale-hunting ban when the government announced that its ships would add ten sperm whales and fifty Bryde's whales to its hunt list. This decision prompted an international protest from fifteen countries that categorize these whales as endangered and see the Japanese move as a bold attempt to resume whale hunting for commercial purposes. There is talk among these fifteen nations of trade sanctions against Japan if it carries out its planned whale hunt. The United States in the past has denied Japan certain fishing rights in its waters as a result of Japanese whale hunting. For their part the Japanese feel that they are the targets of a kind of cultural imperialism as other countries try to change their dietary habits. Prime Minister Mori called the expanded whale hunt "a matter of principle, of national pride." Moreover, Japanese officials stated that protections put in place in 1986 have led to a significant increase in the whale population, particularly among the minke whale population, thereby lessening the impact of the international criticism of the expanded whale hunt.

But countries like the United States, New Zealand, and Great Britain and international environmental organizations like the Greenpeace Whale Project are outraged at the Japanese for expanding the hunt list and for claiming that whale populations are large enough to merit a resumption in the killing of whales. The Japanese position is viewed as consumption driven, and the so-called scientific hunt is ridiculed as a means of circumventing the 1986 restrictions. As Richard Page of the Greenpeace Whale Project stated in an interview with the *Washington Post*, "The primary reasons they [Japanese] are doing this is to sell the meat on the Japanese market and keep the industry alive. There is a difference between counting whales for science and killing them for science. There are whale researchers all over the world who are studying whales without killing them."

For all the international criticism and threat of sanction, the Japanese are undaunted in their push to expand the whale hunt. Already the government has stated that it intends to increase the whale kill in the coming years. There is little effort to be conciliatory with the international community on whaling. In 2002 the Japanese government engaged in a bitter dispute with the United States when Washington sought to reinstate a five-year whale-hunting season for the Alaskan Eskimo, who have long competed with the Japanese. Despite the international opposition and the tensions that have erupted with the United States, the Japanese are convinced that they have an obligation to their fishing industry and their cultural traditions to stand up to the criticism and the sanctions. In this case a public policy issue is driven as much by business consideration as by consumer habits. ⊕

CHALLENGES

Shortly before his death in January 2000, Prime Minister Obuchi's advisory council issued a report entitled *Japan's Vision for the Twenty-first Century.* In that report the advisory council presented a surprisingly pessimistic view of Japan's future, using such terminology as "a sense of urgency," "anxiety" over Japan's decline, and the tendency for the political leadership to keep the system "unchanged." The report reads like a mix of gloom and doom and cheer-leading and talks of the need to be courageous in the face of the challenges that lie ahead. The recommendations in the report were not new as council members called for deregulation, an end to heavy government spending in big ticket public works projects, and a reduction in the influence of the ministries and the special interests that often control the ministries. There was even a recommendation for the direct election of the prime minister as a means of reducing the power of the bureaucracy and weakening the influence of the *keiretsu.*

The advisory council report fits in with the current national dialogue over change and challenge. The Japanese, from the man and woman on the street to the highest levels of party and bureaucracy, are talking about a transformation of the entire national system of leadership and decisionmaking that will take the country into a new era. Much like transformations during the Meiji Restoration that did away with the samurai ruling class and during the American occupation that brought governing reforms, the "third revolution" would be a break with existing power relations and policy process, replacing the past with a more open, competitive, and dynamic system of politics, corporate behavior, and economic development. For a country like Japan that has been wedded to the past and reluctant to make major adjustments to the way it organizes its society and conducts its key decisionmaking processes, the call for a "third revolution" signals deep frustration within Japan and strong support for a fundamental shake-up in national life.

In many respects Japan has already entered the "third revolution" with reforms in the business and financial sectors and new openings in foreign trade and investment. But the kind of change that is revolutionary in character is much broader than that dealing with the economy. A revolution in Japan would include revamping the political elite, changing the relationship between citizen and state, redefining the national political culture, debating military policy and military preparedness, and examining the implications of new regional powers on Japanese security and economic development. Each of these challenges will test the Japanese political and governing system in ways that cut to the heart of what it means to be Japanese.

First and foremost attaining a "third revolution" will require sweeping reform of Japan's de facto one-party system. The ruling Liberal Democratic Party is not a dominant force in Japanese politics and government just because of its superior organization and money-raising capabilities; it has prospered through scandal and recession because the Japanese electorate has been offered no credible alternative. If change is to come to the political elite in Japan, it will come from within the LDP as a new generation of leaders seeks to create a more publicly responsive and politically aggressive ruling organization. Pushing the LDP out of power in a manner akin to the dismantling of the Russian Communist Party is not out of the question, but that is not the Japanese way. With Prime Minister Koizumi at least on the surface committed to change, the LDP and indeed Japan can enter a new period of change where real economic and governing restructuring occurs, not just the usual delay and cautious tinkering.

Koizumi has had and likely will have a difficult time in moving his party and the entrenched interests in the bureaucracy toward meaningful reform. A number of policy initiatives pushed by Koizumi in 2002 such as reducing the bad debt load, revamping the bloated public works sector, and pressing for the privatization of the postal service simply languished in the Diet and the ministries. Koizumi has shown a feistiness and a determination to chart an independent course that puts him at odds with the old-line forces in the LDP and the ministries, but real structural reform continues to elude the prime minister. Old power arrangements and old bureaucratic practices die hard in the Japanese political system.

Economic necessity and external pressures can combine to force change in ways that the LDP is not ready for. The frustration and anger that are present in Japanese society after ten years of economic decline can be a power trigger for leadership change. A poll taken by the Japanese cabinet in 2001 found that the level of dissatisfaction with the quality of life had dropped dramatically since 1995 and that there is little patience with the established system of governance and economic policymaking among wide segments of the population. Moreover, the ever expanding reach of the global economy can be a potent stimulus for internal political reform. Because the economic rules have changed, the political rules will change too.

Another powerful force at work in Japanese politics that will ultimately influence the governing elite is aging leadership. Political parties that hold power for a long time suffer from the effects of political gerontocracy; their leadership ages and is forced by the facts of life to give up power. When Prime Minister Mori accepted the leadership of the LDP he was photographed with his cabinet and other ranking LDP leaders. The picture was a classic example of gerontocracy—scores of aging men in their late seventies and early eighties posing for the cameras perhaps for the last time before they retire or leave the political stage. Revamping the political elite may not be so much a process of forced change as a kind of survival of the fittest.

It is well known that the Japanese bureaucracy is a powerful player in the process of governing. Key ministries and the ministerial elite in those ministries make and enforce public policy. This means that other more democratic institutions in the Japanese political system have little voice in charting the course of national development. The Diet has been weak, the prefecture system of local governance is no match for the power of the central government, opposition politics is fractured, and other nongovernmental players such as the press, the electronic media, and public opinion are much less influential than in other industrialized countries. The Japanese people have come to accept that their system is in large part nondemocratic, with policy being made through the interaction of bureaucracies, special interests, and LDP leadership. If Japan is to truly reform the way it does politics and create a "third revolution," it will have to redefine the manner in which the all-powerful state meets the Japanese people.

The concept of popular sovereignty will have to be clarified and improved on in the Japanese political system. Reforms will have to be instituted that place the popular will in closer contact with the government. Changes such as the direct election of the prime minister are one such reform that would begin the process of true democratization. There are some signs that younger members of the Diet are beginning to challenge the status quo and are using the legislative body to control the ministries. Prime ministerial advisory councils are emerging as a new method of reining in the bureaucracy. Japan will also have to develop a more potent press and civic reform groups that pressure the LDP, and special interests will need to become more visible. Currently there are not enough channels for opposing the power of government in Japan. Because the opposition political parties are forever engaged in petty disputes and realignments, the voice of popular sovereignty will have to come from somewhere else. Without a stronger Diet, a more vigilant press, and the emergence of a vocal citizen reform movement, the power of the ministries will remain unchallenged and democratic practice will be relegated to an electoral process that has been unable to bring about change.

All of Japan's challenges, however, are not solely domestic and associated with the character of the political and governmental system. In the last few years Japan has been forced to articulate a foreign policy that moves beyond the postwar alliance with the United States and its generous foreign assistance programs. The emergence of China as a regional powerhouse has made Japan rethink its reluctance to become involved with its neighbors. In recent years Japan has been at odds with China over incursions into its waters by Chinese naval and intelligence vessels. There is also a long-standing dispute over tiny islands in the East China Sea that each country claims as its own. Underlying these points of tension is the growing aggressiveness of the Chinese in the region and the accompanying expansion of its military establishment. Japan, which in the past has avoided taking steps that would heighten diplomatic tensions with its neighbors, took the unusual step in 2000 of threatening to delay loans to China, a considerable threat since Japan has provided China with over $23 billion in assistance since 1979. Japan's concerns over China have intensified as Russia under Vladimir Putin has talked openly about a "strategic partnership" with the Peking government, an alliance that Liberal Democratic officials would rather not see develop. Then there is North Korea with its emerging nuclear capacity and its test firing of missiles that served as a wake-up call to the Japanese.

Although security issues are now rising to the top of the Japanese priority list, the economy and economic restructuring remain critical. Political leaders like Prime Minister Koizumi cannot avoid the realities of a fourth recession in the last decade, an eighteen-year low for the Tokyo stock market, declining credit ratings from international investor services, and a continuous drop in consumer spending that has now entered its ninth year. Koizumi has stated publicly that he knows the keys to moving Japan out of its economic funk: reducing bank debt, rebuilding confidence in the stock market, expanding credit to small businesses, and encouraging the frugal Japanese to spend more. The challenge is not analyzing the problems or articulating the solutions; rather, it is finding the political will to take major steps, perhaps even radical steps in a national environment that has thrived on tinkering, delaying, and giving the appearance of change.

COMPARISONS

Comparing the Japanese political system to other systems in the world immediately brings up the influence of the United States. In post–World War II Japan it was the United States that laid the governing foundation for a defeated country. Since that postwar constitution Japan has looked to the United States for models of governance as well as numerous other aspects of national life such as business practices, industrial policy, popular culture, and sports. It is not that Japan wants to be like the United States; in fact, Japan has carefully and stubbornly sought to retain its unique way of making public decisions and crafting its own response to domestic and international challenges. But the influence of the U.S. presence after the war profoundly affected the way Japan developed as a democracy.

Japanese history and politics demonstrate that the influence of the United States and other Western democracies on this Asian power has been limited and in a number of areas nonexistent. Japan has shown a masterful ability to maintain the form of Western democratic institutions and processes while holding on to its own ways of governing. Even though Japan is included among the Western industrial powers, it is at heart an Asian industrial power. Japan has been careful to show the Western nations that it resembles them in its governing form and its political ideology, but it remains Asian in the way it responds to problems, solves conflicts, and deals with controversies or threats. The reliance on one political party, the behind-the-scenes power of the ministries, the weakness of the legislature and the courts, the narrowness of civil society, and the perpetuation of a compliant citizenry suggest that Japan is not in the Western governing tradition, and certainly has not evolved into a carbon copy of the American system as General MacArthur had hoped.

Increasingly Japan is accenting its "Asianness" as it pays closer attention to events in its region. There is the economic competition with China, the attempt to establish relations with North Korea, and the growing interaction with the other economic players in Asia. Japanese government officials and business leaders appear to appreciate the importance of looking both to the

West and the East in terms of national development and national security. But it is the newfound attention given its neighbors and its geographic neighborhood that has come to identify modern Japan. Since the time of the Meiji dynasty there has been a tug-of-war within Japan as it has been pushed and pulled between West and East. If history is the guide, Japan will continue to exist as both Western and Eastern, with the governing form from the West and the culture, practices, and values of the East.

CONCLUSION

The answer to the question, What is Japan? unfortunately remains unclear. Japan is moving through a period of uncertainty; its economy is stagnant and its political leadership unpopular. Its once premier position as the world's model for trade, industrial development, and wealth generation is now severely compromised. Japan is under new pressure to follow a "third revolution" but faces entrenched interests fearful of what systemic change will bring to the existing power arrangements.

A distinct generational shift is occurring in Japanese society that has already been the source of some reform in government and in the way government operates. Younger Japanese politicians in the LDP led by Junichiro Koizumi have been much more aggressive and vocal in criticizing past practices and have pushed for reforms in key public policy areas such as deregulation and bank restructuring. These political leaders are responding to growing demands on the part of a Japanese electorate that wants to see a new way of doing the nation's business. They have not always been successful, but they are a force that can no longer be ignored.

There is an evolving political culture in Japan that is likely to force change in the way government operates. The Japanese no longer have confidence in the triumvirate of the LDP, the ministries, and the business networks. The LDP is seen as out of touch, the bureaucracy is no longer a prize career plum, and the business community has lost popular support as a result of recession, unemployment, and the end of the caretaker relationship between worker and management. These breakdowns in support and respect will likely have a major impact on the operation of government. The triumvirate has always depended on a citizenry that is deferential, tranquil, and apolitical. Those traditional values are being attacked today, which will lead to less respect for and toleration of the old governing ways.

In Japan, however, it is not so much a distinct choice between revolution or status quo, but rather whether the Liberal Democratic Party, key ministries, and traditional business groupings can make adjustments to Japan, Inc., and achieve modest change without dismantling the mode of operation that supports the status quo. In this state of domestic flux and international dynamism brought on by the demands of globalization, it is possible that Japan will enter its "third revolution" and usher in a new era of fundamental change. But Japan remains a fundamentally conservative society determined to protect its way of life. Social stability and social cohesion are paramount to the Japanese, and they will resist disruptive revolutions.

A FEW BOOKS YOU SHOULD READ

Gerald Curtis, *The Logic of Japanese Politics: Leaders, Institutions, and the Limits of Change* (New York: Columbia University Press, 2002). An invaluable guide to the workings of the Japanese government and political system.

Yoichi Funabashi, *Alliance Adrift* (New York: Council on Foreign Relations, 1999). A study of U.S.-Japanese relations, including key issues such as the base in Okinawa and key trade issues.

Marius Jansen, *The Making of Modern Japan* (New York: Belknap, 2000). A comprehensive study of Japan's evolution from isolationism during the Tokugawa dynasty to modern times.

Alex Kerr, *Dogs and Demons: Tales from the Dark Side of Japan* (New York: Farrar, Straus & Giroux, 2002). A critical analysis of the current dilemmas facing Japan, with stinging commentary about what is wrong with Japanese society and government.

Masaru Kohno, *Japan's Postwar Party Politics* (Princeton: Princeton University Press, 1997). A key guide to the LDP, its power, and its penchant for scandal.

A FEW WEB SITES YOU SHOULD VISIT

www.ashai.com. A major Japanese newspaper in English provides solid coverage of the current scene.

www.kantei.go.jp. The Japanese prime minister's Web page.

www.shugiin.go.jp. The Web page of the House of Representatives.

www.sunsite.sut.ac.jp. A search engine for all things Japanese.

www.darkwing.uoregon.edu. Council of East Asian Libraries link to a host of sites on Japan.

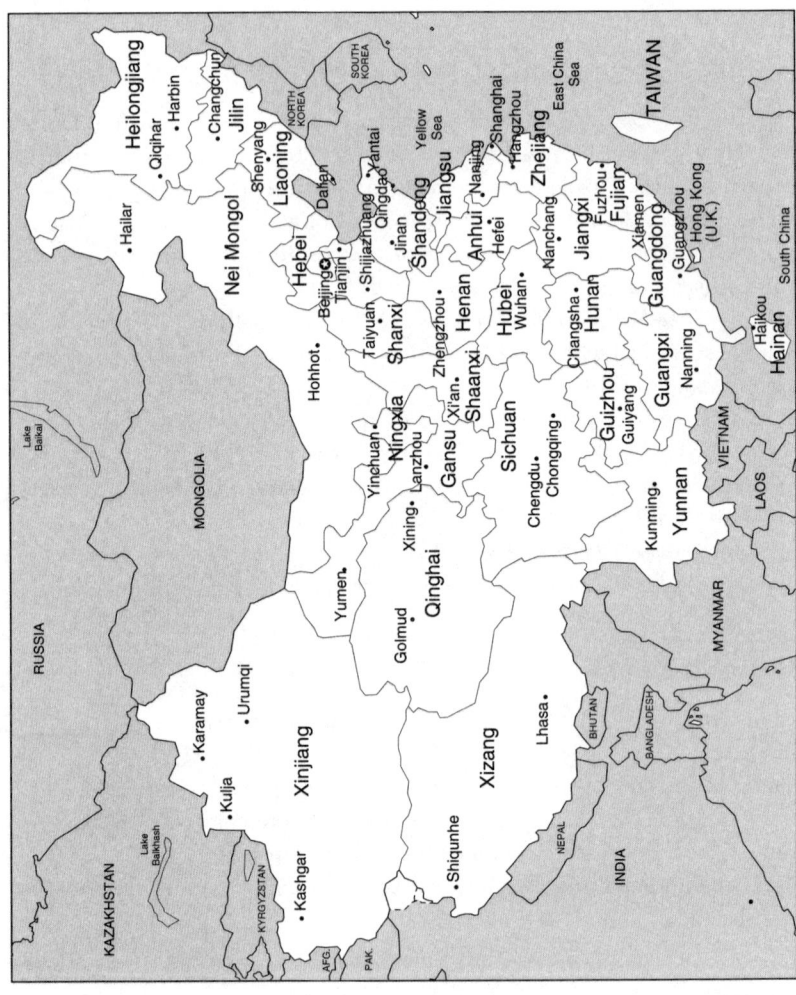

MAP 5.1 China

People's Republic of China

Data Bank

Area: 3.7 million sq. miles
Population: 1.25 billion (1998 est.)
Rural/urban ratio: 71/29
Ethnic makeup: 92 percent Han Chinese, 8 percent other nationalities,
    including Tibetan, Mongolian, Uighur, Manchu, and Korean
Life expectancy: Males, 68 years; females, 71 years
Adult literacy: 82 percent
Form of government: Communist
Head of state: President Hu Jintao
Head of government: Premier Wen Jiabao
Per capita income/GDP: $1,070 (2002)
Exports: $194 billion; imports $165 billion (partners: United States,
    Japan, Taiwan)

Source: United Nations and World Bank

SETTING THE SCENE

China is a country that is hard to ignore. With a population of over 1.2 billion people, China's strengths and weaknesses are tied to its people. China constantly focuses on how it can control demographic growth while at the same time respond to the quality-of-life consequences of having so many people. For example, the Chinese government has for years sought to enforce a one-child-per-family policy that is designed to bring population increases within an acceptable range. Public works projects such as the mammoth Three Gorges Dam seek to harness the power of the Yangtze River to provide electricity to an ever expanding number of consumers. Recently China opened its

261

western regions in Xijiang province to development and the southwestern provinces such as Guangdong to Western-style capitalism. These regions serve as demographic and economic safety valves as millions of Chinese move about the country in search of new opportunities and a better life.

As the world's most populous country, China has become a major force in the global economy. Due to its willingness to embrace capitalist models, China has been enormously successful with yearly GDP growth rates in the 8–10 percent range. As a result of its population and its economic vigor, foreign investors, multinational corporations, and export-import entrepreneurs see the 1.2 billion Chinese as a huge reservoir of consumers who will provide businesses with a bottom line bonanza. Although China currently makes up only 3 percent of world trade, it is anticipated that in the coming years as the economy continues to grow and China begins its membership in the World Trade Organization (WTO), world trade will increase significantly. Corporate executives in the industrial world have visions of new markets and greater profitability from a China that is fully integrated with global markets.

China's population size also has strategic implications. China overshadows its Asian neighbors with its numbers and landmass. Its military has become quite formidable, and its aggressive actions toward Taiwan have unsettled other nations in the region. Regional neighbors, especially Japan, are concerned over China's military spending, which is nearly 26 percent of all spending in Asia, and China's willingness to threaten its adversaries. Many military analysts in the West view China as the next great military threat, in terms of both its conventional weaponry and its development of a nuclear capacity.

But population, size, economic promise, and military expansion are only part of China's uniqueness. China is also hard to ignore because it is a nation that is governed by a communist ideology and a communist political system. While the world has embraced democracy, China has held steadfastly to the ideas of Marx, Lenin, and Mao Zedong. Born in the revolution of 1949, the political leadership of China has sought to preserve and advance Marxism-Leninism even to the extent of turning society upside down with "purifying" movements such as the Cultural Revolution during the 1970s and the stern repressive actions during the Tiananmen Square uprisings in 1989.

Despite its economic changes and openness to Western business models, China remains a country that is revolutionary, statist, centralized, and authoritarian. It is a country of one political party, one political philosophy, one political elite, and one politically defined direction. China still employs the language of communism with its People's Congress, collective farms, and party cells headed by party cadres. China's openness to the global marketplace hides the political reality of a country that even today sternly resists opening up its politics to permit personal freedoms, party competition, and independent institutions. Those who attempt to reform the political process or open the political system, as the Russians did after the fall of communism, face harsh retribution and intimidation from a governing elite that has little interest in popular participation.

Although in recent years harsh images of the tension between democracy and authoritarianism in China have been infrequently disseminated in the Western press, the government continues to exert a high level of control in the country. Examples of this include the brutal crackdown on the Falun Gong sect, a growing opposition group that is seeking to express its spiritual views unimpeded by the government. There are horrible stories of government torture and intimidation of those who seek to offer the Chinese people an alternative to the Communist Party. And finally, there are regular attempts by the Chinese government to control events in Tibet through a sizable military presence.

As a result of its communist foundations and its quasi-capitalist facade, China is a country of stark contrasts that are visible everywhere. There are the constant reminders of Marxism-Leninism with red flags, portraits of Mao, and revolutionary slogans urging the people on toward some social or economic goal. But China is also a country where the Western consumer ethic has begun to emerge. Alongside the visual signs of communism are the accoutrements of a market economy—cell phones, high fashion, and billboards selling everything from Coca-Cola to Nike sneakers. In the bustling cities of the Southwest, China looks much like a newly industrialized country (NIC) that has bought into capitalism without reservation. But in the rural areas peasant life has not changed markedly. There is little farm mechanization, people use bicycles to travel, housing consists mostly of shoddy mud-and-thatch huts, and poverty dominates.

Persons walking the streets of Beijing or Shanghai often experience a startling disconnect as the red communist flag vies for space with the ever present golden arches of McDonald's (as of 1999 there were 235 McDonald's restaurants in China). In the rural areas peasants still wear the traditional Mao jacket, while many of their neighbors dress in the latest fashions from the United States, Japan, and Europe. To reinforce the obvious dual nature of the Chinese economy, former Chinese leader and the architect of modernization Deng Xiaoping once described the country as having a socialist market economy—an apparent contradiction in terms but in reality an apt description of the attempt by the leadership to preserve the old while embracing the new.

China is a nation that political scientists are watching closely to determine when and how the liberalizing character of the economy will affect the political system. Unlike Russia, which moved toward political reform and democratization first and then began dismantling the communist economy, China has chosen to accent Western capitalist techniques and programs first. In the process it has shunned any attempts at democratization. But those who watch closely the impact of economic liberalization know that free trade, foreign investment, business travel, the Internet, and membership in the World Trade Organization will eventually have an impact on political values and political expectations. Chinese political leaders are in a sense trying to shut out the inevitable as they crack down on dissent and limit political participation.

In this chapter we will examine China against the backdrop of impressive economic development and disturbing political control. China is a country that cannot be ignored, but not just because of its population, its communism, and its vast consumer potential. Inside China's boundaries a contest of epic proportions is being waged between authoritarian control and democratic liberalization. How this contest plays out holds the key to the direction that China will take as it seeks to find its place in a new world.

FAMILY PLANNING POLICY

With 1.2 billion people, China desires a public policy that limits births and responds to the economic and social pressures associated with an ever growing population. In the late 1970s, after years of avoiding the ramifications of yearly population growth surges (annual rates of increase nearing 3 percent), the Chinese government made family planning a high priority. What evolved from governing circles, and eventually was included in the Chinese constitution, was the one-child family policy. As administered, Chinese couples are expected to limit their families to one child (and with government approval two children). There are some variations of this policy in urban and rural areas, and some exceptions if the first child is a female, since Chinese culture values male over female babies. Since the policy was implemented, the Chinese authorities responsible for monitoring compliance have had difficulty obtaining compliance in rural areas, where there are few health facilities that can provide birth control and other family planning assistance. The traditional cultural environment values children as farm workers and caregivers for the elderly. When the communes were abandoned in the 1980s, the state lost an institutional system it could use to ensure compliance, and as a result efforts at holding rural couples to the one-child policy were less effective.

Nevertheless, the one-child policy adopted by the Chinese government has not been a failure. In the years immediately following the announcement of the policy and the introduction of family planning measures, population in China decreased significantly. Since that time birthrates have occasionally moved upward, again in the rural areas and as a result of economic down-turns. Overall, however, Chinese population growth rates have settled to an average of 1 percent a year, while fertility rates have plummeted dramatically. The success of the one-child policy has led to the so-called missing girls problem. Because of family planning and the preference for male babies (which fostered infanticide, abandonment, and abortion), China today has a severe shortage of girls. At present the government does not see this as a seri-ous problem since it wants to continue controlling the population, but in the long run the missing girls may lead to negative birthrates.

In terms of policy implementation of the one-child program, the Chinese utilize a number of incentives and controls. The government has set a re-quirement for obtaining a marriage license that stresses late marriage and frowns on early dating and public displays of affection. Once a couple has a child, the mother is required to insert a birth control device. Should a sec-ond child arrive, either the husband or the wife must agree to sterilization. Although these measures appear draconian, the government offers people incentives such as greater opportunities to enter schools and better health benefits. A system of fines is applied to families that break the regulations, but in the current social climate the fines have been relaxed. Government of-ficials often permit couples to continue to have children until they give birth to a son.

The family planning/one child program in China is administered by offi-cials who are expected to meet quotas that are sent down to the grass roots from provincial and ultimately national population bureaucrats. Most of these officials are women who belong to village committees. In recent years these birth planning officials have been the targets of public protests and an-ticorruption actions. Charges that officials have shifted fine revenues col-lected from couples who exceed the established number of births to private accounts are rampant. The corruption of the one-child fine revenue has served to relax the stern climate of compliance that is the backbone of population control. Also, the pro-abortion practices implemented by the birth planning officials have received international criticism. Religious organizations and human rights advocates see the Chinese use of abortion as an ethical issue that is driven by the need for local family planning workers to meet govern-ment-imposed quotas.

In response to the flood of criticism targeting its one-child policy, the Chinese government in 2002 revised its guidelines. In place of fines, families who have so-called unauthorized births will pay a compensation fee that re-flects the social cost of additional children. Moreover, local officials will be re-quired to hand over the fees to the central government. The change is an ad-mission by the government that harsh measures regarding family planning and children do not work and create unnecessary antagonism toward the state. China continues to have a population problem, but it cannot be solved with measures that penalize parents and enrich corrupt officials. ⊕

POLITICAL MILESTONES

The political and governmental roots of China begin some two hundred years before the birth of Christ. In 221 B.C. the Emperor Qin (pronounced Chin, and therefore the derivation of the name "China") brought together a number of small kingdoms and laid the foundation for an imperial system that lasted until 1911, when the Republic of China was established under Sun Yat-sen. During the period of imperial rule China was controlled by a series of long-running dynasties. The longevity of these dynasties has often been attributed to an effective governing system headed by a class of civil servants called mandarins. In their governing role these mandarins, and indeed the imperial system, benefited from an advanced economy that was highly productive and the envy of Asia. A value system based on the teachings of Confucius proved to be conducive to stability, social hierarchy, and support for authority.

But the imperial system could not sustain itself and eventually succumbed to internal unrest and foreign control. China became a country of warlords and foreign occupiers, where the peasant class languished in abject poverty. Slowly the old system gave way to revolution and the communist alternative. Modern Chinese political history begins with the rise of communism and the collapse of governments connected with the West. The forces of social and political change overwhelmed the old regime, which cared little for the rural peasantry and was crippled by corruption. Mao Zedong and his Communist Party tapped into the latent unrest in the rural areas to foment a revolution that transformed China. Despite thousands of years of imperial culture, the Chinese revolution, its roots and its development, provide the focal point of defining what China is today and where it is going in the future.

Chiang Kai-shek, Mao Zedong, and Prerevolutionary China

With the founding of the republic in 1912, China entered a new era as Western-style democracy was introduced. Dr. Sun Yat-sen, founder of the republic, was the most famous and respected political leader in China. Educated in the West and exiled there for over sixteen years, Sun eventually rose to leadership of the KMT-Nationalist Party, better known as the Kuomintang. The fall of the old imperialist regime did not come easily as Sun failed eleven times in his attempts to stage a governing revolution in

China. In the fall of 1911, with Sun out of the country, a new challenge to the imperial throne was launched in the city of Wuhan. This revolution spread quickly, and by the time Sun returned in December, a new government had been formed with him as president. On January 1, 1912, China was formally established as a republic.

Sun was more adept at exile politics than at governing a brand-new democracy. Almost immediately China fell into internal disarray and Sun was forced to cede power to the warlords. While China languished without central authority, an important political relationship was developing between the Kuomintang and the Chinese Communist Party. The Kuomintang, now headed by Chiang Kai-shek, and the communists, led by Chen Duxiu, formed an uneasy alliance in the early 1920s under the guidance of the Comintern, the international arm of Soviet communism. For a time these two organizations had similar aims as they sought to unify the country. But it soon became obvious that the Kuomintang, which was more conservative and tied to the West, and the Communist Party, which had revolutionary ambitions, would not be able to remain allies.

In 1927 the alliance ruptured when Kuomintang forces attacked Communist Party activists in Shanghai, killing thousands. Although the ranks of the communists were decimated, the attack invigorated the remaining leadership elite to fight the Kuomintang and to do so with new methods. A little-known functionary of the Communist Party, Mao Zedong, emerged as a leader with a revolutionary vision that accented rural organization of the peasant class and the use of guerrilla hit-and-run tactics to weaken the urban-based Kuomintang.

At first Mao and his vision were not accepted by the mainstream communist leadership. But after the Kuomintang defeated the communists in a conventional battle in 1934, Mao led the remaining forces on what became known as the Long March. In effect Mao took his communists on a year-long retreat into the hinterlands of China. But rather than merely beat a hasty retreat, Mao used the Long March to develop ties with the rural peasantry. Mao's communist soldiers liberated areas under the control of warlords and broke up large estates. In the process the communists became known for their interest in the needs of the peasant class and their commitment to bringing economic justice to the rural areas. Mao turned the potential destruction of the Communist Party during the Long March into an opportunity to educate and mobilize the largest social and economic sector in China, the peasants.

Within two years of the Long March, Mao had risen to the chairmanship of the Communist Party of China. Mao became a revered leader in the rural areas and the membership of the Communist Party grew dramatically under his tutelage.

Despite the animus that existed between the communists and the Kuomintang, they joined forces to fight a common enemy when the Japanese invaded Manchuria in 1931 and seized control of most of northern China. When World War II broke out, the communists and the Kuomintang together formed the resistance movement against the Japanese.

Once the Japanese had been defeated, Mao and the Kuomintang again severed their relationship and began to compete for power. Fortunately for the communists, the years of developing a power base in the rural areas paid off as the urban-centered Kuomintang were unable to withstand the steady reduction of their territory and a diminution of their influence. By 1949 the communists were threatening Shanghai, the key center of remaining Kuomintang support. With the Kuomintang retreating to its island fortress of Taiwan, the communists claimed control of China. On October 1, 1949, Mao stood in Tiananmen Square in Beijing and declared victory. The Chinese communist revolution had begun.

The Formative Years of the Chinese Revolution

Revolutionary China under Mao was filled with bold ideological pronouncements, grand socialist schemes, and a constant undercurrent of totalitarian governance. Mao was clearly in control and fully committed to transform China into a communist state. Early on there were the now standard five-year plans that sought to centralize economic decisionmaking and move China quickly from an agricultural to an industrial society. A new constitution promulgated in 1954 established the Soviet model of an all-encompassing bureaucratic state controlled by an elite party hierarchy. Mao was fixated on making China the leader of the communist world and replacing the Soviets, who were deemed too unorthodox and too willing to compromise Marxist principles. The Sino-Soviet split in the 1950s was a mirror of what was going on within the Communist Party between supporters of Mao, who advocated a hard-line approach of ideological purity, and more moderate elements who feared that ideology would limit government's ability to move forward with its modernization plans.

As China sought to define its revolution, the first signs of disagreement within the party hierarchy came in 1956 with the Hundred Flowers campaign. Initially Mao felt that communism was secure and popular enough to allow a period of openness. In a speech he used the phrase "let a hundred flowers bloom and a hundred points of view contend." Intellectuals, artists, writers, and others took Mao's statement as a sign that a period of liberalism was sanctioned by the government. But the Communist Party and Mao himself became concerned that the Hundred Flowers campaign would get out of hand and pose a threat to the established order. As a result, the government let it be known that expressions of openness would not be tolerated and that the focus should be on internal economic development, not aspects of individualism. The Hundred Flowers campaign and its early demise signaled that the communist leadership would not tolerate departures from the official ideology or expressions of individual thought.

With the demise of the Hundred Flowers campaign, China under Mao turned its attention to the Great Leap Forward (1958–1960). Mao felt that it was essential for China to move quickly to become a modern nation-state. His plan was to mobilize the masses in the rural communes to build bridges, irrigation canals, roads, and other infrastructure improvements. Although Mao successfully mobilized the Chinese people, the Great Leap Forward failed in large part because of poor planning. The concept of mass mobilization fit nicely with the Marxist theory of using the workers to build a communist society, but putting theory into practice proved to be disastrous. Following the Great Leap Forward China entered a period often called the Three Bad Years, in which there was widespread famine and general economic decline. The domestic situation became so depressed that new policies were introduced to decentralize decisionmaking and foster greater individual initiative, two radical departures from communist ideology.

As China moved into the mid-1960s, the domestic economic situation stabilized and living conditions improved. But Mao and the leadership of the Communist Party feared that the Chinese people would be lulled into a pattern of personal interest rather than ideological commitment. There was concern that the revolutionary orthodoxy would be compromised and that China would forsake its goal of creating a pure communist state. Mao in particular was upset that those in the growing middle class turned away from the grand vision of the Long March and the victory over the Kuomintang. Chinese bureaucrats and youth were singled out as too preoccupied with maintaining the benefits gained since 1949. These opposing points of view—economic stability versus revolutionary upheaval, middle-class prosperity versus mass orthodoxy—served as the backdrop of Chinese politics as the country entered its most chaotic period—the Great Proletarian Cultural Revolution.

The Cultural Revolution

The Cultural Revolution, which lasted from 1965 to the death of Mao in 1976, was a period of enormous upheaval that touched all aspects of Chinese society. In the name of the communist revolution Mao and other ideologues, including his wife, Jiang Qing, systematically purged party functionaries and government bureaucrats. Many of these officials were removed from their jobs and their homes and relocated to reeducation camps, where they were constantly bombarded with Maoist doctrines and forced to confess their sins. Many never made it back to their jobs or homes. It is estimated that 30 percent of the members of the Central Committee were purged during the Cultural Revolution because they failed to show unquestioning support for communist principles and the vision of Mao Zedong. Although Mao professed that his goal was to maintain the ideological purity of the revolution and crush the emerging capitalist ethic in the country, the attack on party and government functionaries is often viewed as proof that Mao was nervous about losing control of power to a new generation of leaders.

Mao's attempt to rekindle the revolutionary spirit and maintain control in China eventually got out of hand. Doctrinaire students known as the Red Guards took the Cultural Revolution to a new level as they went through the countryside intimidating and torturing people they felt were not supportive of Mao and his communist vision. During their peak activity from 1966 to 1969 the Red Guards (who numbered 17 million) destroyed all vestiges of prerevolutionary China, such as monuments, art works, and historical documents. Their goal was to do away with the "Four Olds": old thoughts, old culture, old customs, and old habits. The only truth the Red Guards accepted was found in Mao's Red Book, a revolutionary bible that was credited with hundreds of slogans, chants, and warnings such as "So long as it is revolutionary, no action is a crime" and "To rebel is justified."

Mao tolerated the ideologically motivated chaos instigated by the Red Guards for a while. The Chinese leader believed firmly in constant change and the need to upset the social and political system in order to attain the communist ideal. But as the Cultural Revolution progressed and the Chinese economy came to a standstill, Mao reined in the Red Guards and called on the People's Liberation Army (PLA) to establish order. In this second stage of the Cultural Revolution (1969–1971) the PLA rounded up many of the Red Guards and transported them into the rural areas where Mao believed they would benefit from contact with the peasant class.

As China entered the mid-1970s, the worst excesses of the Cultural Revolution had come to an end. The death of Mao in 1976 and the arrest of the so-called Gang of Four (headed by Mao's wife) put an end to the radicalism of this ten-year period of orthodoxy and political retribution. The Cultural Revolution had fostered little positive development in China. Mao unquestionably shook up the system in his drive to root out bourgeois materialism and political moderation, but in the course of this unrelenting experiment in change, China came perilously close to civil war and economic depression.

Modernization Under Deng Xiaoping

Although Mao and his second in command, Premier Zhou Enlai, died within six months of each other in 1976, and the Gang of Four was in jail, moderates in the Communist Party hierarchy were not able to take immediate control of the policy process. For two years, from 1976 to the critical Third Plenum of the Communist Party in 1978, China was caught in the grip of a power struggle between neo-Maoists led by Hua Guofeng and the more pragmatic wing of the party led by the newly rehabilitated Deng Xiaoping. Hua's faction wanted to continue Mao's emphasis on revolutionary fervor and class struggle against capitalist influences, while Deng's faction accented economic development and openness to Western business and trade models. Deng was convinced that Mao's fanatical attachment to ideology and constant change in the name of the revolution was the root cause of China's malaise. These factional disputes played out in the Third Plenum of the Communist Party Central Committee meeting in November 1978.

At the plenum the forces of Deng Xiaoping emerged triumphant. Party leaders who had been banished to work in agricultural communes by Mao were rehabilitated by the party leadership (Deng himself had spent time in rural areas because of his more pragmatic views), and the neo-Maoists were publicly criticized for their excesses during the Cultural Revolution. Most importantly, the Third Plenum established a new direction in the economy, legal rights, and democratic practice. The watchwords were now "socialist modernization," "socialist legality," and "socialist democracy." Socialist modernization meant that China would take practical measures to advance the economy in a socialist framework. Socialist legality meant that past abuses and excesses of the revolution would be ended, and socialist democracy meant that there would be popular participation in the election of county-level people's congresses and more power for delegates in the National People's Congress. The key change, though, was in the way the Communist Party leadership viewed modernization. There would be greater emphasis on abandoning the Soviet-style centrally controlled economy in favor of a more flexible approach using market mechanisms and a greater willingness to consider opening trade ties to Western capitalist nations.

The key to the shift in Chinese politics and economic development was Deng Xiaoping. Deng became senior vice premier in 1977, but the title masked his real power. Rather than lead in Mao's charismatic and bombastic style, Deng preferred to stay behind the scenes and manipulate the party, the government, and the People's Liberation Army. Although he was seventy-four when he emerged as the most powerful man in China, Deng was able to provide the energy and drive to take China away from the chaos and horrors of the Cultural Revolution. He quickly introduced a new program called the "Four Modernizations," which stressed industrialization, improvements in agriculture, scientific and technical advances, and military modernization. There was little revolutionary sloganeering from Deng, just determination to get China back on track economically. Deng began to break up the agricultural collectives and introduce private sector businesses. Policies were implemented to welcome foreign investment and foreign trade, and personal restrictions were relaxed, as the Maoist insistence on Marxist dogma was replaced with greater respect for the work of artists, musicians, writers, and academics, who had suffered terribly during the Cultural Revolution.

The changes Deng brought to China were well received by the people, and they stimulated an unprecedented period of economic growth. In the 1980s China led the world in GDP growth. Urban and rural incomes rose dramatically, as did foreign investment. As Deng changed China's economic direction, his policies began to change the domestic scene in ways that would eventually bring about his greatest challenge. With the economy liberalized and booming, the Chinese people began to take the next steps toward liberalization of society and politics. Western dress began to replace the drab Mao jackets of the Cultural Revolution. Intellectuals and students were permitted to travel to the West more frequently, and heightened foreign investment and trade meant that Western products and Western market attitudes began to surface in the country. China was slowly but surely beginning to raise a capitalist system on its socialist foundation.

Deng lost his reputation as a reformer during the Tiananmen Square demonstrations in June 1989. In the wake of an inflationary spiral and growing corruption, demonstrations erupted in a number of Chinese cities led in large part by disgruntled workers. In Beijing, students from the prestigious University of Beijing took to Tiananmen Square and protested the lack of democracy in China. For days the students occupied the square and captured the attention of the West as they demanded that the economic reforms advanced by the government be accompanied by democratic reforms. Their calls went unheeded as Deng sent in the PLA to crush the student demonstrations. Hundreds were killed, thousands were jailed, and many students went into hiding and eventually reached the West as political exiles. Deng's actions in putting down the Tiananmen Square demonstrations were roundly criticized in the West, but they came as no surprise to those in China who knew that the party leadership was committed to economic change but not political openness.

Although Deng's repressive steps were supported by the party leadership, his standing in the leadership elite gradually diminished. Later in 1989, one of Deng's closest allies, Zhao Ziyang, the head of the Communist Party, was replaced by Jiang Zemin, a staunch supporter of the crackdown against the students. Jiang later became chair of the key Central Military Commission and president of the People's Republic of China. These moves prompted Deng to retire from government and assume the position of party elder. Deng continued to work behind the scenes to advance the economy, but his influence waned. After 1992 he was seen infrequently in public and in 1997 he died. Deng will be remembered as the guiding force of China's economic revival and push for modernization. His legacy was tainted by his refusal to permit political liberalization to accompany economic liberalization.

Jiang Zemin and Contemporary Chinese Politics

Jiang Zemin's rise to power did not direct China away from the economic direction taken by Deng. Jiang remained firmly committed to the mix of market capitalism, foreign investment, and foreign trade. And on the political front Jiang did not waver from the party's opposition to democratization. While major of Shanghai, Jiang cracked down on dissidents there while Deng was using troops against the students in Tiananmen Square. Once in office Jiang did little to change his image as a hard-line opponent of democracy. In fact democratic rights and political openness actually deteriorated as opposition groups such as the Falun Gong became the target of frequent government attacks and nascent political organizations and social movements were quickly repressed.

Jiang diverted attention away from the harsh internal situation by focusing on regaining the crown jewel of economic prosperity, the return of Hong Kong from the British after nearly one hundred years of colonial rule. With Hong Kong, China gained a center of finance, banking, and business that would further cement the prosperity of its southern provinces and give it an economic gateway to the global economy. Although there were concerns among the population that their political freedoms would be jeopardized, Jiang was able to smooth over the prospect of a new political environment by promising that little would change in Hong Kong.

Jiang became a much more visible head of state as he traveled to Europe and the United States in pursuit of favorable trade relations and membership in the World Trade Organization. Jiang's visit to the United States in 1999 was well received among Washington policymakers and the business community, although he ran into considerable opposition from the exile community that reminded the Clinton administration of China's human rights record. Jiang stressed the importance of continuing China's push for modernization and the opportunities that 1.2 billion people created for American corporations. To show that he was a new kind of leader, Jiang sang songs, wore Western garb, and smiled to the cameras as he toured the country followed every step of the way by Chinese dissidents intent on convincing Washington that political rights were more important than trade opportunities.

Much of the economic success achieved under Jiang's leadership must be credited to Premier Zhu Rongji. Soon after Deng departed, Jiang brought in Zhu to replace conservative premier Li Peng, who was more cautious about moving China further along the road of capitalist development and global interconnection. Zhu was a protégé of Deng who moved quickly up the ladder within the Communist Party with primary responsibility for economic management. Zhu became one of the most popular political leaders in China as he pushed more forcefully for liberalization of the economy and expansion of middle-class prerogatives. Like Jiang, Zhu was no political reformer or advocate of democratization. Furthermore, as the head of the government, Zhu was criticized for permitting extensive corruption. The ever expanding economy tempted many in the party and in government as officials sought to enrich themselves at the public expense.

After taking over national leadership, Jiang Zemin had a difficult time balancing the pressures to further extend the market economy with the concerns associated with liberalizing domestic politics. Jiang had to manipulate party factions while mending fences with liberals, who were still smarting from the Tiananmen Square crackdown. Jiang sought to strengthen his position and carve out a unique identity by appointing new members to the Central Committee and by quietly removing or coopting party adversaries. Following Mao Zedong with his radical communism and Deng Xiaoping with his market reforms, Jiang Zemin struggled to find a middle way. He moved China along the path toward market-based globalism, while not creating circumstances that would weaken the hold of the Communist Party.

At the Sixteenth Party Congress in November 2002 Jiang yielded leadership to Hu Jintao, who represented the so-called Fourth Generation of Chinese leadership. Jiang was reportedly reluctant to give up power, in large part because of suspicion that Hu and his new leadership group would slowly dismantle both the economic and the political system that the Third Generation had put in place. As a result, an arrangement was worked out that allowed Jiang to retain his position as head of the powerful Military Commission and place his allies on the Politburo's Standing Committee, the elite decisionmaking body in the hierarchy of the Communist Party. This compromise permitted a smooth transition of power and created a Chinese version of a check-and-balance system. Remarkably, the Sixteenth Party Congress decided to welcome capitalist entrepreneurs into the membership ranks. Openly seeking capitalists as party activists signaled how far China had moved away from its communist roots to embrace the Western market model of development. What did not change, however, was the commitment of the new leadership to retain strong political control in the hands of the party and a reluctance to open up Chinese society to democratic principles and practices.

Timeline	
1027–256 B.C.	Chou dynasty and the age of Confucius
211–207 B.C.	Ch'in dynasty; the name "China" comes from this period
202 B.C.–A.D. 220	Han dynasty, principal ethnic group, founded
618–906	T'ang dynasty; Confucianism is dominant
1260–1368	Yuan dynasty; era of Kublai Khan
1368–1644	Ming dynasty
1834	Britain granted rights to Hong Kong
1894–1895	Sino-Japanese War
1900–1901	Boxer rebellion
1911	Overthrow of Qin dynasty; republic founded
1931	Japanese occupy Manchuria
1934–1935	Mao's Long March
1949	People's Republic of China established
1958	Great Leap Forward
1966–1976	Great Proletarian Cultural Revolution
1976	Mao dies
1977	Deng Xiaoping assumes power
1989	Tiananmen Square uprising
1997	Jiang Zemin assumes power after Deng's death
2002	Hu Jintao takes power as China's leader
2003	Wen Jiabao named premier

FORMAL GOVERNMENT

In its 1982 constitution the People's Republic of China is defined as "a socialist state under the people's democratic dictatorship led by the working class and based on the alliance of workers and peasants." The character of the governing system in China becomes clearer when the definition of "democratic dictatorship" is presented later in the constitution. The Communist Party of China (CCP) is defined as the "core leadership of the whole Chinese people," or as Mao Zedong stated in the initial 1954 constitution, the CCP is "the highest organ of state power." The People's Republic of China thus is a governing system based on a Marxist-Leninist definition of democracy with workers and peasants being led by one and only one political party, the Communist Party of China.

The structure of government in China is best described as functioning along two tracks. There are the three branches of government—executive, legislative, and judicial—that share some characteristics with Western democracies but are limited in terms of their linkage to the citizenry, their independence, and their ability to make public policy. But alongside these branches is the Communist Party of China, which has its own mission, organizational structure, and power. The leadership elite of the CCP makes critical national decisions. The party leadership controls the vast executive branch ministries, overshadows the work of the National People's Congress, and dictates the interpretation and application of the law by the Supreme People's Court. The CCP in effect controls governing power in China. Although the CCP is a separate entity, Chinese governing institutions do not operate without the leadership and direction of the CCP.

The CCP is organized from grassroots primary party organizations (often called cells) up through local, city, and provincial party organizations to the National Party Congress. The National Party Congress, which meets every five years and consists of over two thousand delegates, is responsible for electing (actually approving the election) the central decisionmaking bodies in the CCP. The Central Committee of the CCP is a body of nearly two hundred party leaders that meets yearly and conducts the affairs of the party during the five-year period after each party congress. The Central Committee is a kind of board of trustees that is charged with the overall direction of the party. It does not have day-to-day powers but serves as a gathering of the party elite. A seven-person secretariat manages the administration of the vast party organization, and a central commission on discipline and inspection ensures that party members follow the ideology and policy direction dictated by the leadership. The central commission on discipline and inspection has the power to investigate and punish party members who stray from the party line. Finally, the Military Commission acts as a liaison with the People's Liberation Army.

At the top of the party power hierarchy is the Politburo, which has twenty-four members and the even more exclusive Standing Committee, which has seven members. The seven members of the Standing Committee are also members of the Politburo. The Central Committee names the members of the Politburo and the Standing Committee after extensive political maneuvering and coalition building. Both the Politburo and the Standing Committee are organized around policy areas with the individual party leader given authority to make decisions in a particular area. The ultraelite

Standing Committee has ultimate authority over the entire policymaking process. Little is known about the inner workings of the Politburo and the Standing Committee because China is a closed society, and political decision-making is often a matter of great secrecy. The top political elite in China does not function as Western democratic leaders do and, except for the president and prime minister, party leaders have little interest in becoming highly visible public figures.

In China the term "government" refers to the State Council, which is a cabinet-like body of forty ministers who represent the vast bureaucracy. The State Council is headed by Premier Wen Jiabao. Like Hu, Wen is a member of the CCP Politburo and Central Committee. Wen Jiabao is assisted in his capacity as premier of the State Council by approximately twelve vice premiers. The State Council, according to article 85 of the Chinese constitution, is the "highest organ of state administration." The State Council is nominally appointed by the People's Congress, but in actuality the Communist Party leadership determines who gets the coveted bureaucratic positions. The administration of government in a communist system like China is guided by what is termed dual rule: that levels below the national ministry are supervised by both the higher ministry and the Communist Party. Ministerial supervision focuses largely on administrative issues, while the party supervision is often concerned with political issues such as ideological interpretations, mobilization of the citizenry, and advancement of national party objectives. Needless to say, dual rule can create complex, confusing lines of authority, but it is designed to serve the Communist Party's desire to maintain centralized control of the governing process.

While centralized party control is exercised in the State Council, the National People's Congress gives the "appearance" of democracy and legislative autonomy. In 1954 Mao called the Communist Party the "highest organ of state power." But the 1982 constitution, as well as major pronouncements by government and party leaders since then, gives the National People's Congress the title "highest organ of state power." The Congress meets once a year. More than 3,000 deputies make up the legislative body and are elected through a bottom-up process that starts at local, then county, then provincial congresses. Deputies hold office for five years.

According to the Chinese constitution, the People's Congress has the authority to elect the president and the vice president of the country. But in reality the deputies rubber-stamp the decision of the Communist Party. On occasion public policy issues have been debated, though open challenges to the wishes of the party leadership are noticeably absent. The legislative branch of the Chinese government is marginally democratic in that there is a process of election which permits a level of participation.

In China judicial authority resides in a hierarchy of "people's courts" under the guidance and control of the Supreme People's Court. These "people's courts" are part of a layered system at various administrative levels. The Supreme People's Court is equivalent to higher courts in a Western democracy, although it plays a largely supervisory role rather than an appellate role. It does not exercise the power of judicial review and cannot overturn acts of the legislature or party dictates. There is also a national network of "people's procuratorates" that deal with local criminal cases. At the village level informal and personal legal arrangements handle disputes without entering the court system.

The key issue in the Chinese judicial system revolves around the independence of the courts. Like the National People's Congress, the judiciary is closely tied to the Communist Party. Justices are often appointed only with the approval of the party hierarchy, especially in matters relating to controversial public policy or political concerns. Greater emphasis has been placed on establishing a more independent judiciary because of the requirements associated with economic development, foreign investment, and trade. In recent years the Chinese have revamped their criminal and civil codes to move away from some of the legal abuses that were prominent during the Cultural Revolution and to assure the foreign community that legal modernization accompanies economic modernization. In many respects the judicial branch of Chinese government has seen the greatest degree of change, a welcome development to those interested in establishing the rule of law and diminishing party control. There is still a long road ahead in terms of creating a judicial system that approaches that found in Western democracies, but the Maoist system of arbitrary application of the law, weak protection of individual rights, and party interference in the judicial system has definitely begun to fade.

In Western democratic countries the military is usually a nonpolitical institution with responsibilities for protecting the nation from foreign threats. In China, however, the People's Liberation Army (PLA) is a vital participant in the political life of the country and a loyal arm of the Communist Party. The military has representation on both the Politburo and the Central Committee of the party, but not on the all-powerful Standing Committee. The PLA uses its position in the party hierarchy to push for greater defense appropriations and influence general military policy. The party oversees the PLA through the Military Affairs Commission and the Central Military Commission. As with other state bureaucracies, the Communist Party monitors military activities and personnel in the lower ranks through its network of committees and political officers, which have responsibility for maintaining civilian control.

As currently constituted, the PLA is the largest army in the world with 3 million men and women in uniform. A reserve militia of an estimated 12 million could be called up for duty during time of crisis. Military service in

China is an integral part of citizenship. Article 55 of the constitution states that it is the "duty of citizens of the People's Republic of China to perform military service." In recent years Jiang initiated efforts to reduce the size of the military and focus on technology rather than mass mobilization. Greater emphasis has been placed on the military using its vast resources to enhance its budget and contribute to the general economy. Introducing an entrepreneurial spirit in the PLA has fostered a climate of corruption as military officers and frontline soldiers engage in black market smuggling and divert profits from military enterprises.

A discussion of Chinese government would be incomplete without mention of the relevant levels of administration in the provinces, cities, counties, and towns. Each of these governing bodies has a People's Congress, which is elected for a five-year term. These representative bodies hold little power. The major administrative decisions and the implementation of national policies are accomplished by the local people's government, which is organized in a tripartite fashion with a governor or mayor, functional bureaucracies, and appropriate courts. As mentioned earlier, each level of government is monitored by both the national government and Communist Party officials to ensure compliance with directives from Beijing. Like many countries China is experiencing some movement toward decentralization, in large part because the liberalization of the economy has brought about the need for speedier decisionmaking and a relaxation of overbearing central control.

From an administrative perspective China is described as being organized into twenty-two provinces and three centrally governed municipalities (Beijing, Shanghai, and Tianjin). Chinese life, however, continues to revolve around the village. China has an estimated 900,000 rural villages where the vast majority of the people reside. Many Chinese continue to have a strong bond to their village, and village life has come to reflect an emerging democratic system. There is evidence of competitive elections for village leaders and examples of village officials seeking out support based on promises made and promises kept. There is also evidence of local officials facing the wrath of local villagers for abuse of power and engaging in corrupt activities. It must be said, however, that the village remains under the watchful eye of the local party official whose job is to promote government initiatives and monitor any movement away from established ideological precepts. The reach of the CCP from Beijing all the way to the village is a long one.

POINT OF FACT
The Chinese government admits that each year over 250,000 of its citizens commit suicide. China accounts for over 55 percent of female suicides in the world.

Constitutional Principles

The Chinese constitution in article 1 uses language that sets it apart from democratic and capitalist nation-states:

The People's Republic of China is a socialist state under the people's democratic dictatorship led by the working class and based on the alliance of workers and peasants.

The socialist system is the basic system of the People's Republic of China. Disruption of the socialist state by any organization or individual is prohibited.

SEX POLICY

In an authoritarian state, especially one that is founded on ideological orthodoxy and revolutionary fanaticism, even the most personal aspects of individual life are controlled. China is currently emerging from a period when sex and intimate personal relations were seen as potential threats to the state. During the Maoist era the Communist Party actively sought to eradicate so-called bourgeois evils such as pornography and prostitution. Furthermore, the government deemphasized sexuality by setting drab clothing standards, requiring husbands and wives to live separately in communes, and promoting passion for the revolution rather than passion for another person. Outward signs of affection and premarital sex were viewed with scorn. Chinese couples had to cloak their intimacy in secrecy.

But with economic liberalization came sexual liberation. Today China is a different country in terms of sexual mores and practices and government regulation of sex and intimate relations. The changes are evident everywhere in China as billboards and adult sex shops peddle everything from Viagra pills to marital videos. The government has even granted permission for China's leading sexologist, Liu Dalin, to open a sex museum as a "cultural offering" in Shanghai. The museum showcases over a thousand items chronicling the history of erotica in China. Although government authorities placed some limits on what the public could see (placed in a room with a sign reading "Experts Only"), the museum has become a major attraction and a further sign that as times change so does government policy. As Liu stated in an interview with the Western press, "Our society has become more and more open because of the Open Door policy, and I think mainly that is a good thing, though maybe some bad things come with it."

Despite the Open Door policy, the Chinese government is not completely open to all facets of sexual liberation. The "bad things" Liu referred to are prostitution and AIDS. During the Mao era prostitution was virtually eliminated as the Communist Party became intolerant of this sordid form of private entrepreneurship. Now, however, prostitution is running rampant in China, and the government has begun to crack down on this "social evil." It has closed over five thousand karaoke bars and massage parlors that catered to the sex trade. Even more serious is the growing AIDS outbreak, which the United Nations estimates has infected 500,000 Chinese, most of whom have engaged in unprotected sex with prostitutes. The government is mounting a health campaign with billboards reminiscent of the revolutionary days when sexually transmitted diseases were a rarity in the country.

A real change related to sex in China is a new openness about expressing affection and an interest in finding out about sex. After decades of government-imposed restrictions, the Chinese sit on park benches in full view of police and steal a kiss. Radio talk shows that cater to questions regarding sex are hugely popular, and the Chinese equivalent of the Kinsey report documents the sexual condition of this once repressed society. Despite its efforts to control what it believes to be the excesses of the sexual revolution, the government has begun to give in to the inevitable. Adult education classes are given in many community centers or workplaces, and sex education, which once was outlawed by Mao, has begun to be reintroduced at the middle school level.

Liberalization in China takes many forms, and the liberalization in the economic and financial sectors often attracts the greatest attention. But liberalization has begun to change the very foundations of Chinese society in everyday areas such as sex and intimate personal relations. Freedom comes in many different forms, but sexual freedom in China has the potential to foster an individual revolution that the government will not be able to control. As with economic and financial liberalization, the Chinese government has accepted the openness and individualism that are essential for a sexual revolution. What they are getting in return is a new generation of citizens who are less and less interested in government control over their private lives. ⊕

THE CITIZEN AND THE STATE

In China the all-powerful state is central to the governing process, and Chinese citizens are incidental members of the state. There is no established principle of popular sovereignty or citizen involvement in national affairs. There is a clear understanding that citizens are to support the state and obey the dictates of party and government officials. The Western democratic tradition of individualism, personal rights, and state responsibility has been turned on its head in China, replaced with what is often termed an organic approach to citizenship stressing the importance of citizens contributing to the overall good of the country and placing their interests below those of the state. In this tradition citizens as individuals are not nearly as important as citizens who are part of a vast nondescript entity called the masses. Individual citizens are not valued; in fact, they may be expended in order to accomplish a particular national objective. Rights are limited and responsibilities are demanded. In short, the citizen exists for the state; the state, on the other hand, defines the duties and responsibilities of the citizen.

Democracy in Marxist-Leninist China means that government is there for the people, but it is not by the people. That is why the Chinese party leadership places so much emphasis on incorporating the term "People's" in the titles of governing, cultural, social, and economic institutions. The Chinese people do not control these institutions, nor do they actively participate in real decisionmaking within those institutions. But the institutions are part of a deeply ingrained belief that China has attained true democracy by destroying its aristocratic and capitalist roots and has replaced the power of the economic elite with that of the revolutionary party leadership acting on behalf of the people. This is what Lenin and the Chinese communist leadership meant by the term "dictatorship of the proletariat"—a workers' state run by the Communist Party in the name of the people.

Once communists gained power in China, they went to work almost immediately to move the people away from the Western value system with its Judeo-Christian beliefs. Using the state-controlled education system and various party propaganda organs, the Chinese leadership sought to inculcate communist values such as the importance of struggle against the enemies of revolution, the need to establish a less hierarchical and more egalitarian social system, and the benefits of rooting out the "evils" in society as defined by Mao. In order to accomplish these objectives, Mao and the various party cadres initiated programs such as the socialist education movement, which was designed to end growing corruption and lack of interest in communist ideology. Mao stressed the importance of education at all age levels and within every aspect of daily life. The "new socialist man" was formed at work, in the neighborhoods, in the schools, and on countless billboards, posters, and larger-than-life pictures that became a regular part of the urban and rural landscape.

After Deng established his dominance in the party, campaigns to create the "new socialist man" were deemphasized. Deng was a pragmatist who focused on internal economic development, although he did not completely break from seeking to establish basic ground rules for citizen-state relations. In 1980 Deng promulgated "four cardinal principles" that were to serve as guidelines for citizen involvement in the post-Mao period. Those principles were

Keeping on the socialist road
Upholding the people's dictatorship
Maintaining the leading role of the Communist Party
Continuing to emphasize Marxist-Leninist and Maoist thought

The communist leadership continued to hold publicly to the Maoist doctrinaire line, but in practice Deng engaged in a kind of mass "formalism." He mouthed orthodox slogans but followed new ways that were aligned with Western democratic practice and capitalist values. During this period the government permitted some newspapers and magazines to express opinions that challenged existing policy. Intellectuals were given freer rein to comment on internal political conditions and the government lifted travel bans, permitting millions of peasants to leave their villages and travel to urban centers. This was the time when groups demanding reform began to evolve. In 1978 the Democracy Wall movement was founded by electrician Wei Jingsheng, who advocated adding a fifth modernization, democracy, to Deng's existing four modernizations. Wei quickly ran up against the entrenched party leadership, which imprisoned him for fourteen years. In 1992 he was released into exile in the United States.

The dissident movement that was born in the post-Mao era continued under the leadership of the noted astrophysicist Fang Li-zhi. Fang used his international scientific connections to travel outside China during this thaw period to drum up support for greater human rights. Fang called for a reform of the Communist Party, stating that the party leaders set a "poor example" and engaged in "unethical behavior." Fang, like Wei, did not call for an overthrow of the Communist Party but rather an improvement in socialist thinking to permit greater freedoms. But like Wei, Fang incurred the wrath of the party leadership and was not allowed to travel or talk openly. He eventually entered exile and continued his teaching and research in the United States.

Despite the repression, the movement to open up Chinese society has not ended. Concern is growing in governing circles over people's increased attraction to organized religion and matters of the spirit. The Communist Party leadership is especially troubled by the participation of high-level officials in religious activities, which is a violation of party rules. There is also growing evidence that party members and government officials, including some at the highest levels of the Standing Committee, are linked to the Falun Gong sect. China in recent years has begun to form a more complex civil society with institutions that are outside the Communist Party and social movements that are based on philosophical and ethical principles not associated with Marx, Lenin, and Mao. Christmas has even made a comeback, with the government permitting a return of St. Nick to the popular culture. The Chinese call him Shengchan Laoren, literally, "The Old Christmas Guy."

The relationship between citizen and state in the current political environment in China is likely to be defined by what model of national power and development holds sway—the model that is present in the capitalistlike south with its growing individualism and weakened ties to the party and government apparatus or the authoritarian-like model of the north with its abiding fear of opening up the political system and accepting competition. This north/south split in political culture and political presence is at the heart of the emerging dilemma over the manner in which citizen-state relations will evolve in the coming years. There is no doubt that Jiang and the Communist Party elite feared what economic liberalization might mean down the road in terms of citizen demands for greater political power and human rights. Yet Jiang and the party needed the economic vitality of the southern provinces in order to enter the global marketplace and become a major player in the new world economy. Those in power in the north limit the challenges to their position and have already cracked down on the Falun Gong and village-level democracy. Furthermore, the Communist Party has begun a campaign to punish those within the government who have engaged in corruption as a sign to the Chinese people that the existing political system can reform and need not be the target of demonstrations and rebellion.

Contemporary history has shown, however, that once economic liberalization has been accepted as a means of improving living conditions and enhancing national development, political liberalization cannot be suppressed for long. Tiananmen Square may have been the first volley fired in the political liberalization of China. The party leadership quelled the demonstration and punished the participants. Since that time there have been no equivalent challenges to the political authority of the government, although in 2002 there were frequent workers' protests as the government sought to privatize its state enterprises, cut back on wages, and limit pension payments to retirees. It may only be a matter of time until a new Tiananmen-like event occurs and the party elite will again have to decide how to rein in the forces of democracy. Until that time the Chinese leadership is banking on the fact that prosperity and economic change will stifle political energy and create an apolitical climate in the country.

Election Data

Although there are no open elections in China, the 2,979 members of the National People's Congress are "elected" by people's congresses in the country's provinces, autonomous regions, and municipalities. Candidates need the approval of the Chinese Communist Party. Candidates represent either the CCP or eight other "democratic parties" that are members of the China People's Political Consultative Conference. The last election process was conducted from October 10, 1997, to March 1, 1998.

TIBET POLICY

"Free Tibet." This is the rallying cry heard at rock concerts and the fund-raisers in the Hollywood community. Tibet has become an international cause célèbre among those who are outraged at the human rights violations and denial of democracy by the Chinese government. Tibet, which is classified as an autonomous region for administrative and governing purposes, has been engaged in a life-and-death tug-of-war with Chinese authorities intent on keeping control of its holdings. The 5 million Tibetans are seeking independence from Chinese rule and are paying the price in terms of Chinese military occupation, repression, and replacement of their culture and way of life. Although much of the attention of the One China policy has been directed at Taiwan, it is Tibet that has become the target of government policies to ensure compliance with centralized control.

The Tibetan push for independence is not new. Since 1911, when the imperial system collapsed, the Tibetan people have thought of themselves as separate from China. The Tibetans are a distinct people (Tibetans are not Han Chinese). Since the thirteenth century they have been fervent followers of the Dalai Lama, a Buddhist priest, who is revered as a godlike religious and spiritual leader. When the communists took over in 1949, there was a move to incorporate Tibet under Chinese domination. In 1951 the Dalai Lama agreed to a level of Chinese involvement in Tibetan affairs, but he remained as the ceremonial authority and the political center of the people. But in 1959, after an internal revolt against growing Chinese hegemony, the People's Liberation Army invaded the country, forcing the Dalai Lama into exile and establishing complete Chinese control. In 1965 China formalized its control by forming the Tibet Autonomous Region. Since that time the Dalai Lama has sought to rally international support to "Free Tibet," while the Chinese have engaged in a program of economic modernization, political intimidation, and cultural imperialism in order to guarantee governmental control and political compliance with its will.

In the absence of the Dalai Lama, much of the Tibetan independence movement is being led by the Buddhist priests and nuns, and most of the repression meted out by the Chinese occupation forces is directed at the Buddhist religious community. Many Buddhist monasteries have been closed and Buddhist monks and nuns sent into exile or forced to attend "patriotic education" programs. In these programs they are often subjected to torture, inadequate food, and lack of basic health services. The common charge levied against the Buddhist leaders is "plotting or acting to split the country or undermine national unity." Although hundreds of monks and nuns have been imprisoned, exiled, or sent to these "patriotic education" programs, their nationalistic spirit has not diminished. They remain ardent supporters of the Dalai Lama and fierce opponents of Chinese attempts to destroy their theocracy and their unique culture.

The Chinese have shown no signs of giving in to the Free Tibet movement. In 1995, in a bold attempt to further weaken the Buddhist opposition, the Chinese kidnapped the six-year-old Panchen Lama, the second-ranking religious leader in the country and the heir apparent to the Dalai Lama. In his place Beijing designated its own Panchen Lama in a clear effort to control the line of succession and ensure that the future religious leader in Tibet will be beholden to the Chinese government. The new Panchen Lama showed his allegiance to the state when he stated, "I thank the party's Central Committee and President Jiang. I will certainly study hard and become a patriotic and religious living Buddha."

The Free Tibet movement is likely to continue despite the harsh methods of the Chinese government. The Dalai Lama has stated that he would support some form of federation whereby Tibet was recognized as semiautonomous with local powers and the preservation of their culture. There is no sign that this proposal will be explored by the Chinese, who continue to put troops in the region. ⊕

PATHWAYS TO PARTICIPATION

Because China is a communist country, popular participation in the political process is severely limited. The avenues of participation all begin with the Communist Party. There is an active dissent movement in and out of the country, which of course is a form of participation, but participation that can have an impact on public policy, social organization, and national life is restricted to the ranks of the party organization. As currently constituted, membership in the Chinese Communist Party is approximately 60 million people, which makes the CCP the largest political party in the world. But that 60 million translates into about 5 percent of a total population of 1.2 billion. Therefore membership in the CCP is akin to elite status and awarded to those who have shown a commitment to the ideals and policy objectives of communism. Members of the CCP must take an oath promising to "fight for communism" throughout their life.

Many CCP members, commonly known as cadres, are low-level functionaries and government supporters. They have little responsibility other than carrying out dictates from higher party authorities and ensuring that the masses are aware of their responsibilities to advance party policies. While the party maintains a visible presence in the urban neighborhoods and the rural areas, the old omnipresent party organization that was in schools, factories, and communes has been replaced with a much less intrusive party organization. Working side by side with the party at the grassroots level is the organizational structure known as the *danwei,* or unit. The *danwei* is the group that the Chinese people are identified with because of their work assignments. It is within the *danwei* that small political study groups called *xiaozu* are formed which serve as links between the people and the party. It is in these *xiaozus* that the Chinese people meet their party leaders and hear about the latest party initiatives and their role in advancing those initiatives.

Although power in the CCP resides at the top levels of the Politburo and the Standing Committee, party leaders have been conscious of developing substantial lower-level institutions, if for no other reason than to keep attuned to the concerns and rumblings of the Chinese people. For example, there is a large youth branch of the party called the Youth League, which has a membership approaching 70 million. Most of the young people in the Youth League attend meetings for social and job-related reasons rather than political interest. The CCP has been able to recruit over a million youths into the regular party organization and has used the Youth League as its eyes and ears on what young Chinese men and women are thinking and saying about their elders in the party.

A number of mass organizations tied to the Communist Party represent key functional groups such as workers and social groups such as women. The All-China Federation of Trade Unions provides the party with insight on key labor issues such as working conditions and worker concerns. The All-China Women's Federation is a highly visible organization that takes positions on a range of domestic and family issues. Since there is only sparse female representation at the highest levels of the CCP (currently no women belong to the

Andra partier:

Politburo or the Standing Committee, but there is one woman alternate), the All-China Women's Federation presses for changes that benefit women.

Interestingly, there are a number of noncommunist political parties in China. These parties are not true opposition organizations, but are tied to the party and represent various segments of society. The role of the noncommunist parties is to provide the CCP with opinions and insights on how the party can improve its policy initiatives and its policy implementation. These parties meet each year in a Chinese People's Political Consultative Conference, which is held during the annual meeting of the National People's Congress. The meeting allows the delegates of these parties to express their views on a range of issues, but always under the watchful eye of party officials. The Consultative Conference allows the CCP leadership to show that noncommunists are permitted to organize and present their view, but nothing substantive comes of these meetings or of the entire non–Communist Party structure.

Attempts to establish a true political opposition free of Communist Party domination have faltered, at least for now. In recent years democratic dissidents have sought to found an independent political party called the China Democratic Party. The CCP quashed the party and sentenced many of its leaders to long jail terms. The repression of the China Democratic Party may only be a temporary detour in what is a slow evolution toward allowing greater political and electoral choice. Communist Party officials from the Ministry of Civil Affairs freely admit that China is moving toward a political system where participation and competition would become commonplace. The term that is heard increasingly in governing circles is "peaceful evolution." Officials recognize that crackdowns against political opposition groups threaten the stability of the nation and the viability of the party.

Democratic participation in China started at the rural village level. Since the late 1980s, when elections were permitted, the Chinese have begun their own participatory revolution in the midst of weakening party influence and control. Spurred on by the collapse of the people's communes, the peasants have used changes in election laws to name representatives to the assemblies that oversee various agricultural issues such as taxation, transportation, price setting, and access to equipment and fertilizers. These elections have all the characteristics of Western democracy, with secret ballots and opposing candidates. The party is still present in the villages, but CCP officials allow the assemblies to play a role in making local decisions and forcing local officials to improve the services they provide. Seen from the perspective of the CCP, village elections are a means of improving its reputation and rebuilding its peasant base. Party leaders are especially concerned that rampant corruption will damage its support and cause peasants to see village democracy as a cosmetic method of developing a favorable democratic image. An estimated 60 percent of Chinese villages have conducted these elections, making local decisionmaking a vital part of rural life.

While elections at the village level reveal growing participation, meaningful decisionmaking at the national, provincial, and national levels remains tightly controlled by the CCP. The party dominates the electoral process as it nominates candidates, runs the elections, and certifies the votes. Elections are held for the express purpose of showing the outside world that China has a democratic framework in place; the more important objective is legitimizing the party leadership. Since Mao's death, there has been some movement away from uncontested elections, with multiple candidates running for office (of course all from the CCP). In 1980–1981 Deng permitted local elections in one Beijing precinct. This democratic opening led to 10,000 candidates being nominated for 316 seats. This explosion of democratic participation forced a quick intervention by the government to manipulate the candidates and the vote. Since that failed miniexperiment in democracy, the CCP has permitted only village democracy. There are examples in recent years of noncommunist candidates running for office and winning, but these candidates have been preapproved by the CCP and are viewed as posing no threat to party domination.

One of the more recent developments in popular participation in China is the formation of nonpolitical interest groups. As Chinese society continues to benefit from economic modernization and expansion, one result is the growth of formal associations. An estimated 200,000 associations have sought permission from the CCP to organize and to function as representatives of particular groups with special interests. Trade and business groups appear to have greater autonomy in large part because they are pursuing goals approved by the governing elite. Controls on cultural groups have been relaxed, but only if they do not engage in open challenges to the political system. Specific issue-oriented groups dealing with environmental concerns, population, and governmental reform have experienced limitations on their ability to function.

Because China has a revolutionary foundation, popular participation occasionally takes an unusual form, such as the widespread placement of wall posters and other visible signs that offer protest statements and antigovernment slogans. In high-intensity periods such as the Cultural Revolution, wall posters were used extensively to rally the party faithful and intimidate the "enemies of socialism." Since the end of the Cultural Revolution wall posters and other symbols have emphasized democratic themes. During the Tiananmen Square period wall posters were used throughout Beijing to inform the Chinese people about the democratic protest. In the time since the Tiananmen Square uprisings wall posters have lost prominence as a means of overt protest and public opinion formation. The Internet, the fax machine, and the cell phone are now the primary methods of communicating political opinions and alerting the populace to government decisions and actions. China, however, remains a closed society with strict government rules on expressing political beliefs. The government has made a concerted effort to control the Internet and restrict the development of Web sites. Nonetheless, officials have found it extremely difficult to shut down modern-day equivalents of the traditional wall poster.

Political participation is at a crossroads in China. There are conflicting signs regarding the direction that China will take in the coming years. Civil society in China has become more diverse and complex. New groups, new associations, and new voices are heard from on a regular basis. The economic liberalization that has changed the face of the country is also having an impact on the structure of the political system. But old habits die hard in China and the political elite remains fearful that increased avenues of participation may threaten its power and authority. That is why groups such as the Falun Gong face harsh repression and nascent political opposition parties such as the China Democratic Party are quickly suppressed. The Communist Party of China seems willing to accept low-level participation away from the centers of power and linked to its objectives of modernization and political consolidation. But the party is not willing to accept direct challenges to its control of the political and governing system by opposition parties or open elections or demonstrations that seek political reform. It is important to note that in 1998 Jiang Zemin talked about the prospect of extending elections to counties and provinces and implementing Deng Xiaoping's projection of national elections by 2050. Those projections have been put on hold, at least in terms of the party leadership. Jiang held that economic and educational development is more important than voting and elections.

THE POWER ELITE

The power elite in the Chinese political system is centered in the highest ranks of the Communist Party, specifically the Central Committee, the Politburo, and the Standing Committee. The membership in the Central Committee political elite represents a wide spectrum of occupations from central party operatives and regional leaders to government and military officials to the heads of mass organizations and special interest groups. What the Central Committee power elite does not include is substantial representation from women and ethnic minorities (thirteen). Political power still resides in senior males who are reluctant to yield power to a new generation of party leaders.

The discussion of the Chinese power elite, however, is not merely a matter of providing a functional and demographic breakdown of the party leader-

PHOTO 5.1 CHINESE
PRESIDENT HU JINTAO.
(REUTERS NEWMEDIA
INC./CORBIS)

*Hu Jintao was born in 1942 in
Jixi, Anhul province. He studied hy-
draulic engineering at the prestigious
Tsinghua University in Beijing.
While a student in 1964, he joined
the CCP. In 1968 he was sent to the
remote province of Gansu as part of
the reeducation program initiated by
the party elite during the Cultural
Revolution. After his stint as a
manual laborer, Hu worked in a
number of engineering and construction positions. During this time he
developed close ties with Song Ping, a
party elder who helped him rise in the party hierarchy. In 1982, at the age of
thirty-nine, Hu became an alternate member of the CCP Central Committee. In
the subsequent years he became president of the All-China Youth Federation and
then the youngest provincial party boss in Guizhou province. In 1988 he became
Tibet's first nonmilitary party boss, a position he used to rise even further in the
CCP hierarchy. In 1992 Deng Xiaoping drafted Hu to organize the Fourteenth
Communist Party Congress, where Jiang Zemin became general secretary.
During Jiang's rule Hu became a member of the Politburo Standing Committee
and in 1998 was named state vice president. In 1999 he was named the vice
chairman of the PRC Central Military Commission. Hu assumed the leadership
of China at the party congress in November 2002.*

ship and the positions they hold in the organizational hierarchy. Key characteristics of leadership include social and educational background, intensity of
commitment to ideological orthodoxy, generational differences, and the
process of promotion and demotion within the ranks. These factors are exem-
plified in the political evolution and leadership characteristics of the former
general secretary of the Communist Party, Jiang Zemin.

   Jiang Zemin emerged from the Tiananmen Square crackdown as the general secretary of the Communist Party. From 1989 to 1994 Jiang served in
the shadow of Deng Xiaoping. Jiang would often defer to Deng and seek his

advice before implementing policy. He would also look to Premier Li Peng for guidance on government issues, careful always not to weaken his support within the aging hierarchy of the party. But while Jiang was cognizant of the power still held by Deng and Li, he was quietly laying the groundwork for his consolidation of power and his emergence as the uncontested leader of China. One of the first steps that he made was to elevate his longtime associate from Shanghai, Zhu Rongji, to executive deputy prime minister, a position just below that of Li Peng. Jiang also began to replace key members of the Central Military Commission who were tied to the Maoist era and to the repression of Tiananmen Square.

Once Deng passed away in 1997, Jiang moved quickly to further consolidate his power. He moved Li Peng out of his position as premier and placed him in the largely ceremonial National People's Congress. Although Li Peng remained at the top of the party hierarchy, it was clear that his power was diminishing. Later Jiang removed another challenger, Qiao Shi, from his party position. Qiao was viewed by many as a potential leadership alternative to Jiang. Jiang benefited from the death of some party elders, which allowed him to appoint loyal allies to the top ranks of the CCP. Jiang further strengthened his hold on power by elevating Zhu Rongji to prime minister and naming longtime aide Zeng Qinghong as head of the party's Organization Department, which deals with many party-government relationships. Jiang established something of a Shanghai connection in the formation of his leadership base. Besides Zhu Rongji, Jiang also named two other former Shanghai mayors to top government positions, Vice Premier Wu Banguo and Party Secretary Huang Ju.

Jiang's consolidation of power involved more than party leaders moving up and down the ladder of importance. He also gained control of the "leading groups" in the party. These groups serve as the link between party and government and define the CCP position on critical national and international issues. By positioning his people as heads of these "leading groups," Jiang was able to control the policy agenda and define party policy on his terms. Jiang also made a determined effort to strengthen his base among the rank-and-file cadres. He stressed better training for the cadres and greater responsibility to implement the party's program. He talked about the need for "developmental dictatorship" in which the cadres would have greater responsibilities in the area of public administration. Jiang's emphasis on strengthening the cadres was about efficiency, but also about improving their status and ultimately their loyalty to him.

One of the most interesting aspects of Jiang's political leadership is the naming of his successor. Since 1999 it was clear that Jiang did not intend to remain as head of the Communist Party beyond the sixteenth party congress in 2002. Jiang and the CCP were intent on having an orderly succession of leadership. A so-called Fourth Generation of party leaders began to emerge in the party hierarchy, with Hu Jintao openly touted as the new leader of the party and the country. Jiang's supporters, who were all in their seventies, were reluctant to relinquish power to Hu and his supporters, who were all in their fifties and early sixties. As the time for the party congress approached, an apparent compromise was reached that permitted a transition of power to Hu and his Fourth Generation while keeping Jiang within the power circle and permitting him and his associates to influence the direction of Chinese policy. Jiang was permitted to be reappointed to the powerful Central Military Commission, making him in effect the commander in chief of the PLA. One of his key allies, Jia Qing Lin, was named to head the Chinese People's Political Consultative Conference, a position with broad powers in the Communist Party organization.

Factional separations based on ideology and public policy approach exist throughout the upper hierarchy of the Communist Party. Historically the Chinese political leadership has been divided along revolutionary and pragmatic lines. The revolutionary or Maoist wing of the party stressed the importance of permanent revolution, ideological purity, mass mobilization, and of course the infallibility of Mao's philosophy. The pragmatic wing, which emerged in the Deng era, accented modernization, economic growth, hierarchical decisionmaking, and a narrow reading and appreciation of Mao's philosophy.

This separation in the party served as the basis for the internal struggles that occurred during the Tiananmen Square uprisings as the two groups and their visions of China clashed over the proper response to the demonstrators. In 2000 the so-called Tiananmen Papers were published in the West, which gave a rare glimpse of the internal debate that occurred within the highest levels of the Chinese government over the proper response to the demonstrations in Beijing. The papers revealed the fears expressed by hard-liners that the demonstrations would weaken the CCP's hold in China and foster alternative sources of political power. After considerable debate the revolutionary vision that was based in the perpetuation of the Maoist philosophy and its adherents won out. The PLA was sent in to crush the demonstrations and the demonstrators.

Under Jiang the pragmatic faction held the upper hand in the party, but only in agreeing on the parameters of economic modernization. In terms of political reform, factional disputes were less visible and divisive. There was a consensus among the power elite that the time for developing an open and competitive political system was well into the future. The government continued to crack down on dissenters and placed numerous limitations on the formation of alternative sources of democratic participation. Although it is still too early to determine the approach of Hu and the Fourth Generation, published reports by the new leaders suggest that they will emphasize domestic economic development and living standards, in particular addressing the plight of the rural and urban poor.

The differences in the party leadership groups are not just ideological and procedural but generational as well. In a communist system the term "gerontocracy" describes a leadership group that holds on to power and the ideological positions of the past in the face of mounting competition from younger party leaders whose views represent a distinct generational divide. In recent years the CCP leadership has been conscious of the generational chasm in its ranks and the problems associated with an aging hierarchy. At the fifteenth party congress in 1997, Jiang Zemin made a concerted effort to address the gerontocracy problem within the Chinese power elite. He called for recruiting and promoting younger cadres and replacing old-line conservatives who opposed his economic reforms and his widening ties to the West.

Although Jiang brought more youthful members into the party hierarchy, especially the Politburo, the average age of the members of the key decision-making body, the Standing Committee, remained in the mid-sixties, with only one of the seven members below the age of fifty-five. Jiang and many of his colleagues on the Standing Committee are from the Maoist generation. But Jiang's successor, Hu Jintao, is a much younger man who has closer ties to the Deng era of pragmatic reform than the Maoist era of revolutionary communism. Age of course does not automatically translate into a predetermined set of beliefs, but it does create generational tensions as younger members, who came to influence within the party in the post-Maoist period, often do not share their elders' reluctance to move forward on economic change and political reform.

The key event in the political hierarchy of the Communist Party was the 2002 party congress, where a generational transition occurred. The turnover was the result of pressure within the party to replace leaders over the age of seventy. At the sixteenth party congress, 180 of the 356 members of the Central Committee were replaced with new members, many of whom were fifty or younger. In the critical Standing Committee, eight new members were appointed, with only Hu Jintao remaining from the previous group. Many of the new members of the Standing Committee had ties to Jiang Zemin, not Hu Jintao. Only Premier Wen Jiabao appears to be closely aligned to Hu. Although many key members of the party elite were replaced in 2002, that did not ensure that factional disputes would end or that the Chinese leadership would speak with one voice. There will always be jockeying for power in the leadership elite in the CCP, and the Fourth Generation group now in power will likely face a new generation of party activists with differing views of how China should develop and how the CCP should move China toward that vision of development.

What the Experts Say

Charles Hutzler, a reporter for the *Wall Street Journal* based in Asia, has followed the new generation of Chinese leadership led by Hu Jintao. He offers his impression of this new leadership:

As a group, these leaders are likely to follow their elders' recipe for economic liberalization: dropping barriers to foreign investment and allowing creeping privatization, while still trying to retain state control over certain strategic industries. But it's in the political realm where some of the biggest problems lie. The bureaucratic, authoritarian government is wrestling with guiding a dynamic economy and diverse society. And it's there that Mr. Hu and his colleagues have left intriguing clues to possible change. They've initiated programs to bring more responsive government if not democracy, by building a professional civil service and encouraging greater transparency.

Wall Street Journal, EASTERN DIVISION, JANUARY 3, 2002, P. I

ENERGY POLICY

One fundamental requirement for China if it is to achieve the critical "breakthrough" from Third World status to newly industrialized country is electrical power. Rapid industrialization, heightened consumer demand as automobile ownership increases, and economic development of the depressed countryside hinge on the development of new sources of energy. At the present time China's energy demand is increasing by 3.5 percent a year, and demand is expected to double over the next twenty years. To meet these needs, China has become dependent on foreign oil, since its own fields are rapidly being depleted. Although China still relies for most of its energy on coal (four-fifths of its supply), it is concerned over the pollution and accompanying health problems associated with burning fossil fuels. China has the most polluted cities in the world, and over 200,000 of its citizens die prematurely each year from illnesses associated with air pollution. As a result China is involved in a massive cleanup of its coal industry that will close down over 18,000 mines and demand that the remaining coal operations install new technologies that will lead to cleaner emissions.

The Chinese government's biggest energy worry is the cost and supply of gasoline. Where in the past China relied on its own reserves and trading relations with only a few countries, it has opened up its purchases to a dozen countries, including the United States and Russia. There also are signs that China is willing to relax its opposition to foreign investment in oil exploration such as Royal Dutch/Shell. Inefficient state enterprises are being pressured to meet the demand, but the inevitability of foreign involvement is apparent to governing circles. Joint ventures have already begun exploring for gas in the Tarim basin of Xinjiang province in western China. Pipelines are being built to transport gas to the more populous southwestern and coastal urban centers. One pipeline will link the Tarim basin with Shanghai, a distance of over 2,600 miles. A major terminal for liquefied natural gas is being built in Guangdong province in the southwest.

Besides shifting from coal to oil and especially natural gas, the Chinese are engaged in a huge hydroelectric power project on the Yangtze River. The Three Gorges Dam is the largest dam projection in the world and the most costly (some estimates place it at $70 billion). When completed in 2009, it will regulate the flow of the Yangtze River and harness its power in order to provide 10 percent of China's electric power needs. But building the Three Gorges Dan has created both human and environmental problems. The dam will displace over a million residents and damage to the fragile ecosystem is anticipated. Over one hundred archeological sites along the river will be destroyed when the area is flooded. Scientists have also called into question the impact of sedimentation on the foundations of buildings after the dam is built.

As for the Chinese government, it is moving with great speed to bring the Three Gorges Dam online as a key link in its drive to expand electric power. Government officials see the Three Gorges Dam as a symbol of modern China and the state's ability to construct a project of enormous size. Former Premier Li Peng was unrelenting in his efforts to advance the dam and purged critics in the party for speaking out against the project. Attempts by scientists and media outlets to weigh the benefits and costs of the project were also suppressed, and environmental activists have run into countless roadblocks as they call into question the necessity of the dam. Even a vote in 1992 in the National People's Congress, where one-third of the delegates either voted against the project or abstained, has not stopped the government from pursuing its ultimate goal.

China needs to expand and diversify its sources of energy. The connection between energy and modernization is fundamental, but to make that connection viable China will be faced with challenges to its state-run system, its environment, and the safety and living standards of its citizens. The Chinese government will be engaged in setting the proper balance between energy and these challenges for some time to come. ⊕

REAL GOVERNMENT

Because the Chinese political system is centered around the Communist Party it therefore follows that public policy decisions would be made within the structure of the Communist Party. Yet the policymaking process is quite diverse and complex, and policy implementation is intricate and fragmented. China is an authoritarian state with central control and little opportunity for opposition. But China is also a state where authoritarianism is tempered by the realities of vertical and horizontal bureaucratic competition and the power ambitions of the party elite at the various levels of the governing structure. In many ways it is a cumbersome decisionmaking system as party and government officials vie for influence alongside national, provincial, and local officials. This competition and complexity is not democratic in nature, but it does foster differences of opinion and limits the ability of the leaders at the top of the governing hierarchy to attain unfettered compliance.

Public policy decisions, as already noted, are centered in the Politburo and the Standing Committee. But the actual formulation of the policies, which includes research, discussion and debate, and political maneuvering, occurs in the leading small groups. The head of a leading small group would likely seek to include a number of top-level experts familiar with the functional area from outside the inner circle of the Politburo and Standing Committee. Below the leading small group is another level, which has responsibility for providing all the relevant data, information, and policy options to the members of the group. These support personnel come from the party secretariat or the State Council ministries.

Since much of this decisionmaking is done in secret, it is likely that the Standing Committee will hear reports from the leader of the small group. The proposal is then debated in the Standing Committee, with the small group members making their case. After the Standing Committee makes its decision, the Politburo receives the policy decision and ratifies the policy at its meeting, which is often held monthly. Because both the Politburo and the Standing Committee are the highest organs of the party, there is often considerable interaction among the members of the two bodies and the leading small group. This interaction can be described as the Chinese version of politics. It is not democratic politics, since there are no representatives from outside the party inner circle and no interest in public opinion, but it is politics as the party elite jockey for position, argue over alternatives, and seek to shape the policy from their perspective.

It is of course one thing to come to agreement in the party hierarchy on a particular policy initiative and another to take that initiative forward into the policy implementation phase. In the Chinese political and governmental system the implementation of public policy decisions is a most difficult proposition in large part because of the labyrinth of power and responsibility that has been constructed in the vast state bureaucracy. The Chinese governing structure is organized vertically from central ministries down through local level departments. The bureaucracy is also organized horizontally in the governing structure at the provincial, county, and town level. The result is a competing bureaucratic system with lines of authority that often are imprecise and create extensive fragmentation. The bureaucratic environment becomes even more fragmented when the party structure, which is organized both vertically and horizontally, is placed in the administrative mix. The result is a huge, octopuslike system that is ripe for inaction, irresolution, and ineffectiveness.

Because policy dictates executed by the party hierarchy must travel through the obstacle course of government bureaucracy, implementation of high-level decisions is often achieved at the local level through informal and personal relationships more than through established procedures. Local authorities recognize that the national governing structure relies on them to implement policy. This allows the local authorities a degree of power as they can ignore a directive or fashion it in a manner of their choosing. There has been considerable concern among party leaders over the extent of bureaucratic delay and confusion in the chain of command. As a result, consolidation, streamlining, and restructuring of the bureaucracy are given high priority. Over the last few years thousands of bureaucratic personnel in the State Council have been relieved of their duties in attempts to simplify the policy labyrinth.

Bringing administrative reform to the bloated Chinese bureaucracy is a top priority of the party leadership. New agencies have been established such as the State Auditing Administration and the Ministry of Supervision to monitor policy implementation and determine where deficiencies lie. There is also evidence that Chinese authorities are willing to employ rudimentary public opinion polls and analytical studies to better understand how the policy process can be improved. There is a realization that the policy process is seriously flawed because of deficiencies at the local level. Party leaders understand that there are too many bureaucratic layers, too many conflicting priorities, and too many examples of local officials "reinterpreting" policies of the national government in order to accommodate special interests or, more likely, advance personal objectives.

A more revealing case study of how policy decisions are made and then put into place involves internal struggles in the top hierarchy of the Communist Party over the Tiananmen Square demonstrations. Even before students and workers took to the streets in June 1989, there was considerable disagreement in the party hierarchy over political reform and the toleration of dissent. In 1987 party reformer and secretary-general Hu Yaobang was removed from his position by conservatives who were critical of his liberal positions. In his place the party named Zhao Ziyang, who was also a reformer but less inclined to support open criticism of the government and more focused on implementing market-oriented changes. To balance the economic liberalization position of Zhao, conservatives appointed Soviet-educated Li Peng as premier. Although Li was effective in limiting the economic reforms of Zhao, he was not able to dampen Zhao's growing interest in political reform, which included steps to weaken the hold of senior party officials and a reexamination of the excesses of the Mao era.

The personnel changes in the party hierarchy took an unusual and fateful turn in April 1989, when Hu Yaobang was permitted to attend a Politburo meeting and present his case for a continuation of political reform. In what was apparently a heated exchange between Hu and conservatives on the Politburo, Hu suffered a heart attack and died. The death of the man who symbolized change and toleration touched off demonstrations and hunger strikes in Beijing and other cities. Conservatives with Deng's support published an editorial in the *People's Daily*, which roundly criticized the demonstrators. The editorial only reinforced the resolve of the students and actually helped expand their ranks. At this point Zhao, who had been in North Korea, sought to have Deng retract the editorial and mollify the demonstrators. Zhao clearly wanted to separate himself from the conservatives and throw his support to the students and their cause. It was clear, however, that Zhao did not have the votes in the Politburo to sustain his position, no matter how popular he was with the demonstrators.

As the demonstrations continued into late May, the students and their supporters became more radicalized and demanded the government institute a series of political reforms, which were expanded to include an end to official corruption and economic policies that would address growing inflation. With the demonstrations growing and the international press taking an interest in this challenge to authority, Deng and his party allies stripped Zhao of his position as general secretary after he refused to be a spokesman for the conservatives. Li

Peng made a half-hearted attempt to speak with the demonstrators on television, but it was becoming obvious that party leaders were not interested in agreeing to any demands of the demonstrators. Deng and Li Peng had already made overtures to the PLA to determine whether military commanders would support martial law and remove the demonstrators from Tiananmen Square. This was not an easy task, since there were divisions in the PLA over how to handle the demonstrations and even which side to support in this political confrontation.

After weeks spent consolidating their position in the Politburo and other key organs of the party, Deng and his conservative allies gave the order to establish martial law and forcefully remove the demonstrators from Tiananmen Square. In the aftermath of the decision to suppress the democracy movement in Beijing and elsewhere, Deng sought to find a suitable replacement for Zhao and reestablish a new level of stability and consensus in the party. His efforts were not immediately successful as the old conservative guard opposed some of his initial nominations, fearful that they were not completely committed to curtailing the political reform movement. Finally, Deng was able to present Jiang Zemin as a compromise candidate. Jiang had successfully dealt with antigovernment demonstrations in Shanghai and seemed to be a hard-line foe of democratization. With the appointment of Jiang Zemin as general secretary of the Communist Party, the short-lived period of liberalization in the top ranks of the party came to an end. Conservatives used their numbers in the Politburo to strip power from political reformers and reestablish a solid front opposed to democratization. Of course the human price for this consolidation of power was enormous and the push for meaningful change in the political system was delayed.

Public policymaking and policy implementation in the Chinese political system is in many respects a high-stakes chess match, with the players making strategic moves against their adversaries as they seek to end the game and establish their philosophy and their position on a particular issue. The process is much more personal and cutthroat than anything in Western nations as the power elite often seek to marginalize if not purge an adversary as they advance their agenda. Since political leaders in China are not removed from office through an electoral process, this behind-the-scenes posturing, maneuvering, and character assassination takes the place of democratic change and provides the Chinese system with new leaders and new approaches. But as this case study of policymaking and policy implementation shows, decisions in the Chinese political system are vigorously debated, all sides in the debate are heard from, coalitions are formed to attain closure, and the final decision is accepted with little hint to the public that a hard-fought chess match has occurred.

POINT OF FACT

The Chinese Communist Party remains a secretive body. At the sixteenth party congress in November 2002, the party leaders were not officially known until they filed out from behind a huge dragon screen and stood in front of the assembled delegates and the world media at the Great Hall of the People.

China in the Global Economy

Shenzhen in southwestern China is the site of the largest state economic zone (SEZ) that caters to foreign investment and produces goods for the international market. Before Shenzhen was declared an SEZ, it was a small outpost with little economic importance. Today, with a population of over 3 million people, Shenzhen is the center of the booming Chinese economy ($1.6 billion in foreign investment in 1998) and an example of how China has changed from a socialist to a capitalist economy (this is where the American popular culture icon, the Barbie doll, is made). Wages are higher in Shenzhen than in the rest of China, goods are more plentiful, prospects for job advancement are better, and the cultural climate is more relaxed and permissive as Western clothes, music, and mores are in evidence.

POLITICAL ECONOMY

Since the death of Mao, the Chinese leadership has sought to move the country away from its socialist foundation and introduce market reforms. These reforms have been designed to make state enterprises more efficient and profitable, encourage privatization of key economic sectors, attract foreign investment and foreign trade, and shift the consumer culture from Marxist sameness to Western diversity. While there is no doubt that the Chinese leadership and growing numbers of the populace are committed to transforming the economy along capitalist lines, the process of transformation has been uneven, divisive, and filled with doubt.

Government officials still pay homage to Mao's socialism and revolutionary slogans. They seek to preserve the state's control of the economy and the communal life of peasants. There is a public revulsion against incentives and wealth accumulation, and a widely promulgated belief that collective economic decisions are far superior to private initiative. But even as the government harks back to the Maoist legacy, it advances Western-style capitalism. State enterprises are sold off, citizens are encouraged to compete in a vibrant marketplace, and slowly but surely the collective ethic is abandoned in favor of individualism.

The efforts to transform the Chinese economy, while not rejecting socialism, are best viewed in terms of the state-owned enterprises (SOEs). There are currently 100,000 of these entities employing more than 100 million workers. The SOEs are responsible for the majority of the industrial output of China and occupy key sectors of the economy such as steel and petroleum. Because the SOEs are part of the old command economic structure, they are inefficient and top-heavy with employees. Because it bases such a large share of its industrial output in unproductive and bloated state enterprises, China has been unable to move quickly and effectively toward a more modern economy that stresses profitability. Instead the state enterprises have been a huge drain on national budgets and the state banking system.

Since the SOEs employ millions, they have been difficult to reform. Jiang Zemin in 1997 announced that he was advocating a massive restructuring of the SOEs. Prime Minister Zhu Rongji made the restructuring of the SOEs one of the centerpieces of his administration. Thousands of SOEs were either shut down or sold to local cooperatives. Those that remained followed Western business practices such as pay incentives, joint ventures with foreign companies, and less government involvement in the day-to-day decisionmaking process. But restructuring has run up against entrenched party and government opposition. Although the SOEs now account for only 29 percent of industrial output, they continue to show signs of inefficiency and waste. There are still too many workers and too much unprofitability. The state continues to pump huge amounts of cash into the remaining SOEs because maintaining inefficient industries is viewed as more acceptable than forcing millions into the unemployment lines or angering recalcitrant party officials. The SOEs are a prime example of the power of party cadres and top leaders to limit market reforms. Bureaucrats continue to wield control over production and distribution networks and are reluctant to accept changes that will weaken their hold on economic policy.

Visible and significant economic reform has occurred in the rural areas. During the Maoist era China was totally committed to a communist model of rural economy. Collective farms that had been introduced in the 1950s were part of a huge state agricultural system in which peasants were paid based on how much they worked and farm products became part of a pricing and distribution schedule controlled by bureaucrats. Later the collective farms were merged into huge people's communes with the intention of achieving better management and more efficient delivery of services. But the grandiose revolutionary schemes of Mao in the rural areas failed miserably as the agricultural economy stagnated under the weight of too much bureaucracy and too little individual initiative.

Again it was not until Mao died and Deng took power that liberalizing change came to the rural areas. Deng advocated the transformation of the communes into what was called a household responsibility system. This new approach to agricultural organization is a Chinese version of the family farm. Peasants are given more responsibility to work the land, produce the crops, and benefit from the sale of their products. Although peasants are not permitted to own the land (they sign long-term lease agreements) and are required to pay taxes and other fees to the local authorities, the household responsibility system has increased agricultural output and improved the living standards of the rural farmers. The increased farm output associated with the household responsibility system has enabled China to keep pace with heightened demands for agricultural commodities in a more consumer-driven economy.

The real transformation in the rural areas of China is associated with the township and village enterprises (TVEs). Under Deng's guidance the government encouraged the formation of rural factories and other commercial enterprises as a means of strengthening the economy outside the urban centers. The TVEs are actually joint ventures with local governments and individual entrepreneurs uniting to form a business outside the control of the state. The TVEs have produced a range of consumer goods such as clothes, small appliances, and even some high-tech components. It is estimated that the TVEs employ 130 million Chinese and contribute 40 percent of China's overall industrial output. Because the TVEs are a relatively new arrival in the economic mix, there are numerous problems with corruption by local officials and growing disinterest among peasants to engage in traditional farming. With the prospects of increasing personal income by starting up a TVE, peasants have neglected the production of traditional commodities, thereby creating shortages of key foodstuffs.

The area of the Chinese economy that has undergone the greatest transformation is foreign trade and investment. In the post-Mao period China has become the world's tenth largest trading nation with over $300 billion in transfers in 1997. Under Deng Xiaoping, China made a concerted effort to use foreign trade as an engine of economic development. The Chinese, modeling their strategy after neighbors such as South Korea and Japan, redesigned their domestic industries for export and opened their economy to the world. Because of low unit costs (largely associated with meager wages paid to its workers) Chinese goods became attractive overseas, especially in the Pacific rim. Today China exports small-scale consumer goods in exchange for heavy machinery and raw materials necessary for its industrial expansion.

Although China has concentrated on trade with Asia, the United States is a crucial partner. Imports and exports have risen steadily in the 1990s and should continue to increase now that China is a member of the World Trade Organization. There is growing debate, however, over the importance of

China as a trading power, despite the growth of imports and exports. Despite its size and its economic potential, China remains no match in terms of trade when compared with South Korea, Japan, and Taiwan. These three nations remain the trade giants of Asia with China still far behind. The key word defining China's trade transformation is "potential." Both the Chinese leadership and Western nations are convinced that China will live up to its billing as the next great trade frontier. The addition of Hong Kong to Chinese sovereignty in 1999, the rapid emergence of Shanghai as the economic gateway to China, and the growing importance of the special economic zones in the southwestern provinces are critical ingredients in the trade transformation.

Attracting foreign investment is crucial to the trade transformation of China. The 1990s were a boom period for foreign investment. In 1997, the peak year for capital infusion, the Chinese attracted $45 billion. Much of this investment came from ethnic Chinese in the Pacific rim, but there has been healthy investment from the United States and Europe. The 55 million ethnic Chinese in Southeast Asia and North America have been critical in providing China with capital. There is a strong kinship between diaspora and mainland Chinese that contributes to a steady flow of capital.

While much of the foreign investment is from the ethnic Chinese, there continues to be significant growth in foreign investment from notable corporate giants such as Coca-Cola, McDonald's, Starbucks, Pizza Hut, and Dunkin' Donuts. There has also been significant investment from high-tech giants such as IBM and Xerox and automobile manufacturers such as Jeep. As of 1999 foreign investment in China was 10 percent of global foreign investment, a figure considered modest but one that harbors great potential. Perhaps the most important figure associated with foreign investment is that capital from overseas has been invested in nearly 250,000 enterprises in China.

China's membership in the World Trade Organization is a critical part of its trade and investment strategy. China wants to move away from being a source of cheap consumer goods (two-thirds of the shoes and more than one-half of the toys sold in the United States are made in China) and begin attracting high technology as a means of expanding its industrial base. WTO membership further opens the prospects for new markets such as the lucrative cell phone equipment and airline markets. There are some important steps that must be taken in conjunction with WTO membership such as the prohibitive tariff schedules on key Western goods such as automobiles, import substitution policies, and controversial access to technology items that have both civilian and military use. Western governments, for example, are concerned the purchase of global positioning system receivers, which could be used to strengthen military capabilities.

While the future ramifications of WTO membership for China remain unclear, there is perhaps no more obvious sign of the impact of the trade and foreign investment transformation in China than in the special economic zones, which are situated primarily in the southwestern provinces and also along the eastern coast. They were set up by the Chinese government for the express purpose of attracting foreign investment and serving as trade gateways to Asia, the United States, and Europe. The SEZs are attractive to foreign investors and traders because of the special incentives and tax breaks provided by the government. The government has spent lavishly in building necessary infrastructure (roads, bridges, water purification, sewage, and housing) in order to attract foreign investors and accommodate the crush of workers who are streaming into the SEZs from the rural areas.

In many ways the most interesting and potentially most system-destabilizing transformation in the Chinese economy is the onset of capitalist culture. The years of double-digit economic growth, privatization, and foreign linkages have combined to create a new value system in China. China under Mao adhered to a state-dependent value system often called the "iron rice bowl" that stressed cradle-to-grave benefits and a governmental image of benevolent concern for the common good. As the Maoist approach faded and was replaced with the market economy, the Chinese quickly came to realize that they no longer could rely on a state safety net. They were increasingly on their own.

Many of the Chinese, particularly the young, urban, and educated, welcomed the shift and eagerly accepted the new value system and Western capitalist culture. Private enterprise expanded, personal wealth skyrocketed, and the Chinese people redefined the way they live and work. In cities such as Shanghai giant skyscrapers, shopping malls, and luxurious apartment complexes have been constructed to accommodate the new wealth and the new desire to live and work like Western capitalists. But many of the old, rural, and uneducated could not cope with the changes. After decades of living under the "iron rice bowl," which offered the Chinese economic stability and predictability but little in creature comforts, they were required to fend for themselves in a more open, competitive system. As a result their living standard declined, medical care in the communes all but disappeared, and unemployment, once rare, became commonplace.

Unfortunately with the energy and prosperity created by the new economic values and culture, China has also experienced the dark side of capitalism. Drugs, prostitution, divorce, and violent crime are now commonplace. Also a wide array of public and private corruption now plagues China. The State Statistical Bureau in a study completed in 1999 reported that 17 percent of all bank deposits, totaling $121 billion, was public money hidden in private accounts. From the high party official who steals millions in smuggled goods to the local official who pockets fines collected from couples who have more than one child to the astounding 70 percent to 80 percent of the

Chinese who pay no tax to the government, the economic environment in China is engulfed in a culture of illegality linked to the expanding opportunities to make money and to grow rich.

Corruption has reached the highest levels of the Chinese Party hierarchy, as evidenced by the house arrest of Chen Xitong, Beijing's municipal head who became Jiang's most visible example of his commitment to root out official misdeeds. There have also been some highly publicized public trials and executions of local party officials found guilty of smuggling and other illegal profit-making schemes. Interestingly, when Deng Xiaoping was seeking to transform the Chinese economy in the early 1980s, he issued a statement in which he urged his people to follow the maxim "To get rich is glorious." Many Chinese, especially in party and government circles, have taken that advice to heart, but often the means used to implement that maxim have been illegal and have created one of China's most serious post-Maoist problems.

While corruption and the social ills that often accompany economic growth pose serious concerns and will need to be addressed in the future, China has now settled into a more normal pattern of growth. Those heady days of double-digit advances are likely over. Moreover, there are signs that the economic data presented by the government on economic growth during the 1990s may not have accurately portrayed existing conditions. The National Bureau of Statistics has come under scrutiny as growth figures from various provinces have not meshed with the national figures. Outside experts are now suggesting that Chinese economic growth, during the years when 7–10 percent increases in GDP were claimed, may in reality have been considerably lower.

The Fourth Generation leadership that took power in November 2002 has an ambitious set of priorities. Initially in order to respond to domestic needs, the new leadership is targeting unprofitable SOEs. Selling off the weaker SOEs and pumping new investment into the profitable ones is viewed as one way of generating more income for the Chinese working class. Many of the unprofitable SOEs have a history of not paying their workers or contributing to their pensions. By speaking so forcefully on behalf of the nation's poor working class, the Fourth Generation leadership has set a lofty goal of economic reform and development. These promises of reform will eventually require evidence of success and likely generate heightened demands for more attention to the needs of the poor. Failure to achieve success could spell disaster for the new leadership.

POINT OF FACT

Taiwan began work in 2003 on an $898 million semiconductor plant in Shanghai. Despite being at odds with Taiwan, China in recent years has welcomed investment from its "rebel" outpost.

HONG KONG POLICY

At midnight on June 30, 1997, the HMS *Britannia* sailed out of Hong Kong harbor as the tiny island protectorate became a special administrative region of China. The British had controlled Hong Kong island, which also included some adjoining territory on mainland China, since 1842 with additional expansion of territory in 1860 and 1898. Britain gained control of Hong Kong as a result of victories over the Chinese in trade wars and used the colony as its gateway to the lucrative China trade. In 1898 Britain agreed to maintain the island and adjoining real estate under a ninety-nine-year lease. British rule transformed the colony into one of Asia's premier financial and service centers. Hong Kong has a per capita income of over $26,000 and a GNP of $164 billion. The British brought to Hong Kong the Western market system, the rule of law, and the protection of civil liberties. Governmental decisions were in the hands of the governor general, who represented the queen and was appointed by the British government. Although there was little in the way of local democratic governance, the 6.5 million residents of the colony seemed unconcerned that major public decisions were made by business elites in consultation with the British.

But as 1997 approached, the British governor general, Christopher Patten, became concerned that the Chinese would quickly strip Hong Kong of its openness and freedom. As a result elections for a Legislative Council were held in 1991 for one-third of the members. In 1995 Patten introduced an electoral reform that provided Hong Kong citizens with the ability to elect all members of the Legislative Council. Because of these electoral reforms, political parties began to form and democratic politicians spoke out more openly about the fear of communist rule. The Chinese saw these British initiatives as last-ditch efforts to compromise their sovereign rights and violate China's Basic Law. They responded by selecting their own legislative body and chief executive, Tung Chee-hwa, a wealthy businessman.

Once the British left, China immediately sent in troops and appointed local administrators who were viewed as supportive of Beijing policies. Since the turnover of power the Chinese have kept to their pledge to keep the capitalist system intact for fifty years. Nor have they dismantled the legal and rights guarantees that were put in place by the British. Democratic elections were held in May 1998, and opposition candidates gained a portion of the directly elected seats, but the vast majority of the delegates were chosen by an indirect method that allows Chinese control of the legislature. There have been growing concerns, however, that China and the pro-Chinese government in Hong Kong are slowly moving away from democratic rule. In 1999 the United Nations Human Rights Committee called on authorities in Hong

Kong to strengthen democratic representation and allow its citizens to have a greater voice in public matters. In particular, the United Nations was concerned about the lack of independent bodies to investigate rights violations and police misconduct. There were also concerns about the independence of the Hong Kong judiciary and its willingness to uphold British legal precedents. There is growing evidence that Beijing is interfering with judicial decisions made by the Hong Kong courts and that its legislative electoral system is in violation of the Covenant on Civil and Political Rights, a document that China signed but did not ratify.

While there are concerns over civil rights and democracy, Hong Kong continues to be a vibrant economic center. Chinese officials recognize that Hong Kong provides it with access to the financial and corporate networks in the United States and Europe. At this time Beijing is not interested in jeopardizing the wealth generated by Hong Kong or the opportunities that it provides the mainland to enhance its global presence. The Chinese have taken the next step up the ladder of capitalism by signing an agreement with the Disney Corporation to build a $3.5 billion theme park by 2005. The agreement is the largest project to be undertaken since the transfer of power. Tung Chee-hwa hailed the agreement as "a vote of confidence in our city and our future." More important than the prospect of having Mickey Mouse in Communist China, the Disney deal is a further example of the "one country, two systems" approach that is at the core of Hong Kong's identity. The fifty-year promise not to change the market-based economy of Hong Kong appears likely to be kept. But whether Chinese officials will continue to chip away at democracy, law, and civil liberties remains uncertain. ⊕

CHALLENGES

A nation such as China with the world's largest population, an economic system that is undergoing fundamental change, and a political hierarchy poised for a massive generational shift is without question faced with enormous challenges. Despite the high levels of economic growth in the 1990s and growing foreign trade and investment interest, China remains a Third World nation with a range of problems endemic to countries that have not reached the level of modernization found in the advanced industrial world. It is important to remember that China's per capita gross domestic product is $1,070, placing it well below Asian competitors such as Singapore ($27,870) and South Korea ($9,040). China's archrival, Taiwan, is considerably more prosperous and advanced with a per capita GDP of $13,832 and much more successful in attracting international trade and investment. Moreover, China's "in-betweenness," as a nation balancing capitalism and socialism in the economic realm and feeling the pressures for more openness and competitiveness in an authoritarian environment, creates internal challenges that must be addressed before they destabilize the overall governing system. Although China has effectively controlled these challenges through its domination of politics and its willingness to dampen opposition, the number of internal challenges has not diminished or lessened in intensity. The to-do list facing the Chinese leadership is considerable and in many respects overwhelming.

The most critical challenge facing the Chinese is responding to the inevitable economic and social dislocations that are likely to occur with membership in the World Trade Organization. The introduction of new trading rules that will force competition and diminish state subsidies are certain to create hardships, especially in the rural areas. Peasants, who are already desperately poor, will be forced to endure greater pressure on their standard of living as foreign farm products enter the Chinese economy. Rural peasants are expected to intensify their migration to the urban areas as the agricultural economy moves through a major transformation. In early response to the changing character of rural life there have been major protests over pricing schedules for commodities and the presence of foreign goods in the marketplace.

Chinese society continues to be buffeted by a wide range of new liberalizing forces. There is a significant debate in the party leadership circle about how best to deal with the growing influence of the Internet as both a commercial and consumer tool and, more importantly for the health of the party, a means of challenging the existing power arrangements. The Chinese government has already sought ways to control content by blocking Web sites, regulating portals through licensing, and attempting to limit the number of English-language sites. Communist Party leaders are conscious that they cannot completely control the Internet, especially since it is one of the primary tools of the global economy, but they also know that they must maintain vigilance over the Internet and use their regulatory power to limit its political and social influence.

The Communist Party will undoubtedly face the issue of how to properly respond to income inequality in the coming years, especially the growing differentiation between urban centers tied to the world economy and cities and rural areas tied to the old Chinese economy. Economic data from 1985–1995 show that in coastal cities such as Shanghai and in the special economic zone cities like Shenzhen there has been a considerable difference in per capita consumption expenditure from inland cities such as Nanking and Wuhan. For example, the gap between the national urban average of consumer consumption and that of Shanghai more than doubled from 1985 to 1990 and then increased fivefold from 1990 to 1995. Similar huge gaps in consumer expenditures were found in SEZ cities such as Shenzhen and Guangzhou, but in internal cities such as Nanking and Wuhan there was little variation from the national average.

The growing disparity between rich cities and regions and the rest of China has not yet created deep resentments among the people. The government wisely has retained many subsidy programs in housing and workplace food distribution, which have made basic necessities affordable. But as China moves further and further away from its socialist roots, workers in cities with a less vibrant economy and stagnant wages will quickly recognize the inequality and press the government for relief. The party leadership's attempt to balance socialism with capitalism hinges on this selective incorporation of a different economic model. But the selectivity has already created pockets of wealth amid a sea of poverty that cannot be sustained indefinitely. At some point in the near future Hu Jintao and Wen Jiabao will have to decide how to deal with the "two Chinas" and the inevitable resentment that will accompany income inequality.

Although many of the challenges faced by the Chinese government and the Chinese people are domestic in nature, important defense and territorial issues are likely to remain at the forefront of the national policy agenda. The expansion of the Chinese military establishment coupled with a more aggressive posture toward Taiwan, and to a lesser extent South Korea and Japan, has propelled the country into a regional and international imbroglio over its strategic intentions. The West views China with increasing unease. Its military spending, its refusal to sign the Nuclear Nonproliferation Treaty, and its arms transfers to high-risk nations such as Pakistan, Burma, and the Sudan have an unsettling character to the major powers as well as China's neighbors. Perhaps most unsettling is China's current initiative to improve the "survivability" of its strategic forces, which are vulnerable to first strikes from the United States. There is also an accompanying initiative (assisted by purchases of advanced weapons from Russia and stolen technology from the United States) to improve the accuracy, guidance, and range of its missiles, all with the intention of making the Chinese nuclear arsenal a force to be reckoned with.

Despite constant criticism from the United States and heightened preparedness in Japan, South Korea, and Taiwan, there is no evidence that the Chinese are interested in putting a halt to military expansionism and nuclear modernization. The Chinese appear to be committed to a plan that moves them into great power status in the decade, and certainly regional power dominance as quickly as possible. Defense analysts are convinced that China has a long way to go in order to become a real threat to the stability of the region and the territorial integrity of a country such as Taiwan. Nevertheless, China has shown that it is not interested in maintaining its current military posture. The political leadership has increased defense spending, modernized its weaponry, and made public pronouncements that have caused its neighbors to formulate new national security strategies.

Much of China's new defense posture has its foundation in the long-standing dispute with Taiwan. In 1945 Chiang Kai-shek took his Nationalist troops out of mainland China and founded the Republic of China on Taiwan, one hundred miles across the China Sea from the People's Republic of China. Since the separation of Taiwan from Communist China, Beijing has made regular attempts to "liberate" the Nationalist-led government. Despite periodic negotiations, there has been no resolution of their disputes nor an agreement that would create a unified China. In recent years tensions have grown between China and Taiwan. The Chinese military in 1999 engaged in live missile firings during its war games, a development that prompted the United States to send warships into the area to stop further escalation. Later in 1999 the Taiwanese president demanded political parity with China by redefining bilateral ties as "special state to state," a code phrase signifying sovereignty that broke off talks and infuriated the Chinese. The election of President Chen Shui-bian and his pro-independence Democratic Progressive Party angered the Chinese, who see the prospect of Taiwan declaring statehood and not engaging in any further talks designed to attain some form of reunification.

The challenges that China faces in the coming years are on the one hand similar to those facing many countries. There are issues of sustaining economic growth, responding to the consumer demands of its citizenry, ensuring political stability in the face of domestic tensions and fragmentation, and dealing with the governmental and societal stresses that accompany globalization. But at the same time while these normal challenges are being played out in China, there are additional challenges that are associated with the unique set of circumstances that come from being a communist country in transition. China is a country poised to make a significant and uncertain overhaul of its top leadership. China is engulfed in ever increasing protests from religious, cultural, and political groups. China is caught between its revolutionary heritage and nascent democracy, a condition that creates deep fissures in the political elite. And China is seeking to find the proper balance between socialism and capitalism at a time when socialism has lost its luster as a development model.

POINT OF FACT
China is preparing for the 2008 Summer Olympics by building seventy-five kilometers of new subway and seven hundred kilometers of new highway, along with a new airport and a new opera house.

DEVELOPMENT POLICIES IN THE FAR WEST

Much attention has been paid to the economic development of the southwestern and coastal provinces where the Chinese government has allowed the market system to flourish. China is committing huge resources to the far western regions, sometimes called the "Wild, Wild West," hoping to transform this dusty backwater into the new frontier of modernization. Calling it the "Western Big Development," Chinese authorities are spending billions of dollars in the nine-province region that encompasses 2 million square miles and is home to 300 million people. At the center of the "Western Big Development" is the province of Xinjiang and its capital city, Urumqi. Daily, thousands of bureaucrats, businessmen, and fortune seekers travel thousands of miles from the poverty of the countryside in search of new opportunities in the rough-and-tumble life of this barren outpost.

These visitors are drawn to the West by a vigorous public relations campaign sponsored by the government, which is intent on creating a balance of development to the length and breadth of China. There is a concern among government officials that too much attention and too many resources have been expended in the southwest and along the coast and that China is fast becoming a dual nation with a developed East and an underdeveloped West. As a result, huge infrastructure projects such as roads, railroads, airports, and pipelines are under construction. Since most of China's oil and mineral reserves are in the far West along with many strategic military installations, the decision has been made that development must be put on the fast track.

There is also mounting concern in leadership circles that the 8 million Uighurs who live in Xinjiang are becoming increasingly rebellious and may seek to begin a movement to break away from Chinese control, like the neighboring Tibetans. There have been regular bombings of public buildings and killings of officials by the Uighurs, a clear signal to the Chinese that if they do not pay closer attention to the region, they will be faced with the prospect of a spin-off of independent states. To head off a breakaway movement the government is encouraging Han Chinese from the eastern provinces to move to the West and establish residency and contribute to its economic development. Calls reminiscent of "Go West, Young Man" are heard repeatedly from government officials. The concept of Manifest Destiny, which served as the guidepost of American westward expansion, has filtered into the public discussion of development. The Chinese army has also been encouraged to settle in the region. Demobilized soldiers have been guaranteed jobs and permission to trade their rural residency permit for one that allows them the freedom to travel to the West.

At present the Uighurs outnumber the Han by about eight to one, and there have been signs that the campaign to relocate in the region has leveled off. The government, however, is not giving up and is offering incentives to keep the flow of Han Chinese going. In order to sustain Han Chinese migration to the region the government's development models clearly favor the Han over the Uighurs. For example, in a move similar to the Oklahoma land settlement of the late 1800s, Han settlers can rent an acre or more of land from the government at low cost and then use the land as they wish. The Xinjiang Production and Construction Corps, which operates farms and factories in the province, has moved 2.4 million people, 90 percent Han, into Xinjiang. Today 40 percent of Xinjiang's residents are Han Chinese.

The Uighurs see such land policies as further proof that the Chinese government is bent on weakening their hold on the land. Policies that favor one ethnic group over another have done little to weaken the rebellious nature of the Uighurs. The region is teeming with discontent. The government is aware that its policies are doing little to stem the rebellion, but by placing the accent on economic modernization, high-paying jobs, and new opportunities, the view from Beijing is that eventually anti-Chinese actions will diminish.

Although the Western Big Development project is only in its infancy and the "Wild, Wild West" is a long way from matching the modernization and prosperity of the southwest and coastal cities, the future of China may very likely be in Xinjiang province and in cities like Urumqi. ⊕

COMPARISONS

The transformation of China and the Chinese economy from Marxist and revolutionary to a mix of socialism and capitalism is best analyzed in terms of a comparison with the former Soviet Union. The Chinese political leadership has made a concerted effort to avoid the internal chaos and economic dislocation that has marked Russia since the collapse of communism. The Chinese have taken a much more gradual approach toward introducing the market system into China and have certainly been reluctant to link economic reform with political change. Besides its gradualist approach, China has also benefited from a number of favorable economic conditions that have not been present in Russia. Deng Xiaoping and later Jiang Zemin got an economic boost from the shift of millions of rural workers from collective farms to jobs in more urban areas where jobs were plentiful. Russia on the other hand was already industrialized, and as a result its labor base was not as plentiful and not as cheap. In addition, China was not saddled with huge short-term debt as was Russia. In part because of Mao's desire to remain self-sufficient, China, unlike Russia, has not had to rely on huge IMF bailouts and thus avoided having to channel precious budgetary resources toward servicing its debt.

The critical difference between the Russian and the Chinese approach to economic modernization has been the ability of the political leadership to maintain control of the reins of power. The Chinese Communist Party hierarchy continues to rule through decree without concern for a multiparty opposition and an intransigent legislature. Because the Russians chose to open up the political system and create independent governing institutions almost immediately after the fall of communism, it fostered an adversarial atmosphere that was democratic in character but not necessarily conducive to formulating and implementing effective economic policies. While the Russian government shifted policy priorities and development approaches on a regular basis in order to respond to domestic crises, the Chinese political leadership moved forward slowly but surely toward its mix of socialism and capitalism. There were and are, of course, internal policy disputes, failures of policy, and growing corruption in the party and governing officialdom, but the Chinese have managed the transition away from communism much better than the Russians have. Russia today is a weak but functioning democracy, while China remains a stern authoritarian state.

CONCLUSION

Future Chinese political leaders will have to deal with a governing climate that is unpredictable and potentially disruptive. Generational differences will play a critical ingredient in defining current and future political development in China. The younger generation that is moving up the party and government ladder has different views on economic modernization and political democracy, and is increasingly antiparty, antistate, and anti-ideology. These cosmopolitans, as they have come to be called, have little tolerance for revolutionary slogans, bureaucratic intransigence, and party factionalism. Many having been educated in the West, these cosmopolitans want China to be modern in political practice as well as in economic models.

Despite the inevitable change that comes with younger leaders moving into positions of political and economic power, China remains a country that is communist, centralized, and authoritarian. While there may be a growing consensus that China cannot turn its back on the global economy and must provide an economic environment that responds to the modern needs and demands of its citizens, China has shown little interest in transforming its political system. China is still a country of human rights abuses, limitations on free speech and assembly, little in the way of real democratic participation, and a lingering reluctance to shed the political culture of Maoist revolution. To break down the old system of politics, the next generation of leaders will likely face intransigence from a generation of elites that is not far removed from the days of the Cultural Revolution. As these two generations seek to consolidate their positions, China and Chinese politics can be expected to continue the breathtaking economic development but in a contentious political environment. In the coming years China may be engulfed in a grand dispute over whether economic modernization will be tied to political development or whether economic modernization will be controlled and limited in order to preserve the governing status quo. This is the future of leadership in China, but in the meantime the transition to that leadership will be contentious.

A FEW BOOKS YOU SHOULD READ

Jasper Becker, *The Chinese* (New York: Free Press, 2000). Personal observations of China by a veteran journalist.

John Fairbank and Merle Goldman, *China: A New History* (Cambridge: Harvard University Press, 1998). The bible of Chinese history.

Joseph Fewsmith, *China since Tiananmen: The Politics of Transition* (New York: Cambridge University Press, 2001). A masterful study of diversity, factionalism, and dissent in the ruling elite in the years since Tiananmen Square.

Bruce Gilley, *Tiger on the Brink: Jiang Zemin and China's New Elite* (Berkeley: University of California Press, 1998). A who's who of modern Chinese politics and government.

Merle Goldman and Roderick MacFarquhar, eds., *The Paradox of China's Post-Mao Reforms* (Cambridge: Harvard University Press, 1999). An essential edited volume on economic changes by two premier China scholars.

A FEW WEB SITES YOU SHOULD VISIT

www.mzdthought.com. Web site for those interested in the words and wisdom of Mao Zedong.

www.insidechina.com. General information site on China and the Chinese.

www.china.org.cn. China Internet Information Center.

www.chinadaily.com.cn. English-language news organization.

www.asiasociety.org. Site of the Asia Society, first-rate think tank on China.

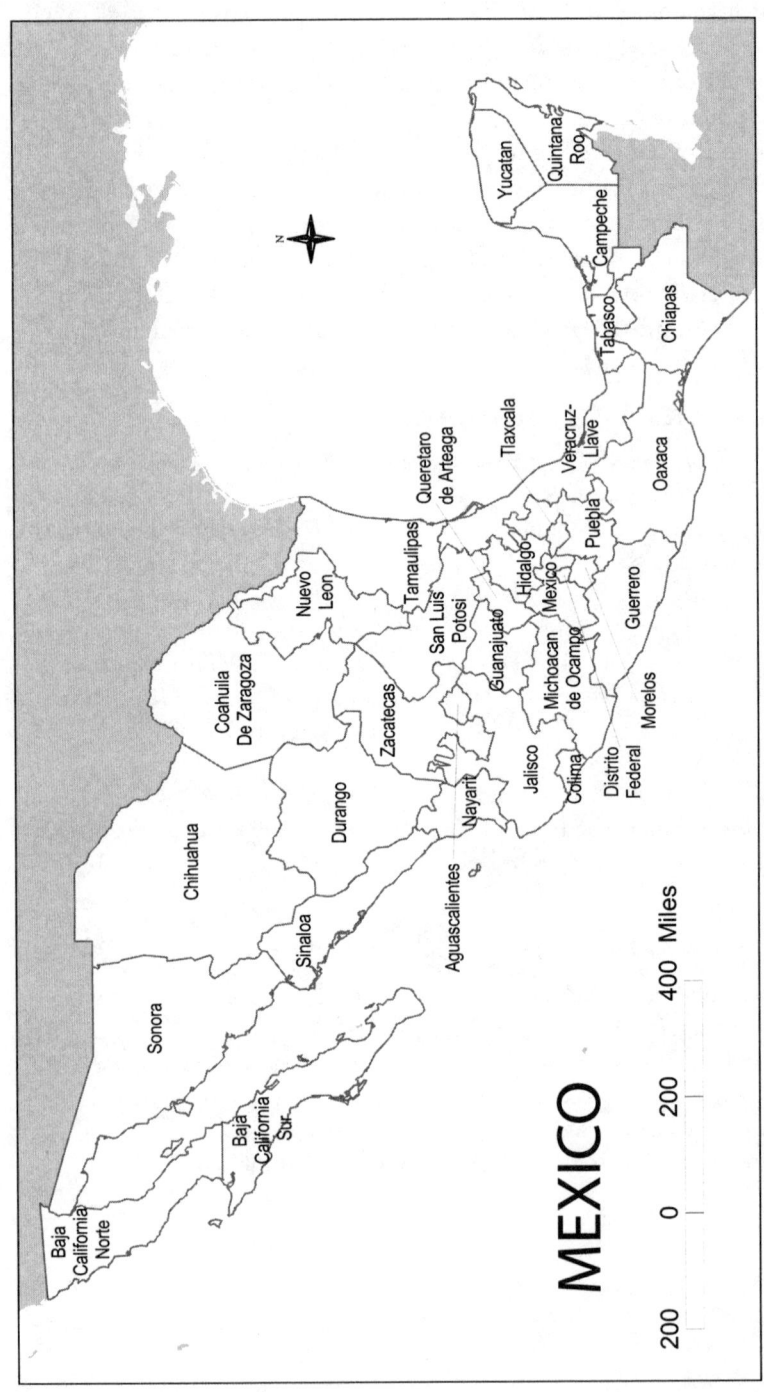

MEXICO

| 200 | 0 | 200 | 400 Miles |

SOURCE: Michigan State University Map Library, Data Source ESRI

MAP 6.1 United Mexican States

United Mexican States

Data Bank

Area: 761,600 sq. miles

Population: 98 million (1999 census)

Rural/urban population ratio: 26/74

Ethnic composition: 60 percent Indian Spanish (mestizo), 30 percent
Indian, 9 percent Caucasian, 1 percent other

Adult literacy: 89 percent

Life expectancy: Male, 73 years; female, 77 years

Form of government: Federal republic

Head of state/government: Vicente Fox

Per capita income/GDP: $6,210 (2002)

Exports: $136 billion; imports $142 billion (partners: United States,
European Union, South America)

Source: United Nations and World Bank

SETTING THE SCENE

In traveling throughout Mexico, my primary purpose has been to become part of another culture and experience life in a way that differs from my American upbringing. In my most memorable trip I traveled through the country by bus and saw Mexico firsthand. As I left the United States and crossed into Nueva Leon on the Mexican side of the border, I recognized that I was entering not only a new country but a new world. On the way from Nueva Leon to the northern city of Monterrey I was struck by the difference between Mexico and the United States. From the window I could see that Mexico was a poor nation struggling to become modern. The rural expanse was dotted by peasant villages with *campesinos* eking a meager existence off the land. In Monterrey I was

317

amazed at the transformation from rural to urban. Monterrey, one of Mexico's industrial centers, epitomized the vibrancy of the Mexican economy with its factories, skyscrapers, and visible consumerism. In a few hours I had seen the fundamental dichotomy of Mexico—the modern world existing side by side with a world that has not changed much in one hundred years.

Next it was down to Guadalajara with its proud colonial past. Magnificent Catholic cathedrals in the center of stately plazas reminded me of Mexico's Spanish heritage, and wonderful museums and art galleries convinced me that I was in a highly cultured society. With one of the most attractive climates in the world, Guadalajara is a mecca for those who want to avoid the hustle and bustle and pollution of Mexico City. In Guadalajara Mexicans can maintain their ties to the Spanish Mexico and experience a life that is slower and more refined.

Then on to the capital city, Mexico City, a demographic behemoth of over 20 million inhabitants. As Mexicans leave the rural areas in search of a new life, Mexico City has become an unplanned and congested urban nightmare. Mexico City is where old and new Mexico meet. There is the cosmopolitan main boulevard, the Paseo de la Reforma, and the wealthy neighborhoods of expensive villas. But there are also countless poverty-stricken barrios where hope is at a premium. Mixed in with the rich and the poor are the perpetual air pollution, the electrical brownouts, and the water sanitation crises brought on by an unending stream of new arrivals and uncontrolled growth.

Finally, I headed south toward Chiapas state and the border with Guatemala, where I experienced Mexico's Indian foundations. I climbed Aztec ruins, mingled with the ancestors of those who fought bravely against the Spanish conquistadors, and learned how generations of these indigenous people have been neglected and exploited by the central government. Looking out the bus window, I realized that in traveling from north to south I had climbed up the social and economic ladder only to be brought down again into the depths of abject poverty.

Traveling through Mexico, I was profoundly moved by the people's struggle to bring about change, to move their country into the modern era. In recent years there have been major changes in the Mexican political system. The seventy-one-year reign of the Partido Revolucinario Institucional (PRI) came to an end in 2000 with the election of Vicente Fox of the opposition National Action Party (PAN). The PRI legacy of total political control, official corruption, and electoral fraud collapsed in an orderly manner as the charismatic Fox won the presidency with ease. Fox has energized the Mexican political system by appointing new faces and promising to take the country away from the practices of the PRI.

Enormous economic changes have occurred as Mexico has emerged as one of the leading industrialized nations in the developing world. Today Mexico has been transformed from a rural outback to the world's eighth largest exporter. Economic growth in recent years has been a solid 5–7 percent, making Mexico one of the standout countries in Latin America for foreign investment. Where once Mexico relied on a state-dominated and protectionist development framework, it now has firmly embraced the liberalized and globalized system of free trade and competitive markets.

What may have changed the most in Mexico is the relationship with the United States. Although there are lingering feelings of animosity and mistrust toward the United States, Mexico has formulated a mature, vibrant relationship with its northern neighbor. The basis of this newfound relationship is the North American Free Trade Agreement (NAFTA), which was negotiated between Mexican President Carlos Salinas de Gortari and George H.W. Bush in 1991. NAFTA has opened up both Mexican and American economies to new areas of trade, expanded capital investment, and stimulated growth in the industrial, service, and high-tech sectors. Mexico is now the second biggest trading partner of the United States (behind Canada, which is also a member of NAFTA) and the repository of the American consumer economy as Wal-Mart, McDonald's, Coca-Cola, and hundreds of other retail brands are found throughout the country. The developing economic relationship between Mexico and the United States is perhaps best seen along the border in the maquiladoras, the Mexican version of low-wage and incentive-laden industrial parks that attract American industries. The maquiladoras have been growing at about 20 percent a year since NAFTA and account for nearly 50 percent of all Mexico's exports.

Significant changes have also occurred in Mexican society. Once a country populated by largely rural people, Mexico has become urban. Three-quarters of the population now live in cities, whereas in 1929, at the beginning of the PRI dynasty, two-thirds lived in the rural areas. Even more significant is the population explosion that has occurred in Mexico. The population of the country is nearing 100 million, a sixfold increase since 1929. Mexico City is now one of the largest population centers in the world along with Tokyo, New York, and São Paulo, Brazil. The burgeoning Mexican economy has produced a new class of millionaires and growing middle and professional classes. Mexico is a nation with Internet cafes, megamalls, chic boutiques, *supermercados*, BMW dealerships, and a consumer ethic that is not that much different from what exists across the border and to the north. The newfound wealth has begun to filter down to the masses as development indices such as infant mortality, nutrition, and education have improved significantly in the past ten years.

Change, however, has not come to all of Mexico or all Mexicans. The southern states of Oaxaca and Chiapas register per capita GDP over $2,000 less than that of more urban and industrialized states. Mexico can be seen as a country with a rapidly advancing north and a poorer and less developed south. PRI leaders over the years shifted resources and encouraged policies that benefited northern states while southern states languished. Whether because the north has the larger population centers or because of its proximity to the United States, the southern states have fallen behind on almost every social and economic indicator.

Nationally there are glaring deficiencies and inequalities. It is estimated that 25 percent of Mexicans lack the financial resources to purchase essential items such as food and clothing. With a minimum wage for most of the working population of less than $4 a day, life is very hard for many of the poor. What jobs are available for the poor are in the informal economy, street vendors hawking cigarettes, shining shoes, and selling flowers and candy. Nearly 16 million Mexicans make their living in the informal economy. A more serious indictment of the Mexican economy is the inequality. A study by the Inter-American Development Bank found that Mexico's wage inequality rose in the 1990s more than that of any other Latin American country.

The unrelenting poverty and inequality in Mexico have contributed to a human exodus north to the United States. Since the days of Texas independence and the Mexican-American War, the 2,000-mile border between the Mexico and the United States has been a gateway for millions of migrants seeking jobs, consumer goods, and a new life. Since the end of World War II, labor needs in the United States and the faltering Mexican economy have led to increased border crossings, largely illegal. It is estimated that 280,000 Mexicans illegally cross the border each year; 400 die trying. For Mexico the movement of people across the border has served as a kind of safety valve easing demands on employment, housing, education, and other services. For the United States, the Southwest (Texas, New Mexico, Arizona, and of course California) has become heavily Mexicanized with dual language, dual culture, and dual lifestyles resulting from countless everyday contacts). New Mexico is nearly 40 percent Hispanic and California is close behind with 26 percent, with much of the total Hispanic population Mexican in origin. Cities such as Los Angeles and El Paso are so Mexicanized that it is difficult to determine whether certain neighborhoods are in Mexico or the United States.

The linkage between poverty and cross-border contact has also contributed to the disturbing rise in drug trafficking. Mexico has become a major source of cocaine, marijuana, and heroin, and Mexican drug gangs have become powerful criminal enterprises with large armylike enforcers, sophisticated methods of delivering drugs, and no hesitation about corrupting public officials or remorse about executing drug enforcement agents. Meeting Americans' drug needs has made these drug lords and the members of their crime organization unbelievably wealthy. Some of them have gained hero status among the Mexican poor because of their shrewd efforts to give back a bit of their illegally gained wealth to the people. These modern-day Robin Hoods have greater legitimacy among the barrio residents than the government, which has often made promises that it failed to fulfill. But for all the public relations strategies employed by the drug lords, Mexico has been hard hit by the narcotics trade as thousands of law enforcement officials have been killed in the line of duty, along with high-level public officials. *Star likhet till USA*

It is difficult to set the scene for the discussion of Mexico and Mexican government and politics without mentioning the United States. Much of what Mexico has become is directly related to decisions made in Washington policy centers and corporate boardrooms. Mexico is a distinct country with its own history, its own identity, and its own unique way of organizing politics and making public decisions. But Mexico has been shaped by its unavoidable connection with the United States. As the great Mexican novelist Octavio Paz has said, "[the North Americans] are always among us, even when they ignore us or turn their back on us. Their shadow covers the whole hemisphere. It is the shadow of a giant. And the idea we have of that giant is the same that can be found in fairy tales and legends; a great fellow of kind disposition, a bit simple, an innocent who ignores his own strength and who we can fool most of the time, but whose wrath can destroy us."

As we move deeper into the discussion of Mexico and Mexican politics and government, it will become clear that living next to the most powerful country in the world has been the source of both enormous opportunity and deep-seated anxiety. Mexico must constantly look over its shoulder, seemingly, to see how the United States will react and to what extent it will interfere. A quote attributed to the nineteenth-century Mexican leader Porfirio Diaz perhaps best sums up the critical and defining relationship with Mexico. Diaz, exasperated with the overwhelming U.S. influence on the Mexican economy, said, "Mexico, so far from God, yet so close to the United States." This overwhelming U.S. influence on Mexico and Mexican affairs serves as the foundation of politics and government. There is a sovereign Mexican state, there is a unique Mexican political system, and there is a clearly defined Mexican policy agenda. But there is also that shadow of the giant looming across the border with the power to shape that sovereignty, that political system, and that policy agenda.

POINT OF FACT
The top three Indian groups in Mexico today are the Nahuatl with 1.1 million people, the Maya with 714,000, and the Zapotec with 403,000.

POLITICAL MILESTONES

Mexican political development is a study in contrasts: periods marked by governmental stability and leadership continuity followed by periods of great flux and uncertainty. Mexican history is full of brave heroes and infamous dictators, visionary thinkers and sinister politicians. There are also grand ideas and important documents that sit side by side with corrupt practices and petty disputes. Impressive acts of national pride too often have been diminished by heinous crimes against humanity. Each country, of course, has its own set of contrasts, but Mexico's contrasts are more extreme and have had a profound impact on the manner in which the country was formed and how it evolved over time.

But these contrasts are characterized by certain constants that provide key insights into what it means to be Mexican. There is the Indian foundation of pre-Columbian times with its great culture and tragic dissolution. There is the Spanish influence and the political-economic model of development that shaped the character of Mexico. There is also the indelible mark of Catholicism with its system of belief and enormous personal power. There is the dominant strain of authoritarianism that pervades not only social relations but also, more importantly, the political realm. And finally, there is the endemic dependency on external forces and institutions that have transformed the Mexican economy and psyche. This is a country whose identity has been shaped by the contrasts and the constants.

The Colonial Era

Before Mexico had a colonial history, it had an Indian history. Hundreds of years prior to the arrival of the Spanish conquistadors, Mexico had an advanced Indian civilization. The Mayans were primarily coastal dwellers and the later Aztecs developed their governing and cultural center at Tenochtitlan, which today is Mexico City. The Aztecs were a sophisticated people who developed hierarchies of courts and administrative systems that were advanced for their time. The Aztecs also built beautiful cities with huge temples, monuments to the gods, and the signature pyramid structures that have become modern tourist attractions and symbols of a once great people.

The Aztec civilization, however, was doomed once the Spanish warships arrived off the Caribbean coast. With powerful weapons, horses, and the belief that they were bringing Christianity to a pagan people, conquistadors like Hernán Cortés moved quickly to subdue the Aztecs. Although Aztec chieftains like Moctezuma and his nephew Guautemoc fought the Spanish, they were no match for the cannons, gunpowder, and bullets of the invaders. The

Spanish decimated the Indian population and pillaged their silver and gold. The Indians were forced into work communities (*encomiendas*) as slaves of the Spanish, who transformed Mexico into a colony designed to enrich the conquistadors and the government in Madrid. Mexico, like most of the colonies settled by the Spanish, was viewed as the source of wealth, land, and prestige. There was little interest in settling the land for farming and economic development. Rather, huge estates (*haciendas*) were built whose purpose was to transfer wealth out of the country to Spain. The Indian population became the human conduits of this transfer of riches, and thousands died in the process. Some Catholic Church leaders such as Bartolome´de las Casas sought to protect the Indians from exploitation by the Spanish authorities and landowners, but these efforts were insufficient to stop what eventually became a decimation of the Aztec people and their way of life.

Although considerable attention has gone to the devastating impact of the Spanish conquest on the Indian population and Indian culture, the governing system put in place by Spain had a significant impact on shaping the political development of Mexico and defining the character of modern politics. The Spanish system of governance was heavily weighted toward centralized control and authoritarian practice. The viceroyalty of Mexico, which served as the administrative arm of the Spanish monarchy, and the hierarchy of local governors and municipal officials were charged with ensuring that the new world economy benefited Madrid and that challenges to the system were quickly repressed. There was no popular base in this governing climate. The Spanish opposed the formation of representative bodies and the establishment of citizen-state relations. This was a top-down system that relied on compliance by the *creoles* (as the colonial subjects were called) and forceful implementation of government policies by the Spanish military.

Inevitably a movement arose to establish *creole* control of Mexico and force the Spanish back to Madrid. That movement began in the early 1800s and was led by two defrocked Catholic priests, Father Miguel Hidalgo and Father Jose Maria Morelos. Hidalgo and Morelos envisioned a democratic Mexico that accented individual rights and land reform for the peasant class. The movement to break from Spain was not embraced by the landed and urban elite, who feared that Hidalgo and Morelos would advocate changes that threatened their position and wealth. After a series of bloody and unsuccessful battles with Spanish forces, the two priests were captured and executed. But the push for independence continued under more conservative leadership. In 1821 the *creole* military leader, Augustin Iturbide, joined forces with other independence-minded groups and struck a deal with the Spanish for independence. Mexico became the first Spanish-based colony in the New World to achieve independence, but the transition from Spanish control to *creole* control was in no way revolutionary. Iturbide declared himself emperor and Mexico remained a country with strong authoritarian roots. The only difference was that the centralized control exercised by Madrid was replaced by incompetent, profligate leadership that weakened the Mexican state and rendered it bankrupt.

The Santa Ana Era

Lacking solid governing institutions and dominated by greedy elites interested only in protecting their land and power, Mexico fell into disorder. There was enormous instability in the postindependence era with over thirty-seven presidential administrations between 1833 and 1855. The only semblance of authority and control was in the hands of General Antonio Lopez de Santa Ana, a crude and vain dictator who led Mexico directly or from the shadows for over thirty years. Santa Ana's governing objective was simple personal aggrandizement. Under his rule he stole from the treasury and impoverished the country. He retained power through repressive methods on one hand and allowing autonomy to rural hacienda owners and urban traders on the other. Thus he was able to continue plundering the country. Amid the chaos, Santa Ana offered Mexicans predictability.

Despite Santa Ana's hold on Mexico and his "savior" status with the Mexican people, he will be remembered as the leader who gave up half of the national territory to the United States. The first loss was Texas. American settlers had been traveling to the Mexican territory called Texas after the Spanish gave up control of Florida and the Jefferson administration bought the Louisiana Purchase. The independent-minded Texans posed a challenge to Mexican sovereignty and authority. Santa Ana sought to end this breakaway movement by overwhelming the upstart Texans at a Spanish mission called the Alamo. The battle at the Alamo between Santa Ana and a badly outnumbered force of Texans, including legendary figures Davy Crockett and Jim Bowie, has entered the pantheon of American and Texan history. The Texans bravely fought to the last man and lost to Santa Ana. But his hero status was short-lived as General Sam Houston defeated Santa Ana's forces at a river junction called San Jacinto and set the scene for the eventual Mexican withdrawal from Texas.

The loss of Texas was a prelude to the next challenge to Mexican sovereignty. The administration of President James Polk was anxious to forge a two-ocean country, and California became the coveted prize. At first the United States sought negotiations with the Mexican government and offered to purchase California ($25 million) along with New Mexico ($5 million). But the Mexicans, fresh from their humiliating loss of Texas, were in no mood to give up land at any price. Polk would not be denied his plan to expand U.S. territory and prepared to go to war. Hoping to avoid a bloody war on Mexican soil, Polk enlisted the support of General Santa Ana, who at the time was living outside the country. Santa Ana, instead of cooperating with Polk, rallied the Mexicans and pledged to fight the United States.

While Santa Ana again captured the loyalty of the Mexican people with his bold promises of stopping the Americans from taking more territory, the U.S. military had the upper hand and moved rapidly to end the war with a minimum of bloodshed. The city of Vera Cruz was shelled and captured and became the entry point for the attack on Mexico. From Vera Cruz the U.S. expeditionary forces moved inland toward Buena Vista in the north and the capital, Mexico City, in the central regions of the country. In ten months Santa Ana's forces were defeated by superior American firepower. The war ended with the humiliating Treaty of Guadalupe Hidalgo in 1848. The Mexican government received $15 million in return for giving up control of California, New Mexico, and what is now Arizona, Nevada, and parts of Oklahoma and Colorado. The treaty is a harsh reminder in Mexico of U.S. hegemony and its willingness to use force to advance its national interests. Much of Mexican nationalism is rooted in its losing nearly half of its territory to the United States.

Santa Ana faced his final defeat in the Mexican-American War. In 1853 he was pushed off center stage by the liberal revolution of Benito Juarez, who sought to bring democratic principles and democratic governance to Mexico. In 1857 Juarez presided over the promulgation of the country's first constitution, whose democratic principles remain in place today. The Juarez era, better known as La Reforma, also weakened the power of the Catholic Church in the areas of land ownership and education. Although Mexico was invaded again in the 1860s, this time by the Hapsburg representatives of France (forcing Juarez to set up a provisional government in exile near the U.S. border), the European monarchs and their Mexican collaborationists were eventually executed and Mexico returned to its democratic reform experiment. Despite La Reforma, Mexico remained enamored of the strongman, the caudillo (man on horseback), who promised order and captured the loyalty of the people with his personal power. Although Santa Ana was gone, there would be others like him.

The Mexican Revolution

After decades of instability, intervention, and insolvency, Mexico began a period of modernization under the dictatorship of Porfirio Diaz, the Porfiriato, which lasted from 1876 to the beginning of the Mexican

Revolution in 1911. Diaz brought Mexico its first glimpses of an advanced industrial economy. Relying on a group of advisers known as the *cientificos,* who were trained in Europe and the United States, Diaz was determined to attract foreign investment, expand trade, and build the critical infrastructure required of a nation that wanted to become modern. Diaz brought modern communication, railroads, and electric power, as well as political stability, to a country in a constant state of flux. There was a price to pay, however, in that Diaz did not hesitate to use his troops to control the population. During his rule millions of rural *campesinos* were pushed off their land and forced to work for large landowners. Attempts at unionization were quickly quelled. Mexico became a haven for foreign investment in mining, petroleum, and ranching. This was the era in which the Guggenheims (silver mining), the Rockefellers (oil), and the Hearsts (ranching and real estate) became major players in the Mexican economy.

The mix of harsh repression and extensive foreign involvement in the economy during the Porfiriato eventually sparked revolution. In the election of 1910 Diaz ran against Francisco Madero, a democratic reformer and a member of a wealthy northern Mexican family that had opposed powerful American investors. Madero was the candidate of free and open elections and limits on presidential power. Diaz, fearing a Madero victory, arrested him. After being released on bail, Madero fled to the United States where he directed the opposition to the Diaz regime. Although Diaz controlled an experienced military, he was challenged in the north by the rag-tag bandit army of Pancho Villa and in the south by horse trainer and *campesino* leader Emiliano Zapata. The revolt against Diaz spread quickly and forced the dictator to resign from office in 1911. Madero returned from the United States and won the presidential election.

Madero may have been a democratic visionary, but he did not possess the tough political skills to remain in office. His election failed to end the jockeying for power or the struggle to control the land. Within fifteen months Madero was removed from office by General Victoriano Huerta and executed. Huerta represented the old elite of landowners, bureaucrats, and foreign interests, but he faced opposition from a range of regional leaders and armies led by Villa, Zapata, and the centrist forces of Venustiano Carranza. For the next six years these armies fought for control of Mexico, with each group carving up a section of the country. In 1914 Huerta resigned amid pressure from the United States, which feared instability on its southern border. With Huerta out of the picture, the fighting continued as Carranza and his superior forces engaged Villa in the north and Zapata in the south. By 1917 Carranza's forces gained the upper hand and brought an end to the fighting.

The crowning achievement of the Mexican Revolution was the 1917 constitution, which for the first time established peasants' and workers' rights in law along with national control of natural resources. Article 123 provided for the right to organize and strike and created a wealth of protections related to the health and welfare of workers. Article 27 expanded national sovereignty to all mineral deposits and sent a clear message that Mexico intended to restrict the role of American companies in the Mexican economy. There were also significant articles that related to education, women's rights, and land reform. In particular, the land reform articles sought the breakup of large estates and the distribution of land to the rural peasantry. The constitutional principles associated with land led to the formation of the *ejido* system, communal land holdings designed to provide landless peasants with new farming opportunities.

The constitution of 1917 ended the Mexican Revolution only in a formal sense. Because Carranza was no radical revolutionary, he did not advance many of the reforms in the constitution. He reneged on land reform, forcing Emiliano Zapata to continue his struggle in the south. Eventually Carranza saw Zapata as a threat and had him assassinated in 1919. As for Pancho Villa, he continued his brand of outlaw revolution in the north and in 1920 signed a peace agreement with the Carranza government. With the fighting over and a government in place, Mexico settled into an era of political stability that was based on conservative policies and practices and directed by military and business elites. The Mexican revolution had its heroes and its high principles, but the eventual victors were more interested in establishing order than introducing major changes to the economic, social, and political systems. Changes in the land system, church-state relations, foreign investment, and workers' rights came later and would depend on the interest of future political leaders.

In retrospect, the Mexican Revolution was not a single movement led by one group, but rather a confluence of regional leaders with their own agendas. These were power contenders seeking to protect or advance their interests but at odds with each other over economic status, allocation of government resources, and a range of social justice issues. But once the Mexican Revolution was over, it had a profound influence on the political psyche of the nation. It served as the modern beginning of Mexican history and a powerful reminder of the values that are the foundation of Mexican society and the Mexican state. While no revolution lives up to its promises and revolutions often disappoint, the Mexican Revolution shaped the political destiny of the nation for generations. What started as a struggle to end a dictatorship and establish liberal democracy ended with conservative military and economic elites in control and only the trappings of democracy. The Mexican Revolution brought change but not a democratic revolution.

The Cardenas Reforms

The presidents who ruled Mexico in the postrevolution era inherited a country in ruins. Over a million people had died in the fighting and a million more suffered serious injuries. There was massive dislocation of the rural peasantry as whole villages were destroyed. Moreover, serious disputes continued to divide the country, especially the relationship between the Catholic Church and the state. From 1926 to 1929, the Cristero revolt was led by Church supporters who opposed the anticlerical policies of President Plutarco Calles. Serious labor strikes affected key industries such as mining and petroleum. Most seriously, political violence continued unabated. Venustiano Carranza was assassinated by his military chief, Alvaro Obregon, who eventually became president. Pancho Villa was murdered in 1923 and Obregon was killed in 1928 after being elected to a second term as president. Scant attention was paid to economic and social reform during this period, although President Calles was instrumental in lessening the influence of the military on national life and in forming the structure of a national political party.

The real change in Mexican politics and public policy occurred in 1934 with the election of Lazaro Cardenas to the presidency. Because a degree of political stability had been achieved, Cardenas began to make serious efforts to fulfill the promises of the revolution. He addressed the land distribution problem that had been one of the key sources of revolutionary fervor among the peasant class. During his six years as president Cardenas distributed 45 million acres of land to 800,000 *campesinos.* Much of this land was placed under the control of the *ejido* system, which ensured that landless peasants would benefit from communally held property. As a result of Cardenas's agrarian reform efforts, the number of landless peasants dropped by over 600,0000. Balancing efforts to reform rural life was Cardenas's initiatives with respect to organized labor. During his presidency the Confederation of Mexican Workers (CTM) was founded, which served as the catalyst for unionization throughout the Mexican economy. Major segments of the workforce from petroleum to education were organized into labor unions. The unions' power created tensions between labor and management and sparked numerous strikes, but wages, benefits, and working conditions improved substantially during this period.

Cardenas's commitment to economic and social reform created an international dispute in 1938. The Mexican president, using article 27 of the constitution as the basis for his action, nationalized the petroleum industry, which was dominated by foreign enterprises such as Standard Oil and Royal Dutch/ Shell. The decision to nationalize foreign petroleum interests was wildly popular in Mexico as thousands demonstrated in the streets of Mexico City to show their support for economic nationalism. The expropriation of the petroleum industry jeopardized relations with the United States. There were calls in the United States for military intervention, but the Roosevelt administration worked quietly to reach a resolution of the dispute. Eventually the World Court worked out an acceptable price for the assets of the petroleum holdings. But for Cardenas and Mexico, the expropriation of the petroleum industry and the formation of Petroleos Mexicanos (PEMEX) was a source of immense national pride and further solidified Cardenas's hold on Mexican politics and public opinion.

While Cardenas is often remembered for his commitment to revolutionary principles and his implementation of key reform programs, his lasting influence lay in the manner in which he organized what became the Party of the Institutional Revolution (PRI). Although President Calles is often viewed as the founder of the modern-day PRI, it was Lazaro Cardenas who developed the corporatist structure of the party around peasants, labor unions, middle-class supporters, and the military. By linking the state to key sectors, the PRI was able to form a huge mass-based political organization that had the ability to shape the demands from these sectors and also allocate the benefits that were directed to these sectors. Under Cardenas the Mexican state through the PRI party apparatus became an efficient and effective machine that controlled the entire political system and as a result weakened other groups or parties that might want to compete with the PRI. It was an ingenious system of control that positioned the PRI as the sole political force in Mexico for the next sixty years.

The PRI in Power

The presidency of Lazaro Cardenas, with its emphasis on social and economic reform, did not set off a sustained period of revolutionary policymaking. The presidents who followed Cardenas were a mix of cautious administrators who concentrated on industrial modernization and expanding economic growth and moderate progressives who made modest efforts to sustain agrarian reform and redistributive policies. The commonality among the Mexican presidents, however, was their commitment to making the Party of the Institutional Revolution the dominant political organization in the country. In 1946 President Avila Camacho changed the name of the party from Party of the Mexican Revolution (PRM) to the PRI. The key change was not in the name but in what the name symbolized. The word "institutional" sent a signal to the Mexican people and opposition groups that the political leadership in the governing party had every intention of maintaining its hold on the reins of government.

From 1940 on, the Mexican presidency changed hands with regularity every six years (the *sexenio*) and remained under PRI control. During that time the Mexican state expanded its involvement in national life and the PRI became entrenched and increasingly distant from the people. While the PRI was able to bring stability to a political system that had endured so much division and violence, it also developed a reputation as a corrupt and reactionary party that would do anything to maintain its central position in the country. Starting in 1968 with the massacre of the protesting college students at the Plaza de Tlateloco during the administration of Gustavo Diaz Ordaz, the PRI saw its popular support dwindle. The presidents who ruled Mexico in the aftermath of the massacre, Luis Echeverria and Jose Lopez Portillo, made some progress in fostering a workable democratic environment, regaining some of the PRI's lost legitimacy. Echeverria recognized the need to introduce populist reforms. In moves that had the potential to weaken the PRI hold, Echeverria lowered the voting age and created new opportunities for opposition parties to win seats in the legislature. But Echeverria remained a man of the PRI and continued to alienate college students and the intellectual establishment with his harsh crackdowns on the press and his toleration of increased corruption in the party.

As Mexico entered the 1980s, the PRI leadership encountered serious economic challenges and growing public dissatisfaction with government corruption. President Miguel de la Madrid (1982–1988) faced major debt problems that forced the government to engage in painful austerity measures. This was a time of deep economic distress in the country, and indeed throughout Latin America. Debt obligations to foreign banks and international lending agencies overwhelmed Mexico's ability to meet interest payments and at the same time establish budgets that addressed the social welfare needs of an expanding population. De la Madrid and his successor, Carlos Salinas de Gortari (1989–1994), began instituting liberal economic reforms that opened the Mexican economy to the emerging global marketplace. Salinas initiated the process of abandoning the statist approach to economic development by selling off government enterprises to private concerns. Salinas rejected long-standing import substitution policies that protected domestic industrialization at the expense of aggressive trade measures. Finally, Salinas took his new economic approach even further by negotiating the

North American Free Trade Agreement (NAFTA) with Canada and the United States. NAFTA created an economic relationship that brought down trade barriers between Mexico, Canada, and the United States and opened up new business opportunities for foreign concerns in Mexico.

Salinas's successor, Ernesto Zedillo (1994–2000), came into office with a distinct disadvantage. He was viewed as a quiet technocrat who lived in the shadow of one of Mexico's more aggressive and high-profile presidents. Moreover, Zedillo entered office at a time when the PRI was in trouble politically because of mounting evidence of official corruption and party nepotism. In fact Zedillo was not the party's choice. Luis Donaldo Colosio, a dynamic and reform-minded leader, was assassinated prior to the election. The assassination opened up the floodgates of PRI corruption as it became clear that elements within the party were associated with the killing and had definite ties to some of Mexico's most notorious drug barons. Carlos Salinas was forced to leave the country after his brother was charged with the murder of PRI general secretary Jose Francisco Ruiz Massieu.

In the wake of Salinas's departure and at the beginning of Ernesto Zedillo's term in office, it was obvious that the PRI was holding on to power only through fraudulent elections, payoffs, and intimidation of the opposition. Zedillo also faced serious economic threats, in particular the peso crisis of 1995, which devastated the purchasing power of the Mexican people and nearly brought the country to economic ruin. A currency devaluation and financial support from the United States enabled Zedillo to bring Mexico back from the brink and usher in a period of economic revitalization. But Zedillo was never able to establish effective political reforms that made the PRI attractive. Despite his honesty and willingness to shed some of the extensive presidential powers, Zedillo presided over the final act in the seventy-year reign of the PRI.

The campaign of 2000 proved to be a key turning point in Mexican history. The disgraced PRI was severely weakened. Its candidate for office was again a party functionary who offered the Mexican voters more of the same. Challenging the huge PRI machine was the charismatic Vicente Fox of the Party of National Action (PAN). Fox offered the Mexican people a new option—a moderate businessman (Fox was a former Coca-Cola executive) who was not a leftist threat to the status quo and who promised to dismantle the PRI system in short order. Fox won in a landslide, along with numerous opposition governors and mayors. The PRI was thrown out of power and was further weakened. While many Mexicans were skeptical about Fox's ability to bring change to Mexico's political system, there was general relief that the PRI had finally left the center stage of government.

THE MEXICAN *EJIDO* AND
AGRICULTURAL POLICY

Agricultural land and the peasants who work the land are an integral part of Mexico's national identity. A fundamental component of land and the peasant class is the *ejido*. The Mexican *ejido* is a system in which peasant communities collectively own agricultural lands. The concept of the *ejido* dates back to the Aztecs, who valued communal land ownership. When the Spanish came, the *ejidos* were divided up and handed over to the conquistadors while the Indians were forced into slave labor on the new estates. During the Mexican Revolution the *ejidos* reemerged as a means of providing land to the peasants. In fact, the Mexican Revolution was largely a response to land inequality and the powerlessness of peasants who had no land. In 1910 at the start of the revolution 1 percent of the landowners controlled 97 percent of all agricultural land, and 92 percent of the rural peasantry were landless.

The constitution of 1917 granted the government the power to expropriate private land to establish *ejidos*. The *campesinos* initially hailed the constitutional provisions that reinstated the *ejido* system as a means of bringing empowerment to the peasant class. But land distribution lagged in the postrevolutionary period as wealthy owners refused to give up their land and the government was unwilling to engage in widespread expropriation. It was not until the administration of Lazaro Cardenas that the *ejido* system became fully operational. When Cardenas entered office, only 7 percent of the available land was held by *ejidatarios*, but in 1940 when Cardenas left the presidency over 50 percent of the land was organized into *ejidos*.

Being an *ejidatario* requires strict compliance with a complex series of rules and regulations. Once the legal process (*dotacion,* or endowment) is finalized, *ejidatarios* are forbidden to sell or rent the land; they can only enter into contracts with other *ejidatarios* with state approval, and they have to promise that only they and their families will work the land. *Ejido* property is managed by state and parastate institutions. Primary supervision is in the hands of the Department of Agrarian Affairs and Colonization, and state-run banks provide the *ejidos* with credit. The *ejidos* have also been part of the PRI agricultural base, and the *ejidatarios* have been encouraged to participate in the Confederacion Nacional Campesina (CNC), which is affiliated with the PRI.

In 1992 the *ejido* system underwent a major reform. A new article in the Mexican constitution restricted peasants from petitioning for land, prohibited expropriation of land, and permitted corporations, investors, stock companies, and commercial associations to hold agricultural land. President Salinas, who advocated the changes, believed that they would encourage productivity through "economies of scale" and the concentration of landholdings. Salinas's position was driven by his attempt to attract foreign investment in agribusiness and thereby increase production.

The agrarian reform immediately set off protests from *ejidatarios*. The peasants feared that the reform, which was designed to privatize the *ejidos* by allowing the sale of the land, would bring back the latifundio system of large agricultural estates in which the *campesinos* became workers, not communal owners. Critics predicted that the change in agricultural ownership would force the *ejidatarios* to sell their land and either work for a foreign investor or move to an urban area, since the large agribusiness corporations introduce advanced farming practices that require fewer hands. Predictions by critics that changes to the *ejido* system would prove disastrous to the *campesinos* have been borne out. Increasingly, *ejidatarios* are selling their lands and working for the big agribusiness concerns, unable to compete effectively with the foreign corporations. NAFTA has also hurt the *ejidos* as agricultural commodities from the United States now compete with locally grown products. There have been calls by peasant groups and critics of the government to reinstate the *ejidos* system under the old rules, but there has been little sympathy shown, as Mexican officials are concerned over the need for greater agricultural productivity and the realities of NAFTA. ⊕

Timeline	
1519	Hernán Cortés lands in Vera Cruz
1810	Mexico declares independence from Spain
1846–1848	War with the United States
1862–1867	Maximilian establishes French monarchy in Mexico
1867	Benito Juarez liberates Mexico and forms democratic government
1876–1910	Porfirio Diaz creates dictatorship and begins modernization
1910–1917	Mexican Revolution
1917	Mexican constitution promulgated
1929	PRI formed
1934–1939	Nationalist Lazaro Cardenas rules Mexico
1938	Mexican oil nationalized
1968	Violent protests during the summer Olympic Games; 200 students killed
1988	Carlos Salinas elected
1994	NAFTA begins implementation
1994	Chiapas uprising begins
1997	PRI loses control of Chamber of Deputies
2000	Vicente Fox elected president

POINT OF FACT

Mexico is the most populous Spanish-speaking country in the world and the second most populous country in Latin America (Brazil is first).

FORMAL GOVERNMENT

As a federal republic, Mexico consists of thirty-one states (each with a constitution, elected governor, and legislative body) and the Federal District of Mexico City. The Federal District has an elected mayor and an assembly made up of 365 councillors. The National Congress is bicameral with a Senate of 128 members and a Chamber of Deputies with five hundred members. In the Senate one-half of the seats are assigned by majority vote from each state, one-quarter by allocation to the top minority party in each of the thirty-one states and the Federal District, and one-quarter by a system of national proportional representation. In the Chamber of Deputies, two hundred seats are distributed by proportional representation among political parties that gain at least 1.5 percent of the vote. The remaining three hundred seats are distributed to the majority party winner. The Mexican judicial branch is headed by an eleven-member Supreme Court with six lower circuit courts and forty-seven district courts. Supreme Court justices are appointed for life with the consent of the Senate. At the local level Mexico is organized into *municipios*, which are equivalent to counties. There are 2,401 *municipios* and they are managed by an *ayuntamiento*, a council that is headed by a *presidente municipal*, a mayor. During PRI rule these mayors served as frontline representatives of the PRI and were responsible for the electoral strength of the party at the local level.

At the pinnacle of government power is the president, who is directly elected by the Mexican people and is permitted to serve one six-year term. The Mexican system of executive power has been termed presidentialism to connote the enormous political power and policymaking latitude in the hands of the president. Presidents since Plutarco Calles have centralized power in their office and have utilized the PRI to ensure that their decisions meet with societal support and smooth implementation. PRI control of the massive union movement, peasant organizations, and many professional groups provided the president with a vast public policy network that can withstand opposition from other parties. Since Fox assumed the presidency, the enormous power of the chief executive has diminished somewhat. With the PRI now an opposition force in the legislature, Fox has had great difficulty dominating the policy process. But despite Fox's problems, the Mexican president has sufficient capability to manage executive-legislative relations. All key legislative initiatives begin with the president and not the congressional leadership. More importantly, past PRI dominance of the Congress assured the president that his legislative agenda would become a reality. On occasion, opposition party strength in the legislature was large enough to force some bargaining and compromise, but in most instances the president encountered few obstacles in formulating and implementing his proposals. In addition to organizational control and legislative power, the president wields patronage power, which is used freely to reward compliance and loyalty. The result is an overwhelmingly one-sided governing system in the hands of one man.

In such a highly centralized and executive-dominated environment the Mexican legislature has been relegated to a passive role and only recently has challenged the president. Although the opposition PRI make up sizable sections of both the Senate and the Chamber of Deputies, they have been reluctant to control those bodies seeking rather to serve as an effective foil to the president. The same is true of the Supreme Court, which, despite having power of judicial review to countermand legislative bills and executive decisions, has been reluctant to take an independent course of action that would put it at odds with the political status quo. Finally, the governors of the states have traditionally been under the thumb of the president. In numerous instances presidents have removed governors who performed poorly or disgraced the government through corrupt practices.

Despite the great power in the hands of the president and the general weakness of legislative, judicial, and local administrative institutions, the Mexican political elite has recognized the need to introduce limited governing reforms that permit greater electoral participation and a stronger opposition voice. In 1990 the PRI-controlled Chamber of Deputies approved a series of reforms that allowed the opposition access to the Electoral Commission's computers and created a mechanism of settling election disputes. Later in 1993 the Congress also passed legislation that increased the number of each state's senators to four, one of whom must come from the most popular opposition party. Also the legislation prevented any party from gaining a two-thirds majority in the Chamber, which limited PRI's ability to push through changes to the constitution.

The introduction of election reforms related to the Chamber of Deputies made some inroads in PRI power and legislative control. As mentioned above, three hundred deputies were elected in "uninominal" or single-member districts. Because of PRI power the vast majority of these seats were won and retained by the governing party. The other two hundred seats in the Chamber were assigned through a "plurinominal" process. This electoral system permits opposition parties to win seats in proportion to the popular vote that they receive in five designated geographical regions. The electoral laws for the "plurinominal" seats favor the opposition parties. Since enactment of the changes, non-PRI parties have dominated this aspect of Chamber allocation. Under the 1993 law the majority party can win no more than 315 seats in the Chamber and no more than three hundred seats if the majority party receives less than 60 percent of the vote.

The electoral law changes contributed to an expansion of opposition visibility and participation in the Mexican Congress. Executive-legislative relations are now more strained and contentious as opposition legislators have become outspoken critics of the government. It is important to emphasize, however, that at no time has the PRI given up control of either body of the legislature. In the 1988–1991 sessions the opposition PAN and PRD parties came close to capturing control but fell a few seats short. Since that time the PRI has maintained its majority hold on the legislature; as a result, the Senate and Chamber have made only minor progress in establishing an independent voice. What has happened in executive-legislative relations is that the PRI successfully engineered a series of electoral reforms that boosted its claim of democratic governance, while not relinquishing ultimate power. With its grassroots organization rallying electoral support, the PRI retained control over the governing institutions with only minor challenges to its authority and its ability to prevail in the policymaking process. Even under PAN president Vicente Fox, the PRI remains the majority in both legislative bodies and in nineteen of the thirty-one states and continues to exercise considerable legislative power.

The PRI has sponsored significant reforms of the judiciary. In 1994 President Zedillo introduced a number of changes to the justice system. Besides shrinking the Supreme Court from an unmanageable twenty-six members to eleven, the reforms raised the qualifications for justices, established a judicial council to relieve justices of many administrative responsibilities, and reduced the term of Supreme Court justices from lifetime service to staggered fifteen-year terms. Furthermore, appointments to the high court must receive support from two-thirds of the Senate, whereas in the past the Senate merely approved the presidential appointments. Because growing opposition membership has changed the composition of the Senate in recent years, it is no longer a given that the president will be able to place his appointees on the Court without a thorough review of the candidate and perhaps spirited congressional debate.

The most important change granted the Supreme Court limited power of judicial review. The Supreme Court may now declare null and void laws and regulations that are disputed between various levels of government. Furthermore, the Supreme Court may utilize judicial review when there is a challenge presented by 33 percent of either the Chamber of Deputies or the

Senate. This is significant in that opposition parties can marshal their numbers and force the Court to act on government laws and regulations. The limited judicial review powers of the Supreme Court are based on the Mexican *amparo* suit. Dating back to 1857 and included in the 1917 constitution, Mexican courts are permitted to restrain the government if they find that the citizens bringing suit have been denied their individual rights. The *amparo* can ensure that Mexican citizens are protected from an all-powerful government. It is important to stress, however, that the *amparo* and the new judicial review are narrow in scope. They do not provide the opportunity to set national policy or to challenge the abuse of power by the government.

Mexico's history of centralized control in the executive branch and strong nationalist sentiment have led to the formation of a large bureaucratic establishment, including a vast array of parastatal enterprises with varying degrees of attachment to the government. Currently there are 1.5 million federal employees, plus an additional million working as national employees in education and a million more employed by autonomous or semiautonomous state agencies. Added to these federal employees are an estimated half million state and local employees providing direct services to the people. Mexico's statist approach, which was a popular trend in the 1960s throughout the less developed world, makes the government the chief employer in the country and contributes to a public sector that is bloated and costly. Although many bureaucrats are low-level staffers who perform menial clerical tasks, they are part of a vast state organization that has been difficult to trim. Various presidents, especially in recent years, have sought to introduce austerity measures that targeted the bureaucracy as a key cost saver for the government, but their efforts have had only marginal impact.

The key ministries in the Mexican bureaucracy have reflected both the long-standing PRI concern for central control and favorable external relations. The most influential ministry is Gobernacion, or the Ministry of Interior, which has responsibility for maintaining internal security and administering elections. Both functions put Gobernacion at the core of government control and make it the target of criticism from human rights groups and from critics of the electoral methods used in Mexico. The Ministry of Foreign Affairs has the prime responsibility of negotiating the relationship between the government and the United States. As Mexico has emerged as a key economic player in the Western Hemisphere and is more interested in expanding its ties to the industrialized world, the Ministry of Foreign Relations has taken on new roles in the government hierarchy. Finally, economy-related ministries such as the Ministry of Finance and the Programming and Budget Ministry have been elevated to prominence within the cabinet. Many of Mexico's technical elite, the *técnicos,* are based in these two ministries and are involved in critical policy matters relating to issues such as currency stabilization, budget allocations, debt management, and economic planning.

Bureaucratic power in Mexico is not confined to the frontline ministries. Because of nationalization policies dating back to the Cardenas government, state enterprises occupy important positions in the Mexican economy and bureaucratic establishment. At one time during the 1980s there were over a thousand parastatal entities controlling everything from petroleum and steel to foodstuffs, fertilizer, and electricity. Since the heyday of state enterprises Mexico has embarked on a privatization policy designed to sell off state assets to private interests. By the mid-1990s the number of parastatal entities had dwindled to just over two hundred, and the trend continues today. As a result of this sell-off, control over Mexico's telephone company, its banks, and its airline has been handed over to private sector investors. Privatization of parastatals like the telephone industry, however, has created new problems of regulation. The new telephone company Telmex has become a private rather than public monopoly with little competition and little concern over regulatory control. It took six years for the Mexican government to establish a regulator, Cofetal, to serve as a counterforce to the powerful telephone company.

While the Mexican bureaucracy, especially the parastatal sector, has been at the center of controversy associated with privatization, the military side of government has been relegated to near obscurity. Unlike many Latin American countries where the military is a force to be reckoned with and often is a power contender with aspirations of holding the reins of governance, in Mexico the military has been depoliticized and its power substantially reduced. Presidents Calles and Cardenas effectively limited the power of the military, and the tradition of civilian dominance has remained in place. By 1946, during the presidency of Miguel Aleman, military representation in the PRI hierarchy was denied. In the modern era the military has been used to put down internal rebellions, such as in Chiapas, but most of its attention has been on drug interdiction, civic action programs designed to enhance development, and responding to natural disasters.

The depoliticization of the Mexican military does not mean that it lacks influence in government. Presidents in the 1980s and 1990s were conscious of the need to keep the military leadership happy by providing ample budgetary resources and pay raises. The military has been content to play a reduced role in Mexican politics and to be satisfied with the budgetary largesse that comes its way from the government. This has not stopped military officials from becoming involved in financial scandals and public corruption. In 1997 General Jesus Gutierrez Rebello was arrested on accusations that he was involved with one of the drug cartels and used his power to protect the cartel from arrest. There were also signs of military unease and unrest, especially over the inability of the Salinas and Zedillo administrations to develop an effective strategy to deal with the Chiapas rebellion. Military leaders were outraged over the government's unwillingness to include them in the negotiations leading up to a cease-fire while bending to the demands of the peasant revolutionaries. Few observers are of the view that the Mexican military will become a political factor in the future and seek to reenter the governing arena, but there is no doubt about the potential of the armed forces to become a power contender in government.

As to the future of governance in Mexico, much depends on the ability of Vicente Fox to usher in a new era of reform and restructuring. In the early days of his administration Fox laid out an ambitious vision of a new Mexican government. He talked about forming a new security and justice ministry to deal with corruption and crime fighting, restructuring the oil parastatal PEMEX so as to permit it to operate as an independent corporation (but not privatize the oil giant), introducing a sweeping tax reform package, and returning more autonomy to the states. In his address to the Chamber of Deputies Fox emphasized his commitment to decentralization and to greater grassroots democracy through wider use of initiatives and referendum.

Fox's ambitious agenda and his desire to move away from the PRI legacy of central control will not be easily accomplished. President Fox is in a weakened state because PRI controls both the Senate and the Chamber of Deputies, and also because the 1917 constitution does not provide him with the kind of executive power necessary to cut through PRI opposition or to meet crises. In 2002 for example, Fox was not permitted to leave the country on a visit to the United States. Both houses of Congress denied him permission to leave.

Fox has limited decree power, but he cannot veto Congress and he does not have the ability to introduce an interim budget document should the Congress fail to support his budget. Faced with these institutional roadblocks, Fox will have to use his persuasive skills in order to work with the PRI to advance his reform and restructuring agenda. The fact that his own PAN party is divided and the leftist PRD cannot be counted on to support his policies will make changing the government structure and practice difficult. As of 2002 Fox had not passed any meaningful legislation through the Mexican Congress.

POINT OF FACT

Mexico is currently debating changing its official name from United Mexican States to Mexico. The PAN government of Vicente Fox feels that "Mexico" better reflects the reality of modern-day nationhood. But changing the name will require amending three articles of the constitution and a redesign of the national currency.

Constitutional Language

Article 27 remains the single most important statement of Mexican sovereignty. The article lays out in great detail (seventeen articles) the position of the Mexican state on control of its natural resources. The key language of article 27 is presented below.

Ownership of the lands and waters within the boundaries of the national territory is vested originally in the Nation, which has had, and has, the right to transmit title thereof to private persons, thereby constituting private property.

Private property shall not be expropriated except for reasons of public use and subject to payment of indemnity.

The Nation shall at all times have the right to impose on private property such limitations as the public interest may demand, as well as the right to regulate the utilization of natural resources which are susceptible of appropriation, in order to conserve them and to ensure a more equitable distribution of public wealth.

INDIAN BILL OF RIGHTS

One of the more unusual events in the early days of the presidency of Vicente Fox was the two-week march of the Zapatista rebels from Chiapas led by the mysterious and charismatic Subcommandante Marcos. Accompanied by two dozen of his fellow rebel commanders, Marcos traveled through twelve Mexican states to rally grassroots support for an Indian bill of rights. The so-called Zapatour was the latest in the public relations campaign that Marcos has developed to call attention to the plight of the Indian population in southern Mexico and to demand autonomy for the Indian people. The march was similar to that conducted by legendary rural revolutionary Emiliano Zapata, who traveled to Mexico City in order to bring attention to peasant land issues in 1914. Thousands of Mexicans lined the march route as the unarmed Zapatistas left their base in the city of San Cristobal and headed north to the capital city. When they reached Mexico City, President Fox welcomed Marcos and his commanders and promised that he would work to have the Mexican Congress pass his legislation granting new rights for the Indians. The rebel commanders entered the chambers of the Mexican Congress with their faces covered in the now famous ski masks popularized by Marcos. The presence of the Zapatista entourage placed enormous pressure on President Fox to win support for the Indian bill of rights.

Fox's bill and his public support for Indian rights, however, ran up against stiff congressional opposition. The bill not only gave autonomy to Indian communities but allowed them communal ownership of land and permission to use traditional customs to choose leaders and dispense justice. Such powers would create parallel electoral and judicial systems that many feared might weaken democracy. Furthermore, congressional opponents viewed the bill as legitimating local bosses, or caciques, and creating special privileges that would lead to a disintegration of national unity. Another concern was that creating an autonomous region for the Indian population would further limit their ability to benefit from private sector investment and global-driven economic growth. But proponents of the bill stated that the 1917 constitution established rights for individuals but failed to provide for the rights of indigenous peoples. Supporters of the Indian rights bill believed that the lack of indigenous rights contributed to the poverty and exclusion of the Indian population in the southern states of Mexico.

The basis for the Indian bill of rights is the so-called Cocopa initiative. Cocopa is the legislative commission that was responsible for the peace process between the government and the Zapatistas in Chiapas. The Cocopa initiative was finished in 1966 and served as the centerpiece of the peace agreement between the government and the rebels. The Mexican government under Zedillo, however, never implemented the agreement and talks between the rebels broke down despite the fact that over 3 million indigenous residents from Chiapas and neighboring states endorsed the Cocopa initiative. Once Fox entered office, he presented the accord to the Mexican Senate as the basis for the Indian rights bill and renewed the peace process between the government and the Zapatistas.

Fox has placed his reputation as a proponent of Indian rights on the line with the legislation that is before the Mexican Congress. He has taken steps to remove military units from Chiapas state and has granted amnesty to rebel leaders. But the core of his attempt to bring peace to the region is the Indian rights bill. Failure to achieve some level of autonomy for the indigenous people and guarantees of massive infusions of assistance may rekindle the fighting in the region and embolden leftists in Mexico to challenge the authority of the government. ⊕

THE CITIZEN AND THE STATE

When the Spanish arrived in Mexico in 1519, they brought with them their language, customs, and Catholic faith. They also introduced into the New World a governing philosophy and method of governance. The Spanish view of government and governing was authoritarian to the core. The Spanish system emphasized the importance of a powerful king and aristocratic court presiding over its possessions and its subjects. There was little in the way of democratic institutions to provide governing balance as was emerging in England. In order to manage this vast imperial domain, the Spanish monarchy devised what has come to be called corporatism, a series of social, political, and economic sectors such as the Catholic Church, the military, the bureaucracy, and the local political authorities that would report directly to the king or queen in Madrid. There were no intermediate institutions or processes such as legislatures, courts, or independent bureaucratic agencies. The Spanish system was top-down, closed, and highly centralized.

Because of the authoritarian, centralized, and corporatist nature of the political environment, Mexico evolved into a nation that was largely devoid of citizen involvement. The governing values were obedience to the political authorities and support for the existing system. The principles of individualism, personal freedom, and guaranteed rights that became the foundation of the American political experience were never part of the Mexican political culture. Instead, the values were devotion to the monarchy, acceptance of the status quo, and the recognition that citizen rights, if any, were bestowed by the monarch. There was no tradition of inherent, inalienable rights that developed elsewhere in North America.

The Catholic Church further contributed to this culture of obedience and support by emphasizing the importance of respect for authority and duty to church and state. As a result, the Mexican people developed a fatalistic approach to their position in society and the state structure. The common view was that little could be done to change their lot in life and that if action was taken to challenge authority, it would likely result in a stern response from the authorities. Citizen-state relations became a one-way street. Government and the governors were distant and the process of governing was hierarchical, formalistic, and rigid. These values and governing characteristics continue to characterize the Mexican political culture. There is in Mexico an underlying respect for the strong leader, a guarded acceptance of democratic institutions, and a lingering fatalism about the ability to achieve meaningful political reform.

The onset of the Mexican Revolution was supposed to change not only the governing structure of the country but also the relationship between citizen and the state. The revolution marked a turning point in Mexican history because it introduced principles such as democracy, social justice, and reform into the national dialogue. Mexicans, even today, have strong intellectual and emotional ties to the events, the heroes, and the governing framework that emerged from that period because they recognize that their country was finally embracing a new governing philosophy. The constitution of 1917 in particular is seen as the crowning achievement of the revolution and the embodiment of the values that formed the basis for the seven-year struggle. There is also strong support for the agrarian reform component of the revolution. The *ejido* system that was developed in the postrevolution period and the distribution of new land titles to *campesinos* is widely seen as one of the great accomplishments of the PRI governments. And labor reforms, from the right to strike to the guarantees of health and welfare benefits, are now firmly entrenched within Mexican society and the labor union movement remains a powerful segment within the political arena. In public opinion polling for their landmark study *Civic Culture* (1959), political scientists Gabriel Almond and Sidney Verba (updated in 1988 and 1991) found that the level of national pride in the Mexican state, the constitution, democracy, and equality had significant support among a wide spectrum of Mexicans.

Although Mexicans have maintained strong linkages to the revolutionary period and its accomplishments, they harbor deep-seated resentment toward the governing system that is the legacy of the revolution. Mexicans view the bureaucrats and the politicians as distant from their everyday needs and more interested in using government as a road to personal enrichment. Although political leaders such as Lazaro Cardenas remain on a pedestal for fulfilling the grand guarantees of the constitution of 1917, most of the presidents in the modern period have been derided by the general public as corrupt, self-serving, and inept. Furthermore, the political system presided over by these presidents was seen as incapable of reform, with entrenched interests opposed to real reform and seeking reelection by any means, including fraud.

PRI longevity in power, however, was not due to a series of electoral flukes but resulted from astute delivery of services to party faithful, cautious reform initiatives, and skillful organization of key constituencies such as rural peasantry and urban labor. The PRI acted as a kind of national patron or father figure providing benefits to its party faithful in return for their vote and their quiet support. The Mexican government developed a range of programs that provided subsidized food, health care, and public sector jobs. PRI strength in the rural areas was based on land titles to peasants and price supports for agricultural products. For many years the PRI also could count on extensive middle-class support, in large part because it provided low taxes, modest but steady growth, and perhaps most importantly political stability.

The breakdown of the PRI support system among the Mexican people can be traced to the Chiapas revolt that began in 1994. The impoverished peasants of this southern Mexican state took up arms and held the state capital of

San Cristobal de las Casas for a number of days in protest of the government's failure to address their concerns over land reform, gross income inequality, and rampant corruption. The rebellion was led by the Zapatista Army of National Liberation (EZLN), which was made up of Indian peasants and led by the ski-masked Subcommandante Marcos. Their goal, as articulated by Marcos, was a return to the principles and the promises of the Mexican Revolution. Social justice for peasants and true democratic reforms that allowed political opposition to effectively challenge the control of the PRI government were their rallying cries. The Zapatistas opposed the newly implemented NAFTA agreement, which they believed would further weaken their agricultural economy in the name of trade barrier reduction and commodity competition.

The Zapatistas were highly successful in packaging their message to the outside world. Foreign journalists and the Mexican press streamed into Chiapas, intrigued by the revolutionary fervor of the Zapatistas and their ability to embarrass the government at a time when it was touting its entrance into NAFTA. Subcommandante Marcos, who became a darling of the local and international press with his skill at offering cogent sound bites and stinging criticism of the PRI government, reminded all who would listen that all was not well in Mexico. Although the Zapatista movement did not gain control of Chiapas, it forced the government to initiate agrarian reforms and allocate new levels development money to assist the peasants. But most importantly, the Zapatistas called into question the legitimacy of the PRI leadership.

While the rural areas remain the "heart and soul" of Mexico and the foundation on which national political power is built, it is in the burgeoning urban areas where a new political culture is being formed and where new definitions of citizen-state relations are emerging. Mexico City is home to the ever expanding middle class, which has prospered in the post-NAFTA era and has formed a social system that is far removed from that found in the rural areas. The new Mexican middle class is more impatient with government, more demanding of its politicians, and less tolerant of the fraud and corruption that have become staples of national life. Mexico City is a hotbed of politics with its headline-grabbing newspapers and magazines such as *Proceso* and *Nexos,* its politicized student population at the National Autonomous University of Mexico (UNAM), and its community of writers, artists, and scholars with their decidedly leftist views. While much of the foreign press focused on the revolution in Chiapas, Mexico City continued to be wracked by regular strikes whether at the universities or among key economic sectors such as teachers, medical personnel, or public employees.

Urban life in Mexico has also fostered growing political activism outside the existing electoral competition. Socially conscious groups have formed to address a range of issues such as the extensive pollution caused by overcrowding and industrialization and the needs for adequate housing, water, and nutrition. In recent years women in Mexico have become more vocal in pressing the government for new rights and protections. Church groups, both Catholic and Protestant, have renewed their involvement in advocating for the poor, who often live in deplorable conditions in the hundreds of neighborhoods (barrios) that dot the urban landscape. But perhaps the best example of the vitality of political life in Mexico's urban centers is the grassroots protest movements that have formed over the years. Starting in the wake of the 1968 massacre, Mexico City's landscape has been populated by a growing number of urban-based organizations committed to improving living conditions for the poor. Often responding to the government's failure to respond to a particular crisis such as the earthquake that hit Mexico City in 1985 or the PRI's uneven distribution of resources, neighborhood organizations have taken to the streets to protest and have become a force to be reckoned with. Mexican cities, particularly Mexico City, have become centers of a new level of political activity that flies in the face of the fatalism that is often associated with life in the rural areas.

Mexicans increasingly view themselves as citizens of a global economy and partners (albeit unequal ones) with their neighbors to the north. NAFTA and the benefits that have accompanied the trade agreement have convinced many Mexicans, especially those in the professional and business classes, that the government has the country on the right track. Of course old ways are not changed easily, and considerable apprehension remains over the ability of the Fox government to institute meaningful reforms. The old PRI system has begun to be dismantled, corrupt officials are being replaced, and members of a new political and bureaucratic elite are moving into positions of authority. The old adage, The more things change the more they stay the same, will be severely tested in the coming years in Mexico. But at the present time, the end of seventy years of PRI rule has brought new life to a relationship between the governed and the government.

POINT OF FACT

In Mexico taxes are 11 percent of the gross domestic product, while in the United States taxes are 30 percent of it. Tax avoidance in Mexico is chronic. It is estimated that over 30 percent of the economy is not reported and that most of the rich and many small businesses do not pay taxes.

PRIVATIZATION OF PEMEX

Who owns the natural resources contained under the ground and the sea? This question was answered unequivocally by the drafters of the Mexican constitution in 1917. Article 27 of the constitution clearly established the nation as holding sovereign rights to the natural resources contained within its national borders. The leaders of the revolution viewed article 27 as sending a message to the world, particularly the United States, that it intended to protect its oil, gas, and mineral wealth.

But times change and political and economic conditions do as well. Today Mexico is in the throes of a major debate over the future of its state-owned oil and natural gas company, Petroleos Mexicanos, better known as PEMEX. Facing cash shortages and in desperate need of investment capital to modernize its infrastructure, the Mexican government is seeking to sell off some PEMEX assets. For Mexicans this idea is as revolutionary as the nationalization of Mexican oil by Lazaro Cardenas in 1938. Since then Mexican government officials have built PEMEX into the engine of national economic development and one of the primary sources of tax revenue. Moreover, PEMEX symbolizes national pride and national control of critical natural resources.

The struggle over the future of PEMEX goes to the heart of the Mexican economy and Mexican national life. PEMEX is Mexico's largest company with sales of $24 billion in 1999. PEMEX produces 3 million barrels of oil a day from proven reserves of 28.3 billion barrels. PEMEX operations are integrated from exploration to refining and marketing to petrochemical production. The production of oil accounts for 20 percent of Mexico's export revenue. As a state-owned entity, PEMEX is required to return 60 percent of its revenues as taxes to the national treasury. Because of the heavy tax burden PEMEX officials have been forced to seek foreign investment in order to carry out drilling and infrastructure programs at its Cantarell field near Tampico and its Burgos natural gas field in northern Mexico.

Despite the pride that Mexico has for PEMEX and the struggle for national control that it represents, the government since 1992 has been seeking to privatize a portion of the company. The administration of Carlos Salinas recognized that PEMEX was cash strapped and unable to adequately modernize its assets. Efforts were undertaken by Salinas and his successor Ernesto Zedillo to offer a number of petrochemical plants for sale as a way of generating cash. In 1999 these efforts came to a head when Alpek (a subsidiary of the Mexican conglomerate Grupo Alfa) withdrew its bid to purchase a 49 percent share in Mexico's third largest petrochemical plant. At the core of the withdrawal was Alpek's reluctance to hold minority control of the plant. Many of the private concerns interested in purchasing various PEMEX assets have stated publicly that the 51/49 percent scheme offered by the Mexican government is an unattractive deal breaker.

The failure of the Alpek deal began speculation that eventually the government might offer to privatize all of PEMEX in order to attract the billions in investment dollars necessary for modernization. But in order to achieve complete privatization, proponents would have to deal with opposition from oil unions, the PRI, and nationalists, who see PEMEX as a symbol of revolutionary control of national resource wealth. In a globalized world where the statist approach to national development has been discredited, the prospect of PEMEX remaining under state control is less and less likely. The current administration of Vicente Fox, which takes a pro-business and pro-globalization approach, will be under heavy pressure to move toward complete privatization. But facing opposition from a coalition of labor, the PRI, and Mexican nationalists, Fox may find moving from nationalization to privatization one of the most difficult challenges of his administration. ⊕

PATHWAYS OF PARTICIPATION

For over seventy years, until the presidential election of 2000, membership in the PRI or the various subgroups that support it was the exclusive channel of political participation. Because opposition political parties were weak and leaderless throughout most of the period of PRI rule, and unions, peasant organizations, and middle-class professional associations were aligned with the party, there were few alternative avenues through which critics of the system could express their views or mount an effective challenge. Even the electoral process was mere window dressing. These democratic events were never more than a public means of measuring support for the PRI. In the 1976 presidential election, for example, PRI candidate Jose Lopez Portillo received 85 percent of the popular vote and faced no opposition party candidate.

PRI political and electoral dominance began to erode during the 1980s. Despite winning the presidency in 1994, the PRI was clearly a party that was barely hanging on. Opposition parties began to make inroads in areas of traditional PRI strength. The National Action Party (PAN) started to achieve electoral victories in key states and the Congress. In 1989 the PAN won its first governorship by winning the state of Baja and its first Senate seat in 1991. Later in 1994 the PAN came in second to Carlos Salinas (PRI) in the presidential vote, gaining 25.9 percent of the vote and winning 119 seats in the Chamber and 25 seats in the Senate. Even more significant was the PAN victory in winning the governorships in the key states of Jalisco and Guanajato and the mayoralty of Guadalajara. The PAN sustained its popularity in the

1997 legislative elections and continued to hold critical governorships and mayoralties.

The problem with the PAN was that it never was able to present an attractive candidate for national office. Despite considerable funding from business and financial groups and the backing of some of Mexico's most visible millionaires from the industrial center of Monterrey, the party's leaders were often locked in debate over whether to support neoliberal policies of less government and free trade or to accent programs that supported Mexico's poor, who were likely to be victimized by a free market approach to national development. In the 1994 presidential election PAN put forth Diego Fernandez as its presidential candidate. Fernandez advocated a more moderate program that placed less stress on advancing the business agenda. The moderation of Fernandez resuscitated the PAN, which placed a solid second in the balloting with 28.6 percent of the vote, and laid the groundwork for the Fox candidacy in 2000.

PRI's declining popularity gave new impetus to the left in Mexico. In 1988 the Democratic Revolutionary Party (PRD) was launched by Cuauhtemoc Cardenas (the son of Lazaro Cardenas) after Carlos Salinas's highly questionable victory. The 1988 election was viewed by many in Mexico and the international community as deeply flawed. Local party bosses utilized a range of tactics such as stuffing ballot boxes and organizing so-called *carruseles,* or flying brigades of party supporters transported to various polling sites to vote more than once. There was also evidence of intimidation of opposition candidates and voters. Cardenas contested PRI vote irregularities in a number of states and pressed for a series of electoral reforms, but to no avail. Eventually the PRD became an electoral force in Mexican politics, placing second in the Chamber of Deputies in the 1997 vote with 125 seats. Despite his loss, Cardenas won the key mayoralty of Mexico City in 1997, an elective position that had always been in the hands of the PRI and is considered the second most powerful political position within Mexico.

For many observers of Mexican politics, the future of opposition to the PRI was in the hands of Cuauhtemoc Cardenas. As heir to the most popular PRI president and sharing his father's populist views, Cardenas and his PRD party moved to the center of opposition politics. But right from its formation in 1988, the PRD was wracked by internal feuding over charges that Cardenas was running the party in an authoritarian manner. Cardenas's appeal lay in his staunch nationalism and his promises to bring real social reform rather than the piecemeal, election-oriented programs offered by the PRI. Cardenas was never able to translate his connection to the past and his leftist programs into national popularity. The fact that the PRD proudly announced its membership in the Socialist International sent fear throughout the business community and among the insecure middle class, while the peasants and workers saw no reason to switch from the PRI to an unknown leftist.

Despite the PRI's enormous organizational advantage and its past record of finding a way to win the presidency, the 2000 election became the ultimate test of PRI political and electoral strength. President Zedillo, sensing that the PRI was in trouble with the Mexican voters, instituted a new form of presidential selection for the party. Instead of continuing *dedazo* ("big finger"), the traditional practice of the outgoing president choosing his successor, Zedillo established the first ever party primary. The primary was a controversial step for the PRI as it bypassed the influence of the president and the inner circle of the party elite. Zedillo was convinced that for the PRI to survive politically and electorally, the parties had to move to a more democratic form of candidate selection. The primary process yielded Interior Minister Francisco Labastida, who was Zedillo's favorite. But his selection prompted criticism from opposition leaders, who reminded Mexican voters that the *dedazo* had not really disappeared.

Although the PRI sought desperately to give the appearance of openness and fairness, the charisma of Vicente Fox coupled with the lackluster campaigning of Francisco Labastida provided the PAN with an unprecedented victory. Fox garnered 42.5 percent of the vote to 36.1 percent for Labastida, with Cuauhtemoc Cardenas coming in a distant third with 16.6 percent. Perhaps just as significant as Fox's electoral victory was declining support for PRI presidential candidates. From the astounding 85.4 percent of support, which Lopez Portillo received in the 1976 election, voter preference for PRI candidates slipped to 69.2 percent in 1982, 48.7 percent in 1988, and 48.8 percent in 1994.

But the 2000 election centered around the victory of the PAN and its businessman/rancher/governor president, Vicente Fox. Although the PAN is a largely middle-class party with strong ties to business and the Catholic Church, Fox was able to turn attention away from the conservative program of his party and concentrate on the importance of replacing the PRI. Fox's victory was a validation of changing electoral dynamics in Mexico. The Mexican voter of 2000 proved to be more urban, more youthful, more affluent than during the heyday of PRI power. The support that Fox received in the 2000 election was a vote to end official corruption, police and military in the employ of drug lords, and a system of politics based on handouts, patronage, and politically motivated social programs.

The PRI will face the difficult process of redefining its role in a vastly different Mexican political system. While the party retains a central role in the governing structure of Mexico (and has evolved into a potent opposition force challenging Fox's policy initiatives and relishing the opportunity to embarrass him), its defeat in the 2000 election brought on an extended period of organizational introspection. PRI strength has shifted away from Mexico City to the nineteen governors and the bosses of the trade unions in petroleum, telecommunications and electricity, and teachers. This organizational base has great potential to revive the party and position it for the 2006 election. But already there are signs of deep fissures in the grassroots organization. At the state and mayoral level the PRI is populated by "dinosaurs," old-line politicians whose style of participation is based on finding jobs or doling out cash to supporters. But the future of the PRI does not lie in old-style politics that seeks to shore up traditional voting groups. The PRI is slowly becoming a party of younger technocrats who want more democracy and an end to the old ways. The PRI is poised to restructure its three-hundred-member national council and look for the emergence of a new leader. That restructuring and new leadership may provide the impetus to regain voter confidence and bring new faces into the party. If not, the PRI will remain a party that functions along an outdated pathway of participation.

As the PRI organization undergoes restructuring, the various subgroups that have provided grassroots support will likely be forced into a similar process. The most visible arm of the PRI at the grass roots is the Confederation of Mexican Labor (CTM). Since the death of its legendary leader Fidel Velazquez in 1997, the CTM has been seeking to regain its prominent place in the PRI corporate system. Even before the loss of the presidency, the CTM was faced with the reality of declining membership, rival confederations, and less attachment to the PRI. Increasingly Mexicans find employment in the service and commercial sectors, not in the traditional labor sectors. These workers are less attracted to the labor model promoted by the CTM with its strict labor-management divide and its strike mentality. With the new Mexican worker less enamored of the CTM, support for the PRI has dwindled. Whereas in the 1980s the PRI could count on nearly 80 percent of union members supporting the governing party, in the 1990s that number dropped to around 50 percent. CTM bosses continue to pressure the government to maintain pro-labor legislation such as a closed shop, exorbitant severance packages, and automatic promotion based on seniority.

The union movement may be forced to develop new strategies in the wake of Fox's victory, but the business sector is likely to enjoy a period of growing influence. Business groups have always operated outside the PRI web of organizations. But now that the PAN, with its ties to commercial and financial sectors, is in power, there is likely to be a heightened level of interest group activity promoting business interests. In recent years the most influential business groups in Mexico have been the National Confederation of Chambers of Industry (CONCAMIN), the National Chamber of Manufacturers (CANCINTRA), and the Confederation of National Chambers of Commerce (CONCANACO).

Besides these confederations, Mexican business is also represented by a number of groups that are aligned with various private industries. The Monterrey Group represents over two hundred families who control most of the industrial output in the northern regions of the country. In the past the confederations and the Monterrey Group were solidly in the PAN camp and contributed heavily to PAN candidates. Although the business community is not aligned with the PRI, it had to deal with the governing party for so long that it is divided on the extent of state intervention in the economy and the proper course to take with respect to privatization and NAFTA. Because President Salinas and President Zedillo followed neoliberal policies, antipathy toward the PRI waned in the 1990s. But with Vicente Fox in the presidency, the business confederations and the groups will operate with greater certainty of receiving a favorable hearing in governing circles.

One sector of Mexican society that is certain to grow in political influence is the Catholic Church. Since the revolution the Catholic Church has been forced into the background of public life. The PRI leaders who led the revolution and then formed governments were fiercely anticlerical, in large part because Church officials aligned themselves first with the Spanish conquerors and later with the authoritarian dictators. In the aftermath of the revolution the Church lost huge tracts of land and clergy were not allowed to wear their clerical garb or perform Masses and other religious services openly. A 1992 constitutional amendment lifted many of these restrictions.

In Vicente Fox the Church had for the first time a practicing Catholic as chief executive and a political party that is staunchly pro-Church. Fox has stated that he would seek changes in Mexican law to allow the Catholic Church to own media outlets, thereby affording new opportunities to educate the public. The Catholic hierarchy has long sought this right and is heartened by Fox's view that religious teaching should no longer be barred from public schools and that Church leaders should be permitted to comment on political matters. Fox, however, ran afoul of the Catholic Church with his divorce and remarriage in 2001. Church leaders were stunned by his actions and the warm relationship was damaged.

Mexico is, at least for the short term, leaving behind the PRI pathway of participation with its central control and paternalistic methods of gaining and maintaining voter allegiance. But no one knows what lies ahead now that a non-PRI president is in power and the old style of politics is in retreat. Traditional electoral practices and tried-and-true forms of shaping voter attitudes are difficult to remove from the body politic, so it is a safe bet that Mexican pathways of participation will evolve ever so slowly. Nevertheless, the victory of Vicente Fox in 2000 was a watershed event of major proportions. Not only did the PRI lose an election, it lost the ability to define the rules of politics. The Mexican people will now be looking for new ways to participate in the political process and will feel less compunction to abide by rules established by the PRI. There will likely be a blending of the old with the new, but above all there will be newness: new avenues of participation, new rules of participation, and new participants. All will combine to remake the Mexican political and electoral process.

Electoral Data

The results from the presidential election of July 2, 2000, were as follows:

Vicente Fox Quesada, PAN	42.5 percent
Francisco Labastida Ochoa, PRI	36.1 percent
Cuauhtemoc Cardenas Solorzana, PRD	16.6 percent
Gilberto Rincon Gallardo, DS	1.6 percent
Manuel Camacho Solis, PCD	0.6 percent
Porfirio Munoz Ledo, PARM	0.4 percent

ANTIPOLLUTION POLICY

Mexico City is the most polluted city in the world. Situated at 7,400 feet and surrounded by mountains, Mexico City is in a basin where cold air is trapped by warmer air. The result is that pollution from human activities collects in the air over four- to six-day cycles, creating periods of air pollution that require health warnings, temporary curtailment of industrial production, and restrictions on the use of automobiles. At one point in the late 1980s Mexican officials devised an antipollution program that asked drivers not to take their car on the road for one specified day during the week.

Seeking a remedy for an environmental and health problem that was causing thousands of deaths each year, the Mexican government made cleaner air a national priority. Cleaning up the air in and around Mexico City was a significant challenge for a country that is focused on industrial development and has scarce national resources. Yet in the last fifteen years Mexico has made enormous strides, including a marked decrease in the levels of carbon monoxide, lead, and sulfur dioxide. In one fifteen-month period between 2000 and 2001 Mexico City went without one smog emergency, an unprecedented milestone. Today in Mexico City it is not uncommon to see the surrounding mountains forty miles in the distance.

The successful antipollution measures in Mexico City are associated with cleaner fuels and catalytic converters. Government policy required that over 4 million private cars be equipped with antipollution devices. Recently the Mexican government, with financial assistance from international agencies and nongovernmental organizations, created incentives to owners of over 2 million older automobiles to replace their cars with newer models that had advanced exhaust systems. Also, new government programs provide subsidies to manufacturers to outfit gas-powered delivery trucks with liquid petroleum gas, which burns more cleanly.

On the horizon in Mexico's program to rid the air of harmful pollutants is a plan to introduce electric engines. One of the leaders of the movement to transform transportation in Mexico is Nobel Prize winner Mario Molina. A professor at the Massachusetts Institute of Technology who gained international recognition for his work on ozone depletion, Molina admits that much more needs to be done to keep pollution within acceptable limits, especially since the population of Mexico City continues to grow and electric cars are still a long way off. But Molina is realistic: "It is not a question of superclean fuels versus clean, but a question of clean versus dirty."

Attacking Mexico City's air pollution problem is ultimately a financial and development challenge. Trading in old cars, buying new fleets of fuel-efficient trucks, using more costly petroleum, and investing in electric cars requires extensive outlays of public and private resources. Despite the costs and the impact restrictions may have on industrialization, Mexico City officials and the national government are determined to put the unwanted reputation as the "world's most polluted city" behind them. The goal is to provide a level of environmental safety that saves lives and improves the quality of life for the residents of the country's largest city. ⊕

THE POLITICAL ELITE

Political and governmental power in Mexico has been concentrated in the PRI since 1929, but characterizing that concentration of power as noncompetitive would be simplistic and inaccurate. Recruiting leaders, appointing key officials, and attaining the ultimate prize, the presidential nomination, are all wrapped up in a complex web of party interrelationships and rival camps. Until the electoral victory of Vicente Fox the power elite in Mexico was formed through a highly personal process based on a patron-client arrangement often termed a *camarilla*, or political clique. The PRI hierarchy was a maze of numerous interlocking *camarillas* made up of high-level officials who

Photo 6.1   Mexico's President Vicente Fox gestures during State of the Nation address. (Reuters NewMedia Inc./Corbis)

Vicente Fox was born in 1942 in Mexico City. As a child he moved with his family to a ranch in San Cristobal. He received his undergraduate degree in business administration from the Mexico City campus of the Ibero-American University. Later he received a diploma in upper management from the Harvard University business school. In 1964 he joined Coca-Cola de Mexico. In 1980 he joined the National Action Party and in 1988 was elected as federal deputy for the Third District of Leon. In 1995 he was elected governor of the state of Guanajuato, and in 2000 was elected president of Mexico as a member of the PAN party.

headed a "family" of supporters. The use of the term "family" in connection with the *camarilla* system reflects the importance of kinship in leadership recruitment and career advancement. Studies have shown that many of Mexico's elite during the PRI reign were in some way related or were linked through the *compadrazgo* rite of godfather sponsorship.

Because of the close-knit nature of the relationships in the political families, the members of these vast *camarillas* were deeply loyal to their party patron, seeing him as someone who deserved their allegiance, if for no other reason than that their future career aspirations were linked to his advancement. The importance placed on the *camarilla* as the primary, if not sole, route to power and position often created an environment of internal politics pitting one *camarilla* against another, all vying for the ultimate goal of the presidency and the key cabinet positions that accompany the office of the presidency. To complicate this personal alliance building, many key party members felt that the best way to ensure their personal success was to become members of multiple *camarillas* in an attempt to establish a series of ties that would benefit their career and their position within the PRI hierarchy.

Much of the personal jockeying for power and influence within and among the various *camarillas* was focused on the *sexenio,* the race for the presidency every six years. Would-be candidates for the presidency, party leaders, and office seekers became entangled in the personal alliance building that was critical to moving up the ladder within the *camarilla* and eventually catching the eye of the presidential nominee. Because the *camarilla* system was built on personal relationships and alliances, forming a political family was a long process of association and loyalty. This emphasis on personal association and loyalty afforded the PRI the ability to maintain its hold on the political system, but it also created the opportunity for intense rivalries and factional disputes among the various *camarillas.*

The remnants of the *camarilla* system continue to operate around state governors and local party bosses, but the career track toward the presidency and cabinet positions has been disrupted. Moreover, reformers in the PRI are more focused on ridding the party of the vestiges of the past and moving toward more modern means of leadership recruitment and career tracking. Many of Mexico's new political elite have been trained in technical and administrative specialties in the United States and Europe and have returned to Mexico with less commitment to the patron-client/personal relationship mentality of party organization. Today in the PRI there is more emphasis on establishing a party meritocracy that is based on education, skill, and talent instead of sponsorship, connections, and placement in a hierarchy of power. Earlier only the top national PRI leaders had a *técnico* background (Salinas, a Harvard-trained economist, and Zedillo, a University of Pennsylvania urban planner). But today *técnicos* have filtered deep down into the party membership to challenge the "dinosaurs" of the old PRI.

While the PRI is suffering from a breakdown in its leadership system and internal disputes over the leadership model best suited for its political resurgence, the PAN and particularly the governing elite formed by President Vicente Fox is bringing not only new faces into government but new approaches to leadership. Vicente Fox came into office with a sense of urgency to remake Mexico and deal with a huge agenda of social and economic problems. Fox's sense of urgency was best encapsulated by his campaign slogan "The time to be in Mexico is today." He regularly harped on the need to act on Mexico's needs: "Today, today, today!" The center of Mexican government has always been the presidency, but Fox was determined to take bold measures that addressed the length and breath of Mexico.

Linked with Fox's sense of urgency and broad policy agenda is his desire to be an accessible chief executive. Reminiscent of Franklin Delano Roosevelt, Fox addresses the nation by radio in Mexican-style fireside chats. Fox moves around the country talking to the poor in barrios, holding court at his ranch (often on his horse "The King"), and mingling with churchgoers at Sunday Mass. The once highly secure presidential estate in Mexico City has been opened up to ordinary citizens in order to meet Fox's desire to make his office *la casa del pueblo*. Fox is an outgoing if not gregarious chief executive, who meets personally with people, hugging them and showing real interest in solving their problems. In many respects Fox is a throwback to the old-style patron who saw his responsibility as personally dealing with the concerns of his people. The difference, however, with his PRI predecessors is that Fox is not inclined to dole out money or appliances to peasants or slum dwellers. Rather, he tries to convince them to find ways to solve their problems on their own or to seek training or guidance from government agencies.

Fox's leadership style has filtered down to the organization of his advisory system. Fox takes his cabinet secretaries and their spouses to a mountaintop lodge near Mexico City for what has been described as a cross between a religious and corporate retreat. During his regular cabinet meetings, Fox is more interested in eliciting ideas from his ministers than issuing orders. The format is open and intense, but it is designed to generate new ideas and new initiatives, not issue directives. A key member of his advisory system is the public opinion pollster. Fox is ever conscious about how his style and his scattershot initiatives are playing with the Mexican people. In his first year in office the polls found clear evidence that Fox's manner of leadership was playing well with the public. Fox's approval rating has consistently surpassed those of PRI presidents, and if communications with the president are a sign of support, then Fox is the first president since Lazaro Cardenas to engender widespread citizen support.

Critical to Fox's success is his team of advisers and cabinet officials. Because of his ambitious programmatic agenda, Fox depends heavily on his ministers to turn his promises into effective policies. Although Fox has brought in a whole new cast of officials who are not tied to the PRI, he has kept the practice of appointing highly trained technocrats to staff his main-line agencies. Most of these officials were educated in the United States, such as Francisco Gil Diaz, the head of the finance and public credit secretariat (Ph.D. in economics from the University of Chicago), and Luis Ernesto Derbez, the trade and industrial promotion secretariat (Ph.D. in economics, Iowa State University). One surprise appointment was naming Jorge Casteneda as secretary of foreign affairs. Casteneda received his undergraduate degree from Princeton and chaired the Latin American Studies Program at New York University. He authored a book highly critical of Mexican-U.S. relations entitled *Limits to Friendship*. Casteneda became the "quiet voice" in Fox's ear as he advised the president on the key relationship with its neighbor to the north. But in 2003 Castenada resigned after a stormy relationship with the media, legislators, and fellow cabinet members.

In addition to appointing a cabinet and advisory team not tied to the PRI, Fox has brought a management approach to the key administrative and revenue-producing agencies of government. For example, he fired PRI political appointees at many bureaucracies and replaced them with distinguished business leaders, charging them to revamp their agencies and bring efficiency, productivity, and if necessary austerity to these bodies. One agency where Fox has implemented this management approach is PEMEX. Fox appointed Raul Munoz Leos, who was the executive vice president of Du Pont Mexico and a board member of a number of major corporations in Mexico including Sears Roebuck S.A. At the critical Light and Power Company Fox appointed Alfonso Caso Aguilar, who had a notable career working as a consultant to international business in Mexico and also as an executive in charge of investment at international agencies such as the Inter-American Development Bank. Fox let it be known that he intends to fully support these executives/bureaucrats as they seek to transform government agencies from inefficient, patronage-laden institutions to modern business enterprises.

With the election of Vicente Fox the political elite in Mexico is changing. But new names and new faces are not the critical ingredients of change at the top layers of political and governmental power. President Fox has transformed both the leadership style and the leadership process in Mexico. Fox seems determined to make the office of the presidency much more visible and populist. He is the first president in seventy-one years who does not wear the PRI label. Fox has decided that it is absolutely necessary to move among the people, build up popular support, and institute reforms that expand democratic opportunities. After decades of PRI leadership that was either distant or driven by electoral concerns, the shift to a more personalistic approach to leadership is a new departure.

Composition of the Mexican Legislature

In the 2000 national elections the Chamber of Deputies with its five hundred members had the following configuration:

The Alliance for Change (PAN and Ecologist Green Party), 223 seats
The Institutional Revolutionary Party (PRI), 209 seats
The Alliance for Mexico (PRD, Labor Party, Convergence for the Democracy, Social Alliance Party, and Nationalist Society Party), 68 seats

---

POINT OF FACT
According to the Latinobarometro polling service, 15 percent of Mexican citizens in 1995 stated that under certain circumstances an authoritarian government would be preferable to a democratic government. In 2001, 35 percent of Mexicans stated that an authoritarian government would be preferable to a democratic government.

REAL GOVERNMENT

Governing in Mexico is not so much a process as a method. The process of governing suggests a step-by-step movement through an institutional setting with a policy being developed through the interplay of powerful institutional leaders following set rules and traditions. A method of governing suggests that the institutional setting is less important and that institutional leaders concentrate on other means such as personal relationships and personal interactions in order to develop public policy. The dominant theme of Mexican politics is that power is defined in personal terms; those who have power advance their policy agenda by effectively employing strategies that maximize their personal ties. The reality of governing in Mexico is that people matter rather than institutions. Public policymaking is not confined exclusively to the democratic institutions—legislatures, courts, and local governments. Instead, the president, key cabinet secretaries, party leaders, and members of the business elite form a working clique of policy formulators and control the process of decisionmaking from agenda setting to implementation. The president is the first among equals and the dominant force in the government.

As a result of the centralization of power in the presidency and the enormous opportunity to control the policy agenda and the policy process, there is little evidence that Mexican presidents are "detached" from the day-to-day operation of government or "out of the policy loop." Instead, Mexican presidents seek to be personally identified with the individual policy initiative and of course receive credit for that initiative. Those who surround the president recognize that this method of making public policy is top-down and ego-driven and is not designed to bring a team approach to the advisory system.

The power that the Mexican president wields in the public policy process varies with each individual chief executive. Carlos Salinas amassed enormous presidential power and was able to control the policymaking agenda and push through legislation with little obstruction. Salinas used his domination of the policy process to negotiate the NAFTA treaty. He also sought unchallenged authority to name and replace governors. During his six years in office Salinas fired seventeen state governors who in various ways displeased him or embarrassed the government and the PRI. In the area of social policy Salinas developed the National Solidarity Program, an antipoverty and public works program. He made sure, however, that the administrative bureaucracy (a prime source of patronage and personalistic favor distribution) remained tied to his office. There was little in Mexican government that did not involve Carlos Salinas.

Ernesto Zedillo, on the other hand, used a different method of governing. Zedillo had less support in the PRI, but he chose to develop a decisionmaking and policy implementing approach that accented power sharing and institutional independence. Zedillo refused to participate in intraparty disputes or influence the direction of disputed elections. He actively sought to devolve more power to the state governors and sought to transform social welfare programs by reducing centralized control. One critical consequence of Zedillo's method of governance was that the percentage of bills submitted by the executive branch dropped from 90 percent under Salinas to 41.5 percent under Zedillo. The legislation proposed by Zedillo passed with little opposition, but in return the Mexican Congress became a working partner with the executive in lawmaking.

Vicente Fox has brought changes to presidential power and to the general method of governance employed by past PRI chief executives. Fox is more willing to make public policy decisions from within a diverse and active advisory system. Following a practice that he used when he was governor of Guanajuato, Fox initially appointed a transition team that was charged with developing new approaches to dealing with corruption, crime, tax reform, and immigration. On taking office Fox moved quickly to restructure government agencies. While pledging to continue Zedillo's plan to devolve more power to the states, he centralized the administration of the federal police and separated the law enforcement and spy agencies from the interior secretariat. This administrative change was designed to send a signal that corrupt practices and abuse of power would not be tolerated. Fox also created new government agencies that were charged with responding to problems long ignored by the PRI such as Indian issues, the status of migrants abroad (particularly in the United States), and the disabled.

Unlike his PRI predecessors, Fox must govern in a contentious political climate. The PRI still controls the legislature, and his own PAN is fraught with internal discord. He must rely on his persuasive skills and his ability to marshal public opinion if he is to address difficult policy issues such as tax reform, utility rate increases, and moving toward a more privately funded energy sector. In the early days of his presidency he was able to present and attain unanimous approval of a lean budget that marked his administration as having interest in efficient use of public resources. He also showed his intention to govern for all the Mexican people with his pledges to guarantee greater Indian rights and Indian autonomy, especially in southern states such as Chiapas. But Fox's early successes were seen as the result of a honeymoon period in Mexican politics and the collapse of the PRI after its first electoral loss in seventy years.

Although there are serious questions about Fox's ability to govern in a PRI-dominated political system and his capacity to successfully deal with the more difficult policy issues facing the country, there is no doubt that he is committed to change and to what he describes as the reform of the state. As he stated in his address to Congress after his inauguration, "The cause of many of our problems lies in the excessive concentration of power. The reform of the state must ensure that the exercise of power in an ever more balanced and democratic manner is reinforced." From all available evidence, Fox appears determined to follow a method that distributes governing power, embraces new governing alternatives, and establishes new governing institutions. The crucial challenge facing Fox as he seeks to advance the reform of the state is whether compromises with the old method of concentration of power used by the PRI will negate his efforts to build a new governing method.

Because of its legacy of colonial corporatism, dictatorial rule, and revolutionary statism, Mexico has evolved into a governing system based on control. At every level of political power there is evidence of control—control by the PRI, control by the president, control by state governors and local political leaders. There is little room for independence, autonomy, and independent action. There are signs that Vicente Fox is seeking to move away from the legacy of control, but it is too soon to determine whether he will be successful in overcoming a method of governance that has been intertwined with Mexican life for generations.

The Mexican government today is functioning on two levels—the official level on which the state, the president, and the bureaucratic system exercise control over the public sector and national life, and the unofficial or informal level, on which drug lords, corrupt officials, revolutionary guerrillas, and all who oppose the government operate outside the sphere of government control. The two-level nature of Mexican government is the most serious problem facing President Fox. He was an outsider who challenged the dominant control of the PRI, but now he is an insider who must reconcile these conflicting and contradicting conditions of national governance. Fox has pledged to change government in Mexico, and that means changing not only the political elite and the policy agenda but also the role of the state, the manner in which the president operates, and the method used for formulating and implementing national policies. This is a Herculean task that will require replacing hundreds of years of history and tradition in six years.

POINT OF FACT
When the PRI was in power, local party officials offered all kinds of bribes for votes, from pencils and tortillas to taxi licenses and land titles. Monetary payments up to $500 were common.

What the Experts Say

Joseph Klesner of Kenyon College, a leading expert on Mexican electoral politics and the emergence of Vicente Fox as Mexico's leader, says the following about the importance of the 2000 election and the end of PRI dominance:

Mexicans took a large step toward consolidating their democracy by electing Vicente Fox. In so doing, they have brought democracy to their nation by a peaceful and constitutional path, a rarity among countries in the region. Redoubts of authoritarianism do remain in the complex Mexican political system and dislodging them will pose a challenge to the new Fox administration. However, Mexicans have much about which to be proud as they open the twenty-first century.

JOSEPH KLESNER, "THE END OF MEXICO'S ONE-PARTY REGIME," *PS: Political Science*, March 2001, PP. 107–114

THE POLITICAL ECONOMY

At the core of Mexico's development strategy is a widely held view that state control of key national assets is essential. Since 1917 Mexico's economy has been firmly under the direction of the state. One of the founding principles of the Mexican Revolution was establishing the state as the protector of natural resources (under article 27). When Lazaro Cardenas nationalized the foreign petroleum industry in 1938, he solidified the role of the state in directing key sectors of the economy. In the post–World War II era the Mexican state continued to direct the economy as President Miguel Aleman established import substitution policies by hiking tariffs to protect domestic industries. Aleman's policies were continued by succeeding presidents because they produced a more vigorous economy with real GDP doubling between 1950 and 1970. By the end of the 1970s Mexico had evolved into one of the more developed nations in the Third World with a per capita income of over $2,000. With this success Mexican leaders felt comfortable in following the strategy of state-directed economic development. As a result the number of state-owned companies increased from 84 in 1970 to 845 in 1977, and the government embarked on a massive public infrastructure program designed to further push Mexico into the upper levels of Third World development.

But there was a price to pay for this sustained period of government intervention and control. By the end of President Luis Echeverria's term in 1976, Mexico was heavily in debt due in large part to the outlays for the state-owned companies and a rising trade deficit caused by long disinterest in exporting and a refusal to open the economy to foreign investment. The Mexican economy began to experience serious weakness as its debt mushroomed and the peso was devalued for the first time since the 1950s. What saved Mexico, at least for a time, were its huge oil reserves, which created an artificial period of prosperity during the presidency of Jose Lopez Portillo. With oil revenues entering the economy, Mexico borrowed heavily to expand its industrial infrastructure. When the oil boom ended in the early 1980s, Mexico was saddled with $80 billion in debt (one of the highest in the less developed world), a prolonged period of inflation (36 percent during the *sexenio* of Lopez Portillo and 159 percent during the presidency of de la Madrid), and a series of peso devaluations that damaged the purchasing power of the average citizen. By 1988, when Carlos Salinas became president, Mexico's peso had lost 97 percent of its value.

The presidency of Carlos Salinas marks a watershed in the direction of the Mexican economy. Salinas put in place a neoliberal model of development that accented a market economy, diminishing trade barriers, reduced state budgets, and active pursuit of foreign investment. Although Salinas attained reductions in state spending and attracted significant foreign investment, both the NAFTA agreement and the privatization of key industries were poorly thought out and implemented, causing short-term dislocations and questionable government practices. In the case of NAFTA, Mexican farmers were ill prepared for the competition, the end of government subsidies, and the lack of productivity that comes with tiny plots of land rather than giant agribusiness estates. In the case of privatization, Salinas was more interested in using the money from the sale of state assets to fill the pockets of his friends and associates and to build the PRI election war chest than in constructing an efficient private sector.

The changes to the Mexican economy instituted by Salinas and the excitement about a "new" Mexico were dashed within days of Ernesto Zedillo taking over power in 1994. The Mexican peso crashed dramatically and the Mexican economy contracted by 6.2 percent in 1995. Within a year Mexican capital flight reached an estimated $10 billion and the government faced the real threat of becoming insolvent as its currency reserves were depleted to dangerous levels. Many who have examined this precipitous fall blame Zedillo as much as Salinas. Besides doing little to reverse the dangerous economic and financial policies of his predecessor, the new president warned Mexican businessmen in advance of the problems, causing extensive capital flight, and then compounded the problem by contracting the money supply and thereby fueling a steep recession.

With the economy in free fall, the Mexican banking system was near collapse and was only revived by a $100 billion bailout, largely from the United States. Fortunately, Zedillo corrected the Mexican economy by opening the country to foreign investment. Zedillo also paid careful attention to inflation and brought it down to single figures. The resurgence of the Mexican economy under Zedillo was aided by a spike in oil prices and growing international demand. Unlike his predecessors, Zedillo used the money to repay international debts rather than squander it on public works projects and party payoffs. Zedillo left office in 2000 with an economy that had achieved a 5 percent growth rate.

Vicente Fox's approach to Mexican economic development has been in line with his general method of governance, which is to inundate the policy process with a steady stream of new initiatives. Speaking early in 2001, Fox laid out an ambitious economic program that emphasized the importance of expanding growth and opportunities to previously neglected regions of the country. Fox introduced the "March South" initiative, which was designed to promote permanent employment in the economically depressed regions of the south. Fox also established a program of regional development dividing the country into five sectors in order to address infrastructure needs and ensure that policies promote sustainable development. In the critical area of energy Fox committed the nation to a full-scale modernization of PEMEX, the Federal Electricity Commission, and individual power companies. Fox pledged to restructure and refocus PEMEX to ensure greater productivity and efficiency of management. This emphasis on modernization was viewed as essential to avoid future power shortages and to enhance Mexico's ability to export both petroleum and electrical power.

Like his predecessors, Fox has shown an interest in encouraging foreign investment, especially with the European Union. There is a noticeable shift in emphasis away from relying on U.S. investment and a desire to diversify the sources of foreign capital. The accent on expanding foreign investment is tied directly to employment opportunities. Fox stated that he wanted to generate 1 million new jobs in 2001 and similar job expansion in future years. Instead of creating public works jobs, Fox called for the development of an entrepreneurial spirit in Mexico that would follow along lines of the foreign corporate presence. Fox has also sought the formation of micro- and medium-sized companies that would build a new job base and make Mexico a nation that moves away from its statist past.

At the core of Fox's vision of a new Mexican economy is his plan to achieve massive fiscal reform. As envisioned by Fox, reform has five objectives: administrative simplification, heightened saving and investment, reduction of tax evasion, integration of the "gray" (untaxed) economy, and increased government revenue to ensure healthy financing of public spending. With this plan in place, Fox believes, the government will have greater revenues available to address a number of long neglected social programs and economic development ventures. Fox views fiscal reform as enabling "a revolution in education, the quality of health services, the fight against poverty, and the rescue of our natural resources." President Fox is committed to linking a more efficient state and a more vigorous private economy with social programs for the young, the poor, and the aged.

Prospects for a successful Fox presidency depend in large part on trade and investment relations with the United States, and on the ability of the NAFTA agreement to continue generating jobs and overall economic growth. Mexico's export sector has been growing by about 10 percent since the NAFTA agreement, and exports from the maquiladora region along the border have been growing at 20 percent a year. The maquiladoras currently employ 1.3 million workers compared to 546,000 when NAFTA began. But the benefits from NAFTA are clearly tied to the U.S. economy. As of 1999, 88 percent of Mexican exports were destined for the United States and 74 percent of Mexican imports came from the United States. The economic growth that Mexico has enjoyed in recent years is definitely tied to the strength of the U.S. economy. For example, while the export economy has been growing by 10 percent, the domestic market has seen a slight 3.5 percent growth rate. Mexico has tied its economic growth to trade and specifically trade with the United States. Any sustained economic downturn in the American economy would do significant damage to Mexico's efforts to further establish itself as a newly industrialized nation.

Economic success will also be judged in terms of whether Fox's economic stewardship will begin to close the ever expanding income gap between Mexicans who have prospered in the post-NAFTA era and Mexicans who have fallen further down the slope of income inequality. A study done by the World Bank in the mid-1990s found that the bottom 40 percent of the Mexican population accounted for only 11 percent of the national income, while the upper 30 percent retained almost 70 percent of the national income. Despite Mexico's strong economic performance in the post-NAFTA period, real wages have declined by as much as 50 percent (the minimum wage calculated for Mexico City is a paltry $4 a day) and unemployment outside the maquiladora region is as high as 40 percent. Many Mexicans have been forced into the informal or gray economy, where an estimated 9 million people make a subsistence living.

Income inequality in Mexico is about more than data. A Mexican university study found that infant mortality among the richest 20 percent of the population was 13 per 1,000 babies born, but among the poorest 20 percent the death rate was 52 per 1,000 babies born. Similar inequality is found in education. Although the number of years that Mexican young people spend in school rose from 2.8 years in 1960 to 7.7 years in the mid-1990s, the difference in school attendance between wealthy and poor children is dramatic. The richest 10 percent of Mexican schoolchildren attend school 12.1 years, while the poorest 10 percent are in school a mere 2.1 years. Most of the income inequality results from huge differences in the economic climate between the rural and urban areas.

Today some 23 million Mexicans live in abject poverty on the *ejidos,* where they work land that often lacks suitable fertilizers and subsist on meager government social welfare programs such as Zedillo's antipoverty program, Progresso. The Zedillo program, which followed Salinas's much heralded antipoverty Program for National Solidarity, ties food and money to the commitment of families to educate their children and mothers to visit health clinics. About five years into the program there is some evidence that infant mortality is down and children are staying in school longer. In one sense Mexico has placed heavy emphasis on its social welfare programs designed to bridge the gap between the rich and the poor. Social spending in recent years has increased to 61 percent of the budget, which is up from just 30 percent in the early 1980s. But the social welfare budget as a percentage of the GDP has actually shrunk by 50 percent because the government has reduced its overall commitment to public sector solutions to national problems. This has left the private sector—churches, nongovernmental organizations, and individual charities—with the daunting task of responding to the needs of Mexico's poor.

Economic indices on economic growth, per capita income, service sector job formation, trade patterns, and industrialization show that Mexico has made significant development strides that place it in a category separate from many other less developed nations. For example, the Mexican economy did not face the kind of economic downturn that its Latin American neighbors Argentina, Brazil, and Uruguay did in 2002. A combination of sound monetary and fiscal policies and a steady stream of foreign investment buoyed the economy.

And yet there remains nagging evidence of a persistent social lag in Mexican development. As with many less developed nations, there are two Mexicos, one that reflects the benefits of a new global economy and the other stuck in the past with only scant evidence of progress in bringing the benefits of the global economy to the poor. Fortunately for Mexico there are a number of promising signs that it indeed belongs in a separate development category. But Mexico still has significant socioeconomic problems that if left without resolution will keep it from moving up into the ranks of the developed nations.

POINT OF FACT
An entry-level worker in a maquiladora factory in Tijuana earns $1.50 an hour. A similar worker in China earns twenty-five cents an hour. Since 2000, over five hundred foreign-owned assembly line factories in Mexico have closed, with much of the work going to China.

Mexico in the Global Economy

McAllen, Texas, is one of the top ten fastest growing metropolitan areas in the United States, largely because of NAFTA's influence on employment opportunities in the maquiladora region. Over 2,000 American factory managers and other professionals cross the border into Reynosa, Mexico, to run the 209 factories that have been built there and to manage the 64,000 workers who have moved from rural areas in search of work. In 1988 there were only twenty factories with 16,000 employees in Reynosa.

THE MAQUILADORAS

Perhaps no other economic development initiative has had as much impact on Mexico as the border industrialization program. Established in 1966, the program led the way for the formation of the maquiladoras, manufacturing facilities located across the border from the United States. The maquiladoras, also called "in bond" or "twin" plants, process imported materials or commodities for reexport to the United States. What the border industrialization program created in effect was a trade and manufacturing system that allowed raw materials from the United States to be sent to Mexican border towns and placed "in bond" so as not to enter the Mexican economy. These materials were processed in Mexico and then exported back to the United States without requiring the U.S. company to pay a Mexican duty. Only on their reentry into the United States were the assembled goods subject to custom duties.

In 1972 the border industrialization program was further modified to permit non-Mexican ownership of maquiladora plants. The modification heightened the movement of U.S. companies across the border enticed not only by the prospect of avoiding Mexican duties but more importantly by the reduced costs associated with low wages, low taxes, and few environmental and industrial regulations. Corporate executives were further convinced to move their U.S. operations across the border because of intense overseas competition and manufacturing practices (often called just-in-time inventory systems) that required quick delivery of products. The maquiladora plants proved to be ideal to compete with Asian competitors.

Since the establishment of the maquiladoras, over 1,800 U.S.-based plants have been built employing over 500,000 workers in border cities such as Ciudad Juarez, Nuevo Leon, Matamoros, Mexicali, and Tijuana. Most major U.S. corporations—General Motors, Zenith, General Electric, Honeywell, Texas Instruments, Chrysler—have built plants along the border. The border industrialization program has worked so well that the Mexican government expanded the maquiladoras to the interior of the country in an attempt to stem the tide of peasants leaving the land in search of jobs in the north. The success of the maquiladoras led to a modification that would allow goods produced in the border plants to enter the Mexican market. As envisioned by the government, a yearly permit would be required and goods allowed entry into the Mexican market would be limited to 20 percent of production or 50 percent of current year production over the previous year production.

A boon to the Mexican economy, the maquiladoras have fostered ill will in the American labor community. It is estimated that over 100,000 American workers have lost their jobs to the maquiladoras. With many Mexican workers in the border plants making $2–$4 a day, compared to $20–$40 an hour in wages and benefits for the American worker, it is not surprising that U.S. corporations are drawn to Mexico. Corporate executives in the United States are quick to point out that the global economy makes competitiveness key to survival; jobs not lost to Mexico would be lost to Asia. The maquiladoras also have fostered tensions in Mexico, as workers in the border plants often complain of poor working conditions, long hours, meager health and safety regulations, and intimidation from managers should they complain or worse yet begin to organize unions. When workers leave the maquiladoras, they walk across the street to shantytowns with few modern amenities, since the corporations accept no obligation to build housing or schools or critical infrastructure to accommodate the thousands of workers who trek north to the plants.

The maquiladoras are visible evidence of how the global economy has touched Mexico. The watchwords of the new world economy are competitiveness and survival. By providing a manufacturing system that keeps cost low and regulations at a minimum and dissuades unionization, the maquiladoras will continue to prosper and attract U.S. corporations along with the Mexican poor anxious for a better life, despite the working conditions and the quality of life in the border towns. Because Mexico exists in a global economy, the maquiladoras are already experiencing competition from even lower wage equivalents in China. The number of maquiladoras has declined, as has the number of workers. Since 2000, over 250,000 Mexican workers, who prospered because of the maquiladoras, have found themselves unemployed, a stark reminder of the realities of the constant shifts in the global marketplace. ⊕

CHALLENGES

A less developed country like Mexico faces enormous challenges. Reaching the next level of development and sustaining that development in an uncertain world requires a number of critical ingredients—great leadership skill, fortuitous economic and financial conditions, competent public sector administration, visionary private sector investment, and a steady social climate free of destabilizing divisions. There is also that critical developmental intangible—luck. For the moment Mexico appears to be on the right track to reach that next level. The presidency of Vicente Fox has restored confidence in the government, the NAFTA agreement has been a positive force for strengthening the economy, and a new generation of educated Mexicans are committed to bringing needed reforms to weaken the hold of corruption, mismanagement, and excessive state regulation. After the devastating impact of the peso crisis and the reign of drug-related violence that stunned the country in the mid-1990s, Mexico now has a more confident look and is slowly but surely taking on the appearance of a nation ready to reach the next level of development.

In order to "break through," however, Mexico will have to address a series of challenges that are by no means insignificant. PRI dominance in Mexican politics and national life has provided the country with stability and predictability, but it also created a system of uneven development, inefficient administration, closed decisionmaking, and a deeply mistrustful, cynical citizenry. Mexico must now take the steps to move away from the PRI system and install a new set of governing approaches and socioeconomic policies that are more in line with the demands of a global economy and Western-style democratic practice.

Mexico is in reality two countries. The northern half is heavily industrialized, better educated, and more prosperous, while the southern seven states below the Tropic of Cancer are largely agricultural, less developed, and poor. There are some obvious reasons for the discrepancies between north and south. Mexican capital was drawn to the north with the express purpose of making a trade connection with the United States. The industrial gap increased with the formation of the maquiladora regions, which catered to U.S. investment along the border. Mexican leaders made key decisions in the 1950s and 1960s to develop a transportation system that benefited the north, with roads linking population centers like Mexico City, Puebla, and Guadalajara to the U.S. border. Few if any roads and no railroads were built with destinations to the southern states. The Mexican government decided to improve irrigation and electricity in the north while the south received few infrastructure improvements.

A regional development program made attempts to address the problem of the two Mexicos in the late 1990s, but the peso crisis and a drop in revenue halted the initiative. President Fox has added regional development to his long list of to-dos, but it remains to be seen whether such a major undertaking moves to the top of the list. In the meantime the problem of northern prosperity and southern poverty continues unabated and is likely to worsen in the coming years. The Chiapas uprising and the push for an Indian bill of rights may be the spark that provides the political energy to finally address the plight of the south. But it remains to be seen whether the Fox government can marshal adequate resources to deal with a problem that was years in the making. Key to regional development is a shift in resources from Mexico

City to the various states. Governors seeking to gain a larger share of budget allocations have formed the National Conference of Governors to lobby the central government to gain the power to raise local revenue and to change the formula for transferring resources to the states.

Despite his popularity Fox faces numerous institutional roadblocks, including minority status in the legislature and partial control of state governors and municipal councils. Moreover, the old PRI system has by no means been replaced; it has only been rendered headless. There is still life among the PRI activists, especially the so-called baby dinosaurs, the younger generation of party faithful and former government officials who want to drive out the old guard so that they can position themselves to retake government. Any attempt by Fox to bring systemic reform to Mexican government will meet with powerful resistance and force compromise, or in the classic Latin American tradition, a facade of grandiose form that masks the weakness of real substance.

There is an old Mexican saying, "Le colgaron muchos milagros" (They hung many miracles from him). This is the predicament that President Fox finds himself in as he seeks to remake Mexican government and the popular perceptions of Mexican government. Expectations of political reform and institutional redefinition are high in post-PRI Mexico. The Mexican people yearn for a different way of running their country and Fox has promised them that he will bring them that different way. So much hangs on Fox and his promises that he will inevitably fail in some of his pursuits and be unable to make good on some of his laundry list of promises.

As seen throughout this chapter, Mexican development is intimately tied to events on the other side of the border. Decisions made in Washington and on Wall Street often set the parameters within which Mexico must operate. President Fox has already laid out a blueprint of how Mexico might be able to establish a new relationship with the United States based on respect and equal treatment. Fox in his first meeting with President George Bush in 2001 suggested that Mexico and the United States create an open border that allows for the free movement of people and dismantle the walls, barbed wire, and Border Patrol units that transform Mexican workers into criminals. While this controversial proposal is not likely to be supported by residents of border states, Fox is serious about moving away from the prevalent mentality in the United States that the movement of Mexicans across the border is a national security threat.

Fox also made it clear to President Bush that he would like to see a quick end to the certification process that yearly grades Mexico on its level of cooperation in the drug war. Mexicans have long seen the certification process as a demeaning exercise that concentrates on the alleged failures of its national drug policy. Fox promised Bush that he would weed out the corrupt officials in his national drug forces, which would obviate any further certification. A visit by former U.S. Senator Jesse Helms to Mexico in 2001 laid the groundwork for an end to the certification process. Helms, who had strongly advocated certification, came away from meetings with Fox and his drug advisers convinced that Mexico was making real progress on the drug corruption front. Helms promised that the U.S. Congress would likely revisit the certification issue and end what has been a humiliating experience for Mexico.

Fox bolstered his antidrug reputation in 2002, when Benjamin Arrelano Felix was arrested and the death of his brother Ramon was announced. For years the Arrelano Felix brothers had been the most notorious and feared drug clan in Mexico. The brothers were responsible for the killings of over three hundred law enforcement personnel. In the late 1990s the United States offered a bounty of $2 million for the arrest of the brothers. Thanks in large part to greater cooperation between Mexican and U.S. drug officials, the arrest and death of the two brothers was presented as an enormous triumph for the Fox administration and a significant blow to the transshipment of illegal drugs across the border. It further enhanced its reputation as relentless in the pursuit of drug lords in 2003, when it captured Osiel Cardenas, the head of the Gulf cartel, for whom the FBI had posted a $2 million reward.

Although migration and drugs form a critical aspect of Mexican-U.S. relations, at the core of establishing a new more positive and mature linkage is NAFTA. Few Mexicans would deny that the free trade agreement with the United States has helped spur economic development and some social mobility. But from the Mexican perspective there is more to NAFTA than whether the United States gains access to the insurance and mutual fund market or what percentage of spare parts are permitted entry into the country. Mexicans look at the maquiladora region, which is often viewed as the embodiment of NAFTA, and see beautiful new plants across the road from shantytowns. Mexicans further see factories drawn by NAFTA opportunities polluting the air and the groundwater and causing unforeseen medical problems. President Fox's pledge to improve the lives of the poor and foster a more evenhanded relationship with the United States will inevitably bump up against the American corporate presence. Fox is by no means a nationalist or foe of foreign presence in his country, but his populist agenda may force him to take measures that combine the free trade components of NAFTA with social responsibility tenets that are grounded in a more statist and socialist approach to national development.

INDEPENDENT FOREIGN POLICY

Living in the shadow of the United States has not stopped Mexican government leaders from seeking ways to exercise a measure of independence, particularly in foreign policy. Mexico prides itself on taking foreign policy positions, especially with regard to hemispheric affairs, that are not in line with the objectives of the United States and in fact run contrary to those objectives. The number one principle of Mexico's foreign policy is national self-determination, not unusual for any sovereign state, but when placed in the context of Mexican-U.S. relations becomes the driving force of its international relations. In a hemisphere in which integration, cooperation, and partnership are the watchwords, Mexico holds firm to its revolutionary nationalism, at least when it comes to responding to the actions and initiatives of the United States.

Mexico's independent foreign policy took shape in the years following the Cuban Revolution. When the United States was pressuring the countries of the hemisphere to fall in place behind its economic and political isolation of Cuba, Mexico resisted the pressure and maintained diplomatic ties with the communist country. Later it supported the Marxist government of Salvador Allende in Chile and openly criticized the United States for its decisions to destabilize the economy and promote a military coup. Mexico was one of the first nations in the hemisphere to break diplomatic ties with the Nicaraguan dictator Anastasio Somoza, a longtime friend of the United States and an arch anticommunist. And finally, when the war in Central America became an obsession of the Reagan administration, the Mexican government broke rank with the United States and lent its support to the aims of the guerrillas. Later as the war intensified and claimed thousands of civilian lives, the Mexican government took the lead and pushed for a peaceful settlement of the dispute.

The support that Mexico has shown communists and guerrilla movements is not only its way of following an independent path from the United States but also a reflection of its revolutionary heritage. Mexican leaders have consistently championed the cause of nonintervention, resolution of internal problems without the use of outside force, and national control of critical resources. Because Mexico has been the target of U.S. military and corporate intervention in the past and has seen the United States meddle in its internal affairs, it is not shy about taking positions in support of groups or movements that challenge U.S. power. Mexican officials who have challenged U.S. dominance in the hemisphere do so with the support of the people. Public opinion polls, especially in the 1970s and 1980s, showed a consistent pattern of anti-American sentiment among Mexicans.

Mexican independence in matters of foreign policy, however, is not blinded by the past or support for revolutionary ideology. Mexico in the era of NAFTA has become much more pragmatic in its relations with the United States and in taking policy positions that may run contrary to U.S. interests. The spirit of cooperation that is inherent in the NAFTA philosophy has become the foundation for a more cordial relationship with the United States. The personal bond between President Fox and President George W. Bush further solidifies a maturing relationship in which both countries view each other as partners worthy of respect and consultation. Fortunately, the foreign policy agenda for Mexico in the hemisphere is similar to that of the United States and there is currently no significant issue that would force the partnership to deteriorate. Yet Mexico and the United States share a history filled with animosity and mistrust. The new level of partnership that has developed in recent years must be viewed as fragile and capable of coming undone. ⊕

COMPARISONS

Although Mexico's linkages to the United States serve as one of the fundamental themes of this discussion, it is important to emphasize that Mexico is a Latin American country with much in common with its neighbors to the south. Like its Latin American neighbors, Mexico is working to strengthen its democratic tradition and build its political and governing institutions in ways that enhance democracy. The countries of Central and South America are ever conscious of political developments in Mexico, as they are of how Mexico's government manages economic modernization and implements trade policies. In many respects Mexico has become the focus of attention in Latin America. While many countries in the region see their democratic systems challenged by both military and revolutionary forces and their economies have suffered through huge indebtedness and financial uncertainty, Mexico has moved from a one-party state to a competitive political environment, and the government has successfully avoided an economic downturn.

Mexico's success in avoiding the political instability of countries like Colombia and Venezuela and the economic chaos of Argentina and Uruguay is in part related to its ties with the United States and the fact that its twenty-five-hundred-mile border provides a kind of economic spillover effect that enhances domestic development. Mexico has been more successful than many of the countries in Latin America in transforming its political system, whether by making elections more competitive, professionalizing the leadership of the national bureaucracy, addressing chronic corruption, or restoring confidence in government. Mexican officials have been more adept than other Latin

American leaders in embracing the rules and requirements of the global economy. NAFTA has been a boon to trade with Canada and the United States, and it has had a profound effect on how Mexico does business.

Like its Latin American neighbors, Mexico is haunted by many of the problems that are endemic to the region. Like Latin America, Mexico is a country where revolutionary activity challenges the authority of the government. Mexico is also a country where income inequality could easily foment unrest and weaken the foundations of democracy. Revolution, social unrest, and a collapse of democracy are not imminent in Mexico, but the seeds of political instability are present and cannot be ignored. Mexico wants to become the leader of Latin America and not fall prey to the political and economic problems of its neighbors. But right beneath the surface of politics and the economy lie the seeds that could easily transform Mexico into a troubled nation much like some of its neighbors.

CONCLUSION

The election of Vicente Fox in 2000 inaugurated a new era in Mexico. There are now new faces in government, new policy initiatives before the Mexican Congress, and a new sense of optimism about government's capacity to bring about reform. Mexico is no longer an afterthought of development in the Western Hemisphere. With its oil reserves, the NAFTA agreement, the industrialization of the maquiladoras and Monterrey, and its burgeoning middle class, Mexico has set itself apart from many of its Latin American neighbors and established itself as one of the "breakthrough" countries in the less developed world. Mexicans see themselves as active participants in the new global economy and a country that can no longer be ignored outside the region. Its selection as a member of the United Nations Security Council in 2001 is another example of how Mexico has been transformed.

But as with all transformations, the past remains a powerful counterforce. Mexico remains a poor country, dependent on the United States for the vibrancy of its economy and mired in dangerous social conditions of inequality and injustice. For all the political change brought on by Vicente Fox, the old PRI system remains in place with its corrupt officials, bloated bureaucracy, and inefficient state enterprises. The governing climate has become even more troublesome now that the PRI is in opposition with the capacity to checkmate Fox's programs and create political gridlock. For all the goodwill and optimism that the Fox victory fostered in Mexico, there remains a vast reservoir of skepticism in the country over the prospects of moving from political change to social and economic change. Where the PRI stranglehold on politics allowed them to easily dismiss dissent and public criticism, Fox has little room for error and enormous pressure to produce results. As Fox finishes his *sexenio* in the presidency, Mexicans will be waiting to see whether he was the president who ushered in transformation or merely a slight shift in the mode of governing.

A FEW BOOKS YOU SHOULD READ

Roderic Ai Camp, *Politics in Mexico: The Democratic Transformation* (New York: Oxford University Press, 2002). The most up-to-date examination of Mexican politics and the condition of Mexican democracy.

Wayne Cornelius et al., *Subnational Politics and Democratization in Mexico* (San Diego: Center of U.S.-Mexican Studies, 1999). Essential study of the role of governors and local political party leaders in the development and retardation of democracy.

Jorge Dominguez and Rafael Fernandez de Castro, *The United States and Mexico: Between Partnership and Conflict* (New York: Routledge, 2001). The most recent discussion of the complex issues that unite and divide these two neighbors.

Enrique Krause, *Mexico, Biography of Power: A History of Modern Mexico, 1810–1996* (New York: HarperCollins, 1997). A highly readable account of the evolution and revolution of Mexico and Mexican politics.

Sebastian Rotella, *Twilight on the Line: Underworlds and Politics at the U.S.-Mexico Border* (New York: Norton, 1998). Distressing page turner about the impact of the drug trade on Mexico and the United States.

A FEW WEB SITES YOU SHOULD VISIT

www.mexonline. The most comprehensive search engine for Mexico.

www.utexas.edu/la/mexico. The University of Texas site that is recognized as having the most wide-ranging sources on Mexico and Mexican politics.

www.presidencia.gob.mx. The Web site of the Mexican president; contains not only speeches but updates on public policy issues.

www.mexicool.com. A site that accents Mexican life.

www.unam.mx/voices. A site from the prestigious National Autonomous University of Mexico.

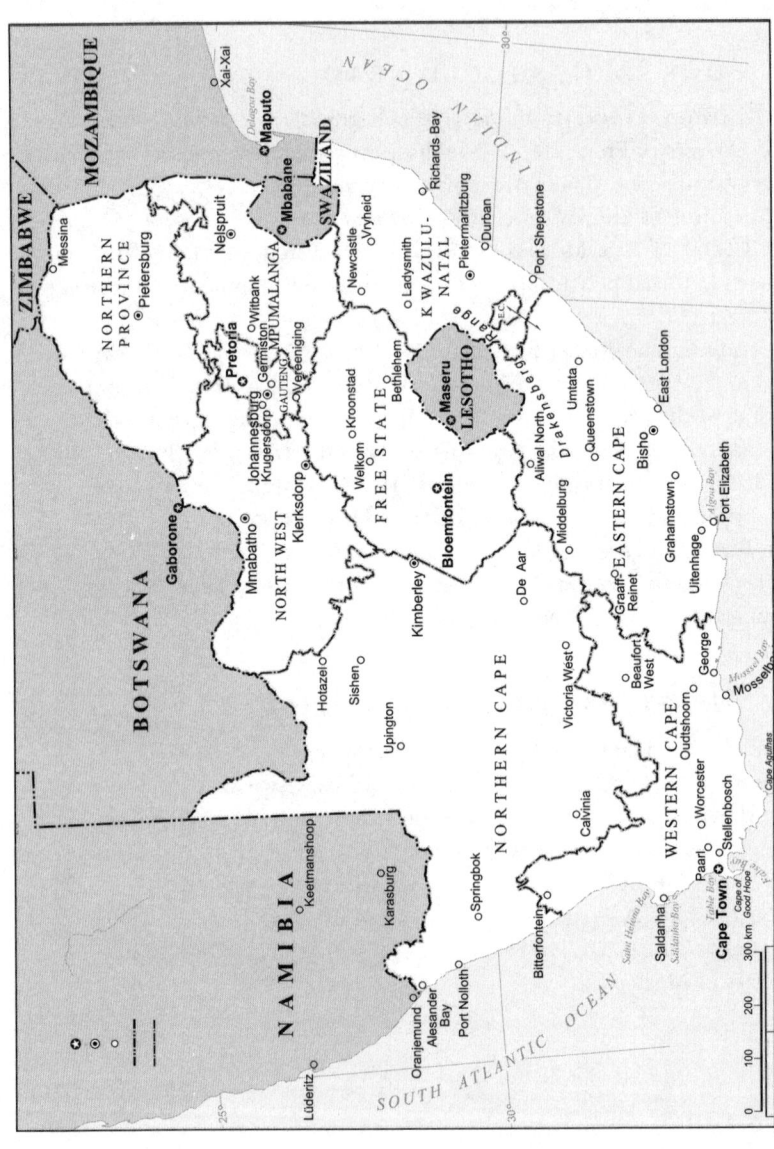

MAP 7.1 Republic of South Africa

7

Republic of South Africa

Data Bank

Area: 470,462 sq. miles
Population: 42 million (1998)
Rural/urban population ratio: 50/50
Ethnic makeup: 78.3 percent black, 12.7 percent white,
    8.8 percent colored, 2.2 percent Asian
Life expectancy: Male, 62 years; female, 68 years
Adult literacy: 85 percent
Form of government: Republic
Head of government: Thabo Mbeki
Per capita income/GDP: $2,200 (2002)
Exports: $32.2 billion; imports $29.5 billion
    (partners: United Kingdom, United States, Germany)
Sources: United Nations and World Bank

SETTING THE SCENE

At his inauguration in 1994 Nelson Mandela, the first black president of South Africa, said the following:

> The time for the healing of the wounds has come. The moment to bridge the chasms that divide us has come. The time to build is upon us . . . we enter into a covenant that we shall build the society in which all South Africans, both black and white, will be able to walk tall, without any fear in their hearts, assured of their inalienable right to human dignity—a rainbow nation at peace with itself and the world.

Mandela's speech was the final chapter in the apartheid era, when the white minority maintained a system of political, economic, and social control while the black majority was subject to laws and procedures that kept them powerless and made them second-class citizens. One year earlier Mandela had been honored for his life and his work against injustice with the Nobel Peace Prize. Mandela shared that prize with F. W. de Klerk, the last prime minister under apartheid, who released him from prison and began dismantling the barriers to racial equality. Mandela's taking the oath of office was not only a personal triumph over oppression but a symbolic event acknowledging that South Africa had started the journey away from its past of racial division and discrimination.

This was a startling reversal of power for a black activist who had spent twenty-seven years in the infamous Robben Island prison on charges of advocating sabotage against the state. Despite enduring the horrors of his imprisonment, Mandela never wavered in his resolve to end apartheid. He became an international hero, celebrity, and moral compass, while the white-dominated South African government became a pariah state that was shunned by the international community. On his release from prison in 1990, Mandela set out immediately to move South Africa toward democratic government. He took command of the antiapartheid party, the African National Congress (ANC), and negotiated with the white majority government to bring an end to apartheid and replace it with a system of free and fair elections, a move that ultimately brought black majority control to South Africa.

Nelson Mandela is no longer the president of South Africa and the infamous apartheid laws that separated whites from blacks are but a sad memory, but the struggle to transform South Africa into a "rainbow nation" based on democracy and equality continues today. The process of shifting from white to black control has forced South Africans to face the fact that holding political power creates new sets of problems requiring strong leadership, skillful compromise, and diplomatic consensus building. Almost immediately after the governmental transition it became obvious that black majority rule engendered resentment among whites who saw their privileged place in South African society threatened. On the other side of the racial equation, blacks in South Africa quickly seized on the change in power to exercise their rights and on many occasions challenged the white establishment.

While the antagonism between newly liberated blacks and the white establishment was not surprising given the years of oppression under apartheid, the reaction from whites led to serious economic problems and growing social tensions. White flight out of South Africa along with capital flight rose dramatically as those who controlled the nation feared becoming targets of black retaliation. Attracting foreign investment was also a problem, with multinational enterprises leery of placing their resources and energy in a country where race hatreds still exist. The most disturbing result of this black-white problem was the attacks against white farmers in the interior regions and random acts of violence against whites, even in their heavily guarded homes. For example, the nation was rocked in 2001 by the savage murder of F. W. de Klerk's wife in her suburban Johannesburg home. These murders, many with racial overtones, have given South Africa the reputation of a nation engulfed in black-white animosity.

As South Africa moves away from the Mandela years, it finds itself facing a reracialization of society. Racial problems and race-based violence are on the increase in South Africa, not only between whites and blacks but also among blacks of varying social classes. Much of the reracialization is the result of income inequality and lack of employment opportunities, but the political leadership in South Africa has also helped fan the flames of division. Current president Thabo Mbeki has made constant reference to "two nations," suggesting that the vast social and economic gulf that exists between the races will prevent them from coming together. Mbeki has been criticized for defining South Africa in purely racial terms and for deepening white fears that racial harmony is unattainable. Mbeki has softened his race-based rhetoric, but fears that deep-seated racial antagonisms are permanent hang over South Africa like a dark cloud.

One of the most visible examples of South Africa's efforts to put to rest its past was the Truth and Reconciliation Commission chaired by Bishop Desmond Tutu. Established in 1995, the commission was convened to examine the human rights abuses that occurred under white rule. Bishop Tutu, a world-renowned symbol of religious opposition to apartheid, viewed the commission as a means of uncovering the details of the oppression that occurred in South Africa. True to his Christian principles, Tutu insisted that the findings lead to a national reconciliation between black and white. Police, military, or government officials found responsible for human rights violations could receive amnesty if they admitted their involvement in human rights abuse and publicly apologized. In 1996 F. W. de Klerk publicly apologized on behalf of his National Party: "We have gone on our knees before God Almighty to pray for His forgiveness. I stand before you today to admit that which was wrong . . . to continue to build bridges in our quest for reconciliation. Reconciliation cannot be achieved unless there is also repentance on all sides. I should like to express my deepest sympathy with all those on all sides who suffered during the conflict."

Although the Truth and Reconciliation Commission mainly focused on white oppression of antiapartheid activists, Bishop Tutu was determined to ensure fairness in this process and demanded that black-against-white oppression also be investigated, even calling Nelson Mandela's wife at the time, Winnie Madikizela-Mandela, to answer charges of murder and torture. When the commission presented its final report to the public in 1998, it documented stories of horrible human rights abuses committed largely by white authorities. But true to his word, Bishop Tutu granted amnesty to 125 officials (although over 7,000 applications were received), leaving the rest to face criminal charges. Although the report caused extensive debate in South African society, Bishop Tutu was adamant in his belief that the only way South Africa could move on after apartheid was to find out the truth of what happened over a thirty-four-year period and then seek ways to attain national forgiveness and reconciliation. As Tutu said at the time, "The truth can be, and often is divisive. However, it is only on the basis of truth that true reconciliation can take place. True reconciliation is not easy, it is not cheap."

Moving beyond a transition of governing power to a national transformation is at once an enormous opportunity and an enormous burden for South Africa. Postapartheid South Africa is a reflection of the racial reality long ignored by the white minority. South Africa is now truly African. Its political leadership and its governing administration are in the hands of officials who represent the majority of citizens. Moreover, its enormous natural resource wealth is now directed by those with roots in South Africa. There is a determination to improve the lives of ordinary citizens and to use the power of the state to close the income and quality-of-life gap that has marginalized millions of people. And, perhaps most importantly, there is a sense of urgency as a nation and a people moving beyond its past and finally charting its own course.

But with every opportunity that freedom and equality afford the South Africans there are burdens to bear. The public policy agenda is brimming with demands for change, but the resources necessary to address these demands are limited. South Africa is a developing nation that has some natural resource advantages over other developing nations, but it remains a nation with serious social and economic impediments. Unlike some its neighbors in Africa, South Africa is a country where hope is not a dream. In many areas of national life progress is being attained and development is occurring. In other areas, unfortunately, South Africa is mired in the Third World condition of despair with scant hope of escaping. This mix of hope and despair defines South Africa today.

RACE AND EMPLOYMENT POLICY

One of the expected developments in postapartheid South Africa was an emphasis on creating job opportunities for blacks. Held back by the white business and professional classes during National Party rule, blacks viewed the ANC's rise to power as a long-awaited opportunity to correct the employment imbalance. For example, in 1994 at the onset of ANC control of government 6 percent of the South African civil service managerial class was black. In the private sector, the percentage of black managers was more difficult to determine but it was believed to be lower than that of the civil service. Faced with such dismal black representation in managerial positions, the Mandela government moved quickly to change the imbalance. In government the percentage of black managers rose to 38 percent by 1997, and in provincial administration it rose to nearly 70 percent. Private sector businesses followed suit by increasing the numbers of blacks in managerial positions in what is believed to be in the 10–20 percent range.

While blacks have moved into midlevel positions in the public and private sectors, government officials contend that racism remains the primary obstacle to a more race-sensitive hiring and job environment. As a result, the government has instituted a number of new laws intended to ensure business compliance with its racial hiring objectives. The Employment Equity Act requires employers to submit annual reports on their efforts to make their workforce "demographically representative." In present-day South Africa "demographically representative" means that businesses must have a staffing mix that is 75 percent black, 52 percent female, and 5 percent disabled. Although employers have the opportunity to justify why they are not in compliance with the legislation, the burden of proof is on the side of the business. If a black candidate for a position charges discrimination in hiring, the business must show why the applicant could not have gained the skills necessary to function in the job. If a business is found to be in violation of the hiring codes, there are large penalties.

The Employment Equity Act was bolstered further in 2000 with a "promotion of equality bill," which bans all forms of discrimination, from race and sex to pregnancy, age, belief, culture, language, and social and economic status. In vague statutory language that has brought opposition from business groups, the legislation prohibits spreading views that might "promote inequality." The law and the broad-based nature of the statutory language means that employees have considerable legal basis for suing their employer or intended employer for discrimination. The law also permits lawyers to accept discrimination cases based on the legislation on a no-win, no-fee basis. Businesses in South Africa are convinced that the legislation will be a boon to lawyers and create a huge explosion of litigation that will cost them large sums of money in an attempt to defend their hiring practices. Many small South African firms are convinced that the legislation will drive them into bankruptcy. Furthermore, reverse discrimination suits are being filed in South African courts as white employees and prospective employees are going to court charging that the new laws are violating the rights of minorities to expect fairness in hiring.

Adjusting to the new reality of black majority rule has turned the employment situation upside down as the government now uses its control to show preferential treatment toward those who suffered discrimination under apartheid. New laws, however, run up against unintended consequences. The efforts to provide blacks with new hiring opportunities have worked among the middle class to the point where there is a shortage of trained black managers and stiff competition by companies to find blacks capable of assuming technical and administrative responsibilities in the workplace. The losers in this national effort to right the wrongs of the past appear to be unskilled blacks who do not possess the educational background necessary to move up the employment ladder. Employment laws and legal guarantees have created a system for ensuring that discrimination against blacks will no longer be an issue in South Africa, which is not to say that all blacks will benefit or that there will not be new employment issues as the white minority encounters new barriers to employment. ⊕

POLITICAL MILESTONES

The historical evolution of South Africa is best understood from two perspectives—the imperialistic designs of the European powers and the desire of white settlers to maintain control of the land, the economy, and the governing structure. Because of its strategic position at the tip of the African continent, South Africa was seen by the world's trading powers as a vital link to the West Indies, in particular Indonesia, and to India and Pakistan. Both the Dutch and the British coveted South Africa as a trading outpost and later a lucrative reservoir of precious metals. But South Africa also was viewed as a rich farming region where Dutch and British settlers could start a new life and own large parcels of land. Concern for the indigenous African tribes was not an issue as the colonists established control of the land and built a white nation on a black continent. South Africa's roots therefore were firmly set as a place where outside domination was the driving force of development and white minority control set the political, economic, and social rules.

In such a race-based environment it was not difficult for South Africa to move toward a political and social system that accented white domination and fostered economic separation. With its abundant resources and personal wealth, South Africa took the path of control and discrimination and created two worlds, one white and rich and the other black and poor. It would take generations for South Africans to reject the concept of a dual society and make the country and its people whole. In the process South Africa became a tragic example of racial segregation, governmental intransigence, and political violence, all in the name of apartheid.

The Boer War

The Dutch founded the Cape Colony (what is today the Western Cape Province) in the 1700s in order to establish a suitable port for trade with the West Indies. By the late 1700s a series of small trading ports and villages had been established. As the Dutch increased their presence in South Africa, the farmers, or Boers, developed the rich land and pushed the indigenous hunters (*khoi*) out. The Boers came to see themselves as the true Africans and any outside settlers as interlopers. Later the British arrived to develop the Cape Colony as a strategic stop in their India trade routes and competed with the Dutch settlers for control of the region. In 1795 the British wrested control of the Cape Colony from the Dutch and set the stage for an extended period of conflict between the two imperialist powers. When the British began sending settlers into the Cape Colony in the early 1800s, it was inevitable that the two countries and their colonists would come to arms.

At first the Dutch challenged the British by staging a number of uprisings, but the Boer leaders decided to move inland away from superior British forces. In 1835 some 12,000 Boers set out on the Great Trek into the Transvaal and the Orange Free State. In an experience reminiscent of the westward movement of pioneers in America, the trekkers encountered harsh conditions and attacks from indigenous tribes such as the Zulus as they sought to establish new communities. A battle with African tribes at the Blood River in 1838, in which the trekkers defeated a larger force of warriors, is memorialized as one of the defining events of the Boer experience. Their decision to move inland proved to be wise, as they prospered away from the coast and the British. Of course indigenous tribes bore the brunt of the new colonization by the Boers. Although the Boers signed land agreements with the tribal chieftains, many of these agreements were broken at the convenience of the land-hungry settlers.

The Great Trek provided the Boers with only temporary control of their destiny. Once diamonds and gold were discovered in South Africa in the late 1880s, the British arrived in waves and reignited tensions with the Dutch settlers. The British governor of the Cape Colony, Cecil Rhodes, encouraged British settlers in 1895 to rise up against the Dutch in Johannesburg and Pretoria and establish complete control of South Africa once and for all. Rhodes and the British high commissioner in the Cape Colony were proponents of imperial control that stretched throughout the African continent from Cairo to South Africa. Rhodes's expansionist actions forced the hand of the Dutch, who feared that the British were poised to destroy their language, traditions, and freedom. President Paul Kruger of the Boer Republic declared war against the British in 1899.

For the next three years the Boers fought the British in a bloody war that claimed thousands of lives, including over 20,000 civilians who were confined in concentration camps to weaken their resolve. The Boer War ended in 1902 with the Boers agreeing to a treaty, although British control of the Boer Republic did not take effect until later. There is evidence that the British were reluctant to establish firm control over the Boer Republic because they felt pangs of conscience for their ferocity in pursuing the Boers and bringing them to submission. The British gained control of the Orange Free State and the Transvaal in 1907. One year later a convention was held in the city of Durban to create a country out of the four colonies. In 1910 the British consolidated the remaining colonies into a dominion creating the Union of South Africa. Strangely, the British were unwilling to follow up their victory over the Boers with administrative control. In effect the Boers were permitted a large measure of self-government in the four colonies of the republic. The Boers, commonly referred to as Afrikaners, were given political rights and moved into positions of governmental authority, while the British shifted their concerns to matters of regional foreign policy and defense. The Afrikaners had indeed lost the battle with the British and were forced to give up formal control of their republic, but eventually they emerged victorious and in control of the political system.

The National Party and the Beginnings of Apartheid

Once the Union of South Africa was formed, it became evident that a gulf was developing between whites of English ancestry and Afrikaners. The English were concentrated in the major urban centers and controlled much of South African business, while the Afrikaners were farmers. The Afrikaners disagreed with the English over issues ranging from preservation of their language and culture to the income inequality that they experienced. The gulf between the English and the Afrikaners widened when blacks were brought in to work in the mines, displacing Afrikaners who had held those jobs for generations. Afrikaners increasingly felt like second-class citizens and took steps to ensure that English domination would not strip them of their identity or their place in the economy. They developed a host of social, educational, economic, and political organizations designed to protect them from the English. Many of these organizations developed a posture that was not only anti-English but anti-black as well. The Afrikaners were turning inward, conscious only of protesting what they felt were threats to their unity as a people.

The backbone of the Afrikaner movement was the National Party, formed in 1914. At first the party built its ideology around cooperation with the

English, but in the 1930s it split. The wing led by Daniel Malan, an un-abashed white supremacist and a vocal spokesman for the Afrikaner cause, became the driving force of Afrikaner politics. During the depression years Malan became an outspoken advocate for employment opportunities for Afrikaners who had lost jobs to the English or to blacks. Malan's organiza-tional skill made the National Party a major political force in South Africa. It played on the fears of the Afrikaner population and their resentment toward the British. The National Party supported Nazi Germany, and many Afrikaners were jailed for publicly taking a position that was contrary to British interests. By the end of World War II the National Party represented a segment of South African society that was at serious odds with the British government and British values.

In 1948 the National Party won the national elections and Daniel Malan became prime minister. The 1948 victory began forty-six years of continuous political control by the National Party, which introduced the apartheid sys-tem. Within years of taking power, Malan and the National Party majority in the legislature passed numerous laws designed to create two societies, one white and privileged and one black and segregated. The leaders of the National Party were convinced that the only way that they could preserve their way of life was to use their political power to limit English influence and completely shut out the black majority from any meaningful role in South African society.

In 1949 the South African government passed the Prohibition of Mixed Marriages Act and one year later the Immorality Act, which outlawed inter-racial marriage and interracial sexual relations. In 1950 the Groups Areas Act was promulgated, which stripped blacks of rights to live in white areas. That act and others passed later established the right of the government to resettle blacks without their permission. In 1953 the government passed the Reservation of Separate Amenities Act, which was the basis for creating sepa-rate facilities for whites and blacks. Finally, in 1959 the Extension of University Education Act was passed, which kept black students from at-tending South Africa's three major universities.

These racist laws and the segregation that occurred as a result were supple-mented by even more egregious violations of basic freedoms and human rights. One example was the so-called pass laws that forced blacks to carry identification papers at all times. The pass laws were used to punish blacks who challenged the apartheid system by denying them work or the privilege to move into white areas of the country. South African police often used the pass laws to intimidate blacks by arbitrarily arresting thousands and detain-ing them for extended periods of time. Everyday harassment by the police using the pass laws fostered intense black opposition to apartheid and frequently led to violence, imprisonment, and death.

The apartheid policies of the National Party moderated somewhat during the late 1950s and early 1960s as the government of Prime Minister Henrik Verwoerd introduced policies that stressed race separation rather than race segregation. The National Party leadership sought to put a more positive face on its racism by establishing separate enclaves in the interior and separate townships outside of the major urban areas. The government provided blacks with land, in effect racial reservations, that was unclaimed by whites for the purposes of forming what were termed "self-governing" homelands. The government encouraged blacks to move to the homelands and establish homes and communities there. The homeland policy was presented to the outside world as a great democratic experiment, when in reality it was just another form of segregation. In the urban areas the government sought to concentrate blacks in large communities such as the Soweto township outside Johannesburg. Again the government presented the townships as separate governing systems, but Soweto and other such communities were nothing more than hastily organized slums designed to keep blacks together and provide the government with the means to better manage the black majority. Soweto at its zenith housed 3 million black South Africans under miserable conditions.

The African National Congress and the Response to Apartheid

As the apartheid system developed in the 1950s and 1960s, the black majority was bound to fight back. The African National Congress (ANC) supplied the political foundation for anti-apartheid. Founded in 1912 as a nonviolent protest party against white rule, the ANC was led by Chief Albert Luthuli, who sought to advance the status of blacks by quietly but firmly working with the established white minority. Luthuli's political activity ultimately led to his banishment to a village in the interior. With Luthuli out of party leadership the ANC swung toward a more militant and leftist ideology. In 1955 the ANC published the Freedom Charter, which established the party as the primary challenger to the authority of the white government. Later the ANC began the Defiance Campaign, a series of highly visible steps designed to show government officials that it would not sit idly by while blacks were harassed, imprisoned, and murdered.

ANC militancy intensified as a result of the Sharpesville massacre in 1960. Black protesters were attacked by police, with over sixty killed. In the protests that followed, ANC leaders were jailed and eventually the ANC was banned. The Sharpesville massacre is often seen as one of the turning points in ANC militancy. Although ANC leaders like Nelson Mandela had already been charged with crimes against the state, after the massacre the party began plotting to overthrow the government and embraced violence as the only means available to rid the country of apartheid. In 1964 Mandela and others were jailed for revolutionary activity. With Mandela in jail and key ANC operatives in exile, the government had struck at the heart of the anti-apartheid movement. But the ANC did not disband or fail to challenge white rule. In fact, the militancy of the ANC intensified as party regulars sabotaged South African military and industrial installations. With assistance from communist countries like the Soviet Union the ANC became an active party of national liberation and took on the ideology and the vision of socialism.

The outlawing of the ANC, the imprisonment of Mandela, and the shift of the party toward leftist revolution placed the primary opposition to white control of South Africa outside the mainstream of national life, but that did not stop others from taking up the gauntlet. One of the most prominent opponents of apartheid outside the ANC was Steve Biko. A former medical student, Biko chafed under the harsh apartheid regime and emerged as the fearless voice of opposition. Biko was one of the key leaders of the Soweto uprisings of June 1976. White police fired on demonstrators in the black township, killing twenty-three people. But protests against the killing exploded and days of rioting ensued. Eventually six hundred people died, and as a result a new generation of anti-apartheid protesters were born. Biko was arrested in 1977 and was tortured and murdered in police custody. Biko became another martyr in the fight against white oppression. His death also helped bring international attention to the human rights violations of the South African government. In response to Biko's death, militant blacks formed the Black Consciousness Movement, which developed into a major opposition force in South Africa. It organized black youth in colleges and high schools and the townships. These militant youths became the foot soldiers in an anti-apartheid campaign that continued into the 1980s, despite frequent attempts by the government to quash the demonstrations and dismantle the movement.

The International Campaign Against Apartheid

The anti-apartheid movement in South Africa gained the attention of the international community. At first, major world powers like the United States and Great Britain were reluctant to come out against apartheid, other than to criticize human rights abuse. Opposition to apartheid began to gather momentum when many universities in the United States were pressured by the student population to divest themselves of stock in companies that either did business with South Africa or maintained a corporate presence in South Africa. Divestment became a rallying cry for students and critics of apartheid, and eventually a set of guidelines was formulated that many companies followed. The divestment campaign forced a number of companies to either cease their contacts with South Africa or take measures to pressure the apartheid government to bring racial reform to the country. As many as two hundred U.S. corporations left South Africa by the early 1980s as a result of the divestment campaign. Major international banks also joined the campaign against South Africa. In 1985 major banks refused new loans to the government, a decision that stung the political leadership.

The pressure against the South African government spread to other areas of national life such as athletics. During the 1970s and 1980s key international sports federations instituted sanctions against South Africa. These sanctions led to boycotts of South African participation in major sporting events. South Africa was banned from participation in the Olympic Games and in sporting events close to the heart of the average citizen such as soccer, rugby, and cricket. Certainly not as influential as the divestment campaign, the sports sanctions reminded South African athletes and fans that there was a price to pay for living in a country that harbored racist policies.

The international campaigns against apartheid eventually forced the hand of governments that had been reluctant to isolate South Africa. On the continent, the South African government was pressured by neighboring black-governed states, especially the Organization of African Unity (OAU). Although the OAU did not possess as much clout as the major industrial powers, it nonetheless provided a regional forum against apartheid. Later the British Commonwealth came out against apartheid and placed pressure on the government in London to take more active measures against South Africa. In 1974 the United Nations stripped South Africa of its membership in the General Assembly and in 1977 voted to impose an arms embargo against it. The United States followed suit when the Carter administration publicly supported majority rule. Later the U.S. Congress overrode a veto by President Ronald Reagan to establish economic sanctions against South Africa when it passed the Comprehensive Anti-Apartheid Act. In Great Britain Prime Minister Margaret Thatcher reluctantly followed similar pressure from Parliament.

By the late 1980s South Africa was increasingly a pariah state with few supporters. The major world powers had taken steps to distance themselves from the government and its apartheid policies. More importantly, the South African government was beginning to feel the pain associated with the loss of the foreign corporate presence and corporate investment. As the Cold War came to an end and the world began to change in countless ways, South

African leaders came to the inevitable conclusion that they had to reenter the international community. The only way to do that was to begin dismantling apartheid.

F. W. de Klerk and the Transition from Apartheid

The beginning of the end of apartheid in South Africa occurred in the mid-1980s with a series of secret meetings between representatives of the African National Congress and a mixed group of Afrikaners, clergy, members of the security sector, and the business community. The white leadership grudgingly came to realize that it must establish some sort of accommodation with the ANC or face further isolation and widening protests. Both sides wanted key concessions in order to achieve a breakthrough agreement. The government was adamant in demanding that the ANC renounce violence, while the ANC insisted that Nelson Mandela be released from prison and resume his leadership of the party. Although these talks, which at one stage involved Mandela and South African President P. W. Botha, did not yield an agreement, they nevertheless provided momentum for a process that would ultimately lead to an end of apartheid.

The critical juncture in the negotiations between the ANC and the government came when President Botha suffered a stroke in 1989 and was replaced by F. W. de Klerk. De Klerk, although himself a staunch Afrikaner, was more amenable to attaining a settlement with the ANC and more willing to release Mandela from prison. In 1986 Mandela was moved from Robben Island and spent the next four years under a form of house arrest and participated in negotiations with the government. During that time Mandela met frequently with white officials to discuss the terms of a settlement. Much of the disagreement centered around Mandela's vision of a power-sharing arrangement with the Afrikaners. The white minority feared that a government including blacks, especially blacks from the hated ANC, would strip them of their power and their unique culture.

In February 1990 President de Klerk announced to the South African legislature that he had released Nelson Mandela from prison and that the African National Congress would no longer be banned. Nelson Mandela emerged from imprisonment as the de facto leader of South Africa. Mandela's release caused celebration in South Africa as blacks got a glimpse of the man who spent the better part of his adult life behind bars as a symbol of resistance to apartheid. Mandela's release, though a moment of high drama and inspiration, was only the beginning of a long process of bringing a formal end to white majority rule and apartheid. For three more years both sides engaged in intense and often heated negotiations. The formal structure of the negotiation was conducted through the Conference on a Democratic South Africa (CODESA), but the critical negotiations occurred between Mandela and de Klerk, two leaders who were willing to talk but harbored deep-seated feelings of mistrust.

The confrontations and violence in the period after Mandela's release cast doubt on the ability of the freed black leader to bring an end to apartheid. Mandela was forced to walk a fine line in the negotiations. As a rebel leader, his effort to bring an end to apartheid by talking with the government and seeking common ground was viewed with suspicion within the ANC and mistrust by the South African government. As a symbol of hope in a new South Africa, moderates, both black and white, were counting on him to bring an end to racialist policies in their country. Gradually the negotiation process began to bear fruit. The white government started to rescind key statutes of apartheid. In 1990 the Separate Amenities Act was repealed, and in 1991 the Lands Act was done away with. With momentum for reform established, both sides were able to reach an accommodation that resulted in a new constitution in 1993 and the promise of the first fully open and multiracial elections one year later.

In the national elections in 1994 the African National Congress with Nelson Mandela as its leader won a crushing victory. The ANC received 63 percent of the vote (a record 22 million South Africans cast their ballots, many voting for the first time) and captured 252 of the 400 seats in the legislature. More importantly Nelson Mandela was chosen president of South Africa by the ANC-dominated legislature. In an effort to reinforce the concept of power sharing, Mandela named de Klerk deputy president. De Klerk remained as deputy president until a new constitution was written by the ANC-dominated legislature in 1996. At that time de Klerk resigned from his position citing the need for an active opposition. With the departure of de Klerk and the National Party from government, South Africa became a nation fully controlled by the black majority. Apartheid had ended.

The ANC victory and Nelson Mandela's ascension to the presidency mark one of the most significant governing transitions in modern time. After spending decades on the fringes of politics and being the target of government-sponsored repression, the ANC and Nelson Mandela were now entrusted with leading South Africa. But victory and the creation of black majority rule carried with it an enormous burden. The new power elite in South Africa would be charged with not only the endless tasks of national development but also the challenge of dealing with the white minority, who were anxious, if not fearful, about their status in a radically different social and political environment. Realizing Nelson Mandela's dream of a "rainbow nation" would be daunting.

Timeline

1652	Jan van Riesbeeck establishes Dutch settlement
1795	British take over Cape Colony from Dutch
1820	British send settlers to South Africa
1835–1840	Great Trek
1838	Battle of Blood River between British and Afrikaners
1867	Diamond mining begins
1886	Gold mining begins
1899–1902	Boer War
1910	Union of South Africa formed
1912	African National Congress created
1948	National Party takes power
1960	Sharpesville massacre
1964	Nelson Mandela imprisoned
1977	United Nations embargo
1986	Apartheid laws abolished
1990	Nelson Mandela released from Robben Island prison
1994	Nelson Mandela becomes president of South Africa
1996	Truth and Reconciliation Commission established
1999	Thabo Mbeki elected president

GUN CONTROL POLICY

South Africa is awash in guns. After years of paying the price in gun-related deaths, the government is taking bold action to curb gun ownership and punish those who use guns in a crime. About 3.5 million South Africans own licensed firearms, but the number of illegal weapons is estimated to exceed 4 million. In 1998, before the South African government passed sweeping gun control legislation, 12,298 deaths were linked to firearms—half of all murders in the country. The explosion of guns and gun deaths in South Africa is a carryover from the apartheid era when guns were regularly smuggled into the country by anti-apartheid forces or distributed by whites with hopes of fomenting black-on-black conflict. Today guns are at the center of the crime wave that has settled into South African national life.

In 1999 the South African government decided to take action against gun use by proposing sweeping legislation. One year later the Firearms Control Act was passed by parliament, despite heavy opposition from gun owners. The act requires gun owners to relicense their weapons every five years. Jail sentences of up to twenty-five years are established for those who possess a firearm illegally. Gun owners are required to take competency tests and a limit of one gun per owner is set. There are also provisions in the act that give police greater powers to prosecute illegal gun owners. The Firearms Control Act replaces a weak set of laws that had been largely ignored or avoided by bribing officials. In 2001 the South African government went one step further by signing a protocol with thirteen other African countries that seeks to control the flow of illegal arms in the region and provides sanctions against countries that violate arms embargoes. The protocol prohibits civilian use of light military weapons, compels member states to monitor gun licenses, and restricts the number of gun owners. South Africa took the lead in pushing for the regional protocol, with Safety and Security Minister Steve Tshwete urging his counterparts in the region to take action against "the biggest menace in our society."

The Firearms Control Act has not been universally embraced. The head of the South African Gunowners Association complained that the legislation did nothing to address the criminal use of firearms, but merely punished law-abiding gun owners. Gun owners, particularly white farmers, fear that the law will hamper their ability to defend themselves from what they view as threats from the black majority. Moreover, the pro-gun lobby is convinced that the South African police will not have the manpower to adequately administer the relicensing process. Their answer to the gun problem is more police and stiffer punishments for those who use a gun in the commission of a crime or possess an illegal weapon. On the other side of the issue is the Gun-Free South Africa group, which hailed the legislation as a necessary step to reduce the enormous growth in murders using firearms. Minister Tshwete echoed the Gun-Free South Africa position by stating that the Firearms Control Act will provide "a decisive blow to violent criminals who have terrorized law-abiding citizens for too long."

The debate over gun control in South Africa mirrors the arguments heard in the United States. But in South Africa the use of weapons to settle minor disputes has become so serious that the government felt only strong regulatory measures and a regional approach could stem the tide of gun-related murders. There are some signs that gun-related murders decreased when the Firearms Control Act was passed, but the debate over relicensing and limitation on gun ownership continues in South Africa. As with many public policies, race and racial animosity have become part of the subtext of the debate as whites fear the loss of protection against perceived threats from blacks, while blacks blame whites for creating the gun culture that was fostered by apartheid and opposition to black majority rule. ⊕

FORMAL GOVERNMENT

South African government is founded on the constitution of 1996, which establishes the nation as a constitutional and republican state. In the preamble to the constitution it is made clear that South Africa is intent on building a nation that is democratic and based on principles of social justice and equality. The preamble sets out four goals:

- Heal the divisions of the past and establish a society based on democratic values, social justice, and fundamental human rights
- Improve the quality of life of all citizens and free the potential of each person
- Lay the foundations for a democratic and open society in which government is based on the will of the people and every citizen is equally protected by law
- Build a united and democratic South Africa able to take its rightful place as a sovereign state in the family of nations

Despite its noble goals, the 1996 constitution was the result of a contentious process in the Constitutional Assembly charged with drafting the document. The ANC-dominated Assembly encountered stiff opposition from its political enemy, the Inkatha Freedom Party (IFP), which was concerned with incorporating federalism into the constitution as well as the ANC's refusal to submit the issue to international arbitration. The IFP position on federalism versus unitary control centered around local control of the KwaZulu-Natal province and the fear of IFP leader Chief Mangosuthu Buthelezi that the ANC government would dominate the provinces and weaken provincial power contenders like the IFP. Other issues also divided the Constitutional Assembly, including protecting property rights in a land reform process, legitimizing the death penalty, establishing the proper balance of freedom of speech and punishment for racial hate speech, and housing of the parliament in Cape Town or moving it to Pretoria or Bloemfontein.

The constitution also established a Constitutional Court that was responsible for protecting stated rights and determining whether actions by the state were in accordance with constitutional provisions. The Constitutional Court played a key role in the formation of the 1996 constitution when it rendered a decision stating that some provisions of the constitution did not comply with principles established in the interim constitution of 1993. As a result, a second version of the constitution was drafted and the amended text was accepted. In its role as protector of rights, the Constitutional Court was given the responsibility of securing a broader range of individual and group guarantees than in most countries. In the South African constitution there is a human dignity provision, a right to the protection of unique languages (eleven languages are given official status), and guarantees regarding property. Most significantly, the constitution provides for broad protection of individual rights (both black and white) in large part because of the legacy of apartheid and the failure of white governments to provide basic human rights. Amending the constitution requires a two-thirds vote of the National Assembly. The two-thirds vote requirement forces members of the National Assembly to achieve consensus on constitutional changes and build coalitions with other political parties.

The South African constitution also requires that legislation be passed to expand the rights guaranteed in the original document. In 2000, for example, the Promotion of Equality and Prevention of Unfair Discrimination Act was passed in order to give full meaning to the intent of chapter 9 of the constitution, which establishes and governs institutions that strengthen constitutional democracy in South Africa. Implementing chapter 9 of the constitution also led to the formation of the Human Rights Commission, which was charged with protecting, monitoring, and assessing the observance of human rights. Chapter 9 led to the formation of the Commission for the Promotion and Protection of the Rights of Cultural, Religious, and Linguistic Communities for the express purpose of promoting "tolerance and the basis of equality, non-discrimination and free association." Clearly the 1996 constitution provides the foundation for the development of institutions to ensure that South Africa sustains its commitment to equality and fairness and never returns to the days of apartheid.

The 1996 constitution made its most significant departure in governance from the past by moving away from a parliamentary system and introducing a hybrid form of a presidential system. Since 1961 South Africa has had a president but that position was primarily ceremonial. With the 1996 constitution the president is still connected to the legislature in that the National Assembly chooses the chief executive, but the South African president was given significant powers in the constitution, in a manner similar to the president of France. While in office President Mandela chose not to exercise exclusive presidential power but shifted policymaking responsibilities to the deputy president, Thabo Mbeki. Once Mbeki became president, he reasserted executive power and centralized authority in his own hands. Despite the expanded powers of the current president, the constitution limits the chief executive to no more than two five-year terms. The president is also subject to a vote of no confidence by the national legislature. The president is assisted by three deputy presidents from each racial grouping: white, black, and mixed (coloured).

One of the more interesting aspects of the South African executive is the seat of governmental power. By law South Africans shuttle their government between the administrative capital in Pretoria, where the president resides, and the legislative capital in Cape Town, where the parliament resides. When parliament is in session, the president leaves Pretoria along with his cabinet ministers and other bureaucrats and travels to Cape Town, only to make the trek back to Pretoria when the legislative session is over. The South African judiciary, including the Constitutional Court, is situated at Bloemfontein, which is midway between Pretoria and Cape Town.

The president of South Africa determines the size and scope of the cabinet. Currently the Mbeki cabinet consists of twenty-seven ministers. It is dominated by ANC colleagues, but the Inkatha Freedom Party holds a few portfolios, including the Home Affairs Ministry headed by Chief Buthelezi. The cabinet reflects some of the unique characteristics of South Africa as a developing nation. The ministries of agriculture and land affairs reflect issues related to the former homelands, while provincial affairs and constitutional development ministries are concerned with issues relating to the power struggle between federalists and supporters of unitary government. There is also a cabinet ministry of welfare and population development that directs South Africa's efforts to contain population growth and respond to the pressures of a growing population on economic growth and social cohesion.

The core of the South African governing system is the parliament. It consists of the National Assembly and the National Council of Provinces, which replaced the Senate under the former constitution. The National Assembly is made up of four hundred members who are elected through a system of proportional representation for terms of five years. Two hundred of the members are elected by proportional representation from national party lists, and the remaining two hundred are elected in a similar fashion from regional lists. The National Assembly is the primary lawmaking body within South Africa. Because of its power to elect the president, it also assumes the responsibility of overseeing executive decisions and actions. The National Council of Provinces (NCOP), with fifty-four permanent members (six from each of the nine provinces) and thirty-six special delegates (four from each province), has a different legislative responsibility. As envisioned by the Constitutional Assembly, the NCOP is charged with providing a voice for the nine provinces and using its position in the legislative system to protect the interests of the provinces. As structured, the South African legislative process places lawmaking power in the National Assembly, although the NCOP can introduce legislation that affects the provinces. The National Assembly controls money bills and can reject amendments attached to legislation by the NCOP. The NCOP was a constitutional means of placating the IFP and provincial chiefs who feared that the ANC would dictate policy without considering local interests.

To further enhance communication between the central government and the provinces, the constitution mandated the establishment of a house of traditional leaders at the provincial and national level. The National House of Traditional Leaders is a 150-member body that advises the national government on customary law of various tribal groups and when necessary conducts its own investigations regarding issues related to traditional leadership and tribal groups. To assist the provincial officials and National Houses of Traditional Leaders, the government has established a chief directorate, which is responsible for determining compensation for the traditional leaders and providing them with the means through which they can better deal with local problems best handled through tribal channels rather than through central government intervention.

A key structure of South African government and the source of great debate during the Constitutional Assembly was provincial governance. One of the first steps taken by the constitution makers was to abolish the four "independent" and six "self-governing" black homelands. The homelands were a racially transparent attempt by white government during apartheid to provide the semblance of democratic governance for the black majority. In their place the constitution replaced the four so-called historic provinces (Cape, Natal, Orange Free State, and Transvaal) and created nine new provinces: Eastern Cape, Eastern Transvaal, KwaZulu-Natal, Northern Cape, Northern Transvaal, Northwest, Orange Free State, Pretoria-Witwatersrand-Vereeniging (PWV), and Western Cape. Each of these provinces is governed by a legislature of 30–100 members and an executive council, which consists of a premier and various members. The premier is elected by the provincial legislature. The provincial legislature has the power to form a constitution for the province provided that two-thirds of the membership agree (although the constitution must not depart from the national constitution and is subject to review by the Constitutional Court). In 1999 President Mbeki created a permanent forum in conjunction with the provincial premiers. The forum is designed to enhance communication and cooperation and improve integration of national policies in the provinces.

The South African governmental system reflects both its racial past and its racial future. The principles, which serve as the foundation for the governing structure, reveal a nation that is committed to eradicating past injustices and dedicated to establishing a political culture that fosters harmony in a multiracial society. The executive-legislative relationship is constructed in a way that balances power between a president with substantial governing capacity and a legislature that possesses the ability to pass laws and remove the chief executive by vote of no confidence. The prominent Constitutional Court gives South African government a strong legal force that guarantees the constitution will be a "living" document capable of interpreting and applying the law. The federal system, with the nine provinces exercising varying degrees of autonomy and the traditional leaders given a role protecting customary law and practices, creates a workable balance between the center and the periphery.

"Workable balance" serves as the governing rationale of South African government. After decades of one-sided rule by the white minority and a governing system that was fashioned with the express purpose of limiting the power of the black majority, the new leaders of South Africa insisted that the public decisionmaking process would be open to all and representative of national diversity. Yet in the postapartheid period the South African government has been dominated by one political party and one political leadership, the African National Congress. Critics point out that the white minority with its narrow governing structure was replaced by the dominant ANC with its black vision of a new South Africa. While there is an element of truth in this observation, South African government is structured in a manner that over time offers racial groupings, traditional leaders, political parties, and civil society much broader opportunities to participate in national political life.

POINT OF FACT
The South African constitution is one of the longest in the world, with 243 sections.

Constitutional Principles

Language is an important part of South African life and is prominently discussed in the constitution. Section 6 of the South African constitution states the following:

1. The official languages of the Republic are Sepedi, Sesothok Setswana, siSwati, Tshivenda, Xitsonga, Afrikaans, English, isiNdebele, isiXhosa and isiZulu.
2. Recognizing the historically diminished use and status of the indigenous languages of our people, the state must take practical and positive measures to elevate the status and advance the use of these languages.

The national government and provincial government may use any official language for the purposes of government, taking into account usage, practicality, expense, regional circumstances, and the balance of the needs and preferences of the population as a whole or in the province concerned. But the national government and each provincial government must use at least two official languages.

THE FUTURE OF KWAZULU-NATAL

KwaZulu-Natal province is home to over 4 million of the 8 million Zulu people. Tucked into the northeastern corner of South Africa, KwaZulu-Natal is a rich agricultural region with great potential. But KwaZulu-Natal has the highest poverty level of any province in South Africa and has been the hardest hit by the HIV/AIDS epidemic. The province is engulfed in a long-running feud between Chief Buthelezi, the primary political figure in KwaZulu-Natal, and the ANC. At issue is local autonomy, and Buthelezi has repeatedly threatened to pull the province out of the South African nation and set up a separate sovereign entity. While the tensions between Buthelezi and the ANC have subsided in recent years, there remains the possibility that South Africa may face a crisis of nationhood similar to Canada's with Quebec province.

As the politics of local control are played out in Johannesburg, the provincial government and the people of KwaZulu are engaged in a concerted effort to revive their economy and deal with a health crisis that many predict will cut their population as much as 25 percent by 2016. At the center of the problems facing KwaZulu-Natal is poverty. Nearly 40 percent of the households in the province are below the poverty level for South Africa. Seventy-two percent of the children under five years live in poverty. Because of high unemployment rates, each working resident of the province supports as many as five other people, creating a vast network of dependency. This endemic poverty has bred widespread crime as the poor prey on the poor and government officials are engaged in corrupt practices that further weaken the authority of the public sector. Add to this the HIV/AIDS crisis, which has attacked over 35 percent of the population, and KwaZulu-Natal is the most troubled of South Africa's provinces.

The political and government leadership of KwaZulu-Natal is engaged in a massive effort to strengthen the economy, which is hoped to have a spillover effect on unemployment, crime, and violence. One of the most highly touted efforts to revitalize KwaZulu-Natal is the development of small, micro, and medium enterprises as engines of economic growth and employment. The government has created a relationship with the Durban Manufacturing Advice Center (DUMACO) to provide those in the province with assistance in forming enterprises, particularly for export. To enhance the prospects of new entrepreneurs the government is following an aggressive road-building program to link rural communities with Durban and other population hubs. The government is convinced that if KwaZulu-Natal is to benefit from the global economy it must be integrated with the major urban areas.

A concerted effort is under way to attract foreign investment to the province. Foreign capital has been declining in recent years in large part as a result of crime and the HIV/AIDS epidemic. Government officials are working to convince South Africans to invest in businesses in the province and reduce the capital flight that has beset the economy. Two new initiatives designed to attract foreign capital and simultaneously revitalize the economy target tourism and gambling. The King Shaka International Airport, currently under construction, will open the region to tourist flights from abroad. A gambling board was appointed by the government and interest is growing in the development of new casinos. Government leaders have stated that gambling is a high priority in its development plans.

The economic revival of KwaZulu-Natal is essential from a development and of course a human standpoint, but it is viewed by many in South Africa as a critical ingredient in lessening the tensions between the provincial government and the ANC-controlled national government. South Africans are seeking to avoid an economically and socially disintegrating KwaZulu-Natal province, which would be a prime breeding ground for separatists. If KwaZulu-Natal declines further and separation becomes a reality, South Africa will face a crisis of major proportions. ⊕

THE CITIZEN AND THE STATE

The first step in defining the relationship between the citizen and the state in South Africa is to answer the question, Who are the South Africans? South Africa is a multiracial nation dominated by blacks; nevertheless, it has substantial populations of other racial groups. At present South Africa comprises 75 percent black/African, 13.6 percent white, 8 percent coloured, and 2.6 percent Indian/Asian. While much of the focus in South Africa has been on the black majority and the white minority, the coloured and Indian/Asian segments of society play a prominent role in the economy and in politics. The coloured or mixed-raced South Africans reside in a kind of no-man's-land. Because they are neither black nor white they do not play a prominent role in national politics. Yet because they make up 8 percent of the population, the coloureds have gained influence in provincial politics. Many coloureds gravitate toward the white minority and have in recent elections supported the New National Party. The attraction of the coloureds to white-dominated parties is based on a fear that the black majority government will not protect their property rights and will see them as a mere racial extension of the Afrikaners. The Indian/Asian population traces its roots to the slaves who were brought to South Africa to cut sugar cane. Over time the Indians became the small shopkeepers and merchants of South Africa and have paid little attention to national politics. Their numbers are still small enough that they are not a factor in the national political equation.

The racial makeup of South Africa can also be viewed from several other vantage points. Perhaps most importantly, the black population is increasing at rates in the 2–3 percent range, while the white population is experiencing less dramatic increases. Consequently, the black majority is deepening in South Africa, while the white minority is becoming less prominent. As a result, whites are increasingly expressing concerns over their status in society and their ability to protect their culture and their economic and political interests. One sign of this concern showed up in a 1997 public opinion poll, which found that only 58 percent of whites were willing to support the concept of "one, united South Africa out of all the different groups who live there." Eighty-seven percent of blacks, 94 percent of coloureds, and 95 percent of Indians supported an inclusive definition of national identity. The survey also found that whites, coloureds, and Indians perceive their racial group as facing unfair treatment by the black majority government. All three minority groups stated that they had experienced a declining level of influence over governmental affairs since the blacks took power in 1994.

Nelson Mandela's dream of forming a "rainbow nation" has had only limited success. During his time as president, Mandela publicly announced his goal to establish a nation that accented reconciliation rather than retribution. Mandela made it clear early in his administration that he would not tolerate a wholesale dismissal of Afrikaner civil servants. Even police and security forces, who were often the source of repression against blacks, were permitted to remain in their jobs. Moreover, Mandela was conscious of symbolic acts of reconciliation such as his much publicized decision not to ban rugby (a largely Afrikaner sport that was segregated) and instead to make an appearance at the World Cup final match in 1995 wearing the jersey of the championship South African team. The act of wearing a rugby jersey at a white-dominated sporting event may have been the high point of Mandela's "rainbow nation" crusade.

Since Mandela left office in 1996 and Thabo Mbeki took over the presidency, progress in achieving the "rainbow nation" has been difficult. Mbeki has taken a different view toward race relations and the role of government in righting the wrong created by apartheid. The view among whites, coloureds, and Indians that their place in South African society has weakened under black majority rule is often connected to the public statements of President Mbeki. On numerous occasions Mbeki linked whites to racism and made broad claims that "racism remains ingrained across all sectors of South African society." Facing extensive criticism from the white community for fueling racial discord, Mbeki backtracked somewhat with a series of speeches in which he stated that whites had been "working very hard" to make a success of the country and that "their good example" should be followed. Despite Mbeki's recent conciliatory tone toward whites, they are concerned about being painted as racists and as the cause of South Africa's inability to become an inclusive society.

The reracialization of South Africa and the growing unease among the country's minority groups toward the black majority government must be balanced by examples of a broad democratic consensus and a commitment among the political elite to make democracy an effective form of governance. South Africans solidly support the electoral process. In the 1999 national legislative elections, 89 percent of registered voters turned out. Participation among racial minorities was high. White turnout, for example, was 80 percent and Indian participation was equal to that of the black turnout. Many expected that participation would drop off after the 1994 election, but enthusiasm for democracy has remained. The turnout of South African voters in 1999 was impressive in that the election was a culmination of a campaign that at times was highly charged and occasionally violent. There is, however, cause for concern regarding the long-term commitment of the South African people to democratic participation. From the 89 percent voter turnout in the 1999 legislative elections, the turnout for South Africa's municipalities in 2000 dropped to less than 50 percent. Although municipal elections do not provide the same intensity as national elections, the heavy drop-off was viewed with considerable concern.

While Mandela stressed the importance of using democracy to end apartheid, Mbeki has worked to convince South Africans that democracy can be the source of economic development and the means through which deep income disparity between social classes can be eradicated. There has been much talk in the Mbeki administration of delivering results and tying those results to democratic governance. Mbeki wants his government to set an example by responding to electoral support from the voters with effective programs that address serious social and economic problems.

The social contract between government and the people was severely weakened during the apartheid era. This breakdown lingered into the Mandela presidency and now the Mbeki presidency with the perception that government is unresponsive and that grassroots viewpoints are systematically ignored. One result of this unresponsiveness is an epidemic of noncompliance by the citizenry as taxes are left unpaid, crimes go unreported, and laws regulating corruption are dismissed. The Mbeki administration has by no means transformed South African government into a responsive channel for grassroots demands, but at least there is official recognition that government must lead the way in making democracy a two-way experiment.

Mbeki has sought to inculcate nation-building principles that are not commonly stressed by leaders anxious to advance a development agenda. Mbeki talks about corporate responsibility, quality of life, and social mobility and directs his rhetoric at white business executives and landowners. He is convinced that whites need to move beyond standard economic development goals of growth, currency stabilization, and trade balances and address the impact of globalization and the market economy on the black working class. In his rush to deal with the huge income gap between white and black and between affluent and poor blacks, Mbeki has challenged the white business community to recognize inequality (and its racial connections) as the top economic development priority and to take bold steps to reduce the gap between rich and poor.

To place his mark on citizen-state relations, Mbeki in 2000 supported the "Home for All" campaign. The campaign was based on remarks made by former ANC head Chief Luthuli in 1962, that South Africa "is not yet a home for all her sons and daughters . . . there remains before us the building of a new land, a home for people who are black, white, brown, from the ruins of the old narrow groups, a synthesis of the rich cultural strains which we have inherited." The core of the Home for All campaign is the declaration of commitment, a statement that white South Africans are asked to sign. The declaration recognizes that "racist attitudes of white superiority and black inferiority continue to shape our lives, communities and institutions." White signers of the declaration in effect acknowledge that as a racial group they have benefited from apartheid and that centuries of racial inequality must be eliminated, but not by words alone. The Home for All campaign seeks to move beyond the declaration to the formation of a development and reconciliation fund that will pool resources to aid in breaking down the social and economic barriers that separate whites from blacks.

President Mbeki has also sought to address the legacy of apartheid through the educational system. At a major educational conference in Cape Town in 2000, Mbeki talked about the importance of "Saamtrek" or "drawing together" as a basis for fostering a new social and political culture in South African schools. Mbeki seeks to establish core values that accent the commonalities of the South African people rather than their racial differences. To achieve this, Mbeki used the conference to begin the process of debating such issues as oaths of allegiance in schools and discussion of the character of patriotism in postapartheid South Africa. While the search for common values through the educational system has been viewed as essential in achieving a "drawing together," whites and opponents of the ANC government are wary of oaths of allegiance and redefinitions of patriotism, which may serve to divide racial groups rather than bring about a commonality.

The future of race relations and the strengthening of democratic governance in South Africa will depend in large part on the further development of civil society. South Africa prides itself on the depth of the groups, associations, and institutions that form civil society and has relied on the various segments of civil society to form a political culture and a political process in which racial tolerance and democracy can flourish. As a result of the resistance movement against apartheid in the 1970s and 1980s, supporters of democracy formed civic organizations, professional bodies, social movements of women, youth, and students, religious organizations, traditional leadership, trade unions, traders associations, cultural and sporting bodies, and nongovernmental service organizations. Although groups such as the Black Consciousness Movement led the way in galvanizing popular opposition to apartheid, civil society was a rich mix of organizations. Traditional institutions such as the Anglican Church and certain factions of the Dutch Reformed Church became highly visible proponents of a democratic solution to ending apartheid. A number of nongovernmental organizations, for example, the National Business Initiative, participated in the transition period from apartheid to democracy. External funding sources such as the Ford Foundation provided seed money to begin the formation of grassroots groups. Together these organizations laid the groundwork for a civil society system that pressured the white minority government to end apartheid while creating the environment for a peaceful transition from apartheid to democracy.

Today there is renewed emphasis on expanding civil society in South Africa to move beyond racial issues and democratization and include responding to current problems such as crime, corruption, women and child abuse, and HIV/AIDS. At a conference in 2001 that kicked off the civil society initiative, leaders from a wide range of civil organizations discussed the next steps to deepening the relationship between citizen and state. There was concern among civil organizations that in the postapartheid era government and nongovernment were blurred. Many leaders of civil organizations feared being coopted by the government and losing their influence. One joke in governing circles is that NGO now stands for "next government official." There is thus a major debate in civil society on the most effective strategies to ensure that the "dual power" of government and civil organizations that existed in the fight against apartheid can be revitalized in the new democratic South Africa.

One of the concluding themes of the civil society initiative that is likely to serve as the foundation for the future relationship between citizen and the state was the importance of organizing South African youths and convincing them of the merits of racial harmony and democratic governance. Organizations such as the South African Youth Council and the National Youth Service Programme have been hailed by the government as models of youth participation in national development. These organizations have linked up South African young people with over 260 community-based projects at hospitals, schools, police stations, and courthouses. These organizations aim to convince young people of the value of serving the nation and the importance of working with the government to solve national problems. South African political leaders and civil society representatives are convinced that partnerships between the government and organizations, particularly among the young, will help to lessen racial animosity and provide the means to enhance the effectiveness of democratic government.

POINT OF FACT

Female parliamentarians in South Africa have developed the South African women's budget, which is designed to "highlight the gender dimensions of the government's budget to ensure that gender equity is better served by the budget process and allocations."

Electoral Data

The June 2, 1999, election for the National Assembly yielded the following results:

African National Congress	66.4 percent
Democratic Party	9.6 percent
Inkatha Freedom Party	8.6 percent
New National Party	6.9 percent
United Democratic Movement	3.4 percent
African Christian Democratic Party	1.4 percent
Freedom Front	0.8 percent
United Christian-Democratic Party	0.8 percent
Pan-African Congress	0.7 percent
Federal Alliance	0.5 percent
Minority Front	0.3 percent
Afrikaner Unity Movement	0.3 percent
Azanian People's Organization	0.2 percent

EDUCATION REFORM POLICY

One of the most significant changes brought about by the demise of apartheid is found in the area of education. Under white minority rule, South African blacks were given an education that suited the needs of the ruling class. So-called Bantu education prepared blacks for menial jobs rather than the demands of a global economy. Worse yet, until 1995, 70 percent of blacks received no education, thereby being sentenced to a life with little opportunity for advancement. Under the new constitution, education is compulsory and universal. Furthermore, the governments of both Nelson Mandela and Thabo Mbeki have committed over 20 percent of the national budget for education, thus guaranteeing that education will rank high on the list of national priorities.

But government commitment and budgetary resources are not enough to overcome long-standing inequities in terms of qualified teachers, books, and equipment. Education in South Africa continues to suffer from institutional racism as white schools have adequate personnel and resources, while black schools have substantially less. Education Minister Kader Asmal summed up the plight of black schools in South Africa: "White schools are one step behind Spain. Black schools are one step behind the Republic of Congo. We face an extraordinary imbalance." But the problem of black education in South Africa is compounded by the lack of commitment that the poor have toward the imbalance in their schools. Education officials see the poor as having an apartheid mentality toward education: they place little emphasis on the advancement of their children and show little interest in changing the status quo.

The South African government approaches the dire situation in education not with an infusion of new books and equipment but with stringent demands on students to prepare for the matric, the national exam that is the key to gaining acceptance into college. President Mbeki gained national attention when he traveled to the northern provinces to castigate educators for not demanding more of their students. Mbeki demanded that students attain higher scores and reminded them that they were last among similarly tested students in Africa (the pass rate in 2000 was 47 percent, the lowest in recent memory). Mbeki even threatened to fire principals who could not make measurable advances in test scores on the matric. The South African government echoed the concerns of President Mbeki when it unveiled a five-year educational strategy to improve student performance. Targets were set for literacy, professional guidelines were set for educators, and new infusions of resources were pledged.

Despite the national strategy and the commitment to provide resources, local educators are taking a different tack as they seek to reform education. There is now in South African education a call for discipline—students and teachers are to arrive on time, work is to be completed with no excuses, parents are expected to push their children toward excellence. In some localities there are even calls for corporal punishment as a way of forcing students to take their studies seriously. Educators are convinced that money for new books and equipment will not compensate for the culture of apathy that is the legacy of apartheid. It may take a new generation of parents and children to overcome the impact of "Bantu education" with its message that there are few opportunities available for blacks and therefore no need to emphasize hard work and discipline.

As with many areas of public policy in a less developed country like South Africa, major reform runs up against scarce resources. South African education will remain mired in second-class status until teachers are paid properly, books are sufficient, and classrooms are built. But in South Africa there is another challenge: the values and behavior patterns of the past must be changed in order for the new education environment to prosper. This challenge may be more difficult to meet than the allocation of budgetary resources. ⊕

PATHWAYS TO PARTICIPATION

South Africa, despite its legacy of narrow politics and closed democracy, has a rich, complex system of popular participation. But certain pathways to participation are wider and more direct than others. The primary pathway to participation is through the African National Congress. The ANC was the dominant resistance organization during apartheid and is the dominant political organization in the postapartheid era. From its inception in 1912 as a black voice against the Land Act, which banned Africans from buying, renting, or using land, the ANC was a voice of opposition against white minority rule and a steadfast proponent of individual rights and political freedoms.

As a resistance party the ANC had one focus—to replace the apartheid system. Imprisoned party leaders like Nelson Mandela and those in exile such as Oliver Tambo and Joe Slovo provided ANC supporters in South Africa with the will to fight on and, more importantly, maintained organizational strength at the grassroots level. Although the ANC was increasingly forced underground, with some elements engaged in guerrilla warfare from Angola, Mozambique, and Zimbabwe, the party also laid the foundation for building key popular organizations such as the Congress of South African Students (COSAS) and the Congress of South African Trade Unions (COSATU).

When the ANC was no longer banned by the white government, the party was well positioned to expand on its grassroots base and begin rebuilding an organizational structure. It quickly established branch and regional bodies and expanded its membership roles. The first national elections in the postapartheid era validated ANC's popularity and organizational strength. It received 62.6 percent of the vote in the 1994 elections. In the first local elections in 1995 the ANC received 66.4 percent of the vote and in the 1999 legislative election the ANC continued its dominance of the South African political system, gaining 65.7 percent of the vote. The ANC has become the equivalent of the Mexican PRI: a party viewed by South African voters as the legitimate political institution of the democratic revolution. The ANC therefore has the potential to remain the sole political force within South African politics, leading a one-party democracy with only token electoral and legislative opposition.

The ANC in the postapartheid era is in many respects a different political party from its days of active resistance. As a governing political party it is responsible for making good on its 1912 promise to bring South Africa together and achieve Nelson Mandela's vision of a "rainbow nation." Moreover, as a governing party the ANC has to prove that it has the capacity to lead the nation and respond to the demands of the people it proudly liberated from white rule. Because it has assumed a new role in South African politics, the ANC has sought to redefine itself from being a black resistance movement to a broad-based political organization with responsibilities to all South Africans. As a governing party the ANC has engaged in consensus politics, which has meant being careful not to alienate the white business class, holding an outstretched hand to the opposition Inkatha Freedom Party, and presenting itself as a responsible global partner to foreign governments and multinational corporations. The ANC also has to respond to growing criticism of its governing policies and its governing failures. In the 1999 national elections the ANC became the target of the opposition for its inability to deal with growing unemployment, illegal immigration from Zimbabwe, Angola, and Mozambique, the exploding AIDS epidemic, and rising levels of violent crime.

In terms of ideology the ANC has tried to maintain a balance between its socialist roots and the realities of the new global environment. When it first took power, the ANC leadership talked about income redistribution, state control of the economy, and dismantling white-owned business conglomerates. But by the end of Mandela's time in office and then under the Mbeki presidency, the ANC has become a mainstream party supporting privatization of state enterprises and attracting foreign investment. The ANC, however, has not forgotten its socialist roots. It still resides on the left of the South African political system, where it advocates using the state to address poverty and development issues. The ANC is thus a political party that walks a thin line as it tries to be all things to all people. It must mollify the white business community and international foreign investors by not appearing statist and anticapitalist. To its black supporters it must promise to use the power of the state to deal with housing, education, land, employment, and health care issues.

Political opposition to the ANC can best be categorized as white dominated and tribal based. In the last legislative elections the largely white moderate Democratic Party emerged as the second most popular party behind the ANC. The Democrats received 9.6 percent of the national vote and earned thirty-eight seats in the National Assembly. Although a far cry from the ANC in terms of voter support, the Democrats have nevertheless made significant progress in attracting support. Formed in 1989 by a merger of three small parties and led by the brother of F. W. de Klerk, the Democratic Party initially aligned with the ANC as a means of deepening its influence within the National Assembly. In recent years the Democrats have become the voice of opposition against racialist policies of the ANC and President Mbeki and also the inefficiency of the government in making good on its public policy promises. Because of its moderation and loose association with the ANC, the Democratic Party has been able to attract whites away from the National Party and advance in the polls.

While the Democratic Party has achieved a measure of electoral success, the National Party, now called the New National Party, slipped in popularity and lost seats in the National Assembly. In the 1999 elections the New Nats received 6.9 percent of the vote and saw their number of legislative seats decline from eighty-two to twenty-eight. The New National Party has suffered from its leadership of the apartheid regime and its inability to make a successful transition in a black majority political system. Roelf Meyer, the well-respected head of the New Nationalists, resigned in 1997 to head his own party, the United Democratic Party, which accented a nonracial platform and presented itself as a bridge between white and black voters. The New Nationalists were stung by Meyer's departure and promptly became embroiled in a series of internal disputes over leadership and ideology. The New Nationals are increasingly viewed as a party that has lost its national character and has become more of a regional party (Western Cape province) headed by conservatives closely aligned with apartheid and race-based politics.

In a remarkable turnaround in 2002 the New National Party announced a comprehensive alliance with the ruling ANC. Under the agreement with the ANC, the New National Party pledged to cooperate "in national government and in all areas of South Africa's political life." By aligning with the ANC, the New National Party received two deputy ministerial positions in Thabo Mbeki's cabinet and positions in several provincial cabinets. The new leader of the New National Party, Marthinus van Schalkwyk, had for months been seeking an alliance with the ANC as a means of revitalizing his party; the ANC sought the agreement as a means of bolstering its support in the Western Cape region. For public consumption the alliance between two parties that less than ten years ago were at opposite ends of the racial spectrum was being presented as a opportunity to advance multiracial cooperation. While this may be so, the underlying motivation for the arrangement between the ANC and the New Nationals was more likely political in nature.

Although the New Nationals have turned the corner with regard to their antipathy toward the ANC, other parties in South Africa remain intransigent regarding race relations and multiracial politics. Despite the fact that it received less than 1 percent of the vote in the 1999 elections and three seats in the National Assembly, the Freedom Front Party cannot be ignored. Founded in 1994 by retired General Constand Viljoen, the Freedom Front is a white separatist organization that seeks to establish a "white homeland." More specifically Freedom Front envisions a confederal South Africa that is based on self-determination for the Afrikaner people. Neither the party nor its goal of self-determination has received wide support from South Africans. It remains an organization that symbolizes ideas that have been rejected. Freedom Front supporters are largely farmers from the interior who fear their land will be taken from them by the black majority government or that the government will stand idly by while blacks engage in terrorist attacks against them. Black-on-white violence in neighboring Zimbabwe in 2000–2001 that was tolerated by the government of President Robert Mugabe (and was not condemned by President Mbeki) further intensified the resolve of Afrikaners in the Freedom Front to continue their political opposition.

The black political opposition is focused on the Inkatha Freedom Party of Chief Buthelezi, which is primarily a political vehicle for the Zulu organization in the KwaZulu-Natal province. Despite its Zulu roots, it has not limited its membership to tribal members. In 1990, for example, the membership changed its focus from a "liberation movement" to a "political party" and opened its roles to all racial groupings. In the postapartheid era the Inkatha Freedom Party has been embroiled in an ongoing and often violent dispute with the ANC. The areas of disagreement with the ANC are constitutional, but there is also deep personal antagonism between Buthelezi and Nelson Mandela. The Inkatha Freedom Party at one point refused to participate in the 1994 elections and even made an alliance with right-wing parties. Eventually it accepted three portfolios in the Mandela government and moderated its opposition and its tacit support of violence. Since 1994 the party has been involved in numerous internal debates over the extent of its participation in the government. In the election of 1999 the party dropped from forty-three to thirty-eight seats as it captured 8 percent of the vote. Although still a force to be reckoned with in South African politics, the Inkatha Freedom Party may become the black counterpart of the New Nats with a regional influence and a declining national presence.

Political party activity in South Africa is not limited to the ANC and the weak opposition organizations. In the 1999 elections 17 percent of the vote went to a list of other parties that span the ideological spectrum from the South African Communist Party on the left to the Afrikaner Resistance Movement on the right. South African electoral politics is an intricate web of party interaction that continues to expand not only because of the open and fair system of democracy that has been put into place but also because of proportional representation. With two hundred of the National Assembly seats awarded from national party lists and two hundred seats awarded from regional party lists, smaller parties have an incentive to remain viable in the political system and compete for a presence in the legislature. Under South Africa's proportional representation system even political parties that receive 0.25 percent of the vote are eligible to win seats in the National Assembly. While by international electoral standards this is an extremely low minimum for eligibility to capture legislative seats, in South Africa it has helped to create a political environment where participation is welcomed.

Despite the proliferation of political parties representing a range of ideologies, tribal affiliations, and racial compositions, politics in South Africa is increasingly marked by electoral and legislative strategies designed to bridge the gap among ideology, tribe, and race. The pathways to participation in South Africa are more inclusive and more moderate in tone. The political parties that have won electoral support and legislative seats have presented themselves as parties of the middle that no longer define themselves in terms of the separations of the past. Although the ANC remains a party that represents the black majority and is not afraid to criticize the white community for foot dragging on jobs and poverty, it nevertheless reaches out to whites at election time and is careful not to create an atmosphere of political exclusion. The same can be said of white-dominated parties like the New National Party and the Democratic Party. These parties reach out to blacks by supporting positions that appeal to them, especially in the areas of affirmative action, job training, and income inequality.

While political participation in South Africa is conducted largely through the party system and particularly the ANC, there are other pathways through which public policy issues can be expressed, shaped, and influenced. One of those pathways is the union movement. South African workers have a powerful voice through COSATU, the Congress of South African Trade Unions. Founded in 1985 after four years of talks between unions opposed to

Facket

apartheid, COSATU today is a nearly two-million-member confederation that bills itself as the "fastest growing trade union movement in the world." COSATU has long been affiliated with the ANC and the South African Communist Party and members of COSATU sit on the executive board of the ANC and are members of governing cabinets. Over the years COSATU has worked tirelessly for worker rights, especially its campaign for a living wage. It was influential in ensuring that a worker lockout clause was excluded from the South African constitution, thereby solidifying the right to strike without retribution from management. COSATU was also instrumental in passing the Basic Conditions of Employment Act in the postapartheid period. The act sets specific limits on working hours and establishes regulations regarding maternity leave and child labor. Currently COSATU is involved in a campaign to soften the effects of the government's privatization initiative in four key state-owned enterprises. Privatization will undoubtedly have a major impact on employment and job security in state enterprises. But perhaps its greatest challenge is in balancing the success that it has attained in gaining jobs for its skilled black members with the ever expanding joblessness of unskilled blacks who are crowding into the cities in search of employment. COSATU's close affiliation with the ANC government has made it a target of unemployed blacks and those in the public sector who feel that the union confederation has sacrificed their interests in order to gain influence in the government.

The most influential South African union in the COSATU network is the National Union of Mineworkers (NUM). Founded in 1982, the NUM is the largest affiliate of COSATU with over 250,000 members. Being a world center for diamond and gold mining and an emerging oil provider, NUM has become an important participant in worker-management relations and government policymaking in regard to natural resource development. The mining sector has experienced numerous clashes over the years between white-owned and -managed mines and black workers who have fought for greater pay and better working conditions. Today NUM focuses less on the mines, which have encountered difficult times, and more on the energy sector where the government has pushed for privatization in order to attract foreign investment. NUM has become a militant force in the public debate over privatization and has used its alignment with COSATU and wildcat strikes to pressure the government to limit the restructuring that becomes inevitable once privatization programs are introduced.

On the business side of the equation, participation in the political process docs not have the kind of high profile and activist organization as labor. The South African Chamber of Commerce and the Small Business Institute represent the corporate sector. Multinationals and international banks have a substantial voice in the political process as South Africa seeks to attract foreign investment and deal with foreign indebtedness. But with the ANC government and in particular President Mbeki still leery of capitalism and globalization, the advocates of business have a harder road to follow as they seek to advance their interests. With the end of apartheid and the ascension to power of the black majority, the pathways to participation have been dominated by parties and organizations that tap into the political and electoral realities of race.

As mentioned above, participants in the political process have recognized the importance of seeking white involvement in their organizations and white support of their policies, but white influence has clearly waned in South Africa since 1994. The political situation in South Africa is based on the understanding that whites are necessary because of their wealth, expertise, and ownership of key business enterprises. Whites in the current political dynamic in South Africa have a consultative role, not a power role; their views and positions are taken under consideration and accommodated as a means to achieve consensus. In the new political world of South Africa, however, whites do not control the pathways of participation. They can use the pathways but they are overshadowed by the black majority that has taken over the pathways and uses them to reach their destinations and on their terms.

POINT OF FACT

According to a study by the Inter-Parliamentary Union, among the emerging nations of the Third World South Africa has the highest proportion of women involved in politics, with 30 percent participation.

THE POLITICAL ELITE

Political power in South Africa is currently undergoing a shift in leadership. Apartheid stalwarts who built the liberation movement and paid the price in terms of exile and prison are slowly but surely giving way to a new generation of leaders who are younger and whose view of governance is less tied to the memory of racial segregation and racial repression. This shift of leadership is not unexpected, since South Africa today is a nation that has moved away from its "struggle mentality" to direct its attention toward economic development and social equity. As a result the leaders of the apartheid period have become something akin to an old guard who are held up as symbols of freedom and democracy but no longer reflect the new South Africa with a new agenda and new goals.

Nelson Mandela has become the elder statesman of South Africa, making public appearances, giving speeches, welcoming foreign visitors, and traveling abroad. After leaving the presidency in 1999, he made it clear that his

PHOTO 7.1   THABO MBEKI
DELIVERS A SPEECH AT THE
WEF IN DAVOS. (REUTERS
NEWMEDIA INC./CORBIS)

Thabo Mbeki was born in the Transkei in June 1942. His parents were both active members of the ANC. At fourteen he joined the ANC Youth League and quickly became active in ANC student politics. He studied economics at London University. On his return to South Africa, Mbeki became embroiled in opposition politics as leader of the African Students Association. In 1962 he left South Africa under orders from the ANC and became active in exile politics in Britain. In 1970 he was sent to the Soviet Union for military training. He returned to Africa and led opposition to the apartheid government from neighboring Botswana and Swaziland. In 1975 he became a member of the National Executive Committee of the ANC. Throughout the 1970s and 1980s he held many positions with the ANC. In 1989 he led a delegation that began secret talks with the South African government over the release of political prisoners. In 1993 he was elected chairperson of the ANC. He became the deputy president of South Africa in the Mandela administration. In 1997 he was elected president of the ANC and in 1999 he was elected president of South Africa.

would be an advisory role and that he would not seek to compete for power with his successor, Thabo Mbeki. Mandela's opinion is solicited and he does not shy away from commenting on public policy matters, particularly with respect to racial matters and the advancement of civil society. His position in South Africa has taken on that of a revered national father figure who brought the country through its most difficult challenges and now has handed over the mantle of power in a mature democratic fashion. Nelson Mandela does not occupy a place in the policymaking circle, nor has he sought one. He appears content in his role as spokesman for racial harmony, democratic participation, and the attainment of his ultimate goal, the rainbow nation. In recent years deteriorating health has limited his public appearances and travel.

Archbishop Desmond Tutu has also taken a less visible role in South African politics. After publishing his report on the Truth and Reconciliation

Commission, Tutu turned his attention toward implementing many of the reforms that were part of the commission's recommendations. He advocates compensation for the victims of repression and he has often commented on the state of race relations in postapartheid South Africa. But like Mandela, Tutu is no longer at the center of the apartheid storm. His role now is to help rebuild racial harmony incrementally, not to engage in major initiatives such as the Truth and Reconciliation Commission. Tutu continues to be the conscience of South Africa and a leader whose views are never dismissed and are always carefully considered.

In some cases the old guard of South African politics simply left the scene because the fight against apartheid took so long. Oliver Tambo, an important leader of the ANC throughout its liberation struggle, was permitted to return to South Africa after thirty years in exile in 1990. Tambo was likely to be the deputy president under Mandela and might have moved up to the presidency after Mandela left the office. Tambo, however, died unexpectedly in 1993. Another member of the old guard was Walter Sisulu, who spent twenty-seven years in prison for his leadership activities with the ANC. Upon his release in 1989, Sisulu assumed a prominent place in the party hierarchy, rising to vice president. But ill health forced Sisulu to give up the position to Thabo Mbeki. Many observers of South African politics were convinced that Sisulu was the heir apparent to Nelson Mandela, but just as with Tambo, age and health interceded to deny him the opportunity to take a more prominent role in postapartheid South Africa. Joe Slovo, leader of the South African Communist Party (SCAP), was the chief of staff of the military wing of the ANC, responsible for anti-apartheid guerrilla activities outside South Africa. Slovo returned from exile in 1990 and eventually became housing minister in the Mandela government. Slovo moved away from his communist roots and made a much publicized speech condemning Soviet President Mikhail Gorbachev. He was an influential figure in South African politics until he died in 1995. The leader of the South African Communist Party after Slovo was Chris Hani, an outspoken critic of apartheid and the more moderate positions of Nelson Mandela. Hani was assassinated in 1993.

The influence of Nelson Mandela's former wife, Winnie Madikizela-Mandela, has fluctuated in recent years. Once viewed as the voice of the imprisoned Nelson Mandela and the de facto coleader of the ANC, Madikizela-Mandela's position in the ANC has deteriorated considerably. Initially Madikizela-Mandela was a deputy minister in her husband's government but she was dismissed in 1995 because her leftist views were seen as detrimental to the new face that the party was trying to present. Later she became embroiled in charges of murder stemming from investigations of the Truth and Reconciliation

Commission. The Mandela United Football Club, with which she was associated, was shown to be nothing more than a "private army" that intimidated political opponents. The publicity surrounding the charges against Madikizela-Mandela served as an obstacle to her advancement in the party. In 1997 she retained her position as head of the ANC Women's League, but her attempts to gain support from the party for the position of deputy president were quashed.

In 1998 she rebounded and used her position on the Executive Committee of the ANC to ensure a high position on the party list for the 1999 legislative elections. Although Madikizela-Mandela is detested by the more cerebral and publicity-shy Mbeki, she has carved out a place in the power elite of South African politics. She has effectively used grandstanding public relations maneuvers such as giving an impassioned speech at the funeral of a young AIDS victim, Nkosi Johnson, and has become the primary voice of the poor in townships like Soweto. She has also mastered the leaked letter to the press (one of which suggested that Mbeki is a womanizer) and regularly castigates the Mbeki government for its failings regarding poverty policy. Despite her reputation as a leftist ideologue and her involvement in the murders of two young boys who crossed paths with the feared United Football Club, Madikizela-Mandela remains an influential force in the ANC. The fact that she is the divorced wife of South Africa's legendary leader and the target of the Truth and Reconciliation Commission has not significantly limited her ability to rise in the party. She is viewed as the leader of South Africa's poor and a potential threat to the established ANC leadership.

While many of the old names of the apartheid era still resonate in South African politics, Thabo Mbeki has engineered a discernible power shift away from the old anti-apartheid guard to a new development-minded elite. Although Mbeki was himself an exile and a target of the white apartheid government, he was of a different generation. The son of an ANC leader who spent his formative years away from the liberation struggle as an organizer and representative of the ANC, Mbeki concentrated his efforts on organizing the underground movement in South Africa and convincing neighboring African countries to support the ANC. As an ANC activist who was not imprisoned, Mbeki developed a broad range of skills and an even broader range of international contacts. While Mandela became a living symbol of opposition to apartheid and a moral compass for all South Africans, Mbeki became the diplomat, organizer, policy expert, and administrative leader of the party, which helped position him for future leadership.

Once apartheid ended and Mandela became president, Mbeki moved into the leadership hierarchy of the party and the government. Mandela recognized Mbeki's experience and made party leaders aware of his support for his protégé. In the party elections that occurred once Mandela announced his intention not to run for president, Mbeki ran unopposed. Clearly Nelson Mandela viewed Mbeki as the right person to lead the ANC and the nation in the postapartheid era and made that known to the ANC membership. Mbeki's emphasis on redistributive policies matched Mandela's vision that South Africans must move from political equality to economic equality or the dream of the rainbow nation would be a mere pipe dream. There were areas of disagreement between Mandela and Mbeki such as the public dispute over the Truth and Reconciliation Commission report citing the ANC for human rights violations. Mbeki condemned the report as "scurrilous" and advocated blocking the report. Mandela chastised Mbeki and the party for these actions and pushed for full disclosure of all human rights abuses.

Although the South African government is firmly in the grasp of Thabo Mbeki, he is joined by a number of key officials. Because the South African governing system has a deputy president, Jacob Zuma plays an important role in the political elite. Like many ANC members, Zuma was imprisoned on Robben Island and later exiled in Mozambique. When he returned to South Africa in 1990, he became minister of economic affairs and tourism in KwaZulu-Natal. Because his roots were in KwaZulu-Natal, Zuma became a key negotiator between the ANC and the Inkatha Freedom Party during their 1993–1994 conflict. Based on his value in the negotiations and his ties to both Mandela and Mbeki, Zuma became the national chairperson of the ANC and later deputy president of the ANC. There is no doubt that Zuma has the inside track to the presidency in 2004 should Mbeki decide to leave office. Because Mandela served only one term, Mbeki may face pressure in the ANC to limit his term in office. If that transpires, then Zuma will be his likely successor.

Although many members of the Mbeki cabinet share experiences as either prisoners on Robben Island or exiled activists, there is a growing reliance on professionals whose connection to the ANC liberation struggle is more distant. Minister of Finance Trevor Manuel worked for the Mobil Foundation in the area of entrepreneurial development and later as head of the ANC Department of Economic Planning. Nkosanzana Zuma, the minister of foreign affairs, has degrees in public health and served as a medical officer in a number of South African hospitals. Lindiwe Nonceba Sisulu, deputy minister of home affairs and member of parliament, has an academic and journalistic background both in South Africa and abroad. Sisulu is often mentioned as a promising future leader in the ANC. Although the Home Ministry portfolio is held by Chief Buthelezi, Sisulu is the ANC "eyes and ears" in this critical administrative department that sets policy for domestic security.

In addition to attracting advisers and ministers with strong professional and technical backgrounds, Mbeki has also made a concerted effort to bring women into his government. Perhaps the most important woman in his inner circle is Mantombazana Tshabalala-Msimang, the minister of health. Tshabalala-Msimang was educated as a medical doctor in Leningrad and received advanced degrees in Brussels and Britain. As minister of health, Tshabalala-Msimang has shaped the policies that underlie South Africa's response to the HIV/AIDS epidemic. She is a frequent and outspoken critic of the international response to the HIV/AIDS crisis and is the primary adviser to President Mbeki on public policies regarding the crisis.

Discussions of the South African political elite naturally focus on the ANC, both in the party structure and in government. But it is impossible to ignore the influence of Chief Buthelezi of the Inkatha Freedom Party and the home minister. Buthelezi has been the home minister and a member of the National Assembly since 1994. Nelson Mandela included Buthelezi in his cabinet in 1994 not only because of the seats that the IFP held in the National Assembly but also because of the importance of bringing peace between the ANC and the IFP in KwaZulu-Natal. Buthelezi sees himself less as a minister in Mbeki's government and more as a tribal leader with an international presence. As the head of Inkatha, which has 1.5 million members, Buthelezi is the primary leader in KwaZulu-Natal and is absolutely essential in any negotiations between the ANC and the government and Inkatha. By placing him in the Home Ministry, both Mandela and Mbeki sought to establish orderly relations in a state that has been the center of violent conflicts.

Because the political elite in South Africa is the ANC elite, leadership carries an extra burden in terms of maintaining a disciplined approach to public policy issues and avoiding the trap of making government decisions in a environment where opposition views and suggestions are marginalized. The ANC leadership has been fortunate that the goodwill and moderation created by Nelson Mandela's presidency have fostered a consensus on critical public policy concerns. But the farther that South Africa becomes removed from the Mandela years, the greater the risk that the political elite will fragment, causing internal party divisions and offering the opposition the opportunity to move into the void and advance its own agenda. The presidency of Thabo Mbeki has already contributed to a breakdown of the governing consensus by his criticisms of whites and his willingness to play the "race card" as a means of generating support from the poor and the unemployed. These actions have divided the party, often pitting government officials against party officials and most importantly calling into question the ability of the leadership elite to manage South Africa's development.

CRIME REDUCTION POLICY

Crime is the number one topic of conversation in South Africa, but government officials have often been reluctant to join the conversation, except to state that crime is coming under control. The explosion of criminal activity in South Africa has been so widespread and so sustained since the ANC took power that citizens live in fear behind closed doors or high walls, major commercial and business sectors in large cities become ghost towns after dark, and criminals are increasingly brazen in their behavior; meanwhile the police seem overwhelmed. The crime wave that has become part of South African national life has gained the attention of the international investment and corporate community. Reluctance to invest in South Africa or to maintain a presence in the country has deepened in recent years.

The extent of the crime wave in South Africa is astounding. In June 2001, after refusing to publicize crime data, South African Police Services told the people what they already knew. From June 2000 to June 2001 there was a 30 percent increase in armed robberies and carjackings, a 32 percent increase in house break-ins, a 24 percent increase in rape, a 70 percent increase in indecent assault, and an astounding 169 percent increase in robberies without arms such as muggings and pickpocketing. Only murder decreased slightly during the study period. Interestingly, the government lifted a ten-month moratorium on crime data after being pressured by the media and opposition parties to inform the nation on the seriousness of crime. Of course South Africans did not have to see the crime data to know what they faced on a daily basis.

While the South African government responded to the crime wave with heightened police presence, stiffer penalties, and overflowing jails, it has also taken public positions that are defensive in nature and appeal to the patriotic spirit of the people. When the crime data was released, Safety and Security Minister Steve Tshwete stated that South Africa was "not out of control" and that the government had "turned the tide" against crime. Deputy President Jacob Zuma, however, took a different tack as he criticized those in society who "orchestrate negativity by harping about crime" and are "sabotaging the progress of the country." Zuma further criticized those who blame the government for the continued high level of crime as having a "lack of patriotism." The government remains on the defensive about crime as many South Africans contemplate leaving the country to avoid what has become a social epidemic.

The South African crime wave has created a civilian response that mixes self-defense and vigilantism. Groups such as People Against Gangsterism and Drugs (PAGAD) were founded in response to the inability of the South African police to adequately curb attacks on citizens by roving drug gangs.

Groups like PAGAD have incurred the wrath of the South African government because of a number of violent encounters between PAGAD members and the police. PAGAD leaders claim that many of the white police officers have ties to right-wing extremist organizations and have little interest in responding to the safety needs of poor black residents in urban areas. The formation of PAGAD and other civilian self-protection groups points to the breakdown of formal police authority. Even the white business and professional classes rely less on police protection and employ private security agencies to guard their homes, offices, and factories.

The South African government links the end of the crime wave to the expansion of employment opportunities. But the level of crime is seen by South Africans as more than job related. A culture of violence grips the country, which many see as one of the sad remnants of apartheid. The apartheid era was marked by violent overthrow efforts, violent revolutionary rhetoric, and violence against thousands of South Africans who dared to challenge the white government. Although the apartheid system is now a memory, the culture of violence remains. Jobs may help, but the culture of violence has to change before the crime wave comes to an end. ⊕

Legislative Composition

As a result of the 1999 elections, the South African National Assembly has the following political party composition:

African National Congress	266 seats
Democratic Party	38 seats
Inkatha Freedom Party	34 seats
New National Party	28 seats
United Democratic Movement	14 seats
African Christian Democrats	6 seats
Freedom Front	3 seats
United Christian Democrats	3 seats
Pan-African Congress	3 seats
Federal Alliance	2 seats
Minority Front	1 seat
Afrikaner Unity Movement	1 seat
Azanian People's Organization	1 seat

REAL GOVERNMENT

Much of the analysis of South African government in recent years centered around President Thabo Mbeki's response to controversial public policy issues. After a year of widespread support for Mbeki and laudatory comments about the South African president's experience and intelligence, the honeymoon period came to an abrupt halt in 2000, when Mbeki and his cabinet took a series of positions that baffled many and caused concern outside the country. Whether the quiet acceptance of the violent invasions of white-owned farms in neighboring Zimbabwe or the strange theories and conspiracies regarding the transmission of HIV/AIDS or the thinly veiled charges of racism made against the business community for their alleged foot dragging on poverty and income inequality, the South African president has been called everything from "bizarre" to "idiosyncratic," and his popularity and that of his ANC government has declined steadily. Although the South African press was reluctant to mount a campaign against Mbeki's leadership style and questionable judgment, there has been substantial debate over why the president and his close advisers have squandered their popularity by adhering to public policy positions that are far from the mainstream.

By 2001 Mbeki had been dubbed the "velcro president," meaning that any mistake he or his ministers made stuck to him and drove him further down in the public opinion polls. Politics in South Africa shifted dramatically from the days of Nelson Mandela, when goodwill and hope for the future created a powerful political culture of support for government and deference for national leaders. Now there is great mistrust of the government and questions about Mbeki's leadership capabilities. He has introduced a tougher brand of politics that harks back to the days of the ANC liberation movement when dissent was not tolerated and discipline was required. Mbeki has supported tough measures by his ministers in using tear gas in a crackdown on street hawkers in Johannesburg and squatters in urban slums; he has attacked judges for their work habits and their sentencing procedures; and he has taken on his allies in the union movement, saying that their criticism of his policies "smacked of revolutionary indiscipline." Mbeki has further eroded support by not rebuking officials in his administration for antidemocratic remarks and by engaging in public tirades against those who question his commitment to democratic practice.

The one area of public policy that has most concerned South Africans, as well as the international community, is Mbeki's position toward the use of the anti-AIDS drug AZT. In 1999 Mbeki announced that he would not approve giving AZT to pregnant women because in his view it is a toxic drug. Mbeki's position on AZT runs counter to international scientific research and is interpreted as his attempt to send a message to the foreign pharmaceutical companies (Glaxo Wellcome makes AZT) that he will not depend on their science to combat the AIDS epidemic. Mbeki's attacks on foreign pharmaceutical companies may be driven by his intense mistrust of the West and Western capitalism. Although the vast majority of the research attests to the reliability of AZT as an anti-AIDS drug, Mbeki and his administration insist on more research into the toxicity issue. Critics of Mbeki's hard-nosed response to AZT state that his policy position has deepened the AIDS crisis in South Africa and delayed the use of a drug regimen that has a proven success rate. But more importantly Mbeki's position has further alienated him from the mainstream medical community in his own country and caused the international community to wonder at how ideology and antagonism toward the West can be allowed to stymie efforts to combat a killer disease.

For decades Mbeki and the ANC fought the white minority government over its failure to adhere to basic human rights standards. Ironically, now he is being castigated by his own citizens for the heavy-handed treatment of those who oppose his rule. The South African Human Rights Commission warned Mbeki of a "deterioration in the human rights environment," and the leader of a watchdog agency charged with ensuring the rule of law in South Africa stated in 1999 that the Mbeki administration would need "closer and more demanding democratic and human rights monitoring." Mbeki dismissed these criticisms as politically motivated and appeared to take a degree of satisfaction in fashioning his administration in a tough, no-nonsense mold. He views dissent as a threat to his power and opposition activity as a form of treason; electoral popularity is transformed into a carte blanche opportunity to exercise power without restraint.

While Mbeki and his cabinet have faced criticism in large part for their divisive policy pronouncements and their failure to deliver on public policy promises, the strains in the South African government have deepened over the use of presidential power to intimidate political rivals and quash investigative efforts concerning corruption and ethics violations. The Mbeki administration became embroiled in a series of controversies in 2001 and 2002 that resulted from party politics and maneuvering associated with the 2004 elections. The most disruptive of these controversies involved Mbeki's charge that three members of the ANC leadership were engaged in a "plot" to do "physical harm" to him. Past ANC secretary general Cyril Ramaphosa, former Gauteng premier Tokyo Sexwale, and former Mpumalanga premier Mathews Phosa were singled out by the president as ringleaders of the alleged plot. The charges against the three were made by a close Mbeki confidant, Safety and Security Minister Steve Tshwete, and were seen as an attempt to preempt growing opposition to the president within the ANC. The alleged plot became even more controversial when press reports stated that Mbeki was using government intelligence units to spy on his party rivals in a clear violation of the constitution. Mbeki has expressed deep concern over the future candidacy of Cyril Ramaphosa. Despite leaving his position as an ANC party leader, Ramaphosa has retained considerable popularity in South African society. He is viewed as a candidate who has ties to the white business community and would attract considerable support should he choose to run against Mbeki in 2004.

The ANC, after maintaining solidarity throughout the Mandela presidency, has shown signs of factionalism and mean-spirited jockeying for political advantage. Mbeki and his ministerial team and ANC activists made it obvious that their intent is to limit future challenges to their political position and to send a message that they are willing to use the power of the state to weaken, if not destroy, intraparty opposition. The power dynamics within the ANC became so tense in 2002 that Nelson Mandela began to reemerge as a political counterforce to Mbeki. Mandela became more vocal in his criticism of Mbeki and worked with the party's National Executive Committee (NEC) to rein in the president and his supporters.

Of particular concern to those opposed to Mbeki is his willingness to remove entire provincial executives of the ANC, who are seen as disloyal or threats to the future political plans of the president and his ministerial supporters. There is also mounting criticism that Mbeki has replaced the concerns of the black working class with those of the emerging black middle class. Mbeki's interest in black economic empowerment has, in the view of pro-ANC organizations such as the Congress of South African Trade Unions, shifted attention away from the needs of poor blacks, the traditional base of ANC support.

The mode of operation in South African government has taken on a definite authoritarian character. Mbeki and his allies in the cabinet and the ANC are using their solid voter base and continued support in the polls to dampen opposition criticism and issue not-so-veiled threats against political enemies. Like the PRI of Mexico, the ANC of Thabo Mbeki is building a "fortress of power" that is designed to be impregnable to those outside its walls. These attacks against perceived political enemies trouble many in South Africa. Since most of the posturing by Mbeki and his supporters is pointed toward the 2004 elections, South Africans fear that Mbeki's ultimate objective is to set up a system of political control that will continue at least until 2009, when his second term, if reelected, ends. There is increasing talk within political circles that Mbeki may be preparing South African politics for a form of "democratic centralism," a term used by communist governments to defend their use of authoritarianism.

President Mbeki has certainly not distinguished himself with his style of governing, but taking on national leadership in post-Mandela South Africa would have been difficult for any politician. Mandela governed in an unreal political environment. With the apartheid system broken, South Africans breathed a sigh of relief and took pleasure in showing the world that black and white could create a new democratic system free of the animosity and mistrust that dominated the country for generations. Mandela entered office with an enormous reservoir of goodwill, and he capitalized on that goodwill to sustain a governing consensus. Moreover, Mandela was an astute student of political perception and made sure that he hit all the symbolic "buttons" of national unity and racial fairness. When Mandela left the presidency, South Africans felt good about their new brand of politics. Public confidence was high and the future looked promising.

But when Mbeki arrived on the political scene, he did not benefit from the Mandela consensus but rather was faced with a quickly deteriorating social scene as crime, unemployment, AIDS, and growing dissatisfaction over income inequality rushed to the surface of national life. Real governing in South Africa began to settle in as it became clear that the euphoria of the Mandela years had ended and the burden of dealing with a host of public policy challenges was unavoidable. Mbeki, despite his errors in judgment and his rough-hewn style, has forced South Africans to face up to the fact that the apartheid system left the country with a poverty-stricken underclass, huge gaps in wealth, and devastating health challenges. Mbeki's task in the coming years will be to move from his reality-based approach to governing to a solution-based approach that addresses the serious problems facing South Africa.

What the Experts Say

Mark Gevisser, a South African journalist who is writing a biography of Thabo Mbeki, writes in *Foreign Affairs*:

Mbeki is a backroom operator who has sold himself as a can-do technocrat far more interested in making things happen than in providing the kind of inspirational imagery at which Mandela excelled. Whereas South Africans loved Mandela unreservedly, they treat Mbeki with a mixture of respect and fear. Whites display more of the latter at Mbeki's avowed intention to accelerate social transformation—which ultimately means giving more of the country's funds and jobs to its black majority.

FROM MARK GEVISSER, "STRANGE BEDFELLOWS,"
Foreign Affairs, JANUARY–FEBRUARY 2000, PP. 173–178

POLITICAL ECONOMY

South African economic policy is shaped by two contradictory perspectives. First, governing leaders are committed to building an economy from the ashes of apartheid, an economy that seeks to close the vast income and service gaps that exist as a result of racial discrimination and racial separation. Second, government officials recognize that in order to expand and sustain economic development, market principles must be adhered to despite their tendency to create income and service gaps. Reconciling these perspectives has posed a difficult dilemma for the ANC and President Mbeki.

Although South Africa has shifted away from a socialist answer to national development in favor of a market approach, it has not completely embraced liberal economic policies. Liberalization has been slow in particular in the privatization of state enterprises. The government has committed itself to complete restructuring of the four major public corporations—Eskom, Transnet, Telkom, and Denel—by 2004. But the restructuring does not include complete privatization. Rather, the government is interested in developing greater private sector participation, particularly in electricity generation and transmission. Government officials are very reluctant to move to a total privatization strategy because of concern over the loss of jobs that often occurs with the sale of state assets and the fear that the delivery of services will be compromised in the name of profit. With unemployment in the mid–20 percent range and a governing philosophy that stresses social responsibility, South Africa has emphasized public-private partnerships as the key to restructuring its state enterprises, rather than placing these assets on the market.

Another reason for the reluctance to move toward privatization is that these state enterprises have provided low-cost services to South Africans. Due to generous state subsidies, the cost of major services such as electricity and water has been quite low. Any effort to move the country away from these subsidies in the name of efficiency and a lower national budget would likely cause a storm of protests. There is also concern over the impact that privatization would have on key labor support. COSATU and other unions have expressed strong reservations over privatization, primarily in terms of the impact that the sale of state enterprises would have on job security. Government officials, however, have sought to defuse criticism of higher prices for services and reduced job security by promising that public-private partnerships rather than privatization will not harm the delivery of low-cost services and will provide more guarantees for employment growth. This middle approach to state enterprises has so far proved an effective means of limiting public criticism, while also moving South Africa toward less reliance on state control of vital resources and services.

An added benefit is that economic restructuring of state enterprises has provided the government with substantial financial proceeds. Those proceeds have been shifted to debt service and spending on social services and infrastructure. South Africa has an estimated 179 billion rand worth ($25 billion) of public assets. Because the Mbeki government is reluctant to engage in wholesale privatization, only 11 billion rand worth has been put up for sale. By 2004 an additional 40 billion rand worth will be transferred into private or private/public hands. But the allure of cash infusion from the sale of state assets is strong. For example, the sale of 20 percent of Telkom, the state telecommunications utility, would raise over 20 billion rand, which could erase the government's borrowing needs for up to two years. Moreover, private economists in South Africa estimate that privatization could increase GDP growth by as much as 2 percent. It is the enormity of the cash infusion plus the impact on economic growth that has made the privatization issue one of the key and controversial economic policy issues facing the Mbeki administration.

While privatization of state enterprises has emerged as the frontline issue, it has often detracted from the considerable progress made by the government in advancing the general economy. In 1996 the government launched its major economic development initiative, called the Growth, Employment, and Redistribution Program (GEAR). GEAR was designed to move South Africa into the new global environment by accenting foreign investment, competitive pricing, stable exchange rates, and efficient public sector enterprises. Economic policies like GEAR have helped bring stability and growth to South Africa. Although economic growth figures have remained in the modest 2–3 percent range, the government has gained a reputation as a competent steward of fiscal and monetary policy. Inflation in 2000 was a respectable 6 percent, budget deficits have declined steadily, and liberalization policies in the area of trade have either matched or exceeded goals set by the World Trade Organization. A free trade agreement between South Africa and the European Union began in early 2001, which will remove tariffs on 86 percent of EU imports and on 95 percent of South African exports.

The positive economic news from South Africa since Mbeki took power has begun to be recognized by the international community, particularly the international banking and lending community. In 2000 Standard & Poor's upgraded South Africa's investment grade rating, citing the country's "unusual strengths." In particular, Standard & Poor's mentioned that the government had pursued prudent fiscal policies, managed the external debt burden successfully, achieved low inflation rates, and fostered a "robust and well-regulated banking sector." The report stressed that South Africa continues to face a chronic current accounts deficit due in large part to excessive consumer demand for imports relative to exports of natural resources such as diamonds and gold. There was also concern over low savings and investment rates. Attracting foreign investment has been a particular concern for the government because of lingering fears that the ANC is not fully committed to market principles and that racial antagonisms will erupt and weaken the fragile social stability that was put in place when Nelson Mandela was president.

One area of the economy that has remained a trouble spot is the labor market. Mbeki and the ANC have long advocated for employment opportunities for blacks. In order to ensure that blacks will have access to the job market, labor laws have been promulgated that require strict hiring practices. As mentioned earlier, labor laws require companies with fifty or more employees to classify those employees to ensure that the firm is "demographically representative." Furthermore, firms are held to a high standard regarding discrimination against blacks. These labor laws have created an employment environment in which firms seek to evade restrictive hiring rules by falsifying the numbers of employees or by hiring contract workers who are not under their control. As a result, there is a growing tension between government and the business community in South Africa over hiring standards and compliance with those standards.

But hiring policy is not the critical issue of employment. The South African government has stated repeatedly that economic growth must hit 6 percent each year in order to have an impact on chronic unemployment and the poverty that accompanies the unemployment. Despite the steady growth of the economy, GDP increases have held steady at around 3 percent, not enough to create the kind of job momentum necessary to make significant inroads on unemployment. The government has followed an aggressive policy of providing assistance to black entrepreneurs through its special development initiatives program and has taken the lead in forming economic enterprise areas in regions where there is serious unemployment and underdevelopment. But these programs run up against devastating job losses in the nonagricultural area. For example, the decline in gold prices has crippled the mining industry, causing mine closings and layoffs. To make inroads with respect to unemployment, the government will have to speed up the creation of enterprise zones and attract even more foreign investment.

While privatization and labor market issues occupy center stage in the political economy, the government has defined a clear set of fiscal, monetary, and developmental objectives for the future. The South African government has targeted three critical areas of economic policy—a reduction in the overall tax burden, a continuing commitment to social, development, and infrastructure expenditures, and reducing the budget deficit relative to the size of the economy. The tax reduction objective is viewed as the primary stimulus for lowering the cost of investment and creating jobs. Tax reduction is seen as a critical ingredient for increasing household spending power, especially in light of growing inflationary pressures. Reducing the budget deficit is seen as a major factor in lowering interest rates and lessening the dependence on domestic and foreign borrowing. But the budget deficits that have arisen in recent years continue to run up against the government's responsibility to provide for the range of social welfare, development, and infrastructure projects. Social services, for example, received nearly 44 percent of the national budget allocation in the 2001–2002 fiscal year, with education receiving 20.5 percent and health care 13.1 percent. Military expenditures dropped significantly under both Mandela and Mbeki, from 4.3 percent of GNP in 1988 to 2 percent in the late 1990s.

As South Africa moves farther and farther away from apartheid and introduces market-oriented strategies and programs, there is growing optimism that the economic and social problems that have beset the country are not insurmountable. South Africa has advantages over its neighbors in the struggle for national development. It is more industrialized, its population is more educated, its resource base is substantial, and the level of economic activity dwarfs that of all other countries on the African continent. Despite its problems with income inequality, unemployment, and poverty, South Africa continues to be the most developed of the African countries. In critical development areas such as per capita income, adult literacy, infant mortality rates, and nutrition levels, South Africa has moved substantially ahead of other countries on the continent. There are, of course, serious problem areas such as life expectancy (a result of the AIDS epidemic), housing shortages (a factor of increasing urbanization), and potable water (a key priority of the Mbeki government). But postapartheid South African economy has benefited from the moderating influence of Nelson Mandela, the willingness of the Mbeki government to push forward with market-based policies, and favorable international economic and financial conditions.

Income inequality continues to be the public policy issue that is driving both politics and racial relations. But even the huge gaps between rich and poor, white and black must be balanced by numerous examples of progress. The black technical and professional class is expanding, the concept of black entrepreneurship is now firmly embedded in the national economic culture, and blacks are becoming more visible as participants in the global economy and the institutions of the marketplace. Black businesspeople, for example, now control nearly 10 percent of the capital assets on the Johannesburg Stock Exchange. In fact, the Mbeki government has been criticized for its efforts to foster the economic and social mobility of blacks. The gradual formation of a black elite in South Africa has met with criticism from poor blacks as creating a new income gap between blacks who have prospered since the end of apartheid and blacks whose lives have changed little or have grown worse.

The primary goal of the Mbeki government in the coming years will be to sustain the level of economic development while chipping away at the gap between the haves and the have-nots. While South Africa remains a less developed nation with many of the problems similar to those of its neighbors, it nonetheless is a country that is markedly different and has the potential to serve as both an engine for growth on the continent and a model of development. For the Mbeki government, economic progress becomes not only a tool for political advantage (in this case a second term for Mbeki) but a source of pressure from a citizenry that expects more and increasingly demands more. The black underclass in South Africa can be expected to vent its frustrations over the speed with which income inequality is addressed, while the white minority can be expected to grow increasingly concerned over policies that redistribute wealth, show preferential treatment toward the black majority, and use racial rhetoric to place blame for failed delivery of services. It is the weight of economic success that in a developing country causes the most serious governing problems. President Mbeki and his ANC government have used the current climate of economic success to advance their political position, but the popular expectations for more (and more quickly) often pose the greatest political danger.

South Africa in the Global Economy

South Africa is often viewed as the only country in Africa that has a chance of "breaking through" into the developed world. Despite the fact that South Africa has a per capita GNP of $2,200 compared to a continental average in sub-Saharan Africa of $490, much of South Africa's future success will depend on how it integrates its economy with the global economy. South Africa is dependent on the export of diamonds and gold, which have suffered from depressed prices for a number of years. Foreign investment is a paltry 1 percent of GDP, and its reliance on foreign aid remains substantial ($540 million in 1999). Moreover, South Africa continues to avoid major restructuring of its domestic economy by protecting its industries and subsidizing its agricultural sector. The volatility of the national currency, the rand, signals that the South African economy is not meshing well with the global economy and that "breaking through" into the developed world is not likely to happen soon.

CHALLENGES

The challenges faced by many countries in the world are largely social and economic with an occasional political or national security crisis. But in South Africa the challenge that has life-and-death potential is the spread of AIDS. In 2000, 250,000 South Africans died of the disease and government estimates put the number of people who are carriers of the disease at 4.7 million, which means that one out every nine men, women, and children is affected by the killer disease. More significantly, the number of persons carrying human immunodeficiency virus (HIV), which causes AIDS, was up 12 percent over 1999. In KwaZulu-Natal province, 36 percent of the pregnant women tested were HIV positive. Some projections suggest that 50 percent of the population could succumb to the disease. As a result of the AIDS epidemic the life expectancy of the South African people has dropped dramatically in recent years. In 1996 life expectancy was in the early sixties; in 2000 the level had dropped to fifty-four years, and in 2010 the forecast is for the level to drop to around forty years. By 2015 South Africa's population is expected to decrease by 23 percent. Estimates place the AIDS death rate at 7 million by 2010.

The South African government has been slow to respond to the AIDS crisis. President Mbeki has been unwilling to take an aggressive role in combating AIDS. His health officials have picked up on Mbeki's foot dragging and have failed to develop a comprehensive program against the disease. The result is that South Africa has been late in addressing this killer disease and is facing the consequences in terms of an explosion of new cases and new deaths.

Because of the lax government response, many South African businesses and nonprofit organizations have begun to deal with the epidemic. Many companies, especially those associated with mining, where the disease is rampant, have begun to install condom machines in company toilets and hand out AIDS prevention literature to their employees. Other companies offer AIDS testing and counseling, and an employee who is found to have the disease is offered low-cost drugs. While such efforts have achieved a degree of success, there is little cause for optimism. AngloGold, one of the top mining companies in South Africa, reported in 1998 that 24 percent of its employees had HIV. Besides the human cost of HIV/AIDS, South African companies must deal with the financial costs of health care bills, lost work time, and the lack of replacement workers, especially in skilled and managerial positions.

Pressured in part by the private sector and the international community, the South African government is beginning to develop the kind of massive prevention and medical program necessary to deal with the epidemic. The government has now launched a public relations campaign with billboards, television ads, and leaflet drops showing the benefits of using condoms and engaging in responsible sex. The conflict between the Mbeki government and the international community has begun to reap some benefits in the form of programs designed to bring down the price of the AIDS drugs and move the drugs quickly into the hands of hospitals and rural clinics. Microsoft's Bill Gates has taken on AIDS as one of his philanthropic endeavors and has pledged billions of dollars to combat the disease in Africa, especially in South Africa. Most significantly, the Mbeki government permitted testing the drug Nevirapine on pregnant women with HIV/AIDS, after the province of KwaZulu-Natal announced that it would defy the government's ban on the testing of the drug.

As a result of these developments public, private, and international, there are some signs that the government's programs to combat AIDS has begun to have some impact. A survey conducted by the government in 1998 found that only 16 percent of young women had used a condom during their last sexual encounter outside of marriage. When the survey was conducted two years later in 2000, the number of young women using a condom had increased to 55 percent. Some critics have questioned the accuracy of the responses, but the government is convinced that its efforts have begun to have an impact. There have also been some encouraging signs in the South African school-age population, which has been the principal target of the government's advertising and education programs. The government is convinced that if the next generation is to be saved from the scourge of AIDS (there are 10.7 million orphans in all of Africa), sex education must begin early and inform young people about the dangers of unprotected sex.

In July 2000 the World AIDS conference was held in Durban, South Africa, and hosted by the Mbeki government. The conference demonstrated that AIDS has become more than a disease. It has become politicized as Mbeki and other government leaders in Africa and the less developed world see the disease as a means to criticize the West, Western capitalism, and Western pharmaceutical companies. There is a climate of denial in South Africa that is only beginning to break down. But once the denial is addressed there will be the even more difficult challenge of changing sexual mores and practices, providing prevention and care, and most of all getting the latest drugs to the millions who are HIV positive. The fact that South Africa has the largest number of HIV cases points to the daunting task that lies ahead for the government and the entire medical community. At this stage in the AIDS crisis in South Africa the answers to ending the epidemic are known; it is instituting policies and implementing those policies that are the real challenges. Failure to institute and implement life-saving policies will have a devastating impact on South Africa is a relatively short period of time.

South Africa is a key country on the African continent. Many nations look to it for guidance on issues of economic development, democratization, globalization, and critical public policy issues such as AIDS, population control, and nutrition. In 2001 President Mbeki took the lead in developing the New Partnership for African Development (NEPAD). As a means of attaining what he calls an "African renaissance," Mbeki, along with President Olusegun Obasanjo of Nigeria and Abdelaziz Bouteflika of Algeria, presented NEPAD to the Organization of African Unity (OAU). NEPAD is a bold attempt to ensure that Africa is capable of meeting the twin goals of globalization and democracy in the twenty-first century. Besides endorsing the basic premises of globalization, NEPAD calls for more democratic government, a commitment to respect human rights, massive investments (and foreign assistance) in health and education, and expanded trade in the region and with the industrial world. South Africa thus has domestic challenges that will require astute and aggressive governmental management, as well as regional ones that will require responsible political leadership. NEPAD is the brainchild of Mbeki and is designed to position himself and South Africa as the leader of African development.

South Africa under Mbeki has begun to play a more active role in using its military in peacekeeping operations. In 2002, after President Mbeki became chair of the new African Union, he offered to send 1,500 South African troops as United Nations peacekeepers into the Congo as a follow-up to the agreement that he brokered between the Congo and Rwanda. Mbeki envisions the 76,000-member armed forces of South Africa as playing an increasing role in bringing stability to the region. Since no other country in southern Africa has the numbers or the capability of Mbeki's troops, the role of peacekeeper may grow in the coming years and with it responsibility for leading the region away from its legacy of conflict and unrest.

Both Nelson Mandela and Thabo Mbeki have emerged as the voice of Africa. What they do or say about expropriation of white-owned land in Zimbabwe or AIDS transmission in Uganda or tribal genocide in Rwanda or peacekeeping operations in Sierra Leone gains the attention of regional leaders and indeed the international community. South African political and governmental leaders thus have a special challenge before them to lead in the domestic arena and in regional affairs. How South Africa develops and how it responds to the challenges before it may become the basis for an African model of public policy response to common problems.

AIDS AND DISCRIMINATION POLICY

Much of the attention in the HIV/AIDS epidemic in South Africa has been on the toll in human lives and the politics surrounding the medical response to the disease. What has been largely ignored as South Africa battles HIV/AIDS is the discrimination that those with the disease face as they seek employment, insurance, mortgages, and the everyday necessities that those without the disease take for granted. The AIDS Law Project was formed at the University of Witwatersrand by a core of dedicated lawyers to ensure that those with HIV/AIDS do not face discrimination and also to pressure the government to pass legislation that protects the rights of those with the disease. Because those with HIV/AIDS bear a stigma in South African society, the AIDS Law Project has faced enormous challenges as it seeks to protect the rights of its clients.

Those who have HIV come to the AIDS Law Project because their employer denied them a job when a mandatory test was performed as a requirement for employment. The AIDS Law Project has sued doctors and hospitals for failing to gain prior consent for HIV screening tests. One of the more controversial suits filed by the lawyers was against the South African military, which requires testing before admission into the armed forces. There are also issues of rights connected to insurance. As a result of a 1988 law, companies are within their rights to deny coverage to HIV-positive workers. Because of the law, companies in South Africa conduct more tests than the medical community and deny basic coverage to thousands of workers. The AIDS Law Project is especially concerned about the insurance issue because banks in South Africa demand coverage in the application for a home mortgage.

The work of the AIDS Law Project has expanded from the complexities of job discrimination and insurance coverage to the protection of HIV-positive individuals from abuse and even murder. In a highly publicized case, a Durban woman who announced publicly that she was HIV positive was murdered by four men. After a perfunctory investigation by the authorities in KwaZulu/Natal province, the four men were released because of insufficient evidence. The AIDS Law Project pressured provincial authorities to reexamine the case and appoint new investigators. The lawyers with the AIDS Law Project are convinced that the woman's death was viewed as inconsequential because she was poor and simply one of thousands who die regularly of the disease. Although the lawyers' efforts to bring justice in this case were ultimately unsuccessful, provincial and national authorities now pay more attention to the manner in which HIV/AIDS victims are treated.

The AIDS Law Project is fighting an uphill battle against corporate and government policies that discriminate. Despite the fact that South Africa's constitution has substantial guarantees of human rights, those with AIDS receive little sympathy from the government and face a wall of restrictions from employers. One of the key objectives of the AIDS Law Project is the inclusion of victim rights in labor and health reform legislation. Unfortunately, the South African parliament has not paid particularly close attention to the need to guarantee that HIV/AIDS victims are protected. But corporate and government roadblocks have not stopped the AIDS law project. As project director Mark Heywood states, "We believe if we challenge discrimination, at the end of the day that will assist effective HIV prevention. We want people to live longer, better, with more dignity. But there are worrying trends: Some practices of discrimination are being alleviated, while others are becoming more restrictive." ⊕

COMPARISONS

As the country representing Africa in this text, South Africa is in many ways not a representative country. While surrounding governments in the Democratic Republic of the Congo, Kenya, Nigeria, and Zimbabwe have experienced internal unrest, authoritarian leadership, and economic decay, South Africa has been able to avoid serious domestic disruptions while maintaining its democratic character.

South Africa, however, has not been without its democratic compromises and its institutional lapses. The South African political system, like its counterparts in the region, has centralized power in the governing ANC; President Thabo Mbeki and his executive office overshadow the legislature and the judiciary; and a disturbing number of human rights abuses and extra-constitutional actions call into question the political elite's commitment to democratic principles and practices. South Africa has transitioned from a one-party apartheid state controlled by the white minority to a one-party democratic-style state controlled by the black majority. As is often the case in the less developed world, the South African government creates the appearance of democratic process, when in reality it is tightly controlled from the president's office and institutions are too often mere window dressing.

South Africa stands out as a model of democratic governance in a challenging social and economic climate. South Africa has been able to sustain its democracy, while other African countries have slipped into authoritarianism or even political chaos. There is no question that South Africa is the leader of Africa. Its neighbors in the region and the international community of nations recognize that South Africa remains an exception to the rule on the continent. South Africa may have been blessed with natural resources and in a strange way may have been assisted in its economic and institutional development by first colonial and then white minority rule. Since the end of apartheid, South Africa has built on the positive contributions of the past and has not forsaken democratic governance in the present. The future direction of South African politics will help determine the prospects for democracy among all the people of Africa.

CONCLUSION

Erasing the memory of decades of race-based public policies supported by race-based economic and social institutions is a daunting and perhaps impossible task. But the South Africa of the twenty-first century has developed to a place where race and national modernization have converged. South African leaders have decided that it is essential to right the wrongs of the past through stern admonitions to the white business and professional elite and public policies that benefit the black majority.

To many outside South Africa, particularly in Europe and the United States, this racial strategy of national modernization holds the potential for fomenting dangerous black/white antagonisms that could easily destroy the fragile political and social balance and wreak havoc with the national economy. In a strange political twist, modern-day South Africa and the black majority leadership will be judged in part on how they respond to the needs and the rights of the white minority. After decades of chafing under white minority rule, the white minority holds the key to a positive evaluation of black majority rule. President Mbeki and the ANC naturally are concentrating their policymaking energies on the problems that affect the vast majority of the nation, but in South Africa it is the minority, a very wealthy and powerful minority, that cannot be ignored or worse yet be subjected to race-based retribution.

As noted throughout this discussion, much of governing is a process of balancing contending forces, whether political, social, or economic. Since 1994 South Africa has been viewed as a nation that has successfully balanced the highly charged legacy of apartheid with the promise of starting anew. South Africa has indeed started anew but it has not been able to shed the memory of the past. Recent positions taken by the government that perpetuate past racial antagonism jeopardize the delicate balance. In coming years the process of South African development will continue to be played out against this theme of balance, with both South Africans and the international community hoping that racial conditions do not impede the goals of national modernization.

POINT OF FACT

The South African national anthem is a moving song of national pride. The words of the anthem are as follows:

> *God bless Africa*
> *Let her glory be held high*
> *Please listen to our prayers*
> *God bless*
> *We her children*
> *Spirit please come down*
> *God bless*
> *Holy spirit please come down*
> *Bless us*
> *We her children*

God protect our nation
Please bring down an end to our wars and pain
Protect us
Protect our nation, Africa
Amen, so be it
Forever and ever.

A FEW BOOKS YOU SHOULD READ

Alex Boraine, *A Country Unmasked: Inside South Africa's Truth and Reconciliation Commission* (New York: Oxford University Press, 2001). Boraine was a key figure in the formation of the TRC and presents an insider view of the proceedings and the behind-the-scenes politics.

Murray Faure and Jan Erik Lane, *South Africa: Designing New Political Institutions* (Thousand Oaks, Calif.: Sage, 1996). A record of how South Africans formed a new constitution and new governing institutions.

Marais Hein, *South Africa: Limits to Change: The Political Economy of Transformation* (Cape Town: University of Cape Town Press, 1998). Essential reading for those interested in the modern South African economy and the challenges that lie ahead.

Anthony Sampson, *Mandela: The Authorized Biography* (New York: Knopf, 1999). Definitive biography of the father of South African democracy.

Leonard Thompson, *A History of South Africa* (New Haven: Yale University Press, 1995). Although this history only takes the reader to the early presidency of Mandela, it is the best account of South African development.

A FEW WEB SITES YOU SHOULD VISIT

www.parliament.gov.za. Web site of the South African parliament. Good for day-to-day policy discussions.

www.anc.org.za. Official Web site of the African National Congress. Invaluable for current politics.

www.gov.za. South African government Web site, a one-stop search engine on all things government in South Africa.

www.natweb.co.za. Web site of the opposition New National Party. Alternative views of politics and government

www.truth.org.za. Web site of the Truth and Reconciliation Commission. Essential history of the apartheid years.

MAP 8.1 Iraq

8

Iraq

Data Bank

Area: 438,000 sq. kilometers
Population: 22.7 million (1999)
Rural/urban population ratio: 23/77
Ethnic makeup: 75 percent Arabs, 15 percent Kurds, 10 percent other
Life expectancy: Male, 66 years; female, 68 years
Adult literacy: 58 percent
Form of government: Interim Administration of the United States and
    the United Kingdom
Head of government: United States and United Kingdom
    administrators with Iraqi elites
Per capita income/GNP: $1,060 (2002)
Exports: $21.8 billion (Russia, France); imports $13.8 billion
    (Egypt, Russia)
Source: United Nations and World Bank

Iraq is the ultimate example of a nation in transition. The invasion by U.S.
and British troops that began in March 2003 was designed to remove Iraqi
dictator Saddam Hussein from power, dismantle his repressive regime, and
disarm his military. All three objectives were met. The invasion, called
Operation Iraqi Freedom, was criticized by key countries in the United
Nations such as France, Germany, and Russia. Many countries in the Middle
East lashed out at the invasion (despite lukewarm support for Saddam) as another example of American hegemony in the region. President Bush and
Prime Minister Tony Blair were adamant that removing Saddam was long
overdue and that Iraq's defiance of U.N. resolutions to disarm legitimized

437

their decision to send over 300,000 troops to end authoritarian rule. In the following pages the regime of Saddam Hussein will be discussed as it existed before the invasion, with updates that discuss the shape and direction of postwar Iraq as it moves from dictatorship to democracy.

SETTING THE SCENE

It is difficult to separate Iraq from Saddam Hussein. His mark is everywhere in the country. After becoming president in 1979, Saddam Hussein turned Iraq into his own personal fiefdom. He and his family control all the important levers of state power, and the Baath political party that propelled him to power has become an extension of his rule. Saddam Hussein demands complete obedience and loyalty from those around him. Those who remain obedient and loyal are rewarded and allowed to remain in their positions; those who challenge him or work against him are eliminated. Iraq has a very simple governing system with one all-powerful dictator at the center of power, making policy, issuing orders, punishing adversaries, and enriching those who bend to his will.

Saddam Hussein has been so successful at consolidating his power and developing a governing regime in his image that he has been able to deflect every challenge to his authority and develop a modicum of public allegiance. It would be incorrect to describe him as popular, since support is based on fear rather than respect or admiration. Saddam has been able to present himself as a symbol of Iraqi nationalism, a bold leader who took on the United States, the United Nations, and the Western world and fought them to a standstill. Even though his ruthlessness and megalomania have devastated the economy and depressed the standard of living for most Iraqis, he nevertheless has been able to convince his people that the real culprits are outside the country. In particular, he has assigned blame for the collapse of the domestic economy on United Nations sanctions put in place after the Gulf War and attempts by the United States to topple him from power. Saddam has effectively turned the sanctions against the West through astute public relations ploys (pictures of sickly children in hospitals without medicine and schoolchildren denied milk) to galvanize national opinion and further consolidate his power.

Saddam's ability to shift blame onto his adversaries and his skill at creating divisions among those opposed to him have made it difficult to launch a concerted effort to remove him from power. Ever since the Gulf War, when Allied forces stopped short of ousting him after liberating Kuwait, Saddam has successfully held off attempts to dismantle his regime. Despite economic sanctions imposed by the United Nations and so-called no-fly zones that restrict Saddam's control of the skies, the Iraqi leader has maintained his control of the levers of national power and frustrated those in the West who have sought his removal. Saddam has shown a remarkable capability to foster dissension and caution among those who want to push him out of power.

Although Saddam's ability to remain in power is the source of constant annoyance to countries like the United States, the Western allies have come to understand that his resilience is founded on a dictatorial system that matches that of other infamous dictators of the twentieth century such as Hitler and Stalin. Saddam's power is built around a near totalitarian system where internal regime change is almost impossible. A few examples are sufficient to show the system of terror and control that Saddam has built up around him to ensure his security.

- In 1983 and 1988 Saddam used mustard gas on at least nine occasions during his war with Iran and in 1988 used a variety of nerve agents to kill five thousand Kurdish civilians in northern Iraq. By the end of 1988 an estimated 182,000 Kurds and other non-Arab people had been massacred by Saddam's troops.
- In 1996 Saddam executed his two sons-in-law, who had left Iraq with their wives and sought asylum in Jordan. While the move to Jordan was precipitated by a dispute between one of the sons-in-law, Lieutenant General Hussein Majid, and Saddam's son Uday over the distribution of wealth and internal power struggles, the two families made the fateful mistake of returning home when they were told that Saddam would grant them "forgiveness." Within days of their return Saddam had the men shot. Following a failed 1996 assassination attempt against Uday (who was seriously wounded) and a 1997 attempt on Saddam's other son, Qusai, Saddam rounded up hundreds of prisoners with known opposition proclivities and executed them without trial.
- The Iraqi dictator never sleeps in the same place for more than one night. He moves around, making it nearly impossible for his enemies to develop an assassination plot. Saddam is said to travel in a motorcade of similar-looking Mercedes Benz limousines to make an accurate attack on him more difficult. There are even reports that he has employed Iraqis who impersonate him when he visits areas thought to be hotbeds of opposition.
- Saddam's secret police agents are so pervasive that most Iraqis are reluctant to talk about their living conditions and politics. Informers are present throughout Saddam's Iraq. Even children are encouraged to relate information about government critics, including family members, to the authorities.

- In a 1995 referendum designed to provide Saddam with electoral legitimacy, he received 99.96 percent of the national vote with over 99 percent of the eligible voter turnout. In that referendum Saddam received only 3,300 negative votes, with most observers convinced that those who bravely challenged his regime likely faced some sort of retribution. A similar referendum was conducted in 2002. This time Saddam claimed to receive 100 percent support for his continued leadership of the country. To show their allegiance to Saddam, some Iraqis voted by drawing their blood and using it to mark the ballot.

The regime developed by Saddam Hussein in many respects falls within the parameters of the classic definition of a totalitarian state. Iraq under Saddam has one and only one political party—the Baath Party; there is only one guiding ideology or programmatic plan—the dictate of Saddam; a brutal secret police monitors every political move of the citizenry; and the state controls all information, all access to weapons, and most critical sectors of the economy. In such a totalitarian atmosphere there is little opportunity to challenge the regime or its leader, and those who do are quickly dispatched. With total control Saddam Hussein not only has the capability to run Iraq unimpeded, but also he has little concern about anyone questioning his authority and his judgment. In short, Iraq is Saddam and Saddam is Iraq.

POINT OF FACT
Saddam built seventy-eight presidential palaces, fifty-seven since the end of the Gulf War. The largest is the Sijood palace, with seven hundred structures.

POLICY ON INTERNALLY DISPLACED PERSONS

It is estimated that there are 500,000 internally displaced persons (IDPs) living in the three northern governorates of Iraq and nearly 100,000 IDPs living in the central and southern governorates. The IDPs in the north have been seeking resettlement since the Gulf War and Saddam Hussein's campaigns after the war to crack down on Kurdish separatist actions. The IDPs in the central and southern governorates have been seeking resettlement since the Iran-Iraq war and the Shiite uprisings since the immediate post–Gulf War period. Most of these people live in deplorable conditions in "collective towns," which is a euphemism for internment camps controlled by the government where the basic necessities of life are provided by international relief organizations.

For most of these people, largely women and children, the prospects for returning to their homes, their lands, and their previous way of life are remote.

The Iraqi government has paid little attention to the plight of the IDPs and in fact has contributed to the problem through pure neglect. In the southern governorates the IDPs come from villages ravaged by the Iran-Iraq war. Villagers in this area lost their homes and their prized palm groves, and the government drained part of the marshland in the area in order to place land mines and other protective devices to control infiltration from Iran. After the war the government began a modest agricultural program designed to resettle displaced families in this region. It was interrupted by a shortfall in budgetary resources, as money was shifted to military priorities and self-serving projects tied to Saddam and his family. Many of these IDPs were forced to move to urban areas such as Amarah and Basrah, where they settled in abandoned buildings. There is no evidence that the government has taken any steps to provide housing for these squatters. Rather the government has been content to allow international aid agencies and nongovernment organizations (NGOs) to provide the bare necessities for this growing population.

The plight of the IDPs is but one tragic example of the Iraqi government's failure to address the impact of its wars and its military policies on the general population. Displaced Iraqis have had to rely almost exclusively on U.N. agencies, particularly the settlement and rehabilitation sector, to care for these desperate people. With only scant cooperation from the government, U.N. agencies have sought to rebuild villages, provide rudimentary infrastructure such as sanitation, and offer financial assistance to IDPs. In many cases the international relief community faces an overwhelming challenge since the IDPs require not just shelter, but windows and doors, communal toilet cubicles, cooking and washing facilities, and basic home utensils.

There have been some examples of success in the southern governorates as the United Nations and various NGO-managed trust funds have built shelters and sanitation facilities in the Basrah, Amarah, and Nasiriya areas. While progress is being made, the plight of the IDPs remains the single most serious humanitarian challenge facing Iraq and the international community. The situation is compounded by the fact that the number of displaced Iraqis continues to grow as a result of sanctions, coalition bombing, and most importantly repressive government measures. With Saddam Hussein's regime showing little interest in addressing the needs of the IDPs, in large part because they challenged his rule, they will have to depend on the international community for help. Unfortunately, the efforts of the United Nations and NGOs will certainly be overwhelmed by the enormity of the Iraqi people's resettlement needs. ⊕

POLITICAL MILESTONES

Iraq's roots go back to biblical times, when it was known as Mesopotamia or "land between the rivers." The rivers of Mesopotamia are the Tigris and the Euphrates, which form a valley where the city-states of Sumer were founded. The Sumerians were highly educated and cultured people who are often recognized as producing the first calendar. Over time Iraq became a force in the Middle East. Baghdad evolved into a center of trade, culture, and political power. With the rise of the Ottoman Empire, Iraq came under the control of the Turks and its regional influence declined. When the Ottoman Empire collapsed, Iraq further declined in power and influence as it became a pawn in the hands of European powers like England and France. The British eventually came to control Iraq under a League of Nations mandate. Iraq gained its independence in 1932, but British influence remained under a monarchical system that favored European powers. It was not until 1958 that a military coup ousted the monarchy and placed Iraq on a path toward real independence.

After 1958 Iraq gradually regained the regional dominance it had during the heyday of Sumerian rule. But that dominance came at a horrible cost as both nationalism and militarism led to the rise of Saddam Hussein and the installation of one of the world's most tragic dictatorships. Throughout the modern period Iraq would be guided by the twin forces of nationalism and militarism. After Saddam's rise to power in 1979, the themes of nationalism and militarism became anchored deeply in the Iraqi political system and political psyche and helped advance Saddam's development of unquestioned power in a totalitarian state. The influence of nationalism and militarism under the repressive eye of Saddam Hussein became a sinister and tragic mix for Iraq and the Iraqi people.

Military Coups and the Kurds

Although Iraq gained its independence in 1932, the pro-Western Hashemite dynasty that ruled the country maintained close ties with Britain and generally followed policies that supported European, particularly British, interests. But Western influence waned as the twin forces of nationalism and militarism emerged in Iraq. The relative stability of the Hashemite monarchy ended abruptly in 1958, when King Faisal II was killed in a military coup led by nationalist General Abd al-Karim Qassim. Faisal's death ushered Iraq into a period of instability and uncertainty as a series of military officers jockeyed for power. For nearly ten years Iraq was caught in the grip of military intrigue as rival groups in the armed forces vied for power. The bloody competition among nationalist generals ended in 1968, when Major General

Ahmad Hasan al-Bakr staged a bloodless coup. Bakr was a former premier and leader of the Arab Socialist Renaissance Party, commonly referred to as the Baath Party. Bakr quickly promulgated a new constitution and assumed the key governing positions in Iraq, including the new post of chairman of the Revolutionary Command Council (RCC).

Bakr wasted no time in consolidating his power when he moved against opposition challengers such as Colonel Nazim Kazzar, the head of national security. Bakr laid the groundwork for a terrorist state through frequent arrests and executions of dissenters and opposition groups. Bakr used the threat of plots against him to liquidate his opponents and ensure that he would remain on top of the Iraqi state. During this time of political consolidation Bakr cemented his relationship with the Baath Party and transformed it into a tool of his dictatorship. Although often beset with internal factionalism and petty disputes, the Baath Party became the primary source of popular mobilization and policy implementation.

In this period of instability and political consolidation Bakr faced a challenge from the Kurdish minority as it began a long period of conflict. Iraq had for centuries been populated by diverse people, cultures, and religions. When the British formally established Iraq, the diversity served as the basis for deep-seated competition and antagonisms between the various occupants of this new country. The Kurds, who lived in northern Iraq (with substantial spillover into Turkey and Iran), had resisted domination by the Baghdad government. From 1961 to 1975, the Kurds openly rebelled against Iraq, receiving extensive military assistance from Iran. In 1970 there was a brief period of stability in the Iraqi-Kurdish relationship, which culminated in an agreement whereby the Kurds were formally recognized as an Iraqi people and their language officially accepted. Provision was also made for Kurdish involvement in the Iraqi government.

The agreement, however, quickly broke down over oil revenue issues and boundaries. With the failure of diplomacy, the Iraqi government resorted to a military solution and staged a major assault on the Kurds, driving over 100,000 back into Iranian territory. Iraq and Iran attempted to settle their differences over the Kurds and reached another settlement in 1975. Iran gained control of the strategic Shatt al-Arab waterway in the south in return for breaking all ties with the Kurds. With Iran pledging to withdraw support from the Kurds, the Iraqi government resumed its long-standing policy of ruthlessly blocking the creation of an autonomous Kurdistan in northern Iraq. By 1976 Iraq was engaged in attacks against the Kurds. Thousands of Kurds were deported to southern Iraq, and Arab settlers replaced them in northern Iraq.

After over ten years in power President Bakr resigned and handed over power to Saddam Hussein. Saddam had already been recognized as the force behind the presidency of Bakr, and most sources familiar with Iraq were convinced that Saddam engineered the resignation. But Saddam's ambition to rise to the pinnacle of Iraqi governing power did not hide the fact that opposition to Bakr's rule was growing. There was displeasure in the Revolutionary Command Council (RCC) over Bakr's inability to deal with ongoing Kurdish uprisings and new unrest among the Shiite Muslim community in the wake of the Iranian revolution. There was also opposition to Bakr's proposed Iraq-Syria unification plan and his firing of cabinet ministers who were members of the Iraqi Communist Party. Once in power, Saddam moved quickly to consolidate his authority by purging Communists from his government and removing challengers from the RCC.

The Iran-Iraq War

After the period of consolidation Saddam centered his attention on Iran and various points of disagreement with the government of the shah and later the Ayatollah Khomeini. Saddam was angered by Iran's continued support of the Kurdish rebels, sponsorship of a 1970 coup attempt, and occupation of three islands in the strategically important Gulf of Hormuz in 1971. Tensions heightened between the two countries when Saddam abrogated the 1975 Algiers treaty between Iraq and Iran, allegedly over the Kurdish issue but more likely to challenge the Khomeini government's growing regional influence and its support for Shiite opposition to his regime. (Iraq is controlled by Sunni Muslims, while the Iranians, who are Persians, have a ruling elite dominated by Shiite Muslims.) Saddam feared that Khomeini's Iran would encourage the Shiites in Iraq to overthrow him.

The points of contention between Saddam's Iraq and Iran were tangential to his quest for dominance in the region. Saddam had his own vision of Iraq's place as a strategic power in the region and his place as the most powerful and feared Arab head of state. Iraq and Iran had long competed for power and influence in the region but were restrained by British influence. But with the United States supporting the shah of Iran and Saudi Arabia, Saddam would not accept second place. He sought assistance from the Soviet Union and built his military into the fourth largest in the world. When the Iranian revolution began to show signs of internal discord and a lessening of fervor toward Khomeini's rule, Saddam saw the opportunity he had been waiting for and gave the order to invade Iran's Khuzistan province, long a haven for Kurdish rebels. Saddam was certain that he had calculated the weakness of the Iranian revolutionaries and would end their influence and achieve his dream of regional domination.

The invasion of Iran began an eight-year war of attrition between the two countries. Although Saddam's military had a decided advantage over Iran, particularly in terms of air superiority, Iran's armed forces fought back against the Iraqi troops with a religious zeal inspired by dedication to Khomeini and his fanatical Islamic Republic. The war quickly settled into a stalemate with both sides losing hundreds of thousands of troops and billions in equipment. One estimate put the loss of military and civilian life on both sides at a million people. Saddam sought various cease-fire agreements from the Tehran government, but his overtures were rejected because the Iranians sought $150 billion in reparations and his ouster. For the Iranians and the Ayatollah Khomeini, the war was a "holy war" against Saddam and his Baath Party. But for Saddam the war was essential to establish himself and Iraq as the dominant political and military force in the region. Saddam was not about to relinquish his hold on Iraq as a prerequisite for peace with Iran. Better to sacrifice thousands of his troops and impoverish his country with war than agree to a peace that left him out of power.

The protracted war ended in 1988, when both sides fought over the key city of Basra near the disputed Shatt al-Arab waterway in southern Iraq. For months the Iraqis and Iranians battled each other with artillery fire and suicide attacks. It was not until the government of Ayatollah Khomeini faced internal pressure over the costly battle that the two sides were able to reach a cease-fire. But, even after the agreement was reached, Saddam did not approve the ending of hostilities until 1990.

Saddam and the Invasion of Kuwait

Saddam's decision to take aggressive action against Kuwait was the result of a July 17 Revolution Day speech in which he charged that the Kuwaiti government was producing oil in violation of OPEC quotas and was stealing oil from Iraq by engaging in so-called slant drilling, a procedure in which oil wells are dug on the Kuwaiti side of the border but the drilling actually takes the oil from reserves in Iraqi territory. The charges were viewed as a facade for the Iraqi dictator's desire to use an invasion of Kuwait as a stepping-stone to increased influence in the region, leading to his complete domination.

But Saddam miscalculated the international response to his invasion and the ability of the United Nations to respond with one voice. Within hours of the invasion the United Nations Security Council demanded an immediate withdrawal of Saddam's troops and within days it passed a trade embargo. On November 29, 1990, the United Nations approved the use of any methods needed to force Iraqi compliance by January 15, 1991. Saddam met these measures with characteristic intransigence and bravado. Although he sent foreign minister Tariq Aziz for face-to-face discussions with U.S. and U.N. diplomats, there was no movement on the part of the Iraqis, only bold claims of a jihad against the United States and calls for Arab retaliation against Israel. The Iraqi leader clearly enjoyed the international limelight and the prospect of taking on the United Nations and particularly the United States.

While the Western coalition prepared for a land invasion of Iraq, Saddam's forces systematically pillaged Kuwait. Saddam had long coveted the oil-rich but weakly defended Kuwait, and his forces wasted no time in claiming Kuwaiti property as theirs. The homes of wealthy Kuwaitis were broken into and their possessions stolen, women were savagely raped and the men who resisted were executed. Saddam's cousin, Ali Hassan al-Majid, better known as "Chemical Ali" for his involvement in the gassing of the Kurdish people in 1998, turned up in Kuwait and coordinated the pillaging and human rights abuse.

In January 1991 the United States led a large international coalition of over 600,000 troops to remove Iraqi troops from Kuwait. Although the coalition victory over Saddam's troops was quick and devastating (the miles and miles of destroyed Iraqi trucks, tanks, and artillery became the visual proof on the nightly news of the enormity of the loss), Saddam was not driven from power. He agreed to disarmament terms with the United Nations that limited his air control to the center of the country (the so-called no-fly zones) and accepted severe economic sanctions, but he quickly sensed that the Western powers were not going to intervene on behalf of the opposition Kurds in the north or the Shiites in the south. As a result, Saddam moved to crush the rebellion of the Kurds and Shiites as the United Nations and the Bush administration stayed in the background and gave only lip service and some humanitarian aid to both groups.

Saddam and Postwar Iraq

Saddam Hussein's leadership of postwar Iraq focused on responding to the economic dislocations connected with the trade sanctions, the constant pressure from UNSCOM (the U.N. weapons inspection unit), and American and British domination of the skies over the no-fly zones. During 1994 and 1995 Saddam made numerous changes in his cabinet and often resorted to the tried and true practice of appointing family members or cronies whose loyalty was unquestioned. This consolidation of power and concentration on loyalty achieved its zenith with the Revolutionary Coordinating Council's decision in 1995 to change the Iraqi constitution to permit a national referendum that would allow Saddam to confirm his popular support. In an extraordinary move, the National Assembly officially named Saddam as its nominee for a seven-year term as president of the country. A few weeks later the national referendum was held with Saddam gaining overwhelming voter support.

Although Saddam used the national referendum to remind his opponents that he could marshal considerable popular support, his problems dealing with the sanctions, the weapons inspections, and the no-fly zones continued and intensified. In May 1996 the U.N. Security Council approved the "oil for food" program despite Saddam's objection that it was a violation of national sovereignty (and a loss of control over oil revenues). After some delays related to U.S. concern over program monitoring and Saddam's resistance, the oil for food policy was implemented in December, with Iraq permitted to sell $2 billion in oil over a six-month period. The proceeds were to be distributed to Kuwaiti victims of the 1990 invasion, Kurds in northern Iraq, and children and those needing medical attention in Iraq. Eventually the oil for food arrangement raised $5.2 billion, amid mounting charges of misuse of the funds and illegal sale of additional oil.

Tensions between Saddam and the West escalated in 1997, when the Iraqi government stated that it would block weapons investigations under the auspices of UNSCOM unless the economic sanctions were lifted. The head of the UNSCOM team was former Australian ambassador to the United Nations Richard Butler. Butler was a outspoken critic of Saddam and a relentless force in pushing for expanded weapons inspections. Butler was convinced that his inspectors had made significant progress in uncovering weapons of mass destruction, but they were also convinced that Saddam was hiding caches of biological and chemical agents and nuclear materials that could be used to develop weapons of mass destruction. In response to UNSCOM pressure, Saddam threatened to expel the inspectors, especially the American inspectors. Over the next two years Saddam, the United Nations, and the United States played a game of diplomatic maneuvering and high-stakes confrontation, with Saddam seeking to force UNSCOM out.

During this period Saddam often relented in the face of U.N. and U.S. pressure and permitted the UNSCOM inspectors to remain in Iraq. But in December 1998 Saddam resisted the continued presence of the weapons inspectors. Richard Butler and the international team of inspectors were convinced that Saddam refused to cooperate with UNSCOM because inspectors were making progress in finding the sources of weapons production. As tensions escalated between the two sides, the U.S. and British air forces subjected Saddam's military targets to four days of bombing, with the objective of destroying his bomb-making factories and storehouses of lethal biological and chemical agents. Although the air raids destroyed some of Saddam's military command posts and weapons factories, there was general agreement that the bombing did not destroy Iraq's capacity to build weapons of mass destruction.

In the years after the bombing, Saddam and the Iraqi leadership focused on devising ways to circumvent the economic sanctions and weaken the resolve of the Western coalition. Despite regular confrontations with American and British fighter jets in the no-fly zones, Saddam tried to convince Arabs that the U.S.-led efforts to strangle Iraq were punishing innocent civilians. The United States and Britain, however, were unmoved and continued the air war policy, citing Saddam's acquisition of sophisticated radar from the Russians and fiber optic communications from the Chinese, both designed to improve the Iraqi capacity to challenge American and British fighters.

Despite claims by the United States and Britain that Saddam remained a threat to the region and was seeking ways to bolster his military capacity, the Iraqi leader developed stronger ties with neighboring countries, even though many Arab nations remained mistrustful of him and his regime. Egyptian President Hosni Mubarak criticized the continued air raids as doing nothing but "complicating matters." Syria's vice president broadened its criticism of the United States by saying that the bombing was a means of dividing Arabs while the Israelis were crushing the Palestinians.

What unified the region and played into Saddam's hands was concern over U.S. policy that continued the sanctions and the air war more than ten years after the invasion of Kuwait. Saddam was able to convince Arab nations that the attempt to maintain an economic stranglehold on Iraq threatened his nation's sovereignty and impoverished his people. Saddam also benefited from the growing anti-American climate in the Middle East during the war in Afghanistan. In 2002 during the Israeli-Palestinian conflict Saddam offered to give $25,000 to each family of a suicide bomber and encouraged other countries to engage in an oil boycott of the United States.

Although the United States worked to convince moderate Middle Eastern nations of the need to move against Saddam and his weapons of mass destruction, there was little regional interest in attacking him. Despite his authoritarian regime and past destabilizing policies, he was not viewed as an immediate threat. Saddam carefully crafted his response to threats from the Bush administration to elicit support from neighboring Middle Eastern countries and to cast the United States as an overzealous and hegemonic power bent on revenge.

Despite Saddam's efforts to generate support in the region and the world community, in November 2002 the Bush administration forged an international coalition of support that led the U.N. Security Council to pass a unanimous resolution (Resolution 1441) to establish a strict timetable for onsite inspections leading ultimately to the disarmament of Saddam's weapons of mass destruction. Although the resolution was a compromise in order to win the support of Russia and France, two of Iraq's trading partners, there was no mistaking the message of the United Nations: Saddam would have to disarm or be disarmed by U.S. and British armed forces. The resolution led to a renewal of onsite inspections in Iraq by U.N. personnel. From December 2002 to March 2003 the U.N. inspectors sought to document Iraq's compliance (or lack of it) with disarmament resolutions from the Gulf War era that required destruction of all weapons of mass destruction. But once the United States and Britain failed to get U.N. approval to take military action, the U.N. inspectors were removed. Diplomacy had failed and the road to war was open.

Timeline

1919	Britain given mandate over Iraq
1958	Monarchy is overthrown
1968	Baath Party takes power
1979	Saddam Hussein assumes presidency
1980–1988	Iran-Iraq War
1990	Kuwait is invaded
1991	Operation Desert Storm to liberate Kuwait
1995	Saddam wins overwhelming presidential victory in national referendum
1998	United Nations weapons inspectors leave Iraq
1999–2002	Ongoing air strikes by Americans and British in Iraq
2002	Campaign by the Bush administration to gather international support for an attack on Iraq
2003	United States and Britain invade Iraq

FORMAL GOVERNMENT

Examining the formulation and implementation of Iraqi public policy under Saddam Hussein suggests that the government is Saddam Hussein. Saddam's official title is President and Prime Minister of the Republic, Chairman of the Revolutionary Command Council, and Secretary General of the Regional Command of the Baath Party. The titles cover much of governing power in Iraq. However, despite the fact that Saddam controls all the key positions, Iraq is not without a formal structure of governance. The formal structure is inextricably connected to the personalist leadership of Saddam, his extended family, and loyal supporters in the Baath Party, the secret police, the military, and key ministries.

Much of the government in Iraq was created by the 1968 provisional constitution. It clearly stated that the Arab Baath Socialist Party governs Iraq through the Revolutionary Command Council (RCC), which holds both executive and legislative authority. The RCC is defined as Iraq's highest governing authority. Saddam decreased the number of seats in the RCC, stripped it of anyone who might challenge his authority, and transformed it into an institution that ratifies and ultimately legitimizes decisions that he and he alone makes. As initially established, the RCC was viewed as a collective institution charged with making public policy decisions and then overseeing the work of the various ministries. But when Saddam consolidated power after Bakr resigned, the RCC's role as collective decisionmaker was downgraded.

Despite Saddam's control, the RCC has continued to serve as a monitor of government policy implementation. In a real sense the RCC is Saddam's administrative supervisor, ensuring that the Council of Ministers (the governing cabinet) carries out his dictates. By using the RCC in this role of policy monitor, Saddam has created the appearance of broad-based decisionmaking. The RCC issues decrees (with Saddam's approval) that have the force of law and therefore do not move through the legislative system. The composition of the RCC fluctuates based on Saddam's political objectives, but membership in the body is limited to activists of the Baath Party. Membership in the RCC is coveted by the party elite and is a sure sign of loyalty to Saddam.

Domination of public policymaking by Saddam and the RCC has diminished the role of the legislature. The Iraqi National Assembly is made up of 250 members who come from fifty-six constituencies. There is no other body in the Iraqi legislature, since bicameralism was abandoned with the overthrow of the monarchy in 1958. All candidates seeking to run for seats in the National Assembly require the approval of the government and must declare their allegiance to Saddam Hussein. By law candidates for the National Assembly must "believe in God, the principles of the July 17–30 revolution, and socialism." Most of the members of the National Assembly are from the Baath Party, but there are some independents. In the 1996 election there was an element of competition as 689 candidates vied for the 220 seats. The remaining thirty seats from the Kurdish provinces were filled directly by Saddam Hussein, since no election was held in the autonomous regions. There was no evidence of opposition parties or candidates challenging any of these 689 candidates. In the 2000 election, five hundred candidates participated in the election process, again with no real opposition alternative. One of the only significant changes in the 2000 election was that twenty-five women candidates were victorious and now hold seats in the National Assembly. Although elections for the National Assembly are held every four years, the actual functioning of the Iraqi legislature is much less regular. The National Assembly meets for only a few weeks each year, and Saddam controls the agenda. The lawmaking function is confined to ratifying decisions made by Saddam and the RCC.

Because the Kurdish minority has remained a powerful force inside Iraq, Saddam has sought to control the Kurds and limit their separatist ways by creating autonomous governing institutions. In 1980 Saddam agreed to the formation of a Kurdish legislative council that had little if any power. But after the Gulf War, with Saddam effectively cut off from air superiority over Kurdish territory, genuinely democratic institutions gained an opportunity to function and mature. The Iraqi Kurdistan National Assembly was established in 1991 with responsibility for selecting a prime minister and serving as the representative body of the Kurdish people. The unicameral body contains 105 seats, and power is split between two political parties, the Democratic Party of Kurdistan and the Patriotic Union of Kurdistan.

Although Saddam is the center of governing power and controls all the levers of governance, he has formed a vast bureaucracy that reaches into all facets of Iraqi national life. The Council of Ministers is larger than in most developing countries and certainly in most democracies. Some of the unique bureaucracies are the Ministry of Religious Affairs, Ministry of Irrigation (the centuries-old foundation of Iraqi agriculture), and Ministry of Oil. The primary requirement for these ministers is loyalty to Saddam. In return, they are well compensated and despite the economic sanctions have access to the latest Western clothing, technology, and transportation. Within the ministerial circle Saddam has established three deputy prime ministers, who serve as his closest advisers. He has also established two ministers of state who provide counsel on military and strategic matters.

The Iraqi judicial system has little power and functions in a manner that solidifies Saddam's position. The judiciary is headed by a Court of Cassation, which comprises five courts of appeal, a court of first entry, and various religious and revolutionary courts. Saddam uses the religious courts to gain support among Islamic leaders, particularly the Shiites. Saddam has shown little interest in advancing Islam in Iraq and views Muslim religious leaders as a political threat. The revolutionary courts are often employed in cases involving security threats to Saddam's regime. These revolutionary courts serve as venues to publicly try those involved in coups against the regime or those who have committed crimes against the state. There is little in the religious and revolutionary courts that approaches Western-style due process and defendant rights.

In terms of internal administrative organization Iraq is organized into fifteen governorates with Baghdad being the largest and Basra in the south the second largest. While these governorates have some degree of power regarding local services, real governing power flows from Baghdad. Iraq is formally described as having a unitary system of local administration, but in this case unitary is best understood as centralized. Saddam uses the governors of these administrative units as one of his links to the citizenry. He rewards them handsomely for their loyalty and punishes them harshly when they are unable to maintain control. The governorate of Basra with its Shiite ethnic composition has been most difficult for Saddam to control. As a result he has stationed a large contingent of troops in and around Basra in case of an uprising.

Three governorates are associated with the Kurdish Autonomous Region. Kurdish autonomy was established in 1970, when the government legally recognized the Kurds' right to a level of control of their homeland in northeastern Iraq. In 1976 the Iraqi government expanded autonomy by creating the Kurdish Autonomous Region, which was made up of the three governorates. The recognition of Kurdish autonomy and the creation of the Kurdish Autonomous Region, however, was largely a public relations maneuver meant to contain a separatist movement by more militant Kurdish leaders. After the Gulf War Baghdad began more substantive negotiations regarding the Kurdish region. But discussions broke down and today the Kurdish Autonomous Region is described as a safe haven protected by American and British fighter jets. It is a highly contentious area where Iraqi and Kurdish troops clash and where Saddam has pledged to regain complete control.

Iraq's formal governing structure, unlike countries influenced by Western democratic values and practices, encompasses more than just the standard three branches of government and the relationship between center and periphery. The authoritarian and therefore centralized nature of the Iraqi political system requires a more expansive discussion. In particular, the Baath political party must be included in the description of formal government. Founded in 1947 as a party that advocated Arab nationalism, the Arab Socialist Renaissance Party (Baath) grew in influence with branches throughout the Middle East. With the 1968 coup that brought General Bakr to power, the Baath became an integral part of Iraqi government. Later, with the promulgation of the National Action Charter, Bakr made the Baath into the centerpiece of his regime. Saddam Hussein's rise to Iraqi strongman in 1979 was through the Baath, which further underscored the status of the party as the core of the authoritarian regime and the primary recruiting stepping-stone for the Iraqi political and governmental elite.

Once in power, Saddam transformed the Baath into a mass-based party with the mission of ensuring state control. While the leadership of the party is closely regulated and loyalty is essential, the party organization is used as the primary state mechanism for political socialization, popular mobilization, and general societal organization. Although membership rolls in the party are not made public, it is estimated that up to 8 percent of the Iraqi population is associated with the Baath. The Baath Party has cells, similar to

Communist Party cells, throughout Iraqi society. Neighborhood, school, factory, union, youth, and other sectors are tied into the Baath Party, which uses these linkages to monitor everyday life and ensure that Iraqis do not stray from the established doctrine set by Saddam and his government.

Baath Party domination of Iraqi politics and national life means that the process of governing often becomes a competition between bureaucratic authority within the ministries and party authority that is in the RCC and throughout society. Of course Saddam remains the ultimate authority and he has been known to play his bureaucratic ministers against his Baath officials to ensure that one does not become powerful enough to threaten him. After falling out of favor with Saddam in the late 1980s and early 1990s, the Baath organization played a key role in the 1995 national referendum and 1996 National Assembly elections. The party was seen as critical in achieving the huge turnout for Saddam and one year later in dominating the list of candidates for the legislative elections.

Along with the Baath Party the Iraqi military is part of the formal governing structure. Again, the authoritarian nature of the Iraqi political system depends on the armed forces not only to protect the nation from outside threats and advance the foreign policy objectives of the government but also to provide the regime with the means through which it can survive challenges to its existence. In the case of Saddam's regime, the military has not been the foundation of government stability. In fact, the Iraqi military has been the source of assassination plots and coup attempts against Saddam and his inner family and advisory circle.

The Iraqi military at present has an estimated 400,000 men organized in twenty-three divisions. The raw numbers and the divisional composition, however, are misleading. Western intelligence sources generally agree that only twelve of the twenty-three divisions would respond to Saddam's call to arms. The elite Republican Guards and the Special Republican Guards numbering 100,000 troops are well equipped with over 2,000 tanks and 2,100 artillery pieces. The Republican Guards and the Special Republic Guards remain zealously loyal to Saddam and can be counted on to obey his orders. The remainder of the Iraqi military is poorly trained and equipped and its commitment is based more on fear than professional pride and loyalty.

Saddam has kept his military in line by a mixture of generous financial rewards, expensive Western goods, and other privileges. He moves officers around, demotes those who pose a challenge, and promotes those who show unquestioned loyalty. He has also kept fresh leadership in areas critical to the defense of the nation and his survival, such as the air force and the Republican Guards. Despite all this maneuvering, Saddam faces a military that has a history of behind-the-scenes planning against him. Observers of Iraqi politics openly admit that they cannot be certain about the extent to which the military has tried to remove Saddam, since many assassination attempts and coups never become public. Scheming officers are summarily executed without mention in the strictly state-controlled press.

The final piece of the Iraqi governing structure is the secret police and paramilitary apparatus that Saddam has carefully developed over the years. There is no doubt that Saddam's resiliency in power is directly associated with his skill at building an internal security system and spy network. The best known and influential unit of the security system is the General Intelligence Apparatus, or Mukhabarat. The Mukhabarat's mission is to monitor most of the key government sectors: Baath Party officials, bureaucratic ministers, and military officers. The general security directorate keeps a close eye on civilian threats to the regime and a military intelligence unit has responsibility to monitor Iraqi opposition groups abroad and gather intelligence in foreign countries. There is also the special security unit, al-Himaya, which is Saddam Hussein's personal security force. Al-Himaya handles special intelligence matters such as monitoring Saddam's close associates and is often called on to mete out punishment to Saddam's enemies. Saddam has also assembled a complex web of semiofficial and paramilitary units that maintain order, intimidate opponents of his regime, and serve as frontline guerrilla units in the face of invaders. Al-Istikhbarat is the main military intelligence unit. It spies on foreign countries and engages in clandestine operations. Fedayeen Saddam, or "Saddam's Men of Sacrifice," make up an elite force dedicated to protecting Saddam and his regime at all costs. Many of the Fedayeen are from Tikrit, Saddam's hometown. Al-Quds Army is a civilian militia of civil servants formed in 1998 to prepare the nation in case of invasion. Finally, Ashbal Saddam are the "Lion Cubs of Saddam," boys from ten to fifteen years of age who are trained in summer camps to fight for Saddam. Many join the Fedayeen.

The complexity of the Iraqi spy system is a clear sign of Saddam's fear of traitors. By creating competing security agencies and then charging them with the task of ferreting out "enemies of the state," Saddam has increased the chances that assassination or coup plots will be discovered. Developing an elaborate secret police and internal security system is one of the foundations of classic totalitarian government. With thousands of agents looking into the private affairs of Iraqi citizens and creating an internal atmosphere of fear and intimidation, Saddam has taken out a political insurance policy against threats to his life and position. But for Iraqi citizens, whether in government or out of government, the secret police and the security agents are responsible for a complete breakdown in trust, freedom, and openness.

Constitutional Principles

Article 37 of the Iraqi constitution lays out the supremacy of the Revolutionary Command Council with the following language:

The Revolutionary Command Council is the supreme institution in the State, which on 17 July 1968 assumed the responsibility to realize the public will of the people, by removing the authority from the reactionary, individual, and corruptive regime, and returning it to the people.

POINT OF FACT

Article 39 includes the official oath of office for the president, vice president, and major officials of government:

I swear by God Almighty, by my honor and by my faith to preserve the Republican system, to commit myself to its Constitution and laws, to look after the independence of the Country, its security and territorial integrity, and to do my best earnestly and sincerely to realize the objectives of the Arab Nation for Unity, Freedom, and Socialism.

POLICIES DESIGNED TO RESPOND TO DISABLED PEOPLE

The constant state of war in Iraq has substantially increased the number of people with disabilities, particularly injuries associated with combat or land mines. The World Health Organization (WHO) estimates that more than 2 million Iraqis can be categorized as suffering from a war-related disability. The number of Iraqis with disabilities is most pronounced in the northern governorates and the southern region, which were hard hit by either the war with Iran or the Gulf War. As with the plight of displaced persons, disabled children and adults suffer from scarce resources and a government that shows a declining level of interest.

Government policies regarding the disabled were not always marked by resource allocation and inattention. In 1980, prior to the Iran-Iraq War, the government enacted a social welfare law that was generally viewed as progressive. In fact, Iraq was the first Middle Eastern nation to take an active role in providing medical, educational, and economic rights to the disabled. As a result of the law, over thirty education and rehabilitation institutes were established that dealt exclusively with disabled children and adults. Furthermore,

Iraqis passed labor legislation requiring every employer in the country to put aside at least 3 percent of job positions for the disabled. The Iraqi model for dealing with the disabled and providing job opportunities was so successful that it was used in other countries such as the United Arab Emirates.

But by 1991 most of the programs put in place by the government were in a state of disarray or were simply abandoned. Many of the education and rehabilitation centers were deprived of funds and had to suspend operations. Transportation, a vital link for bringing children and adults to the centers, was severely cut back. By the 1990s international agencies such as WHO reported that the number of centers for the disabled had declined by as much as 30 percent. Without these centers many families with disabled children and adults have had to fend for themselves in an ever harsher economic climate.

The economic collapse of Iraq after the Gulf War and the shifting of resources away from social welfare priorities have also affected the work opportunities of the disabled. The Iraqi Ministry of Labor and Social Affairs reported after the Gulf War that 80 percent of disabled adults had lost their jobs. Disabled women were hardest hit by the layoffs, as the ministry admitted that upward of 95 percent had been laid off, never to be rehired. Since the early 1990s there has been no appreciable increase in employment of the disabled as the Iraqi economy remained mired in deep depression. The sad result is that disabled have joined the long lines of vagrants begging on the streets in order to stay alive. Many have had to leave their families who cannot afford to take care of them.

International agencies, most associated with the United Nations, are working to provide a modicum of relief to the disabled. The United Nations Development Program, the International Labor Organization (ILO), UNICEF, and WHO have set up programs to provide vocational training and employment opportunities for the disabled. These, however, are small efforts that in no way address the hundreds of thousands of disabled children and adults who have lost what was once a prized safety net. The Iraqi government is making no concerted effort to restart programs that provide basic services and opportunities for the disabled. The situation continues on a downward slide and is compounded by growing numbers of disabled, due in large part to land mine explosions. ⊕

THE CITIZEN AND THE STATE

In Iraq there is little in the way of a relationship between citizens and the state. The state dictates policy and the citizens are expected to obey. The Saddam

Hussein regime is not based on values such as openness, communication, involvement, and toleration. Instead, Saddam demands that Iraqi citizens be loyal servants of the state and unquestioning supporters of their supreme leader. There is little room to maneuver in this closed society. Those who are bold enough to question authority are quickly punished and those who seek to introduce an alternative relationship between citizens and the state are executed.

The simple formula of citizenship that Saddam created in Iraq has had devastating consequences on the body politic. Throughout the country there is widespread distrust, not just of foreigners but of neighbors and colleagues. When approached by outsiders, Iraqis are ill at ease and refuse to get involved in conversations that steer toward their opinions of the government and Saddam. Although participation is high in terms of the 1995 and 2000 national referenda and the elections for the National Assembly, there is a noticeable sense of forced involvement and fear of failure to participate. There was credible evidence during the 1995 referendum that five hundred persons were arrested in three provinces for casting ballots against Saddam, and a member of the intelligence service was reportedly executed for voting against Saddam.

If there is any civic value that does not appear to be forced or required by Saddam, it is national pride. As a result of the Gulf War and the subsequent sanctions and regular bombing raids, Iraqis have developed an us-versus-them mentality that has affected the ability of the general population to deal with scarcity and suffering. The Iraqi people, at least publicly, do not blame their leader for the deaths of thousands of babies and elderly. Instead, they see the sanctions as an attempt by Western powers to punish them as a people. There is obvious anti-American sentiment in Iraq, especially among those who have lost loved ones to the lack of medicine or infant formula or other basic necessities of life.

There is no question that the relationship between citizen and state in Iraq is defined by Saddam Hussein. One of the more obvious manifestations of the domination of Iraqi political culture by Saddam Hussein is the extent to which he has developed a cult of personality around himself. His picture is displayed prominently throughout the country. Huge monuments that glorify his accomplishments attest to his limitless megalomania, and state-controlled media provide a constant stream of his image, his words, his policies, and his promises.

Much of Saddam's contact with the Iraqi people is designed to further the cult of personality. There are regularly televised speeches on key holidays such as the anniversary of the 1968 revolution and the "liberation" of Kuwait in 1990. On these occasions Saddam takes credit for the development of Iraq or for Iraqi leadership of the Arab world. But Saddam has not been limited to the standard modes of public relations. In 1996 he swam (many say that it was a double posing as Saddam) in the Euphrates River along with a contingent of bodyguards to prove to his fellow Iraqis that he remained vigorous despite rumors of ill health. He also ventures out regularly (again under heavy armed protection) dressed in various types of garb from the standard military uniform to traditional ethnic dress to an informal tweed jacket. He is usually accompanied by his family and almost always brings along children to play up the father-figure image.

Saddam's efforts to shape the national political culture to his advantage have distinct religious and ethnic overtones. Saddam regularly invokes the name of God in his speeches and public pronouncements. The 1998 speech celebrating the thirtieth anniversary of the revolution began with "In the Name of God, the Compassionate, the Merciful" and ended with "God is Great." Although Saddam is committed to maintaining Iraq as a secular state, he rarely misses an opportunity to prove his religious inclinations. With neighboring Iran under the control of religious leaders (mullahs) and the Shiites in the southern regions of the country always threatening him and his regime, Saddam recognizes the importance of incorporating religion into the political culture and using it as a basis for building public support. Saddam often is portrayed in the press or on television praying in Muslim mosques. He has provided public resources to renovate key Shiite shrines. There is even evidence that Saddam sought to link his ancestry with the prophet Muhammad, although Shiite leaders dismissed the ancestral exercise as highly questionable. After coalition forces gained the upper hand in the invasion, Saddam, showing his ties to the Muslim religion, called on Iraqis to engage in a holy war, a jihad, to repel the invaders.

The economic and social gulf between the minority Sunni Muslims, who dominate the business and governmental elite, and the Shiite majority, who have experienced extensive discrimination at the hands of the Sunnis, has been a source of continued concern for the regime of Saddam Hussein. Since taking power, Saddam has sought to incorporate more Shiites into the governing inner circle. The move to broaden Shiite involvement in the Baath Party and even in the Revolutionary Command Council was motivated primarily by fear. Isolating the highly religious and outwardly hostile majority might prompt their leaders to grow increasingly threatening to the regime. But such overtures to the Shiites mask the general policy of systematic repression by Saddam and his government.

During the 1970s there were a number of uprisings in Shiite enclaves in the south, including rioting that broke out in 1979 when religious leaders staged a march to Iran to congratulate Ayatollah Khomeini on his victory over the shah. The Iraqi government responded swiftly to this march by imposing martial law and deporting hundreds of thousands of Shiites. The unlucky ones were summarily executed. With the onset of the Iran-Iraq War, Saddam began to rethink his policy of oppressing the Shiites. This despite the fact that religious leaders openly incited rebellion against the government, and the underground Shiite group the al-Dawah (Islamic Call) was nearly successful in assassinating Deputy Prime Minister Tariq Aziz in 1980. What precipitated the change in policy was the fact that the vast majority of Saddam's army fighting the Iranians was Shiite. If Saddam was to sustain the war, he needed to show a level of tolerance toward the Shiites and their religious leaders.

Although the Shiites remained loyal to Saddam during the Iran-Iraq War, their support for him and his government ended with the allied liberation of Kuwait. As Saddam's troops retreated toward Baghdad, Shiites in and around the southern city of Basra began a movement to push the Iraqi government and the Baath Party organization out of the region. With the United States and Great Britain providing a no-fly zone in the south, the Shiite rebels were successful for a time. Gradually, Saddam's Republican Guards gained the upper hand by using a wide range of terror methods, even draining the marshes created by the Tigris and Euphrates Rivers that provided hiding places for the rebels. There was evidence that Saddam's troops used chemical warfare to subdue the Shiite rebels and to instill fear in the civilian population. Since Saddam engaged in the terror campaign against the Shiites in the south, there have been only sporadic opposition and no real concerted effort to challenge the authority of the Baghdad government.

Since coming to power, Saddam Hussein has defined his relationship to his people in very simple terms: submit to my authority or experience the full wrath of my power. One former Iraqi diplomat who is now living in exile summed up the simplicity of that relationship in a BBC interview: "Saddam is a dictator who is ready to sacrifice his country, just so long as he can remain on his throne in Baghdad." There are no limits to his power and no limits to the use of violence to retain power. Saddam has created a civic climate that is devoid of citizenship. As a result, in Saddam's Iraq there is nothing that can be described as civic virtue or civic involvement or civic responsibility; there is only civic obedience and fear of challenging the civic authority.

POINT OF FACT

A French filmmaker in 2001 traveled with Saddam to the Iraqi countryside where he lectured a local mayor on the importance of both oral and personal hygiene. Saddam's concern for cleanliness was not based on a belief in the benefits of a national hygiene policy. Rather, he feared contamination by his people and had an obsession with security. Anyone seeking an audience with Saddam must shower and have his or her body completely searched.

What the Experts Say

Robert Kaplan, a distinguished writer on international affairs, particularly in the less developed world, provides a clear-headed view on what Iraq after Saddam might look like and what the West can realistically expect:

Iraq is a one-man thugocracy, so the removal of Saddam would threaten to disintegrate the entire ethnically riven country if we weren't to act fast and pragmatically install people who could actually govern. Therefore we should forswear any evangelical lust to implement democracy overnight in a country with no tradition of it. . . . Our goal in Iraq should be a transitional secular dictatorship that unites the merchant classes across sectarian lines and may in time, after the rebuilding of institutions and the economy, lead to a democratic alternative.

ROBERT KAPLAN, "A POST-SADDAM SCENARIO,"
Atlantic, NOVEMBER 2002, PP. 88–89

Electoral Data

At the last elections, which were held on March 27, 2000, participation in the vote for the 250-person National Assembly was restricted to members of the National Progressive Front, which is in reality an organization representing the Baath Party and nonpartisans supporting the Baath government. There was a turnout of 83.6 percent.

LAND MINE POLICIES

The threats to the life and health of Iraqi citizens are overwhelming and include the U.N. sanctions and the repressive actions of the Hussein regime. In addition, land mines take a toll on human life. Since the Iran-Iraq War, an estimated 2,386 minefields spread out over 212 kilometers have been identified by teams of inspectors associated with the United Nations and other nongovernmental organizations devoted to protecting civilians from the ravages of antipersonnel mines. Mines were placed throughout northern and southern Iraq by the military to fend off invading armies and separatist groups. A cheap and effective means of protecting territory, land mines have had a devastating impact on the civilian population.

Since 1991 almost 3,000 deaths due to land mine explosions have been reported, as well as 5,400 injuries, mostly loss of limbs. Iraqis who are injured by land mines face a life of hardship. The government has been slow to develop programs to provide land mine survivors with prosthetic devices and rehabilitative services. Many amputees have had to rely on international foundations and care workers for assistance. Children are especially vulnerable as they often wander off while playing only to end up as victims of hidden antipersonnel mines.

The presence of land mine fields forces an exodus from the region as the civilian population leaves to avoid death and dismemberment. Rural farmers and sheepherders have been especially hard hit as they have had to move out of dangerous areas. Mines have also hindered the development of needed infrastructure projects related to electricity and water. With large tracts of land set off-limits by the presence of land mines, many Iraqis go without electricity or access to safe water.

The Iraqi government has done little to remove the mines and has allowed international agencies to begin clearing known mine fields. The United Nations has trained over seven hundred land clearance personnel and has added an additional two hundred staff members with responsibility for surveying and mapping areas and providing rehabilitative care. As of 1999 the mine clearance project had removed antipersonnel devices from 500,000 meters of Iraqi territory and assisted 2,700 civilians. As a result of the mine clearance, farming and grazing territory has been returned to productive use. Unfortunately the U.N. teams have only begun to de-mine Iraq and further injuries to the civilian population are a certainty.

Because of the enormity of the problem, the United Nations has developed a three-pronged program to deal with land mines. The program accents threat avoidance, heightened awareness through educating the civilian population, threat prevention—clearly marking dangerous areas—and threat elimination—continuing removal of land mines. The future of land mine removal and the rehabilitation of the victims of land mines depends on funding by the United Nations and nongovernmental organizations such as the United States Campaign to Ban Land Mines. Paying independent contractors to conduct the hazardous work and health professionals to provide the necessary prosthetics and amputee training is costly, and funding is often uncertain and uneven.

Because of the enormous territory in Iraq with land mines and the sheer numbers of land mines, the United Nations estimates that it may take thirty-three years to make the civilian population safe. This of course is contingent on the Iraqi government's not placing additional land mines in new areas. The threat that land mines pose to innocent Iraqis must be viewed as a long-term, if not generational, challenge. ⊕

PATHWAYS TO PARTICIPATION

The discussion of political participation in Saddam Hussein's Iraq presents a contradiction. The system of centralized control created by Saddam is specifically designed to diminish, if not destroy, participation in matters of politics and governance. Although Saddam and his supporters in the Baath Party hail the turnout in the national referendum for president and for the legislative elections as proof of substantial citizen involvement, there is little evidence that any real political organization is encouraged by the regime or that opposition political activity is tolerated. In 1991 the RCC published a law authorizing the formation of political parties not associated with the Baath Party. The law, however, is used to screen parties that do not support Saddam. A new party must be based in Baghdad, verify that it has at least 150 members over the age of twenty-five, and prove that it "takes pride" in the 1958 and 1968 revolutions. No political parties that have an ethnic or religious character are permitted, and some parties are officially banned, membership in them becoming a capital offense. In 1999 Saddam ordered government officials to consider the formation of political parties within a multiparty system, but two political parties that sought to organize were refused recognition allegedly because of insufficient numbers.

Despite the overwhelming control exercised by Saddam, there is a wide array of opposition parties and groups offering alternative viewpoints and seeking to create a governing system that provides open and fair elections. The critical difference, however, is that Iraqi opposition groups operate in exile. The Iraqi Communist Party has the longest history of resistance to Saddam. It was declared an enemy of the state by the then RCC vice chairman, Saddam Hussein. Since that purge the Iraqi Communist Party has operated in exile from London, Turkey, and northern Iraq. In exile the Communist Party has declined in influence and has been replaced as the most prominent opposition group by the umbrella organization known as the Iraqi National Congress (INC).

Founded in Vienna, Austria, in 1992 as a largely Kurdish opposition front, the INC has developed into a broad-based organization devoted to the overthrow of Saddam and his regime. It has gained the support of the United States and has been the beneficiary of $97 million in political and military assistance through the Iraqi Liberation Act, legislation passed by the U.S. Congress designed to provide "seed money" to initiate the end of the current Iraqi government. The political head of the INC is Ahmed Chalabi. Chalabi has worked tirelessly to form a viable opposition movement, but his inability to unify the three main military groups in the organization has made him a weak figurehead. Instead, Kurdish political leaders such as Mustafa Barzani and his Kurdish Democratic Party (DPK), Jalal Talabani and the Patriotic

Union of Kurdistan (PUK), and the Supreme Assembly of the Islamic Revolution (SAIRI), led by Muhammad Bakr al-Hakim, often act alone in their fight with Saddam. All these organizations have agreed to coordinate their activities with INC but not follow its dictates.

Chalabi and the INC have often been praised by the United States as the democratic alternative to Saddam Hussein. In 1996 Saddam's troops entered the northern city of Salahuddin and ransacked the headquarters of the INC and killed many members of the organization, fearing that the threat from the opposition was real and growing. Despite the repression by Saddam's security forces, the INC is in large part a "paper" opposition that is used by the United States for propaganda purposes. Iraqis do not tend to see it as an organization with the potential to bring Saddam Hussein down. Chalabi has developed elaborate plans in conjunction with the Central Intelligence Agency to liberate Iraq, but he has little credibility outside of his base in Kurdistan and the corridors of power in Washington.

Because the DPK and PUK often engage in deadly competition, the most influential opposition organization is the Supreme Council for the Islamic Revolution in Iraq (SCIRI). Founded in 1982 as an umbrella organization representing a number of Shiite groups in southern Iraq, SCIRI includes the Holy Warriors or al-Mujaheddin, who have direct ties to Iran; the Islamic Call (al-Dawah), which in 1997 claimed responsibility for the assassination attempt on Saddam's son Uday; and the Islamic Action Organization, a splinter group that broke off from Islamic Call. SCIRI has remained viable in large part due to organizational ties and funding from Iran. SCIRI gained greater legitimacy as an opposition force when the Clinton administration entered into negotiations with the group to seek ways to destabilize the Iraqi government and remove Saddam. SCIRI has what the INC does not: organization cohesiveness and popular support.

In recent years a new opposition movement has developed that is being closely watched. The Iraqi National Accord is made up of Sunni Muslims, with considerable membership from defecting members of the Iraqi military. Its leader is Major General Tawfiq al-Yassiri, a naval officer who was wounded in an uprising against Saddam in 1991. The National Accord has financial support from Saudi Arabia and has been described by the Central Intelligence Agency as the "most promising" of the Iraqi opposition groups. The National Accord opened its offices in Amman, Jordan, in 1996 with the support of King Hussein, who was growing increasingly fearful of Saddam's aggressive attempts to lead a pan-Arab movement. The National Accord moved its headquarters to London and in recent years has established a formal organizational structure claiming to represent all sectors of Iraqi society. The National Accord has operated in Kurdish territory but has stayed out of the competition between the

DPK and the PUK. Like the other opposition groups, the National Accord remains an exile organization and its influence inside of Iraq is unknown.

As the Bush administration moved toward implementing a military policy designed to remove Saddam Hussein from power, it placed more emphasis on creating a united opposition. In 2002 the State Department launched an initiative that would put in place a new opposition force. With $5 million in seed money, State Department officials began showing more support for what came to be known as the Group of Four, a coalition of the Iraqi National Accord, the two Kurdish political movements, and the Shiite opposition. The Iraqi National Congress was noticeably absent from the Group of Four membership, a sign of the Bush administration's disappointment with the ability of the INC to fashion a workable opposition force in Iraq. Forming and funding the Group of Four signaled that the United States was actively courting Iraqi opposition organizations and seeking to convince them to move forward with actions to destabilize and eventually destroy Saddam Hussein's regime.

Significant difficulties in developing a potent exile or external opposition to Saddam Hussein do not mean that there is no domestic opposition to the Iraqi leader and no effort to create opposition organizations based on democratic principles. Some of the more active groups opposed to Saddam in Iraq are lawyers. There is evidence that lawyer groups have formed with the purpose of developing an antiregime network. There have been reports of leaflets being distributed and underground newsletters being circulated. There are also signs that lawyer groups are beginning to gain the attention of Saddam and his family. In 2001 Saddam's son Uday accused the country's lawyers of defending "criminals" and making deals with judges to win cases. "Criminals" has become a code word for Iraqis who challenge the authority of the government and engage in subversive activity. Of course lawyers who engage in antiregime activity risk the full weight of the government's repression. Numerous lawyers have been tried in Iraqi courts and sentenced to execution.

Regular reports are published in Kuwaiti and Saudi newspapers describing demonstrations against the government over issues ranging from maldistribution of food to access to water to failures to provide medicine. The government may send out its supporters to blame Western sanctions for the shortages, but especially in the southern Shiite regions protests and antiregime graffiti on public buildings are common. In fall 2002 there was a major public demonstration in Baghdad when Saddam opened the prisons and let hundreds of inmates out as a means of generating public support in light of invasion threats by the United States. The move backfired in that many Iraqis with relatives in jail found that their loved ones were not among those released, the likely victims of execution or death while in prison. The extent and intensity of the demonstrations pointed up Iraqis' underlying anger at the regime. It is important to note that protests like those that occurred in 2002 often do not hold Saddam responsible for all of Iraq's ills. Rather, members of the Baath Party and local officials have become the targets of protests and even physical harm. Many of these protest gatherings and attacks on officials are orchestrated by SCIRI and by various religious leaders. These events almost always trigger a repressive response from the government.

In Iraq public protests and underground activities are necessary because the government has a lock on media. The government and the Baath Party own all print and broadcast media. The Iraqi media are utilized solely to advance propaganda. RCC decree 840 (1986) requires the death penalty for anyone insulting the president or high government officials. There is even a section in the penal code that prohibits singing a song that could cause public unrest. And a public law promulgated in 1968 prohibits writing articles on twelve designated topics that are deemed detrimental to the president, the RCC, and the Baath Party.

The Iraqi government's control of the media severely restricts the ability of journalists to report on public affairs or engage in news analysis that would reflect negatively on the Hussein regime. Freedom of speech and the press is officially protected by the constitution but only "in compliance with the revolutionary, national, and progressive trends." This language forms the basis for the government's frequent crackdowns on freedom of speech and press and for prosecuting dissenters in journalism and in sectors where such freedoms are essential, such as academia. As the U.N. special rapporteur stated in his report on Iraqi human rights, the government had "effectively eliminated" the freedoms of thought, expression, association, and assembly.

Demonstrating the extent of government control of journalists, the Iraqi Union of Journalists is headed by Uday Hussein. In recent years Uday has dismissed hundreds of journalists for not sufficiently praising Saddam. He bestows financial awards on journalists who openly support Saddam. The Ministry of Culture and Information also plays an important role in controlling journalists and monitoring their work. The ministry provides guidelines for the press and controls the access of foreign correspondents. It also controls the publications of all books in Iraq, including educational texts. Finally, the government takes extraordinary steps to jam foreign news broadcasts and to ensure that satellites and fax machines remain in the hands of pro-Saddam officials. Although restrictions on journalists and the ownership of satellites and fax machines were relaxed somewhat, stiff penalties remain, including imprisonment for illegal possession of these technologies.

Saddam's restrictions on speech and the press have not completely silenced Iraqis desperate for a democratic opening in their nation. In northern Iraq a number of independent newspapers have appeared since the end of Operation Desert Storm. There have also been radio and television broadcasts originating from the northern regions. Attempts by the Ministry of Education to publish textbooks containing pro-regime propaganda have been met, primarily in the northern Kurdish enclaves, with systematic efforts to remove the propaganda. And journalists and academics have resisted the government by not accepting positions in the government-controlled media or by refusing to engage in aggressive monitoring of their colleagues. In one highly publicized action in 1999, Uday Hussein jailed members of the Iraqi National Student Union for not disciplining a group of student journalists who had openly criticized the government and its policies.

Clearly the pathways to participation in Saddam Hussein's Iraq are limited. Under these conditions it is a wonder that any form of independent participation exists in Iraq. Regular protests over religious issues, ethnic restrictions, shortages related to the sanctions, and human rights violations are a testament to the bravery of Iraqis who dare to challenge the government. While most Iraqis remain frozen in the climate of fear that engulfs the country, there is a growing hunger among an ever widening citizenry who express their displeasure with Saddam and his regime.

POINT OF FACT

Saddam perceives himself as something of an author. He has written two books, Zabibah and the King *and* The Fortified Castle. *Both books are must reading in Iraq.*

WATER POLICY

In the poor countries of the world something as simple as water can hold the key to development or poverty. In Iraq water has not been a major policy concern in large part because of the Tigris and Euphrates Rivers, which cut through the center of the country and supply the famous Iraqi irrigation system. But in recent years a decision by neighboring Turkey to build a series of dams has begun to threaten the water supply and further damage Iraq's attempts to rebuild its economy.

Turkey has begun building a huge network of twenty-two dams under what it calls the Southeastern Anatolia Project (the Turkish acronym is GAP). The Turks hope to capture the water from the snows in the eastern part of the country in the reservoirs behind the dams as a means of guaranteeing supplies for agricultural sectors and electrical power. The problem with the GAP project is that the water the dams are controlling normally flow into the Mesopotamian plains of Syria and Iraq. The Iraqi government has complained vigorously to Turkey that the level of water in the Tigris and Euphrates has dropped dramat-

Photo 8.1   Former Iraqi President Saddam Hussein
addresses the nation in a televised broadcast in
Baghdad. (Reuters NewMedia Inc./Corbis)

*Saddam Hussein was born in 1937 to a poor farming family in Tikrit. In
1955 Saddam moved to Baghdad and became involved in Baath Party politics. He worked his way up the ranks of the party, performing a number of duties associated with opposition to the military president of Iraq, Abdul Karim
Kassem. In 1959 Saddam was involved in the assassination attempt on
Kassem. He was wounded in the attempt and fled to Cairo. In Cairo he studied
law and continued his involvement with the Baath movement. In 1963 he returned to Baghdad, where he became the assistant secretary general of the Baath
Party. In 1968 the Baath Party took power. Saddam served as the powerful
aide to the new president, Major General Ahmed Hassan al-Bakr. In the early
1970s Saddam emerged as the real power holder in the government of al-Bakr
and in 1979 he forced al-Bakr to resign and took over the presidency.*

ically as each new dam is built. In 1998 Iraq claimed that the water level in the
Tigris dropped to a third of its previous level. The Turks defend their dam and
reservoir network by stating that dropping water level is due to climatic
changes that have caused dry winters with little snow.

Over the years Iraq has signed treaties with its neighbors regarding the movement of water from Turkey in the Mesopotamian plain. But as demand for water expands in Iraq and water levels drop, tensions are developing over the control and distribution of what has become a precious commodity. Iraqi farming has been especially hard hit by the lack of water as its wheat crop has withered during the peak growing season. Iraq has had to purchase food from abroad in order to make up for the shortfall that is directly related to lack of water.

The situation is not expected to improve in the future, since the GAP project is far from completion. When it is finished, Turkey will likely shift more water from the two rivers for its use, thus precipitating an agricultural crisis in both Iraq and Syria. Moreover, because Turkey controls the water flow it has used water availability as a political tool to extract concessions from Syria regarding Kurdish insurgents. Iraqi officials are concerned that Turkey may use the same strategy to win concessions from Saddam Hussein.

Currently Iraq is not in a position to challenge the Turks on water availability. It has problems with its water distribution system, which has been devastated over the past twenty years. The combination of war, economic sanctions, and a depressed economy has wrecked the irrigation system. Foreign water consultants who examine the irrigation system find the channels are caving in, pumps are not working due to a shortage of spare parts, and salt deposits coat many of the fields. It will take years to rebuild the irrigation systems and billions of dollars. But even if the Iraqi government does shift resources into the water infrastructure, the issue of availability and the negotiations with Turkey remain.

For now Turks, Syrians, and Iraqis are holding talks about joint study commissions and cooperative efforts to use the water from the Tigris and Euphrates in an equitable manner. But if climatic changes persist and water is at a premium, many in the region feel that Turkey will decide to control supply and availability while Iraq may be forced to make concessions. ⊕

THE POLITICAL ELITE

There is a political elite in Iraq outside of Saddam and his closest family members that, although narrow, wields considerable power and controls the process of governing. Membership in the Iraqi political elite is part clan association, part extended family, and part loyal members of the Baath Party. Saddam, of course, is at the center of the decisionmaking apparatus in Iraq, but he has distributed power to those who have also shown the ruthlessness and brutality that are his trademark governing modus operandi. Needless to say, members of the political elite who show disloyalty or are unwilling to exercise power in the manner of their leader are quickly dispatched.

Saddam's boyhood roots lie in his hometown of Tikrit, north of Baghdad. Saddam was the son of poor parents. When he was ten, Saddam was sent to Baghdad to live with his uncle, Khayrallah Tulfah, an Iraqi army officer who was a strong advocate of Arab unity. As a student Saddam immersed himself in anti-British and anti-Western literature and became increasingly attracted to radical solutions to the colonial presence in his country and in the Middle East. It is believed that Khayrallah encouraged the young Saddam to commit his first murder, killing a prominent communist and backer of the military ruler Abdel Karim Qassim. Two years later Saddam was involved with another assassination attempt, this time on Qassim himself. The attempt failed and Saddam escaped to Egypt.

When Saddam returned from exile four years later after the coup that removed Qassim from power, he quickly moved into the circles of political influence, serving as the interrogator and torturer in the Palace of the End, the royal residence in Baghdad. In the period of military coup and countercoup Saddam was imprisoned from 1964 to 1966, but by then he had developed a reputation as the leading member of the Baath Party and a revolutionary hero with impeccable credentials. When his cousin, General Ahmed Hassan al-Bakr, became president and head of the RCC, Saddam was named deputy chairman of the council. Years later Saddam would not hesitate to push his cousin out of power in order to become Iraq's president.

Once securely in power, Saddam built his regime by retaining ties to his ancestral home and to family members who resided there. It is often said that the "mob from Tikrit" runs Iraq. While this is an exaggeration, Saddam has brought many of his friends and family into the centers of power. Saddam named his Uncle Khayrallah mayor of Baghdad, and he proceeded to become one of the most corrupt, repressive officials in the regime. Saddam later removed him from power. Khayrallah's son and Saddam's cousin, Adnan Khayrallah, was Saddam's closest relative growing up. Once Saddam gained power, he named Adnan defense minister during the Iran-Iraq War. When Adnan became a very popular army general, Saddam gradually stripped him of key responsibilities. Adnan died in 1989 in a helicopter accident under very suspicious circumstances. Another key member of the "mob from Tikrit" is Saddam's half-brother, Barzan. For years Barzan was a shadowy hanger-on in Saddam's inner circle. He was believed to be responsible for purchasing many of Iraq's weapons of mass destruction. In the 1990s Barzan mysteriously left Iraq in a likely power struggle with Saddam. For many years Barzan lived in Switzerland, but now he and his brother Watban are listed as presidential advisers to Saddam.

Saddam continues to depend on clan members from Tikrit as functionaries in his government, but in recent years he has closed the circle of the power elite and relied more heavily on his two sons, Uday and Qusai. Uday, the older of

Saddam's sons, has played a less influential role in the governing regime. He runs the major television network in Iraq and has regulatory power over journalists. Uday has concentrated his interests in a variety of business ventures, always relying on his ties to his father as a means of ensuring profitability. Uday's political influence declined markedly when he became involved in a scandal in which he and his bodyguards clubbed to death his father's personal valet. The valet was apparently arranging sexual liaisons for Saddam, and Uday feared that one of those liaisons, which ended up as Saddam's second wife, would jeopardize his power position in the family. Saddam put Uday on trial for the murder but settled for a short exile in Switzerland. When he returned, Uday kept a low profile until an assassination attempt in 1966 nearly cost him his life. Although Uday is viewed as a hothead playboy with little capacity to govern, the fact that he is Saddam's older son makes him a force behind the scenes and a real contender to succeed his father.

Saddam's youngest son, Qusai, may be the second most powerful person in Iraqi government. Qusai is much more serious and power savvy than his older brother. A law graduate, Qusai has supervised the Republican Guards, the Special Security Guards, and the Fedayeen, a 40,000-member special unit designed to control popular uprisings. At key periods of external threat Saddam has also placed Qusai at the head of the Iraqi armed forces to ensure loyalty and guarantee that should Saddam die Qusai would be in a position to move quickly into power.

In terms of day-to-day influence in the small circle of Saddam's family members, advisers, and hangers-on, there is general agreement that Deputy Premier Tariq Aziz is second in command in Iraq. The only Christian in Saddam's Muslim leadership clique, Aziz has been a mainstay of Iraqi government since the early 1970s. As an editor of the Baath Party newspaper, Aziz gained the attention of Muhammad el-Bakr, and in 1974 he was named minister of information. Once Saddam rose to power, Aziz moved up quickly in government, first as vice prime minister and then minister of foreign affairs during the Gulf War. After the war Saddam named him deputy prime minister. At each stage of his career Aziz became a key player in Saddam's regime, concentrating primarily on presenting Iraq's foreign policy position to the world and negotiating with Western nations and the United Nations over issues related to the economic sanctions and UNSCOM weapons inspectors.

Tariq Aziz has been the most visible member of the Iraqi inner circle. While Saddam never leaves the country and rarely speaks to the foreign press, Aziz travels widely and has been the main conduit for official Iraqi domestic and foreign policy positions. It was Tariq Aziz who stared down Secretary of State James Baker in the last negotiating session before the Gulf War; it was Tariq Aziz who laid out the arguments against the UNSCOM inspections on the *Larry*

King Show; and it was Tariq Aziz who moved around the Middle East seeking support for a united front against the continuation of Western-imposed economic sanctions. Although it is nearly impossible to determine the decision-making relationship between Saddam and Aziz, Iraqi government defectors acknowledge that Aziz has been given free rein to chart foreign policy and has unlimited access to Saddam.

Also holding considerable power in the inner circle is Vice President Taha Yasin Ramadan. A military man who has a distinguished record from the Iran-Iraq War and the Gulf War, Ramadan, in most observers' view, ensures that Saddam's public policies are implemented correctly. The vice presidency is often viewed as merely ceremonial, but in recent years Ramadan has become the point man in pressing the West to lift the economic sanctions against Iraq and to gather support in the Middle East against the sanctions. Ramadan's credentials as a loyal Saddam supporter are unquestioned. He has been active in targeting opposition groups in London that are seeking to topple the Saddam regime. His fanatical zeal against the United States is revealed in an oft quoted promise: "I tell you all that Iraq will continue to defend its land, policy, and dignity. We will fight until the last citizen." Other persons of influence include Ali Hassan al-Majid al-Tikriti (Saddam's first cousin and chief enforcer) and Izzat Ibrahim al Douri, the deputy head of the RCC. Ibrahim's daughter is married to Uday.

It is also important to identify who is not part of the political elite. In a highly centralized authoritarian regime, it seems likely that the military high command would play a prominent role in national decisionmaking, particularly since Saddam himself is a military man. But Saddam is wary of the military, in large part due to the history of coup attempts developing within the leadership ranks of the armed forces, and few members of the general staff have become trusted advisers. For public consumption Saddam is often seen presiding over a meeting of his key staff, many of whom are military officers. But Saddam regularly shifts these officers around or changes their job descriptions to deprive them of the opportunity to build an independent power base. Saddam has made a conscious choice that rather than admit the generals into the power elite, it is better to keep the military high command well paid and well supplied to lessen the chances of challenges to his rule.

Iraq remains in the hands of one man. Those around him serve at his pleasure and survive at his whim. Saddam may distribute responsibility to others and may listen to the counsel of his advisers, but there is little apparent delegation of authority in Iraq. There is a recognizable political elite in Iraq but it is not a power elite. Power remains with Saddam and he doles out power at his discretion and takes it away, often with cruel ruthlessness.

POINT OF FACT
Saddam is commonly referred to in Iraq as the Great Uncle.

POLICIES REGARDING IRAN

The war between Iraq and Iran has long been over, but the resumption of normal relations has not gone smoothly. Iraq and Iran remain hostile neighbors with numerous points of dispute. Neither government has any real interest in achieving a breakthrough settlement. Iraq is seen by the Iranian government as a dangerous military threat that could unleash its considerable arsenal of weapons of mass destruction at any time. Iran, on the other hand, is seen by the Iraqi government as a fanatical religious state that could marshal its Shiite population in an attack that would destabilize the current Iraqi regime. There is little evidence of either country taking steps to form a new era of good relations and forget the past.

Of the many disputes that remain between Iraq and Iran, the Iranian government has been most vocal in denouncing the repression of Shiites in the south of Iraq, particularly the assassinations of key Shiite clerics. The Iranian government was especially enraged in 1998 when a key cleric, Sheikh Ali al-Gharavi al-Tabrigzi, was assassinated. The sheikh was a key figure in the Supreme Assembly of Islamic Revolution, which has ties to the Tehran government. The Iranians accused Iraq of the assassination and the Baath Party for immediately suppressing the protests in Baghdad that occurred after the assassination. The murder of the sheikh was one of many attacks on key clerics that have caused Iran to seek support in the Middle East to condemn the actions of the Iraqi government.

Another area of dispute between Iraq and Iran is the status of prisoners that each country has held since the end of the war in 1988. There have been periodic releases of prisoners by both countries but both Iraq and Iran have been reluctant to make a final exchange of prisoners. Both governments have used the prisoner issue as a potential bargaining chip over other issues. Iran has been especially unwilling to end the prisoner exchange unless there is some resolution of the damage Iraq caused to eleven border cities, as well as the destruction of key refineries and industrial plants. Although the numbers of prisoners held by both sides are not easily determined, Iran appears to hold more prisoners and is reluctant to release all of them until the war damage issues are addressed and some form of compensation from Iraq is forthcoming.

Despite the animosity between Iraq and Iran, the two governments have made some progress toward resolving their differences. Both countries have agreed to form several joint committees for the purpose of developing more positive trade and economic relations. High-level trade delegations met in

1998 and signed an agreement that would build on the U.N. oil for food program. Both countries pledged their support for maintaining regional security and peaceful resolution of disputes, and in an expected move castigated the Israeli government for its handling of the Palestine issue. The 1998 agreement set in motion a series of other trade contacts that brought Iraq-Iran relations back to a more normal setting.

The attack on the World Trade Center in September 2001 had a chilling effect on Iraq-Iran relations. Iran, in an apparent attempt to curry favor with the United States, pledged to work against terrorism and against countries that harbor terrorism. The position taken by the Iranian government set in motion a cooling of the normalization of relations with Iraq that had been building for a number of years. The United States made no effort to hide its desire to end the regime of Saddam Hussein and actively sought Iran's support. As the international war on terrorism progresses, Iran may distance itself from its neighbor and Iraq may become further isolated in the region. Although Iraq and Iran are not likely to develop a secure relationship, the targeting of Saddam by the United States and the emergence of a more moderate government in Iran put a stop to any further normalization. ⊕

REAL GOVERNMENT

Of all eight countries examined in this text, Iraq stands out as the one in which there is little if any connection between the formal governing structure and the realities of how public policy decisions are made and implemented. Because Saddam Hussein exercises overwhelming control and is willing to use a range of punishments for disloyalty and failure to heed his instructions, describing what is called real government, as applied to Iraq, is not a matter of detailing a complex process of institutional competition and group dynamics. Rather, the focus must be on Saddam Hussein, the manner in which he operates, the way in which he leads the nation, the approaches he uses when interacting with his staff and ministers, and the steps he takes to ensure compliance with his wishes. The explanation of how government really works in Iraq revolves around one man and, as we will see, the explanation is not terribly complicated or difficult to comprehend.

Westerners see Saddam as a cruel dictator who will use any means at his disposal to stay in power. While this is certainly true, Saddam's policy decisions are nonetheless often based on a clear-headed analysis of costs and benefits. Saddam has shown an uncanny talent for using delay, short-term compromise, and public relations ploys to achieve his objectives. These tactics have allowed him to survive coup attempts to befuddle his opponents in the West. Saddam

Hussein is not a crazed dictator who has been lucky to remain in power. He is a wily manager of power and personnel and an astute student of the limits of international intervention.

A key to understanding the manner in which Saddam rules Iraq is how he was able to frustrate the UNSCOM weapons investigators and eventually force them out of the country. United Nations Security Council Resolution 687 and a series of implementing resolutions passed immediately after the Gulf War stipulate that Iraq must provide "full, final and complete disclosure of all aspects of its nuclear, chemical, biological, and long-range missile programs, allow unconditional inspection access by international monitors, cease any attempt to conceal, move, or destroy any material or equipment related to these activities, and cooperate with UN monitoring of relevant Iraqi facilities and trade activities." Since the promulgation of those resolutions Saddam and his government have engaged in a systematic program to hide weapons and major components of advanced weapons of mass destruction (WMD). UNSCOM has described Saddam's efforts at thwarting weapons inspectors as a vast "concealment mechanism."

From the initial arrival of the weapons inspectors associated with UNSCOM in 1991, Saddam reluctantly and selectively complied with UNSCR 687. Although he destroyed a number of older weapons and provided access to certain areas requested by UNSCOM inspectors, he did everything possible to limit and control the work of the United Nations. For example, Saddam ordered that military and government officials engage in a cynical version of hide-and-seek as WMD were moved about the country and concealed in presidential palaces and underground bunkers to avoid detection. Saddam also engaged in a series of other noncompliance tactics, including seizing incriminating records from weapons inspectors, denying the weaponizing of VX nerve gas agents despite UNSCOM verification, refusing to permit access to Ministry of Defense sites, and destroying incriminating documents related to projects regarding the use of biological weapons or SCUD missile components.

In October 1998 Saddam ended this cat-and-mouse game with UNSCOM and abruptly announced that he would prevent U.N. weapons inspectors from entering Iraq. The announcement called for lifting economic sanctions, firing UNSCOM chairman Richard Butler, and distancing UNSCOM from the "espionage, deliberate harm and agentry of the United States." Both the United States and Great Britain described the announcement as "totally unacceptable." British Foreign Secretary Robin Cook accurately portrayed Saddam's motives when he stated that the Iraqi leader was "gambling that the world would grow weary of constant confrontation."

This is the modus operandi of Saddam Hussein in his dealing with the United Nations, UNSCOM, and the Western powers: agree to cooperate, limit the extent of cooperation, delay when pressed to cooperate, engage in methods designed to cover up real intent, create a crisis situation as a means of weakening Western resolve, and resist any attempts to reveal the extent of noncompliance and remain confident that this regimen of intransigence will eventually wear down the opposition. This modus operandi has allowed Saddam to avoid giving up his weapons while keeping his adversaries at bay.

A complete discussion of the way in which government works in Iraq and the manner in which Saddam makes decisions and controls power must include the system of terror that has been put in place by the regime. The documentation regarding human rights violations conducted against assassins, political opponents, coup makers, religious leaders, protesters, and innocent citizens who in some way angered the governing elite is overwhelming. But cold statistics and general categories of abuse are not sufficient to show how Saddam, his family, and his henchmen use force as a political tool to punish, to intimidate, and to remain in power. A few examples will suffice to show how Saddam and his regime employ terror.

- Amnesty International reported in 1999 that authorities executed a seventy-year-old blind man and seven of his eight sons after stating that the eighth son, who went into exile, was suspected of participating in the attack on Uday Hussein. The families of those executed were required to retrieve the bodies one by one over a ten-day period. The houses of those executed were demolished after the ten-day period.
- Iraqi intelligence chief Rafa Daham Mujawwal al-Tikriti, Saddam's second cousin, was killed three days after he was removed from his post. The Iraqi government stated that Rafa died in a car crash and then said that he died from a heart attack. Opposition sources in Kuwait believe that Rafa was killed either because he had failed to protect information about Iraq's military deals with Russia or had in some way crossed paths with Uday Hussein.
- Iraq's chief architect, Husam Bahnam Khuduri, suffered a slow death from thallium poisoning. As chief architect, Khuduri had intimate knowledge about the construction of Saddam's palaces, tunnels, and bunkers. Although the official obituary did not list the cause of death, Khuduri showed signs of the slow-acting poison that has become a staple of Saddam's terror methods.
- Former Iraqi soccer players described torture at the hands of Uday Hussein for failing to qualify for the 1994 World Cup. One player, Sharar Haydar Mohamad al-Hadithi, was beaten on the soles of his feet, dragged shirtless through a gravel pit, and forced to jump into raw sewage to increase the chances of infection. Other members of

the team were forced to kick a concrete ball around the grounds of Radwaniya prison, again under orders from Uday Hussein.

- In 2001 Saddam's Fedayeen beheaded two hundred women, supposedly in a campaign to stop prostitution. But many observers outside the country felt it was another cruel attempt to quash dissent.

The use of terror by Saddam Hussein, his sons, and the various organs of state security is so common in Iraq that it is difficult to separate its use from the process of governing. The slightest hint of challenge to those in power elicits a violent response. Moreover, the use of violence, as evidenced in the above examples, stretches the limits of cruelty. Of course the purpose of using terror and particularly heinous forms of violence is to shock opponents of the regime into silence and conformity. The regular use of terror by the regime can only be described as successful, since the vast majority of Iraqi citizens are apolitical and are not involved in public activity that could be perceived as antigovernment. And yet reports from outside Iraq detail a continuation and expansion of opposition to the regime of Saddam Hussein. Military coup making, Shiite religious activity, Kurdish separatism, exile political organization, and intellectual and professional criticism have pushed the regime to rely more heavily on terror to retain political control of the country.

Iraq in the Global Economy

According to data from the United Nations and other sources, there is a general consensus that the Iraqi economy will not regain its presanction size for a year after the conclusion of the war. Of course much of the economic decline experienced by Iraq is the result of international sanctions and the impact of the invasion, but the regime of Saddam Hussein is not interested in playing by the new rules of globalization. Like many dictators, including Cuba's Castro and Syria's Assad, Saddam Hussein is content to keep Iraq isolated from the world and the world economy, relying on the sale of oil as the chief source of foreign currency. Basic tools of the global economy—computers, satellite dishes, and fax machines—are either banned or confined to a narrow circle of pro-Saddam elites. Foreign travel and foreign cultural exchanges are strictly controlled, and of course the government control of the press and media keep news from the people. Isolation and control are the opposites of the rules that guide globalization, and so until Iraq reenters the global marketplace and relaxes its controls, there will be little that approaches a global economy in Iraq.

WEAPONS OF MASS
DESTRUCTION POLICY

Iraq was decisively defeated in the Gulf War and its military infrastructure was damaged, but it remains a serious regional and global
threat because of its ability to protect a range of weapons of mass
destruction. Based on data from the U.N. weapons inspection team, Iraq has a
nuclear, biological, and chemical capacity that could be used against its neighbors and U.S. assets in the region. These weapons of mass destruction could
also be transferred to various terrorist cells and used to attack Western interests throughout the world. The fact that U.N. weapons inspectors were not allowed into the country from 1998 to 2003 gave the Iraqis free rein to further
develop their stockpile of nuclear, biological, and chemical weapons.

Iraq is known to have engaged in clandestine efforts to procure special nuclear weapons–related equipment along with black market uranium and plu-
tonium, the critical ingredients for bomb making. If Iraq acquires the equipment and ingredients, it retains a sufficient number of nuclear scientists to
develop a nuclear device. Iraq also has the capacity to equip its al-Hussein
ballistic missile with a 300-kilometer range or more advanced version of the
al-Hussein with a potential of 650-kilometer range.

In the area of biological weapons U.N. inspectors believe that Iraq has an
extensive stockpile of over 150 aerial bombs and missile warheads that could
carry biological agents. Iraq's Mirage fighter jets likely have the capacity to
spray biological agents. There is also evidence from the United Nations that
Iraq has mobile production facilities with the ability to produce "dry" agents,
which have a longer shelf life and can be widely disseminated. What is most
disturbing about Iraq's biological weapons of mass destruction is that
weapons inspectors were unable to account for seventeen tons of biological
weapons growth media that could be used to resume production of anthrax,
botulinum toxin, and gas gangrene.

Iraq's chemical weapons stockpiles and capabilities also are cause for concern. It is thought that Iraq has retained upwards of twenty-five special
chemical ballistic missile warheads, 2,000 aerial bombs, and at least 30,000
rockets and artillery shells that could be equipped with chemical agents. Iraq
also has the capability to produce mustard gas, VX, and other nerve agents,
as it did during the Iran-Iraq War and its campaigns against the Kurds. As
with its nuclear and biological capacity, Iraq has sufficient scientific and technical expertise to develop effective chemical weapons agents along with the
delivery systems.

Although each of these weapons of mass destruction poses a severe danger, Iraq's biological weapons cause the most concern in the West. Despite

the fact that UNSCOM destroyed a biological weapons production factory at Al Hakam (the Iraqis said it produced animal feed) along with equipment and materials used in manufacturing biological agents, it is believed that Iraq continues to work in the area of biological warfare. The program is headed by Dr. Rihab Taha, a British-educated scientist who has been dubbed "Dr. Germ." The danger in nonnuclear weaponry is that in the absence of monitoring both biological and chemical weapons could be produced in a matter of weeks, while nuclear weapons would take up to five years of uninterrupted development and would require materials that are difficult to acquire. With seventeen tons of biological and chemical agents unaccounted for, Iraq remains a serious threat, especially since it showed little reluctance to use chemical weapons in the past on its enemies as well as its own people. ⊕

POLITICAL ECONOMY

Consistent with the rest of Iraqi national life, the economy is marked by government control of all major industries and a highly centralized approach to economic decisionmaking and implementation. Saddam maintains a firm grip on all aspects of the economy and of course ensures that the financial rewards generated by the economy pass through his hands. As with many dictatorial regimes, Iraq is run like a family business with economic decisions being made to generate family wealth as well as advance political aims. Under such a business model there is little room for private initiative or innovation, except when approved by the governing regime. A dictatorship like that created by Saddam is always reluctant to foster a more open economic and financial environment. Such openness would seriously hamper Saddam's ability to maintain control and would create opportunities for outsiders to expose the corruption of the political elite.

The foundation of the family business and the source of the family wealth in Iraq is oil. Since the oil industry was nationalized in 1972, the political elite has used the revenues from oil exportation to fuel the economy and provide personal wealth and ostentatious public works projects. During the oil boom days of the mid-1970s, when the price of crude oil increased dramatically, Iraq found itself awash in oil revenues. These revenues allowed the state to engage in a wide range of modernization projects. Roads and bridges were constructed along with airports and irrigation projects. Some of the wealth actually began to filter down to the citizenry as the government expanded the national electricity grid, which supported the greater use of household appliances. Housing units were built and a range of social and educational programs were introduced strengthening the middle class and offering the opportunity for poor Iraqis to rise up the social and economic ladder.

The Iran-Iraq War and the Gulf War ended the period of oil-based wealth and modernization. The connection between war, oil production, and economic decline is clearly highlighted in the course of national development since 1980. The eight-year Iran-Iraq War caused severe damage to the economy because the military expenditures necessary to sustain the fighting, coupled with damage to the oil-producing infrastructure, forced the government to impose a harsh austerity program, borrow extensively abroad, and restructure debt. The war debt in 1988 was estimated at $70 billion—seven years of oil revenues. In total the Iran-Iraq War cost the country $100 billion, which it has never been able to recoup. After the war the Iraqi economy rebounded somewhat as the country returned to normalcy and oil production bounced back. But the Gulf War and the devastating military defeat at the hands of coalition forces again pushed Iraq into economic decline. From 1990 to 1999 Iraq's gross domestic product dropped from $60 billion to $5.7 billion. During this period the value of the Iraqi currency, the dinar, fell so steeply that a monthly salary of 5,000 dinars barely covered the cost of two chickens. And the infant mortality rate rose from 25 per 1,000 births in 1990 to 92 per 1,000 births in 1994.

For much of its history Iraq was predominantly an agricultural economy (Iraq is the world's largest producer of dates). Even today agriculture contributes 11 percent of the GNP and employs 30 percent of the workforce. But oil exploration and extraction have transformed the economy and the country. The Iraqi economy depends almost exclusively on oil to generate foreign exchange earnings. It is estimated that as much as 95 percent of Iraq's foreign exchange comes from the oil sector. During those times when Iraq has not been at war or under Western sanctions, oil exports have fueled the economy and lined the pockets of the political elite. But for most of the last twenty years, since the Iran-Iraq War, oil production has been restricted, causing economic depression and the accompanying steep decline in the standard of living. Throughout the postwar sanction period the Iraqi oil industry has been functioning at one-tenth its normal capacity.

In recent years a revamped U.N. oil for food program (U.N. Resolution 1284) has allowed Iraq to export oil to about three-fourths of pre–Gulf War levels. The easing of the sanctions by U.N. head Kofi Annan, which gave Iraq permission to sell 5.2 billion barrels of oil every six months, translated into $3.6 billion to buy food and other critical supplies. This arrangement to modify the oil for food program eased domestic shortages and improved the key inflation and unemployment indicators. As a result, Iraq made some marginal gains in strengthening its per capita output levels and its standard of living. Imports of food increased, along with medical supplies and health care services. Nevertheless, Iraq continued to struggle economically. In 2001 estimates placed the real growth of GDP at -5.7 percent.

The Iraqi government has sought ways to move the economy forward despite the sanctions and their broad impact on the standard of living. There has been some diversification of the economy with the introduction of chemicals, textiles, cement, construction materials, leather goods, and machinery. There has even been small-scale formation of start-up electronic component firms. But the diversification of the economy has been seriously hampered by both the U.S.-British bombing raids and the U.N. sanctions. Moreover, diversification is foundering as the Iraqi government continues to accent oil exportation while lashing out at Western powers for the continuing sanctions.

The closed nature of the Iraqi political system makes it difficult to obtain accurate economic data or develop a precise description of the Iraqi economic system. Some general information is available about the current state of the Iraqi economy. Because of the sanctions and the misallocation of resources, Iraq suffers under an annual inflation rate of 60 percent, with unemployment equaling that figure. It has a trade deficit of 68 percent and foreign debts that are 330 percent of the gross national product, which translates into a per capital foreign debt of $3,900 (most of the foreign debt is owed to Saudi Arabia and Kuwait, two of Iraq's archenemies). Inflation and unemployment have had a detrimental effect on the Iraqi worker. State workers often have to wait months to receive their salaries; smuggling is rampant along with the black market. Many Iraqis sold their valuables in open-air markets. When staple goods are available, most Iraqis have a difficult time purchasing them.

Iraq does not have a positive record of employing neoliberal economic policies in the manner of other less developed countries. Some halfhearted attempts were made in the late 1980s to privatize the economy, follow a deregulation program, and entice foreign investment. But the centralized nature of the Iraqi economy and a poor business environment proved to be a drag on implementing these initiatives. Even when there has been heightened interest by foreign investors and signs of increased trade opportunities, countries and businesspeople hesitate to participate in the Iraqi economy for fear of corruption, confiscation, and aggressive foreign and military policies that could lead to war.

The future direction of the Iraqi economy will be guided by U.N. sanctions and the shape that the oil for food program takes in the coming years and the shape of the postwar government. The oil for food program provides a window into how Saddam Hussein has survived despite enormous pressure from the outside world. Faced with the economic embargo, the government developed an elaborate smuggling system to transport truckloads of oil overland to Turkey. Iraq required its illicit oil customers to pay a forty-cent surcharge on every barrel of oil received. This arrangement, which was a clear violation of the embargo, has generated $500,000 daily in revenue for Saddam. The money coming in from these clandestine sources not only permitted Saddam to continue lining his own pockets and building public monuments but also allowed him to "buy" allegiance from the Iraqi middle class. Members of the bureaucracy, military, security forces, and Baath Party had access to the latest in Western goods, from luxury cars to electronic gadgets. But the lower class felt the full brunt of the sanctions as expressed in shortages of basic commodities.

Saddam ended the surcharge policy because of pressure from the United Nations and a desire to attract Western interest in Iraq's 110 billion barrels of proven reserves. As a result, French, Italian, and Spanish oil firms have signed bilateral agreements with Saddam. Iraq has also signed agreements with Russian companies for drilling and service contracts that some estimates place at $90 billion. Although the U.N. sanctions forbid foreign countries from investing in Iraqi oil, countries have nevertheless signed contracts in hopes that once Iraq loses its pariah status, access to the oil reserves will open up. French, Chinese, Indian, and Dutch companies have entered into these future agreements, which if implemented will provide a huge boost to the Iraqi economy.

All this behind-the-scenes activity in connection with Iraq's oil potential has helped relax the sanctions governing spare parts and other infrastructure necessities. Although the U.N. Security Council at first denied the request for an increase from $300 million to $600 million for spare parts to bolster the heavily damaged and antiquated oil industry, there was growing pressure in the West to begin the process of rebuilding Iraq's infrastructure as the foundation for its economic revival. There was also an emerging consensus in the West that a series of "smart" sanctions should be put into place. These "smart" sanctions would permit a more realistic and humanitarian approach to what goods are permitted into Iraq and would thus greatly alleviate the suffering of the people.

In 2002 the U.N. Security Council, after intensive behind-the-scenes negotiations, voted 15–0 to overhaul the economic sanctions. Under the new sanctions, which were approved by the United States, only items on a "dual use" schedule must be examined by a U.N. committee to determine whether they have a military potential. All other goods will be permitted to enter Iraq unimpeded. It is estimated that these new "smart sanctions" will allow Iraq to begin building a more normal domestic economy, while allowing the United Nations to continue controlling the movement of goods and materials that Saddam could use to rebuild his military or engage in aggressive actions in the region.

Despite the "smart sanctions," there is little sympathy for Saddam and his regime and little interest in creating a massive effort to bring the Iraqi economy back to its pre–Gulf War state. There is, however, a growing consensus in the U.N. Security Council that the old sanctions and the oil for food program so crippled the economy in Iraq and caused such massive human suffering that changes had to be made. The United Nations and the Western powers must walk a fine line, trying to help the Iraqi people while not providing Saddam with the means to strengthen his hold on political power.

Most of the attention regarding the Iraqi economy is on post-Saddam development. Although access to oil reserves will certainly benefit the country as revenue will not be diverted into palaces, weapons of mass destruction, and the pockets of Saddam's entourage, nonetheless an enormous challenge awaits the Iraqi economy after years of war, sanctions, and the megalomania of the national leadership. The United States in 2002 stated that removing Saddam from power would require a huge infusion of economic assistance to rebuild the devastated economy (estimated at $200 billion). Aid will be necessary to meet the immediate needs of a country that suffered a military invasion, as well as neglect and decay caused by Saddam's dictatorship and the U.N. sanctions. The challenge will be daunting, to say the least.

CHALLENGES

The challenges that Iraq will face in the coming years can be viewed from a number of perspectives, but in the end all hinge on Saddam Hussein. Iraq is a war-torn nation with a decrepit economy, a downtrodden people, and a disintegrating political environment. Saddam Hussein, his family, and his supporters in the Baath Party hold what is left of Iraq together through sheer terror.

What scant progress Iraq has made in the past few years to return to normalcy and reenter the world of international trade has once again been shattered. Where the Western alliance and the United Nations were reaching agreement on relaxing sanctions and adopting a more humanitarian stance associated with the oil for food program, there is now only condemnation of Saddam Hussein as a threat to international security. There is no longer the view that the West must somehow tolerate Iraq and accept Saddam Hussein for what he is.

Whatever happens in the war against terrorism and against Saddam Hussein's regime, Iraq remains a shambles. In 1998 the World Health Organization (WHO) conducted a study of the mental health of the Iraqi people to determine the effects of years of almost ceaseless war and deprivation. A summary of their findings provides a sad look into the psychosocial condition of the Iraqi people and the challenges ahead as the nation seeks to return to some semblance of normalcy.

- The number of mental health patients attending the health facilities rose by 157 percent from 1990 to 1998.
- The total number of hospital admissions for mental disorders rose from 6,736 in 1990 to 15,996 in 1998.
- The number of young children and adolescents suffering from mental disorders increased by 124 percent between 1990 and 1998.
- Between 30 percent and 50 percent of medical or surgical cases were found to be mentally ill.
- The number of university students who drop out or request postponement of studies has steadily increased over the sanction years.

In a companion study done by UNICEF the researchers who talked with hundreds of Iraqis reported the following findings regarding the impact of war and sanctions on children:

Today's young children in Iraq grow up with a deep sense of insecurity about the satisfaction of their basic survival and development needs, and children as young as 4 years are already involved in income-generating activities in order to contribute to the family income, most of them working in the streets. . . . The family atmosphere also suffers from persistent psychological distress. . . . An increase in family conflicts and child abuse has been observed. Other reports indicate an increase in family breakups, resulting in an increase of the number of orphans. Families whose resources for loving care are depleted through long-term multiple distress can no longer provide their children with a sense of belonging.

The real challenge facing Iraq in the post-Saddam era will be rebuilding a country that has been under totalitarian rule since 1979. The military action taken against Saddam will likely cause extensive damage to the country's infrastructure, in addition to the loss of life and further destruction of the economy. The United Nations, for example, estimates that since the Gulf War 50 percent of Iraq's sewage treatment plants are inoperable and another 25 percent are polluting the environment. Of Iraq's twenty generating plants, thirteen were damaged or destroyed. Even today only 4,400 megawatts of electric power are available, when the actual need is for 6,200 megawatts. Many areas in rural Iraq face ten-hour blackouts.

When Saddam is gone, Iraq will be a country with a daunting task. Despite the damage that has already been done to Iraq and the prospects of new damage associated with regime change, Iraq has some cause for optimism in a post-Saddam period of reconstruction. There are huge oil reserves (second only to Saudi Arabia's), a competent middle class, and a general population that is thirsting for some semblance of normality. These sources of optimism, however, have to be balanced against Iraq's deep ethnic and religious divisions, lack of modern technology (other than military technology), weak social and political institutions, and a general population that has little understanding of how to live in or operate an open society.

A post-Saddam Iraq will have to deal with thousands of refugees and hundreds of thousands of hungry citizens. Civil order will need to be maintained while a national leadership that was not tied to Saddam is identified. Forming a government will also be a painstaking process of coalition building among groups vying for control. The prospect of a partition of Iraq with the Kurds in the north, the Shiites in the south, and the middle regions un-

---

Key U.N. Resolutions Against Iraq

Resolution 660 (1990)	Condemns the Iraqi invasion of Kuwait
Resolution 661 (1990)	Imposes economic sanctions on Iraq
Resolution 687 (1991)	Establishes special commission on weapons (UNSCOM)
Resolution 986 (1995)	Establishes the oil for food program
Resolution 1284 (1999)	Establishes U.N. Monitoring, Verification, and Inspection Commission to replace UNSCOM
Resolution 1409 (2002)	Modifies the oil for food program, institutes smart sanctions
Resolution 1441 (2002)	Declares that Iraq is in "material breach" of earlier weapons restrictions and gives the regime a "final opportunity" to comply with U.N. agreements

der Sunni or sectarian control is a real possibility and a serious threat to territorial integrity. Getting the country back to some semblance of normality after years of decay and decline will be an enormous task.

COMPARISONS

The dictatorial governing regime established and sustained by Saddam Hussein is one of only a few in the world community of nations. Although a number of authoritarian governments are headed by a family dynasty, religious clerics, or military generals, few governments have been designated as "pariah" regimes that exist on the very fringes of accepted political behavior. North Korea, Libya, and Cuba are often mentioned along with Iraq as nations that pose a danger to regional and international interests. Iraq and these other "pariah" states refuse to follow fundamental rules of governance and state-to-state relations accepted widely in the world. Like Iraq, these countries shun international agreements, threaten neighboring countries, and engage in a wide array of practices that violate basic tenets of human rights and freedoms.

At the core of pariah states like Iraq is a dictator who has mastered the arts of popular control and regime longevity. Unfortunately for the Iraqi people, Saddam Hussein has learned much from the likes of dictators Josef Stalin and Mao Zedong and current compatriots Kim Il Sung of North Korea, Muammar Qaddafi of Libya, and Fidel Castro of Cuba. These dictators have survived in power through ruthless use of violence, shrewd management of domestic affairs, and an ingenious capability to fend off threats from outside forces. Dictators in the mold of Saddam Hussein do not survive as king of the hill because they are lucky but because they have expert survival skills.

But dictators like Saddam Hussein are not invulnerable. They overplay their hand, they antagonize their supporters, they threaten the wrong enemy, they grow sick and old and infirm. Yet dictators like Saddam Hussein do not leave power easily or in a peaceful manner. They have to be pushed out of power either by external military means or by a domestic coup d'état. Unfortunately, when dictators are pushed out of power they leave behind a legacy of death, destruction, and plunder that takes generations to overcome. Because the Saddam Husseins of the world stay in power so long, they have the time and the capability to ruin countries and peoples. When Saddam Hussein is pushed out of power, the Iraqi people will likely rejoice in his departure while facing up to the realization that removing the effects of his legacy will be a monumental task.

CONCLUSION

One of the unfortunate realities of history is the kind of strange status that is given to dictators. Adolf Hitler, Benito Mussolini, Josef Stalin, Mao Zedong are the subjects of endless studies and scholarly debates. Their despicable acts of terror and the excesses of their megalomania continue to fascinate many. They become larger-than-life figures who revolt us even as they intrigue us as the manifestation of evil in our midst. The outrageousness of their governing style and the horrific treatment they give their own citizens combine to keep these men at the center stage of history. While quiet, competent democratic leaders enter and leave politics with nary a hint of notoriety, these dictators build reputations that hold our attention long after they exit the world stage.

Sadly, Saddam Hussein has become an authoritarian icon destined to be remembered for his cruelty and examined for clues to the sources of his tyranny. Like most dictators, Saddam has weathered many attacks on him and his regime. His intelligence and protective systems have provided him with the means to sustain his rule despite overwhelming external pressure and growing internal threats. But as a dictator, Saddam's control and survival are not guaranteed. There is always someone out there who will challenge his power or seek to remove him or end his life. This is Saddam's fate.

A FEW BOOKS YOU SHOULD READ

Ofra Bengio, *Saddam's Word: Political Discourse in Iraq* (New York: Oxford University Press, 1998). Compendium of Saddam's speeches and Baath publications. Insights into how Saddam has retained power and societal support.

Richard Butler, *The Greatest Threat: Iraq, Weapons of Mass Destruction, and the Growing Crisis in Global Security* (New York: Public Affairs, 2000). Observations on Iraq from the outspoken head of UNSCOM. An unsettling discussion of the threat posed by Saddam.

Mariya Kanan, *Cruelty and Silence: War, Tyranny, Uprising, and the Arab World* (New York: Norton, 1993). An Iraqi exile tells the story of the regime of repression under Saddam.

Martin Kelly, *Martyr's Day: Chronicle of a Small War* (New York: Random House, 1993). Of the many Gulf War books, this is one of the best, in part because it looks at the impact of the war on Iraq.

Charles Tripp, *A History of Iraq* (New York: Cambridge University Press, 2000). The most recent and therefore updated history of Iraq. Solid historical analysis of the Saddam years.

A FEW WEB SITES YOU SHOULD VISIT

www.iraqfoundation.org. Nonprofit organization that is "working for democracy and human rights in Iraq."

www.menic.utexas.edu. Site of the Center for Middle Eastern Studies at the University of Texas. A wealth of information.

www.rferl.org/Iraq-report. Iraq Report provides regular reports on developments inside Iraq.

www.arabicnews.com. News from the region with substantial information on current events in Iraq.

www.inc.org.uk. Web site of the Iraqi National Congress, the main opposition organization currently operating outside Iraq.

9

The Last Comparison

Just as the world is changing, so is the study of comparative politics. Although the study of nation-states still requires close examination of institutions, processes, and policies, there is growing interest in examining within and among nation-states the relationship of political culture to public policy formation, the effect of technological sophistication on citizen–state interactions, the impact of religion on political stability, the influence of corporations on national development, and the status of key social issues such the role of women, immigration pressure, and the level of racial and gender discrimination in the general political arena. These new approaches to comparative politics show that examining nation-states and making connections among and between nation-states constitute a vital and dynamic field of study. The community of nations in the twenty-first century is larger in terms of numbers, as well as linkages among these nations in an ever more complex global environment.

The eight nation-states examined in this text already have been and likely will be affected in the future by some of these new forces at work in the field of comparative politics. The discussion in each chapter incorporates information about and analysis of how these new forces influence the conduct of politics and governance in the United States, the United Kingdom, Russia, Japan, China, Mexico, South Africa, and Iraq. But much more needs to be done. In the future it will be absolutely necessary to understand how these new and dynamic forces are connected to the structures of politics and government. The core of power and decisionmaking in a political system remains critical to an understanding of a nation-state and essential in order to clarify comparisons and contrasts. But increasingly the work of comparative politics centers on how the political arena and the governing process respond to people as individual actors, as members of social and economic organizations and users of modern technology, and as part of a popular culture.

In the future we may want to know more about how the political values that serve as the foundation of the United States have affected neighboring Mexico. We may also want to know more about the ways in which the Russian and Japanese governments manage economies where there is a history

489

of central control and large influential bureaucracies. There will also be a need to know more about how Britain, as a former colonial power, deals with its own racial problems compared with its former colony South Africa, which now is being accused of racialization of national politics and public policy. And in the future we may want to know more about how China and Iraq respond to pressures from women wanting a larger role in national life. The connections and interactions among countries are growing at a rapid pace as globalization and technological advances foster ever changing domestic conditions that require new approaches to analysis. Since all or most of these connections and interactions will eventually end up within the political and governing arena, students of comparative politics will never be at a loss for new areas of research. In short, the future is bright for those who want to engage in one of the oldest forms of political science, comparison.

Index